Windows® Server 2003:
A Beginner's Guide

Martin S. Matthews

McGraw-Hill/Osborne

New York   Chicago   San Francisco
Lisbon   London   Madrid   Mexico City
Milan   New Delhi   San Juan
Seoul   Singapore   Sydney   Toronto

The *McGraw·Hill* Companies

McGraw-Hill/Osborne
2100 Powell Street, Floor 10
Emeryville, California 94608
U.S.A.

To arrange bulk purchase discounts for sales promotions, premiums, or fund-raisers, please contact **McGraw-Hill**/Osborne at the above address. For information on translations or book distributors outside the U.S.A., please see the International Contact Information page immediately following the index of this book.

Windows® Server 2003: A Beginner's Guide

   34567890 FGR FGR 0198765

ISBN 0-07-219309-3

Publisher   Brandon A. Nordin
Vice President & Associate Publisher   Scott Rogers
Acquisitions Editor   Jane Brownlow
Senior Project Editor   Betsy Manini
Acquisitions Coordinator   Tana Allen
Technical Editor   John Cronan
Copy Editor   Robert Campbell
Proofreader   Stefany Otis
Indexer   Valerie Perry
Computer Designers   Carie Abrew, Tabitha M. Cagan
Illustrators   Melinda Moore Lytle, Michael Mueller, Lyssa Wald
Series Designer   Jean Butterfield
Series Cover Designer   Sarah F. Hinks

This book was composed with Corel VENTURA™ Publisher.

To Dick and Pat Shepard,
the world's greatest neighbors and wonderful friends.
Thanks Dick and Pat, for always being there, no matter what the need.

About the Author

Martin Matthews (Marty) has used computers for over 30 years, from some of the early mainframe computers to recent personal computers. He has done this as a programmer, systems analyst, manager, vice president, and president of a software firm. As a result, he has first-hand knowledge of not only how to program and use a computer, but also how to make the best use of the information a computer can produce.

Over 20 years ago, Marty wrote his first computer book, on how to buy minicomputers. Nineteen years ago, Marty and his wife Carole began writing books as a major part of their occupation. In the intervening years, they have written over 50 books, including ones on desktop publishing, web publishing, Microsoft Office, and Microsoft operating systems from MS-DOS through Windows Server 2003. Recent books published by **McGraw-Hill**/Osborne include *Windows XP Professional: A Beginner's Guide, FrontPage 2002: The Complete Reference,* and *Windows 2000: A Beginner's Guide.*

Marty, Carole, and their son live on an island in Puget Sound where, on the rare moments when they can look up from their computers, they look west across seven miles of water and the main shipping channel to the snow-capped Olympic Mountains.

Contents

PART I
The Windows Server 2003 Environment

Acknowledgments

It takes a number of people to create a book like this and especially to make it a really good book. The following people, and others I do not know, have added much to the book and have made my job manageable.

John Cronan, technical editor, corrected many errors, added many tips and notes, and generally improved the book. John is also a great friend. Thanks, John!

Jane Brownlow, acquisitions editor, provided the needed support, as well as a lot of latitude. Thanks, Jane!

Betsy Manini, project editor, added to the readability and understandability of the book while listening to my considerations and being great to work with. Thanks, Betsy!

Tana Allen, acquisitions coordinator, kept the project organized and on track while correcting formatting problems and identifying lost screen shots. Throughout it all, Tana has been a delight to work with. Thanks, Tana! (Tana had the audacity to go off and get married during this book. I wish her and her husband a great many years of happiness and that 31 years from now she can write as I have next.)

Carole Matthews, my life partner for over 31 years, my very best friend, and sharer of our parenting adventure, provided the necessary support without which this book would not have been possible. Thanks, my love!

Introduction

Windows Server 2003 is the full blossoming of the Windows server operating system. What began as Windows NT, went through a major transition in Windows 2000 Server to become in Windows Server 2003 a full-featured, fully capable server operating system. The net result is a server operating system that is more reliable, easier to install, faster, and more scalable. It also has an excellent directory service, supports most current hardware, is easier to manage, provides better security, and delivers exceptional web support.

The purpose of this book is to show you how to use these features and many others, and get the attendant benefits.

How This Book Is Organized

Windows Server 2003: A Beginner's Guide is written the way most people learn. It starts by reviewing the basic concepts and then uses a learn-by-doing method to demonstrate the major features of the product. Throughout, the book uses detailed examples and clear explanations with many line drawings and screenshots to give you the insight needed to make the fullest use of Windows Server 2003. *Windows Server 2003: A Beginner's Guide* has five parts, each providing a complete discussion of one major aspect of Windows Server 2003.

Part I: The Windows Server 2003 Environment

Part I introduces you to the Windows Server 2003 environment, and what's new about it. This part establishes the foundation for the rest of the book.

- **Module 1, Exploring Windows Server 2003,** provides an overview of Windows Server 2003 and serves as a guide to the more in-depth discussions that take place in the later modules.

- **Module 2, Migrating to Windows Server 2003,** explores the pros and cons of migrating to Windows Server 2003 and how an organization might go through the evaluation for themselves.

Part II: Deploying Windows Server 2003 and Windows XP Professional

Part II covers planning for and deploying Windows Server 2003 and Windows XP across an organization. The purpose of this part is to assist you in going though the planning process and then actually doing a detailed installation.

- **Module 3, Preparing for Installation,** looks at all the steps that must be carried out prior to installing Windows Server 2003, including the possible pitfalls to stay clear of.

- **Module 4, Installing Windows Server 2003,** takes you through the various steps necessary to install the Server from different starting points, as well as if you are upgrading or doing a clean install.

- **Module 5, Rolling Out Windows XP Professional,** describes both the manual and automated approaches to the installation of Windows XP Professional.

- **Module 6, Remote Installation Services,** describes how to use the Remote Installation service to install both Windows Server 2003 and Windows XP Personal.

Part III: Networking Windows Server 2003

Part III devotes three modules to networking, the single most important function within Windows Server 2003.

- **Module 7, Windows Server 2003 Networking Environment,** provides a comprehensive foundation on networking by describing the schemes, hardware, and protocols or standards that are used to make it function.

- **Module 8, Setting Up and Managing a Network,** describes how networking is set up and managed in Windows Server 2003.

- **Module 9, Using Active Directory and Domains,** looks at how domains are used in Windows Server 2003 and the central role that Active Directory plays in managing networking.

Part IV: Communications and the Internet

Part IV covers the ways that you and your organization can reach out from your LAN to connect to others or allow others to connect to you, both on the Internet and through direct communications.

- **Module 10, Communications and Internet Services,** provides an overview of communications and how to set it up, including using a dial-up connection with the Remote Access Service (RAS), and using an Internet connection with Internet Explorer and Outlook Express.

- **Module 11, Internet Information Services Version 6,** describes Internet Information Services (IIS) and how is it set up and managed.

- **Module 12, Virtual Private Networking,** explains VPN: how it works, how it is set up both with PPTP and L2TP, and how it is used.

- **Module 13, Terminal Services and Remote Desktop,** describes Terminal Services, how it is set up, and then how to use Application Server Mode, Remote Administration, and Remote Desktop.

Part V: Administering Windows Server 2003

The purpose of Part V is to explore the numerous administrative tools that are available within Windows Server 2003 and discuss how they can best be used.

- **Module 14, Managing Storage and File Systems,** looks at the extensive set of tools that are available in Windows Server 2003 to handle the various types of storage systems and the files and folders they contain.

- **Module 15, Setting Up and Managing Printing and Faxing,** describes what constitutes Windows Server 2003 printing and faxing, how to set it up, how to manage it, how to manage the fonts that are required for it, and how to use faxing.

- **Module 16, Managing Windows Server 2003,** discusses the system management tools and user management tools that are not part of setting up, networking, file management, and printing.

- **Module 17, Controlling Windows Server 2003 Security,** describes each of the security demands and the Windows Server 2003 facilities that address that demand, as well as the ways to implement those facilities.

Conventions Used in This Book

Windows Server 2003: A Beginner's Guide uses several conventions designed to make the book easier for you to follow:

- **Bold type** is used for text that you are to type from the keyboard.

- *Italic type* is used for a word or phrase that is being defined or otherwise deserves special emphasis.

- A monospaced typeface is used for command listings either produced by Windows Server 2003 or entered by the user.

- SMALL CAPITAL LETTERS are used for keys on the keyboard such as ENTER and SHIFT.

When you are expected to enter a command, you are told to press the key(s). If you are to enter text or numbers, you are told to type them.

Part I

The Windows Server 2003 Environment

Module 1

Exploring Windows Server 2003

Windows Server 2003 is the latest Microsoft Windows operating system for servers in a client/server network. It comes in several editions, ranging from simple web servers to complex datacenter servers. All editions include built-in support for the .NET technologies that allow the connection among people, systems, and devices for the exchange of information and computer resources using Extensible Markup Language (XML) web services, which are building blocks of applications that can be used together or with other applications. The .NET technologies, which is what is meant by ".NET," operate over local area networks as well as the Internet to support the integration of people and computers working together in a single organization, as well as across many organizations to provide a high level of connectedness and interoperability.

CRITICAL SKILL
1.1
Understand the Reasons for Windows Server 2003

Windows Server 2003 is a significant and worthwhile upgrade from Windows 2000 Server, and most especially from Windows NT Server 4. There are many reasons for saying this, but here are some of the more outstanding ones:

- **It is more reliable** My own experience confirms what numerous sources outside Microsoft have said about Windows Server 2003: it is more reliable than Windows 2000 and a lot more reliable than Windows NT 4.

- **It is easier to install** Automated Server configuration in addition to improved Plug and Play capability, an enlarged driver database, and enhancements to the Setup Program make Windows Server 2003 significantly easier to install than Windows NT Server 4 and an improvement over Windows 2000 Server.

- **It is faster** Across the many ways that processing speed can be measured, outside sources and my experience show that Windows Server 2003 is definitely faster than Windows NT 4, and under most circumstances it is faster than Windows 2000. Windows Server 2003 can make better use of memory and the newest processors, such as the Intel 64-bit Itanium, further improving the speed.

- **It has a better directory** Windows Server 2003's Active Directory is a significant improvement over Windows NT's limited domain structure, and it is a step up from Windows 2000's Active Directory, including improvements in group membership replication, synchronization, and an enhanced Users and Computers snap-in.

- **It supports more hardware** Windows Server 2003 provides support for many new hardware devices over Windows 2000 Server, including CD writers for burning CDs, new keyboard buttons, high-resolution monitors and printers, multifunction printing/fax/copying devices, and expanded AutoPlay capability.

● **It is easier to manage**   Windows Server 2003 includes enhancements in the Microsoft Management Console (MMC) and IntelliMirror, which enables settings and files to follow a user from machine to machine across a network; and file management improvements including encrypting of offline files, using FAT32 on DVD-RAM, and an improved disk defragmenter.

● **It offers better security**   Windows Server 2003 security enhancements include support for a secure wireless local area network (LAN); extended error handling in Kerberos, IPSec (Internet Protocol–based security) monitoring; public and private key archival and recovery; enhanced certificate features; and numerous improvements in creating and managing Group Policy, including improvements in administrative templates, new policy settings, and folder redirection.

● **It offers enhanced services**   Windows Server 2003 provides a number of enhanced services, including capacity planning and Internet Authentication Service (IAS) in Internet Information Services (IIS); many new features in Dynamic Host Configuration Protocol (DHCP) and Domain Name System (DNS); and remote desktop, service redirection, load management, and standby power support in Terminal Services.

● **Incorporation of .NET**   Windows Server 2003 incorporates Microsoft's new .NET technologies, which embed within the operating system the means to use XML to link applications, services, and devices together in a single online solution. For example, while you are shopping at an online store, the store could check a Smart Card in a reader on your computer to verify who you are and your credit card number; you could access your credit card provider to check the credit available to you; and then you could access the air freight company to check on their delivery schedule, all while making a decision to buy something at the store.

The purpose of this book is to show you how to use these features and many others, and get the attendant benefits. In this module, I will provide a quick overview of Windows Server 2003, looking briefly at each area of the product, including a description of its function and how it relates to the rest of the product.

CRITICAL SKILL
1.2 Compare Windows Server 2003 Editions

Windows Server 2003 comprises four independent and separately sold editions:

● **Windows Server 2003 Web Edition**   A server for hosting smaller web sites and running Internet Information Services (IIS)

- **Windows Server 2003 Standard Edition**   A network server operating system that is meant for smaller to moderate-sized organizations and is an upgrade for Windows 2000 Server and Windows NT Server 4 (with Service Pack 5 or later)

- **Windows Server 2003 Enterprise Edition**   A network server operating system that is meant for larger organizations, especially those involved in e-commerce, and is an upgrade for Windows 2000 Advanced Server and Windows NT Server 4 Enterprise Edition

- **Windows Server 2003 Datacenter Edition**   A network server operating system that is meant for the largest organizations, especially those involved in data warehousing and online transaction processing, and is an upgrade for Windows 2000 Datacenter Server

Hardware Differences

The hardware that can be used differs significantly among the versions of Windows Server 2003, as shown in Table 1-1.

This book will focus on the Windows Server 2003 Standard Edition and touch a bit on the Web Edition and the Enterprise Edition.

Progress Check

1. What is XML and how is it used?

2. What are some of the reasons to upgrade from Windows NT Server 4 or Windows 2000 Server to Windows Server 2003?

3. What are the hardware characteristics of Windows Server 2003 Standard Edition?

---

1. XML stands for Extensible Markup Language, which uses web services to create building blocks that can be used together to create an application or to link applications, services, and devices together in a single online solution.

2. The predominant reasons to upgrade to Windows Server 2003 is that it is more reliable, is easier to install, is faster, has better directory services, supports more hardware, is easier to manage, provides better security, and incorporates .NET technology.

3. Windows Server 2003 Standard Edition can use up to two processors, works with a maximum of 4GB and a minimum of 128MB of memory, runs only on a 32-bit platform, and does not provide for clustering.

Windows Server 2003	Concurrent CPUs	Max. Memory	Min. Memory	Platforms	Clustering
Web Edition	2	2GB	128MB	32-bit	None
Standard Edition	2	4GB	128MB	32-bit	None
Enterprise Edition	8	32/64GB*	256MB	32 and 64-bit	8-node
Datacenter Edition	32	64/128GB*	512MB	32 and 64-bit	8-node

* With the 64-bit platform

Table 1-1   Hardware Difference Among Windows Server 2003 Editions

CRITICAL SKILL

1.3

Understand Windows Server 2003 Components

Windows Server 2003 is a complex operating system with numerous components that work together to perform the necessary functions. Figure 1-1 shows the key components of

Ask the Expert

Q: We are a moderate sized company with two Windows NT Server 4 computers and are thinking of upgrading to Windows Server 2003. How do we make the decision between the Standard and Enterprise Editions?

A: The easy answer is to say that since you have been getting along with Windows NT Server 4, Windows Server 2003 Standard Edition will more than serve your needs with greater reliability and much improved performance, plus many new features such as Active Directory. The real answer, though, has to do with where you see your company going. If you see it continuing the pattern of business you've had over the last several years, then most likely Standard Edition is your best choice. If you see major growth in the business or a major change in the way you do business to one that is more computing intensive, such as doing much more business online, then you probably need to take a look at Enterprise Edition.

Windows Server 2003 in an idealized block diagram. The central square marked "Kernel Mode" is the kernel of the operating system and interfaces with the outside world of users, applications, and hardware through the components in the remaining shaded area or gray area labeled "User Mode." User Mode has five main component areas. These are, going clockwise from the upper left in Figure 1-1, as follows:

- Networking over a local area network (LAN)
- Communications and the Internet over a wide area network (WAN)
- User and application interface
- Storage and file management system
- Printing system

The intent of this book is to help you understand how to use these components in the User Mode plus Windows Server 2003 Setup. The components in the Kernel Mode are discussed only to the extent to which you need to understand them to be able to use the User Mode components.

The User Mode components are the foundation of a user's experience with Windows Server 2003 and are the foundation of this book. The remaining sections in this module provide an introductory look at the major areas of the User Mode components that provide for the following functions:

- Deploying Windows Server 2003
- Networking Windows Server 2003
- Communicating and Using the Internet with Windows Server 2003
- Administering Windows Server 2003

The sections discussed here correspond to the remaining parts of this book, so you can easily jump from this overview to the details later in the book.

CRITICAL SKILL
1.4 Deploy Windows Server 2003

Successfully bringing Windows Server 2003 into an organization means not only that the operating system is installed, but also that its performance is optimized and it looks and works the way you want it to. It may also mean that you have successfully installed Windows XP Professional throughout the workstations in your organization. To meet this objective, you must plan and then carry out the deployment, both for servers and workstations.

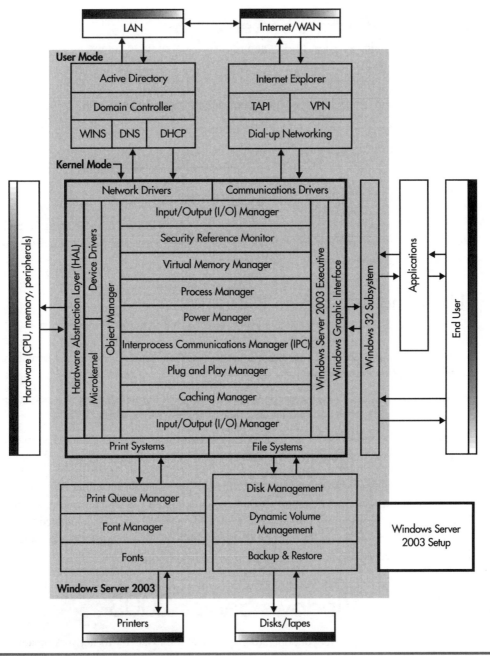

Figure 1-1 Central components of Windows Server 2003

Prepare for Windows Server 2003

To prepare for Windows Server 2003, you must make sure of these points:

- Your computers meet the requirements of Windows Server 2003.

- Windows Server 2003 supports all the hardware in your computers.

- You know the choices that provide the best operating environment for each of the installation decisions.

- Your computers have been prepared for an operating system installation.

- You have a solid plan for carrying out the installation.

Module 3 helps you to prepare for installation by looking at each of these areas for both Windows Server 2003 and Windows XP Professional, and it discusses what you need to know to make the installation as smooth as possible.

Set Up Windows Server 2003

Windows Server 2003 can be installed in a variety of ways, which fall into three categories:

- **Manually**   Someone sits in front of the computer to be installed and, in real time, installs the software on that machine.

- **Automated**   A script or answer file is used to carry out the installation, so a person has only to start the installation on a computer and can then let the script finish it.

- **Remotely**   A person sits in front of a server and performs the installation on another computer across the network. This installation can be manual or automated.

Module 4 explains in detail how to use the manual approach for installing Windows Server 2003 with many variations, the start of which is shown in Figure 1-2. Module 5 describes the manual approach for installing Windows XP Professional, along with the automated approach for installing Windows Server 2003 or XP Professional. Module 6 discusses the Remote Installation service used to remotely install either Server or Professional.

CRITICAL SKILL
1.5 # Network Windows Server 2003

Windows Server 2003 is a network operating system, and it exists for its networking ability. This allows it to connect with other computers for the purpose of performing the following functions:

- Exchanging information, such as sending a file from one computer to another

- Communicating by, for example, sending e-mail among network users

- Sharing information by having common files accessed by multiple network users

- Sharing resources on the network, such as printers and backup tape drives

Networking is important to almost every organization of two or more people who communicate and share information. It is a primary ingredient in the computer's contribution to improved productivity and, from the viewpoint of this book, is the single most important facility in Windows Server 2003.

Networking is a system that includes the physical connection between computers that facilitates the transfer of information, as well as the scheme for controlling that transfer. The scheme makes sure that the information is transferred correctly and accurately while many other transfers are occurring simultaneously. Thus, a networking system has these components:

- A networking scheme that handles the transfer

- Networking hardware that handles the physical connection

- A networking standard or protocol that handles the identification and addressing

Module 7 describes the networking schemes that are available in Windows Server 2003, the hardware that can be used, and the protocols that are common in the industry. Module 7

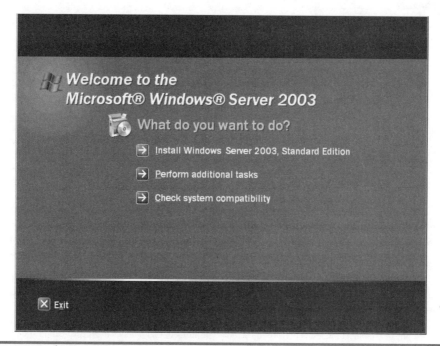

Figure 1-2 Windows Server 2003 initial Setup page

then reviews the wide spectrum of networking alternatives that are available to provide the networking environment best suited to your needs. Module 8 provides a detailed description of setting up basic networking in either Server or Professional and then looks at setting up Server to support the rest of the network—for example, setting up a DNS server, as shown in Figure 1-3. Module 9 explores domains and how Active Directory provides a single access to and management of many different network-related functions.

Progress Check

1. What is required to successfully bring Windows Server 2003 into an organization?

2. What are the three ways in which Windows Server 2003 can be installed?

3. What are the three components of a networking system?

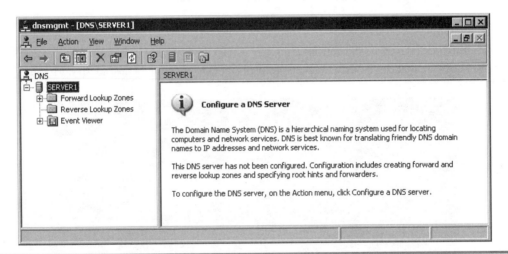

Figure 1-3 Setting up a DNS server

1. To successfully bring Windows Server 2003 into an organization requires that you carefully plan and carry out the server installation, then optimize its performance so it looks and works the way you want it to, and possibly successfully install Windows XP Professional throughout the workstations in your organization.

2. The three ways in which Windows Server 2003 can be installed are manually, where someone sits in front of the computer to be installed; in an automated fashion, where a script or answer file is used to carry out the installation; and remotely, where a person sits in front of a server and performs the installation on another computer.

3. A networking system has these three components: a networking scheme that handles the transfer, networking hardware that handles the physical connection, and a networking standard or protocol that handles the identification and addressing.

CRITICAL SKILL
1.6
Communicate and Use the Internet with Windows Server 2003

"Networking" in the preceding section referred to using a LAN. In this age of the Internet, Windows Server 2003 networking has taken on a much broader meaning that includes all the types of connections that you make outside of your LAN using what was classically called "communications." Windows Server 2003 offers a single window, Network Connections, shown in Figure 1-4, from which you can set up both LAN and external connections.

The types of external connections include these:

● Leased-line and private-line WAN

● Dial-up line computer-to-computer communications using a modem

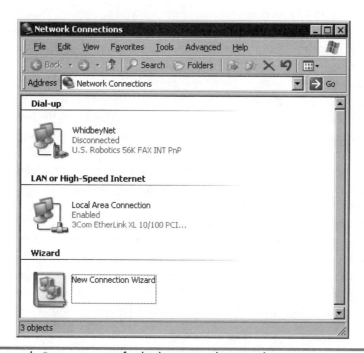

Figure 1-4 Network Connections is for both LAN and external connections.

- Direct computer-to-computer using serial, parallel, or infrared ports

- Remote Access Service (RAS) for accessing a LAN over a dial-up, leased, or private line

- Dial-up, leased, and private line connections to the Internet

- Virtual private networking (VPN) to securely access a LAN over the Internet

Windows Server 2003's communications ability includes the following possible ways to interchange information:

- Computer to computer

- Computer to LAN

- LAN to LAN

- Computer or LAN to WAN

- Computer or LAN to the Internet

Communication may include a modem or other device to connect a single computer to a method of transmission, or it may use a router or other device to connect a network to the method of transmission. Communications can be over copper wires, fiber-optic cable, microwave, ground wireless, infrared, or satellite transmission.

Windows Server 2003 includes a number of programs that control or utilize communications, among which are Internet Explorer for web browsing, Outlook Express for e-mail, Fax, HyperTerminal for computer-to-computer communications, and both the Internet Connection Wizard and the Network Connection Wizard to establish connections. In addition, Windows Server 2003 networking includes programs to set up and manage RAS and VPN forms of networking over communications lines, as well as the Remote Desktop Connection to link two remote computers. Finally, IIS can be used to publish web pages on either the Internet or an intranet.

Module 10 provides an overview of communications and how to set up the various Windows Server 2003 communications features. It then discusses establishing an Internet connection, using Internet Explorer, and setting up and using e-mail over the Internet. Module 11 looks at IIS, how it's set up, and how it's managed, including its administrative window, shown in Figure 1-5. Module 12 describes how to set up and use VPN, while Module 13 discusses Terminal and Application Services, the foundation for Remote Desktop Connection and other remote operations.

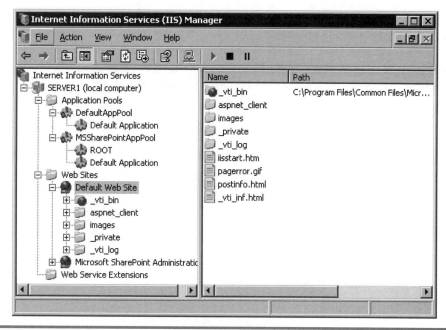

Figure 1-5 Internet Information Services administrative window

CRITICAL SKILL
1.7 Administer Windows Server 2003

The job of administering a Windows Server 2003 network, even one as small as a single server and a few workstations, is a significant task. To assist in this, Windows Server 2003 has a number of system management tools that can be used to monitor and tune the system's performance, both locally and remotely. These tools can be categorized into the following areas:

- File system management

- Printing management

- General system management

- Security management

File System Management

Windows Server 2003 is designed to work in a wide range of computing environments and with several other operating systems. As a result, the structure of its file storage has to be flexible. This is manifest in the types of storage that are available, and in the file systems that Windows Server 2003 can utilize.

Prior to Windows 2000 Server, only one type of storage was available, called *basic storage,* which allowed a drive to be divided into partitions or volumes only before it was reformatted. Windows 2000 Server and Windows Server 2003 add *dynamic storage,* which allows the dynamic creation of and changes to volumes. You must choose which type of storage you want for a given drive, but you can have both types in a computer with two or more drives.

The Windows Server 2003 file system extends well beyond a single drive, or even the drives in a single machine, to all the drives in a network, and it even includes volumes stored offline on tape or disk. The management of this system is significant, and Windows Server 2003 thus has a significant set of tools to handle system management, which are described in Module 14. Among these tools are:

- Disk Management
- Dynamic Volume Management
- Distributed File System
- Removable Storage Manager
- Remote Storage Service
- Disk Backup and Restore

Figure 1-6 shows the Disk Management window.

Printing Management

The ability to transfer computer information to paper or other media is still important, and the ability to share printers is a major network function, as you can see in Figure 1-7. Both Windows Server 2003 and Windows XP Professional can serve as print servers. Module 15 describes what constitutes Windows Server 2003 printing, how to set it up, how to manage it, and how to manage the fonts that are required for printing.

General System Management

Windows Server 2003 has a variety of general system management tools to control many facets of the operating system. Module 16 looks at the system management tools and user management tools that are not part of setting up, networking, managing files, or printing.

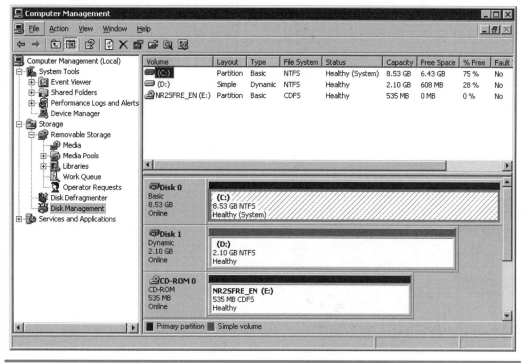

Figure 1-6 Disk Management within the Computer Management window

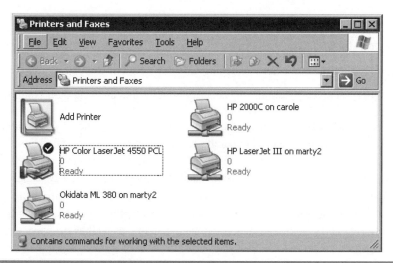

Figure 1-7 Printers window with three network printers and one local printer

System management tools facilitate running parts of the operating system that are not discussed elsewhere. These tools include:

- The Control Panel
- The Task Manager
- The Microsoft Management Console
- The Registry
- The boot process

Managing computer users with their varying needs and peculiarities, both in groups and individually, is a task to which Windows Server 2003 has committed considerable resources. These are addressed in terms of group policies and user profiles. Figure 1-8 shows the window in Active Directory in which you manage users and groups who are allowed entry to the computer. (If you are not using Active Directory, there are other means to manage users and groups through the Computer Management window.)

Security Management

The demands for security in a computer network include:

- **Authenticating the user**   Knowing who is trying to use a computer or network connection.
- **Controlling access**   Placing and maintaining limits on what a user can do.
- **Securing stored data**   Keeping stored data from being used even with access.
- **Securing data transmission**   Keeping data in a network from being misused.
- **Managing security**   Establishing security policies and auditing their compliance.

Windows Server 2003 uses a multilayered approach to implementing security and provides a number of facilities that are used to handle security demands, such as policies for logging on and accessing resources, as shown in Figure 1-9. Central to Windows Server 2003's security strategy is the use of user accounts to provide authentication. Other security features are available with Active Directory, which provides a network centralization of security management that is beneficial to strong security. Module 17 describes each of the security demands and the Windows Server 2003 facilities that address each demand, as well as the ways to implement those facilities.

1

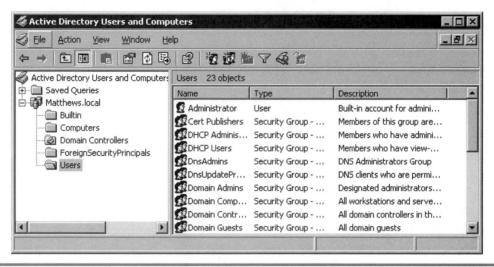

Figure 1-8 Managing users and groups through Active Directory

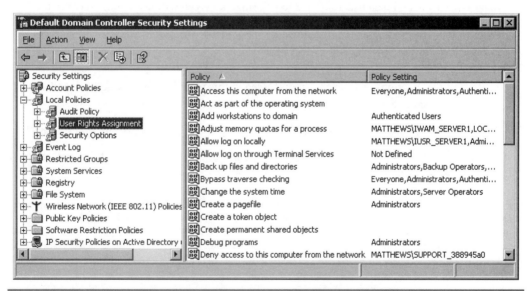

Figure 1-9 Policies are used to determine what users and groups can do.

Progress Check

1. What are the possible ways to exchange information with Windows Server 2003 communications?

2. What are the two types of storage available in Windows 2000 Server and Windows Server 2003?

3. What are the general system management tools in Windows Server 2003?

Project 1 Identify the Functions You Need

This module has described a number of functions that can be performed with a server operating system and has briefly discussed what each function is, how it is performed in Windows Server 2003, and what components of the operating system will do that task. No installation uses all these functions. Most have ones that are critical to what they do and other functions they hardly ever use. The purpose of this project is to identify what functions are most important to you and then use Table 1-2 to prioritize how you will learn about them in the following modules.

Step by Step

1. Review the functions that have been discussed in this module. Possibly go back and scan what was said in earlier sections to recollect what the function does.

2. Determine which functions are most important to you and assign a priority order for each.

3. Use Table 1-2 to lay out a schedule based on your priority and read the related modules in the order given by that schedule.

---

1. The possible ways to exchange information with Windows Server 2003 communications include computer to computer, computer to LAN, LAN to LAN, computer or LAN to WAN, and computer or LAN to the Internet.

2. The two types of storage available in Windows 2000 Server and Windows Server 2003 are basic storage, which allows a drive to be divided into partitions or volumes only before it is reformatted, and dynamic storage, which allows the dynamic creation of and change to volumes.

3. The general system management tools in Windows Server 2003 include the Control Panel, the Task Manager, the Microsoft Management Console, the Registry, and the boot process.

Function	Modules	Priority (Dates)
Deciding to Migrate to Windows Server 2003	Module 2	
Planning for and Installing Windows Server 2003	Modules 3 and 4	
Automating the Installation of Windows Server 2003 and XP Professional	Modules 5 and 6	
Networking	Modules 7 and 8	
Domains and Active Directory	Module 9	
Communications	Module 10	
Web Hosting	Module 11	
Virtual Private Networking	Module 12	
Remote Services	Module 13	
File Handling	Module 14	
Printing and Faxing	Module 15	
Managing Windows Server 2003	Module 16	
Security	Module 17	

Table 1-2 Prioritization of Functions and the Modules That Relate to Them

Project Summary

After you have completed the prioritization project, you will have a schedule for reading the rest of the book. There are two exceptions to this. First, if you have not already installed Windows Server 2003, go through Modules 2, 3, and 4 and do the planning and installation as described there. The remaining modules assume that Windows Server 2003 is installed and running in front of you as you read. There are many instances where you will want to try for yourself what you are reading about. Second, after you have installed Windows Server 2003 and before diving into your priority modules, if you do not have a strong understanding of networking, quickly go through Module 7, which will give you a good networking foundation that will be useful in the rest of the book.

1

Exploring Windows Server 2003

Project 1

Identify the Functions You Need

Module 1 Mastery Check

1. What does ".NET" mean?

2. What are the four editions of Windows Server 2003 and how do they differ?

3. What makes Windows Server 2003 faster to install and support more hardware?

4. What are three of the five component areas of User Mode Windows Server 2003?

5. What must you do to prepare to install Windows Server 2003?

6. What are some of the purposes of networking?

7. What are the types of external connections that can be made with Windows Server 2003?

8. What are the programs in Windows Server 2003 that control or utilize communications?

9. What are the tools in Windows Server 2003 for handling file system management?

10. What are the primary demands for security in a computer network?

Module 2

Migrating to Windows Server 2003

You most likely are wondering whether you and/or your organization should migrate to Windows Server 2003. There are, of course, many answers to that question depending on various factors. The purpose of this module is to look at those factors and discuss how to evaluate them so that you can make the right decision. Part II of this book, which begins with Module 3, will then describe how to perform the actual migration.

Each of the following sections will discuss one of these Critical Skills and look at how you should evaluate it with regard to your situation.

CRITICAL SKILL
2.1

Evaluate Your Organization's Size

As a general statement, the bigger the organization, the more obvious the decision to migrate to Windows Server 2003. And conversely, with a home office or a small office, it is less likely that migration should occur. Of course, these generalizations have many exceptions. The pros and cons of each statement are discussed next.

Larger Organization Migration

Many features in Windows Server 2003 are aimed at larger organizations and therefore will encourage them to migrate. Among these features are the following:

- The scalability of Windows Server 2003 enables it to go from a single computer with a single processor to a cluster of eight computers each with 32 processors in Windows Server 2003 Datacenter Edition, which can be a major plus for a large organization or those expecting to grow large quickly.

- The capability of Windows Server 2003 to handle large data storage volumes better than Windows NT handles them can prove valuable to larger organizations. The Windows Server 2003 facilities for large data storage include Dynamic Volume Management, Remote Storage Service, Removable Storage, and Quota Management. See Module 14 for a discussion of these facilities.

- Windows Server 2003's Active Directory is more useful for a large organization because it can provide a central reference to shares and other services, such as printers, on a number of servers and clients. Module 9 explores Active Directory.

- Windows Server 2003 management features, such as the Computer Management window shown in Figure 2-1, are more valuable to larger organizations because they make handling a large number of users, large storage volumes, and multiple servers easier. Also, the addition of organizational units (OUs) to the domain's hierarchical structure allows system administration to be more broadly distributed, which would benefit a large organization. Windows Server 2003 management features are discussed in Module 16, while domains are covered in Module 9.

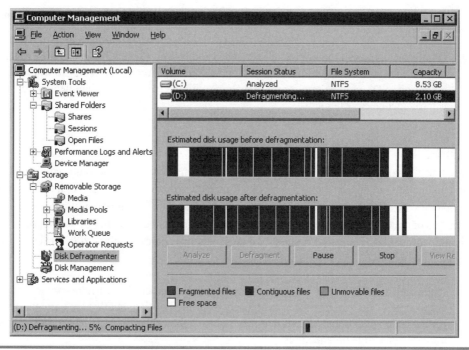

Figure 2-1 Computer Management window

● Windows Server 2003's significant security features, including Kerberos authentication, full implementation of a public key infrastructure (PKI), and file encryption, may be of more interest to larger organizations that tend to have more security concerns. The information in the section "Evaluate Your Security Demands," later in this module, provides an overview of these features, and Module 17 discusses security in depth.

After considering the preceding features that favor migration, you must also consider the following roadblocks that may discourage a large organization's implementation of Windows Server 2003:

● The size of the migration task in a large organization requires lengthy planning, considerable staff training, and a lengthy transition period, all of which equates to a significant expenditure. This, at a minimum, means that a large organization must go slow in its migration. Part II of this book describes the deployment process.

● A heterogeneous environment of mainframe, UNIX, and other non-Windows systems will reduce the benefits available from Windows Server 2003, especially Active Directory. This may mean that the return on investment (ROI) of a migration will not be acceptable.

The considerations needed in a heterogeneous environment are discussed primarily in Part III.

● Organizations heavily using Novell NetWare and Novell Directory Services (NDS) may not see enough advantage in Windows Server 2003 and Active Directory to warrant the migration. NDS may be seen as more mature, with the capability to handle a more heterogeneous environment.

Smaller Organization Migration

The size and complexity of Windows Server 2003, along with the effort required to set it up and maintain it, are major stumbling blocks for smaller organizations (although this book will go a long way toward alleviating that problem). Also, scalability, the capability to handle large amounts of data, Active Directory, and improved security may or may not be as important to smaller companies. There are, though, two areas where Windows Server 2003 provides some major benefits for smaller organizations:

● In the area of reliability and manageability, Windows Server 2003 provides some substantial enhancements that are beneficial to all users regardless of size, but that are particularly beneficial to small organizations that may not have the caliber of experienced staff that's available in a large organization.

● If you share or want to share an Internet connection line, such as a digital subscriber line (DSL) or other high-speed line, Windows Server 2003 provides several features to facilitate this. It includes a built-in router that enables you to install a line termination (a modem, or an ISDN or DSL adapter) in a server and allow anyone on the network to access the Internet over that line. Also, in Windows Server 2003 a modem can be set up to automatically dial an Internet service provider (ISP) whenever the modem is accessed. Finally, Internet Connection Sharing using network address translation (NAT) allows multiple users to share an Internet connection by mapping multiple local area network (LAN) addresses to one IP (Internet Protocol) address, which is what the ISP sees. Module 10 discusses communications and the Internet.

CRITICAL SKILL
2.2 Evaluate Your Hardware and Software

Windows Server 2003 is much more hardware-friendly than Windows NT 4, and it is even slightly better than Windows 2000. It is also more software-friendly than either NT or 2000, but some software glitches are still present.

Windows Server 2003 Hardware Friendliness

Windows NT 4 was a constant headache when it came to dealing with hardware components. Windows 2000 added a number of features aimed at relieving that headache, and Windows Server 2003 has improved on that. Among the Windows 2000 Server and Windows Server 2003 improvements are the following:

- Full implementation of Plug and Play, which allows for virtually pain-free installation of Plug and Play–compliant hardware. (Older, non–Plug and Play hardware can still be a problem, but the following points mitigate that a bit.)

- An extensive set of hardware drivers that are stored in compressed form on the computer, so that you don't need the Windows Server 2003 CD to install a new device.

- Online access to the latest drivers at the Microsoft site and a program to check whether you need them. This is accessed by choosing Start | All Programs | Windows Update, which opens the Microsoft Windows Update web site shown in Figure 2-2.

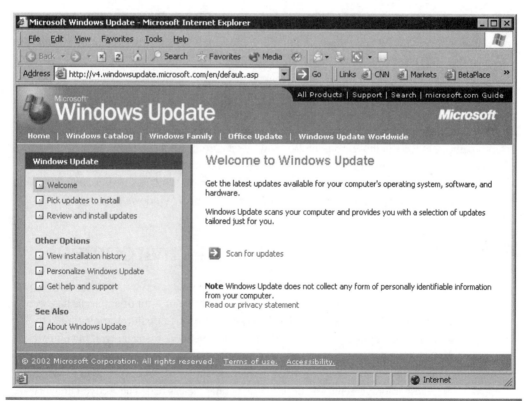

Figure 2-2 Updates of both drivers and the operating system are available online.

- Built-in support for recent hardware developments, including new keyboards, high-resolution monitors, universal serial bus (USB), and Institute of Electrical and Electronics Engineers (IEEE) 1394 (FireWire) ports. USB ports can be used with keyboards, mice, and many other devices, whereas FireWire is a high-speed port used by video cameras and other video devices.

- Efficient use of memory, but demands for a fair amount of it. Although you can run Windows Server 2003 on 128MB, running it on 256MB is really the minimum practical system, and with any significant load, you can easily use more memory. In all cases, the operating system makes good use of added memory.

- Ability to use the FAT32 file system, which was not available in Windows NT 4, although Windows Server 2003 loses a lot of capability if NTFS (NT file system) is not used. Module 14 discusses FAT32 and NTFS file systems.

- Built-in support for recording on CDs through the new Recording tab on the CD's Properties dialog box. This allows you to drag and drop files to the CD-R icon.

Windows Server 2003 Software Considerations

Windows Server 2003 Standard and Web Editions provide a 32-bit software platform, while the Enterprise and Datacenter Editions provide both 32- and 64-bit platforms. All editions provide a lot of protection for the operating system from programs that "misbehave." This means that the first priority is to protect the operating system and keep it running, so a number of applications that step outside the prescribed "box" will not operate. These tend to be hardware-related programs, such as faxing, scanning, CD writing, and gaming software. A number of these types of programs, especially those from the Windows 98 environment, have been upgraded to work under Windows 2000 and therefore for the most part work under Windows Server 2003. Older 16-bit programs, especially DOS-based games, will not run on Windows Server 2003. Hopefully, new versions of those programs will be created that work under Windows Server 2003.

Evaluate Your Networking Environment

Windows Server 2003 is a client/server network operating system, so how well it performs that function is one of the primary measures in the migration decision. A lot of emphasis has been placed on networking Windows Server 2003, and many powerful features are included to support it. Primary among these are Active Directory and network management. In comparison to Windows NT 4 and its domain services, Windows Server 2003 and Active Directory are a substantial improvement and a big plus for migration. From Windows 2000 Server to Windows Server 2003, those improvements are more subtle, but nontheless real. The Active Directory and Domain Name System (DNS) enhancements stand out. Modules 7 and 8 discuss networking, DNS, and other components of networking.

Windows Server 2003 and Active Directory depend heavily on DNS, and Windows Server 2003 wants to be the DNS server on the network. If you use UNIX, Linux, or Solaris servers, they also want to be the DNS server, and the conflict can be difficult to resolve.

You can mix Windows Server 2003 and NetWare, but you want to think through that choice first to make sure that you'll get the benefits that you want.

Progress Check

1. As a general statement, is there more reason for a bigger organization or a smaller organization to migrate to Windows Server 2003.

2. What Windows Server 2003 editions support a 32-bit software environment, and which support a 64-bit environment?

3. What kind of network operating system is Windows Server 2003?

Ask the Expert

Q: We have been using Novell NetWare for some time and are looking at whether to upgrade to NetWare 6 or to move to Windows Server 2003. What are your thoughts on this?

A: The choice between Novell NetWare with NDS and Windows Server 2003 with Active Directory is a difficult decision. NDS is a mature product in NetWare 6 and supports a heterogeneous environment, neither of which is true in Windows Server 2003 Active Directory. Also, Novell's ZENworks gives you a mature set of management features that is just appearing in Active Directory. On the other hand, NetWare does not have the scalability of Windows Server 2003, and reliability is a toss-up. Also, it looks like Microsoft is winning the war on having other products support their product.

---

1. As a general statement, the bigger the organization, the more obvious the decision to migrate to Windows Server 2003. The reason is that many features in Windows Server 2003 are aimed at larger organizations and therefore will encourage the migration.

2. All Windows Server 2003 editions support a 32-bit software environment, while the Enterprise and Datacenter Editions also support a 64-bit environment.

3. Windows Server 2003 is a client/server network operating system.

2.4 Evaluate Your Security Demands

For organizations that require a high level of security (and that is a fast-growing number), Windows Server 2003 offers a lot of support, and security could even be the reason for migrating. The big security pluses in Windows Server 2003 over Windows NT 4 are Kerberos authentication, public key infrastructure, file encryption, and Smart Cards. Between Windows 2000 Server and Windows Server 2003 the pluses are certificate, Kerberos, and IPSec (Internet Protocol–based security) enhancements; secure wireless LANs; and key archival and recovery.

NOTE

Many of the security benefits in Windows Server 2003 require that NTFS and Active Directory be used.

Kerberos Authentication

Kerberos, which was developed at the Massachusetts Institute of Technology (MIT), provides the means to transmit secure data across unsecure networks and is the primary means of authentication on the Internet. As a result, the same authentication routines in Windows Server 2003 can validate both a local Windows client and an Internet-connected UNIX client. Other benefits of Kerberos are listed here:

- **Transitive trusts**   Trust relationships transfer from computer to computer. For example, if computer A has a trust relationship with computer B, and computer B has a trust relationship with computer C, then computer A has a trust relationship with computer C.

- **Kerberos tickets**   Once authenticated, these tickets stay with the user throughout a computer session and allow the user to be quickly authenticated anywhere, without having to query an authentication server each time.

- **Mutual authentication**   This feature allows the user to authenticate a service or server, while also allowing the service or server to authenticate the user. This prevents impersonation, which was possible in Windows NT 4, and is done using the Kerberos ticket.

Public Key Infrastructure

PKI incorporates all the facilities necessary to create, distribute, authenticate, and manage public key encryption. Module 17 provides a complete description of how this works. Briefly, the steps are as follows:

1. A user who is known to the security system is given a certificate.

2. Either the certificate contains public and private keys that are unique to the user, or the user is given keys based upon the certificate.

3. When the user wants to exchange information with either a service or another user, he or she exchanges public keys.

4. The public keys are used to encrypt information to be sent to the owner of the key.

5. Upon receipt of the encrypted information, the private key is used to decrypt it.

This is the process (and it is greatly simplified here) handled by PKI. Windows Server 2003 and Windows 2000 Server are the only Windows operating systems in which it has been fully implemented.

File Encryption

File encryption allows you to encrypt individual files so that if someone gets access to your disk, he will not be able to read the file. This is particularly important for laptop or notebook computers, which are frequently stolen. Once in possession of the machine, the thief can use a variety of techniques to access the hard disk, but if critical files are encrypted, they will be unavailable to the thief.

To encrypt a file, the user, who must be the registered owner of the file, simply selects the encryption attribute in the file's or folder's Advanced Attributes dialog box. The file will be encrypted with a symmetric key (the same key is used for both encryption and decryption). The symmetric key is itself encrypted with the public keys of both the creator and a recovery agent administrator and is then stored with the file. In the normal process of opening the file, the file system will see that it is encrypted and then check to see whether the Kerberos ticket of the user has a private key that will open the file. If so, the file is opened. The only other person able to open the file is the recovery agent administrator. When the file is resaved, it is again encrypted. The entire process of encrypting and decrypting a file or folder occurs in the background, and the user is aware of it only if the file cannot be decrypted.

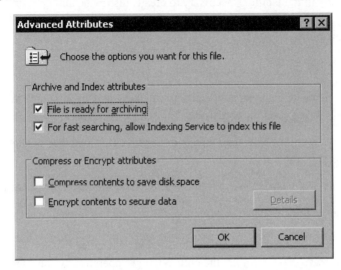

Both Windows 2000 Server and Windows Server 2003 handle file encryption, but only Windows Server 2003 allows encryption of offline files and key archival and recovery.

Smart Cards

Smart cards are like credit cards with an embedded electronic circuit that stores an ID and an encryption key. Smart cards are particularly valuable for remote entry to a network over the Internet using virtual private networking (VPN). Smart cards are also frequently used in the issuance of certificates of authenticity for documents.

Windows Server 2003 fully supports smart cards and their use to log on to a computer or network or to enable certificate-based authentication for opening documents or performing some function like a calculation. Smart cards require a reader attached to the computer through either a serial port or a Personal Computer Memory Card International Association (PCMCIA) slot. With a smart card reader, the user needs to insert her card, at which point she is prompted for a PIN. With a valid card and PIN, the user is authenticated and allowed on the system in the same way she would be by entering a valid username and password.

Windows Server 2003 and Windows 2000 Server support several Plug and Play–compliant smart card readers, and the drivers are included on the Windows Server 2003 CD. Windows NT 4 required third-party software and support for smart cards.

CRITICAL SKILL
2.5 Evaluate Support for the Internet

Windows Server 2003 continues the trend to ever-greater support for the Internet and intranets, although most of the change is incremental to existing capabilities in Windows 2000 Server but significantly changed from Windows NT 4. This is seen in these areas:

- Built-in communications infrastructure

- Internet Explorer version 6 and Outlook Express version 6

- Internet Information Services (IIS) version 6.0

- Built-in support for VPN

Built-In Communications Infrastructure

Support for a modem has been included in operating systems for a long time, but Windows Server 2003 has gone beyond that traditional support with the following features (Module 10 discusses communications and the Internet):

- A built-in router that provides Internet access for an entire network over a single ISDN or DSL line

- Automatic dialing of a modem whenever the modem is accessed over the network

- Network address translation that allows multiple users to share an Internet connection by mapping multiple LAN addresses to one IP address

- A built-in Personal Firewall to provide a first level of protection from unwanted Internet intrusion onto a LAN

- A new Connection Manager and enhanced connection sharing to improve a LAN's access to the Internet using a server as a router.

Accessing the Internet

Accessing the Internet has become a high priority for most organizations, as an increasing number of business-to-business as well as business-to-consumer functions are handled there. To support this, Windows Server 2003 has fully integrated web browsing, e-mail, and a way to set them up with the following tools, all described in detail in Module 10:

- **Internet Connection Wizard**   Leads you through all the steps necessary to set up a modem, obtain an ISP, and configure a connection to that ISP for World Wide Web service, e-mail service, and news service.

- **Internet Explorer** Enables you to search for and go to a web site, as shown in Figure 2-3 (where I searched on "Toshiba"), navigate within a web site, securely send to and receive information from a web site, store a web site's address in a list of favorites or in a links toolbar, print a web page, and maintain a history of the web sites you have visited.

- **Outlook Express** Provides one-on-one communications through the sending, receiving, and storing of e-mail; participation in newsgroups through sending and receiving linked messages; and maintaining and using one or more address books.

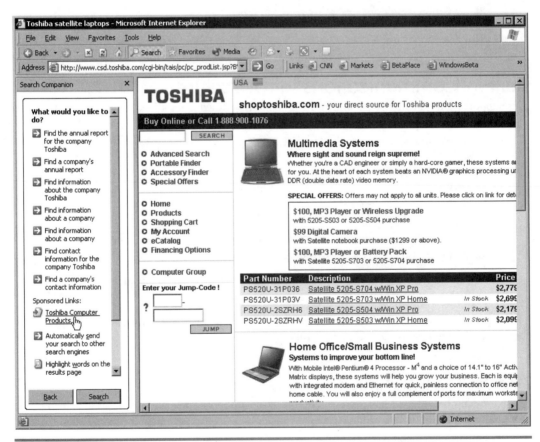

Figure 2-3 Searching in Internet Explorer

Internet Information Services

IIS, the web server for both intranets and the World Wide Web of the Internet, has been included in Windows NT since Windows NT 3.51. IIS 6 is included in Windows Server 2003 and incorporates a number of performance, stability, and security enhancements. Among the features in IIS 6 or in Windows Server 2003 that support web hosting are the following:

- Certificate and Permissions Wizards greatly simplifies the process of issuing security certificates and assigning the appropriate user permissions.

- Enhanced Active Server Pages (ASP) uses scripts to generate a custom web page based on requests received by the server. It includes further enhancements, which in total are called ASP.NET.

- Distributed Authoring and Versioning (DAV) enables greater and more direct control of web pages on a server from such tools as Microsoft FrontPage and Netscape Composer.

- Hypertext Transfer Protocol (HTTP) compression speeds the transmission of a Hypertext Markup Language (HTML) document, which is the text part of a web page.

- Processor Accounting and Throttling enables you to monitor, control, and bill the processor time used by a particular web page. Prior to Windows 2000 Server, there was no way that a Windows server could bill for processor time or prevent a web page from taking over all processor time.

- Integrated Streaming Media Delivery allows the reliable and controllable distribution of industry-standard streaming audio and video directly from Windows Server 2003 without using third-party software.

- Windows SharePoint Services provides a comprehensive set of tools to build and manage an intranet site aimed at team collaboration within an organization.

- Full 64-bit architecture for use on the 64-bit Intel Itanium processor.

Built-In Support for Virtual Private Networking

VPN allows a person to securely use the Internet to access a private network. For example, an employee on a business trip can use the Internet to access the LAN in his or her home office and do so with a high degree of security for the transactions that are being sent over the Internet as well as those crossing the home office network. This is done using one of two tunneling protocols to create a secure path across the Internet. VPN, which is discussed in Module 12, is set up using the Connection Manager Administration Kit (CMAK) Wizard.

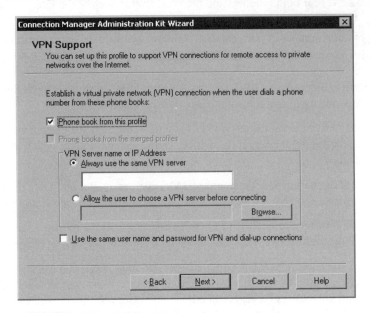

Progress Check

1. What is required to achieve many of the security benefits in Windows Server 2003?

2. What is a smart card and what is it used for?

3. What is VPN and what does it do?

Project 2   Deciding Whether to Migrate

So how do you sum this module up? Everybody will do it differently, but there are some common questions that everyone can use to help answer that question. In the Step by Step

---

1. Many of the security benefits in Windows Server 2003 require that NTFS and Active Directory be used.

2. Smart cards are like credit cards with an embedded electronic circuit that stores an ID and an encryption key. Smart cards are particularly valuable for remote entry to a network over the Internet using virtual private networking (VPN). Smart cards are also frequently used in the issuance of certificates of authenticity for documents.

3. VPN is virtual private networking, which allows a person to securely use the Internet to access a private network. For example, an employee on a business trip can use the Internet to access the LAN in his or her home office and do so with a high degree of security for both the transactions that are being sent over the Internet and those over the home office network.

section, ask yourself the stated question and on a tally sheet note your response. You might use a scale of 1 to 5, with 1 being strongly opposed to migrating and 5 being strongly in favor of migrating. When you are done, add up the responses and see what the result says.

Step by Step

1. Are you are currently using Windows NT 4 domains? Upgrading to Windows Server 2003 Active Directory will provide significant added benefits that will make the migration worthwhile.

2. Is security a major concern? If so, the addition of Kerberos authentication, PKI, file encryption, and smart card utilization are powerful reasons to migrate.

3. Are you are looking at significant network growth? If so, the scalability of Windows Server 2003 is a major asset, and when added to the capability to manage larger networks, these factors could be a reason to migrate.

4. Do you have a fairly large network to administer? System and network administration have taken significant strides in Windows Server 2003 and are strong support for migration.

5. How do you feel about implementing a new operating system? Probably the biggest single strike against Windows Server 2003 is its newness. Any new system demands caution, but a new major network operating system demands it even more because so much depends on its smooth operation. It is probably prudent to wait for at least one if not two Service Packs to be released before migrating.

6. How tight are budgetary concerns? Migrating an organization to a new operating system is a significant expenditure. Probably the smallest part of the cost is the new software. The major expenses are the people costs associated with training for, planning, and implementing the migration, as well as the costs associated with the disruption to the organization.

7. Are you currently using NetWare and NDS in a significant way, and are you satisfied with the results? If so, you probably have less reason to switch in the short term.

8. Do you have a heterogeneous mix of computers, especially one that uses UNIX, Linux, or Solaris in the network with Windows servers? If so, your benefits, especially from Active Directory, will be reduced substantially.

9. Are you currently doing or are you planning to do significant work online either with an intranet or on the Internet? Windows Server 2003 brings many capabilities to the table including IIS 6, streaming server capability, SharePoint Services, and enhanced VPN support.

(continued)

Project Summary

Only you can determine how to weigh these factors for your own situation. The balance of this book, though, will provide substantially more insight into Windows Server 2003, which will help you to make your migration decision.

Module 2 Mastery Check

1. What features in Windows Server 2003 encourage larger organizations to migrate?

2. What are the two areas where Windows Server 2003 provides benefits for smaller organizations?

3. What are the hardware improvements in Windows 2000 and Windows Server 2003?

4. What are the security improvements in Windows Server 2003 relative to Windows 2000 Server?

5. What are the principle benefits of Kerberos?

6. What is the simplified process in Public Key Infrastructure (PKI)?

7. What are the primary Internet tools in Windows Server 2003 and what do they do?

8. What is IIS and what does it do?

9. What is SharePoint Services and what does it do?

Part II

Deploying Windows Server 2003 and Windows XP Professional

Module 3

Preparing
for Installation

Deploying Windows Server 2003 and Windows XP Professional is a significant undertaking that requires thorough planning and careful attention to details. The purpose of this part of the book is to assist you in going through the planning process and then carrying out the detailed installation. Module 3 looks at the steps that must be carried out prior to installing these newest Windows versions for business users, including ways to handle possible pitfalls. Module 4 takes you through installing Windows Server 2003 from different starting points, including upgrading and performing a clean install. Module 5 describes both the manual and automated approaches to the installation of XP Professional. Module 6 shows how Remote Installation Service can be used to remotely install either Windows Server 2003 or XP Professional.

CRITICAL SKILL

3.1 Consider Installation Needs

The installation of Windows Server 2003 and Windows XP Professional is, on the surface, a simple procedure: you put the Microsoft distribution CD in the drive or access the files over a network and follow the instructions on the screen. However, below the surface, the installation isn't necessarily that simple. Before you can actually install the software, you must consider the following:

- Your computers must meet the requirements of Windows Server 2003 or Windows XP Professional.

- You must be sure that Windows Server 2003 or Windows XP Professional supports all the hardware in your system.

- You must know the choices that provide the best operating environment for each of the installation decisions.

- Your computers must be prepared for the operating system installation.

- You must have a solid plan for carrying out the installation.

This module helps you prepare for installation by looking at each of these areas for both Windows Server 2003 and Windows XP Professional. I'll discuss what you need to know to make the installation as smooth as possible.

CRITICAL SKILL

3.2 Check System Requirements

Windows Server 2003 has significant hardware requirements. Review Table 3-1 to make sure your systems meet the minimum requirements.

System Component	Windows Server 2003	Windows XP Professional
Processor	133 MHz Pentium minimum, 550 MHz Pentium II recommended, two processors maximum	133 MHz Pentium or higher, two processors maximum
RAM	128MB minimum, 256MB recommended, 4GB maximum	64MB minimum, 128MB recommended, 4GB maximum
Hard disk space	1GB minimum free space with 2GB recommended in a 10GB hard drive	650MB free space with 1GB recommended on at least a 4GB drive
CD-ROM drive	If CD installation, a CD-ROM or DVD drive is needed	If CD installation, a CD-ROM or DVD drive is needed
Floppy disk drive	Is optional and no longer required for any installation.	3.5-inch high density; optional if CD is bootable
Video display system	VGA or higher resolution	VGA or higher resolution
Input devices	Keyboard and mouse (both optional)	Keyboard and mouse (both optional)
Network device	Compatible network card	Compatible network card

Table 3-1 System Requirements for Installation

NOTE

In this and the remaining modules of this book, when you see Windows Server 2003 without identifying an edition, I am speaking about Standard Edition in the few instances where it makes a factual difference, as it does here with the system requirements. Module 1 shows the differences in hardware requirements among the four editions, and additional information is provided in the following sections.

About System Requirements

The requirements in Table 3-1 are generalized; special situations do exist for which various requirements apply. These special situations are noted in the following paragraphs.

Processors

Both Windows Server 2003 Standard Edition and Windows XP Professional support up to two processors in a single computer, in what is known as two-way *symmetric multiprocessing (SMP)*. Both Windows Server 2003 Enterprise and Datacenter Editions support up to eight processors in a single computer (8-way SMP). This allows a wide range of scaling in a Windows Server 2003 installation, from a single computer with a single processor to many computers, each with a number of processors.

Random Access Memory (RAM)

Windows XP Professional and Windows Server 2003 Standard Edition support up to 4GB (gigabytes) of memory, while Windows Server 2003 Enterprise Edition supports up to 32GB, and Datacenter Edition supports up to 64GB of memory on a 32-bit platform and 64GB and 128MB respectively on a 64-bit platform.

System Bus

Only Industry Standard Architecture (ISA), Extended ISA (EISA), and Peripheral Component Interconnect (PCI) can be used for the general-purpose system bus, with the PCI bus strongly recommended.

Hard Disk Space

The amount of free hard disk space required is dependent on a number of factors, especially in Windows Server 2003. Among these factors are the following:

- The Windows components that are installed. Different components require different amounts of space, and they are *additive,* so depending on what you choose to install, the amounts of necessary disk space will vary.

- The type of file system used. NT file system (NTFS) and FAT32 (file allocation table 32) are more efficient and are assumed in the minimum requirement. An additional 100–200MB of free disk space is required to use FAT.

- A network-based installation requires 100–200MB of additional free disk space to store additional files.

- An upgrade requires more space than a new installation to expand an existing user accounts database into *Active Directory,* which consolidates the access to all the resources on a network into a single hierarchical view and a single point of administration.

NOTE

The space required during Setup (as shown in Table 3-1) will probably be greater than the space used after installation.

CD-ROM and Floppy Disk

A CD-ROM is not required if a network-based installation is used. Windows Server 2003 no longer supports a floppy disk–based start for Setup, and so a floppy disk drive is not required under any circumstances.

Networking

A network card is not required if networking is not desired and a network-based installation is not used. If a network-based installation is used, it requires a suitable server to deliver the files.

Check Hardware Compatibility

After you have checked and determined that your system meets the minimum requirements for installing Windows Server 2003, you need to determine whether the particular brands and models of computer and component devices are compatible with the operating system. You can do this to a limited extent through the Microsoft web site at http://www.microsoft.com/hwdq/hcl/. In addition, the Setup.txt folder and the Read1st.txt file in the root folder, both on the Windows Server 2003 CD, contain late-breaking information on hardware usage and other information you need before you install.

TIP

You can save a lot of problem-resolution time by checking for hardware compatibility and making any necessary adjustments before installing Windows Server 2003.

When you check your hardware compatibility, you need to know the makes and models of all the devices in your systems, and when you do the actual installation, you may need to know the settings on those devices. Even if you are fairly certain you know this information, it is a good idea to take an inventory of your systems before you start the installation, including a physical look at the devices and an online look at how the system sees them.

Take a Physical Inventory

To take a physical inventory, you open the computer case and identify the circuit boards, disk drives, and other components. Because a great many types of computers, circuit boards, and disk drives are available and used, it is not possible to describe exactly how to do a physical inventory that will necessarily fit your system. If you don't know how to do a physical inventory, you can skip it; the online inventory will have to suffice. If you do a physical inventory, you need to consider the following information. (See "Take an Online Inventory," the next section, for a complete list of topics that you need to handle with the system inventory.)

TIP

If you have all the manuals and brochures or flyers that came with your equipment, you may be able to answer many of the physical inventory questions without opening the computer case.

- Type of adapter card (network interface card, sound card, video adapter)

- Make and model of the adapter card (3Com Etherlink XL PCI Combo, Creative Labs CT3930 Sound Blaster 32, Matrox Millennium II)

- Type and position of card slot (ISA, EISA, PCI, or AGP; first, second, or third slot)

- Settings on the adapter cards (interrupt request line, or IRQ; I/O port address; direct memory address, or DMA)

NOTE

The newer Plug and Play cards may not have settings on the card because they are all handled with software.

- Type, make, model, and size, if applicable, of disk drive (hard drive, IBM, DGHS-39110, 9.1GB; CD-ROM, Yamaha, CDRW6416SZ; floppy, Teac, 1.44MB)

- Type and position of disk drive interface (Small Computer System Interface [SCSI], position 0 through 7 or 15; primary or secondary Integrated Device Electronics [IDE], master or slave)

Take an Online Inventory

The online inventory is done by recording information about your system that can be displayed on the screen or printed using your old operating system. The type and completeness of information that is available to you depend on the operating system you are using. In most cases, you get an initial startup message generated by the BIOS (basic input/output system) that provides a lot of information.

In Windows 98 or Windows Me, you can get further information by choosing Start | Settings | Control Panel and then double-clicking System. Then open the Device Manager tab, click Print, select System Summary, and click OK. This prints out a comprehensive report of the devices in your system, the resources (IRQs, I/O ports, DMA, and so on) they use, and the types and sizes of your disk drives. The first page of this report for one of my computers is shown in Figure 3-1.

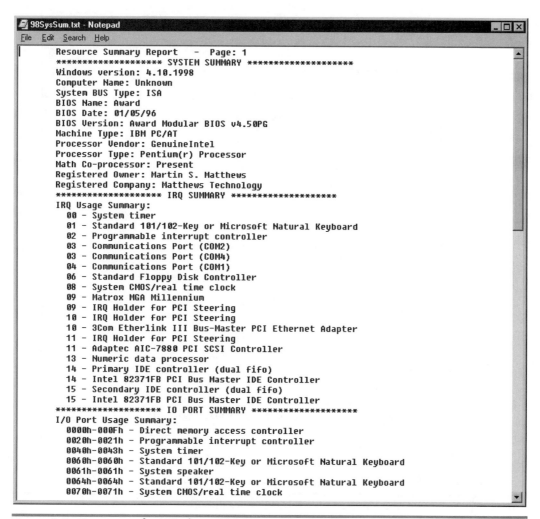

Figure 3-1 First page of a Windows 98 Resource Summary Report

In Windows NT 4, you can get additional information by choosing Start | Programs | Administrative Tools | Windows NT Diagnostics, and then clicking Print. Make sure All Tabs and Summary are both selected, and then click OK. This also provides a comprehensive report, although not as clear and to the point as the Resource Summary Report generated in Windows 98 and Me. The first page of this report for one of my computers is shown in Figure 3-2.

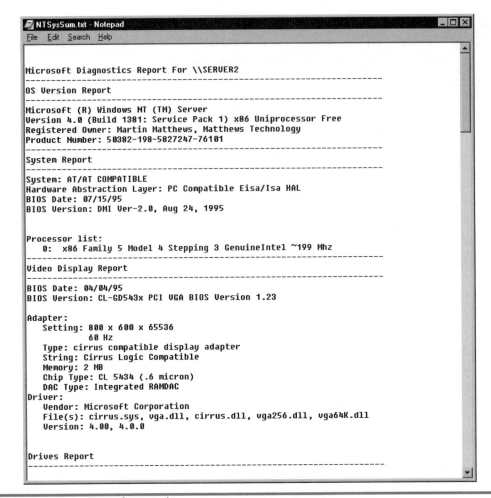

Figure 3-2 First page of a Windows NT 4 Diagnostics Report

In Windows 2000 Server, you can print a Resource Summary Report similar to, and possibly improving on, the Windows 98 Resource Summary Report. This report is available by choosing Start | Settings | Control Panel | System | Hardware | Device Manager | View | Print. The first page of the report for my server is shown in Figure 3-3.

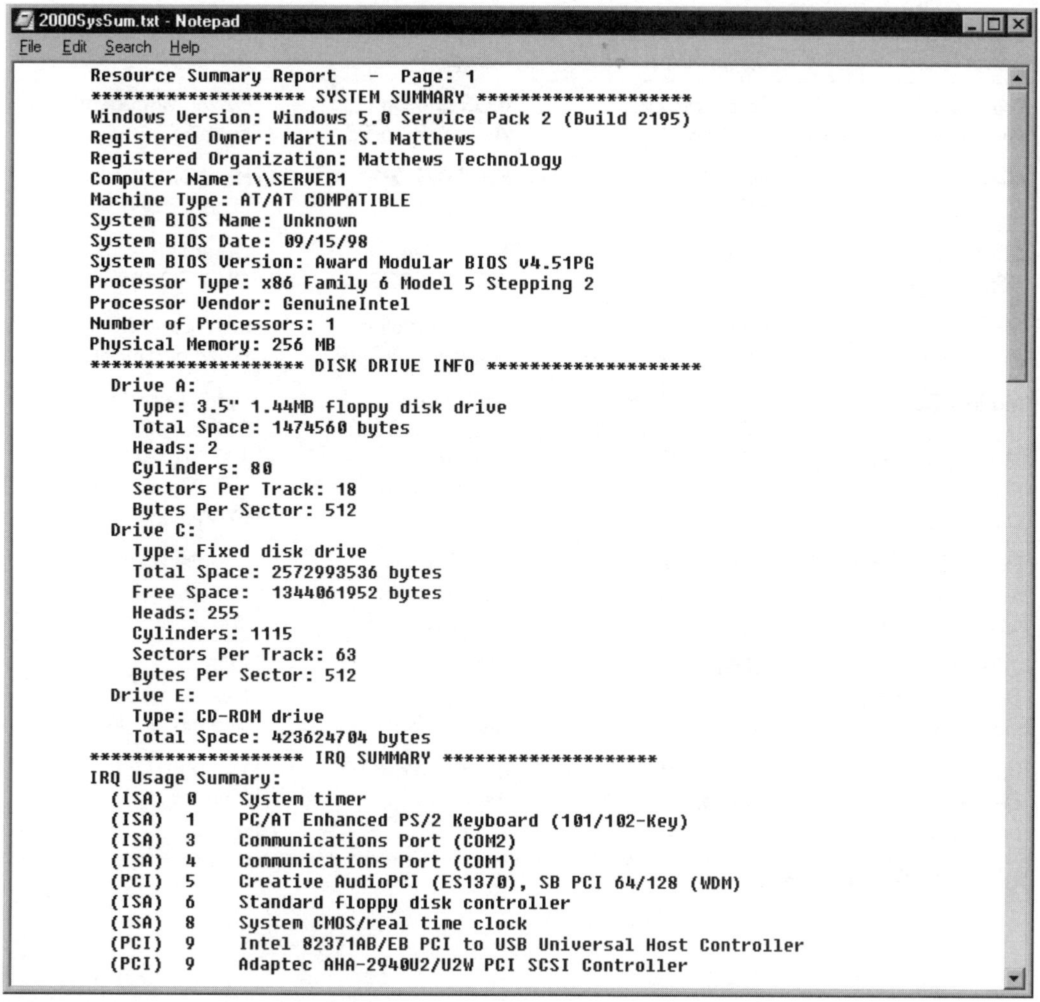

```
2000SysSum.txt - Notepad                                                    _ □ ×
File  Edit  Search  Help

    Resource Summary Report    -   Page: 1
    ******************** SYSTEM SUMMARY ********************
    Windows Version: Windows 5.0 Service Pack 2 (Build 2195)
    Registered Owner: Martin S. Matthews
    Registered Organization: Matthews Technology
    Computer Name: \\SERVER1
    Machine Type: AT/AT COMPATIBLE
    System BIOS Name: Unknown
    System BIOS Date: 09/15/98
    System BIOS Version: Award Modular BIOS v4.51PG
    Processor Type: x86 Family 6 Model 5 Stepping 2
    Processor Vendor: GenuineIntel
    Number of Processors: 1
    Physical Memory: 256 MB
    ******************** DISK DRIVE INFO ********************
     Drive A:
       Type: 3.5" 1.44MB floppy disk drive
       Total Space: 1474560 bytes
       Heads: 2
       Cylinders: 80
       Sectors Per Track: 18
       Bytes Per Sector: 512
     Drive C:
       Type: Fixed disk drive
       Total Space: 2572993536 bytes
       Free Space:  1344061952 bytes
       Heads: 255
       Cylinders: 1115
       Sectors Per Track: 63
       Bytes Per Sector: 512
     Drive E:
       Type: CD-ROM drive
       Total Space: 423624704 bytes
    ******************** IRQ SUMMARY ********************
    IRQ Usage Summary:
     (ISA)  0      System timer
     (ISA)  1      PC/AT Enhanced PS/2 Keyboard (101/102-Key)
     (ISA)  3      Communications Port (COM2)
     (ISA)  4      Communications Port (COM1)
     (PCI)  5      Creative AudioPCI (ES1370), SB PCI 64/128 (WDM)
     (ISA)  6      Standard floppy disk controller
     (ISA)  8      System CMOS/real time clock
     (PCI)  9      Intel 82371AB/EB PCI to USB Universal Host Controller
     (PCI)  9      Adaptec AHA-2940U2/U2W PCI SCSI Controller
```

Figure 3-3   First page of a Windows 2000 Resource Summary Report

The end result of both the physical and online inventory should be a system inventory form containing the information shown in Table 3-2 (example answers are in italics).

For your systems, you may need to add or remove fields from those shown in Table 3-2, but creating and using such a form will help you prepare for the installation of Windows Server 2003 and Windows XP Professional.

System Name: Server1	System Type: Server/Workstation	Domain Name: Domain1	Date: 4-5-2003
Processor 1: Pentium II 600	Processor 2: Model and speed	BIOS and Date: Award, 9-15-98	Power Management: Enabled
Memory: 256MB	Hard Disk 1: SCSI-0, 20GB	Hard Disk 2: SCSI-1, 10GB	Hard Disk 3: Interface and size
CD-ROM Drive: SCSI-1, 32x	Floppy Drive: 1.44MB	Tape Drive: SCSI-3, 20GB	Other Drive: DVD, CD-RW
Mouse: PS/2, Serial, or USB	Keyboard: PS/2, Serial, or USB	SCSI Controller: Adaptec AHA-2940	RAID Controller: Make and model
Modem Card: U.S. Robotics 56K Fax, ISA, COM2, IRQ 3, I/O Port 3E8-3EF DMA—no	Network Card: 3Com Etherlink III PCI, IRQ 9 I/O Port B800-B81F DMA—no	Sound Card: Creative PCI128 PCI, IRQ 5 I/O Port B400-B43F DMA—1	Video Card: Matrox G200 AGP, IRQ 10 I/O Port 3B0-3DF DMA—no
External Modem: Make and model COM1-3, USB	PCMCIA Slot 1: Device, make and model	PCMCIA Slot 2: Device, make and model	Parallel Port: Device, make and model, ECP?
COM1: Device, make and model, IRQ	COM2: Device, make and model, IRQ	COM3: Device, make and model, IRQ	COM4: Device, make and model, IRQ
USB Port 1: Device, make and model	USB Port 2: Device, make and model	Infrared Port: Yes/No	Video In/Out: Yes/No

Table 3-2 System Inventory Information

Handle Incompatible Devices

If you find devices in your inventory that are not discussed on the Microsoft hardware compatibility web site and not mentioned in Read1st.txt or other files, they will probably work fine using general-purpose drivers in Windows Server 2003. The only way to know for sure whether they are compatible is to try to install Windows Server 2003 and see what happens. If you encounter a problem, you may be told about it while running Setup, or the device may simply not work when you are done. If this is a boot device, such as a SCSI (Small Computer System Interface)

Ask the Expert

Q: I can understand the desirability of taking the physical and online inventory, but with over a hundred computers to upgrade there is no way I can do that. Can't I just fix any problems that occur after installation?

A: It is certainly possible to operate that way, but what you are doing is trading time after installation for time before installation. This can lead to repeating the installation or even not being able to complete an installation without replacing parts of the system.

or RAID (redundant array of independent disks) controller, you will not be able to finish the installation. The solution is to contact the manufacturer and obtain a Windows Server 2003 driver from them (you may be able to download it from the Internet).

If you want to use a third-party driver for hard drives with Windows Server 2003, watch for a prompt early in the installation process that asks you to press F6. Then follow the onscreen instructions to load and install the drivers. Module 5 will further discuss using third-party drivers.

Progress Check

1. What are the recommended hardware requirements for Windows Server 2003 Standard Edition?

2. Will the hard disk space required by Windows during Setup differ from the disk space required after installation?

3. What is a good way to save a lot of problem resolution time with hardware compatibility?

---

1. The recommended hardware requirements for Windows Server 2003 Standard Edition are a 550 MHz Pentium II processor, 256MB of memory, 10GB hard disk, CD-ROM drive, VGA monitor, keyboard, and mouse.

2. Setup requires more hard disk than the space required after installation.

3. You can save a lot of problem-resolution time with hardware compatibility by checking the Microsoft hardware compatibility web site and making any necessary adjustments before installing Windows Server 2003.

CRITICAL SKILL
3.3 Make Correct Installation Choices

During the installation process, Setup gives you a number of choices about how you want to install the software. If you consider these choices before you perform the installation and take the time to determine which choices will be best for your operation, you will probably end up better satisfying your needs. Some of the choices depend on earlier decisions and may not be available on certain decision paths.

Decide to Upgrade or Perform New Installation

The first decision that you must make during the setup process is deciding which type of installation you want to perform, as shown in the Windows Setup Wizard screen in Figure 3-4. An *upgrade,* in this case, means replacing a currently installed operating system with Windows Server 2003 or Windows XP Professional in the same disk partition. A *new installation,* on the other hand, will load Windows Server 2003 or Windows XP Professional to a newly formatted disk or a separate disk partition without an operating system, where either the OS has been removed or the partition has never had one (this is also called a *clean install*).

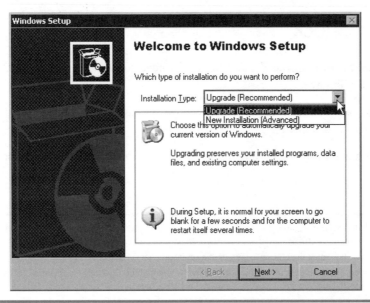

Figure 3-4 Making the first decision between an upgrade and a new installation

You can upgrade to Windows XP Professional or Windows Server 2003 only from the following operating systems:

- **Windows XP Professional:**
  Windows XP Home Edition
  Windows 2000 Professional (all Service Packs)
  Windows Me
  Windows 98 (all versions)
  Windows NT 4 Workstation (all Service Packs)

- **Windows Server 2003 Standard Edition:**
  Windows 2000 Server (all Service Packs)
  Windows NT Server 4 or Terminal Server (all Service Packs)

NOTE

If you are using Windows NT Server 4 Enterprise Edition, you can upgrade to Windows Server 2003 Enterprise Edition, but not Standard Edition.

If you are not currently running one of the identified upgradable products, you can either upgrade to one of those products and then upgrade to Windows Server 2003, or you can perform a clean install.

The major reasons to upgrade, if you can, are the following:

- To preserve all the current settings (such as users, rights, and permissions), applications, and data on your computer. Your current environment is preserved intact while upgrading to a new operating system.

- To make the installation of Windows Server 2003 simpler. Most of the installation decisions are made for you, using the settings in the current operating system.

The major reasons to do a clean install are these:

- To get around an operating system that cannot be upgraded.

- To dual-boot into both the old operating system and Windows Server 2003. This allows you to use either operating system. Windows Server 2003 would be its own partition.

- To clean up your hard disks, which makes them more efficient, gets rid of unused files, and gives you back a lot of disk space.

If you can either upgrade or do a clean install (setting aside dual-booting for a moment; which will be discussed in the next section), this decision is between preserving your current system with all of its settings, applications, and inefficient and wasted space, and doing a clean install. The clean install gives your new operating system an environment not hampered by all that has been done on the computer in the past, *but* it is a *lot* more work. With a clean install, you have to reinstall all your applications and reestablish all of your settings. This is not an easy decision. It may seem like a "no-brainer" to keep your current environment and forgo all the extra work, but you should ask yourself whether you're really *that* happy with your current environment. Installing a new operating system is an excellent opportunity to clean house and set up your system the way it should be, even if it takes a fair amount of extra time. Consider this decision carefully.

Decide Whether to Dual-Boot

Dual-booting allows you to choose from among several operating systems each time you start your computer. If you are unsure whether you want to switch to Windows Server 2003, or if you have an application that runs only on another operating system, dual-booting gives you a solution. For example, if you want to keep Windows NT Server 4 on your computer to use it after installing Windows Server 2003, or if you have an application that runs under Windows 98 but not Windows XP Professional, dual-booting provides the means to do what you want. If you are thinking of dual-booting as a disaster recovery strategy for those instances in which you can't boot Windows Server 2003, that is not a good reason, because Windows Server 2003 has a number of built-in disaster recovery tools, such as the Recovery Console and Safe Mode, that assist in repairing the problem that caused the disaster. The Recovery Console, Safe Mode, and other disaster recovery tools are discussed in Module 16.

You can dual-boot Windows Server 2003 with MS-DOS, Windows 3.*x,* Windows 95, Windows 98, Windows Me, Windows NT 3.51 or 4, and Windows 2000. In all cases, you must have installed the other operating system before installing Windows Server 2003. If you are installing Windows Server 2003 on a computer that already has a dual-boot environment, Windows Server 2003 Setup will create a dual-boot environment with the *last operating system used.* So if you currently dual-boot between Windows 98 and MS-DOS, and MS-DOS was the last operating system used, Windows Server 2003 Setup will install dual-booting between Windows Server 2003 and MS-DOS.

Dual-booting also has significant drawbacks:

- You must install Windows Server 2003 in a separate partition so that it doesn't overwrite any of the files belonging to the original operating system. This means that you must reinstall all the applications you want to run under Windows Server 2003 and you must reestablish all your settings.

- You must handle some complex file-system compatibility issues and you can't share files that use the latest features of Windows Server 2003. See the discussion following this list of bulleted items.

- Windows NT 4's Defrag and Chkdsk utilities won't work on Windows Server 2003's NTFS partition.

- In a dual-booting situation, the Plug and Play features of Windows 95, Windows 98, and Windows Server 2003 could cause a device not to work properly in one operating system because the other operating system reconfigured it.

- Windows NT 4's Emergency Repair Disk won't work after installing Windows Server 2003.

- Dual-booting takes up a lot of disk space with two complete operating systems.

- Dual-booting makes the operating environment much more complex than it would be otherwise.

- You cannot use dynamic disks, a feature that allows you to adjust the partitioning without reformatting the disk, if you use dual-booting.

When you dual-boot, both operating systems must be able to read the files that you want to share between them. This means that the shared files must be stored in a file system that both operating systems can use. When you install Windows Server 2003, you have a choice of NTFS, FAT, and FAT32 file systems. (See the next section, "Choose the File System," for more information.) NTFS has significant features in Windows Server 2003, such as Active Directory, improved security, and file encryption, but these features are not usable by Windows NT. In addition, Windows NT 4 can access only the latest NTFS (NTFS 5) files if you have installed Service Pack 4 or later, and you still cannot use all the features of NTFS 5. Therefore, if you choose NTFS as your common operating system, you run the risk of Windows NT not being able to access the files. On the other hand, if you choose FAT, the lowest common denominator, you give up many of the benefits of a more powerful file system, such as file-level security and large disks; plus FAT32 cannot be used by Windows NT.

NOTE

Windows Server 2003 can't be installed on, or directly access files on, a volume that has been compressed with DoubleSpace or DriveSpace.

One possible file system solution when dual-booting Windows NT and Windows Server 2003 is to use FAT for the Windows NT partition where all shared files are stored and use NTFS for the Windows Server 2003 partition, knowing that Windows NT probably will not be able to access the files in the NTFS partition.

Dual-booting is a compromise and doesn't give you all that you can get out of Windows Server 2003. It is therefore not recommended unless you have a need that is not handled any other way, such as a needed application that does not run under Windows Server 2003—and even in this case, you might leave the application on a dedicated server and move most of your work to another server running just Windows Server 2003.

NOTE

Although Windows NT may not be able to access some NTFS files on the same computer in a dual-boot situation, it, along with all other operating systems, can access those same files if the access is over a network (the server translates the files as they are passed to the network).

Choose the File System

If you just read the preceding section on dual-booting, you might think that choosing the file system to use with Windows Server 2003 is too complex. In fact, it is not. In all but the dual-booting circumstance just described, you do want to use NTFS because it provides many significant advantages that far outweigh any consideration for FAT or FAT32. NTFS provides the following benefits:

- It allows and fully supports the use of disk volumes up to 2TB (terabytes), and files can be as large as the total disk volume. Files on FAT are limited to 2GB, and files on FAT32 are limited to 4GB.

- It provides much more efficient large file and volume handling than does FAT or FAT32.

- It allows the use of file-level security, where you can identify how individual files are shared. In FAT and FAT32, this cannot be done below the folder level.

- It supports Active Directory and domains for improved security, flexibility, and manageability. This is not available with FAT and FAT32.

- It allows the encryption of individual files as well as offline files for a very high level of security, a feature that is not available with FAT and FAT32.

- It provides for *sparse files,* which are very large files that take up only the disk space needed for the portion of the file that has been written.

- It supports disk quotas that control how much space an individual user can consume.

Unless you have to dual-boot a system, you'll want to choose to use NTFS. You can convert existing files to NTFS during installation, or you can do it after installation by using the Convert.exe file, which you must expand from Convert.ex_ in the i386 folder on the Windows Server 2003 installation CD.

1. Start the expansion process by choosing Start | Programs | Accessories | Command Prompt to open the Command Prompt window.

2. Type the letter of the drive with a colon on which you have mounted the Windows Server 2003 CD, press ENTER, type **cd\i386**, and then press ENTER to change the current folder to i386.

3. Finally, type **expand convert.ex_ c:\convert.exe** and press ENTER to place the Convert.exe file in the root directory of the C drive in the computer you are working on.

4. To perform the conversion to NTFS, while still in the Command Prompt window, type the letter of the drive with a colon on which you copied Convert.exe, press ENTER, and type **convert** *drive*: **/fs:ntfs**, where *drive* is the letter of the drive to be converted.

Decide on Partitioning

Partitioning divides a single hard disk into two or more partitions, or *volumes*. These partitions are given drive letters, such as *D, E,* or *F,* and so are called *logical drives.* When you do a clean install of Windows Server 2003, you are shown the current partitioning of the boot disk and asked whether you want to add or remove partitions. When you have configured the partitions the way you want, you can determine on which partition you want to install Windows Server 2003.

There are two main reasons for partitioning: to have two different file systems on the same drive, and to provide a logical separation of information or files. If you dual-boot, you need to use at least two different partitions to keep the two operating systems separate so that the Windows Server 2003 installation does not replace any of the original operating system's files. Another reason for a separate partition is if you want to use the Remote Installation Service (RIS) to remotely install Windows XP Professional on workstations.

When you are considering the partitioning options, you also need to consider the size of each partition. You need to allocate at least 2GB for Windows Server 2003 by itself, and it is wise to leave yourself some extra space. If you are working on a large, active server, you should allocate around 10GB for such things as Active Directory information, user accounts, RAM swap files, optional components, and future Service Packs.

Under many circumstances, you'll want only a single partition on a hard disk to give yourself the maximum flexibility to use up to the entire disk. You can also manage your partitioning after you complete installation (see Module 14).

Choose the Type of License

When you install Windows Server 2003, you are asked whether you want to use Per Seat or Per Server licensing. If you choose Per Server, you must specify the number of Client Access Licenses (CALs) you want assigned to the server.

Per Server Licensing

Per Server licensing determines the number of the *concurrent connections* to the server. Any workstation can use one of the connections, but you can have only so many connections at any one time. Each connection requires one CAL. The individual workstations do not need their own CAL; they can share several so long as they are not all connected at the same time, but they do need a license for their own operating system, such as Windows XP Professional or Windows 98. Per Server licensing is usually used for smaller businesses that have only one server, and it should be used if you don't know which licensing option to use. You can switch from Per Server to Per Seat without penalty, but you can't go the other way. You should also use Per Server licensing for Internet or remote access servers, where the users are probably not licensed as Windows Server 2003 clients.

Per Seat Licensing

Per Seat licensing is licensing each *individual computer* that accesses the server. This means that each workstation has its own CAL in addition to its own operating system license and can use the CAL to access any number of servers. The servers can have any number of concurrent connections, so long as each connection has its own CAL. Larger companies with more than one server normally use Per Seat licensing. If you are going to install Terminal Services, you'll want to use Per Seat licensing unless you are going to use the Terminal Services Internet Connector.

The licensing decision is based purely on what you will be doing with the system. If you have only one server or are going to use the server being installed primarily for Internet services, you'll want to use Per Server licensing. If you have multiple servers or you're going to use Terminal Services, you want Per Seat licensing.

Choose Optional Components

You can no longer choose to install optional components while you are installing Windows Server 2003, but you can after installation is complete. It is a good idea to know what the default selections are and how they compare to your needs, so that you know what you need to install— after you have completed the Windows installation—using Add or Remove Programs in the Control Panel to open the wizard shown in Figure 3-5. Although additional components add capability to your system, they also take up disk space and possibly utilize resources such as memory and CPU cycles if they are running. It is therefore important to install only the components that you are certain you will need.

The first step is to look at the major services that are available within Windows Server 2003, as shown in Table 3-3, and determine which are required on the server you are installing.

The next step is to look at the details of the major services that you selected and determine which of the installation options fit the needs of the system you are installing. Following is a list of all the options in Windows Server 2003.

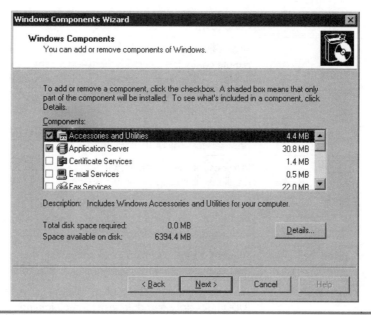

Figure 3-5 Adding or removing Windows components

Service	Function
Application Server	Provides Internet Information Services (IIS), Application Server Console, ASP.NET, and Message Queuing Services
Certificate Services	Provides the means to authenticate e-mail and Internet web transactions
E-mail Services	Provides the Post Office Protocol 3 (POP3) service and Simple Mail Transfer Protocol (SMTP) for an e-mail server
Fax Services	Allows the sending and receiving of facsimile transmissions
Indexing Service	Provides the means to index the text in documents on a hard disk so that full text searches can be performed quickly
Management and Monitoring Tools	Provides the means to develop communications applications with client dialers and centrally updated phone books (includes Simple Network Management Protocol [SNMP] and Windows Management Instrumentation [WMI])

Table 3-3 Major Optional Services Available in Windows Server 2003

Service	Function
Networking Services	Allows the transfer of information among both local and remote computers; includes many other services such as Internet authentication service, DHCP (Dynamic Host Configuration Protocol), DNS (Domain Name System), and WINS (Windows Internet Naming Service)
Other Network File and Print Services	Provides file and print services for Macintosh computers and print services for UNIX computers
Remote Installation Services	Provides for the remote installation of Windows XP Professional on clients that support remote booting
Remote Storage	Provides for the use of removable media and the automatic transfer of infrequently used information to removable media, such as tape and removable disks
Terminal Server and Terminal Server Licensing	Allows the use of minimal workstations or "thin clients" that run their applications on the server, similar to a time-sharing system
UDDI Services	Provides a Universal Description, Discovery, and Integration (UDDI) directory and database for maintaining the infrastructure for XML web services in an intranet
Update Root Certificates	Provides for automatically downloading the most current root certificates from Windows Update
Windows Media Services	Provides for the delivery of streaming audio and video over the Internet or an intranet

Table 3-3 Major Optional Services Available in Windows Server 2003 *(continued)*

Accessories and Utilities

These tools and small applications make use of the computer easier:

● **Accessibility Wizard**   Sets up the system for special vision, hearing, and mobility needs.

● **Accessories**

  ● *Calculator*   Provides an on-screen calculator where both scientific and general math functions may be performed.

  ● *Character Map*   Provides special characters and symbols that can be inserted in documents.

  ● *Clipboard Viewer*   Allows you to look at the information on the Clipboard.

  ● *Desktop Wallpaper*   Provides background images that can be used for the desktop.

- *Document Templates*   Provides document templates for the most common programs.
- *Mouse Pointers*   Provides alternative mouse pointers.
- *Paint*   Provides the means to create and edit simple bitmapped pictures.
- *WordPad*   Provides the means to create and edit short documents.

- **Communications**

  - *Chat*   Allows text communications with other Windows users over a network.
  - *HyperTerminal*   Allows direct connection with other computers using a modem and phone line.

- **Multimedia**

  - *Windows Media Player*   Allows you to play audio and video files on a properly equipped computer.
  - *Sample Sounds*   Provides sounds that can be played back on a properly equipped computer.
  - *Sound Recorder*   Allows you to record sound on a properly equipped computer.
  - *Volume Control*   Allows you to control the volume.

- **Automatically Installed Accessories**

  The following accessories and utilities are automatically installed:

  - *Accessibility Wizard*   Allows you to configure the accessibility options to hearing, vision, and mobility assistance.
  - *Activate Windows*   Provides a registration of the computer and Windows with Microsoft and optionally registers the primary user and her company.
  - *Address Book*   Provides a searchable file in which contacts can be entered and managed.
  - *Backup*   Provides a method for copying files, with or without compression, from a computer's disks or network disks to removable media (tape or removable disk) and back again.
  - *Calculator*   Provides both normal and scientific calculators to perform mathematical computations.
  - *Character Map*   Allows you to copy and paste special characters in any installed font.
  - *Command Prompt*   Opens a window from which DOS-like commands can be entered.
  - *Disk Cleanup*   Deletes unused or unneeded files at the direction of the user.
  - *Disk Defragmenter*   Takes files that are fragmented over the disk and makes them contiguous.

- *Magnifier*   Provides a draggable window that magnifies the section of the screen it is over.
- *Narrator*   Provides voice narration of selected areas of the screen, such as dialog boxes and menus, using the computer's sound system.
- *Network Connections*   Allows you to set up connections to other computers and the Internet.
- *New Connection Wizard*   Allows you to set up a new connection to a LAN, the Internet, or a remote computer.
- *Notepad*   Provides for basic text creation and editing.
- *On-screen Keyboard*   Displays a keyboard on the screen on which individual keys can be selected by the mouse or other pointing device.
- *Paint*   Provides the means of producing simple drawings.
- *Program Compatibility Wizard*   Assists you in configuring older programs to run with Windows Server 2003.
- *Remote Desktop Connection*   Allows you to remotely run applications on another computer's desktop.
- *Scheduled Tasks*   Allows the scheduling of tasks, such as Backup, so that they happen on a prescribed basis.
- *Synchronize*   Allows the network copy of a document, calendar, or e-mail message to be updated when that item is edited offline.
- *Utility Manager*   Provides a single dialog box from which all the accessibility options can be configured and started.
- *Windows Explorer*   Displays files and folders that are on disks of either the local computer or one on the network.
- *Windows Media Player*   Provides for the playing of audio and video files on the computer, on CDs and DVDs, and downloaded from the Internet, including Internet radio.
- *WordPad*   Provides a simple word processor.

Application Server

This provides for the installation and management of several services:

- **Application Server Console**   Snap-in for the Microsoft Management Console (MMC).
- **ASP.NET**   Provides for the running of Active Server Pages (ASP) in the .NET Framework.

- **Enable Network COM+ Access**   Allows the hosting of Component Object Model (COM+) components of distributed applications.

- **Enable Network DTC Access**   Allows a Distributed Transaction Coordinator (DTC) to monitor and utilize network transactions.

- **Internet Information Services (IIS)**   Allows the distribution of web pages over the Internet or an intranet—a web server.

  - *Background Intelligent Transfer Service (BITS) Server Extensions*   Provides for control of data transfer.

  - *Common Files*   Provides files required by other IIS components as well as documentation.

  - *File Transfer Protocol (FTP) Server*   Allows the transfer of files over the Internet or an intranet using FTP.

  - *FrontPage Server Extensions*   Provides server support for many of FrontPage's features.

  - *Internet Information Services Manager*   Allows the management of IIS from the Microsoft Management Console (MMC).

  - *Internet Printing*   Allows printing over the Internet or an intranet and web-based management of it.

  - *NNTP Service*   Allows the use of the Network News Transfer Protocol (NNTP) in IIS to handle Internet or intranet newsgroups.

  - *SMTP Service*   Allows the use of the Simple Mail Transfer Protocol (SMTP) in IIS to handle Internet or intranet mail service.

  - *World Wide Web Service*   Provides for the publishing of web pages on the Internet or an intranet.

- **Message Queuing**   Provides the messaging services needed by applications that are distributed over a network, even when part of the network is down.

  - *Active Directory Integration*   Uses Active Directory when the computer is part of a domain.

  - *Common*   Provides the core components of Message Queuing Service.

  - *Downlevel Client Support*   Allows downlevel clients to be recognized by and to access Active Directory.

  - *MSMQ HTTP Support*   Allows Microsoft Message Queuing Services (MSMQ) to use the Hypertext Transfer Protocol (HTTP) to send and receive messages.

  - *Routing Support*   Optimizes the routing of messages.

  - *Triggers*   Notifies an application when a message arrives in a queue.

Certificate Services

These provide the means to authenticate e-mail and Internet web transactions:

- **Certificate Services CA**   Creates a certification authority (CA) that can issue digital certificates for use with public key encryption of files sent over a network.

- **Certificate Services Web Enrollment Support**   Provides the means to request, receive, and authenticate digital certificates from others.

E-Mail Services

These provide the support for an e-mail server:

- **POP3 service**   Provides for the retrieval of e-mail and includes SMTP.

- **POP3 Service Web Administration**   Provides for the web-based administration of POP3 and SMTP.

Fax Services

This allows the sending and receiving of facsimile transmissions.

Indexing Service

This provides the means to index the text in documents on a hard disk or web site so that full text searches can be performed quickly.

Management and Monitoring Tools

These allow network performance monitoring and improvement:

- **Connection Manager Administration Kit**   Provides for the creation and distribution of custom remote access connections to clients.

- **Connection Point Services**   Provides support for Phone Book service and the updating and distribution of phone books using IIS to clients.

- **Network Monitor Tools**   Allows the analysis of information transferred over a network.

- **Simple Network Management Protocol (SNMP)**   Allows the monitoring and reporting of activity in network devices.

- **WMI SNMP Provider**   Uses WMI to allow applications to access SNMP information.

- **WMI Windows Installer Provider**   Provides access to Windows Installer information by applications using WMI.

Networking Services

These allow the transfer of information among both local and remote computers:

- **Domain Name System (DNS)**   Allows the use of server names instead of IP (Internet Protocol) addresses by relating the two.

- **Dynamic Host Configuration Protocol (DHCP)**   Provides the dynamic assignment of IP addresses as they are needed so that clients do not need a permanently assigned IP address.

- **Internet Authentication Service (IAS)**   Provides the accounting and authentication service needed for dial-up networking and virtual private networking (VPN).

- **RPC Over HTTP Proxy**   Allows remote procedure calls (RPCs) based on the distributed component object model (DCOM) to use IIS to travel over an intranet or the Internet.

- **Simple TCP/IP Services**   Provides the Character Generator, Daytime Discard, Echo, and Quote of the Day services used in TCP/IP.

- **Windows Internet Naming Service (WINS)**   Allows the use of NetBIOS names in place of IP addresses for older versions of Windows networking.

Other Network File and Print Services

Allows Macintosh and UNIX users to access a Windows Server 2003.

- **File Services for Macintosh**   Allows connected Macintosh users to access files and folders on Windows Server 2003s.

- **Print Services for Macintosh**   Allows connected Macintosh users to send print jobs to printers on Windows Server 2003s.

- **Print Services for UNIX**   Allows connected UNIX users to send print jobs to printers on Windows Server 2003s.

Remote Installation Services

These provide for the remote installation of Windows XP Professional on clients that support remote booting.

Terminal Server

This sets up the server to host multiple workstations running applications on the server using Terminal Services.

Terminal Services Licensing

This allows the registration and tracking of Terminal Services clients and is required with Terminal Services.

UDDI Services

These provide a Universal Description, Discovery, and Integration (UDDI) directory and database for maintaining the infrastructure for XML web services in an intranet:

- **UDDI Services Administration Console**   Provides an administration console for UDDI Services.

- **UDDI Services Database and Web Server Components**   Provides the actual UDDI directory and database and the ability to use it with IIS.

Update Root Certificates

This provides the automatic downloading of the latest certificates for use on the Internet, with e-mail, and new software.

Windows Media Services

These provide streaming of multimedia (audio and video) to users on a network:

- **Multicast and Advertisement Logging Agent**   Provides the means to log multicast and advertising events using Windows Media components.

- **Windows Media Services**   Creates a Windows Media server.

- **Windows Media Services Administrator for the Web**   Provides the means to manage Windows Media Services in a web browser.

- **Windows Media Services Snap-in**   Provides the means to manage Windows Media Services in the Microsoft Management Console (MMC).

Choose Network Naming Conventions

In a network, each server and workstation requires a name with which to address other systems. With TCP/IP, which is used in most local area networks (LANs), forms the basis of the Internet, and is strongly recommended with Windows Server 2003, each server and workstation has a numeric IP address as well as an alphabetic name. When you set up Windows Server 2003, you can choose how to assign IP addresses and how to translate a name into an IP address (called *name resolution*).

Assign IP Addresses

IP addresses can be either automatically and dynamically assigned by the DHCP server, which may also be identified as the domain controller, or manually assigned by an administrator. The Properties dialog box for a LAN connection's Internet Protocol (TCP/IP) allows you to specify the automatic assignment of an IP address or the entry of a static number, as shown in Figure 3-6. If you want to use the automatic assignment, a server on the network must have the generation of IP numbers enabled. To do this, you must install and configure DHCP, which then will provide an IP address to each server and workstation on the network each time they log on. The domain controller itself, though, needs a static IP address, which is assigned during installation.

If yours is a small network, the manual assignment of IP addresses is not a problem. You can either get a series of IP addresses from an Internet service provider (ISP) or use a series of IP addresses not used on the Internet, such as 10.0.0.1 to 10.255.255.255. Thus if you have a five-member network, your machines could be assigned 10.0.0.1 through 10.0.0.5.

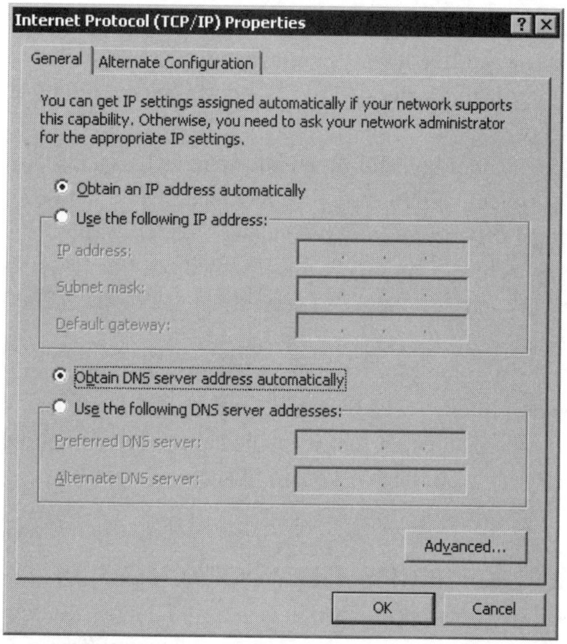

Figure 3-6 Automatically obtain or manually enter an IP address in TCP/IP properties

Ask the Expert

Q: Is installing and enabling DHCP part of installing Windows Server 2003, and if not, how is it installed?

A: Installing DHCP is not part of running Windows Server 2003 Setup. After Setup is complete, the Configure Your Server wizard opens and asks you if you want to install and enable a number of server components, including DHCP. This process is described in Module 8.

For a network of any size, especially one that is growing, it makes a great deal of sense to install and enable DHCP and allow it to assign IP addresses dynamically. This greatly simplifies adding and removing workstations and servers, from an IP address standpoint.

Resolve Network Names

Name resolution allows easily remembered names to be used to refer to workstations and servers; it automatically translates the name into an IP address that is used by TCP/IP. This is particularly important when IP addresses are dynamically assigned, and thus changed, every time the computer logs on to the network. In Windows Server 2003, name resolution can be done using the DNS or WINS.

WINS is an older technology, and if you have clients using Windows NT or an earlier Microsoft operating system, WINS should be included in a domain controller. WINS is installed as an optional networking component (see "Choose Optional Components," earlier in the module). The server on which WINS is installed must have a static IP address. WINS is not required for workstations, clients, or servers using Windows 2000, Windows XP, or Windows Server 2003.

DNS is needed for Windows 98, Me, XP, 2000, or 2003 workstations, clients, and servers, or for Active Directory, Internet web browsing, and e-mail. DNS is automatically installed when a domain controller is created, and it can be installed as an optional component. DNS also requires the server it is on to have a static IP address.

Decide to Use Domains or Workgroups

During the installation of networking, which is part of Windows Server 2003 Setup, you are asked whether you want to use domains or workgroups. A *workgroup* is a simple networking structure used to share folders and printers with a minimum of security. In a workgroup, there is no server structure and little difference between servers and clients. Workgroups are used only in the smallest networks.

A *domain* has a much more sophisticated structure that groups networking resources and user accounts under a domain name, provides for three levels of servers that can keep automatically replicated copies of the same information, and generally provides a high level of security. Windows Server 2003's Active Directory requires one or more domains.

Unless you have a very small network, under ten users, and little potential for growth, choosing to use a domain is strongly recommended.

Progress Check

1. You can upgrade to Windows Server 2003 Standard Edition from what operating systems?

2. What is dual-booting and what operating systems can you dual-boot with Windows Server 2003?

3. What are partitioning and logical drives and why use partitioning?

4. What is the difference between workgroups and domains?

---

1. You can upgrade to Windows Server 2003 Standard Edition from Windows 2000 Server (all Service Packs) and Windows NT Server 4 or Terminal Server (all Service Packs).

2. Dual-booting allows you to choose from among several operating systems each time you start your computer. You can dual-boot Windows Server 2003 with MS-DOS, Windows 3.*x*, Windows 95, Windows 98, Windows Me, Windows NT 3.51 or 4, and Windows 2000.

3. Partitioning divides a single hard disk into two or more partitions, or volumes. These partitions are given drive letters, such as D, E, or F, and so are called logical drives. There are two main reasons for partitioning: to have two different file systems on the same drive, and to provide a logical separation of information or files.

4. A workgroup is a simple networking structure used to share folders and printers with a minimum of security. In a workgroup, there is no server structure and little difference between servers and clients. Workgroups are used only in the smallest networks. A domain has a much more sophisticated structure that groups networking resources and user accounts under a domain name, provides for three levels of servers that can keep automatically replicated copies of the same information, and generally provides a high level of security. Windows Server 2003's Active Directory requires one or more domains.

Prepare Systems for Installation

Installing an operating system entails a moderate risk that you could lose some or all the information on the computer, which makes it a good idea to back up the hard disks before the installation. Installing an operating system is also a great opportunity to clean up and make the system more efficient. In addition, you need to make certain adjustments to the system to make sure that the installation runs smoothly. All of these tasks are included in the following steps to prepare for an operating system installation:

● Back up all hard disks.

● Inventory current software.

● Clean up current files.

● Upgrade hardware.

● Disable conflicting hardware and software.

Back Up All Hard Disks

In a server environment, backing up is probably better disciplined than it is for a client workstation, unless the server also takes charge of backing up the workstation. Therefore, backing up may or may not be a routine task. In any case, it is important that you perform a thorough backup prior to installing a new operating system. This should include backing up all data files, including mail files, address books, templates, settings, My Documents, favorites, cookies, and history. Backing up application files not only is unnecessary (usually), because you should have copies on the distribution disks, but it is also difficult, because the application files are distributed in several folders.

The best technique for backing up data files if you don't already have a file list is to work down through a hard disk, folder by folder, looking at each of the files within each folder. This is definitely a tedious task, but it's worthwhile not only for backing up, but also for the following cleanup and application inventory tasks. In many cases, you can back up entire folders if you know all the files are data files. In other cases, many of the files in a folder are application files, and you do not need to back them up—although a few files might be custom templates, settings, or data files that you do want to preserve.

The tools (hardware and software) that you use to do a backup depends on what you have available. Backup within Windows NT 4 is fairly crude, while Windows 98, Me, and 2000 have reasonable backup programs. (Windows Server 2003 is better yet, but you need to back up before installing it.) The best choice is one of several third-party programs, such as VERITAS (previously Seagate Software) Backup Exec (**http://www.veritas.com/**). Backup media can include tape, removable hard disks, Zip drives, writable or rewritable CDs, DVDs, optical drives, or even a different hard disk on another system. Whatever you use, make sure that you can read it back in your Windows Server 2003 system.

TIP

With the low cost of large hard disks, it might be worthwhile to get one just to hold the latest backup of one or more systems, although you should still also use removable media so that you can store a copy of your data away from the computer in a fireproof container.

Another way to perform a backup is to make a mirror copy of a hard disk onto another hard disk using products such as PowerQuest's Drive Copy for a one-to-one copy, or Drive Image for a compressed copy (http://www.powerquest.com). This way, if you have a problem with the installation, you can simply swap drives or restore a compressed image of the drive.

Another technique of keeping data handy and easy to back up is to put all of your data files in folders within My Documents. This is the default practice of Windows 98, Me, XP, 2000, and 2003, and it makes it easy to determine which folders contain data. Similarly, if you create a separate partition on your hard drive in which you store only data, you not only can easily determine your data folders, but you can also reformat the partition with your operating system and application files without disturbing your data.

Inventory Current Software

As you are going through the hard disks to back them up, you should also take an inventory of the applications on the disk, in case you need to reinstall anything. Separately from the disk review, note what is on the Desktop, the Start menu, the All Programs menu, and the taskbar if the system you are upgrading from is Windows 98, Me, 2000, or XP. Additionally, open Add or Remove Programs on the Control Panel and note what programs it shows as currently installed, as well as the Windows components that are currently installed. For each application, note the installed version, whether it is still used, what its supporting files are (such as templates and settings), and where the files are stored on the hard disk. (This latter information needs to be fed back to the backup process to make sure these files are included.) Finally, you need to make sure you still have the distribution disks for each application and note where they are kept. These steps will assure that you have the knowledge, application files, and data files necessary to restore the applications that were running on the computer before Windows Server 2003 was installed.

Clean Up Current Files

Most of us intend to clean up the disks we are responsible for, to get rid of the files and applications that are no longer used, but few of us get around to it. It is a difficult chore, and who is to say that an application or file will never be needed again? Also, we have all had the experience of either needing a file we recently removed or finding a file that has gone unused for some time.

Given that you have done a thorough job of backing up your data files and have a complete inventory of applications, the question of whether a file will be needed again is moot, because you can always restore the file or application if you need it. That leaves only the objection that it is a long, arduous task—and it is.

The best way to clean up a hard disk is also the easiest and the scariest because it is so final—reformatting the hard drive and reloading only the applications and files that you know will be immediately used. This puts a lot of pressure on backing up well and making sure you have a good application inventory, but given that you do, reformatting the hard drive is a good solution. Still, it is a fair amount of work because of the time to reload what you want on the hard drive.

Cleaning up a server adds another dimension covering the entire user- and permission-related information. Basically, the users and permissions database must be audited and unused, and duplicate entries must be removed. Even harder is cleaning up the user and shared folders on the server. Again, these are the kinds of tasks that often get put off, but they are truly necessary if you are going to have a clean and efficient system. Explaining to users that you have a safe backup, and that if they really need a file you'll add it back, helps convince them that it is okay to remove from the server the *lightly used* (no one will admit it is *never* used) information.

Upgrade Hardware

Like cleaning up a hard disk, performing hardware upgrades often gets put off because it can disrupt a system. So again, use the "new operating system" excuse to get it done. Use the inventory that you took earlier to determine what hardware you need or want to upgrade, and purchase and install the hardware before installing Windows Server 2003, so the new operating system has the benefit of the new hardware. In doing this, consider upgrading the BIOS on the motherboard by checking the manufacturer's web site to determine whether an upgrade is available and, if so, whether it would benefit you.

Disable Conflicting Hardware and Software

Certain hardware and software, if it is running, can cause Setup to fail. For that reason, you need to take the following steps on each computer to prepare for a Windows Server 2003 installation:

- Disable any UPS (uninterruptible power supply) device connected to the computer's serial port by removing the serial cable from the computer. The UPS can cause problems with Setup's device-detection process. You can reconnect the cable after Setup is complete.

- If you are using disk mirroring, it needs to be disabled prior to starting Setup. You can restart disk mirroring when Setup completes.

- Windows Server 2003 cannot reside on or access either DriveSpace or DoubleSpace volumes, so if you want to use such volumes with Windows Server 2003, they must be uncompressed. Make sure you have backed up and inventoried the volume first, because it is possible that uncompressing will lose information.

- Stop all programs that are running, especially any virus-detection programs, before starting Setup. These programs may give you spurious virus warning messages while Setup is writing to the disk. Sometimes these programs are automatically started when the system is booted, so you may have to go to some lengths to find and stop them. Here's how:

  a. Choose Start | All Programs | Startup, and remove any programs you see there. Similarly, remove any program in the Autoexec.bat file.

  b. Restart your computer, right-click any icons on the right side of the taskbar, and select Close, Disable, or Exit if one of those options exist.

  c. Press CTRL-ALT-DEL, and click Task Manager to open the Windows Task Manager shown in Figure 3-7.

  d. Select each of the programs in the Applications tab that are running and click End Task. You may also want to go to the Control Panel Add or Remove Programs and remove any remaining programs that automatically start.

Figure 3-7 Applications can be stopped in the Task Manager

Prepare a Windows NT Domain

If your systems currently include a Windows NT domain, in addition to the preceding backup and other preparatory steps, you need to take two additional steps to ensure the domain's integrity:

- You must upgrade the primary domain controller (PDC) first. To protect the domain, select a backup domain controller (BDC) that can be promoted to PDC, and remove it from the system by disconnecting its network cable. If the upgrade to Windows Server 2003 fails, you can reconnect the BDC and promote it to PDC. If the upgrade succeeds, you reconnect the BDC and upgrade it as you will any other BDC.

- When a Windows NT domain is upgraded to a Windows Server 2003 domain, it will greatly expand the user accounts database to handle the requirements for Active Directory. For this reason, you want to leave plenty of extra disk space for this expansion. While the minimum free disk space for a Windows Server 2003 upgrade is roughly 2GB, having between 4GB and 6GB available, or even more, is not unreasonable, depending on the size of the network.

CRITICAL SKILL
3.5 Plan a Windows Server 2003 Migration

Going through the tasks described so far in this module for a server and several workstations is a fair amount of work; doing it for a number of servers and many workstations is a major undertaking. In both cases, having a solid plan for how it will be accomplished is most helpful, and in the large installation case, it is mandatory.

A migration plan must reflect the organization it is designed for, but most plans should cover the following steps:

1. Identify what computers are to be upgraded or installed with Windows Server 2003 or Windows XP Professional and the order in which their upgrades will be completed.

2. Identify the hardware that needs to be acquired and installed so that Step 1 can be accomplished.

3. Assign someone the task of developing a detailed list of tasks needed to complete Steps 1 and 2.

4. Develop a timeline for completing the tasks in Step 3.

5. Determine a set of installation dates that will provide the minimum amount of disruption to the company's normal activities. A long weekend is often a good idea for everyone except those doing the changeover.

6. Develop a budget for the software, hardware, and labor specified in the preceding steps.

7. Identify realistically the possible disruptions to the company's business and the cost of such disruptions.

8. Identify the benefits of changing over to Windows Server 2003 and how those benefits translate into reduced costs and improved revenues.

Most organizations of any size require a plan such as this, and upper management will look long and hard at the results of Steps 6–8. It is, of course, not a simple numerical comparison. The dollars in Step 6 are hard, out-of-pocket funds, and the dollars in Steps 7 and 8 may be hard to identify. The real question is whether the benefits of Windows Server 2003 are worth the costs, and how well could the company get along without the changeover. Every organization has to answer that question for itself.

Carrying out a changeover from one operating system to another is a serious undertaking. Companies have been significantly harmed when upgrades were poorly done, and they have benefited greatly when they were done correctly. Here are the three key elements to success:

- Have a detailed knowledge of your current computers and networking system and what you want to achieve with Windows Server 2003.

- Create a detailed plan of how you are going to carry out the conversion with minimal cost and disruption to the organization.

- Communicate continually and exhaustively with everyone involved.

Progress Check

1. What are the steps you need to take to prepare a system for installation of an operating system?

2. What are some of the techniques you should use to take a complete inventory of applications?

3. What is the best way to clean up a hard disk?

---

1. The steps you need to take to prepare a system for installation of an operating system include backing up all hard disks, inventorying the current software, cleaning up current files, upgrading hardware, and disabling conflicting hardware and software.

2. The techniques you should use to take a complete inventory of applications include a complete disk review; noting what is on the Desktop, the Start menu, the All Programs menu, and the taskbar; opening Add or Remove Programs on the Control Panel and noting what programs it shows as currently installed, as well as the Windows components that are currently installed. For each application, note the installed version, whether it is still used, what its supporting files are (such as templates and settings), and where the files are stored on the hard disk.

3. The best way to clean up a hard disk is to reformat it and reload only the applications and files that you know will be immediately used.

Ask the Expert

Q: Is Windows Server 2003 really worth the very substantial cost to an organization to install it?

A: It is my opinion that Windows Server 2003 provides significant benefits to most organizations, as discussed in Modules 1 and 2. Only you can determine whether those benefits are worth the cost to your organization; then make sure that the installation process does not erode the net value.

Project 3 Complete an Installation Check List

Use this exercise to fill in the accompanying checklist to prepare for the installation of Windows Server 2003.

Step by Step

1. Determine for each system on which you are installing Windows Server 2003:

   a. Processor: Number _____, Type _____, Speed _____ MHz

   b. RAM memory: Amount _____ MB

   c. Primary hard disk: Total size _____ GB, Available Size _____ GB

   d. CD-ROM installed: Yes/No

   e. Floppy disk installed: Yes/No

   f. Network card installed: Yes/No

   g. Keyboard installed: Yes/No

   h. Mouse installed: Yes/No

2. Compare the results in Step 1 with the system requirements and determine if the system can support Windows Server 2003. Yes/No

3. Inventory for each system on which you are installing Windows Server 2003:

   a. Processor 1: _____, Processor 2: _____

   b. Memory: _____ MB,

   c. Hard Disk 1: Type: _____, Size _____ GB
   Hard Disk 2: Type: _____, Size _____ GB

d. CD-ROM Drive: Type: _____, Speed _____ X

e. Floppy Drive: Type: _____, Size _____ MB

f. Tape Drive: Type: _____, Size _____ GB

g. Other Drive (DVD, CD-RW) Type: _____, Speed _____ X

h. Mouse: Type: _____, Keyboard: Type: _____

i. Disk Controller: Type: _____, RAID Controller: Type:_____

j. Modem Card: Type: _____, Speed _____ Kbps

k. Network Card: Type: _____, Speed _____ Mbps

l. Sound Card: Type: _____

m. Video Card: Type: _____

n. External Modem: Type: _____, Port _____

o. PCMCIA Slot 1: Device: _____

p. PCMCIA Slot 2: Device: _____

q. Parallel Port: Device: _____

r. COM1: Device: _____, COM2: Device: _____

s. COM3: Device: _____, COM4: Device: _____

t. USB Port 1: Device: _____, USB Port 2: Device: _____

u. Infrared Port: Device: _____, Video In/Out: Device: _____

4. Compare the inventory prepared in Step 3 with Microsoft's hardware compatibility list and determine if all the components are compatible.

5. Make the following installation choices:

a. Decide to upgrade or do a clean install _____

b. Decide whether to dual-boot _____

c. Choose the file system: _____ FAT, _____ FAT32, or _____ NTFS

d. Determine the number of partitions: _____, size of each: _____

e. Choose the network naming convention _____

f. Decide to use _____ domains or _____ workgroups

(continued)

6. Carry out the following installation preparation steps:

    a. Back up all hard disks: _____ Done

    b. Inventory current software: _____ Done

    c. Clean up current files: _____ Done

    d. Disable conflicting hardware and software: _____ Done

7. Prepare a migration plan that reflects the organization it is designed for; include the following steps:

    a. Identify what computers are to be upgraded or installed.

    b. Identify the hardware that needs to be acquired and installed.

    c. Develop a detailed list of tasks needed to complete Steps 1 and 2.

    d. Develop a timeline for completing the tasks in Step 3.

    e. Determine a set of installation dates.

    f. Develop a budget for the installation.

    g. Identify the disruptive costs to the company's business.

    h. Identify the benefits of changing over to Windows Server 2003 and how those benefits translate into reduced costs and improved revenues.

Project Summary

Preparing for many tasks is harder than actually carrying them out, but the preparation assures that the task will go smoothly. Such is the case with the installation of Windows Server 2003, but in its case the preparation not only makes it go smoothly, but it also assures it is a success.

Module 3 Mastery Check

1. What are some of the major considerations before installing an operating system?

2. What are the factors that determine the amount of free hard disk space required in Windows Server 2003 installation?

3. What information do you need to collect when you take a physical inventory?

4. What are the major reasons to upgrade during an installation, and what are the major reasons to do a clean install?

5. What are some of the drawbacks of dual-booting?

6. What are some of the reasons to choose NTFS over either the FAT or FAT32 file systems?

7. What are the differences between Per Server and Per Seat licensing?

8. What are some of the techniques and media you can use to back up hard disks?

9. What are the steps needed to prepare a computer for a Windows Server 2003 installation?

10. What are the common steps in preparing a migration plan for installing Windows Server 2003?

Module 4

Installing Windows Server 2003

With the preparation described in Module 3 completed, you are ready to start the actual installation of Windows Server 2003. If you have not read Module 3 or completed its preparatory steps, I strongly recommend you do that before continuing here.

CRITICAL SKILL
4.1 Choose a Setup Method

There are a number of ways that Windows Server 2003 can be installed, but they fall into three categories:

- **Manually**   A person sits in front of the computer where the OS is to be installed and, in real time, does the installation on that machine.

- **Automated**   A script or answer file is used to carry out the installation, so a person does not have to stay in front of the computer being installed.

- **Remotely**   A person sits in front of a server and performs the installation on a computer across the network. The installation can be manual or automated.

In this module, the manual approach, with many variations, is described in detail. In Module 5, the automated approach will be described along with the manual approach for Windows XP Professional. Module 6 describes the remote approach using the Remote Installation Services, which requires remotely bootable network interface cards and motherboards that support them, as well as a dedicated server or volume (partition) on a server.

The process of installing Windows Server 2003, independent of the approach, has three distinct phases, each of which needs its own discussion:

- Start Setup
- Run Setup
- Configure a server

CRITICAL SKILL
4.2 Start Setup

Setup can be started either over a network or locally, again independent of the approach. They both have a lot in common, but manually starting over a network is discussed first.

NOTE

Installing over a network is different than installing remotely. Installing over a network reverses the positions. You are in front of the machine being installed, accessing the network to get the installation files. With remote installation, you are in front of the server installing on a machine across the network.

Start over a Network

If you are active on a network where you can access a hard drive or CD-ROM drive on another computer, you can install Windows Server 2003 using files on that computer. Use these steps to do that:

1. On a server or any other computer on the network (I'll call this the "Setup server"), insert the Windows Server 2003 distribution CD in the CD-ROM drive.

2. Either copy the contents of the Windows Server 2003 distribution CD to a new folder on the hard disk on the Setup server and then share that folder, or share the CD-ROM drive on that computer.

3. On the installation computer, using the tools available in its operating system, locate the other computer over the network and either the folder in which the I386 contents were placed or the I386 folder on the CD-ROM drive.

4. If you are in DOS or Windows 3.*x* and viewing the I386 folder on the Setup server, run Winnt.exe.

5. If you are in Windows 95, 98, Me, or XP; Windows NT 3.51 or NT 4; or Windows 2000 and viewing the I386 folder, double-click Winnt32.exe, as shown in Figure 4-1.

NOTE

You can upgrade to Windows Server 2003 Standard Edition from Windows 2000 Server (all Service Packs), and Windows NT Server 4 or Terminal Server (all Service Packs). Windows NT Enterprise Server 4 and Windows 2000 Advanced Server cannot be upgraded to Windows Server 2003 Standard Edition; you must use Windows Server 2003 Enterprise Edition.

Figure 4-1 Starting Setup using files on a computer across a network

Start Locally

There are a number of ways to start Setup locally, depending on whether:

- You want to boot Windows Server 2003 Setup directly or start it from an existing system
- Your system can boot from a CD
- You want to start from DOS, Windows 3.*x*, or a newer version of Windows

These alternatives and their resultant starting steps are shown in Figure 4-2 and are further described in the next few sections.

NOTE

After starting by directly booting into Setup, you can only do a clean install. If you start Setup from an existing operating system, you can either do a clean install or upgrade from a compatible system (see the preceding Note).

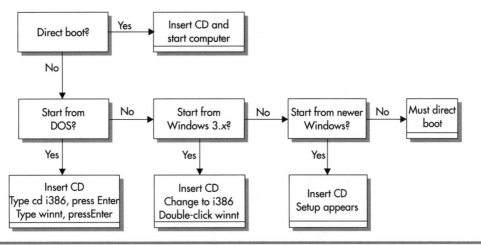

Figure 4-2 Choices in starting Windows Server 2003 Setup

Starting by Directly Booting Setup

If you want to directly boot Setup, you can do so with a new unformatted hard drive or one that has any other OS on it. The only questions are whether you can boot from a CD, which is required, since Windows Server 2003 does not have boot floppies available.

If the system on which you want to do the installation can boot from a CD, then you can start Setup simply by following these steps:

1. Insert the Windows Server 2003 CD in the CD-ROM drive.

2. Restart the computer.

3. If necessary, press ENTER or "any key," as suggested, to boot from the CD.

4. Windows Server 2003 Setup will begin to load.

If you can't boot from a CD but believe you should be able to (most computers made after 1996 can boot from the CD), you may need to change one or more settings in the system BIOS (basic input/output system) at the very beginning of the boot process. Depending on the computer, the BIOS can be changed in a number of different ways. Recent BIOSs from the two most popular third-party BIOS manufacturers, Award and American Megatrends, Inc. (AMI), as well as two Dell Dimension computers, and IBM and Toshiba laptops are changed as follows:

- **Award Version 4.51PG**   Press DEL right after memory check; select BIOS Features Setup; select Boot Sequence; press PGUP until "A, CDROM, C" is displayed; press ESC to quit; select Save & Exit Setup; press ENTER; press Y; and press ENTER.

- **AMI BIOS Version 2.4**   Press DEL right after the memory check, select Advanced Setup, select 1st Boot Device, choose CDROM, select 2nd Boot Device, choose Floppy, select 3rd Boot Device, choose IDE-0, press ESC twice, select Save Changes And Exit, press ENTER.

- **Dell Dimension 4100**   Press and hold DEL as the system is first booted until you see Loading Setup, use the arrow keys to first select Boot and then 1st Boot Device, press ENTER, select ATAPI CDROM, press ENTER, similarly choose Floppy for 2nd Boot Device and IDE-HDD for the 3rd Boot Device, press F10 to save and exit, select Yes, and press ENTER.

- **Dell Dimension 2300**   Press and hold F2 as the system is first booted (when you see the Blue Dell screen), use the arrow keys to first select Boot, press ENTER, and then 1st Boot Device, press ENTER, select CD-ROM, press ENTER, similarly choose Floppy for 2nd Boot Device and Hard Disk for the 3rd Boot Device, press F10 to save and exit, select Yes, and press ENTER.

- **IBM 770 Laptop**   Press and hold F1 as the system is first booted (when you see the initial memory check), use the mouse to first click Start Up, click Power-On, click Reset, click CDROM for the first boot device, click Floppy for the second boot device, and HDD-1 for the third boot device, click OK, click exit, click Restart, and click OK again.

- **Toshiba Satellite 1400/1405 Laptop**   Press and hold ESC when you first turn on the computer. Press F1 when told to do so, use the arrow keys to select Boot Priority, press the SPACEBAR until you see CD-ROM – LAN – FDD – HDD, press END to save and exit, and select Y to indicate you are sure.

NOTE

If you have two CD-ROM type of devices, such as a DVD or CD-RW, try them both; one may work and the other not.

If you can't boot from a CD, then the only other alternative is to install another operating system that can boot from floppies, and then start Windows Server 2003 Setup from that other operating system (see the next section).

Starting from Another Operating System

You can start Windows Server 2003 Setup from these other operating systems ("starting" Setup from these OSs doesn't mean you can "upgrade" from them):

- MS-DOS

- Windows 3.1, Windows 3.11, or Windows for Workgroups

- Windows 95, 98, or Me, any version

- Windows NT 3.51, Windows NT 4 (any service packs), Windows 2000 (any service packs), or Windows XP either edition

Starting from DOS   With DOS running on the computer on which you want to install Windows Server 2003, use these steps to do the installation:

1. Insert the Windows Server 2003 CD in its drive.

2. At the DOS prompt, make the CD-ROM drive current by typing, for example, **d:** and pressing ENTER.

3. Type **cd** and press ENTER. The directory will be changed to I386.

4. Type **winnt** and press ENTER. Windows Server 2003 Setup will begin to load.

TIP

Running Setup from DOS or Windows 3.x is much slower than either directly booting from the CD or starting from a newer version of Windows. See the section "Running a Clean Install Started in Other Ways" later in this module, where it discusses using SmartDrive to speed up DOS and Windows 3.x installs.

Starting from Windows 3.x   With Windows 3.x running on the computer on which you want to install Windows Server 2003, use these steps to do the installation:

1. Insert the Windows Server 2003 CD in its drive.

2. Start File Manager and open the CD-ROM drive.

3. Browse to and open the I386 folder.

4. Browse to and double-click Winnt.exe.

5. Windows Server 2003 Setup will begin to load.

Starting from a Newer Windows   With Windows 95/98/Me, Windows NT 3.51/4, or Windows 2000/XP running on the computer where you want to install Windows Server 2003, use these steps to do the installation:

1. Insert the Windows Server 2003 CD in its drive.

2. The Autorun feature, if active, will load the CD, and a Welcome message will appear, as shown in Figure 4-3.

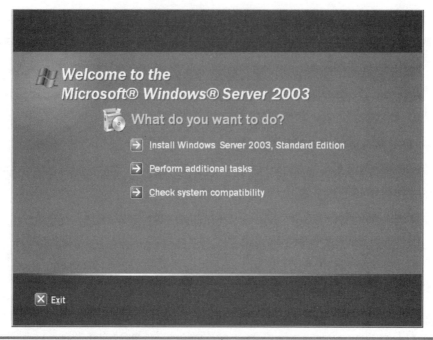

Figure 4-3 This Welcome message will automatically appear when you insert the Windows Server 2003 CD in a newer version of Windows.

3. If you see the Welcome message, click Install Windows Server 2003, Standard Edition.

4. If you don't see the Welcome message, use Windows Explorer to open the CD-ROM drive and double-click Setup.exe.

The Windows Server 2003 Setup Wizard will launch (as shown in Figure 4-4), asking whether you want to upgrade or do a new installation.

CRITICAL SKILL
4.3 Run Setup

Setup has two distinct phases: a character-based phase called the Setup Program, and a GUI (graphical user interface) phase called the Setup Wizard. Also, if you start Setup from an upgradable Windows OS (Windows NT Server 4 or Windows 2000 Server), several GUI dialog boxes (beginning with the one shown in Figure 4-4) are used to gather some information that is otherwise done in the character-based process. Also, Setup is slightly different depending on whether you are doing an upgrade or a clean installation. All of these different aspects of running Setup are covered in the following sections:

- Running a Clean Install Started from a Newer Windows Version

- Running a Clean Install Started in Other Ways

- Running an Upgrade

Run a Clean Install
Started from a Newer Windows Version

If you started Setup in a newer version of Windows, Setup has three phases:

- An initial GUI phase

- An intermediate character-based Setup Program phase

- A final GUI-based Setup Wizard phase

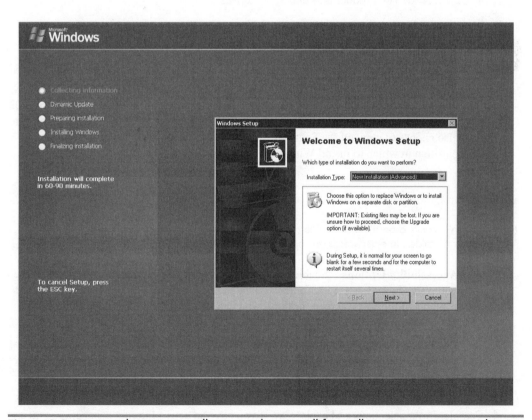

Figure 4-4 You can do a new installation or clean install from all operating systems and an upgrade from Windows NT Server 4 or Windows 2000 Server.

CAUTION

By definition, a clean install means that anything that was previously on the hard disk partition or volume will be removed and therefore lost during a reformatting process, to give you a clean hard disk partition.

Initial GUI Phase

Having started from a newer version of Windows, you should have the dialog box previously shown in Figure 4-4 on the screen. The steps to continue from this point with Setup are as follows:

1. In the dialog box shown in Figure 4-4, choose New Installation (see the discussion in Module 3) and click Next. The License Agreement dialog box opens.

2. Click I Accept This Agreement (or forget about installing Windows Server 2003) and then click Next. The Product Key dialog box opens.

3. Enter the product key located on the Windows CD envelope or case, and click Next. The Setup Options dialog box opens, as shown in Figure 4-5. This allows you to change the way files are copied and installed, select special accessibility options, and change the language used by Windows Server 2003. The specific choices you have are as follows:

    ● **Advanced Options** Enables you to specify the location of the Windows Server 2003 Setup files and the folder in which you want Windows Server 2003 installed. You can also choose to copy all the Setup files from the CD to the hard drive, and choose the partition in which to install Windows.

NOTE

If you don't specify a partition and folder, the default is to install in the currently active partition and folder; in other words, to copy over the existing operating system.

    ● **Accessibility Options** Enables you to turn on a Magnifier to enlarge portions of the Setup screen for those with limited vision, and/or turn on a Narrator to read aloud the contents of the Setup screen for those who cannot see it (you must have a sound card and speakers).

    ● **Language Options** Enables you to select a primary language and one of the areas of the world that language is used. This determines not only the language to use, but also the formats for dates, times, currency, and numbers, as well as character sets and keyboard layouts. You can also choose to install support for East Asian languages.

4. Complete your selections and click Next. If you have an active Internet connection, you are offered the opportunity to get updated Setup files. If you want to do this, accept the option

Figure 4-5 Selecting Setup options

Yes, Download The Updated Setup Files (Recommended) and click Next. You will be told as the dynamic update connects with Microsoft's web site, downloads the necessary file, and finally updates the necessary files.

5. Setup will begin copying files. This is fairly fast from a CD but can take a while over a network, depending on the speed of the network and the traffic on it. When the copying process is complete, the computer is rebooted and the character-based Setup Program is started.

Intermediate Character-Based Setup Program Phase

The intermediate character-based Setup Program phase continues with these steps:

1. Upon restarting, you are given a choice of which operating system you want to start. Do nothing or press ENTER to choose the default Windows Server 2003 Setup.

2. Setup inspects your hardware configuration and gives you a chance to press F6 to install a third-party Small Computer System Interface (SCSI) or redundant array of independent disks (RAID) mass-storage driver. If needed, press F6, press S when asked, and follow the instructions for installing the driver. Setup then loads the files that you need. Upon completion, you are asked whether you want to continue with Setup or Quit Setup.

NOTE

You need to press F6 rather quickly if you want to install a driver. You have only about ten seconds to make the decision and press the F6 key. If you are unsure about whether you need to make the decision, press F6. You can always exit without installing a SCSI or RAID driver.

3. Press ENTER to continue Setup. If you are installing over an existing copy of Windows, you will be asked if you want to set up Windows now (if so, press ENTER); repair the existing Windows (if so, press R); or to quit Setup without installing Windows (if so, press F3). Press ENTER. You are next shown the existing partitions and asked which you want to use for the current installation.

Use the UP ARROW and DOWN ARROW keys to select the partition you want to use. You then can press ENTER to install in that partition, press C to create a new partition in unpartitioned space, or press D to delete an existing partition other than the one from which you booted and create a new one in its place.

NOTE

You will not be able to delete the partition from which you originally booted the computer. You will be able to do this if you boot into Windows Server 2003 Setup from the CD and follow the preceding instructions. You can also delete or repartition a hard disk by booting from the Windows Server 2003 CD, start Setup, follow the initial instructions through restarting of the computer, then choose Repair ("R") and Recovery Console ("C"). Here you have a DOS-like interface where you can get a list of commands by typing **help**. Use the Diskpart command to remove partitions (type **help diskpart** to learn how to do to this). Also, see "Use the Recovery Console" in Module 16. Type **Exit** to leave the Recovery Console and reboot.

4. If you want to install into an existing partition, select that partition and press ENTER. Otherwise, select the unpartitioned space you want to use and press C. If you use unpartitioned space, you are next asked whether you want the new partition formatted using NTFS or the FAT (file allocation table) file system. Choose an option and press ENTER. The new partition will be formatted as you directed.

If you are installing Windows Server 2003 into a partition with another operating system, you will get a message that says the older operating system will no longer work and that this practice is not recommended. If you in fact want to do this, press C to continue and then press L to delete the existing Windows. The existing Windows will be deleted.

In all cases, Setup then copies the necessary files to the computer. When this is completed, Windows Server 2003 restarts and the graphical Setup Wizard starts.

NOTE

Not using NTFS severely limits what a server can do. Most importantly, it cannot be a domain controller and cannot use Active Directory.

Final GUI-Based Setup Wizard Phase

When the Windows Server 2003 Setup Wizard starts, you see a window somewhat similar to the one shown around the dialog box in Figure 4-4. Setup tells you it is detecting and installing the hardware devices on the computer. Continue through Setup with these steps:

1. After a bit of time, the Regional and Language Options dialog box appears. This allows you to choose a system or user locale that determines which language is the default, which other languages are available, and how numbers, currencies, time, and dates are displayed and used for the system in general, as well as for the current user. You can also choose which keyboard layout to use and several keyboard options.

2. Select the regional settings that you want, and click Next. The Personalize Your Software dialog box will appear.

3. Enter the person's name and organization to be associated with the computer, and click Next. The Licensing Modes dialog box appears.

4. Either click Per Server and enter the number of concurrent connections (five is the default), where each *connection* must have its own Client Access License, or click Per Seat, where each *computer* must have its own Client Access License. (See the discussion in Module 3.) After making the selection, click Next, and you'll see the Computer Name And Administrator Password dialog box.

5. Enter a unique name for the computer (it can be up to 63 characters long, but pre–Windows 2000 computers will see only the first 15 characters) and enter and confirm a password to be used by the system administrator. Click Next. If you don't enter a password, you are reminded that without a password, you will not be able to log on over a network. Also, if you enter a simple password, you will get a recommendation to use a strong one (at least six characters long and a combination of upper- and lowercase letters, special characters, and numbers). Click Yes to continue without a password or a simple one or No to go back and enter a strong one.

6. If you have a modem connected to an active phone line, you will next see the Modem Dialing Information dialog box. Select the country/region are you in, enter the local area or city code, enter the number to dial to get an outside line, and check whether the phone system uses tone or pulse dialing. When you are done, click Next. You'll see a dialog box for Date And Time Settings.

7. If necessary, set the current date and time, and click Next. The Windows networking components will be installed. This allows you to connect to other computers, networks, and the Internet. When the networking software is installed, if you have an operating network interface card (NIC), you are asked to choose either Typical settings, which is the default and creates network connections using the Client for Microsoft Networks, File and Print Sharing for Microsoft Networks, and the Transmission Control Protocol/Internet Protocol (TCP/IP); or Custom settings, which allows you to manually configure networking components. Choosing Custom allows you to add or remove clients, services, and protocols, such as the Client Service for NetWare or the AppleTalk protocol.

8. Choose the network settings you want to use, and click Next. The Workgroup Or Computer Domain dialog box appears, asking whether you want this computer to be a member of a domain.

9. If you click No and the computer is part of a workgroup, enter a workgroup name. If you click Yes, type the domain name. In the latter case, you need to enter a username and password. Click Next when you are done with the domain settings. Setup will install the components that you have selected with the settings you specified.

When component installation is done, Start menu items are installed, components are registered, settings are saved, all temporary files are removed, and the system is restarted.

10. When the system is restarted, upon request, press CTRL-ALT-DEL, enter the Administrator's password you first entered in Step 5, and click OK. If you installed the Client Service for NetWare, you will be asked to identify the NetWare server to which you want to connect. If you have none, leave None displayed and click OK.

When loading is complete, the Windows Server 2003 desktop will appear with its default icons and the Manage Your Server window, shown in Figure 4-6. This window and the steps to configure Windows Server 2003 are discussed later in this module under "Configure a Server."

A Display Settings balloon may appear pointing to an icon on the right of the taskbar. Clicking this icon or in the balloon will bring up a dialog box asking if you want Windows to automatically correct the screen resolution and color. Click Yes to do that or No to ignore the issue for the moment.

Another balloon will eventually appear reminding you that you have 30 days to activate Windows Server 2003. See the section later in this module entitled "Activate and Register the Software."

Figure 4-6 The initial Manage Your Server window displayed the first time Windows Server 2003 is started

Progress Check

1. Can you update the current operating system when you directly boot the Windows Server 2003 CD?

2. Can you keep your program and data files in the same partition in which you do a clean install?

3. When asked to choose the file system you want to use, why should you choose NTFS?

---

1. When you directly boot the Setup CD, you can only do a clean install. If you start Setup from an existing operating system, you can do either a clean install or an upgrade from a compatible system.

2. By definition, a clean install means that anything that was previously on the hard disk partition or volume will be removed and therefore lost during a reformatting process, to give you a clean hard disk partition.

3. Not using NTFS severely limits what a server can do. Most importantly, it cannot be a domain controller and cannot use Active Directory.

Run a Clean Install Started in Other Ways

When you boot from a CD, or start from DOS or Windows 3.*x,* you have only two phases: the character-based Setup Program and the GUI-based Setup Wizard. You see none of the startup GUI dialog boxes but go right into the character-based Setup Program.

Character-Based Setup Program

Having started Setup, begin the character-based Setup Program with the following steps:

1. If your boot device does not contain your Setup files, you need to confirm the drive and folder where those files exist. Often, the CD-ROM drive is drive D:, in which case the correct response would be **D:.** When the correct drive and folder are displayed, press ENTER.

2. If you are starting from an older version (5.*x* or 6.*x*) of DOS or Windows 3.*x* and don't have the DOS SmartDrive disk-caching system loaded, you will be reminded that having it will greatly improve the performance of Setup (although it is still slow compared to other ways of starting Setup). SmartDrive is started with the program Smartdrv.exe that was included with DOS 6.*x* and Windows 3.*x.* If you look at the original distribution diskettes for these products, you will see the file Smartdrv.ex_. This is a compressed file that must be expanded with Expand.exe, also on the distribution diskettes (type **expand a:\smartdrv.ex_ c:\smartdrv.exe**, assuming that you are in the directory with Expand.exe). With Smartdrv.exe in the root directory of the hard disk, add the line **smartdrv.exe** to the Autoexec.bat file. After you have started DOS, you can check to see if SmartDrive is loaded by typing **smartdrv** and pressing ENTER. If loaded, you will see a report of the version, cache size, and status. An initial set of files is copied to the hard disk, which can be a very slow process if you started from DOS or Windows 3.*x,* and your system is rebooted.

3. Setup inspects your hardware configuration and gives you the opportunity to press F6 to install a third-party SCSI or RAID mass-storage driver. If needed, press F6 and follow the instructions for installing the driver. Press F2 for an Automatic System Recovery (ASR, see Module 16). Setup then loads the files that you need.

NOTE

You need to press F6 rather quickly if you want to install a driver. You have only about ten seconds to make the decision and press the F6 key. If you are unsure about whether you need to press F6, press it. You can always exit that question without installing a SCSI or RAID driver.

4. Setup asks whether you want to repair the existing installation of Windows (even if there isn't one installed) or set up a new Windows Server 2003 installation. Press ENTER for a new installation.

5. The Microsoft License Agreement is displayed, and you are asked to press F8 if you agree to it or ESC if you don't. If you want to install Windows Server 2003, press F8.

6. If there is an existing Windows installation, you'll be asked again whether you want to repair that installation, which you can do by pressing R, or install a fresh copy of Windows Server 2003 by pressing ESC.

7. You are next shown the existing partitions and asked which you want to use for the current installation.

8. Use the UP ARROW and DOWN ARROW keys to select the partition you want to use. You then can press ENTER to install in that partition, press C to create a new partition in unpartitioned space, or press D to delete an existing partition and create a new one in its place.

9. If you truly want to do a clean install, press D. Confirm that you want to delete a system partition by pressing ENTER and then pressing L. To set up Windows Server 2003 in the unpartitioned space, press ENTER (a partition will automatically be created for you).

10. Select whether you want the new partition formatted using NTFS (recommended) or the FAT file system, whether you want a quick or normal format (if you want to really make sure you have cleaned off all the old material from the disk, choose the normal format; otherwise, choose quick, which is much faster) and then press ENTER. The new partition will be formatted as you directed.

11. If you have an existing FAT or FAT32 partition, you will be asked whether you want to convert it to NTFS (recommended) or leave the current file system intact. Select Convert and press ENTER. Confirm that you want to convert the partition by pressing C.

When the conversion or formatting is done, the remaining files are copied to the hard disk. Upon completion, the computer is restarted and the GUI-based Windows Server 2003 Setup Wizard is started.

GUI-Based Setup Wizard

When the Windows Server 2003 Setup Wizard starts, you will see the window shown in the background of Figure 4-4 and installation continues by detecting and installing the hardware devices on the computer. When that is done, the Regional And Language Options dialog box appears. This allows you to choose a system or user locale that determines which language is the default; which other languages are available; and how numbers, currencies, time, and dates are displayed and used for the system in general, as well as for the current user. You can also choose which keyboard layout to use and several keyboard options. Continue through Setup with these steps:

1. Select the regional settings that you want, and click Next. The Personalize Your Software dialog box will appear.

2. Enter the person's name and organization to be associated with the computer, and click Next. The Product Key dialog box appears.

3. Enter the 25-character product key that appears on the Windows Server 2003 envelope or case. When you are finished, click Next. The Licensing Modes dialog box appears.

4. Either click Per Server and enter the number of concurrent connections (five is the default), where each *connection* must have its own Client Access License, or click Per Seat, where each *computer* must have its own Client Access License. (See the discussion in Module 3.) After making the selection, click Next, and you'll see the Computer Name And Administrative Password dialog box.

5. Enter a unique name for the computer (it can be up to 63 characters long, but pre–Windows Server 2003 computers will see only the first 15 characters) and enter and confirm a password to be used by the system administrator. Click Next. (If you don't enter a strong password, you will be encouraged to do so.)

6. If you have an active modem, you will be asked for the country/region you are in, the local area or city code, the number to dial for an outside line, and whether the phone system uses tone or pulse dialing. When you are done, click Next. You'll see a dialog box for Date And Time Settings.

7. If necessary, set the current date and time, and click Next. The Windows networking components will be installed, and if you have a working NIC, the Networking Settings dialog box will appear. This allows you to connect to other computers, networks, and the Internet.

   When the networking software is installed, you are asked to choose either Typical settings, which creates network connections using the Client for Microsoft Networks, File and Print Sharing for Microsoft Networks, and the TCP/IP protocol with automatic addressing, or Custom settings, which allows you to manually configure networking components. Choosing Custom allows you to add or remove clients, services, and protocols, such as Client Service for NetWare and the NWLink IPX/SPX/NetBIOS Compatible protocol.

8. Choose the Network settings you want to use, and click Next. The Workgroup Or Computer Domain dialog box appears, asking whether you want this computer to be a member of a domain.

9. If you answer No and the computer is part of a workgroup, enter a workgroup name. If you answer Yes, type the domain name. In the latter case, you need to enter a username and password that has administrator privileges on the domain. Click Next when you are done with the domain settings. Setup will install the components that you have selected with the settings you specified.

   When component installation is done, Start menu items are installed, components are registered, settings are saved, and all temporary files are removed.

10. When the Setup Wizard is finished, the system is restarted; upon request, if you are part of a domain, press CTRL-ALT-DEL, enter the Administrator's password you first entered in Step 5, and click OK. If you installed the Client Service for NetWare, you will be asked to identify the NetWare Preferred Server to which you want to connect. If you have none, leave None displayed, and click OK. Otherwise, select the server and, if needed, enter the default tree and context and click OK.

When loading is complete, the Windows Server 2003 desktop will appear with its default icon and the Manage Your Server window, shown in Figure 4-6. This dialog box and the steps to configure Windows Server 2003 are discussed later in this module, under "Configure a Server."

Running an Upgrade

An upgrade to Windows Server 2003 must be done from either Windows 2000 Server or Windows NT Server 4. That means that it must be started from one of those products. Also, many of the settings for Windows Server 2003 are taken from the earlier system. There are still three phases, but they are abbreviated, although if you are upgrading a Windows 2000 Active Directory domain, you must prepare it for Windows Server 2003.

Preparing Active Directory

Windows Server 2003 contains a number of changes to Active Directory and the organization of the domain, called its *schema*. To get ready to install Windows Server 2003, both the Active Directory forest and its domain need to be prepared. Do that with the following set of steps:

1. If you have already started Setup, you need to click Cancel, Yes, and Finish to get out of it, and click Exit to close the Welcome To Setup window.

2. Open Start | All Programs | Accessories | Command Prompt, make the drive containing Windows Server 2003 Setup current by typing its drive letter (for example **D:** if Setup is on a CD in drive D:) and pressing ENTER, and change the directory to \i386 by typing **cd\i386** and pressing ENTER.

Ask the Expert

Q: I don't see any place to choose the optional components such as Internet Information Services (IIS), HyperTerminal, and Fax Services?

A: These are now installed after you complete running Setup. IIS is installed as a part of installing the Applications Server in the Configure Your Server Wizard, and the other items you mention are installed with Add Or Remove Programs.

3. Type **adprep \forestprep** and press ENTER. When you are asked if you want to continue, type **c** and press ENTER. The forest preparation tasks will be carried out—it will take a while, and you will be told when it is finished.

4. When forest preparation has completed, but while still at the command prompt and the \i386 directory, type **adprep \domainprep** and press ENTER. The domain preparation tasks will be quickly carried out and you will be told when they are finished.

5. At the command prompt, type **exit** and press ENTER to close the command prompt window. You can now restart Setup and do an upgrade.

Initial GUI Phase

Having started from a newer version of Windows, you should have on the screen the Upgrade vs. Install dialog box, which was shown earlier, in Figure 4-4. The steps to continue from this point with Setup are as follows:

1. In the Upgrade vs. Install dialog box, choose to upgrade, as shown in Figure 4-7 and click Next. The License Agreement dialog box opens.

2. Click I Accept This Agreement (or forget about installing Windows Server 2003) and then click Next. The Product Key dialog box will open.

3. Enter the product key that is shown on the Windows Server 2003 CD envelope or case and click Next.

4. The Get Updated Setup Files dialog box will open. Click Yes to download the latest Setup files and click Next. You'll be connected to the Microsoft web site, any updates will be downloaded, and the Setup programs will be updated.

5. If Setup finds one or more programs that are not compatible with Windows Server 2003, you will be told about them, as shown in Figure 4-8. In actuality the two programs shown here are replaced in the upgrade. Click Details to learn more about the problem and click Save As to save a text file listing of the problems. When you are ready click Next.

Setup will begin copying files. This is fairly fast from a CD but can take a while over a network, depending on the speed of the network and the traffic on it. When the copying process is complete, the computer is rebooted and the character-based Setup Program is started.

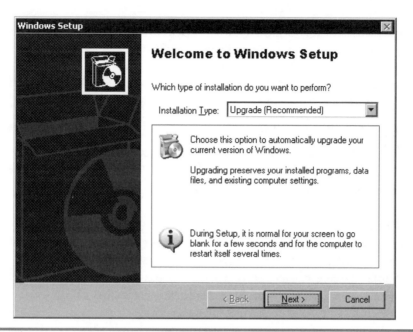

Figure 4-7 Choosing to upgrade an existing system

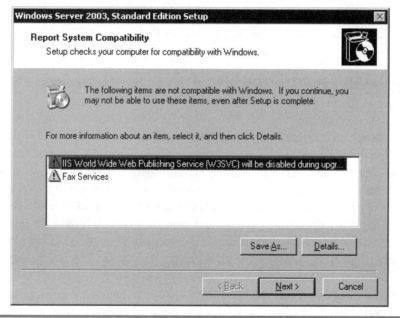

Figure 4-8 Identifying incompatible programs

Intermediate Character-Based Setup Program Phase

The intermediate character-based Setup Program phase continues with these steps:

1. Setup inspects your hardware configuration and then copies the files that you need. Upon completion, you are told that Setup will restart your computer.

2. You are given a choice of which operating system you want to start. Do nothing to choose the default Windows Server 2003 Setup.

3. Setup then begins installing the hardware devices on the computer. When this is completed, the Windows Server 2003 Setup Wizard is started.

Final GUI Phase

In a normal upgrade, the final GUI phase is just a series of messages telling you how great Windows Server 2003 is and what is happening. No installer interaction is needed. Setup will load and install the components that were in the previous system with their original settings. When component installation is done, Start menu items are installed, components are registered, settings are saved, and all temporary files are removed.

When loading is complete, if you are part of a domain, you will be asked to press CTRL-ALT-DEL, enter a username and password, and click OK. In any case, the Windows Server 2003 desktop will appear with the desktop icons you had previously, and the Manage Your Server window (discussed later in the module) will open; if you are upgrading from Windows 2000 Server, it will show the components, such as File Server, Application Server, and Domain Controller, that you previously had installed.

CRITICAL SKILL
4.4 # Activate and Register the Software

Windows Server 2003 and Windows XP Professional require that the software be activated if you want to use it more than 30 days (not the 14 days noted in Figure 4-9). The purpose of activation is to make sure that the copy of operating system installed is a legitimate copy and to tie that copy to a particular computer or hardware signature, so that it can be used on only one computer. Microsoft says that activation, which is done over the Internet, does not include the transfer of any personal information or any information about the software or data that is on the computer. If you wish, as a purely optional item you may also register the installation with Microsoft. Registration ties an installation with its copy of the software to a particular name (personal and/or business), address, and other facts, and it allows you to be notified when updates, bug fixes, and other notices are published by Microsoft.

The Windows Product Activation dialog box shown in Figure 4-9 will appear after you have completed installation, started Windows Server 2003 or Windows XP Professional, and used the product for a while. You may also open it through the Start menu, as described in the steps that follow, or you may open it by clicking the "keys" icon on the right of the taskbar that appears with the reminder notice in a balloon. In any case, complete the activation and optionally the registration by using Step 2 and on.

1. Open the Start menu and click All Programs | Accessories | System Tools and click Activate Windows. The Activate Windows dialog box will open as shown in Figure 4-9.

2. Choose whether you want to activate Windows over the Internet, using the telephone (a very laborious task), or at a later date, and click Next.

3. If you also want to register the product, which is optional but recommended, click Yes, I Want To Register…, and then click Next.

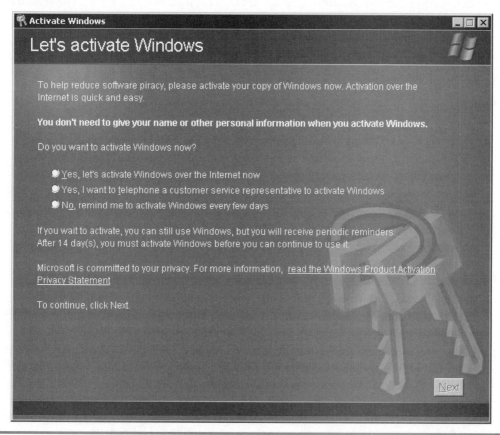

Figure 4-9 Windows Server 2003 and Windows XP Professional must be activated.

4. If you choose to register, fill in the form that appears next and then click Next. Given that you are connected to the Internet, Windows will activate itself and register you. You may go through several dialog boxes to get connected to the Internet.

5. When you are told that you have successfully activated and optionally registered this copy of Windows, click OK.

CRITICAL SKILL
4.5 Configure a Server

The Manage Your Server window, which was shown in Figure 4-6, provides access to the primary configuration tasks needed to get a usable server. Much of the rest of this book is spent on the discussion and fine-tuning of these settings. For that reason, the discussion here is brief and limited to what is necessary to do an initial configuration of a server. The areas that will be covered, out of those available in the Manage Your Server window, and the order in which they will be discussed are as follows:

- Active Directory with DNS
- DHCP Server
- File Server
- Print Server

Other items are left for the appropriate section later in this book (Application Server, which includes IIS, is discussed in Module 11, Terminal Server is covered in Module 13, and the advanced topics, which include support tools and optional components, are largely discussed in Modules 14 and 16).

Before You Configure

Before you start configuring the server, take a quick look at how the server is configured coming out of the Setup. The amount of initial configuration that you have to do will depend on whether you did a clean install or an upgrade. Since an upgrade maintains the previous settings, and even Active Directory is set up if the server is a domain controller, there may be very little for you to do in the next several sections. To check that out, take a quick look at the system before starting into the configuration, with the following steps:

1. Open the Start menu and click Windows Explorer. When it appears, open the Local Disk and My Network Places for a view of your system similar to Figure 4-10.

2. Open the hard drives and the folders on those drives by double-clicking them, to see what is on the disks.

Figure 4-10 Looking at the files and folders in a new installation

3. Right-click your boot drive or volume and choose Properties to see how much room you have after installing Windows Server 2003.

4. Open My Network Places, the Entire Network, the Microsoft Windows Network, and the workgroup or domain that you have there (if you do) to see if you are connected to the network and if you can see other computers to which you can link.

5. Open the Start menu and point at Administrative Tools. Note that you can restart Manage Your Server there, as shown in Figure 4-11. (Your Administrative Tools menu may be different than that shown in Figure 4-11, depending on whether you did an upgrade or not and the options you selected during installation.)

6. Again open the Start menu and click Printers And Faxes to see what is installed. Close Printers And Faxes, once more open the Start menu, and point at the Control Panel to see what is available there.

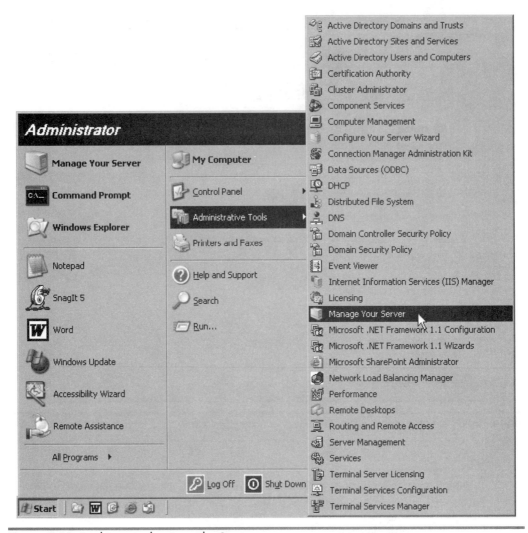

Figure 4-11 Looking at what is on the Start menu

7. With the Control Panel open, point at Network Connections, and then, if it is available, click Local Area Connection. If you have a Local Area Connection, its Status dialog box will open. This will tell you if you are connected and the speed, like this:

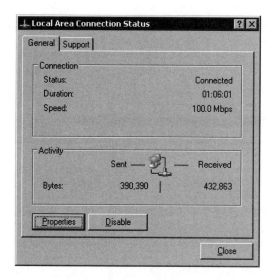

8. Close the Local Area Connection Status dialog box and then look around at anything else that you want to explore. When you are done, close all dialog boxes and open Manage Your Server (Start | Administrative Tools | Manage Your Server).

This gives you a very brief overview of your server, but it should give you an idea of what needs to be done to configure it.

Server Roles

In the Manage Your Server window, click Add Or Remove A Role to choose the role(s) you want the server you are installing to play in the network. After verifying that the server has been properly set up and everything is turned on, click Next. The Server Role dialog box will open, as shown in Figure 4-12, and let you select one or more roles for your server.

Selecting a Role

The roles you can choose to install with the Configure Your Server Wizard are described in Table 4-1. You can run through the Configure Your Server Wizard several times to have your server handle several roles.

Setting Up a Domain Controller

When you choose to set up a domain controller in the Server Role dialog box, you are also choosing to set up Active Directory and the Domain Name Service (DNS). Active Directory, which consolidates the access to all resources on a network into a single hierarchical view and a single point of administration, is a major focal point of Windows Server 2003 and a topic this

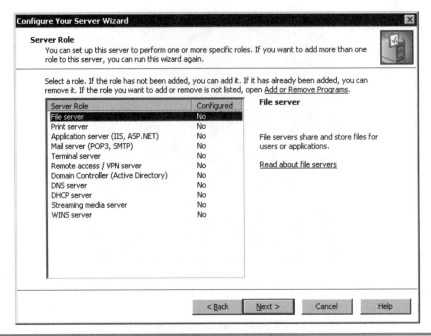

Figure 4-12 Select the role(s) to be fulfilled by a new server.

Server Type	Description
File Server	Stores and manages files that can be accessed by clients.
Print Server	Provides access to and management of network printers.
Application Server	Installs and provides access and management services to IIS, ASP.NET, XML Web Services, web applications, and programs that clients with a license can use.
Mail Server	Installs POP3 and SMTP services to allow the handling and management of e-mail services.
Terminal Server	Installs a service that allows a client to run an application on the server as if it were on their client computer.
Remote Access/ VPN Server	Installs a service that allows a remote client to connect to the local area network (LAN) via a dial-up connection over a local phone line or over the Internet using virtual private networking (VPN).
Domain Controller	Sets up a domain controller with the Active Directory service to store and manage directory information and logon processes. If this is the first domain controller on the network, DNS is also installed with the domain controller.

Table 4-1 Options for Server Types

Server Type	Description
DNS Server	Sets up the Domain Name System (DNS) to translate computer names and their domains to Internet Protocol (IP) addresses.
DHCP Server	Sets up the Dynamic Host Configuration Protocol to assign IP addresses to clients on the network.
Streaming Media Server	Provides web services for transmitting audio and video media over the Internet or an intranet. Automatically installed with Windows Media Services.
WINS Server	Provides the foundation web services for delivering web files over the Internet or an intranet. Automatically installed with Internet Information Services.

Table 4-1 Options for Server Types *(continued)*

book spends most of a module on (Module 9). Here, suffice it to say that if you have multiple servers, you will want to use Active Directory, if for no other reason than that it consolidates the username and password logon for the entire network. Active Directory requires NTFS and must be resident on a domain controller. Part of configuring Active Directory will mean checking for these requirements and setting up the domain controller. Set up a domain controller and Active Directory now with these steps:

1. In the Configure Your Server Wizard Server Role dialog box, choose Domain Controller, click Next, and then click Next again to start the Active Directory Installation Wizard.

2. In the Active Directory Installation Wizard Welcome dialog box click Next. In the Domain Controller Type dialog box shown in Figure 4-13, select whether you want this domain controller to be for a new domain to be created now, or have this domain controller be for an existing domain.

Ask the Expert

Q: In Windows 2000 Configure Your Server one of the roles that you could assign to a server is that of Net Server. Where is that role in Windows Server 2003? Isn't that a basic requirement?

A: Yes, it is such a basic requirement that it is installed by default and you no longer have to select it as an option. All the servers for Windows Server 2003 have networking facilities installed while running Setup.

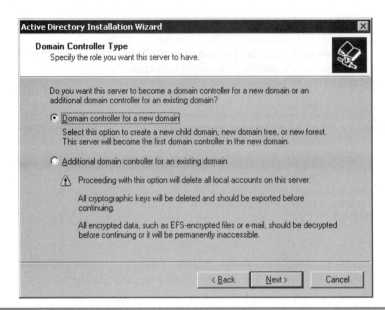

Figure 4-13 Deciding whether to create a new domain to be a part of an existing one

CAUTION

Read carefully and think about the cautions under making this domain controller an additional controller for an existing domain. The consequences, such as deleting all cryptographic keys and making all encrypted files and e-mail unreadable, are pretty drastic, unless you have done a clean install.

3. Click Next. If you decide to create a new domain, choose if you want to create a new domain in a new forest, a new child domain in an existing domain tree, or a new domain tree in an existing forest. Click Next, enter the full DNS name for the new domain, and click Next again.

If you choose a simple name such as "Sales," which is certainly acceptable, you will be warned that the name does not appear to be a full domain name. It is nonetheless acceptable. Click Yes to go ahead and use it, or No to go back and change it.

You are told what the NetBIOS name will be, which is used by older operating systems and is limited to 15 characters. You can change it if you wish. Click Next when you are ready. The Database and Log Folders dialog box will open. Here, you can specify where to keep these files; it is suggested that they be kept on separate hard disks.

4. Make the necessary corrections to these paths and click Next. The Shared System Volume dialog box will open and ask where you want to store this folder, which contains the server's copy of the domain's public files.

5. Enter the folder location and click Next. The DNS Registration Diagnostics dialog box will open. If the current server is the first domain controller for a domain and is not a DNS server, you will be told that under those circumstances the DNS client will not be able to use dynamic updating. You can change the DNS name, make the current computer a DNS server, or ignore the problem.

6. Click Next when you have made your choice. If you choose to make this a DNS server, the Permissions dialog box will open. Choose between pre–Windows 2000 and Windows 2000/2003 permissions. After making the choice, click Next.

7. Enter and confirm a password for an administrator to enter Directory Services Restore Mode, and click Next.

8. Review the summary of actions you have chosen for the new domain and Active Directory, similar to what is shown in Figure 4-14. If you want to change anything, use Back to go back and make the changes. When you are ready, click Next. The domain and Active Directory will be configured.

9. If the computer on which you are installing Windows Server 2003 is not already a DNS server, it will be made one and you may be told that you need to insert the Windows Server 2003 CD and assign a static IP address (refer to Module 3) and that you now have the option to do that. Click OK. The Local Area Connection Properties dialog box appears, from which you should do the following:

   a. Select Internet Protocol (TCP/IP) and click Properties. The Internet Protocol (TCP/IP) Properties dialog box opens.

   b. Click Use The Following IP Address and enter an IP address. If you don't have an IP address, you can make one up using the number range 10.0.0.0 through 10.255.255.255. For example, 10.0.0.9 is a legitimate number, and if it isn't used by another computer on your network, it will work fine. This range of numbers is not used on the Internet.

   c. Press TAB to go to Subnet Mask. Subnet mask 255.0.0.0 should be filled in for you. Change the 0's in the second and third positions to **255** so that you have a subnet mask of 255.255.255.0.

   d. Click OK twice. The installation of components will continue.

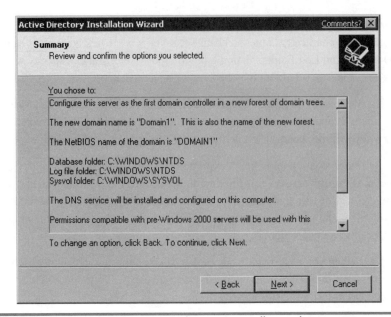

Figure 4-14 Actions to be taken to set up a domain controller and Active Directory

10. When installation of Active Directory, the domain controller, and DNS are completed, you are informed of that. Click Finish. You are told that you need to restart the computer. Click Yes to do that now. When the computer restarts, you are told that this server is now a domain controller. Once more click Finish.

Managing Active Directory, as well as a lot more on how to configure it, will be covered in Module 9.

Setting Up a DHCP Server

If the server that you are setting up is the first server in a network and you don't want to manually assign IP addresses to all the computers in the network, you need to set up the Dynamic Host Configuration Protocol (DHCP) to automatically assign and manage IP addresses for all the other computers on the network. Do that next.

1. In the Manage Your Server window, click Add Or Remove A Role, click Next in the Preliminary Steps dialog box, and click DHCP Server and click Next in the Server Role dialog box. Click Next again in the Summary Of Selections dialog box; after the necessary files are copied, the New Scope Wizard will open.

A DHCP *scope* is a set of IP addresses with a given set of properties, such as the duration that they can be assigned, that have been grouped together for an administrative purpose, such as for the use of one department.

2. Click Next. Enter the scope name and description, and click Next. Enter the starting and ending IP addresses that will belong to this scope, for example, 10.0.0.11 to 10.0.0.19. Enter the subnet mask that tells the server how much of the IP address has to be searched to determine its uniqueness. In the IP range just described, a subnet mask of 255.255.255.224 or a length of 27 is adequate. This says that the last five bits of the 32-bit IP address are all that the computer needs to look at (the server can ignore the first 27 bits), as shown in Figure 4-15.

NOTE

If you try to create a subnet mask that is too small for the range of addresses that you want to use and then click Next, you will get a message that you cannot do that and be asked if you want to create a superscope to contain the range you specified. In most instances, you should go back and increase your subnet mask.

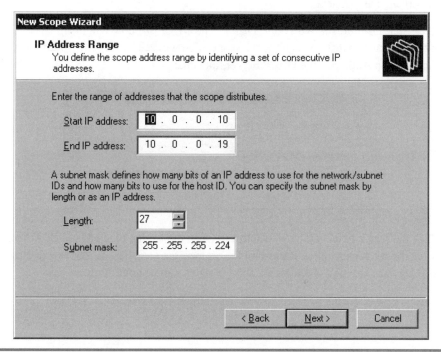

Figure 4-15 Identifying the IP range and subnet mask for a DHCP scope

3. Click Next. Enter any part of the IP range that you want to exclude from being assigned to computers in the network, such as those addresses reserved for other servers and routers, and then click Next.

4. Enter the duration of the addresses' leases and click Next. You are asked if you want to configure other DHCP options or wait for another time. Click Yes and then Next. Enter the address of the router used as the default gateway to the network, either from other networks or the Internet. You can enter more than one. When you are done, click Next.

5. Enter the parent domain and DNS server to be used by this domain. After entering a server name, click Resolve to get the server's IP address and then click Add. When you have entered all the servers, click Next.

6. If you have a Windows Internet Naming System (WINS) server to convert NetBIOS names to IP addresses, enter those and click Next. Click Yes, you want to activate this scope now, and click Next.

7. When you are told that you have successfully completed the New Scope Wizard, click Finish. You will then be told that the server is now a DHCP server. Click Finish again. After creating and even activating a new DHCP server, it cannot be used until it is authorized. Do that next.

8. Click Start | Administrative Tools | DHCP. The DHCP window will open. Open the server in the left pane so that you can see the scope. You will see a (red) downward pointing arrow and a note to Authorize the DHCP Server, like this:

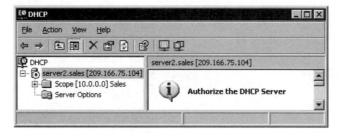

9. Click the server in the left pane to select it. Open the Action menu and click Authorize. After about a minute, click Refresh in the toolbar; the arrow on the server will change to an upward pointing green arrow, and the status will become Active.

10. Close the DHCP window. You now have a fully operational DHCP server.

Setting Up a File and Print Server

With the general-purpose nature of the server described here, a file server and print server also need to be installed. You may need to install others for your purposes. Here are the steps for a file server and print server:

1. In the Manage Your Server window, click Add Or Remove A Role, click Next in the Preliminary Steps dialog box, and click File Server and click Next in the Server Role dialog box.

   The Disk Quotas dialog box will be displayed, where you can determine whether to set limits on clients' use of disk space, what those limits are, and how you want the exceptions logged.

2. Make the desired disk quota choices and click Next. The Indexing Service dialog box will open, where you can turn Indexing Service on or off. If the server you are installing will have a lot of searches performed on it, Indexing Service will speed up the searches, but it will slow down the overall performance of the server.

3. Choose whether Indexing Service should be on or off and click Next. You are shown the choices you have made that change any of the settings. Click Next. The Share A Folder Wizard will open. Click Next.

4. Enter the folder path that you want to be the root of the shared folder or folders (this may be the root directory of the drive), and click Next. If you choose the root directory, you will be told that for security reasons this may not be the best choice. Click Yes to continue or No to go back and change your choice.

5. Enter the share name and description and click Next. Select the basic share permissions and click Finish. You are shown your choices and told that sharing was successful. If you want to share another folder, click that check box, and then in any case, click Close.

6. You are told that the server is now a file server. Once more, click Finish. You are returned to the Manage Your Server window. Click Add Or Remove A Role and then click Next. Select Print Server and once more click Next.

7. Select the type of clients, Windows 2000 and 2003 only or all Windows clients, for which you want to install print drivers, and click Next. You are shown the choices you have made that change any of the settings. Click Next. The Add Printer Wizard will start. Click Next.

8. Choose between a local printer, one connected to the server you are configuring, and a connection to a printer on the network, and click Next. Choose among finding a printer in the domain directory, connecting or browsing to a printer on your LAN, and connecting to a printer on the Internet. If you choose the second option, you can immediately click Next to open Browse For Printer, or enter a path and printer name for a printer on the LAN or a URL for a printer on the Internet and click Next.

NOTE

If you have a local printer, one connected to the computer you are setting up, and that printer is Plug and Play, it will automatically be found and you will not have to browse to it.

9. If you open the Browse For Printer dialog box, select the computer and printer that you want to use and click Next. If you are asked if you want to install a newer driver for the printer, click OK.

10. If this isn't your first printer, you will be asked to choose whether you want this printer to be the default printer. Make this choice, click Next, and then click Finish. You are brought back to the start of the Add Printer Wizard, from which you can add another printer or click Cancel.

11. You are told that the server is now a print server. Once more, click Finish. You are returned to the Manage Your Server window. If you have additional roles to install, proceed as you did for the first. If not, click Close.

When you activated and registered the software, and when you configured the server as a domain controller, DHCP server, file server, and print server, many detail components that in the past required their own configuration steps got automatically set up with Windows Server 2003. If you followed the instructions here, you will have set up and configured DNS, DHCP, TCP/IP, and Active Directory.

Although several facilities within Windows Server 2003 may still need to be configured, such as the web server, which is discussed in Module 11, this module has provided a fully operational network server connected to the Internet. A good starting position.

Progress Check

1. What is the purpose of product activation?

2. What are the typical network settings that are installed by default when you choose Typical?

3. What is a DHCP scope?

---

1. The purpose of product activation is to make sure that the copy of the operating system installed is a legitimate copy and to tie that copy to a particular computer or hardware signature, so that it can be used on only one computer.

2. The typical network settings that are installed by default when you choose Typical are Client for Microsoft Networks, File and Print Sharing for Microsoft Networks, and the TCP/IP protocol with automatic addressing.

3. A DHCP *scope* is a set of IP addresses with a given set of properties that have been grouped together for an administrative purpose.

Project 4 Prepare an Installation Plan

Use this project to prepare an installation plan for deploying Windows Server 2003. This plan will help you navigate through the many steps required for a successful installation.

Step by Step

1. Determine the method of installation that you will use:

   a. Manually, sitting at the computer to be installed (this module)

   b. Automated, using a script (see Module 5)

   c. Remotely, doing the installation across the network (see Module 6)

2. Determine the way that you will start Setup:

   a. Over the network (Setup files are on the server)

   b. Locally (Setup files on the local computer) and started by:

      i. Booting the Setup CD

      ii. Booting from another operating system:

         ● MS-DOS

         ● Windows 3.*x* and Windows NT 3.51

         ● Windows 9*x,* Me, and Windows NT 4

         ● Windows 2000 and XP

3. Determine how you will run Setup:

   a. Run a clean install started from a newer version of Windows

   b. Run a clean install started in other ways

   c. Run an upgrade

4. Activate and register Windows

5. Determine the initial server configuration steps you need to perform:

   a. Review what was done during Setup, including:

      i. Open hard drives and folders to see the contents

      ii. Open the boot drive Properties to see the space left

      iii. Open My Network Places to see if you are connected

(continued)

    iv. Open Start | Administrative Tools to see what is installed

    v. Open Start | Printers And Faxes to see what is installed

    vi. Open Start | Control Panel | Network Connections | Local Area Connection to see if your network connection is functional and at what speed

b. Select the roles to be performed by the server:

    i. File server

    ii. Print server

    iii. Application (web) server

    iv. Mail server

    v. Terminal server

    vi. Remote Access /VPN server

    vii. Domain controller

    viii. DNS server

    ix. DHCP server

    x. Streaming media server

    xi. WINS server

c. Set up a domain controller and Active Directory:

    i. For a new domain:

        ● Create a new domain forest

        ● Create a domain tree in an existing forest

        ● Create a child domain in an existing tree

    ii. For an existing domain

    iii. Set up a DNS server

    iv. Assign a static IP address

d. Set up a DHCP server

e. Set up a file server

f. Set up a print server

Project Summary

Preparing this installation plan will allow you to go through the setup process much more smoothly and with a higher chance for a successful installation.

Module 4 Mastery Check

1. What are the three ways that Windows Server 2003 can be installed, and how do they differ?

2. Is there any difference between installing over a network and installing remotely? If so, what is the difference?

3. What are the ways you can start Setup when sitting in front of the machine on which you want to perform the installation of Windows Server 2003?

4. With a newer version of Windows running on the computer on which you want to install Windows Server 2003, what do you have to do to start Setup?

5. What are the options that are available in the Setup Options dialog box?

6. What program is strongly recommended if you are starting from an older version of DOS (5.x or 6.x) or Windows 3.x?

7. What are some of the items that you should look at before starting into the server configuration?

8. What are some of the roles you can assign to a server with the Configure Your Server Wizard?

9. What is a subnet mask and how can you determine what it should look like?

10. Will a DHCP server begin handing out IP addresses after it is created and activated? If not, what must you do to get that to happen?

Module 5

Rolling Out Windows XP Professional

A client/server environment typically has a large number of clients and a small number of servers. As a result, the installation of the clients, such as Windows XP Professional, cries out for an automated approach. This module covers both manual and automated ways of installing Windows XP Professional. The automated approaches work equally well with Windows Server 2003, if you have a number of servers to install.

The manual installation of Windows XP Professional is very similar to that for Windows Server 2003. As a result, you need to read the "Start Setup" section of Module 4 if you want to install Windows XP Professional manually, because starting Setup for Windows XP Professional is exactly the same as it is for Server. You can start over a network or locally, you can boot from the installation CD-ROM, and you can start from MS-DOS or any version of Windows. All of this is described in Module 4's "Start Setup."

Because running Setup for Windows XP Professional is somewhat different from running it for Windows Server 2003, the routine is presented again here, using the same section structure presented in Module 4:

- Run a Clean Install Started from a Newer Windows Version

- Run a Clean Install Started in Other Ways

- Run an Upgrade

CRITICAL SKILL
5.1 Run a Clean Install Started from a Newer Windows Version

If you start Setup in a newer version of Windows, Setup has three phases:

- An initial GUI phase

- An intermediate character-based Setup Program phase

- A final GUI-based Setup Wizard phase

CAUTION

By definition, a clean install means that anything that was previously on the hard disk partition or volume will be removed and therefore lost during a reformatting process, to give you a clean hard disk.

Initial GUI Phase

Having started from a newer version of Windows, you should have the dialog box shown in Figure 5-1 on the screen. The steps to continue from this point with Setup are as follows:

1. In the dialog box shown in Figure 5-1, choose New Installation (Advanced) (see the discussion in Module 3 under "Decide to Upgrade or Perform a New Installation") and click Next. The License Agreement dialog box opens.

2. Click I Accept This Agreement (or forget about installing Windows XP) and then click Next. The Product Key dialog box opens.

3. Enter the product key located on the Windows CD envelope or case, and click Next. The Setup Options dialog box opens, shown in Figure 5-2. This allows you to change the way files are copied, select special accessibility options, and change the language used by Setup. The specific choices you have are as follows:

   - **Advanced Options** Allows you to specify the location of the Windows XP Setup files and the folder in which you want Windows XP installed. You can also choose to copy all installation files from the CD to the hard disk and then complete the

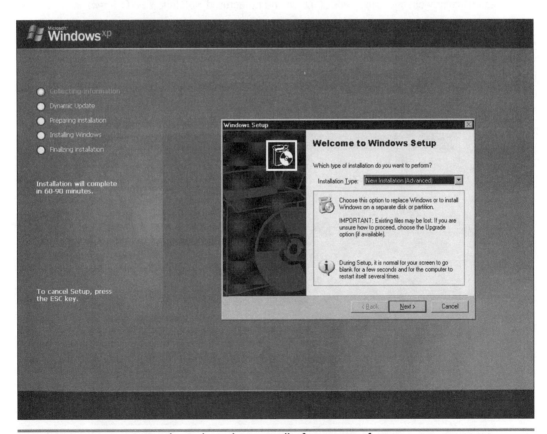

Figure 5-1 You can upgrade or do a clean install after starting from a previous version of Windows.

installation from the hard disk, and you can choose the installation drive and partition during Setup.

- **Accessibility Options**   Allows you to turn on a Magnifier to enlarge portions of the Setup screen for those with limited vision, and/or turn on a Narrator to read aloud the contents of the Setup screen for those who cannot see it (you must have a sound card and speakers).

- **Language Options**   Allows you to select a primary language and one of the areas of the world that language is used. This determines not only the language to use, but also the formats for dates, times, currency, and numbers, as well as character sets and keyboard layouts. You can also choose additional languages you want to use, including support for East Asian languages.

4. Complete your selections and click Next. You are asked if you want to get the most recent Setup files from the Microsoft web site. If you are connected to the Internet, it is a wise idea to utilize any changes since your CD was manufactured, so click Yes. Otherwise, click No.

5. Click Next if necessary. Setup will go over the Internet and download the latest files, if you chose that option. Then it will begin copying files. From a CD, this is fairly fast, but over a network, it can take a while, depending on the speed of the network and the traffic on it. When the copying process is complete, the computer is rebooted and the character-based Setup Program is started.

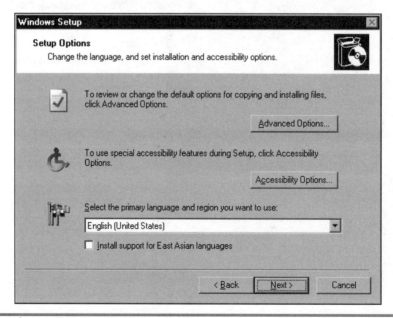

Figure 5-2 Selecting Setup options

Intermediate Character-Based Setup Program Phase

The intermediate character-based Setup Program phase continues with these steps:

1. Setup inspects your hardware configuration and gives you a chance to press F6 to install a third-party Small Computer System Interface (SCSI) or redundant array of independent disks (RAID) mass-storage driver. If needed, press F6 and follow the instructions for installing the driver. Setup then loads the files that you need. Upon completion, you are told that Setup will restart your computer. (If you don't press F6, the computer doesn't restart at this point.)

NOTE You need to press F6 rather quickly if you want to install a driver. You have only about ten seconds to make the decision and press the F6 key. If you are unsure about whether you need to press F6, press it. You can always exit without installing a SCSI or RAID driver.

2. If you pressed F6, press ENTER to restart. You are given a choice of which operating system you want to start. Press ENTER to choose the default Windows XP Professional Setup. You are asked whether you want to set up Windows XP or repair an existing Windows XP installation.

3. Choose Set Up Windows XP by pressing ENTER. You are next shown the existing partitions and asked which you want to use for the current installation.

4. Use the UP ARROW and DOWN ARROW keys to select the partition you want to use. You then can press ENTER to install in that partition, press C to create a new partition in unpartitioned space, or press D to delete an existing partition and create a new one in its place.

NOTE You will not be able to delete in this manner the partition from which you originally booted the computer. You should be able to do this if you boot into Setup from the Windows XP CD. In that case, you can choose "D" at this point.

5. If you have chosen to do a new installation and you are using an existing partition, you will get a message that you are installing on a partition that contains another operating system and doing so might cause the other operating system not to function properly. Press C to continue.

6. If you truly want to do a clean install and you did not boot from the partition from which you want to install Windows XP, press D. Confirm that you want to delete a system partition by pressing ENTER and then pressing L. To set up Windows XP in the resulting unpartitioned space, press ENTER (a partition will be created for you).

7. If you created a new partition, select whether you want the new partition formatted using NTFS or the FAT (file allocation table) file system, and press ENTER. If you select NTFS, you are cautioned that it will not be able to be read by the older operating systems. Press C to convert the drive. The new partition will be formatted as you directed, and if you choose NTFS, the computer will be restarted.

Setup then copies the remaining files and begins detecting and installing the hardware devices on the computer. When this is completed, the final GUI-based Windows XP Setup is started.

Final GUI-Based Setup Phase

When Windows XP Setup starts, you see the Windows Setup window. Setup completes installing devices, and you see a moving bar indicating the progress. When that is completed, the Regional And Language Options dialog box appears. This allows you to choose a system or user locale that determines which language is the default; which other languages are available; and how numbers, currencies, time, and dates are displayed and used. Continue through Setup with these steps:

1. Select the regional settings that you want, and click Next. The Personalize Your Software dialog box appears.

2. Enter the person's name and organization to be associated with the computer, and click Next. The Computer Name And Administrator Password dialog box appears.

3. Enter a unique name for the computer (it can be up to 63 characters long, but it cannot contain spaces and pre–Windows 2000 computers will see only the first 15 characters) and enter and confirm a password to be used by the system administrator.

4. Click Next. If you get the Modem Dialing Information dialog box, enter the requested information and again click Next.

5. You'll see a dialog box for date and time settings. If necessary, set the current date and time, and in any case, click Next. The Windows networking components will be installed. This allows you to connect to other computers, networks, and the Internet.

When the networking software is installed, if you have a network card and Setup sees it, you are asked to choose either Typical settings, which creates network connections using the Client for Microsoft Networks, File and Print Sharing for Microsoft Networks, and the TCP/IP protocol with automatic addressing; or Custom settings, which allows you to manually configure networking components. Choosing Custom allows you to add or remove clients, services, and protocols, such as Client Service for NetWare and the IPX/SPX/NetBIOS protocol.

6. Choose the Network settings you want to use, and click Next. The Workgroup Or Computer Domain dialog box appears, asking whether you want this computer to be a member of a domain.

7. If you click No and the computer is part of a workgroup, enter a workgroup name. If you click Yes, type the domain name. Click Next when you are done with the domain settings. If you selected Domain, you will need to enter a username and password and click OK. Setup will install the needed components with the settings you specified.

   When component installation is done, Start menu items are installed, components are registered, settings are saved, and all temporary files are removed. The computer is restarted.

8. If the computer is not part of a domain, the Welcome To Microsoft Windows message will appear. Click Next. If the computer is not already connected to the Internet, you will be asked how the computer will do that. Click Yes if the computer will connect through a network or No if the computer will connect directly to the Internet through a modem. Click Next. You are then asked if you want to activate Windows. See activation details in the following section.

9. If you are connected to a domain, the Network Identification Wizard will appear. Click Next. You are asked if you want to add a user to the computer. If you want to add a user (you have already made Administrator a user) and this computer is part of a domain, enter the username and the user's domain, or click that you do not want to add a user. Enter the name(s) of the person or persons who will use this computer and click Next.

10. If you chose to add a user in a domain, you are asked to specify the level of access for that user: Standard, Restricted, or Other. Choose a level of access and click Next.

11. Whether or not you added a user, click Finish to complete Network Identification. Startup will continue by asking you to press CTRL-ALT-DEL; if requested, enter the user's name and password you first entered in Step 3, and click OK.

When loading is complete, the default Windows XP desktop will appear and one or more notes ("balloons") will appear in the lower right of the screen. You may be told that you can automatically adjust the screen resolution by clicking the icon being pointed at. You will be told that you can take a tour of XP by clicking its icon, and you will be told that you have 30 days to activate Windows, if you didn't activate earlier.

Activate Windows XP

You can activate Windows immediately or you can do it later by clicking the keys icon on the right of the toolbar or by opening Start | All Programs | Accessories | System Tools | Activate Windows. The activation process attaches the copy of the operating system to the set of hardware on which it is installed and then registers that combination with Microsoft. The purpose of this is to prevent one copy of the operating system from being installed on several computers. You may decline to register your name and address if you wish (Microsoft says that no personal information is collected during activation). Windows activation is started:

● As a part of concluding Setup, where it starts automatically

● By clicking a balloon message that appears in the lower right of the screen after Setup has completed and Windows has loaded

● By opening Start | All Programs | Accessories | System Tools | Activate Windows after Setup has completed and Windows has loaded

In each of the last two cases, the Activate Windows window opens, as you can see in Figure 5-3. Use the following steps to do the activation in that window.

1. Choose between activation over the Internet and over the telephone and click Next. You are asked if you want to also register with Microsoft by giving them your name and address so that they can tell you about updates and new products as they come out. This is optional, and there is no problem if you don't want to do it. In most instances, though, it is worthwhile to register.

2. Choose between registering or not, and click Next. If you choose to register, you will be asked for your name and address. Do that and click Next. The activation program will then connect to Microsoft over the Internet and both activate and register your installation, given that is what you want. When you are told the process was successful, click OK.

If you choose to activate over the telephone, you will be asked to select your location, which will give you one or more telephone numbers. You will then be given an installation ID number that you must give to the service representative on the telephone. The service representative in turn will give you a confirming number that you must enter to complete the activation process.

Ask the Expert

Q: I really don't want to give my name and address to Microsoft when I activate Windows XP. How can I avoid that?

A: You do not give your name and address to Microsoft at the time of activation, and they say that no personal information is collected at that time. They do ask you to register, which collects your name and address, but that is optional and you can skip it.

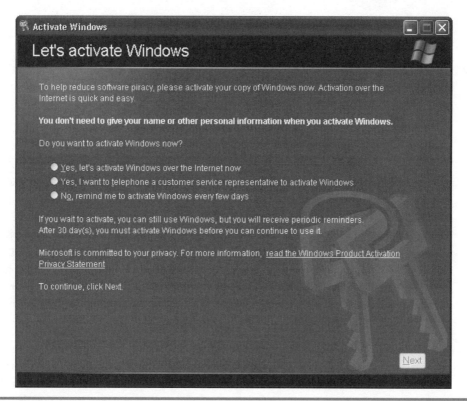

Figure 5-3 Activating Windows

CRITICAL SKILL
5.2 # Run a Clean Install Started in Other Ways

When you boot from a CD or start from DOS or Windows 3.*x,* you have only two phases: the
character-based Setup Program and the GUI-based Setup Wizard. You see none of the startup
GUI dialog boxes but go right into the character-based Setup Program.

Character-Based Setup Program

Having started Setup (see the various ways you can do that in Module 4), begin the character-
based Setup Program with the following steps:

1. If your boot device does not contain your Setup files, you need to confirm the drive and
   folder where those files exist. Often, the CD-ROM drive is drive D:, in which case the

correct response would be **D:\i386**. When the correct drive and folder are displayed, press ENTER.

2. If you are starting from an older version (5.*x* or 6.*x*) of DOS or Windows 3.*x* and don't have the DOS SmartDrive disk-caching system loaded, you will be reminded that having it will greatly improve the performance of Setup (although it is still slow compared to other ways of starting Setup).

   SmartDrive is started with the program Smartdrv.exe that was included with DOS 6.*x* and Windows 3.*x*. If you look at the original distribution diskettes for these products, you will see the file Smartdrv.ex_. This is a compressed file that must be expanded with Expand.exe, also on the distribution diskettes (type **expand a:.ex_ c:.exe**, assuming that you are in the directory with Expand.exe). With Smartdrv.exe in the root directory of the hard disk, add the line **smartdrv.exe** to the Autoexec.bat file. After you have started DOS, you can check whether SmartDrive is loaded by typing **smartdrv** and pressing ENTER. If it's loaded, you will see a report of the version, cache size, and status. An initial set of files is copied to the hard disk, which can be a very slow process if you started from DOS or Windows 3.*x*. A screen tells you the MS-DOS portion of Setup is complete; remove a floppy if there is one in the drive and then press ENTER to restart.

3. Setup inspects your hardware configuration and gives you the opportunity to press F6 to install a third-party SCSI or RAID mass-storage driver. If needed, press F6 and follow the instructions for installing the driver. Also, you are quickly asked if you want to press F2 to do an Automated System Recovery (ASR, see Module 16). Setup then loads the files that you need.

NOTE

You need to press F6 rather quickly if you want to install a driver. You have only about ten seconds to make the decision and press the F6 key. If you are unsure about whether you need to press F6, press it. You can always exit that question without installing a SCSI or RAID driver.

4. Setup asks whether you want to repair an existing installation of Windows XP or set up a new Windows XP installation. Press ENTER for a new installation.

5. If you do not have the Windows XP CD in the drive, you will be asked to insert it.

6. The Microsoft License Agreement is displayed, and you are asked to press F8 if you agree to it or ESC if you don't. If you want to install Windows XP, press F8.

7. If there is an existing Windows XP installation, you'll be asked again whether you want to repair that installation, which you can do by pressing R, or install a fresh copy of Windows XP by pressing ESC.

8. You are next shown the existing partitions and asked which you want to use for the current installation.

9. Use the UP ARROW and DOWN ARROW keys to select the partition you want to use. You then can press ENTER to install in that partition, press C to create a new partition in unpartitioned space, or press D to delete an existing partition and create a new one in its place.

10. If you want to do a clean install on a previously used partition, press D. Confirm that you want to delete a system partition by pressing ENTER and then pressing L. To set up Windows XP in unpartitioned space, press ENTER (a partition will automatically be created for you).

11. Select whether you want the new partition formatted using NTFS (recommended) or the FAT file system and whether you want to use quick formatting or the normal formatting (recommended), and then press ENTER. The new partition will be formatted as you directed.

12. If you have indicated you want to use an existing FAT or FAT32 partition, you will be asked whether you want to convert it to NTFS (recommended) or leave the current file system intact. Select Convert and press ENTER. Confirm that you want to convert the partition by pressing C. When the conversion or formatting is done, the remaining files are copied to the hard disk. Upon completion, the Windows XP Setup GUI window will open.

GUI-Based Setup Wizard

When the Windows XP Setup GUI window opens, you see several messages telling you that Windows XP is loading files and then detecting and installing the hardware devices on the computer. When that is done, the Regional And Language Options dialog box appears. This allows you to choose a locale that determines which language is the default; which other languages are available; and how numbers, currencies, time, and dates are displayed and used for the system in general, as well as for the current user. Continue through Setup with these steps:

1. Select the regional and language settings that you want, and click Next. The Personalize Your Software dialog box will appear.

2. Enter the person's name and organization to be associated with the computer, and click Next. The Product Key dialog box opens.

3. Enter the Product Key that is on the Windows XP CD envelope or case. The Computer Name And Administrative Password dialog box appears.

4. Enter a unique name for the computer (it can be up to 63 characters long but cannot contain spaces, and pre–Windows XP computers will see only the first 15 characters) and enter and confirm a password to be used by the system administrator.

5. Click Next. If you get the Modem Dialing Information dialog box, enter the requested information and again click Next. You'll see a dialog box for Date And Time Settings.

6. If necessary, set the current date and time, and click Next. The Windows networking components will be installed, and if you have a network card and Setup sees it, the Networking Settings dialog box will appear. This allows you to connect to other computers, networks, and the Internet.

7. When the networking software is installed, you are asked to choose either Typical settings, which creates network connections using the Client for Microsoft Networks, File and Print Sharing for Microsoft Networks, and the TCP/IP protocol with automatic addressing, or Custom settings, which allows you to manually configure networking components. Choosing Custom allows you to add or remove clients, services, and protocols, such as Client Service for NetWare and the IPX/SPX/NetBIOS protocol.

8. Choose the Network settings you want to use, and click Next. The Workgroup Or Computer Domain dialog box appears, asking whether you want this computer to be a member of a domain.

9. If you answer No and the computer is part of a workgroup, enter a workgroup name. If you answer Yes, type the domain name. Click Next when you are done with the domain settings. If you entered a domain name, you need to enter a username and password, and then click OK. Setup will install the necessary components and the settings you specified.

When component installation is done, more files are copied to the hard drive, Start menu items are installed, components are registered, settings are saved, and all temporary files are removed. The computer is restarted. If the computer is not already connected to the Internet you will be asked how the computer will do that. Answer Yes if the computer will connect through a network or No if the computer will connect directly to the Internet through a modem. You are then asked if you want to activate Windows. See "Activate Windows XP" earlier in this module.

Whether or not you were asked about connecting to the Internet, the Network Identification Wizard will appear.

10. Click Next. Depending on whether you are a member of a workgroup or a domain, you are asked either if you want to add a user to the computer or if you want to identify who will use the computer. This may continue through several screens. Enter the usernames that you want to add, as well as the additional information requested, clicking Next as needed.

11. Whether or not you added a user, click Finish to complete the user identification. Startup will continue.

12. Upon request, press CTRL-ALT-DEL, enter the Administrator's password or select another user and enter the global password for all users, and click OK.

When loading is complete, the default Windows XP desktop will appear and one or more notes will appear in the lower right of the screen. You may be told that you can automatically adjust the screen resolution by clicking the icon being pointed at. You will be definitely told that you can take a tour of XP by clicking its icon, and you will eventually if not immediately be told that you have 30 days to activate Windows and you can do so by clicking its icon, if you didn't activate earlier. See the "Activate Windows XP" section earlier in this module.

CRITICAL SKILL

5.3 Run an Upgrade

An upgrade to Windows XP Professional may be done from Windows Me, Windows 98, Windows 2000 Professional, or Windows NT Workstation 4. (MS-DOS, Windows 3.1*x*, Windows 95, Windows NT Workstation 3.51, and OS/2 require a clean install.) It therefore can be started from any of the upgradable products. Many of the settings for Windows XP are taken from the earlier system, so there are fewer steps and only two phases, both using a GUI.

Initial GUI Phase

Having started from a newer version of Windows, you should have displayed onscreen the Upgrade versus Install dialog box shown earlier in Figure 5-1. The steps to continue from this point with Setup are as follows:

1. In the dialog box shown in Figure 5-1, choose Upgrade and click Next. The License Agreement dialog box opens.

2. Click I Accept This Agreement (or forget about installing Windows XP) and then click Next. The Product Key dialog box will appear.

3. Enter the product key that is shown on the Windows XP CD envelope or case and click Next.

4. You may be told that Setup will check your hardware and software for compatibility with Windows XP Professional and prepare an upgrade report, as shown next. Choose if you want to see only hardware and other serious issues, to see all known issues, or not see the report at all, and click Next.

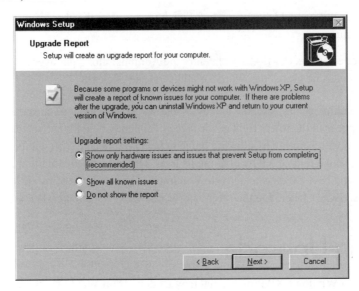

5. You will be asked if you want to get updated Setup files by downloading them from Microsoft. It is a good idea to do this by clicking Yes and then Next. If you are connected to the Internet, you will be connected to the Microsoft site and the latest files will be downloaded. If you cannot be connected to the Internet, you will be told and Setup will continue. After a bit, if there are issues that need to be addressed, the Upgrade Report will be displayed, as you can see here.

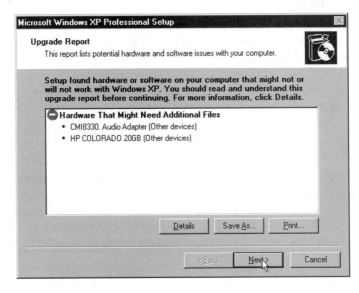

6. Decide how to handle any incompatible items, as necessary (for example, you may be told that a piece of hardware needs an upgraded driver, which you can install after installation).

7. After you have handled all the issues on the Upgrade Report, click Next. More of the installation files will be copied to the hard disk, and then the computer will be restarted.

Final GUI Phase

A new Setup window will appear and you are told that Setup is preparing for the installation. Setup will continue copying files. From a CD, this is fairly fast, but over a network, it can take a while, depending on the speed of the network and the traffic on it. When the copying process is complete, the computer is rebooted and the same Setup window reappears, now telling you that it is installing Windows.

In a normal upgrade, the final GUI phase is just a series of messages telling you about Windows XP and indicating what is happening. No installer interaction is needed. Setup will load and install with their original settings the components that were in the previous system. When component installation is done, Start menu items are installed, components are registered, settings are saved, and all temporary files are removed. The computer is restarted, and Windows XP Professional will start to load. After adjusting your screen resolution, if you are part of a domain, you will be asked to press CTRL-ALT-DEL to begin, to log on with a username and password, and then in all cases the Welcome To Microsoft Windows message appears asking you to spend a few minutes setting up your computer.

1. Click Next. You are asked if you want to activate Windows now over the Internet. If so, click Yes and then Next.

2. If you activate now, you are asked if you want to register with Microsoft. See the discussion under "Activate Windows XP" earlier in this module. If you do want to register, click Yes and Next, enter the registration information requested, and again click Next.

3. If you are not already connected to the Internet, you will be asked if you want to do that. If so, follow the instructions on the screen and click Next as needed.

4. If asked, enter the names of the users of this computer and click Next. If you indicated you wanted to activate the computer and you are connected to the Internet, you will be told that you have completed activating and, if selected, registering Windows. Click Finish. If you are part of a domain, you are asked to enter and confirm an initial password that will be used for all users. These can be changed after starting Windows. Do that and click OK. Windows XP Professional will continue to load.

When loading is complete, the Windows XP default desktop will appear with the Start menu open, as shown in Figure 5-4.

Figure 5-4 Initial Windows XP window

Progress Check

1. Can you do a clean install and preserve any of your current files or settings?

2. How do you change the location of the Setup files and where to install Windows XP?

3. What are some of the notes that pop up in the lower right of the screen immediately after Setup completes?

---

1. No, a clean install by definition cleans off all files on your hard disk, which means that you must reinstall all current applications and copy back all data files that you have backed up.

2. Advanced Options in the Setup Options dialog box allows you to specify the location of the Windows XP Setup files and the folder in which you want Windows XP installed.

3. When loading is complete, you may be told that you can automatically adjust the screen resolution, you can take a tour of XP, and you have 30 days to activate Windows.

CRITICAL SKILL
5.4 Automate Windows XP Installation

Automating installation means to run Setup without intervention, to execute a command on a computer and walk away while Setup installs or upgrades to Windows XP. The end objective is to run Setup on a number of machines with a minimum of effort. Microsoft has developed two major ways of handling this:

- Command-line parameters
- Disk imaging

NOTE

When you perform an unattended Setup, there is a legal assumption that you and the organization for which you are installing Windows XP have read and accepted Microsoft's End User License Agreement (EULA).

Command-Line Parameters

Setup is started by one of two commands, depending on where you start it. From MS-DOS or Windows 3.1*x,* Setup is started with the command **winnt**, and from more recent versions of Windows and Windows NT, Setup is started with **winnt32**. Both Winnt and Winnt32 have a series of parameters and switches that allow them to be run with little intervention, as described in the next two sections.

Winnt Parameters and Switches

Winnt.exe can be run from any 16-bit OS running on an Intel-based computer that meets the minimum requirements for installing Windows XP Professional (see "Check System Requirements" in Module 3). You can simply type **winnt** at a command prompt (DOS prompt or in the Windows Run command), but if you do, you must stay in front of the system for an hour or more and answer questions as Setup presents them. To remove the need for you to answer questions, you can use Winnt's parameters and switches to answer the questions. The full Winnt command has the following syntax, with the parameters described in Table 5-1:

winnt [/s:*sourcepath*] [/t:*tempdrive*] [/u:*answer file*][/udf:*id* [,*UDB_file*]]
[/r:*folder*][/r[x]:*folder*][/e:*command*][/a]

Parameter or Switch	Description
/s:*sourcepath*	***Sourcepath*** is the full path to the location of the Windows Setup files. You can have multiple **/s:***sourcepath* parameters, but Setup will stop if the first one is not available. For example: **/s:d:\i386** if you are directly accessing the installation CD on drive D:, or **/s:\\server\c:\winxppro** if the I386 folder on the CD has been copied to the Winxppro folder on drive C: of a computer named "Server."
/t:*tempdrive*	***Tempdrive*** is the drive on which Setup will store temporary files during installation and will install Windows on that drive. If this isn't specified, Setup will use the first available hard drive, normally drive C:. For example: **/t:e:**.
/u:*answer file*	***Answer file*** provides some or all of the answers needed by Setup for an unattended operation. This requires **/s**. For example: **/u:answers.txt**.
/udf:*id* [,*UDB_file*]	***Id*** identifies the value in an answer file (see the preceding description) that Setup is to override with a value in a Uniqueness Database (UDB) file. If **UDB_file** is not specified, you are prompted to insert a disk with the $Unique$.udb file. For example, **/udf:ComputerName,unique.udb** overrides the **ComputerName** value in the answer file with the **ComputerName** value in Unique.udb.
/r:*folder*	***Folder*** is an optional folder to be installed and kept on the installation drive after Setup finishes. For example: **/r:c:\foldername**.
/rx:*folder*	***Folder*** is an optional folder to be copied to the installation drive and then deleted when Setup finishes. For example: **/rx:c:\foldername**.
/e:*command*	***Command*** is executed at the end of the final GUI-mode Setup. For example, **/e:c:\path\program** to launch a program named "program."
/a	Turns on the accessibility options.

Table 5-1 Winnt Command Parameters and Switches

NOTE

Microsoft is in the process of changing the name of the file used for identifying multiple computers from Uniqueness Database File (UDF) to Uniqueness Database (UDB) file. UDF and UDB files are the same and a reference to one is a reference to the other. In the Windows XP version of these files they are consistently called UDF files. In the Windows Server 2003 version, you will see references to both UDF and UDB files, and the actual files created by the Setup Manager wizard have a .udb extension.

NOTE
Windows XP Winnt does not create floppy disks as Windows NT did, so the **/x** and **/b** switches for not creating floppies and for floppyless operation, respectively, are now gone.

Each of the Winnt parameters eliminates a possible user input during the running of Setup. The **/t** parameter is also used if there are multiple partitions on the hard disk or multiple hard disks. The answer file and UDB file are discussed further under "Create Answer Files," later in the module.

Winnt32 Parameters and Switches

Winnt32.exe can be run from any 32-bit version of Windows (Windows 95/98/Me, Windows NT 3.51/NT 4/2000, or Windows XP) running on an Intel-based computer that meets the minimum requirements for installing Windows XP Professional (see "System Requirements" in Module 3). You can simply double-click Winnt32 in Windows Explorer or type **winnt32** in the Windows Run command, but, (as you do when using Winnt) you must then stay in front of the system for an hour or more and answer questions as Setup presents them. To remove the need to answer questions, you can use Winnt32's parameters and switches to answer the questions. The full Winnt32 command has the following syntax, with the parameters (which are somewhat different from those for Winnt) described in Table 5-2:

winnt32 [/s:*sourcepath*] [/tempdrive:*drive*] [/unattend[*num*]:[*answer file*]]
[/udf:*id*[,*UDB_file*]] [/checkupgradeonly] [/cmdcons] [/cmd:*command*]
[/copydir:i86*folder*] [/copysource:*folder*] [/debug[*level*]:[*filename*]] [/dudisable]
[/duprepare:*folder*] [/dushare:*folder*] [/m:*folder*] [/makelocalsource] [/noreboot]
[/syspart:*drive*]

Parameter or Switch	Description
/s:*sourcepath*	**Sourcepath** is the full path to the location of the Windows Setup files. You can have multiple **/s:*sourcepath*** parameters, but Setup will stop if the first one is not available. For example: **/s:d:\i386** if you are directly accessing the installation CD on drive D:, or **/s:\\server\c:\winxppro** if the I386 folder on the CD has been copied to the Winxppro folder on drive C: of a computer named "Server."
/tempdrive:*drive*	**Drive** is the drive on which Setup will store temporary files during installation and will install Windows on that drive. If this isn't specified, Setup will use the first available hard drive, normally drive C:. For example: **/tempdrive:e:**.
/unattend	Used only with upgrades from a previous version of Windows (98, Me, NT 4, and 2000) in which all answers to Setup questions are taken from the previous installation.

Table 5-2 Winnt32 Command Parameters and Switches

Parameter or Switch	Description
/unattend[*num*]:[*answer file*]	**Answer file** provides some or all of the answers needed by Setup for an unattended operation. If you are upgrading from Windows NT or Windows 2000, you can use **num** to indicate the number of seconds between Setup finishing copying files and restarting the computer. For example: **/u30:answers.txt**.
/udf:*id*[,*UDB_file*]	**Id** identifies the value in an answer file (see the preceding description) that Setup is to override with a value in a UDB file. If **UDB_file** is not specified, you will be prompted to insert a disk with the $Unique$.udb file. For example: **/udf:ComputerName,unique.udb** overrides the **ComputerName** value in the answer file with the **ComputerName** value in Unique.udb.
/checkupgradeonly	Produces the Compatibility Report after checking the upgrade compatibility with Windows. The report is named Upgrade.txt in the Windows installation folder for Windows 98/Me upgrades, and is named Winnt32.log in the installation folder for Windows NT 4 and Windows 2000 upgrades.
/cmdcons	Adds a Recovery Console option to the operating system selection screen to repair a failed installation after exiting Setup.
/cmd:*command*	**Command** is executed at the end of the final GUI-mode Setup. For example, **/cmd:c:\path\program** to launch a program named "program."
/copydir:*folder*	**Folder** is copied to the folder in which Windows is installed, normally Winnt. You can have multiple copies of **/copydir:folder**. For example, **/copydir:Newdrivers** copies the folder Newdrivers to the Windows folder, probably C:\Winnt\.
/copysource:*folder*	**Folder** is temporarily copied to the folder in which Windows XP is installed, normally Windows or Winnt, and then deleted when Setup is finished. You can have multiple copies of **/copysource:folder**. For example, **/copysource:Newdrivers** temporarily copies the folder Newdrivers to the Windows XP folder, probably C:\Windows\ or C:\Winnt\. When Setup is finished, the folder is deleted.
/debug[*level*]:[*filename*]	**Filename** is the name of a debug log created by Setup at the **level** specified. The levels are: 0-severe errors; 1-errors; 2-warnings; 3-information; and 4-detailed information. Each level includes lower levels. The default is C:\Winnt\Winnt32.log, at level 2. For example: **/debug3:C:\MySetup.log**.
/dudisable	Disables Dynamic Update and therefore uses only the original Setup files, even if the answer file specifies that Dynamic Update should be run.
/duprepare:*folder*	Prepares **folder** so that it contains the Dynamic Update files downloaded from the Windows Update web site. This folder can then be used while installing multiple copies of Windows.

Table 5-2 Winnt32 Command Parameters and Switches *(continued)*

Parameter or Switch	Description
/dushare:*folder*	Uses **folder**, which contains the Dynamic Update files placed there by **/duprepare**, instead of going out to Windows Update web site for each install.
/m:*folder*	**Folder** contains replacement files that Setup will use instead of the default files if the replacement files are present. For example: **/m:\\server\c:**.
/makelocalsource	Copies the installation source files to the hard drive on which Windows is being installed from either a CD or over a network, so that the files are available when the CD or network is not available.
/noreboot	Prevents restarting the computer after Setup's file-copy phase, so that another command can be executed.
/syspart:*drive*	**Drive** is a secondary hard drive onto which Setup is to copy the boot or startup files and mark the drive as active. When the drive is installed in another computer and that computer is started, Setup automatically starts at the next Setup phase. This requires **/tempdrive**. For example: **/syspart:e:**.

Table 5-2 Winnt32 Command Parameters and Switches *(continued)*

You can use Winnt32 parameters **/syspart** and **/tempdrive** to refer to the same secondary hard drive (not the boot drive in the current computer), and then use **/noreboot** to stop Setup after the file-copy phase. If you then remove the drive, place it in a different computer, and start that computer, Setup will continue with the Setup Wizard in the GUI phase. In this way, Setup can be started for a number of different types of machines by creating a disk image that can be customized after being restarted in the final machines.

CAUTION

In the just-described process of preparing a drive for another computer, don't reboot the original computer with the prepared secondary drive still installed. The computer will not boot and will hang because two boot devices are at the same level.

Creating Answer Files

Answer files are obviously the key to running Setup unattended. They are, by their nature, complex files with many parameters. To help you understand and create answer files, Microsoft has included five tools on the Windows Server 2003 CD:

NOTE

Use the deployment tools on the Windows Server 2003 CD, since they are newer than the tools on the Windows XP CD.

- A sample answer file named Unattend.txt in the \i386 folder

- A guide to all the possible parameters in an answer file, along with more sample files in a Help file named Deploy.chm in the \Support\Tools\Deploy.cab file

- Articles in Readme.txt in the Deploy.cab file that are a last-minute update to Deploy.chm

- A GUI program called Setup Manager wizard to create answer files based on answering questions in Setupmgr.exe in the \Support\Tools\Deploy.cab file

- A general help file for automated and custom installations in Ref.chm in the Deploy.cab file

NOTE

Deploy.cab is a compressed file that contains the preceding items, as well as other items. You can simply double-click this file to unpack and see the files it contains, which you can then drag to another folder. You use the Suptools.msi in the \Support\Tools folder to unpack and install the tools in Support.cab.

You can see that Microsoft takes this area seriously, as it should and as is needed due to its complexity. The best measure of this complexity is the 160-plus pages needed in Unattend.chm to document all the parameters and their options that can be in an answer file. This should not discourage you, because the vast majority of all answer files use only a small percentage of these parameters. Take a look at Unattend.txt, the sample answer file in the \i386 folder on the Windows Server 2003 CD. Figure 5-5 shows it, but open it on your own screen where you can see it better. At the same time, open Ref.chm in the \Support\Tools\Deploy.cab file so that you can switch back and forth between Unattend.txt and Ref.chm. You'll want to look up the meaning of parameters and their possible values.

From the sample file, you can see a number of conventions, among which are the following:

- Comments begin with a semicolon (;). Even if you don't need to be reminded about what you were doing, it is a good idea to use lots of comments so that someone else can clearly understand what you were doing.

- The file is broken up into sections, each with a heading in square brackets.

- Within each section is a list of parameters that relate to that section.

- Parameters are assigned values by placing an equal sign (=), which may or may not be surrounded by spaces, after the parameter and before the value. For example, **Parameter = value**.

- If a value includes spaces, it must be enclosed in quotation marks ("), and other literal values may or may not have quotation marks.

NOTE

The [Unattended] section is required for the answer file to be used by Setup.

```
UNATTEND.TXT - Notepad                                                    _ □ X
File  Edit  Format  View  Help
;  Microsoft Windows
;  (c) 1994 - 2001 Microsoft Corporation. All rights reserved.
;
;  Sample Unattended Setup Answer File
;
;  This file contains information about how to automate the installation
;  or upgrade of windows so the Setup program runs without requiring
;  user input.  You can find more information in the ref.chm found at
;  CD:\support\tools\deploy.cab
;

[Unattended]
Unattendmode = FullUnattended
OemPreinstall = NO
TargetPath = *
Filesystem = LeaveAlone

[UserData]
FullName = "Your User Name"
OrgName = "Your Organization Name"
ComputerName = *
ProductKey= "CKY24-Q8QRH-X3KMR-C6BCY-T847Y"

[GuiUnattended]
;  Sets the Timezone to the Pacific Northwest
;  Sets the Admin Password to NULL
;  Turn AutoLogon ON and login once
TimeZone = "004"
AdminPassword = *
AutoLogon = Yes
AutoLogonCount = 1

[LicenseFilePrintData]
;  For Server installs
AutoMode = "PerServer"
AutoUsers = "5"

[GuiRunOnce]
;  List the programs that you want to launch when the machine is logged into for

[Display]
BitsPerPel = 16
XResolution = 800
YResolution = 600
VRefresh = 70

[Networking]

[Identification]
JoinWorkgroup = Workgroup
```

Figure 5-5 A sample answer file, Unattend.txt in \i386 on the Windows Server 2003 CD

One way to create an answer file is to copy and modify Unattend.txt. In many instances, the parameters, and even some of the values, will be the same. Listing 5-1 is an example answer file created by copying and modifying Unattend.txt. The purpose of this example answer file is to do a clean install to a new hard disk. You can see that very little modification was needed to make this file work. The primary changes were to repartition the hard drive with NTFS, personalize the file, and adjust it for my monitor. In "Use Setup Command Lines and Answer Files," later in the module, you see how this answer file can be used.

Listing 5-1 Modified Sample Answer File

```
[Unattended]
; Delete all partitions on the boot drive, create one new partition,
; and reformat it with NTFS
Unattendmode = FullUnattended
OemPreinstall = NO
TargetPath = WINNT
Repartition = Yes

[UserData]
FullName = "Martin Matthews"
OrgName = "Matthews Technology"
ComputerName = "MTech1"

[GuiUnattended]
; Sets the Timezone to the Pacific Northwest
; Sets the Admin Password to NULL
; Turn AutoLogon ON and login once
TimeZone = "004"
AdminPassword = *
AutoLogon = Yes
AutoLogonCount = 1

[Display]
BitsPerPel = 16
XResolution = 1024
YResolution = 768
VRefresh = 60

[Networking]
; When set to YES, setup will install default networking components.
InstallDefaultComponents = YES

[Identification]
JoinWorkgroup = Matthews
```

Use the Setup Manager Wizard

If you want to do more with an answer file than what is done with the sample Unattend.txt, it becomes very laborious, both from having to look up in Ref.doc the many parameters and the values that are allowed, and from having to manually enter everything while not making a typing and/or spelling mistake. The answer for this is to use the Setup Manager wizard, which, in a GUI environment, creates an answer file for you based on your responses in its dialog boxes.

The Setup Manager wizard prompts you to enter the information needed for the type of setup you are automating and the degree of user interaction you want. If you specify a fully unattended installation, the Setup Manager wizard prompts you to enter all the necessary information. If you select a higher level of user interaction (there are five levels), the Setup Manager wizard prompts you accordingly, and you can leave more questions unanswered in the answer file, forcing the end user to answer them in Setup.

Start the Setup Manager wizard and create an answer file with the following steps:

1. Create a new folder called **Deployment** on your hard drive. Then, open the \Support\Tools folder on the Windows Server 2003 CD, double-click Deploy.cab to open it, and drag its contents to your new Deployment folder.

2. In the Deployment folder, double-click Setupmgr.exe. The Setup Manager wizard's welcome message will appear.

3. Click Next. You are asked whether you want to create a new answer file or modify an existing one, as shown here:

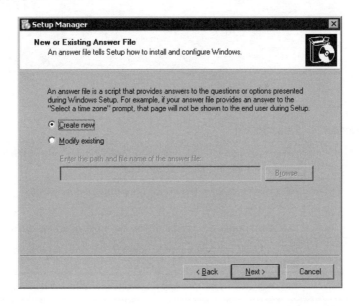

4. Leave the default Create New selected (or click it if it's not selected) and click Next. You are asked what the answer file will be used for: an Unattended Setup; Sysprep Setup, which is explained later in the module, under "Create and Use Disk Images;" or Remote Installation Services (RIS), which is discussed in Module 6.

5. Again, leave the default Unattended Setup selected and click Next. You are asked to select the Windows product that the answer file will install; choose Windows XP Professional and click Next.

You are then asked to choose one of the five levels of user interaction, as shown next. Look at the description under each. Table 5-3 provides another description of them.

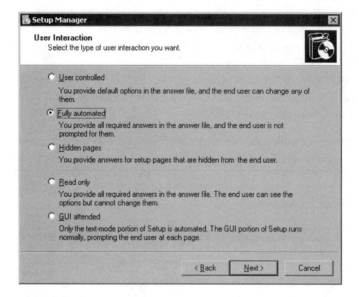

Level of Interaction	Description
User Controlled	Defaults are provided to the end user, but users must make their own choices for the installation questions
Fully Automated	All answers to Setup's questions are provided in the answer file and the end user has to do nothing
Hidden Pages	The Setup pages are hidden if you have provided the answers
Read Only	The end user can see but not change questions that are answered in the answer file
GUI Attended	The final GUI Setup Wizard questions are left for the end user

Table 5-3 Levels of User Interaction

6. Select the level that is correct for you (Fully Automated is used in the following steps), and click Next. You are then asked if you want to create or modify a distribution share or folder on the server's hard disk, or whether this answer file will reside on a CD. Leave the default of creating a new share, and click Next.

7. Specify the location of the Setup files, either the Windows XP Professional CD or a location on a hard drive to which you have copied the files from the \i386 folder on the Windows XP Professional CD. The files at this location will be copied to the distribution folder. Click Next. Accept the default path, name, and share name of the folder or enter a new one and click Next.

NOTE

If you choose a fully automated installation, you must accept Microsoft's End User License Agreement before you can continue with the Setup Manager wizard.

8. Accept the license agreement and click Next. You are presented with a hierarchical list of questions that are necessary for a comprehensive answer file on the left of the dialog box, and the particular questions for a given area on the right, as you can see in Figure 5-6.

9. Provide the answers to the Setup Manager wizard that are correct for the installation you want to perform, clicking Next at the bottom of each dialog box. When you have made all

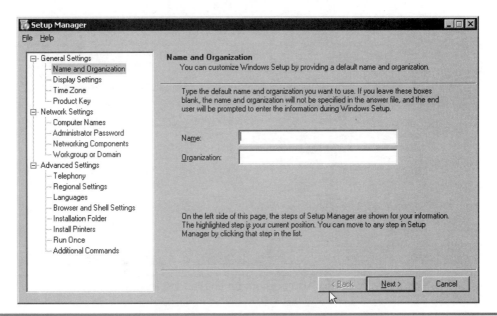

Figure 5-6 The hierarchy of questions for creating an answer file

the entries you want and are at Additional Commands, click Finish. You are shown the location where the Unattend.txt file will be stored, which you can change if you wish. Then click OK. The installation files will be copied to the folder you specified earlier.

10. When the Setup Manager is done copying the Setup files, you are shown a summary of what it has done for you. Click the close button in the upper-right corner of the window (not the Cancel button) to exit the Setup Manager.

NOTE

If you specify multiple computers, a UDB file is created to modify the answer file for each computer. Also, a BAT file is created to start the winnt32 command with the answer file.

These steps should have created the following four or five objects in locations that you specified, plus the distribution folder, as shown in Figure 5-7:

- **Windist** A distribution folder with all the files and folders necessary to do an unattended installation (you may have named yours differently)

- **I386** Setup files from the I386 folder on the Windows XP installation CD

- **Unattend.txt** The answer file that was your original objective

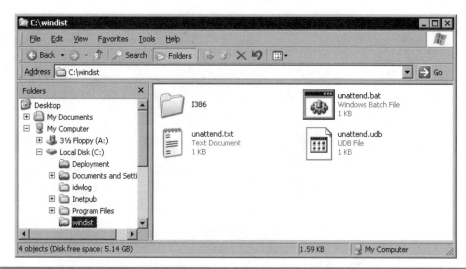

Figure 5-7 A distribution folder for carrying out an unattended installation

● **Unattend.bat**   A sample batch file that implements both the answer file and the distribution folder

● **Unattend.udb**   If you have multiple computers, this file is included to supply the names of the computers

The folder and three files within your distribution folder (Windist is the default shown here) are discussed next, in turn.

I386 Folder   The I386 folder is a copy of the folder of that name on the Windows XP Professional CD with the addition of the OEM subfolder, as shown in Figure 5-8. Possible uses for the OEM folder and its subfolders are described in Table 5-4.

NOTE

The OEM folder is created for you; you must create the subfolders below OEM as you need them.

NOTE

OEM1 and OEM are the same if drive C: is the system drive on which Windows is installed. OEM1 just gives you the flexibility of installing on any drive.

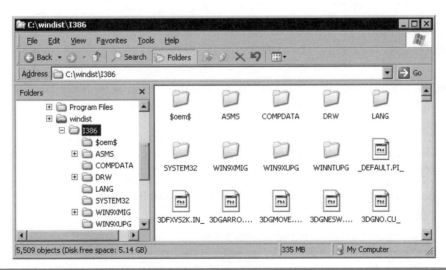

Figure 5-8 I386 folder with the OEM subfolder

Folder	Description
OEM\	Holds files, folders, and applications that you want placed on a newly installed hard disk. A Cmdlines.txt file in the OEM folder can contain a list of commands, such as application-setup and .inf commands, that will be run at the end of the final GUI phase of Windows XP Setup.
OEM\$$\	Holds files and folders that you want copied into the Windows folder (normally named Windows or Winnt) on the computer being installed. You must follow the structure of the Windows folder, so fonts must be in OEM\$$\Fonts.
OEM\$$\System32\	Holds files, such as DLLs, that you want copied to what is normally named \Windows\System32 or \Winnt\System32.
OEM\$1\	Holds files and folders that you want copied to the root directory of the system drive on which Windows is installed. The actual drive letter is assigned by Setup during installation, providing flexibility over multiple systems.
OEM\$1\Drivers\	Holds additional device drivers not included in Windows.
OEM\C\	Holds files and folders that you want copied to the root directory of drive C:.
OEM\D\	Holds files and folders that you want copied to the root directory of drive D:.
OEM\Textmode\	Holds hardware-related files, such as SCSI and fiber channel device drivers, that are used in the early character-based or text mode of Windows Setup.

Table 5-4 Purpose and Contents of the OEM Folder Tree

You can extend the OEM folder structure to include other folders, as necessary, for both Windows and other applications, to mirror the drive(s) in the computer being installed.

Unattend.txt Answer File   The answer file that is produced by the Setup Manager wizard (shown in Figure 5-9) has some sections, parameters, and values not seen earlier:

● The [Data] section, used when booting from a CD, contains the **AutoPartition** parameter, which with the value 1 tells Setup to eliminate all current partitions and reformat the hard drive with NTFS.

● The parameters **OemSkipEula**, **OemPreinstall**, **OemSkipRegional**, and **OemSkipWelcome** customize how Setup looks to the user.

● The **ComputerName** parameter has the value you gave it or a value of *, which will be substituted with the names in the UDB file (see the later section "Unattend.udb Alternative File").

- The [TapiLocation] section provides the home area code.

- The [SetupMgr] section contains the two options for the computer name and the location of the distribution folder.

- The [GuiRunOnce] section contains two commands to install different printers.

- The [Identification] section contains a parameter and value to join a domain or workgroup.

Unattend.bat Batch File   The Unattend.bat batch file, shown in Figure 5-10, is used to implement the answer file and the UDB alternative file, as well as to identify the location of

```
; SetupMgrTag
[Data]
    AutoPartition=1
    MsDosInitiated="0"
    UnattendedInstall="Yes"

[Unattended]
    UnattendMode=FullUnattended
    OemSkipEula=Yes
    OemPreinstall=Yes
    TargetPath=\WINDOWS

[GuiUnattended]
    AdminPassword=*
    EncryptedAdminPassword=NO
    AutoLogon=Yes
    AutoLogonCount=2
    OEMSkipRegional=1
    TimeZone=4
    oemskipwelcome=1

[UserData]
    ProductKey=*|
    FullName="Marty Matthews"
    OrgName="Matthews Technology"
    ComputerName=*

[TapiLocation]
    CountryCode=1
    Dialing=Tone
    AreaCode=360

[SetupMgr]
    ComputerName0=Mtech1
    ComputerName1=Mtech2
    DistFolder=C:\windist
    DistShare=windist

[GuiRunOnce]
    Command0="rundll32 printui.dll,PrintUIEntry /in /n \\Marty2\HPLJIII"
    Command1="rundll32 printui.dll,PrintUIEntry /in /n \\Carole\HPL2000C"

[Identification]
    JoinWorkgroup=Matthews

[Networking]
    InstallDefaultComponents=Yes
```

Figure 5-9 Answer file produced by the Setup Manager wizard

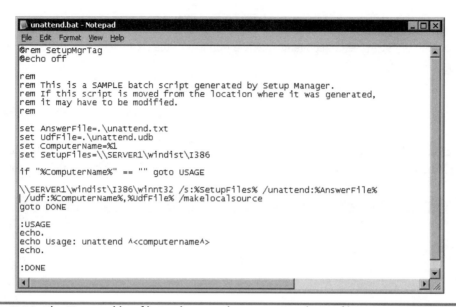

Figure 5-10 The Unattend.bat file implements the answer and UDB files.

the distribution folder created by the Setup Manager wizard. It provides a basic command line that starts Winnt32 from the distribution folder using the answer and UDB files. The batch file is started by typing its name at a command prompt followed by the name of the computer on which the installation is being performed; for example, **unattend mtech1**, if the computer name is Mtech1. The Winnt32 command line included in Unattend.bat has only a few of the many parameters and switches that are available, so any of the others may be added as you wish.

NOTE

To open Unattend.bat, right-click the file in Explorer and choose Edit. Choosing Open or double-clicking will execute the file.

The contents of Unattend.bat follow the standard syntax for batch programs dating back to DOS. This syntax is briefly reviewed in Table 5-5.

Unattend.udb Alternative File   The Unattend.udb alternative file (called Unattend.udf in Windows XP), shown next, is a simple file that supplies the computer name to the answer file.

Batch Command	Description
@	Prevents the current line from being displayed.
Rem	Treats the following text as a remark.
Echo off	Prevents following lines from being displayed.
Set (DOS command)	Defines an environment variable, such as AnswerFile, to be the string on the right of the equal sign.
%1 (one of nine input variables)	Stands in for the first string typed on the command line following the batch filename and a space. Additional spaces are used to separate additional strings.
If	Performs a test of a condition and executes a command if the condition is true, to implement branching in a batch command. The command is ignored if the condition is false.
%string%	Defines *string* to be an environment variable.
==	Generates a true condition if the strings on either side are the same. The strings can be variables or literal strings.
Goto	Transfers execution to the label that follows the **Goto** command.
:string	Defines *string* to be a label, which can contain up to eight characters, but no spaces or separators.
Echo	Displays onscreen the message that follows it.

Table 5-5 Batch Command Syntax

Since both the index and the data for the Unattend.udb file are the same, and there are only two alternatives, there seems to be little reason for it. If you were to have several variable fields, like the addition of FullName and OrgName, it might make more sense.

You can easily add a FullName field, since it is in the [UserData] section, as shown next. It will replace the value that is in the answer file.

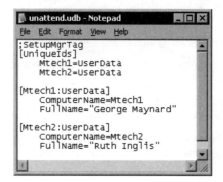

Progress Check

1. How is Setup started from a command prompt?

2. What is Deploy.cab and how is it used?

3. What are two easy ways to create an answer file?

Use Setup Command Lines and Answer Files

The Setup command lines and answer files can be implemented in a number of ways, among which are the following:

- Type a Setup command with appropriate parameters and switches at a command prompt (a DOS prompt or Windows Run command).

- Create a batch file with a Setup command in it and execute the batch file by typing its name at a command prompt or double-clicking it from Windows.

- Copy a batch file with a Setup command in it to another computer and execute it from that computer. You may refer to Setup's files either in a distribution folder or on the Windows XP CD, and either on a server or on a local drive.

---

1. Setup is started by one of two commands, depending on where you start it. From MS-DOS or Windows 3.1*x*, Setup is started with the command **winnt**, and from more recent versions of Windows and Windows NT, Setup is started with **winnt32**.

2. Deploy.cab is a compressed file that contains many of the items that are provided to help you create and use answer files. You can simply double-click this file to unpack and see the files it contains, which you can then drag to another folder.

3. An answer file can be easily created by copying and modifying the sample answer file named Unattend.txt, and with a GUI program Setup Manager wizard (Setupmgr.exe) that will create answer files based on answering questions.

● Copy a batch file with a Setup command in it to a floppy disk. If the floppy is bootable, the Setup batch file can be started from the Autoexec.bat file on the floppy. Alternatively, the batch file on the floppy can be executed at a command prompt or by double-clicking it on the computer to be installed.

● If you can create a CD, especially a bootable one, you can include the batch file, the answer and UDB files, and the complete distribution folder. The batch file then can be started from the Autorun.inf file on the CD.

You can probably think of other ways to use these files and folder. The batch file just mentioned, in all but the last scenario, can be very simple, or it can be even more complex than what you saw with the Setup Manager in Figure 5-10. You can decide whether or not the Setup command (Winnt32 or Winnt) refers to answer and UDB files, and whether or not you want to use the distribution folder. Look at a couple of examples that follow.

Simple Typed Command
A simple situation would be to upgrade Windows 2000 Professional to Windows XP Professional. Suppose you have several workstations running Windows 2000 Professional and you want to upgrade them to Windows XP Professional. To do that, unattended (meaning that all the current settings would come from the current installation), with the CD in drive D: and the current installation in C:, you would use these steps:

1. Place the Windows XP Professional CD in its drive. Click Exit to close the Welcome To Windows XP install window.

2. Open the Start menu and choose Run.

3. In the Open command line, type: **D:\i386\winnt32.exe /s:d:\i386 /unattend**.

4. Press ENTER. Setup will start and its screen will appear. You'll see several dialog boxes flash by, and you'll be asked to enter the product key and press ENTER.

   The message stating that files are being loaded will briefly appear, and then the computer will automatically restart in the second GUI phase with Preparing Installation highlighted. The file copying takes place, the previous configuration is used to create a new configuration, and the computer is again restarted. The second GUI phase reappears, now with Installing Windows highlighted. You'll see several messages onscreen giving you status information, and then Setup completes and, for a third time, reboots your system. Windows XP will appear.

5. Remove the CD, because you're done.

Okay, so that was too simple, but it indicates how simple Setup can be when done unattended.

Use an Unattended File   The easiest way to use an unattended file is by starting Setup from a newer version of Windows using the Run command with the Unattend.txt file. You might do this if you had a number of computers with, say, Windows 98, on which you want to do a clean install of Windows XP Professional. You would create the Unattend.txt file using the Setup Manager wizard as you did earlier in this module. The only change might be to leave the Setup files on the Windows XP CD to keep from having to create and use a deployment folder. When you have created the Unattended.txt file, which we'll assume has that name in the C:\Deploy folder, make sure the Windows XP CD is in its drive, assumed to be D:, and then open the Run command by opening the Start menu and choosing Run. In the Run dialog box type:

D:\i386\winnt32 /s:d:\i386 /unattend:c:\deploy\Unattend.txt

and press ENTER. The only attention that is required is to confirm that you want to do a new installation replacing the existing Windows installation.

To make this even easier, when the Setup Manager creates Unattend.txt, it also creates a batch file named Unattend.bat, which contains the command you just typed, as shown next. So long as this batch file and the Unattend.txt answer file are in the same folder, all you have to do is open that folder in Windows Explorer and double-click the batch file. Setup will be started, and the answer file will lead it through the entire process.

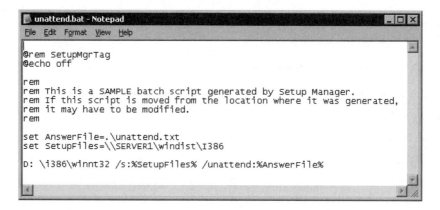

Batch Command on a Floppy   One of the most common forms of distributing Windows within a company is to accompany the Windows CD with a company floppy that installs and configures Windows for the company's environment. Suppose you want to install Windows XP Professional on a number of workstations, and you are going to use the Setup Manager wizard to prepare the answer file and batch file. Here are the steps:

1. On a server, start the Setup Manager wizard, choose to create a new answer file for an unattended installation of Windows XP Professional. It will be Fully Automated, but you do not need to create a distribution folder, since you will be installing from a CD.

2. After accepting the license agreement, make the detail entries that support the fully automated installation you want to do. If you are going to install multiple computers, be sure to enter all of the computer names. Name the answer file something other than Unattend.txt (and if you start it from DOS, it must be eight characters or less; use **Unatt.txt** for purposes of this example) and finish the Setup Manager wizard.

3. Double-click the Unatt.txt answer file and, under [Data], change the value of MsDosInitiated to "1," as you can see in Figure 5-11. Save and close the Unatt.txt file.

4. Right-click the Unatt.bat batch file, choose Edit and delete "32" after "winnt," and change "/unattend:" to "/u:," so that Unatt.bat can be started from DOS, as shown next. Save and close Unatt.bat.

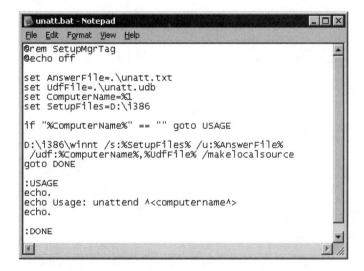

```
@rem SetupMgrTag
@echo off

set AnswerFile=.\unatt.txt
set UdfFile=.\unatt.udb
set ComputerName=%1
set SetupFiles=D:\i386

if "%ComputerName%" == "" goto USAGE

D:\i386\winnt /s:%SetupFiles% /u:%AnswerFile%
 /udf:%ComputerName%,%UdfFile% /makelocalsource
goto DONE

:USAGE
echo.
echo Usage: unattend ^<computername^>
echo.

:DONE
```

5. Using a DOS or older Windows system, format a floppy disk, include the system files so that it will boot, and then copy the answer and setup batch files to it. Create the necessary Config.sys and Autoexec.bat files needed to activate your CD drive, which vary from computer to computer. Toward the end of Autoexec.bat file, add the following line:

Unatt.bat *computername*

where *computername* is the name of the computer a particular floppy will be installing (given that you are installing multiple computers); for example, I typed **unatt.bat mtech1**.

6. Windows XP Setup strongly recommends that Smartdrv.exe be loaded in order to complete running in a DOS environment. See the discussion in Module 4 about locating, expanding, and using Smartdrv.exe. Here, you should add it to this Autoexec.bat file above the CD-ROM driver command. Close and save the Autoexec.bat file.

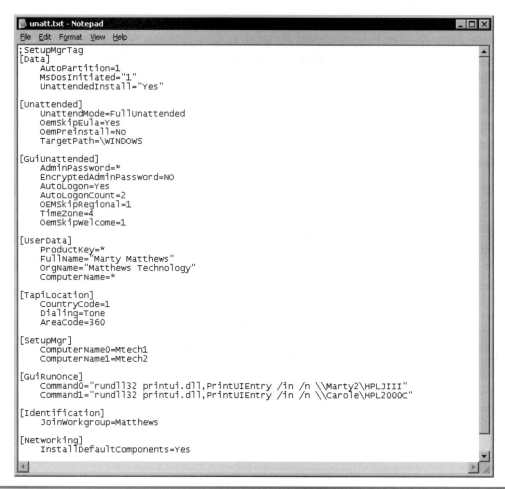

Figure 5-11 Answer file for installing from a floppy disk and a CD

7. Place the floppy you just created and the Windows XP Professional CD in their respective drives in the computer to be installed, and start the computer, making sure it is booting from the floppy, not the CD or hard disk. You'll see the initial character mode screen telling you that files are being copied to the hard disk.

8. While the copying is underway, remove the floppy so the computer does not reboot from it. Upon completion of the initial copying from the CD to the hard disk, the computer will automatically restart and continue copying, really installing the files from their compressed image to their final working image.

When the second phase of copying is complete, the computer will restart a second time with the GUI-based Setup. You will see several messages as Setup goes through the PreInstall, Install, and Final phases. Then, Setup will complete and for a third time reboot the system. Windows XP Professional will appear.

9. Remove the CD, because you are done.

Custom Bootable CD   Creating custom bootable CDs is very handy if you have a "CD burner" available to you. You can use the full set of objects produced by the Setup Manager wizard, including the distribution folder. The distribution folder should contain a subfolder named **I386**, which needs to be copied intact to the CD. In addition, you need to change the batch and answer files for the disk drives being used, and copy both of them and the UDB file to the root directory in the CD.

My CD creation software, Roxio's Easy CD Creator 5.3, requires a bootable image, either a bootable floppy disk, a bootable hard disk, or another bootable CD from which to take the booting information. I used the floppy that I used in the previous "Batch Command on a Floppy" section and copied the Autoexec.bat, Config.sys, Smartdrv.exe, Unatt.txt, and Unatt.bat files from that floppy to the root directory on the CD. There are several different types of CD creation tools, so my comments will be generic in that regard, although I assume your CD creation tool has a Windows Explorer–like capability in which you can create folders. Here are the steps to create a custom bootable CD (these instructions assume that your CD drive is drive D:):

1. Create the answer, batch, and UDB files and the distribution folder, as you did previously.

2. Open the answer file (Unattend.txt) and, under the [SetupMgr] section, change DistFolder to point to where the files will be on the CD (probably **D:\i386**). Also change DistShare to be **i386**. Save and close the answer file.

3. Edit the batch file: change the value for SetupFiles to **D:\i386**, and change the path and program for Setup to **D:**. Save and close the batch file.

4. Make any changes you want to the OEM folder structure and then copy the files you want into that structure.

5. Insert a blank CD-R disk in its drive and start your CD creation program. Specify that the disk is to be bootable, and point to where the program can find the system files necessary for booting. Name the CD something like **UnAttWinXP**. (In Easy CD Creator 5.3, you open the File menu, choose New CD Layout | Bootable CD, select the emulation you want [floppy, hard disk, or CD], identify the source of the bootable image, and click OK.)

6. Copy the contents of the distribution folder to the CD including the batch file, the answer file, the UDB file, and the Autorun.inf file, as well as the I386 folder. At this point in Easy CD Creator 5.3, it looks like the following illustration; note the two BIN files used for booting.

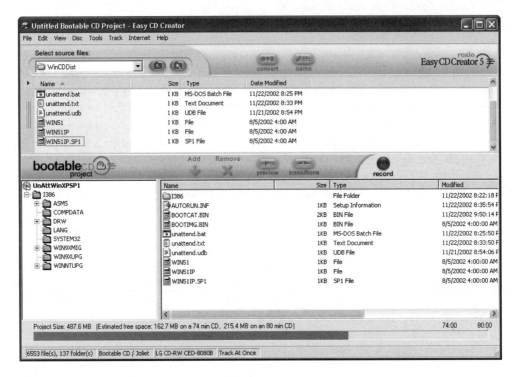

7. Write the CD.

8. Place the CD in a computer on which you want to install Windows XP Professional, and restart the machine. Setup will start and run as you have seen before when booting from a CD.

NOTE

On some of the early computers on which you could boot from a CD, you are not asked if you want to do that; the computer just automatically boots from the CD if there is a bootable CD in the drive. This means that you must remove and reinstall the CD each time the system is rebooted during installation.

CRITICAL SKILL
5.5 Create and Use Disk Images

Another major way of distributing Windows XP is *disk imaging,* the process of creating and duplicating a standardized disk image or set of contents that is to be placed on the hard disks of multiple computers. This image can include—in addition to the OS—applications, data sets, and custom settings. Windows XP has a special tool, called the System Preparation tool, or SysPrep, for preparing the master image that will be cloned. In the master image, SysPrep places another program, Setupcl.exe, which, when a clone of the master image is first started, assigns a unique security ID (SID) to that computer and runs a five- to ten-minute GUI-mode Setup to personalize the computer with such information as the user, company, and computer names.

NOTE

For disk imaging to work, the systems must be nearly identical. The following items must be identical: the Hardware Abstraction Layer (HAL), which is where the programming code is turned into machine language at the processor level; the Advanced Configuration and Power Interface (ACPI) for power management; the type of disk controller; the number of processors; and the platform (32-bit versus 64-bit). These items can differ: the processor model (Intel Pentium 200, PII-350, or PIII-800), RAM size, and Plug and Play devices, such as network interface cards, video cards, modems, and sound cards.

The process of creating and using disk images involves five steps:

1. Create the master image of the operating system and applications that you want to replicate.

2. Prepare a special answer file and distribution folder for creating a disk image, using the Setup Manager wizard.

3. Prepare the master image for copying, using the SysPrep tool.

4. Copy the master image onto other disks using a third-party product, either hardware or software, such as PowerQuest's Drive Image or Symantec's Ghost.

5. Start the clone for the first time and run through it in Mini-Setup.

Look at each of these steps and the part they play in creating and using a disk image to deploy Windows XP Professional.

NOTE

Sysprep.exe and Setupcl.exe together replace Rollback.exe, which was used in Windows NT 4 to perform a similar function.

Create a Master Image

Disk image duplication begins by installing Windows XP Professional on the hard disk that will serve as the master image. This is a normal installation, except that it should be done using a distribution folder, answer file, and command line (batch file) so that the master image has a consistent look and feel, and you can purposefully leave such things as the username, computer name, and so on blank. Once you have the OS installed the way you want to replicate it, install the applications, such as Microsoft Office, that you want to replicate. Finally, go through the settings, shortcuts, Start menu, and desktop and make them the way you want the system replicated.

When the master image is configured the way you want it, create or copy a Deployment folder on the master disk, as you did in Step 1 of "Use the Setup Manager Wizard." This folder should contain at least Setupcl.exe, Setupmgr.exe, and Sysprep.exe.

Prepare Control Files for Drive Image Creation

The Setup Manager wizard has a special set of features that prepares a unique answer file and distribution folder for use in image file creation. The following steps show how this works:

1. From the Deployment folder on the master image disk, double-click the Setup Manager wizard (Setupmgr.exe) and click Next on the welcome message.

2. Select Create New and click Next to display the list of alternative end uses: Unattended Setup, Sysprep Setup, and Remote Installation Services.

3. Select Sysprep Setup and then click Next. This will generate an answer file that can be used with the System Preparation tool. Continue on and answer the remaining Setup Manager wizard questions as required to create the disk image you need, clicking Next as necessary.

4. When you are done, you are shown a dialog box asking where you want to store the Sysprep.inf file created by the Setup Manager wizard. This is the equivalent of the answer files created earlier. The default is the Deployment folder that you created from Deploy.cab earlier in this module, which is where you want it. Click OK. My Sysprep.inf is shown in Figure 5-12.

On your computer, you should find the new Sysprep folder, like the one shown in the following illustration. This has the I386 and OEM folder structure that you saw earlier in the normal Windows XP distribution folder, as well as the Sysprep.inf answer file.

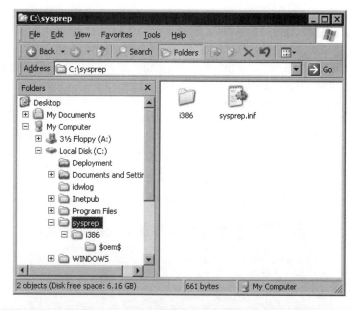

Figure 5-12 Answer file for use with Sysprep

Prepare a Disk Image

Preparing a disk image is accomplished by running Sysprep.exe. Before doing that, make sure that Sysprep.exe, Setupcl.exe, and Sysprep.inf are together in the Deployment folder and that it is that copy of Sysprep.exe you use to begin the preparation. Once you are sure of the correct location, use the following steps to run Sysprep:

1. In Windows Explorer, open the Deployment folder and double-click Sysprep.exe. A message appears stating that some of the security parameters may change and that the computer will be shut down when Sysprep is finished.

2. Click OK. After a brief time the System Preparation Tool dialog box will appear like this:

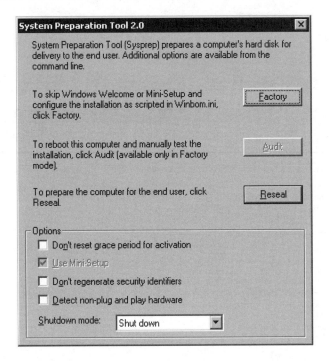

3. When you are ready, click Reseal. You are told that the next time you boot this hard disk, you will regenerate the SIDs on it. Click OK. You see several brief messages that Sysprep is working and then Windows will shut down. Depending on your computer, either it will shut itself off or you'll see a message saying it is now safe to do so.

4. If necessary, shut off your computer, and then remove the master image hard disk.

CAUTION

It is very important that you do restart the original or another computer by booting off the master image hard disk. This is set up to be replicated, and when it or one of its clones is booted, a one-time setup process is run and then the Sysprep folder and its contents are deleted.

Copy a Disk Image

Once you have a master image disk, it can be duplicated in several ways. Hardware duplicators are available that copy a disk image to many disks at the same time. In addition, at least two software products, PowerQuest's Drive Image and Symantec's Ghost, can copy a disk image from one disk to another. In any case, the master hard drive must be removed from its former position as a boot device and its image (not just files) must be copied to another device. One way around having to remove the master image disk is to boot from a floppy. PowerQuest's Drive Image has the capability to make a set of floppies that you can use in this way.

The process of actually copying in PowerQuest's Drive Image is very simple. Once started, it tells you that it needs to run in DOS and asks whether that is OK. If you agree, Windows will be shut down and Drive Image will appear in its own GUI screen with mouse support. You will be asked whether you want to create a drive image, restore a drive image, or copy an image from one disk to another. After choosing the disk-to-disk copy, you'll need to select the From disk and which or all of its partitions, and then select the To disk and its partitions, which can be resized. If the To disk is formatted, you'll be asked if it is OK to remove the existing formatting. With your agreement, the process begins by checking the integrity of the data and the quality of the To drive, which is followed by the copying, and finally by verification. When it's done, you have an exact, bootable clone of the master image.

Start Up a Clone for the First Time

When the end user first starts a computer in which one of the clone disks is installed, Windows goes through a miniature version of Setup that takes 5 to 10 minutes (versus 40 to 60 minutes for the full Setup). The Mini-Setup goes through the following steps after loading the GUI environment:

1. A full hardware and Plug and Play detection is carried out.

2. The Windows XP Setup window appears, and after a short time, the system is restarted and the full Windows XP window comes up. After a few minutes, the Windows activation window appears. Click Next.

3. The End User License Agreement is displayed and the end user must accept it and click Next.

4. Enter the Product Key and click Next.

5. The end user must enter the computer name and description and click Next.

6. Enter the administrator's password, and click Next.

7. Determine if the computer is a member of a domain or a workgroup, enter the corresponding name, and click Next.

8. Identify whether the computer connects to the Internet using the local area network or more directly using phone lines and a modem, and click Next.

9. Choose whether to activate the computer, click Next; consider whether to register, click Next; if registering enter the needed information and click Next; enter the names of the computer's users, and click Next and then Finish.

10. Windows is restarted, any printer connections will be made, and the normal Windows XP screen appears.

The process is very straightforward and much less annoying than the full Setup. If you use My Computer or Windows Explorer to look at the hard disk, you'll see that the Sysprep folder and its contents are gone.

Progress Check

1. What is a common form of distributing an unattended Windows installation within a company?

2. What is disk imaging?

3. What must you not do when creating a disk image?

---

1. One of the most common forms of distributing unattended Windows installations within a company is to accompany the Windows CD with a company floppy that installs and configures Windows for the company's environment.

2. Disk imaging is the process of creating and duplicating a standardized disk image or set of contents that is to be placed on the hard disks of multiple computers.

3. When creating a disk image, it is very important that you not restart the original or another computer by booting off the master image hard disk. This is set up to be replicated, and when it or one of its clones is booted, a one-time setup process is run and then the Sysprep folder and its contents are deleted.

Project 5 **Prepare an Installation Plan II**

Similar to what you did in Module 4, use this project to prepare an installation plan for deploying Windows XP Professional. Also, this plan will help you sort through the various ways of automating the installation of either Windows Server 2003 or Windows XP Professional.

Step by Step

1. Determine the method of installation that you will use with Windows XP:

   a. Manually, sitting at the computer to be installed (this module)_____

   b. Automatically, using a script (this module)_____

   c. Remotely, doing the installation across the network (see Module 6)_____

2. Determine the way that you will start Setup of Windows XP:

   a. Over the network (Setup files are on the server)_____

   b. Locally (Setup files on the local computer) and started by:

      i. Booting the Setup CD_____

      ii. Booting from another operating system:

      - MS-DOS_____
      - Windows 3.x or Windows NT 3.51_____
      - Windows 9x, Me, or NT 4_____
      - Windows 2000_____

3. Determine how you will run Setup of Windows XP:

   a. Run a clean install started from a newer version of Windows_____

   b. Run a clean install started in other ways_____

   c. Run an upgrade_____

4. Activate and register Windows XP_____

5. Determine the type of automated installation to use:

   a. Command-line parameters_____

      i. Started from DOS or Windows 3.1x (Winnt)_____

      ii. Started from a newer Windows (Winnt32)_____

Rolling Out Windows XP Professional

Project 5

Prepare an Installation Plan II

(continued)

    b. Answer files_____

        i. Copy and modify the example file_____

        ii. Use the Setup Manager wizard to create an answer file_____

    c. Disk images_____

  6. Determine what Setup Manager will create:

    a. What is the end objective of the answer file:

        i. Windows unattended installation_____

        ii. Sysprep installation_____

        iii. Remote Installation Service_____

    b. What is the platform to be installed:

        i. Windows XP Home Edition_____

        ii. Windows XP Professional Edition_____

        iii. Windows Server 2003 Standard Edition_____

        iv. Windows Server 2003 Enterprise Edition_____

        v. Windows Server 2003 Web Edition_____

    c. What is the level of user interaction desired:

        i. User controlled_____

        ii. Fully automated_____

        iii. Hidden pages_____

        iv. Read Only_____

        v. Final GUI attended_____

  7. Determine how command lines and answer files will be used:

    a. Type a Setup command with parameters at a command prompt_____

    b. Create a batch file with a Setup command and parameters in it_____

    c. Copy a batch file with Setup to another computer and execute it_____

    d. Place a batch file with Setup on a floppy and boot that floppy_____

    e. Place a batch file with Setup on a CD and boot that CD_____

Project Summary

This installation plan will not only allow you to go through the Windows XP setup process more smoothly, but it will also help you think through how to use the Setup automation techniques.

✓

Module 5 Mastery Check

1. While running Setup, can you delete a partition from which you booted? If not, how can you do this?

2. From what Windows products can you upgrade to Windows XP Professional?

3. Where can you specify what languages are installed on the computer and which one is the primary language of the computer?

4. What does automating installation mean, and what are two ways of handling it?

5. What is an answer file, how is it used, and what are some of the tools to help you understand, create, and use one?

6. What does Setup Manager create?

7. What are some of the possible uses for the OEM folder and its subfolders?

8. What are some of the ways that Setup command lines and answer files can be used?

9. What is the critical element that must be true for disk imaging to work, and what are some of the specifics about it?

10. What are the steps in the process of creating and using disk images?

Module 6

Remote Installation Services

Remote Installation Services (RIS) is used to install Windows XP Professional and other software, such as Office, on clients from a server running RIS. This allows you to set up a server to automatically install XP Professional on clients without ever seeing the client computer. This is a substantial improvement over having to visit and spend over an hour in front of each computer on which XP is being installed. RIS can also be used to install other operating systems, except a server, in addition to XP, and to install a number of applications.

Several requirements must be met to run RIS, as follows:

- You must have Administrator privileges.

- The server must meet the minimum requirements for running Windows Server 2003, either Standard or Enterprise Edition, as described in Module 3.

- The server must have a separate NT File System (NTFS) version 5 or later drive or partition (volume) with at least 2GB free (recommended) where RIS can be installed. The RIS volume cannot be the boot drive or partition and cannot have any of the system files stored on it (normally kept in the \Windows\System32\ folder).

- Either the RIS server or other servers on the network must have Domain Name Service (DNS), Dynamic Host Configuration Protocol (DHCP), and Active Directory (AD) running.

- The Windows XP files and applications programs that you want to install on the client computer must be on the RIS server.

- The client that will be installed by RIS must meet the minimum requirements for the operating system being installed.

- The client must have an NTFS version 5 or later formatted drive on which RIS will install the operating system and other desired software. This drive cannot use the Encrypted File System (EFS) or the Distributed File System (DFS), and all previous information on the drive will be lost (you can only do a clean install with RIS).

- The client must either have a network interface card (NIC) that supports the Preboot Execution Environment (PXE) protocol version .99C or later or have a NIC that will work with a special boot floppy that can be created with RIS, as described later in this module.

NOTE

If you are not comfortable with the concepts and operation of DNS, DHCP, and AD, it is recommended that you read Part III of this book on networking (Modules 7, 8, and 9) first and then return to this module.

It turns out that only the latest laptop computers with built-in NICs or the very latest Personal Computer Memory Card International Association (PCMCIA) card (PC card) meet the last requirement, because PXE requires the Peripheral Component Interconnect (PCI) interface, which has not been normally incorporated in the PC cards that are so often used for NICs on laptops. A number of NICs in desktop computers that were manufactured in the last several years (since 1998) and use the PCI interface will work with at least the RIS boot floppy. NICs that allow remote booting and management normally comply with the PXE version .99C protocol. The list of supported NICs as of the date this is written (Fall 2002) is shown next (later in this module, you'll see how to look at a current list of supported NICs):

3Com 3C90*x* family	3Com FEM656C PC Card
3Com MiniPCI	Accton MPX5030
Allied Telesyn 2500TX	AMD PCnet Adapters
Compaq NetFlex 3, 100, 110	DEC DE450, 500
HP DeskDirect 10/100TX	Intel Pro Family
RealTek 8139	SMC 1211 TX EZCard 10/100
SMC 8432 EtherPower 1	SMC 9332 EtherPower 10/100
SMC 9432 EtherPower II 10/100	SMC EN1209D-TX5

CRITICAL SKILL

6.1

Install and Set Up Remote Installation Services

RIS is not installed as part of the normal Windows Server 2003 Standard or Enterprise Edition installation, and therefore, in most cases it must be separately installed and set up.

Install Remote Installation Services

RIS is installed with the Windows Components Wizard entered through Add Or Remove Programs. Use these steps:

1. On the server that you want to contain RIS, open the Start menu, choose Control Panel, click Add Or Remove Programs, click Add/Remove Windows Components. The Windows Components Wizard will open.

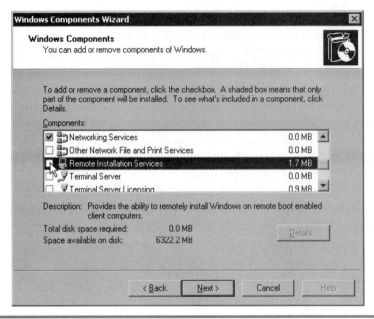

Figure 6-1 Using the Windows Components Wizard to install RIS

2. Scroll down the list of components until you see Remote Installation Services, as shown in Figure 6-1. Click Remote Installation Services, click Next, and then click Finish when it appears.

3. Close the Add Or Remove Programs window and restart the computer.

Set Up Remote Installation Services

To make a server a Remote Installation Services server, you must run its Setup program. Do that next.

1. Open the Start menu and choose All Programs | Administrative Tools | Remote Installation Services Setup. The Remote Installation Services Setup Wizard will open, as you can see here. Notice the requirements.

2. Click Next. The Setup Wizard will search your drives and partitions for one that meets its requirements (NTFS version 5 or later, not a boot drive or partition, and without any system files), and display what it thinks is the best choice or tell you if there isn't one.

TIP

If you need to format a drive or partition, a quick way is to right-click My Computer, choose Manage, open Storage | Disk Management, right-click the drive or partition to be formatted, and choose Format. You can also create a partition from free space as well as format a drive/partition.

3. Accept the recommendation or change it and click Next. You are told that normally the server will not respond to client computers until it is turned on after running Setup, but you can change that.

4. Leave the default of not immediately responding and click Next. Browse to the location of the XP Windows installation files (those that originated on the Windows XP Setup CD) that you want to install on the client computers.

5. Click Next. Enter the name of the folder in which the Windows installation files will be stored on the server ("Windows" is the default) and click Next again. You are shown the friendly description and Help text that will be displayed to users of the Client Installation Wizard if you enable that for the user, similar to what you see here:

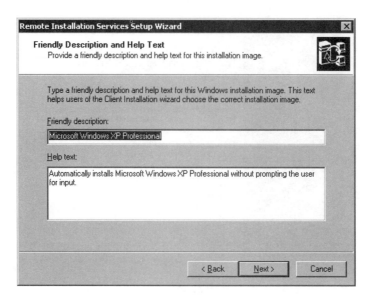

6. Change the description and Help text as you see fit and click Next. You are shown a list of the settings you have chosen. If these are not correct, click Back and make the necessary changes.

7. When the list is correct, click Finish. The RIS Setup Wizard will create the necessary folders, copy the installation files, and create or start the other necessary components to complete the set up of RIS, as shown next. This will take a fair amount of time.

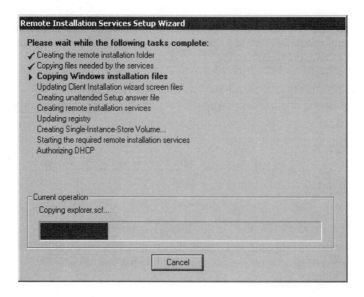

8. When the RIS Setup Wizard has completed all of its tasks, click Done.

NOTE

One of the components set up with RIS is a Single-Instance Store (SIS) volume. If you create several installation images for different combinations of operating systems and applications, there will probably be a lot of overlap among the files in the various images. SIS is a neat capability (called by Microsoft the "SIS groveler agent"!) that searches out and eliminates duplicate files, replacing them with a pointer to a single instance of the file stored in the SIS volume.

CRITICAL SKILL

6.2 Configure Remote Installation Services

While most of the RIS default settings are acceptable, you do need to turn RIS on so that it responds to remote installation requests and then configure it to your needs. Also, you will need to create an RIS boot floppy disk.

Configure RIS to Your Needs

Look at how RIS can be configured with the next set of steps:

1. If you have installed RIS on a domain controller, then open the Start menu and choose Administrative Tools | Active Directory Users And Computers. If RIS is not on a domain controller, then open the Start menu, choose Run, type **dsa.msc**, and press ENTER. In either case, the Active Directory Users And Computers window will open.

2. Within the domain in which the server exists, select either the domain controller or the computer on which RIS has been installed, right-click that computer, and choose Properties.

3. In the Properties dialog box click the Remote Install tab, which will open as shown in Figure 6-2. Select Respond To Client Computers Requesting Service to turn on RIS and then click Verify Server. The Check Server Wizard will start.

4. Click Next. If all is well, you will be told that Setup did not detect any problems. Otherwise, the problems that were found will be described along with what you need to do to fix them. Click Finish. RIS will be restarted, and DHCP will be reauthorized. Click Done to return to the server's Properties dialog box.

5. Click Advanced Settings. Here you can specify how clients will be named and where you want the client accounts kept. Unless you have some reason to change them, leave the defaults. (If you wish to use something other than the username, the Media Access Control

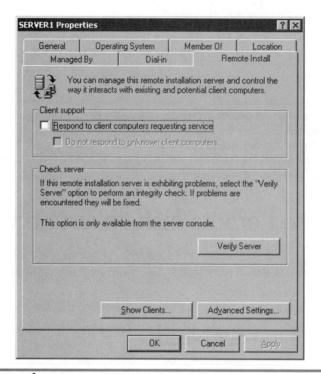

Figure 6-2 Properties of a RIS server

(MAC) address, which is hard-wired onto every NIC by the manufacturer, is a good alternative, but it doesn't give you a user-friendly name by which to identify the computer.)

6. Click the Images tab. You should see the image that you created when you set up RIS. Click the Tools tab. There should be nothing listed (this is for third-party remote installation tools). Click OK twice to close both the Advance Settings and the server's Properties dialog box.

NOTE

Usually the RIS server knows about only the very latest computers that have a globally unique identifier (GUID) / universally unique identifier (UUID) stored in the computer's basic input/output system (BIOS). Therefore, if you click Show Clients you normally will not see anything. Also for that reason, you don't want to select Do Not Respond To Unknown Client Computers, because the only known ones are those with GUID/UUIDs.

Create a Remote Installation Boot Floppy

Since the majority of computers and their NICs are not compliant with the PXE protocol, to use RIS the computers must be started with a special remote installation boot floppy. This boot floppy not only starts the computer, but it also requests an Internet Protocol (IP) address from the DHCP server and then broadcasts that IP address, asking that the RIS server respond. The RIS boot floppy is created with the Rbfg.exe program added to the RIS server when RIS is installed. See how to use this program with these steps:

1. Open the Windows Explorer, locate and open the C:\Windows\System32\RemInst\ folder, and then double-click Rbfg.exe (assuming that C: is the drive on which Windows is installed and you have used the default naming conventions in a clean install). The Remote Boot Disk Generator dialog box will open as shown next.

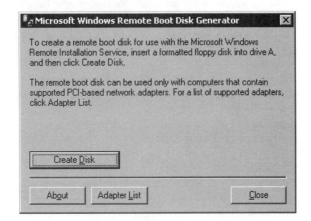

2. Click Adapter List and a list of the NICs that are supported by the remote boot disk will be displayed. Close the Supported Adapters list. If the NIC in the computer you want to install is not shown on the Supported Adapters list, it is still worthwhile trying the remote boot disk process because many NICs emulate those on the list, especially the NE 2000 PCI.

3. Insert a formatted floppy disk in its drive and click Create Disk. The disk will be verified and the files written. When the process is complete, you are told that the floppy has been created and you are asked if you want to create another. Click Yes or No.

4. When you are done creating the floppies you want, click Close to close the Remote Boot Disk Generator dialog box, and remove the floppy disk from its drive.

6.3 Test and Troubleshoot Remote Installation Services

With a floppy boot disk in hand; DHCP, DNS, and Active Directory all running and properly configured; and a valid username and password available, you are ready to test RIS and if necessary troubleshoot it.

Test Remote Installation Services

The following set of steps will show you how to do that:

1. On a client computer on which you want to use RIS, insert the newly created floppy disk and restart the computer. Given the appropriate boot sequence (a floppy boot is enabled and takes place before a hard disk boot), the floppy should boot and give you a series of messages like this:

```
Microsoft Windows Remote Installation Boot Floppy
(C) Copyright 2001 Landworks Technologies Co. a subsidiary of 3Com
Corporation
All rights reserved.
3Com 3C90XB/C 10/100 Ethernet NIC

Node: 0050DABCFF2B
DHCP...
TFTP..............
Press F12 for network service boot
```

Your fourth and sixth lines on the NIC and Node (fifth and seventh lines above) will of course reflect your NIC and its address, but if you do not get all of the last three lines but instead get an error message, you'll need to see the Troubleshooting section following these steps to figure out your problem—there are a number of possible causes.

2. Quickly press F12. If you do not do it within approximately five seconds, you will get a message "Exiting Remote Installation Boot Floppy." In that case, simply reboot with the floppy still in the drive and more quickly press F12. If you press F12 in time, the Client Installation Wizard will appear and the client will be able to log on to the network and install Windows.

3. Press ENTER to continue. Enter a username and password needed to log on to the network. A domain name and the server you are connected to should be displayed. Press ENTER to continue. You are warned that all data on the hard drive will be deleted.

4. Press ENTER again. (If more than one installation image is available, you will be given the choice of which to install; if only one is available, it is assumed and there will not be a

choice.) An account name, a globally unique ID, and the RIS server name that will be used for the installation are shown. If these are not correct, restart the process with Step 1; otherwise, press ENTER to continue. The normal Windows XP Professional Setup should start in character mode and begin copying files.

5. Remove the floppy disk while the character mode file copying is in process. After that completes, the system will restart (why the floppy has to be removed) and the graphic user interface (GUI) setup mode will continue the setup process. In this default installation, the client user will be asked to enter two items, the user's name and the product key (later in the module you'll see how to get around that).

6. When asked, enter the name of the person to use the client and press ENTER. Similarly, enter the product key and press ENTER. Setup will complete the installation, the computer will be restarted, and Windows XP Professional will be started for the first time, where the user will need to go through the activation and registration pages.

Troubleshoot Remote Installation Services

There are obviously a number of things that can go wrong during the RIS test. These are the most common problems:

- Not being able to boot from a floppy

- Network card unsupported by the RIS boot floppy

- Not being able to connect to the RIS server

  Look at each of these next.

Not Able to Boot from a Floppy

Given that you do not have a bad floppy drive or diskette, then the most common reason for not being able to boot from a floppy disk is that that capability has been disabled in the computer's BIOS. Use the next set of steps to look at the BIOS and, if it is okay, to see if there might be a problem with the diskette and then the drive.

NOTE

Not all computers access their BIOS the same way, and not all BIOSes operate the same. The following steps are based on the 1998 and 2000 Award Software BIOS, the 1997 AMI (American Megatrends, Inc.) BIOS, the 1999 IBM ThinkPad 770 BIOS, the 2000 and 2002 Dell Computer BIOS, and a 2002 Toshiba Satellite BIOS. Most computers use some derivative of either the Award or AMI BIOS (Dell is very similar to Award), so it is very possible that even though you aren't working with one of the BIOSes mentioned, you will be able to relate what is said to the computer you are working with.

1. Reboot the computer. Immediately after the memory check that occurs very early in the start up process, press DEL or DELETE on the Award, AMI, and older Dell machines; press F2 on newer Dell machines; press F1 on the IBM ThinkPad; or press ESC and then F1 on the Toshiba. This will open the BIOS Setup utility.

2. *In the older Award BIOS,* use the DOWN ARROW to select BIOS Features Setup; press ENTER; use DOWN ARROW to select Boot Sequence; press PGDN or PGUP to select the A,CDROM,C boot sequence; make sure Boot Up Floppy Seek is Enabled; press ESC; and then press F10 to Save, Exit, and reboot.

   In the newer Award BIOS, use the RIGHT ARROW to select Boot; use DOWN ARROW to select Removable Device; press ENTER to open the choices; use DOWN ARROW to select Legacy Floppy; press ENTER to make it the removable boot device; press the + key to move the Removable Device to the top position; and then press F10 to Save, Exit, and reboot.

   In the older Dell BIOS, use the RIGHT ARROW to select Boot; use DOWN ARROW to select First Boot Device; press ENTER to open the choices; use DOWN ARROW to select Floppy; press ENTER to make it the first boot device; similarly make the second and third boot devices the ATAPI CDROM and IDE hard drive respectively; and then press F10 to Save, Exit, and reboot.

   In the newer Dell BIOS, use the arrow keys to first select Boot; press ENTER; and then 1st Boot Device; press ENTER; select Floppy; press ENTER; similarly choose CDROM for 2nd Boot Device and Hard Disk for the 3rd Boot Device; press F10 to save and exit; select Yes; and press ENTER.

   In the late 1990's-era AMI BIOS, use the RIGHT ARROW to select Advanced; press ENTER; press ENTER again to open the first boot device, use DOWN ARROW to select Floppy; press ENTER to make it the first boot device; similarly make the second and third boot devices the CDROM and IDE-0 respectively; press ESC; select Save Changes And Exit; and press ENTER.

   In the recent IBM ThinkPad BIOS, use the RIGHT ARROW to select Start Up; press ENTER; press ENTER again to select Power-On; click Reset to clear the startup sequence; click FDD-1 to make the floppy disk the first boot device; similarly click CDROM and then HDD-1 to make them the second and third boot devices; and click OK, Exit, Restart, and finally OK to complete setting up the BIOS.

   In the Toshiba Satellite, use the arrow keys to select Boot Priority; press the SPACEBAR until you see FDD – CDROM – LAN – HDD; press END to save and exit; and select Y to indicate you are sure.

3. When you have completed setting up the BIOS so that the floppy can boot, try booting the RIS boot disk again.

4. If the boot disk still does not work, try another boot floppy disk such as an older Windows or DOS boot disk. If these work and the RIS boot disk does not, then the RIS boot disk is

bad. Use a different piece of floppy media and recreate the RIS boot disk using the steps earlier in the module. If the other (Windows or DOS) boot floppy does not work, then most likely the floppy drive is bad and needs to be replaced.

Network Card Not Supported

If you get a message "Error: Could not find a supported network card," then either your NIC is in fact not supported or you have a bad NIC. The only real solution is to get a new NIC. These are not very expensive and are easy to find. For example, the 3Com 3C905CX-TX-M, which is a remote-manageable 10/100 NIC that adheres to the PXE protocol and therefore does not require a RIS boot disk, is available from reputable dealers online for under $40. Go to http://www.pricescan.com or http://www.pricewatch.com and look up network adapter cards from 3Com for the PCI bus.

Not Able to Connect

If you get the message "No reply from a server, press a key to reboot system," then for some reason the server is not replying to the queries from the RIS boot disk for an IP address. This is quite common and normally occurs because Active Directory, DNS, and DHCP are not installed or configured properly, or that the policies and permissions are getting in your way. Module 8 talks in detail about setting up DNS and DHCP, as well as introducing policies and permissions, and Module 9 talks about Active Directory. Overall, the tasks are these:

● Set up networking, making sure that TCP/IP is installed and that the DNS and DHCP server(s) have a fixed IP address.

● Set up DNS and DHCP, making sure that DHCP is running on a domain controller, that it is authorized for the RIS server, and that a scope has been created covering the clients to be installed by RIS. A correctly set up DHCP server should have the components shown here:

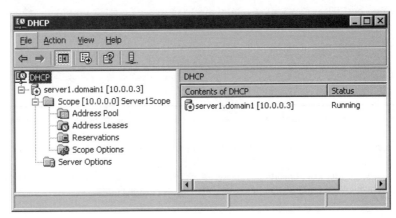

- Set up Active Directory such that the RIS server is a domain controller in the same domain in which the clients to be installed are members.

- Review the policies and permissions for the RIS server and for the client(s) and make sure that nothing stands in the way of doing the remote installation.

- Make sure the person logged on to do the RIS installation (you) has domain administrator privileges.

Progress Check

1. Can you use RIS to install Windows Server 2003?

2. What is the unique hardware requirement of RIS that can be a significant stumbling block to its use?

3. What is a quick way to format a drive or partition?

Ask the Expert

Q: Okay, that was a neat little test, but it certainly wasn't hands free, and only the typical Windows XP Professional was installed. What I really want is to have a complete suite of operating system and applications configured to an organization standard, and installed as close to hands free as possible. Can RIS do that?

A: You bet! RIS gives you several ways to improve on what you have seen already. Keep reading.

---

1. No. RIS can be used to install other operating systems, but not a server, in addition to XP, and to install a number of applications.

2. The client must have either a NIC that supports the PXE protocol version .99C or later or a NIC that will work with a special boot floppy.

3. A quick way to format a drive or partition is to right-click My Computer, choose Manage, open Storage | Disk Management, right-click the drive or partition to be formatted, and choose Format.

CRITICAL SKILL

6.4 Extend Remote Installation Services

RIS allows you to install a complete suite of operating system and applications configured to an organization standard, and to have this as hands free as possible by using

● RIPrep to create an image for remote installation using a completed model installation, including applications and custom settings

● Custom Scripts to automate more or less of the installation process

Each of these capabilities addresses different areas of the installation process and will be described in the following sections.

Use RIS to Install More Than the Operating System

RIS allows you to create a model computer with all the applications and settings that you want to make the standard for your organization and then use the Remote Installation Preparation Wizard or RIPrep to create an image on the RIS server of the model computer. This image can then be used by RIS to replicate it on a number of other computers. The steps to do this are as follows:

NOTE

When you do multiple installations of a specifically configured operating system and set of applications, you are assuming that the computers on which you are doing the installation are close to identical in terms of hardware. This is particularly important for newer laptops with the Advanced Configuration and Power Interface (ACPI), which must use their own image.

1. On the client that you installed using RIS, configure the Start menu, desktop, and other settings to conform to your standard. Then install and configure the applications and utilities that you want on the standard, and do any other setup and configuration activities to have the machine be the prototype you want to replicate.

NOTE

You must use the copy of the operating system that was installed by RIS. Otherwise, RIPrep will not function correctly.

2. Do a Full System Backup on the client using a medium, such as another hard disk or a tape, that is at least as large as the disk being backed up. It is possible that if RIPrep fails during its process of copying the image to the server, the client disk files may be destroyed in the process. Use the Windows XP Backup or Restore Wizard (Start | All Programs | Accessories | System Tools | Backup), choose All Information On This Computer, and a boot/recovery floppy disk will be created that will allow you to fully recreate this prototype.

3. On the prototype client, use Windows Explorer to browse to the RIS Server RemoteInstall (assuming you used the default folder name)\Admin\i386\ folder and double-click RIPrep.exe. The Remote Installation Preparation Wizard will start as shown here:

4. Click Next, confirm that the name of the RIS server is correct, and click Next again. Enter a name for the folder that will contain the new image.

NOTE

If you get a message that the current user does not have permission to do the operation being attempted, you need to go to the server and establish a user account for the client user and give that user domain Administrator privileges.

5. Click Next. Enter a friendly description and Help text of the image you are about to create, and once more click Next. If there are multiple user accounts on the client, you will get a warning message that all user-specific data will be removed when the image is created.

If that is okay, click Next. Otherwise, click Cancel, remove any needed user data, and restart RIPrep.

6. You are told that a number of services will be stopped, such as Help, Messenger, COM+, Task Scheduler, and others. Given that you are working on the prototype client, stopping all of them is okay, so click Next. The services will be stopped. A summary of the settings you have chosen will be displayed.

7. Click Next. You are told that when you click Next again, RIPrep will prepare the client, create the replication image on the server, and then shut down the client.

8. Click Next. The client is checked, its files are copied to the server, and then the client is shut down.

Since all user-specific data has been deleted, when the client is restarted a mini-Setup will be run to restore the computer to a usable configuration. This Setup does no copying, so it runs very quickly, asking you only to accept the license agreement, enter your name and organization, enter the product key, and answer several setup questions. These settings are entered into the Registry, Setup completes, and the system is restarted. Upon restarting, you are asked if you want to set up new network user accounts, and you must reactivate and optionally register the system.

In the RIS server, you can use the Windows Explorer to browse to the RIS volume, then to the \RemoteInstall\Setup\English\Images*yourimagename*\ folder, and see the custom image you just created. In Figure 6-3 you can see I have two images, WINXPPro, the original standard Windows XP Professional installation, and WinXP-OffXP, the new custom installation that contains both Windows XP and Office XP.

The new custom image is used in the same way as you used the standard image described in Testing Remote Installation Services earlier in this module. Boot with the Remote Install floppy or a PXE-compliant NIC, press F12, and after the first two familiar screens, the OS Chooser appears and allows you to choose between the original standard Windows XP and the new custom Windows XP with the applications you added. Choose the custom installation. Continue with the remaining familiar screens. Shortly Setup will start and copy the necessary files, and after you remove the boot floppy, the system will reboot and complete the installation with the entry of a username and product key.

When the new installation finally opens, you may need to change the resolution of the screen, rearrange the order of the desktop, and reactivate the products. The applications are all installed and fully usable.

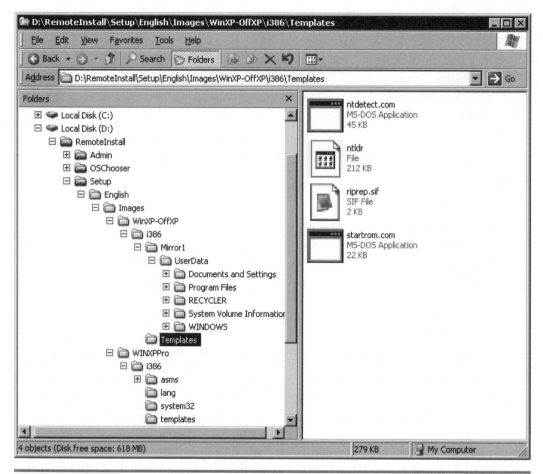

Figure 6-3 The new custom image WinXP-OffXP

Customize the Remote Installation Script

If you want more or less automation, the next step is to edit the setup information file (SIF) that is automatically created for you when the installation image is saved to the RIS server. This file is in the \RemoteInstall\Setup\English\Images*imagename*\i386\Templates folder and has either of two names, depending on how it was created. If the SIF was created by a standard RIS installation as was described early in the module, then it is named Ristndrd.sif. If the file was created by RIPrep, then it is named Riprep.sif. Figure 6-4 shows the Riprep.sif file that was created in the previous section ("Using RIS to Install More Than the Operating System").

```
[data]
floppyless = "1"
msdosinitiated = "1"
OriSrc = "\\%SERVERNAME%\RemInst\%INSTALLPATH%\%MACHINETYPE%"
OriTyp = "4"
LocalSourceOnCD = 1

[SetupData]
OsLoadOptions = "/noguiboot /fastdetect"
SetupSourceDevice ="\Device\LanmanRedirector\%SERVERNAME%\RemInst\%INSTALLPATH%"
SysPrepDevice="\Device\LanmanRedirector\%SERVERNAME%\RemInst\%SYSPREPPATH%"
SysPrepDriversDevice="\Device\LanmanRedirector\%SERVERNAME%\RemInst\%SYSPREPDRIVERS%"

[Unattended]
OemPreinstall = no
FileSystem = LeaveAlone
ExtendOEMPartition = 0
TargetPath = \WINDOWS
OemSkipEula = yes
InstallFilesPath = "\\%SERVERNAME%\RemInst\%INSTALLPATH%\%MACHINETYPE%"
LegacyNIC = 1

[UserData]
FullName = "%USERFIRSTNAME% %USERLASTNAME%"
OrgName = "%ORGNAME%"
ComputerName ="%MACHINENAME%"

[GuiUnattended]
OemSkipWelcome = 1
OemSkipRegional = 1
TimeZone = %TIMEZONE%
AdminPassword = "*"

[Display]
BitsPerPel = 16
XResolution = 800
YResolution = 600
VRefresh = 60

[Networking]

[NetServices]
MS_Server=params.MS_PSched

[Identification]
JoinDomain = %MACHINEDOMAIN%
DoOldStyleDomainJoin = Yes
```

Figure 6-4 Setup information file used by RIPrep, which can be customized

NOTE

There are actually two copies of the SIF, one in the ...\i386\ folder and one in the
...\i386\Templates folder. Always edit the copy in the ...\Templates\ folder because
the copy in the ...\i386\ folder gets copied over by the copy in the ...\Templates\
folder each time RIS is run.

As you saw in Module 5 with the various script files used to automate Setup, there are
many items that you can customize; for example, you can do these things:

● Allow the use of OEM folders to include your data and drivers in the installation.

- Add a product key so that does not have to be entered.

- Add a user's name so that does not have to be entered.

- Use your own computer name instead of the one generated by RIPrep.

- Add a strong password to better protect the system.

- Correct the display resolutions to match those desired.

- Add a domain administrator username and password.

There are, of course, many other things you can do with the setup information file, such as turn system components on or off, but look at how to do the seven items just mentioned:

1. Using the Windows Explorer, locate the RIS volume and open the \RemoteInstall\Setup\ English\Images*imagename*\i386\Templates folder. Use the image created by RIPrep, and double-click Riprep.sif. If requested, click Select The Program From A List, click OK, and double-click Notepad. Your Notepad window should look similar to Figure 6-4.

2. In Notepad, open the File menu, choose Save As, and save the file as Riprep.org. That gives you the original file to return to should you want it again. Close that file and reopen Riprep.sif, which you will now change.

3. Locate the [Unattended] section and the line that reads OemPreinstall = no. Change that to read **OemPreinstall = yes**. This allows you to add OEM folders, as discussed in Module 5.

NOTE

The OEM folders must be at the same level in the RIS folder structure as the i386 folder and *not* inside the i386 folder as shown in Module 5. So in the current RIPrep example being discussed here, the path to the OEM folders would be \RemoteInstall\ Setup\English\Images*imagename*\OEM.

4. Locate the [UserData] section and immediately under the title add a new line that reads: **ProductID=*aaaaa-11111-bbbbb-22222-ccccc*** where *aaaaa-11111-bbbbb-22222-ccccc* is the 25-character product key you need to use.

5. Also in the [UserData] section, change as desired the strings within the quotation marks for FullName, OrgName, and ComputerName.

6. In the [GuiUnattended] section, locate AdminPassword = "*" and replace the * with the password you want to use. In the [Display] section, change the values for XResolution, YResolution, and VRefresh to values that are correct for the monitor(s) being installed.

7. In the [Identification] section, change JoinDomain = %MACHINEDOMAIN% to
JoinDomain = *domainname,* delete the line DoOldStyleDomainJoin = yes, and replace it
with these two lines:

DomainAdmin=*administratorname*

DomainAdminPassword=*administratorpassword*

This change is required because you must have an identified domain administrator to create
your own machine name in place of the automatically generated name.

8. Save the file under its original name in its original location. It should now look like the next
image, which shows the changes in bold (yours will not be bold).

```
[data]
floppyless = "1"
msdosinitiated = "1"
OriSrc = "\\%SERVERNAME%\RemInst\%INSTALLPATH%\%MACHINETYPE%"
OriTyp = "4"
LocalSourceOnCD = 1

[SetupData]
OsLoadOptions = "/noguiboot /fastdetect"
SetupSourceDevice ="\Device\LanmanRedirector\%SERVERNAME%\RemInst\%INSTALLPATH%"
SysPrepDevice="\Device\LanmanRedirector\%SERVERNAME%\RemInst\%SYSPREPPATH%"
SysPrepDriversDevice="\Device\LanmanRedirector\%SERVERNAME%\RemInst\%SYSPREPDRIVERS%"

[Unattended]
OemPreinstall = yes
FileSystem = LeaveAlone
ExtendOEMPartition = 0
TargetPath = \WINDOWS
OemSkipEula = yes
InstallFilesPath = "\\%SERVERNAME%\RemInst\%INSTALLPATH%\%MACHINETYPE%"
LegacyNIC = 1

[UserData]
ProductID=aaaaa-11111-bbbbb-22222-ccccc
FullName = "Martin Matthews"
OrgName = "Matthews Technology"
ComputerName ="Station2"

[GuiUnattended]
OemSkipWelcome = 1
OemSkipRegional = 1
TimeZone = %TIMEZONE%
AdminPassword = "someword"

[Display]
BitsPerPel = 16
XResolution = 1024
YResolution = 768
VRefresh = 72

[Networking]

[NetServices]
MS_Server=params.MS_PSched

[Identification]
JoinDomain = Domain1
DomainAdmin=Administrator
DomainAdminPassword=someword
```

9. Once again, start the test client using the RIS boot floppy disk or PXE NIC, using the custom installation you most recently used in the previous section. The Setup will go exactly the same, except that you should not have to enter the product key or the username and you should not have to change the display resolution. Also, you will get all the custom components from your model image.

CRITICAL SKILL
6.5 Customize the Client Experience

The last bit of customizing RIS is to tailor what the customer sees on the screen and must do to start the remote installation process, and to allow RIS to do custom and restarted installation.

Customize the Client Installation Wizard

The initial set of screens that appear when you do a RIS installation, called the Client Installation Wizard, are stored in the \RemoteInstall\OSChooser\English\ folder on the RIS volume. These screens are similar to (but not exactly the same as) HTML-based web pages, and they can be easily modified using Notepad. For example, the content for the initial Welcome screen is shown in Figure 6-5. As in HTML, there are tags enclosed in angle brackets, and there is always a beginning tag and often an ending tag. Text outside of the angle brackets is displayed as is on the screen. You can therefore modify the text outside the angle brackets at will, making it anything you want. The trick is to understand and use the tags to do the things you want. Many are, of course, obvious, but the action tags are not always so.

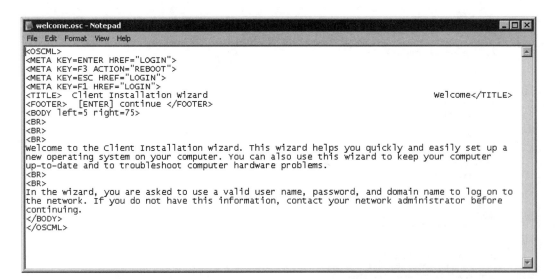

Figure 6-5 The content for the Welcome screen of the Client Installation Wizard

If you look at the four <META> tags in Figure 6-5, you'll see that they all relate a keystroke to something. In three of the four cases, the keystroke is related to HREF="LOGIN". HREF says to open another screen whose name is contained in quotation marks, so the three <META> tags in the Welcome screen with HREF say that if you press ENTER, ESC, or F1, the Login screen should be opened. ACTION says to perform whatever task in the quotation marks, so the ACTION="REBOOT" tag says that if you press F3, the computer should be restarted. The primary purpose of the Welcome screen is to get you to press ENTER, which will open the Login screen.

Open the Login.osc screen, which is shown in Figure 6-6. The <META KEY> tags are similar to what you saw in the Welcome screen except there is no <META> tag for the ENTER key. The <META ACTION="LOGIN"> tag says to take the information on this screen and log in to an Active Directory domain. The <FORM ACTION="CHOICE"> tag begins a form in which the user is to enter a username, a password, and a domain name. The values that are entered are stored in the variables in quotation marks ("USERNAME", "*PASSWORD", and "USERDOMAIN"), the password has its own variable type, and the domain name has a default value contained in an environment variable passed from the server. When the user has made the requested entries and pressed ENTER, there is no obvious next screen. This must be determined by some combination of the LOGIN and CHOICE actions.

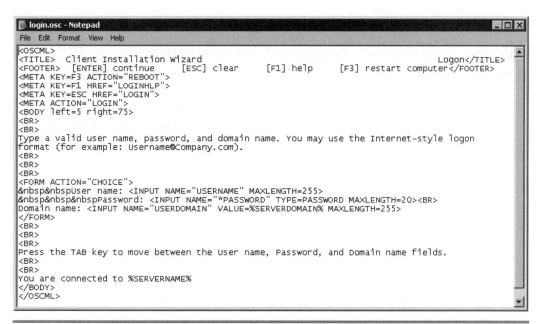

Figure 6-6 The content for the Login screen of the Client Installation Wizard

If you look at the other .osc screens, you will encounter ones that you have already seen and a number that you probably have not. Many of the screens are error messages or help screens. Some of the other commonly used screens are

- Oschoice.osc, used when there are multiple images from which to choose

- Choice.osc, used to choose among custom, automated, and restarted installations

- Custom.osc, used with a custom installation where the user must enter a computer name and a directory service path

- Install.osc, the final screen showing the choices made and used to start Setup

The variables that are entered in the Client Installation Wizard screens are available as environment variables in the setup information files Ristndrd.sif and Riprep.sif. That means that you can gather information in the Client Installation Wizard and pass it to setup information. For example, "MACHINENAME" in the Custom.osc screen is picked up as the %MACHINENAME% environment variable in the .sif files.

The action commands, such as LOGIN and CHOICE, obviously call programs that perform a number of functions that we can only guess about. Therefore, changing the Client Installation Wizard screens requires a trial-and-error process to see what works and what doesn't. If you are rolling out enough systems, though, it may be worth your time to see what you can do with these screens.

Allow Custom and Restarted Installations

In all the examples so far in this module, the running of Setup on the client has been very automated, with you at most only having to enter a username and a product ID. This is normally what is desired, and it is therefore the system default. If you wish, you can change this to allow a custom setup and to allow Setup to be stopped and restarted. The domain's group policies control this, as you can see in Figure 6-7, so they need to be changed to allow custom and restarted Setups. Here's how to do it:

1. Open the Start menu and choose All Programs | Administrative Tools | Active Directory Users And Computers. Right-click the domain containing the RIS clients and choose Properties.

2. Open the Group Policy tab, in the Group Policy Object Links area choose the Default Domain Policy, and click Edit. The Group Policy Object Editor window will open.

3. Open Default Domain Policy | User Configuration | Windows Settings | Remote Installation Services and double-click Choice Options. The resulting window and dialog box are shown in Figure 6-7.

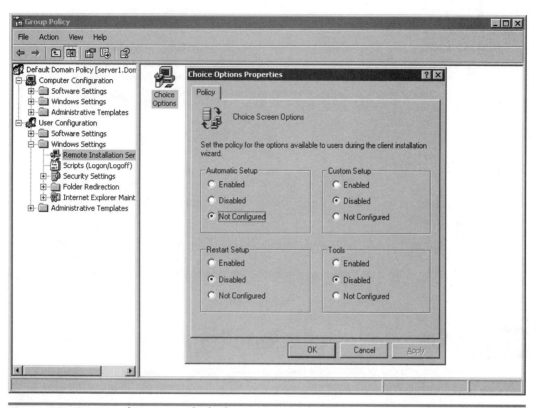

Figure 6-7 Group policies control whether a remote installation is automated or custom.

4. Click Enabled for both Custom Setup and Restart Setup, click OK to close the Choice
Options Properties dialog box, and then close the Group Policy Object Editor window, the
domain Properties dialog box, and the Active Directory Users And Computers window.

Having made this change, if you now use the RIS boot floppy or a computer PXE NIC to
boot, the third screen to appear (the one after logging on with your username) now allows you
to choose an automatic setup, to choose a custom setup, or if a previous setup attempt is
detected, to restart it. If you choose Custom Setup, you can specify a computer name and the
directory service path (typically *domainname*/computers) for the computer account.

NOTE

If you ran the preceding steps on the same client computer used earlier in this module and named the computer something other than the automatic name given to it earlier, you will get a warning that you are creating a duplicate GUID entry in directory services. You can continue with Setup and manually remove the automated entry afterward from Active Directory Users And Computers.

Progress Check

1. When making an image to use with RIPrep, can you use the OS files you earlier copied to the RIS server?

2. What do you do if you want more or less automation with RIS?

3. How can you allow a custom setup and allow Setup to be stopped and restarted?

Project 6 Remote Installation Plan

Similar to what you did in Modules 4 and 5, use this project to prepare a remote installation plan for deploying Windows XP Professional and possibly other applications.

Step by Step

1. Determine if you have the minimum requirements to run RIS:

   a. You have administrative privileges

   b. The server meets minimum requirements for running Windows Server 2003

   c. The server has a separate NTFS drive or partition of at least 2GB

   d. The LAN has DNS, DHCP, and Active Directory running

   e. The Windows XP and application files are available to the server

   f. The client computer(s) meet the minimum requirements for XP

---

1. No, you must use the copy of the operating system that was installed by RIS. Otherwise, RIPrep will not function correctly.

2. If you want more or less automation with RIS, edit the setup information file (SIF) that has been automatically created for you when the installation image is saved to the RIS server.

3. You can allow a custom setup and allow Setup to be stopped and restarted by changing the domain's group policies that control this.

    g. The client must have a drive over 2GB and formatted with NTFS 5

    h. The client must have a NIC that supports the PXE protocol, or the NIC must work with the boot floppy

2. Install Remote Installation Services

3. Set up Remote Installation Services:

    a. Determine the drive or partition to use for RIS:

        i. Formatted with NTFS

        ii. Not a boot drive

        iii. No active system files

    b. Determine the name of the folder to store the installation files

    c. Determine the friendly name and Help text for this installer

4. Configure Remote Installation Services:

    a. In the domain properties Remote Install, select Respond To Clients

    b. In the domain properties Remote Install, verify the server's capability

    c. Determine how you want the clients named

    d. Determine where you want the clients' accounts kept

    e. Verify that the installation image is available on the RIS server

5. Create a Remote Installation Services boot floppy:

    a. Start the Remote Boot Disk Generator

    b. Verify that the client NIC is on the Supported list

    c. Write the boot floppy

6. Test Remote Installation Services:

    a. Start the client either with the boot floppy or over the LAN

    b. Choose the installation image to use

    c. Determine the globally unique ID and RIS server to use

    d. Complete the remainder of the installation

7. Troubleshoot Remote Installation Services:

    a. Not able to boot from a floppy:

Project 6

Remote Installation Plan

(continued)

        i. Floppy not in BIOS boot list

        ii. Bad media

        iii. Bad drive

    b. Network card not supported—get a new card

    c. Not able to connect—assure DNS, DHCP, AD:

        i. Set up networking

        ii. Set up DNS and DHCP

        iii. Set up Active Directory

        iv. Review policies and permissions

        v. You have domain administrator privileges

8. Use Remote Installation Services to install more than an OS:

    a. Create a client prototype with settings and applications

    b. Do a full backup of the client

    c. Run Riprep.exe on the server from the client

    d. Run an install as before, but with the new image

9. Customize the Remote Installation Services script to:

    a. Allow the use of OEM folders

    b. Add a username and product key

    c. Add a computer name

    d. Add a strong password

    e. Correct the display resolution

    f. Add a domain administrator name and password

10. Customize the Client Installation Wizard screens

11. Enable custom and restarted installations

Project Summary

This remote installation plan will enable you to more easily use RIS to set up Windows XP and possibly other applications.

Module 6 Mastery Check

1. What are the requirements that must be met to run RIS?

2. What is a Single-Instance Store (SIS) volume?

3. What are the most common items that can go wrong during a RIS installation?

4. Why, if you click Show Clients, do you normally not see anything?

5. What are the summary set of tasks to set up a domain controller for a RIS installation?

6. What are two ways RIS provides to customize the remote installation process?

7. What is the major assumption when you do multiple installations of a specifically configured operating system and set of applications?

8. What is SIF, is there more than one copy of it, and if so, which do you use?

9. Should the OEM folders be at the same level in the RIS folder structure when used with RIS as was shown in Module 5 for the simple automation of Setup with an answer file?

10. How can you change the initial set of screens that appear when you do a RIS installation?

Part III

Networking Windows Server 2003

Module 7

Windows Server 2003 Networking Environment

etworking is the single most important function within Windows Server 2003. It is its reason for being. The ability to connect computers and allow them to share information and resources is at the forefront of today's push for improved productivity. In line with that importance, this part devotes three modules to networking. Module 7 provides a comprehensive foundation on networking by describing the schemes, hardware, and protocols or standards that are used to make it function. Module 8 describes how networking is set up and managed in Windows Server 2003. Module 9 looks at how domains are used in Windows Server 2003 and the central role that Active Directory plays in managing networking.

CRITICAL SKILL
7.1 Define Networking

Windows Server 2003 is a *network operating system.* This allows the interconnection of multiple computers for the purpose of:

- Exchanging information, such as by sending a file from one computer to another

- Communicating by, for example, sending e-mail among network users

- Sharing information by having common files accessed by network users

- Sharing resources on the network, such as printers and backup tape drives

Networking is important to almost every organization of two or more people who communicate and share information. Exchanging information allows multiple people to easily work from and utilize the same data and prevent errors caused by not having the latest information. E-mail communications facilitate the fast and easy coordination among people of current information, such as meeting arrangements. Sharing information allows multiple people to update and maintain a large database. Sharing resources allows an organization to purchase better (more capable and expensive) devices (for example, a color laser printer) than if they purchased one for each user. Networking is a primary ingredient in the computer's contribution to improved productivity, and from the viewpoint of this book, networking is the single most important facility in Windows Server 2003.

Networking is a system that includes the physical connection between computers that facilitates the transfer of information, as well as the scheme for controlling that transfer. The scheme makes sure that the information is transferred correctly (to the correct recipient) and accurately (the data is exactly the same on both the receiving and sending ends) while many other transfers are occurring simultaneously. To accomplish these objectives while other information is being transferred—generally, a lot of other information—there must be a standard way to correctly identify and address each transfer, and to stop one transfer while another is taking place. A networking system then has these components:

- A networking scheme that handles the transfer

- Networking hardware that handles the physical connection

- A networking standard or protocol that handles the identification and addressing

Windows Server 2003 supports several different networking schemes, works with a variety of hardware, and handles several protocols. The purpose of this module is to look at the possible networking options provided for in Windows Server 2003 in enough detail for you to choose which of these options is best for your installation. Module 8 will then look at how to set up and manage networking with Windows Server 2003, and Module 9 will look at Active Directory and domains in greater depth.

NOTE

While this section of the book provides a great deal of networking information, it pales in comparison with Tom Sheldon's *Encyclopedia of Networking & Telecommunications* (McGraw-Hill/Osborne, 2001). If you find you need more information than is presented here, see Tom's book. He also maintains an active web site at http://www.linktionary.com.

CRITICAL SKILL
7.2 Identify Networking Schemes

The schemes used to transfer information in a network substantially determine the hardware that is used, are integral to the software, and must implement the standards or protocols desired. It is therefore difficult to talk about just the schemes, just the hardware, or just the protocols. They are very interrelated. This is further complicated by the networking scheme being a function of both the type of networking and the technology it employs.

Network Types

The network type is determined by whether the network is confined to a single location or is spread over a wide geographic area.

A network that is spread over a wide geographic area is called a *wide area network (WAN)*. WANs can use telephone lines, both shared and private, satellite links, microwave links, and both shared and dedicated fiber-optic or copper cabling to connect nodes across a street or on the other side of the world. WANs with reasonable amounts of bandwidth (1 Mbps and above) are expensive, on the order of one to several thousand dollars per month, and demand sophisticated technology. They are therefore a major undertaking for a larger organization. A simpler and less expensive, although still not cheap, use of WANs is to interconnect smaller networks within a building or within a campus of closely located buildings. This use of intracampus WANs is discussed in several other places in this module.

NOTE

Many companies are using the Internet to do what WANs once handled, such as e-mail and private information exchange using virtual private networking or VPN, which is discussed in Module 12, so the growth in WANs is very modest.

A network that is confined to a single location is called a *local area network (LAN)*. LANs use dedicated cabling or wireless channels and generally do not go outside of a single building; they may be limited to a single floor of a building or a department within a company. LANs are much more common than WANs and are the type of network primarily discussed in this and the next two modules. LANs have two subcategories, peer-to-peer LANs and client/server LANs, which are distinguished by how they distribute networking tasks.

Peer-to-Peer LANs

All computers in a peer-to-peer LAN are both servers and clients and therefore share in both providing and using resources. Any computer in the network may store information and provide resources, such as a printer, for the use of any other computer in the network. Peer-to-peer networking is an easy first step to networking, accomplished simply by joining existing computers together, as shown in Figure 7-1. It does not require the purchase of new computers or significant changes to the way an organization is using computers, yet resources can be shared (as is the printer in Figure 7-1), files and communications can be transferred, and common information can be accessed by all.

Peer-to-peer LANs tend to be used in smaller organizations that neither need to share a large central resource, such as a database, nor need a high degree of security or central control. Each computer in a peer-to-peer LAN is autonomous and often is joined together with other computers simply to transfer files and share expensive equipment. As you'll read later in the

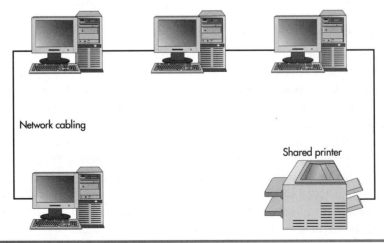

Figure 7-1 A peer-to-peer LAN with bus topology

module, under "Understand Networking Hardware," putting together a peer-to-peer LAN with existing computers is fairly easy and can be inexpensive (less than $50 per station).

Client/Server LANs

The computers in a client/server LAN perform one of two functions: they are either servers or clients. *Servers* manage the network, centrally store information that is to be shared on the network, and provide the shared resources to the network. *Clients,* or workstations, are the users of the network and are normal desktop or laptop computers. To create a network, the clients and server(s) are connected together, possibly with stand-alone network resources such as printers, as shown in Figure 7-2.

NOTE

The difference in network cabling between Figures 7-1 and 7-2 is not a function of one network being peer-to-peer and the other client/server, but rather is a function of the cabling topology used. See "Use Network Topologies" later in this module.

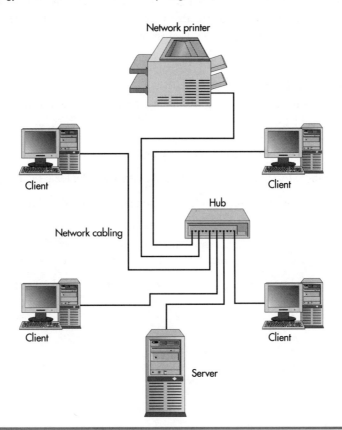

Figure 7-2 A client/server LAN with a star topology

The management functions provided by the server include network security and managing the permissions needed to implement security, communications among network users, and management of shared files on the network. Servers generally are more capable than clients in terms of having more memory, faster (and possibly more) processors, larger (and maybe more) disks, and more special peripherals, such as large, high-speed tape drives. Servers generally are dedicated to their function and are infrequently used for normal computer tasks, such as word processing.

Clients generally are less capable than servers and, infrequently, may not even have a disk. Clients usually are normal desktop and laptop computers that perform the normal functions for those types of machines, in addition to being part of a network. Clients can also be "miniservers," by sharing out some or all of their disk drives or other resources. Therefore, the principal difference between peer-to-peer networks and client/server networks is the addition of a dedicated server.

Windows XP and Windows Server 2003 work together to form a client/server network operating environment, with the Windows Server 2003 performing its function and Windows XP Professional being the client. Several Windows XP Professional workstations or Windows XP Home Edition computers can operate in a peer-to-peer network, but the general assumption throughout this book is that you are principally interested in client/server networking using Windows Server 2003 and Windows XP Professional.

The Networking Task

The task performed by the networking system is substantial and complex. At a minimum, the task includes these elements:

- Identifying each of the computers in a network

- Identifying the information to be transferred as an individual *message*

- Adding to each message a unique identification and the address of the sending and receiving computers

- Enclosing the message in one or more moderate-sized *packets,* similar to envelopes, with the sending and receiving addresses and where the packet belongs within a message

- Encapsulating packets into *frames* that are transferred over the network

- Monitoring network traffic to know when to send a frame so as to avoid colliding with other frames on the network

- Transmitting a frame over the network (depending on the interconnection devices that are used, the frame may be opened and the packets put in new frames while en route)

- Providing the physical means, including cabling and electronic devices, to carry the frame between computers

- Monitoring network traffic to know when a frame is to be received

- Receiving a frame that is on the network

- Extracting the packets in one or more frames and combining the packets into the original message

- Determining whether the message belongs to the receiving computer and then either sending the message into the computer for further processing if it belongs to the computer, or ignoring the message if doesn't belong to the computer

Ask the Expert

Q: At what point should we give up peer-to-peer networking and go play in the big leagues of client/server?

A: There is no one answer for that; it really depends on the demands of the organization. The reasons for using client/server are a need for a large centralized database and its attendant processing, as would be needed for a central accounting, ordering, or personnel system; and/or the need for centralized control of shared files and permissions. One indication that you are nearing the time to make the switch is that one or more computers in your peer-to-peer network is being so heavily used for group functions that it can no longer be used by an individual as a workstation. This computer should be designated a server.

NOTE

Names for pieces of information, such as messages, packets, and frames, are discussed further under "TCP" later in this module; Figure 7-20 in that section shows these pieces of information pictorially.

To better describe the networking task, the International Organization for Standardization, or ISO (a U.N. organization incorrectly referred to as the International Standards Organization; the acronym ISO comes from the Greek word *isos,* meaning equal), developed a reference model for networking. This model is called the Open Systems Interconnection (OSI) model.

NOTE

The OSI model is useful for describing networking and for relating its various components. It does not necessarily represent Windows Server 2003 or any other networking implementation, but it is a widely known and accepted reference.

The OSI Model

The OSI model describes how information in one computer moves through a network to another computer. It defines networking in terms of seven layers, each of which performs a particular set of functions within the networking task, breaking the networking task into seven smaller tasks. Each layer can communicate with the layers above and below it and with its opposite layer in another networked computer, as shown in Figure 7-3. The communication between computers goes down through the lower layers, across the physical connection, and back up the layers in the other computer.

In the OSI model, the lower two layers are implemented in a combination of hardware and software, while the upper five layers are all implemented in software. The software in the lower layers is dedicated to networking and may be burned into silicon. The software in upper layers is a part of the operating system or an application to which networking is only one of its tasks. For example, an e-mail client application wishing to get its mail off the server passes its request to the Application layer of the network system in its computer. This information is passed down through the layers until it reaches the Physical layer, where the information is placed on the physical network. The Physical layer in the server takes the information off the physical network and passes it up through the layers until it reaches the Application layer, which passes the request to the e-mail server application.

Each of the OSI layers can add, if necessary, specific control information to information being transferred over the network. The control information can be for other layers in its own stack or for its opposite layer in the other computer and can be either requests or instructions. The control information can be added either as a header at the beginning of information being transferred or as a trailer at the end. The header or trailer added at one layer becomes part of

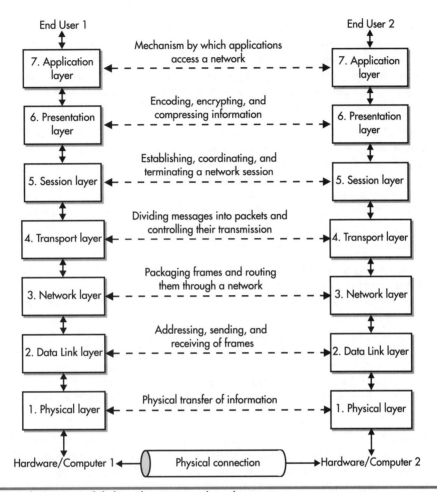

Figure 7-3 The OSI model describing networking between two computers

the basic information being transferred at another layer. The next layer may add another header or trailer or, if an existing header or trailer is intended for that layer, remove the header or trailer. The following lists the type of control information and function defined for each layer:

- **Physical layer**   Defines the physical specifications, such as voltages and timing, to make the network interface function as intended. These specifications are implemented in networking hardware.

- **Data Link layer**   Defines the addressing of frames and the sending and receiving of frames between two linked computers. After passing a frame to the Physical layer to be sent, the Data Link layer waits for acknowledgment that the frame has been received, before it sends another frame; if the acknowledgment is not received, the Data Link layer resends the first frame. The Data Link layer provides point-to-point linkage between itself and the receiving computer by using physical addresses. The physical address at the Data Link layer is called the *media access control (MAC)* address. The Data Link specifications are implemented in a combination of hardware and dedicated networking software.

- **Network layer**   Defines the packaging of packets into frames and the logical addressing (as opposed to the physical addressing used in the Data Link layer) necessary to provide internetwork routing through multiple, connected networks. Packets, which may be larger or smaller than frames, are broken up or combined to create a frame in the sending computer, and are reassembled or disassembled in the receiving computer to reproduce the original packets. The Network layer's internetworking commonly uses the Internet Protocol (IP) addressing to identify where frames should be sent. The Network layer specifications are implemented in dedicated networking software.

- **Transport layer**   Defines the division of a message into packets, the identification of the packets, and the control of the packet transmission to know whether the packets are being sent and received correctly, and if not, to pause and resend a transmission. The Transport layer creates, regulates, and terminates a flow of packets by using a *virtual circuit* between the sending and receiving computers (the flow is still down through the other layers, across the physical connection, and up the other side, but it occurs as if the two Transport layers were directly talking to each other). The Transport layer commonly uses the Transmission Control Protocol (TCP) to start, regulate, and terminate the flow of packets. The Transport layer specifications are implemented in networking-related OS software using networking protocols.

- **Session layer**   Defines the dialog between computers so that they know both when to start and stop transmission, creating a *session,* and when to repeat a session if it is not correctly received. The Session layer also handles security-related issues and has its roots in the mainframe/terminal timesharing environment. The Session layer specifications are implemented in network-related OS software.

- **Presentation layer**   Defines the encoding of information so that it is easily and securely transmitted and read by the receiving computer. This includes the conversion of character, graphic, audio, and video information into common data representation, the encryption and compression of information, and the return of the information to its native form upon receipt. The Presentation layer specifications are implemented in OS software.

- **Application layer**   Defines the mechanism by which applications access the network to send and receive information. This includes the two-way handling of information, as well as the identifying, locating, and determining of the availability of the partner for an information exchange. The Application layer specifications are implemented in OS and application software.

Keep the OSI model in mind as you read the remainder of this and the next several modules. It will help you relate the various components used in networking. Later in this module, under "Interconnection Device Summary," you'll see how the OSI model relates to hardware devices such as hubs and switches, and under "Implement Networking Protocols," you'll see how the OSI model relates to networking protocols and data-naming conventions.

LAN Technologies

LAN technologies are standards that span hardware and software, to handle a large part of the dedicated networking task. LAN technologies handle the entire Data Link layer and some of both the Physical and Network layers. In Windows Server 2003 LANs, you have a choice of three technologies: Ethernet, Token Ring, and Fiber Distributed Data Interface (FDDI).

Ethernet

Ethernet was developed in the early 1970s at Xerox PARC (Palo Alto Research Center) by Bob Metcalfe and others, and was made into a standard (called the DIX standard) by Digital Equipment, Intel, and Xerox about ten years later. The Institute of Electrical and Electronics Engineers (IEEE, pronounced "eye, triple e") made slight modifications to the DIX standard and came out with its IEEE 802.3 standard for Ethernet. This is often referred to as Ethernet 802.3. Since Ethernet 802.3 has been adopted by ISO, making it a worldwide standard, and has become what most people and vendors mean when they say "Ethernet," it is what this book means by the term. There are now three IEEE 802.3 Ethernet standards: IEEE 802.3, the original Ethernet standard operating at 10 Mbps; IEEE 802.3u Fast Ethernet, operating at 100 Mbps; and IEEE 802.3z Gigabit Ethernet, operating at 1,000 Mbps. These will be referred to as "Ethernet," "Fast Ethernet," and "Gigabit Ethernet," respectively.

Ethernet is relatively inexpensive, works well interconnecting many different computer systems, and is easy to expand to very large networks. It therefore has become the dominant LAN technology by a wide margin, completely eclipsing some other early technologies, such as ARCnet, and significantly overshadowing Token Ring. As a result, Ethernet-related equipment and Ethernet support in software, including Windows Server 2003 and Windows XP, has become pervasive. This has brought many vendors into the market to supply equipment, causing the pricing to become most reasonable. As a result, Ethernet (and more recently, Fast Ethernet) has become the technology of choice for almost all new networks.

Ethernet technology covers three specifications:

- A media-access method that describes how multiple computers share a single Ethernet channel without getting in each other's way

- An Ethernet frame that describes a standardized bit structure for transferring information over an Ethernet network

- A hardware specification that describes the cabling and electronics used with Ethernet

Ethernet Media Access Method The objective of Ethernet is to have multiple computers operate independently of each other over a single connecting channel without interference. This is accomplished using a media-access method called Carrier Sense Multiple Access with Collision Detection (CSMA/CD). CSMA/CD works like this:

1. A networked computer wishing to transmit information listens to the network to determine when it is idle.

2. When the computer determines the network is idle, it puts its information on the network with the destination address, making it available to all other computers on the network.

3. Each computer on the network checks whether the address is its own, and if it is, that computer pulls the information off the network.

4. When the network is again idle, all other computers have an equal chance of being the next one to transmit information.

5. If two computers simultaneously begin transmission, a *collision* will occur and be detected. All information on the network is ignored, and the network will be returned to its idle status. The two sending computers then choose a random time to wait before resending their information, thereby minimizing the chance of repeated collisions.

Collisions are a normal and expected part of network transmission, even repeated collisions that result in data errors, which is why the higher levels of the OSI networking model put such emphasis on error detection and correction.

Ethernet Frame The Ethernet *frame* is the standard format used for transferring data over an Ethernet network. The frame defines a specific layout that positions header information, source and destination addressing, data, and trailer information, as shown next. The specific definition and use of each field is as follows:

Preamble 62 bits	SFD 2 bits	Destination 6 bytes	Source 6 bytes	Length 2 bytes	Data 0–1500 bytes	Padding 46–0 bytes	CRC 4 bytes

- **Preamble** A series of alternating 1's and 0's that is used by the receiving computer to synchronize the information in the frame.

- **SFD (start of frame delimiter)** A pair of 1's that is used to mark the start of the frame.

- **Destination and Source addresses** Two 48-bit numbers representing the MAC address of the receiving and sending computers. These numbers are assigned by the IEEE to manufacturers and contain a 24-bit unique manufacturer number and a 24-bit number unique to a specific network interface card (NIC). This means that every NIC comes with a unique address, and the end user does not have to worry about it. If a message is to be broadcast to all stations on a network, the destination address must contain all 1's.

- **Length**   The number of bytes in the data field. In earlier Ethernet standards, this was a type code, which were all greater than 1,500 to avoid getting in the way of the length, which is 0 to 1,500.

- **Data**   The data being transmitted, which can be from 0 to 1,500 bytes long.

- **Padding**   Required if the data is less than 46 bytes, so if the data field contained 38 bytes, 8 bytes of padding would be included.

- **CRC (cyclical redundancy check)**   Also called a Frame Check Sequence (FCS), it is a 32-bit (4-byte) number derived from all the bits in the transmission by using a complex formula. The sending computer calculates this number and stores it in the frame sent to the other computer. The receiving computer also calculates the number and compares it to the number in the frame. If the numbers are the same, it is assumed that the transmission was received without error. If the numbers are different, the transmission will be repeated.

The principle difference between the original DIX Ethernet standard (called Ethernet II—Ethernet I was the original specification prior to DIX) and Ethernet 802.3 is that Ethernet II has a type code in place of the length in the frame. The type code is used to adapt Ethernet to different computer environments, which is done outside of the frame in 802.3. In the Internet protocol TCP/IP (see "Implement Networking Protocols" later in this module), the Ethernet frame is used with a type code that identifies the Internet protocol.

Ethernet Hardware   Ethernet LAN technology defines seven alternative hardware standards that can be used with Ethernet. Each hardware standard uses a specific type of cable and cable layout, or *topology,* and provides a rated speed on the network in Mbps, a maximum segment length, and a maximum number of computers on a single segment. The hardware standards are as follows:

NOTE

In the IEEE names for the Ethernet hardware standards, such as 10Base5, the "10" is the speed in Mbps, the "Base" is for baseband, a type of transmission, and the "5" is the maximum segment length in hundreds of meters. In more recent standards, such as 10BaseT, the "T" stands for the type of cabling (twisted-pair in this case).

- **10Base5 (also called Thicknet)**   The original hardware specification in the DIX standard. It uses a thick coaxial cable in a bus topology (see Figure 7-1) with a fairly complex connection at each computer to produce a 10 Mbps speed over a 500-meter (1,640-foot) maximum segment with up to 100 computers per segment and three segments. 10Base5 is expensive and cumbersome to use, and is seldom used today.

- **10Base2 (also called Thinnet or Cheapernet)**   Uses RG-58 A/U thin coaxial cable in a bus topology (see Figure 7-1) with a simple BNC barrel type of connector to produce a 10 Mbps speed over a 185-meter (606-foot) maximum segment with up to 30 computers per segment and three segments. Until only recently, Thinnet was the least expensive form of Ethernet networking for small (30 or less nodes) organizations.

- **10BaseT (also called Twisted-Pair)**   Uses unshielded twisted-pair (UTP) telephone-like cable in a star topology (see Figure 7-2) with a very simple RJ-45 telephone-like connector to produce a 10 Mbps speed over a 100-meter (328-foot) segment with one computer per segment and 1,024 segments. Recently, 10BaseT has come down in price to that of 10Base2, and with its exceptional expandability, it has become very attractive for many organizations.

- **10BaseF**   Uses fiber-optic cable in a star topology running at 10 Mbps to connect two networks up to 4,000 meters (13,120 feet, or about 2.5 miles) apart. This is often used to connect two or more buildings on a campus.

- **100BaseT (also called Fast Ethernet)**   Has the same specifications as 10BaseT except that the cabling requirements are a little more demanding (requires Category 5 cable in place of Category 3) and it goes ten times as fast. 100BaseT is not a whole lot more expensive than 10BaseT, and with its significant added speed, it has become the Ethernet hardware standard of choice. With the appropriate connecting hardware (see "Understand Networking Hardware," later in the module), you can mix 10BaseT and 100BaseT hardware in the same network to slowly upgrade a 10BaseT network. There are two subspecifications to 100BaseT: 100BaseTX, the most common, which runs over Category 5 UTP using two twisted pairs, and 100BaseT4, which runs over Category 3 UTP using four twisted pairs.

- **100BaseFX**   Uses fiber-optic cable running at 100 Mbps to connect two networks up to 412 meters (1,351 feet) apart or, if full-duplex (separate fibers for sending and receiving) is used, up to 2 kilometers (over 6,500 feet, or a mile and a quarter). Like 10BaseF, 100BaseFX is primarily used to join two networks.

- **1000BaseT and F (also called Gigabit Ethernet)**   Uses standard Category 5 or fiber-optic cable to run at 1,000 Mbps. There are several distance standards, ranging from 25 meters (82 feet) to 100 meters (328 feet) for copper UTP, and 550 meters (1,800 feet) for fiber. In the Fall of 2002, Gigabit Ethernet equipment is on the market at about three times the price of high-quality, name-brand 100BaseT equipment for ten times the speed. If this follows the pattern of 100BaseT, these prices will drop by 40 to 50 percent in the next few years.

"Understand Networking Hardware," later in this module, goes into more detail about the Ethernet hardware standards and the options that are available to connect Ethernet networks.

Token Ring

As Digital Equipment, Intel, and Xerox were promoting their DIX Ethernet standard in the mid-1980s, IBM was promoting Token Ring, which became the IEEE 802.5 standard. Although Token Ring started out at 4 Mbps (called Type 3), it very quickly jumped ahead of Ethernet's 10 Mbps with its 16 Mbps (called Type 1). For an eight- to ten-year period ending in 1997, Token Ring was held in high esteem as the Rolls Royce of networking. It was fast, it was reliable, it could connect personal computers, minicomputers, and mainframes, and it had the backing and name tag of IBM. It was also very expensive, as much as three to five times the cost of high-quality name-brand Ethernet equipment. Then, in 1997, 100BaseT became widely available and Token Ring became an also-ran. There is fiber-optic 16 Mbps Token Ring and some talk about a 100 Mbps Token Ring, but it is lost in the shouting about Gigabit Ethernet.

Token Ring Media Access Method   The Token Ring LAN technology is based on a media-access method that uses an electronic token to carry information and to tell the networked computers when the network is free. It works like this:

1. A networked computer with data to transmit watches the network for a free token.

2. When a free token is acquired, it is *burdened* with the destination address and the information to be transmitted, and sent on to the next computer in the ring.

3. Each computer that is not the destination receives and passes on the burdened token.

4. When the destination is reached, the computer removes the information and returns an acknowledgment to the sending computer.

5. Upon receipt of the acknowledgment, the original sending computer places a free token on the network.

One computer on the network (generally the first computer to come up) is designated the *active monitor,* which watches the network for abnormal conditions such as multiple tokens, missing tokens, and broken tokens. When these conditions are found, the active monitor removes all information on the network and places a free token back on.

Token Ring Frame   The Token Ring frame provides a standard format for transferring data over a Token Ring network. The frame layout, shown next, uses the following field definitions:

Starting Delimiter 1 byte	Access Control 1 byte	Frame Control 1 byte	Destination Address 6 bytes	Source Address 6 bytes	Data variable	CRC 4 bytes	Ending Delimiter 1 byte	Frame Status 1 byte

- **Starting Delimiter**   Uses a unique code to indicate the beginning of a frame

- **Access Control**   Identifies whether the frame is a token and what its priority is

- **Frame Control**   Indicates the type of frame and how it is to be processed

- **Destination Address**   Identifies the address of the intended recipient

- **Source Address**   Identifies the address of the sender

- **Data**   Contains the information being transmitted

- **CRC (frame check sequence)**   Contains a calculated number used for checking the integrity of the frame (see "CRC" earlier in the bulleted list under "Ethernet Frame")

- **Ending Delimiter**   Uses a unique code to indicate the end of the frame

- **Frame Status**   Indicates to the sending computer that the frame has been received

The frame for a free token has only three fields: Starting Delimiter, Access Control with the token identifier, and Ending Delimiter.

Token Ring Hardware   In Token Ring technology, information travels only one direction in a cable, requiring that the ends of the cable be connected together to form a ring. It also means that every computer must have two cables and connections to it, one incoming and the other outgoing. To make this easier, the cables, each a twisted-pair cable, are bundled together and use a single connector. Unlike Ethernet's 10BaseT UTP cable, Token Ring's cable is shielded twisted-pair (STP), and the connector is more complex, both of which add to Token Ring's cost. (The newer Token Ring NICs and other equipment have gone to the same Category 5 cable and RJ-45 connectors used by 10BaseT Ethernet.) To make the ring concept easier, Token Ring uses a *multistation access unit,* or MAU (also called MSAU, by purists, but MAU is the common usage), from which computers can be connected in a star fashion similar to an Ethernet hub, although a MAU is several times more expensive than an Ethernet hub. A MAU can function as a ring itself in a small network or be part of a larger ring as shown in Figure 7-4.

As shown pictorially in Figure 7-4, a MAU contains relays on each port that open when a computer or inter-MAU connection is live, but close when they are not powered. This allows the ring to maintain its integrity when a line is broken or a computer is disconnected.

Token Ring Type-1 cabling uses STP cable in a star-configured ring topology (see Figure 7-4) with an expensive connector to produce a 16 Mbps speed over a 100-meter (328-foot) segment with 1 computer per segment and a total of up to 260 computers in a ring.

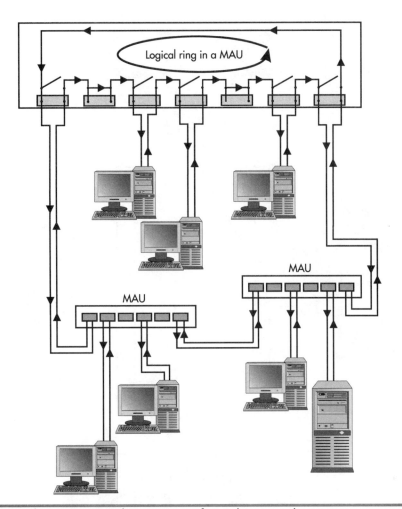

Figure 7-4 A Token Ring network in a star-configured ring topology

Fiber Distributed Data Interface

FDDI is a token-passing, dual-ring LAN technology that operates at 100 Mbps. Originally, FDDI was designed to be used with fiber-optic cable, but newer implementations, called CDDI, use copper Category-5 UTP, although at much shorter distances and with more interference. FDDI has several similarities to Token Ring, in that both pass a token and use a ring topology.

FDDI, unlike Token Ring, has two complete rings, called Primary ring and Secondary ring, that operate in opposite directions, as shown in Figure 7-5. There are two types of FDDI

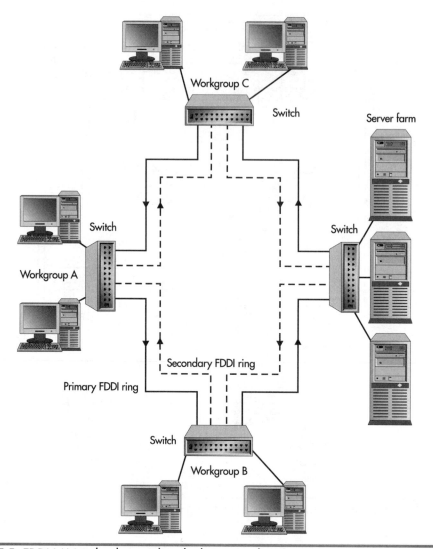

Figure 7-5 FDDI LAN technology with a dual-ring topology

devices, both of which are used to connect to other networks. The FDDI device types are the *single attached station (SAS),* which attaches to only one ring, and the *dual attached station (DAS),* which attaches to both rings. The pair of rings provides substantial fault tolerance. If one ring is broken, the other can take over, and if one segment of both rings is broken, or one device is not working or removed, the two rings can join to reestablish the integrity of the ring.

FDDI is primarily used to link other networks in what is called a *backbone,* both within a building and between buildings. FDDI, using fiber-optic cabling in a ring topology (see Figure 7-5), can run at 100 Mbps over a total distance of 100 kilometers (62 miles) with no one segment longer than 2 kilometers (1.24 miles). In this configuration, FDDI can connect up to 500 network devices. CDDI is limited to 100 meters (328 feet). Fiber offers several advantages over copper: fiber is not susceptible to electromagnetic interference, is more difficult to tap and therefore more secure, does not attract lightening, and most importantly, has a higher quality of transmission.

FDDI has another similarity to Token Ring in that it's a "Rolls Royce technology." It is fast and reliable, but it is also expensive in comparison to 100BaseF. Since 100BaseF shares the Ethernet technology with the very popular 10/100BaseT and is cheaper, 100BaseF is getting the lion's share of the business that FDDI might otherwise have received.

Wireless Networking Technologies

Wireless networking technologies cover a broad spectrum of networking capabilities without wires, including:

- Broadband wireless topologies used in WANs and metropolitan area networks (MANs)

- Cellular wireless networking

- Microwave communications used in WANs

- Satellite communications systems

- Wireless LANs

Broadband wireless and microwave are used between buildings to connect LANs, are fairly expensive, and generally used only by larger organizations. Satellite communications are relatively expensive, slow, and still quite a ways outside any mainstream use. Cellular systems are just starting to get interesting. For some time cellular networking was very slow, 9.6 to 16 Kbps. Recently this has been increased to 64 Kbps, and technologies just coming into use, including Qualcomm's HDR (high data rate), will offer data rates of up 2.4 Mbps.

Wireless LANs or WLANs have become well implemented, widely available, and reasonably priced. They are based on a standard, IEEE 802.11b, that uses the 2.4GHz band, provides data transfer of up to 11 Mbps, and use a transmission scheme that is reasonably secure. A WLAN uses a fixed *access point* that is connected to the wired network through, for instance, a hub, a switch, or a DSL router. This access point is a transceiver (transmitter and receiver) to communicate wirelessly with a card that is added to each computer wishing to use the WLAN (see Figure 7-6). These computers operate on the network in exactly the same way as they

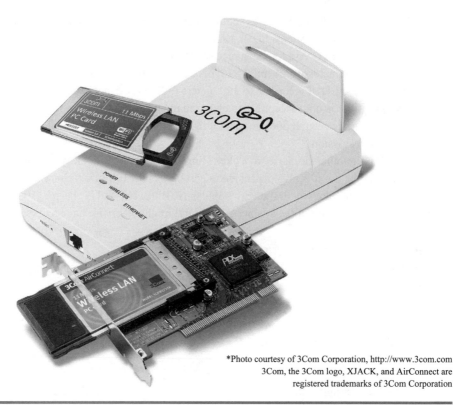

*Photo courtesy of 3Com Corporation, http://www.3com.com
3Com, the 3Com logo, XJACK, and AirConnect are
registered trademarks of 3Com Corporation

Figure 7-6 A selection of 3Com® 11 Mbps Wireless LAN products, including the Access Point 6000, PC Card with XJACK® Antenna, and the AirConnect® PCI Card*

would with a NIC and a cable connection. There are some significant benefits to a WLAN over a normal wired LAN:

NOTE

In addition to the WLAN standard, there is a WIFI wireless fidelity standard that makes sure that the hardware from different manufacturers is compatible; thus, you can walk into any office, airport, or other building with a WIFI standard wireless system and be able to connect if you have the appropriate permissions.

- You do not have the expense of cabling and the even higher expense of installing and maintaining cabling.

- It is extremely easy to add and remove users to the network.

- It is very easy for users to move from office to office.

- Users can roam within an area, say carrying their laptops to a meeting.

- Visitors can easily get on the network.

The downside is of course cost and speed. A good 10/100 NIC costs, on the high side, $20, a cable for one station, again being generous, is $10, and its installation is $20 (averaging the cost of installing a number of stations). So all the cost of connecting a computer by wire to a network is at most $50. An inexpensive access point is about $150 (they go over $300) and, remembering that you are dividing up 11 Mbps of bandwidth, is good for at most ten people or $15 per station. The connecting cards for each computer are $75 to $150, so the total wireless cost of connecting a computer to a network is $90 to over $180, two to three times the cost of using a wire. The speed difference is not just the difference between the 11 Mbps access point and a 100 Mbps NIC, it's the net rate of dividing the 11 Mbps access point by the number of people trying to use it at any instant. Despite these drawbacks, there is a great amount of interest in WLANs, and a number of systems are being sold for both offices and homes.

NOTE

Wireless technology is changing rapidly. As this book is being written, two new wireless standards are being promulgated that allow transfer rates up to 22 Mbps and 55 Mbps respectively and, possibly more importantly, wideband access points that connect at up to 100 Mbps and therefore do not reduce the individual communication rate of each user to some fraction of 11 Mbps. These are of course more expensive, and I would be a slow adopter until a number of manufacturers have accepted the new standard and built compatible systems at these higher speeds.

Home Networking Technologies

Home networking technologies (which can also be used in small offices, especially home offices) generally share one of two types of existing cabling in a home, either telephone cabling or power cabling. In both cases, the objective is to get around installing separate network cabling.

Home Phone-Line Networking   Networks using telephone lines simply plug into the phone jacks already installed in many homes and transmit over a frequency that does not interfere with voice communications, so they can be used at the same time a phone conversation is going on. An industry group, the Home Phoneline Networking Alliance (HPNA) (http://www.hpna.com) has developed a set of specifications and two versions of a standard, HPNA 1.0 and HPNA 2.0. HPNA 1.0 operates at a slow 1 Mbps, while HPNA 2.0 operates at the more standard rate of 10 Mbps. HPNA 2.0 allows up to 25 devices in a network, up to 1,000 feet between any two devices, and not more than 10,000 square feet of total area covered.

Ask the Expert

Q: How many people can you realistically get on a wireless access point?

A: This depends on how much each user is using the network. With light use, like several times a day checking for e-mail or occasionally transferring smaller files, you can get quite a few users, say 20 to 25. At the other extreme, where the average user is working full time transferring information to a central application across the network, then two or three users might max it out. Remember that the normal wireless access point has a single 11 Mbps connection to the wired network and so all users going through that access point share that 11 Mbps (although this is changing, see the preceding note). In a normal wired network connection, each user has full 10 or 100 Mbps.

Home phone-line networking uses a special NIC that plugs into the computer and uses a cable that plugs into a telephone outlet, similar to an internal modem. Alternatively, you can use a USB adapter that plugs into a computer's USB port on one side and into a telephone outlet on the other. A home phone-line network does not need a hub or switch, just the NICs or USB adapters, cables to connect to a telephone outlet, and software drivers. Once installed, they look and operate like any other type of networking. The home phone-line NICs cost two or more times what standard Ethernet NICs cost, and the USB phone-line adapters cost about twice what the phone-line NICs cost. Several of the normal network equipment manufacturers, including 3Com, D-Link, Intel, and SMC, make home phone-line networking equipment.

Considering the cost of hubs, cabling, and the installation of cabling, the cost of a home phone-line network is about the same as an Ethernet network and it does not require the physical disruption caused by installing the cable. On the other side, the most commonly installed Ethernet today is ten times as fast and very readily available and serviced.

The word "home" has been included in the last several paragraphs because most homes have two to four pairs of wires that run throughout a house so that any jack in the house can get on any of the lines. This allows phone-line networking to work anywhere in the house. Most business phone systems are not wired in that way but instead have a separate line or lines run to each office, which has its own phone number(s). These lines are tied together at a local switch, which would block phone-line networking.

Power-Line Networking Power-line networking uses the existing power lines that are throughout almost all buildings for networking. While there may be rooms or areas in rooms without phone lines, very few are without power lines. As in the case of phone lines, there is a manufacturer's group called HomePlug Alliance; it has set a new technology standard called

PowerPacket that is just now being implemented. There is also an older technology available called Passport that is very slow (under 500 Kbps), works only in Windows, has security problems, and is susceptible to power fluctuations. Passport, though, was very cheap, in the neighborhood of $25 per computer. The new PowerPacket runs at 14 Mbps, has improved security, can work with other operating systems, and is not as susceptible to power fluctuations.

The PowerPacket uses a NIC-like card that plugs into a computer and an ordinary looking power cord to plug into any power socket. The cost of the PowerPacket NICs is not yet known (the first ones are just beginning to ship), but they are expected to initially cost around $75; given enough interest, this will come down. If PowerPacket has truly solved the power fluctuation problems (whereas with PassPort, if a garbage disposal was turned on, the network was liable to be scrambled), and if the price per station can come down well under $50, then power-line networking will really take off. It will easily surpass phone-line networking because of the ubiquity of power outlets. When we get to the point of networking refrigerators, microwaves, and dishwashers, power-line networking will be the way to go.

Progress Check

1. What are the two types of networks, and how do they differ?

2. What are the two types of LANs, and how do they differ?

3. What are the two most common Ethernet hardware standards, and what are their predominant characteristics?

CRITICAL SKILL
7.3 Understand Networking Hardware

In its simplest form, computer networking needs only a cable to join two computers, and two NICs that plug into the computers and onto which the cable connects, as shown in Figure 7-7.

---

1. The two most common network types are LANs for local area networking within a single building or organizational unit, and WANs for wide area networking outside the bounds of a LAN. The Internet is a WAN.

2. The two types of LANs are peer-to-peer LANs and client/server LANs. In a peer-to-peer LAN, all computers are both clients and servers and share all functions on the network. In a client/server LAN, some computers are servers, which serve as the network controllers and depository of large databases, and others are clients, which utilize the resources of the servers.

3. The two most common Ethernet hardware standards are 10BaseT and 100BaseT. 10BaseT operates at 10 Mbps, uses UTP Category 3 or higher cabling, and has a maximum segment length of 100 meters, or 328 feet. 100BaseT operates at 100 Mbps, uses UTP Category 5 or higher cabling, and has a maximum segment length of 100 meters, or 328 feet.

Ask the Expert

Q: From the comments here, it sounds like phone-line and power-line networking are not really that much of a benefit over either wireless or standard cable networks. Is that a correct assumption?

A: That certainly was the case a year or so ago. There are now products here or almost here that could change that. A lot depends on how important it is to you to avoid cabling. I happen to not mind the cabling running in the three rooms of my house where I have computers. Also, I happen to think that wireless networking provides a better solution at a reasonably close price, because it is a much more widely used product that is on a developmental fast track.

For both the NICs and the network cable, you have several choices of types and features, and when you go beyond two computers, there are additional components for which there are multiple choices. The first and major decision in making these choices is the LAN technology you are going to use, because that, in many cases, will determine your cabling and NIC, or at least put you in a certain category of cabling and NIC. Therefore, begin this look at hardware with a summary, shown in Table 7-1, of what has been described earlier in this module regarding the alternative LAN technologies.

In choosing a LAN technology, Ethernet 10BaseT and 100BaseT are the predominant choices. Probably well over 98 percent of buyers choose it, with 100BaseT getting the lion's share of new installations and many upgrades. There probably have been no new installations of 10Base5 for many years, and very few legacy installations remain. 10Base2 is also all but gone, since there is no longer a cost advantage over 10BaseT. While there may be some used 10Base2 equipment available that costs next to nothing, it is questionable whether it is worthwhile going down that dead-end path.

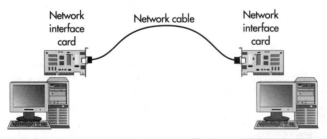

Figure 7-7 Components needed for simple networking

Technology	Max. Speed (Mbps)	Type of Cabling (See Note)	Max. Network Nodes	Max. Nodes/ Segment	Max. Segment Length	Min. Segment Length	Max. Network Length
Ethernet 10Base5	10	Thick coax	300	100	1,640 ft	8.5 ft	8,200 ft
10Base2	10	Thin coax	90	30	606 ft	2 ft	3,035 ft
10BaseT	10	UTP-Cat 3	1,024	2	328 ft		
10BaseF	10	Fiber-optic		2	2.5 mi		
100BaseT	100	UTP-Cat 5	1,024	2	328 ft		
100BaseF	100	Fiber-optic		2	1,351 ft		
1000BaseT	1,000	UTP-Cat5		2	328 ft		
1000BaseF	1,000	Fiber-optic		2	1,800 ft		
Token Ring Type 1	16	STP or UTP-Cat5		260	328 ft		
Type 3	4	UTP-Cat3		72	148		
Fiber	16	Fiber-optic			2.5 mi		
FDDI Fiber	100	Fiber-optic	500		1.24 mi		60 mi
Copper	100	UTP-Cat5			328 ft		

Table 7-1 LAN Technology Specification Summary

NOTE

UTP categories are further explained later in this module, under "UTP Categories." Also, a node is a workstation, a server, or a stand-alone network printer.

The decision between 10BaseT and 100BaseT has almost been erased by the steep decline in the prices for 100BaseT components, where in some cases, 100BaseT components are actually cheaper than 10BaseT components. Also, you can always get 10/100 NICs and use them with 10 Mbps hubs and upgrade those at a later time. 100BaseF increasingly is being used to interconnect networks, buildings, and floors within a building. The following hardware alternatives focus on the needs of these technologies.

Network Interface Cards

Even though you have decided on Ethernet over Token Ring and between 10BaseT and 100BaseT, the decision on which NIC to buy still has several considerations:

● Which bus will the card use?

● What type of card to use?

● Do you want it to be able to wake up the computer?

● Which brand should you buy?

Which Card Bus

NIC manufacturers provide NICs that plug into either ISA (Industry Standard Architecture) or PCI (Peripheral Component Interface) card slots, although most today use the PCI bus. (Figure 7-8 shows a 3Com 10/100 Managed Network Interface Card [3C905CX-TX-M] that is used with either 10BaseT or 100BaseT and that plugs into the PCI bus.) You may not have a choice on which bus to use in the computers you are adding to the network, but if you do (most computers

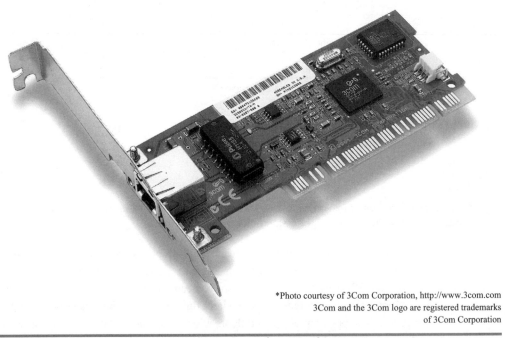

*Photo courtesy of 3Com Corporation, http://www.3com.com
3Com and the 3Com logo are registered trademarks
of 3Com Corporation

Figure 7-8 3Com 10/100 Managed Network Interface Card (3C905CX-TX-M)*

built in the last five or six years have both ISA and PCI slots), you want to choose PCI. ISA slots are either 8 or 16 bits wide (NICs generally use 16 bits), whereas PCI slots are 32 bits wide and thus have a wider data path and are noticeably faster. Another of PCI's major benefits is that you don't have to worry about the IRQ (interrupt request line), because it is uniquely handled in PCI slots. In ISA slots, you have to figure out what IRQs other cards are using, and hopefully have one left over for the NIC. So if they are available, you want to choose PCI-bus NICs.

What Type of Card to Use

Most manufacturers, especially the larger name brands, make several different types of 10/100BaseT NICs in addition to cards for different buses and special features. These differences include whether a NIC is full-duplex or half-duplex, whether it is made for a server, and whether it is multiport. All of these features add to the speed and efficiency of the board, but they also add to the cost, so you need to give them some consideration.

Half-Duplex vs. Full-Duplex
Half-duplex means that when a card is receiving it can't transmit, and vice versa. *Full-duplex* allows the card to transmit and receive at the same time. Obviously, full-duplex is faster, but it does not double the speed as you might expect; rather, it offers 30–50-percent improvement over half-duplex. Currently, most name-brand 10/100 NICS are full-duplex, but it wouldn't hurt to check this factor when you are researching which ones to buy.

Using Server NICs
Server NICs are developed for use in servers, and they supply several features to support that role. Among these features are higher reliability and greater intelligence. The higher reliability is usually a combination of better parts and higher quality control. The greater intelligence means that there is a processor and even memory on the NIC so that it doesn't have to go out to the computer's CPU and memory to handle its processes. This makes the card faster, allowing it to handle a higher volume of information. These features, of course, cost money, so you need to determine whether they are worthwhile. The higher-reliability cards cost about 30–50 percent more than a normal name-brand NIC. The intelligent NICs cost two to three times the cost of a normal name-brand NIC. While that sounds like a lot, it translates to less than $100 additional per card, and you do not have to buy very many of them. When you compare this to the cost of upgrading a CPU, it's reasonable. My recommendation is that an intelligent NIC made for a server is worth the price.

Multiport NICs
NICs are available for servers that have two or four ports, the equivalent of two or four NICs in the server. Given that PCI card slots are generally at a premium in most

servers, these multiport boards may be attractive. The problem is that a dual-port NIC costs over two times the cost of a name-brand server NIC, and a four-port NIC costs over four times the cost of a name-brand server NIC. If you don't have the PCI slots, then this might be a solution, but another solution is to use an interconnection device in front of the NIC (see "Interconnection Devices," later in this module). This is one of those situations in which there is no one right answer. It depends on the network design you are trying to construct.

Wake on LAN and Other Special Features

Several manufacturers, 3Com and Intel among them, have NICs with a "Wake on LAN" feature that will power up a computer to full operating status after it has been turned off. This allows a network administrator or support person to update a computer after hours. Wake on LAN requires a *motherboard* (the main system circuit board in a computer where a NIC plugs in) that implements the PCI bus standard 2.2 or later. Most computers produced in the last two to three years use this standard.

There are at least two other special features that are in some NICs and may prove useful: remote management and remote booting. Remote management allows a network administrator on a server with the appropriate software to monitor the activity and do remote management on a computer across a network. Remote booting allows a server to start a computer without depending on the operating system in the computer. This is important for diagnosing problems in the computer and for the remote installation of Windows and other applications (see Module 6 on Remote Installation Services). Remote booting also requires PCI bus standard 2.2 or later.

If these features are of interest to you, look carefully before buying a NIC and make sure the motherboard you are intending to use it with supports the feature(s) you are getting on the NIC. Remote booting in particular may require special support on the motherboard that is *not* included on most motherboards.

Which Brand

If you look at most catalogs (such as the Data Comm Warehouse catalog used in the previous pricing examples) and online, you will see that there are at least three approximate pricing levels of NICs:

- Name brand (3Com, Intel) with the special features previously mentioned: $60 to $100

- Name-brand basic boards (without the special features): $30 to $75

- Generic basic boards (without the special features): $15 to $35

Although some of the price range in each of the three levels is caused by differences in features, much of the differential is caused by differences in what suppliers charge for the same board. You can see that by looking at PriceWatch (http://www.pricewatch.com) and PriceScan (http://www.pricescan.com), which compare the prices of the same item from different suppliers. In any case, make sure you know what you are buying and what the handling and freight charges are.

The pertinent question is whether the name-brand boards are worth the $15 to $30 differential. From my viewpoint, the answer is clearly yes. In the ten-plus years I have been working with PC networking, I have worked with approximately an equal number of generic and name-brand NICs. I have had troubles with both, but I have had to throw away several of the generic boards, while I have always gotten the name-brand boards fixed or replaced. The backing and support of a name brand is comforting (3Com's lifetime warranty in particular), and sometimes they have added features such as diagnostics that may be valuable. Granted, the lower prices of the generic boards are also attractive, but when a network goes down, that price may not look so good. If you buy a generic from a better supplier to get the supplier's support, your price is very close to the name brand. My recommendation is to choose the name-brand board with the thought that it is going to be more easily recognized in software, such as Windows Server 2003, and provide better support should it be needed. (As was mentioned in Module 6, 3Com wrote the software included with Windows Server 2003 that handles the remote booting needed for remote installation, so it does not take much to figure out whose NICs are guaranteed to support this function.)

Cabling

The primary networking technologies use one of three types of cabling, each of which has several considerations:

- Thin coax for 10Base2

- Unshielded twisted-pair for 10BaseT and 100BaseT

- Fiber-optic for 10BaseF and 100BaseF

Thin Coax

The cable used for 10Base2 networking is a coaxial type and is smaller in diameter than the cable used for 10Base5, 10Base2's predecessor, which was thick and hard to handle. Coaxial cable has an inner wire, surrounded by a plastic insulator, covered by a braided metal outer conductor, and finally a plastic outer jacket, as shown next. There are several types of coaxial cable, or "coax." Among these are the following:

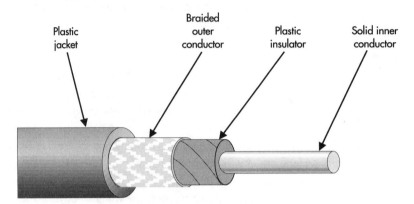

Plastic jacket

Braided outer conductor

Plastic insulator

Solid inner conductor

- RG-8A/U and RG-11A/U is the "thick" coax used with 10Base5 and has a 50-ohm impedance.

- RG-58A/U is the "thin" coax used with 10Base2 and has a 50-ohm impedance.

- RG-59/U is used with cable TV systems and has a 75-ohm impedance.

- RG-62/U is used with ARCnet networking and has a 93-ohm impedance.

It is very important to use the correct cable for an intended function. Even though TV coax cable looks almost identical to thin coax, it will not work, because its impedance is different.

Thin coax uses twist-to-lock barrel connectors on each end of the cable and connects to a NIC using a T connector, as shown in Figure 7-9. Stringing computers together in this manner forms a long line called a *bus topology*. At each end of this network is a 50-ohm terminator, and *one* of these terminators, and only one, needs to be grounded by connecting it to a screw on the case of the computer to which it is connected.

Thin coax and its connectors are slightly more expensive (see the upcoming "Cabling Cost Comparison" section) and a little harder to handle than the UTP used with 10/100BaseT, but thin coax is less susceptible to radio-frequency and electrical interference. Cabling is probably not the reason to make the decision, but it adds weight to 10BaseT.

Unshielded Twisted-Pair

UTP cable used in 10/100BaseT is similar to, but generally not the same as, telephone wiring. For 10BaseT, this cable contains two pairs of wires, or four wires, first twisted in pairs, and then the pairs are twisted together. An RJ-45 modular connector is placed on each end. Although only two pairs are used, the actual cable in both Category 3 and Category 4 cabling has four

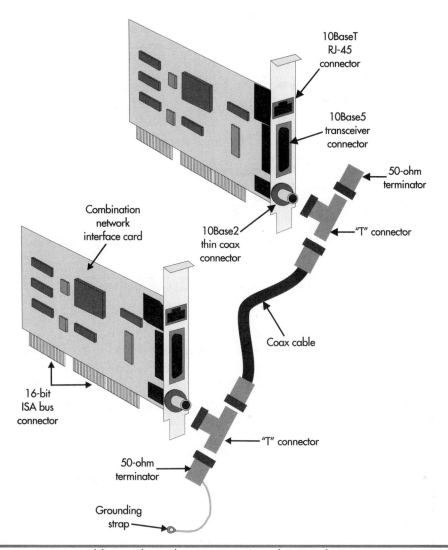

Figure 7-9   10Base2 cabling with combination NICs in a bus topology

pairs, as shown in Figure 7-10. The RJ-45 connector, which can handle four twisted pairs of wires, is similar to but slightly larger than the RJ-11 connector, which can handle two pairs of wires and is used in a normal phone connection. 100BaseT and 1000BaseT use four pairs or all eight wires in Category 5 cable and the same RJ-45 connector.

The pairs of wires in a UTP cable are twisted because that reduces the electrical interference that is picked up in the cable. The number of twists per foot has become a very

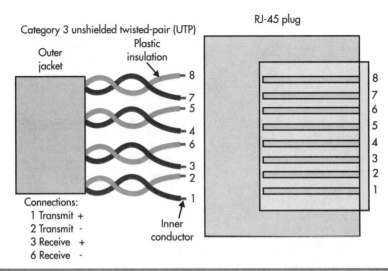

Figure 7-10 Unshielded twisted-pair (UTP) cabling used with an RJ-45 plug

exact science, and it is important to keep the cable properly twisted up close to the connector. An alternative to UTP is STP, with various degrees of shielding: shielding around each pair, shielding around both pairs, or shielding around both the individual pairs and around the combination. STP is considerably more expensive than UTP and is more difficult to handle. To handle the interference problem, there are several rules to follow when running the cable:

● Don't run the cable near a fluorescent light fixture.

● Don't run the cable near an electrical motor, such as those in machines, fans, water coolers, and copiers.

● Don't run the cable alongside a power cable.

● Don't make tight turns that can crimp the cable.

● Don't use a staple gun, which can crimp the cable.

NOTE

Crimping network cabling can change the spacing between individual wires and therefore change its electrical characteristics and performance.

Between voice and data (phone and network), a number of different types of UTP cable exist. The differences are in the degree of fire resistance, in the type of inner core, and in the grade or category of cable, which also specifies the number of twisted pairs.

Degree of Fire Resistance   UTP cables come in two degrees of fire resistance: *plenum* cable, marked "CMP" on the side of the cable, and *PVC* or *riser* cable, marked "CMR." Plenum cable is more fire resistant and doesn't give off dangerous fumes if it does burn. PVC or riser cable, while reasonably fire resistant, is made with polyvinyl chloride (PVC), which gives off potentially dangerous fumes if it does burn. Plenum cable costs between two and two and a half times what PVC cable costs, but it can be used in air passages such as raised floors and suspended ceilings, while PVC cable can be used only in walls and out in the open (check your own local codes for the type of cable you should use).

Type of Inner Core   The inner core of UTP cable can be stranded or solid. Stranded wire is more flexible and less prone to breaking when bent a number of times. It is used in situations where it is frequently moved, such as in a patch panel and between a wall outlet and a computer. Solid wire has lower signal loss and therefore is better for longer runs where it won't be moved frequently, such as in walls and ceilings.

UTP Categories   The following are the seven categories of UTP cable that are used with voice and data communications:

- **Category 1**   Used in telephone installations prior to 1983, it has two twisted pairs.

- **Category 2**   Used in telephone installations after 1982, it has four twisted pairs; used in some early data networks with speeds up to 4 Mbps.

- **Category 3**   Used in many data networks and most current phone systems, it has four twisted pairs, generally has three twists per foot (not in the specs), and easily handles speeds of 10 Mbps.

- **Category 4**   Used in Token Ring networks, it has four twisted pairs and can handle speeds up to 16 Mbps.

- **Category 5**   Used in most networks until recently, it has four twisted pairs, has eight twists per foot, can handle 100 Mbps, and in bulk (1,000 feet) is about 8 cents per foot for solid PVC, about 13 cents per foot for stranded PVC, and 21 cents a foot for solid plenum.

- **Category 5e (enhanced Category 5)**   Used in almost all current network installations, it has the same physical characteristics as Category 5 but with a lower error rate, and in bulk (1,000 feet) is approximately 9 cents per foot for solid PVC, about 12.5 cents for stranded PVC, and 20 cents a foot for solid plenum.

- **Category 6 (really STP)**   Used where electrical interference is a problem, it has four twisted pairs with a foil wrap around each pair and another foil wrap around all pairs. It is planned to handle Gigabit Ethernet, and in bulk (1,000 feet) it is approximately 13 cents per foot for solid PVC and 36 cents a foot for solid plenum.

Connect UTP   UTP cabling simply plugs into a NIC and then into a wall outlet or hub, making 10/100BaseT installation very simple, as you can see in Figure 7-11. For UTP to work between two computers without a hub, the wires must be *crossed over*—the transmitting wires on one computer must become the receiving wires on the other computer. This is one of the functions of a hub, so the wires connecting a computer to a hub must be the same on both ends. When two computers are directly connected to each other, a special cable must be used that has the end connections reversed.

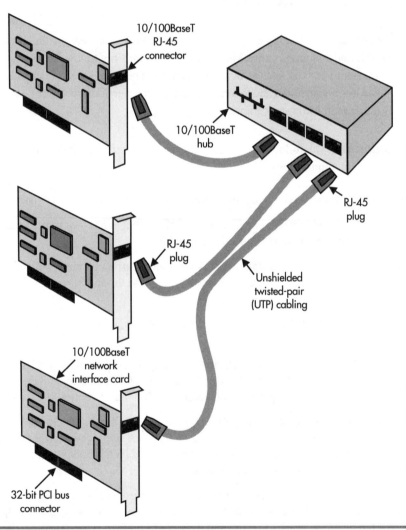

Figure 7-11 10/100BaseT cabling in a star topology

TIP

The rules of thumb used to stay within the 328-foot (100-meter) limit for a 10- or 100BaseT segment are to keep the cable run from the wiring closet to the wall outlet at less than 300 feet, the run from the wall outlet to the computer at less than 20 feet, and the patch panel at less than 8 feet.

Fiber-Optic Cable

Fiber-optic cable transmits light over a very pure strand, or *fiber,* of glass less than the thickness of a human hair. The glass is so pure that there is very little loss of light in a very long cable. The light source is either a light-emitting diode (LED) or a laser. Information is transmitted by turning the light source on and off to produce digital ones and zeros. At the other end of the cable is a light detector that converts the light back to electrical pulses. Fiber-optic cable is immune to electrical and electromagnetic interference and does not radiate energy itself. This means that it is very hard for someone to tap undetected a fiber-optic cable and get the information it is carrying. The result is that fiber-optic cable is a very secure and efficient means of quickly carrying information over a long distance.

Fiber-optic cable, shown next, has a central core of transparent glass (or for short distances of a few meters, it can be plastic). This is surrounded by a reflecting glass called *cladding* that redirects any light coming out of the core back into it. The cladding is covered by one or more layers of plastic and other strengthening materials to make a sheath or jacket. There are two kinds of fiber-optic cable:

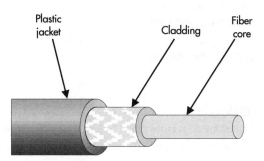

Plastic jacket   Cladding   Fiber core

- **Single-mode or monomode fiber**   Uses a laser with a very small inner glass core (4 to 10 microns for the core and 75 to 125 microns for the core and cladding combined, written 4/75 to 10/125). Single-mode fiber carries the light, in essence, straight down the fiber. This has a high efficiency, allowing for longer distances—as much as ten times the distance of multimode fiber—but it is also the most expensive, costing up to twice the cost of multimode fiber. Single-mode fiber is used in long-distance WANs, in wiring campus networks, and less frequently in building backbones.

● **Multimode fiber** Generally used with an LED, this has a much larger glass core (the FDDI standard is 62.5 microns for the core and 125 microns for the core and cladding). Multimode fiber allows the light to bounce off the walls, thus giving it a lower efficiency but at a substantially lower cost. Multimode fiber is used in *premise* wiring, wiring within a building.

The most common fiber-optic cable is multimode fiber with the FDDI dimensions of 62.5/125. It comes with a single fiber (*simplex*); with two fibers (*duplex* or *zipcord*); or with 4, 6, 12, or more fibers. Like UTP cable, fiber-optic cable comes with PVC (riser) and plenum outer jackets. Since most systems require two fibers, one for transmitting and one for receiving, the two-fiber zipcord is encountered most often. At this time, FDDI PVC zipcord costs between 28 and 36 cents a foot, while plenum zipcord costs between 30 and 40 cents, both in 1,000-foot spools.

Gigabit over fiber (1000BaseF) requires the use of lasers (LEDs are not fast enough) and as a result has a longer maximum distance than 100BaseF (1,800 feet vs. 1,351 feet), which standard is based on LEDs. The standards for 1000BaseF are as follows:

Type of Fiber	Core Size	Maximum Distance
Multimode	50 or 62.5 microns	1,800 feet
Single-mode	10 microns	16,000 feet, or 3 miles

The cost of fiber-optic cabling has decreased only slightly over the last couple of years, but nonetheless it is being used more and more frequently for the backbone and even some of the horizontal wiring in a building (see the following section). Up to a few years ago, all of the backbone wiring was 10Base5, but that has all but been replaced by fiber-optic, which is faster and cheaper.

TIA/EIA Cabling Standards

The Telecommunications Industry Association (TIA) and the Electronic Industries Association (EIA) together have defined a set of wiring standards for telecommunications and computer networking in a commercial building. The purpose of the standards is to provide a common set of specifications for cabling data, voice, and video in a building that provides the users and owners of the building quality, flexibility, value, and function in their telecommunications infrastructure while allowing diverse manufacturers to build equipment that will interoperate. The most applicable of these standards are the following:

● **TIA/EIA-587-A** For data, voice, and video cabling in a commercial building

● **TIA/EIA-569** For the areas and pathways that hold telecommunications media in a building

- **TIA/EIA-606**   For the design and management of a telecommunications infrastructure

- **TIA/EIA-607**   For the grounding and bonding requirements in telecommunications equipment and cabling

These standards define the rules and limitations for each part of the telecommunications and networking infrastructure in a building. The standards break this infrastructure into a defined set of areas and wiring types within a building, as shown on the inside back cover of this book, and defined as follows:

- **Entrance Facilities**   Where the telecommunications services and/or a campus backbone enters a building

- **Main Cross-Connects**   The central facility within a building to which all the equipment rooms are connected with backbone wiring; there may also be a main cross-connect for a campus that ties together all the building main cross-connects

- **Backbone Wiring**   The fast, heavy-duty wiring that runs, generally vertically, from the main cross-connects to the equipment rooms in a building or between main cross-connects on a campus

- **Equipment Rooms**   The areas located on each floor of a building that provide the connection between the backbone wiring going to the main cross-connect and the horizontal wiring going to the telecommunications closets

- **Horizontal Wiring**   The second-level wiring that runs, generally across a drop ceiling, from the equipment rooms to the telecommunications closets, as well as the third-level wiring that runs across a ceiling and down a wall from the telecommunications closets to the wall outlets

- **Telecommunications Closets**   The areas located in several places on a floor of a building that serve a contiguous group of offices and provide a connection between the horizontal wiring running to the equipment rooms and the horizontal wiring running to individual wall outlets

- **Work Area Wiring**   The external (not in a wall or ceiling) wiring that provide a connection between the termination of the horizontal wiring in a wall outlet and the computer or other device connected to the network

NOTE

The TIA/EIA standards discuss both telecommunications and computer networking, and in reading them, you need to make sure what a given topic is discussing. For example, UTP for voice can run up to 800 meters, or 2,624 feet, whereas UTP for data can only run up to 100 meters, or 328 feet.

You can get more information on the TIA/EIA standards from the TIA web site at http://www.tiaonline.org or from Hubbell (a connector manufacturer) at http://www.hubbell-premise.com/technical/ANSI568B.htm.

Cabling Cost Comparison

Table 7-2 provides a comparison of the cost of various types of network cables. This should be used only as a relative comparison between types and not as an indication of the current cost, which changes frequently. Also, there are significant differences in suppliers and quantity discounts.

NOTE

In Table 7-2 you can see that the cost of Category 5e solid cable plenum is actually below the cost of Category 5 due to all the volume in Category 5e.

Interconnection Devices

If you have more than two computers in a 10/100BaseT network, you need some device to which you connect the additional computers. The simplest of these devices is a hub, but you might also use a switch, a router, or a bridge, depending on what you want to do. Each of these devices has a particular use, although there is overlap, and each has several variations. These devices act as building blocks that allow you to expand a network segment and interconnect multiple segments. While reading about these interconnection devices, look at the network configuration on the inside back cover of this book to see how the various devices can be used.

Cable Type (1,000-foot prices 11/02*)	Cost/Foot for PVC	Cost/Foot for Plenum
Thin coax	12 cents	35 cents
Category 5 Solid	8 cents	21 cents
Category 5e Solid	9 cents	20 cents
Category 5e Stranded	12.5 cents	NA
Category 6 Solid	13 cents	36 cents
Fiber-optic FDDI zipcord	28 cents	30 cents

*Data Comm Warehouse, http://www.warehouse.com/dc

Table 7-2 Cabling Cost Comparison

Hubs

Hubs are used to connect other devices on the network. Normally these are workstations, but they can also be servers, printers, other hubs, and other interconnection devices. A hub is a repeater device that takes whatever comes in on one line and puts it out on all other lines without any filtering or intelligence applied to the information stream or where it is going. This means that every station can hear what every other station has put on the network. As the traffic grows, the number of collisions between frames will increase, causing significant degradation in the network throughput. Hubs operate at the Physical layer of the OSI model, simply repeating the information they receive. There are three types of hubs: stand-alone hubs, stackable hubs, and modular hubs.

Stand-Alone Hubs   *Stand-alone* hubs, shown in Figure 7-12, are used in smaller networks and the final workgroup segment of larger networks. Stand-alone hubs come in 4-, 8-, 12-, 16-, and 24-port models for 10BaseT, 100BaseT, and auto-switching 10/100BaseT. 10BaseT hubs are $8 to $10 per port, 100BaseT hubs are $10 to $20 per port, and 10/100BaseT hubs are $26 to $34 per port. There is a lot of variability in this pricing, but generally speaking, the price per port goes down with more ports in the hub.

Most stand-alone hubs are simple devices into which you plug in the 4 to 24 other devices and that's it. If you want to make a change in the configuration, you have to physically unplug and replug in the devices as needed to make the change. You can get smart stand-alone hubs with a management capability that is most often found in stackable and modular hubs. This allows a hub to be monitored and configured remotely using a software package that normally comes with the hub and either SNMP (Simple Network Management Protocol) or RMON

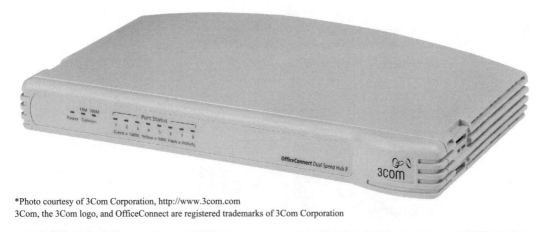

*Photo courtesy of 3Com Corporation, http://www.3com.com
3Com, the 3Com logo, and OfficeConnect are registered trademarks of 3Com Corporation

Figure 7-12 3Com OfficeConnect® Dual-Speed Hub 8 (3C16753)*

(Remote Monitoring). The software generally works with only one brand of hub, so it might be worthwhile to standardize on one brand if you are getting the additional management capability. Stand-alone hubs that can be managed cost $5 to $10 more per port, and then have a separate charge for the management capability of $250 to $450.

Stackable Hubs   As you build a network with 10/100BaseT's star topology, you do so with a hierarchical structure, as shown in Figure 7-13. Such a structure has a maximum of four

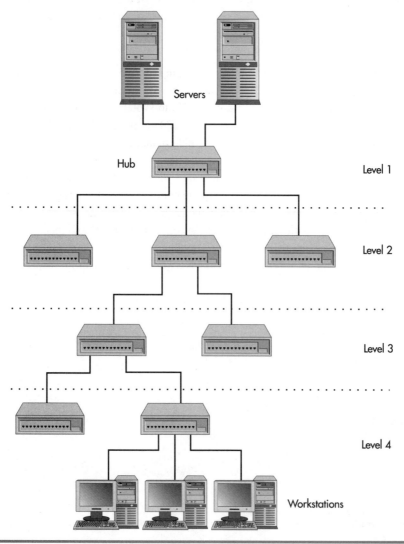

Figure 7-13 Hierarchical structure of a 10BaseT network

hubs (called "repeaters") or levels and five cable lengths between any workstation and the server for 10BaseT, and a maximum of two hubs or levels and three cable lengths for 100BaseT. When you daisy-chain one stand-alone hub to another at any level to simply attach more workstations at that level, each hub counts as an additional level, and you can't exceed these limits. To get around this limitation, *stackable* hubs were developed, which add ports at the same level by joining the backplanes of the hubs as if they were one hub. Therefore, any two devices connected anywhere in the stack have only a single hub between them.

Stackable hubs, shown in Figure 7-14, are similar in appearance to stand-alone hubs, and the only real difference is that the backplanes of stackable hubs can be connected. Stackable hubs can be stacked six to eight hubs high and cost from $30 to $50 per port. These hubs include the option to be managed with the additional management capability, which costs $300 to $1,050 for the stack.

Modular Hubs   A *modular hub,* also called an *enterprise hub,* a *modular switch,* or an *enterprise switch,* is really a large chassis or cabinet with a power supply and backplane into which you can plug many different boards, including hubs, switches, bridges, and routers, as shown in Figure 7-15. By using a single backplane, modular hubs get around the two- or four-layer limit, as do stackable hubs. Modular hubs actually preceded stackable hubs, and in the less-demanding roles (where all you need are the hub functions), stackable hubs are now being used where modular hubs once were, because a stackable hub is much cheaper.

There are many forms of modular units, because you can buy the modules you want to use (hubs, switches, bridges, or routers) and plug them in to a modular backplane that can span one network segment, multiple network segments, or multiple networks. Basically, you buy a

*Photo courtesy of 3Com Corporation, http://www.3com.com
3Com, the 3Com logo, and SuperStack are registered trademarks of 3Com Corporation

Figure 7-14 3Com SuperStack® 3 Baseline Dual-Speed Hub (3C16592B)
(12- and 24-port models)*

Figure 7-15 3Com Switch 4007R Chassis (3C16817)*

chassis with power supply and then buy the modules you need to build the device that fits your network requirements. Modular hubs provide a lot of flexibility, but at a steep price.

In addition to flexibility, modular switches provide another very significant benefit, called a *collapsed backbone.* If the modules were separate devices, you would connect them with a high-speed backbone running at a minimum of 100 Mbps or 1 Gbps, and maybe double those figures if you run at full-duplex. If you move all of these devices into a single modular hub where they are connected by the backplane, what in a stackable switch is a backbone connection is now collapsed onto the backplane and runs at between 100 Gbps and 600 Gbps (that's a "G" not an "M").

Bridges

A *bridge* is used to either segment a network or join two networks, as you can see in Figure 7-16. A bridge looks at the physical or MAC address in a frame on one side of the bridge, and if the frame has an address on the other side of the bridge, the frame is passed on to the other side. If the frame has an address on the originating side of the bridge, the bridge ignores the frame, because all devices on the originating side already can see the frame. Since a bridge looks at a

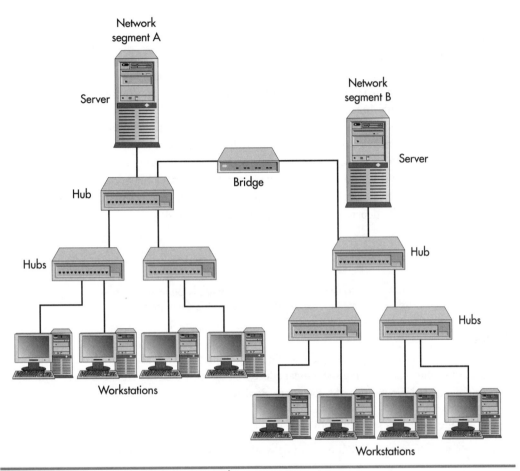

Figure 7-16 A bridge joining two network segments

frame's physical address, it is operating at the Data Link layer of the OSI model, one layer above where a hub operates.

The purpose of the bridge is to reduce the traffic in a network by segmenting it, although it is still one network. If a hub replaced the bridge, the entire network would have all the traffic on both sides of what was the bridge, increasing the collisions and decreasing the throughput.

When you join two networks with a bridge, the result is one network with two segments, but only the traffic that is addressed to the other segment gets through the bridge. Traffic that is addressed within the originating segment stays within its segment. A bridge also lets you have additional hub layers above the four-hub limit in a simple Ethernet network. A frame can travel through four hubs, cross a bridge, and then travel through four more hubs.

The bridge, in essence, takes a frame from one side and, if it is properly addressed, recreates it on the other side.

The bridging discussed so far has described local bridging within a single facility. Bridges can also be used to connect a local network with a remote one and, in so doing, produce a single network with two segments where the traffic between them is limited to that destined for the other network. In this remote scenario, there would be a bridge on either side of the line connecting the two segments so that the local traffic in each segment stays in that segment.

Bridges are basically simple devices and are limited to a single network (both the source and destination addresses must be in the same network) and to a single cabling or media type. Theoretically, a 10BaseT network cannot be joined to a 10BaseF network with a bridge, but by building converters into the bridge, you can join them. Bridges range in price from around $300 to over $1,500, depending on their capabilities and brand.

NOTE

Bridges are becoming hard to find because you can generally perform the same function, plus others with a router or a switch for close to the same price.

Routers

A *router* can perform the same segmenting and joining functions as a bridge, but at a higher level of sophistication, using the logical address of the OSI model's Network layer. The resulting added capabilities of a router are significant:

- Routers connect separate networks, leaving them independent with their own addressing.

- Routers connect different types of networks; for example, 100BaseF and 100BaseT.

- Routers select from among alternative routes a path through a complex network in order to get to an end destination.

- Routers clean up network traffic by checking if a frame is corrupted or lost (traveling endlessly in the network); if so, the frame is removed from the network.

For these reasons, routers are routinely used to connect to the Internet and within the Internet, and to connect a WAN to a LAN. Routers generally are intelligent devices with a processor and memory. With this capability, a router unpacks every frame that comes to it, looks at each packet within the frame, recalculates its CRC, checks to see how many times the packets have been around the network, looks at the logical destination address, determines the best path to get there, repackages the packets into a new frame with the new physical address, and sends the frame on its way. In addition, routers talk to other routers to determine the best path and to keep track of routes that have failed. Routers do all of this at amazing speeds. At the low end, routers process over 250,000 packets per second, and they go above several million packets a second on the upper end. Routers begin at around $400 and go up to many thousands, depending on what they do.

Switches

A *switch*, like a hub, has a number of ports, from 2 to 24, and takes information that comes into one port and sends it out to one or more other ports. Unlike a hub, which does no filtering or processing on the information that flows through it, a switch is an intelligent device that looks at the physical destination address of the frame flowing into it and directs the frame to the correct port for that destination. This removes that frame from the rest of the network, since the frame goes over only the part of the network that connects the sending and receiving devices. This is similar to the maturing of the telephone system from the original party-line system to the modern direct-dial system.

Switches, like bridges and routers, segment a network to reduce the traffic and collisions, and ultimately improve the throughput. Switch segmentation can be done at any level where you would otherwise have a hub, a bridge, or a router. Such a switch functions as a multiport bridge and is therefore operating at the Data Link layer of the OSI model. Further intelligence can be added to some switches so that they become multiport switching routers that unpack frames and operate on the logical address in the packets. Such switching routers operate at the Network layer of the OSI model. For this reason, they are called *Layer 3 switches*.

NOTE

If the top two hubs in Figure 7-16 were switches, you could join the two network segments without a bridge simply by running a cable between the two switches, getting the same segmentation.

Ask the Expert

Q: When should a switch replace a hub?

A: There are two situations where a switch should be used in place of a hub. First, when the traffic on the network reaches such a level that collisions are starting to really slow down the network, then you need to add a switch to keep traffic just to the links that actually need to be crossed. Second, if you need more than four levels of hubs in a 10BaseT network or more than two levels in a 100BaseT one, you can use a switch to add more levels.

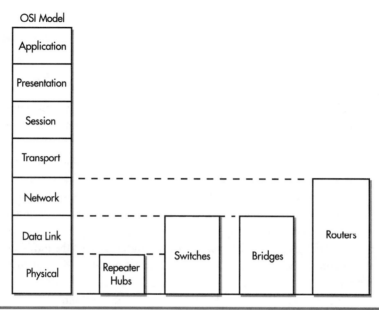

Figure 7-17 Interconnection devices and the OSI model

Switches, like hubs, come in stand-alone and stackable models with and without management capability. The simplest switches cost under $10 a port, whereas a layer 3 switching router may go over $200 a port.

Interconnection Device Summary

When you are building a network, you have many choices regarding interconnection devices. You not only have the choice between hubs, bridges, routers, and switches, but you also have a number of choices within each of those categories. You can get some insight into an answer by looking at where in the OSI model each of the devices operates, as shown in Figure 7-17. Another aspect is the cost of each of the devices, shown in Table 7-3.

Interconnection Device	Cost 7/01 (various sources)
10/100BaseT hubs	$8 to over $30 per port
10/100 Managed Hubs	$14 to over $200 per port
10/100 stackable hubs	$15 to over $50 per port

Table 7-3 Cost Comparison of Interconnection Devices

Interconnection Device	Cost 7/01 (various sources)
10/100 switches (unmanaged to managed)	$10 to over $200 per port
Bridges	$300 and up
Routers	$400 and up

Table 7-3 Cost Comparison of Interconnection Devices *(continued)*

CRITICAL SKILL
7.4 Use Network Topologies

Topology is the design of a network, the way it is laid out. In the figures in this module, you have seen several different topologies. 10Base2 and 10Base5 both use a *bus* topology, wherein all the network devices are attached to a single long cable, as you saw in Figures 7-1 and 7-9. 10BaseT and 100BaseT both use a *star* topology, where the network devices fan out on separate cables from a central hub, as you saw in Figures 7-2, 7-11, and 7-13. FDDI uses a *dual-ring* topology, like the one shown in Figure 7-5, and Token Ring uses a *star-configured ring* topology, shown in Figure 7-4. Finally, when the backbone cabling is added to a 10/100BaseT network, you have a *star/bus* topology, shown on the inside of the back cover of this book.

The bus topology was the original Ethernet topology, but it has the major disadvantage that a break in any part of the network brings the entire network down. In a star topology, a break in a line takes out only those parts of the network connected to the line, potentially only one station. In a self-correcting topology, such as the star-configured ring of Token Ring, if a station is disabled or removed or if a line is broken, the system re-forms a ring and continues operating.

There are disagreements as to whether a bus or a star is easier to cable, but although a star takes more cable, it is cheaper cable, and it is easier to manage. You can put the cable for a star topology in the wall and not connect it to a hub or switch if it is not being used. Also, it is easy to move a station from one network segment to another simply by changing a jumper cable that connects the station from one hub to another.

Lay Out a Network

Once you have decided on the network technology and the type of NIC, cabling, and interconnection devices that you want to use, you still have to figure out how to lay out the network. This includes a lot of questions, such as:

- Which workstations are grouped with which hubs?
- Do you stack several hubs, or immediately use a switch?

- Should the servers be centralized in one location or decentralized in each department?

- When do you need a switch, a router, or a bridge?

- How do you connect two buildings separated by 1,500 feet or more?

There is no one right answer to any of these questions, and there is a lot of difference between the impact of the first question and that of the last question. You can easily alter the connections to change how workstations are grouped, but setting up a wide area network is a job for professionals because you are talking about serious money to purchase the equipment and install it, and significant expense if you want to change it. Inside the front cover is an example network layout showing one way a number of network components might be connected.

In an Ethernet 10BaseT or 100BaseT network, there are several rules that should be followed in a layout. These vary slightly with different manufacturers, but the general rules of thumb are shown in the following table:

Rule of Thumb	Ethernet 10BaseT	Fast Ethernet 100BaseT
Maximum cable length between hub and workstation	100 meters, or 328 feet	100 meters, or 328 feet
Minimum cable type	Category 3	Category 5
Maximum number of hubs between two workstations or a switch and a workstation	Four hubs	Two hubs
Maximum number of cable segments between two workstations or a switch and a workstation	Five cable segments	Three cable segments with a maximum total distance of 205 meters, or 672 feet

There is a great tool for both planning the layout of a network as you are building it and maintaining the network after it is installed. This is Visio Enterprise Network Tools. With Visio, you can easily design the network layout that you want to use, quickly communicate that design to others, create a bill of material, and have a ready reference during installation. After a network is completed, Visio will search the network and automatically discover and document all of the network devices at the Data Link (layer 2) and Network (layer 3) layers. Visio, a Microsoft Office product, can be found at http://www.microsoft.com/office/visio/.

CRITICAL SKILL
7.5

Implement Networking Protocols

Protocols are the standards or rules that allow many different systems and devices to interconnect and operate on a network, be it a small office network or the worldwide Internet. Protocols specify *how* and *when* something should happen, and *what* it is that should happen.

Protocols are developed in many different ways, but for one to become widely used, it must be accepted by a number of organizations, most importantly those building networking software and networking devices. To gain this acceptance, protocols are initially circulated as draft protocols, using documents called Requests for Comments (RFCs). If someone or some organization wants to change a protocol, a new RFC gets circulated with a higher number than the original RFC. The Information Sciences Institute (ISI) of the University of Southern California classifies RFCs as being approved Internet standards, proposed Internet standards, Internet best practices, and For Your Information (FYI). ISI also maintains a web site that lists RFCs and their classification (http://www.rfc-editor.org/) from which you can get copies of the RFCs. You can determine how a piece of software has implemented a protocol by looking at which RFCs are supported. For example, in Windows Server 2003, you can look up the topic "TCP/IP RFCs" in Help and see a list of RFCs that are supported.

Numerous protocols deal with computer networking, but "networking protocols" normally refers to the logical addressing and transfer of information. These protocols deal with the Transport and Network layers of the OSI networking model, as shown in Figure 7-18. In this area, Windows Server 2003 supports three protocols:

- **AppleTalk**   For communicating with earlier Apple Macintosh systems

- **IPX/SPX**   For communicating with Novell NetWare

- **TCP/IP**   For communicating with the Internet and most newer systems

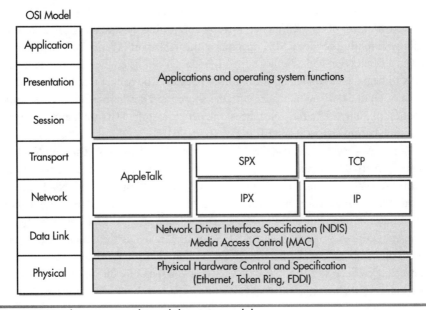

Figure 7-18 Networking protocols and the OSI model

NOTE

Support for the DLC protocol, which was used in communicating with earlier IBM mainframes, and the NetBEUI protocol, which was used in communicating with earlier Microsoft networking systems, has been removed from Windows Server 2003, all editions. Also, support for IPX/SPX is not available in Windows Server 2003 Enterprise and Datacenter editions for Intel Itanium 64-bit systems.

AppleTalk

AppleTalk is a networking protocol that appeared early in the history of the Macintosh. It originally worked with the Macintosh's LocalTalk network, but was subsequently enhanced to work with Ethernet, Token Ring, and FDDI. AppleTalk was designed for small local workgroups, not for large complex networks. With AppleTalk installed in Windows Server 2003 and the appropriate permissions established, a Mac can browse a Windows Server 2003 network. While Apple and newer operating systems such as Windows Server 2003 still support AppleTalk, newer Macintosh systems now can also use TCP/IP (see the upcoming section "TCP/IP").

IPX/SPX

Internetwork Packet Exchange/Sequenced Packet Exchange is Novell NetWare's networking protocol and is included in Windows Server 2003 to allow internetworking with NetWare. IPX/SPX is a very capable networking protocol and is fully routable (able to operate across networks by accessing the logical address at Network layer), unlike AppleTalk. IPX operates at the Network layer of the OSI model, thereby controlling the assembly of packets and providing the routing services. SPX operates at the Transport layer, which establishes and maintains a connection with another network node. Once this connection is established, SPX tells IPX to begin assembling and transmitting packets. The packet that IPX assembles has a data area of up to 64KB and a header with the source and destination address and other control information of 30 bytes. In most instances, the network at the Data Link and Physical layers will limit the packet size to around 1.5KB.

In Windows Server 2003, IPX/SPX is implemented in NWLink. Through NWLink, a Windows Server 2003 computer using Client Services for NetWare can access information on a NetWare server or print on a NetWare-controlled printer. Similarly, with NWLink, a NetWare client can access information on servers or print to printers connected to a Windows Server 2003 computer running File and Print Services for NetWare. NWLink can directly use IPX, called *direct hosting,* or it can use NetBIOS over IPX, which is the default. Either technique works for all combinations of clients (MS-DOS, Windows for Workgroups, Windows 95, Windows 2000, Windows XP, and Windows Server 2003) and for the same list of servers *except* that a Windows XP client cannot access a Windows Server 2003 using direct hosting.

TCP/IP

Transmission Control Protocol/Internet Protocol is a set of networking protocols that grew out of the Internet and has been refined over 15 years to be an excellent tool for transmitting large amounts of information reliably and quickly over a complex network. The two components, TCP and IP, were originally combined and later were separated to improve the efficiency of the system.

IP

The Internet Protocol, like IPX, operates at the Network layer of the OSI model controlling the assembly and routing of packets (called *datagrams* in IP). To send a datagram to a remote node across a complex network, such as the Internet, these are the steps that take place:

1. The datagram is assembled at the Network layer, and the IP address of the destination (which is a logical address, not a physical address) is added.

2. The datagram is passed to the Data Link layer, which packages the datagram in a frame and adds the physical address of the first router that starts the datagram on its way to its destination.

3. The datagram is passed to the closest router, which unpacks the frame, looks at the logical address on the datagram, repackages the datagram in a frame, and adds the physical address of the next router that continues the datagram on its way to its destination.

4. Repeat Step 3 for each router along the path.

5. At the last router before the destination, the destination physical address is added to the frame and the frame is sent to its destination.

This technique allows the information to follow any path through the network, with the decision on which path to take made by the local router, drawing on its knowledge of the local situation. IP is a connectionless service. It sends the datagram on its way not knowing whether it is received or what route it took. Determining whether it is received and replacing the packet if it isn't is the function of TCP at the Transport layer. The route that the datagram takes is a function of the routers at the Data Link layer. The datagram that IP assembles has a maximum of up to 64KB, including a variable header with the source and destination addresses and other control information. The header, which is always a multiple of 4 bytes, is shown in Figure 7-19 and has these fields:

- **Version**   Protocol version number

- **IHL**   Header length in 4-byte words (five-word minimum)

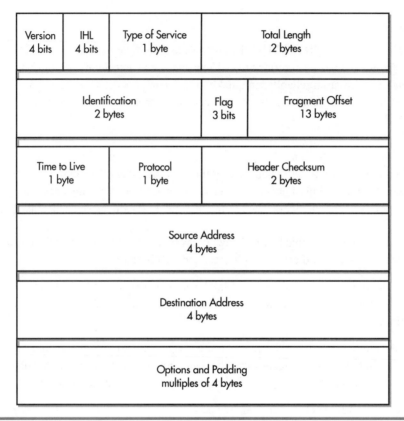

Figure 7-19 IP datagram header

- **Type of Service**   The speed and reliability of service requested

- **Total Length**   Total datagram length in bytes or "octets"

- **Identification**   Fragment identification, so it can be reconstructed

- **Flags**   Fragmentation indicator (DF: 0 = may fragment, 1 = don't fragment, MF: 0 = last fragments, 1 = more fragments)

- **Fragment Offset**   Number in a set of fragments; the first is 0

- **Time to Live**   The remaining number of times through a router before the datagram is discarded

- **Protocol**   The protocol to use at the Transport layer

- **Header Checksum**   Number to check the integrity of the header only

- **Source Address**   The source computer's IP address

- **Destination Address**   The destination computer's IP address

- **Options**   Security, routing, and other optional information

- **Padding**   Ensure that header is in multiples of four bytes

IP Addressing

The source and destination addresses in the IP header are the logical addresses assigned to particular computers, as compared to the physical address on a network card. These 32-bit or 4-byte numbers, called *IP addresses,* can have one of three formats, which vary the sizes of the network and host segments of the address. The leftmost ("high order") bits identify the particular format or "class." All of these classes have a network segment and a host segment that allow for locating a particular computer or router (*host*) within a particular network, as described here:

- Class A can identify up to 16,777,214 hosts in each of 126 networks

- Class B can identify up to 65,534 hosts in each of 16,382 networks

- Class C can identify up to 254 hosts in each of 2,097,150 networks

NOTE

The general IP specification is in RFC 791, while addressing is additionally discussed in RFCs 790 and 796. All of these RFCs are available from http://www.ietf.org/rfc.html.

The IP address is commonly represented as four decimal numbers separated by periods. For example: 127.168.105.204. Each number is one byte in the address. To assist in identifying how to parse (or divide) an IP address into a network segment and a host segment, you must specify a *subnet mask* that serves as a template for this purpose. The subnet mask for class A is 255.0.0.0, for class B it is 255.255.0.0, and for class C it is 255.255.255.0. The subnet mask focuses the attention on local hosts within the current network. If you are working within the current network, the subnet mask can speed up the processing of the IP address.

The majority of IP addresses have been assigned, and there is much discussion on how to handle the growth caused by public acceptance of the Internet. A number of temporary measures have been taken that fit within the current version (version 4) of IP. The long-term solution is a major revision of IP, as proposed in RFCs 1883 and 1887, for IP version 6 (IPv6) that lengthens the address space from 4 bytes to 16 bytes. This allows enough room for every person on earth and every device, including refrigerators, VCRs, and cars, to have an IP address!

7

Windows Server 2003 Networking Environment

NOTE

IPv6, which is just on the verge of implementation, includes many other changes besides lengthening the address field. Among the other changes are the following: cleaning up the header fields to reduce the processor cost; special labeling of real-time audio and video to improve their flow; and adding more capability for authentication and privacy.

TCP

The Transmission Control Protocol, like SPX, operates at the Transport layer, which handles connections. Its purpose is to assure the reliable delivery of information to a specific destination. TCP (like SPX) is a connection-oriented service, in contrast with IP, which is connectionless (like IPX). TCP makes the connection with the final destination and maintains contact with the destination to make sure that the information is correctly received. Once a connection is established, though, TCP depends on IP to handle the actual transfer. And because IP is connectionless, IP depends on TCP to assure delivery.

The sending and receiving TCPs (the protocol running in each machine) maintain an ongoing, full-duplex (both can be talking at the same time) dialog throughout a transmission to assure a reliable delivery. This begins with the sending TCP making sure that the destination is ready to receive information. Once an affirmative answer is received, the sending TCP packages a data message into a *segment* containing a header with control information and the first part of the data. This is then sent to IP, and TCP creates the remaining segments while watching for an acknowledgment that the segments have been received. If an acknowledgment is not received for a particular segment, it is recreated and handed off. This process continues until the final segment is sent and acknowledged, at which point the sender tells the receiver that it's done. In the process of transmission, the two Transport layers are constantly talking to make sure that everything is going smoothly.

NOTE

Different and sometimes confusing names are used to refer to pieces of data being transferred through a network, depending on where you are in the OSI model and the protocol you are using. Assuming the TCP/IP protocol and Ethernet, as shown in Figure 7-20, are at the top of the OSI model, applications create messages to be sent over a network. The message is handed down to the Transport level, which divides the message into segments that include a segment header with port addresses. The segments are passed down to the Network layer, where IP packages the segments into datagrams with logical IP addresses. The datagrams are sent down to the Data Link layer, where Ethernet encapsulates them into a frame with a physical address. The frames are passed to the Physical layer, which sends them over the network to the physical address, where the reverse process takes place. Alternatively, in the Transport and Network layers, a piece of information is generically called a packet of information.

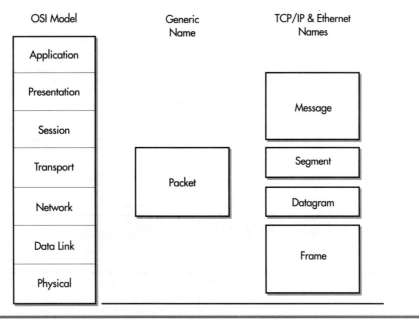

Figure 7-20 The OSI model and the names used for pieces of information

The communication between the sending and receiving TCPs takes place in the segment header, which is shown in Figure 7-21 and explained in the following list. The two protocols use the sequence number, the acknowledgment number, codes, sliding window size, urgent pointer, and options to carry on a very complex conversation about how a transmission is progressing. And all of it is happening in very small fractions of a second.

- **Source Port**   The port number in the Session layer, called a *socket,* that is sending the data

- **Destination Port**   The port number in the Session layer, or socket, that is receiving the data

- **Sequence Number**   A number sent to the receiver to tell it where the segment fits in the data stream

- **Acknowledgment Number**   A number sent to the sender to tell it that a segment was received; the sequence number increments by one

- **Header Length**   The length of the header and therefore the offset from the start of the header to the data

- **URG**   The Urgent field; if 1, the Urgent Pointer is valid

- **ACK**   The Acknowledgment field; if 1, the Acknowledgment Number is valid

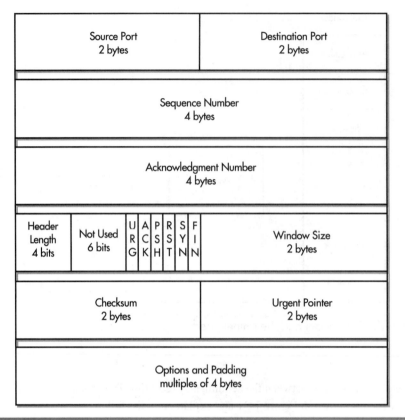

Figure 7-21 The TCP segment header

- **PSH**   The Push field; if 1, the receiver is not to buffer data, but instead to send it directly to the application, as with real-time audio and video

- **RST**   The Reset field; if 1, the communication must be interrupted and the connection reset

- **SYN**   The Synchronize field; if 1, a connection is requested by the sender; if accepted, the receiver leaves SYN = 1 and makes ACK = 1

- **FIN**   The Finish field; if 1, the transmission is to be terminated

- **Window Size**   The number of bytes that the receiver can accept in the next transmission

- **Checksum**   A number with which to check the integrity of the segment

- **Urgent Pointer**   If URG = 1, this is a number used as an offset to point to an urgent piece of information the receiver should look at

- **Options**   Used for special circumstances; normally absent
- **Padding**   Used to ensure that the header is in multiples of four bytes

NOTE

The general TCP specification is in RFC 793, which is available from http://www.ietf.org/rfc.html.

The functions performed by TCP and IP—the packaging, addressing, routing, transmission, and control of the networking process in a very complex environment—are mind-boggling. When you add to that the ease and reliability of networking, it is truly stunning. Now that you know all the networking ingredients presented in this module, isn't it amazing that networking works even in a small workgroup, let alone the Internet? That the Internet is such a worldwide success has to be one of the great wonders of the modern world.

At the beginning of this module, I stated that networking is the single most important facility in Windows Server 2003. Having read this module, I think you can see that the job of networking is a very complex task with many demands, and for Windows Server 2003 to handle it well is a tall order. In the next module, you'll see how Windows Server 2003 tackles these demands, and how to control what Windows Server 2003 does. I think you'll conclude that Windows Server 2003 is well suited to this most important function.

Progress Check

1. What are some of the important characteristics to look for in NICs?

2. What type of wire would you install today for a 100BaseT network to run in the wall, in the ceiling, and from the wall to the computer?

3. In a 100BaseT network, how many levels of hubs (hubs plugged into hubs) can you have?

---

1. Some of the important characteristics to look for when buying a NIC are that it be 100BaseT, for the PCI bus, full-duplex, and name brand.

2. In all cases, you should use Category 5e. In the wall, you should use solid-core PVC, in the ceiling, solid-core plenum, and from the wall to the computer, stranded-core PVC.

3. You can have two levels of hubs in a 100BaseT network.

Project 7 Planning a Network

You have seen in the preceding pages that a great many variables are involved in setting up a network. Use this project to work through the variables and decide what the right choices are for you.

Step by Step

1. Determine the type of network to use:

   a. Peer-to-peer LAN

   b. Client/server LAN

2. Determine the LAN technology to use:

   a. Ethernet

   b. Token Ring

   c. Fiber Distributed Data Interface (FDDI)

   d. Wireless networking

   e. Home networking technology:

      i. Home phone-line networking

      ii. Power-line networking

3. Determine the NIC you will use:

   a. Determine the speed the card will operate at:

      i. 10 Mbps

      ii. 100 Mbps

      iii. 10/100 Mbps

   b. Determine the card bus to use:

      i. ISA

      ii. PCI

   c. Determine the special features it will have:

      i. Half-duplex

      ii. Full-duplex

      iii. Server NIC

iv. Wake on LAN

v. Managed

d. Determine the kind of brand to use:

i. Name brand

ii. Non–name brand

4. Determine the type of cabling to use:

a. Thin coax

b. Unshielded twisted pair (UTP):

i. Category 5

ii. Category 5e

iii. Category 6 (STP)

c. Fiber Optic:

i. Mono-mode fiber

ii. Multimode fiber

5. Determine the amount of cable for each type of fire-resistance.

a. PVC

b. Plenum

6. If using UTP cable, determine the amount for each type of the inner core.

a. Solid

b. Stranded

7. Lay out the network with the required topology:

a. Bus

b. Star

c. Ring

8. Determine the number of each of the following interconnection devices:

a. Stand-alone hubs with _____ ports

b. Stackable hubs with _____ ports

c. Modular hubs with _____ ports

(continued)

     d. Stand-alone switches with _____ ports

     e. Stackable switches with _____ ports

     f. Modular switches with _____ ports

     g. Bridges

     h. Routers

9. Determine the networking protocol to use:

     a. AppleTalk

     b. IPX/SPX

     c. TCP/IP

Project Summary

This project will get you started on determining the network you will set up and give you a check list to help you through the process.

✓ Module 7 Mastery Check

1. What are three purposes of a network?

2. What is the dominant networking technology, and what are some of the reasons for its dominance?

3. What are two reasons in favor of wireless networking and two reasons against it?

4. What are two small office / home office networking technologies, and how do they compare?

5. What are the two primary card buses used with NICs, which should you use, and why?

6. What are three different types of interconnection devices, and how do they differ?

7. What is the primary topology used today, and what are its components?

8. What are the rules of thumb for laying out a 100BaseT network?

9. What is the primary protocol used in Windows networking, and what do its components do?

10. What levels of the OSI model do hubs, switches, and routers operate at and what is the portion of a message called that is being handled at the Transport, Network, and Data Link levels of the OSI model?

Module 8

Setting Up and Managing a Network

When you installed Windows Server 2003, a basic set of networking services was installed and configured using your input and system defaults. This setup may, but doesn't always, provide an operable networking system. In any case, you have a wide spectrum of networking alternatives to review and set to provide the networking environment best suited to your needs. The purpose of this module is to do just that, first by looking at how to set up basic networking in either Windows Server 2003 or Windows XP Professional, and then by looking at how to set up Windows Server 2003 to support the rest of the network.

Basic networking means that the computer can communicate with other computers in the network. To do that, you must

1. Assure the network interface card (NIC) is properly set up

2. Install the networking functions that you want to perform

3. Choose and configure a networking protocol

CRITICAL SKILL
8.1 Set Up Network Interface Cards

In a perfect world, the computer you are setting up has a NIC that is both supported by Windows Server 2003 and fully Plug and Play compatible. If this describes your computer, then your NIC was installed by Setup without incident and you don't need to read this section. As is known by anyone who has installed an operating system on more than two computers, this is an imperfect world. Therefore, this section looks at how to install a NIC and what you need to do to make it fully operational.

If you installed Windows Server 2003 using the instructions in Module 4, and if you went through the section "Configure a Server," then you can skip this section if you believe your NIC is operating correctly. If you had problems with that section of Module 4 or did not go through it, then this section will be worthwhile to you.

Assuming that a NIC *is* properly plugged into the computer, any of these three things could be causing it to not operate:

- The NIC driver is either missing or not properly installed.

- The required resources are not available.

- The NIC is not functioning properly.

Look at each of these possibilities in turn in the next several sections.

Check the NIC Driver

During installation, you may have gotten a message stating that a driver could not be found (although Setup often completes without telling you it skipped network setup because of the lack of a driver). Use the following steps to check whether you have a driver installed and, if you don't, try to install one:

NOTE

The following instructions, as with most in this book unless specifically noted otherwise, are based on the Windows Server 2003 user interface. There are differences both in the steps and in the figures and illustrations between Windows Server 2003 and Windows XP Professional.

1. Open the Start menu and choose Control Panel | Network Connections. The Network Connection menu opens. If you have Local Area Connection as one of your options, you probably have the NIC driver properly installed and you can go on to the next major section, "Install Network Functions and Configure Protocols."

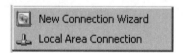

TIP

You can change the name Local Area Connection (for example, if you install two NIC cards, you can give each of them a descriptive name), so it may be named something else in Step 1; you cannot rename New Connection Wizard.

2. If you do not have a Local Area Connection on, you cannot create one by clicking New Connection Wizard. You must first install the NIC and its driver using the Add Hardware Control Panel.

At this point, it is highly likely that you will need a Windows Server 2003 driver for the NIC, so it is best to get it before proceeding. If one did not come with the NIC, then you need to get onto another computer, bring up the manufacturer's web site, locate and download the driver (you need to know the make and model of the NIC), and then copy the driver onto a floppy disk or CD.

NOTE

I went through the process of downloading a driver for an older 3Com card and found it painless. The hard part is figuring out what the card is, because often it is not written on the card, so you have to locate purchase records or documentation—if you know which records go with the card.

3. Again open the Start menu and click Control Panel | Add Hardware. The Add Hardware Wizard opens.

4. Click Next. When asked if the hardware is connected, click Yes (given that the NIC is already in its slot), and click Next again. A list of installed hardware will appear. You may or may not see your NIC on the list (with or without a problem icon—an exclamation point), as shown here:

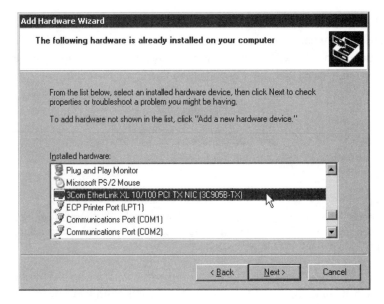

If you see your NIC and it doesn't have a problem icon, then Windows thinks that it is installed and running properly. If you double-click the device, you should get a message saying that "This device is working properly," and you can click Finish to close the Add Hardware Wizard. Your problem may be in software.

5. If you don't see your NIC, double-click Add A New Hardware Device at the end of the list of Installed Hardware. Choose Install The Hardware That I Manually Select From A List— you don't want Windows to search for new hardware (if it was going to find it, it would have)—and click Next. Skip to Step 7.

6. If you see your NIC with a problem icon, double-click it and you will most likely get a Device Status telling you that a driver was not installed. Click Finish to close the Add Hardware Wizard and start a troubleshooter. The Upgrade Device Driver Wizard opens. Click Next. Choose Display A List Of Known Drivers, and click Next.

7. Independent of whether you saw your NIC, double-click Network Adapters in the list of Common Hardware Types. A list of network adapters appears. If your NIC had been on the list, Setup would have found it, so you need to insert and use the floppy disk you made in Step 3, or a CD or floppy disk that came with the NIC.

8. Click Have Disk. Accept the default of the A: drive (assuming that is the floppy drive and you want to use a floppy) and click OK. When it is displayed, select the driver for your adapter, and click Next. When told that the device will be installed, click Next again.

9. You may get a message stating that the driver you are about to install does not have a Microsoft digital signature. Click Yes to go ahead and install it anyway. The driver and its necessary supporting software will be installed.

10. Click Finish. If you now open Start | Control Panel | Network Connections, you should see the Local Area Connection option. If you see the Local Area Connection option, go to the next major section, "Install Network Functions and Configure Protocols."

If you still do not have a Local Area Connection, or some other problem occurred in the preceding process that does not point to an obvious solution, continue through the next two sections to see if a solution is presented.

Check NIC Resources

Most interface or adapter cards in a PC require dedicated resources in order to operate. The resources include interrupt request (IRQ) lines, I/O ports, and direct memory access (DMA) lines. Generally, two devices cannot share the same resources, except that PCI devices can share IRQs. Therefore, if two devices are assigned the same resource, a conflict occurs and the device will not operate properly. This will cause a NIC to not function and the Local Area Connection icon to not appear in the Network Connections window. Check the resources used by the NIC, with these steps:

1. Open the Start menu and choose Control Panel | System. The System Properties dialog box opens.

2. Click the Hardware tab and then click Device Manager on the right of the middle section. The Device Manager window opens as shown next. If you see a problem icon

(an exclamation point) on your network adapter, then there is probably a problem with the resource allocation.

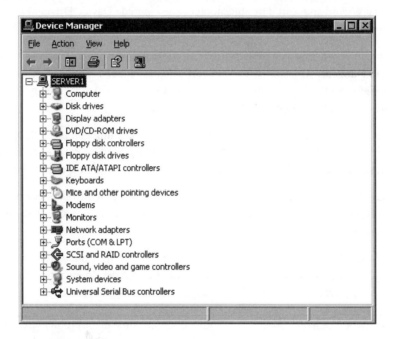

3. Open the Network Adapters category and double-click the particular network adapter that is being researched. The Properties dialog box for that device will open and give you a device status. If there is a resource problem, then it should show up here.

4. Click the Resources tab. In the Conflicting Device List at the bottom of the dialog box, you will see the specifics of any resource conflicts.

5. If you have a conflict, click Use Automatic Settings to turn that setting off, and then go through each of the configurations in the Setting Based On drop-down list to see if any of them cure the problem.

6. If none of the canned configurations cures the problem, click the problem resource and click Change Setting. Click the up or down arrow to change the setting, and then click OK to see if that fixes the problem. Try several settings.

7. If you are having a hard time finding a solution, go back to the Device Manager (you can leave the NIC Properties dialog box open), open the View menu, and choose Resources By Type. Here, you can see all of the assignments for a given resource, as shown for interrupt request lines next, and find an empty resource to assign to the NIC.

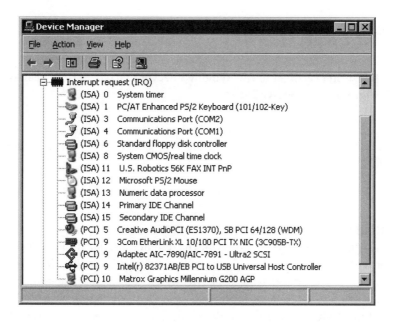

8. If you find an unassigned resource, go back to the NIC Properties dialog box and assign it to the NIC. If you cannot find an unassigned resource, you may have to make a tough choice between the NIC and a conflicting device. Networking is a pretty important service, and if it is conflicting with a sound card, for example, you may have to remove the sound card to get networking. If both of the cards are ISA cards and you have PCI slots available, you may be able to get a new PCI card and remove the conflict.

9. If none of the previous suggestions works, return to the NIC Properties dialog box, click the General tab, and then click Troubleshoot. Windows Server 2003 Help will open and lead you through a series of steps to try to resolve the problem.

10. When you have solved the resource problem as best you can, close the NIC Properties dialog box and close the Device Manager. If you made changes in the resources, you may be told that you need to restart your computer and asked whether you want to do it now. Click Yes, and the computer will restart.

11. If you successfully made a change to the resources, you should now see a Local Area Connection icon in the Network Connections window. If you do, go to the next major section, "Install Network Functions and Configure Protocols." If you don't see a Local Area Connection icon, continue with the following section.

Ask the Expert

Q: If my NIC is not certified to run Windows Server 2003, does that mean it won't work with Windows Server 2003?

A: No, it just means that Microsoft hasn't checked it out. Most older cards are not certified for the newer operating systems but run just fine. Check with the manufacturer to see if they believe it works with Windows Server 2003.

NIC Not Functioning

If neither installing a NIC driver nor changing its resource allocation caused the Local Area Connection icon to appear, it is very likely that the NIC itself is not functioning properly. The easiest way to test that is to replace the NIC with a known good one, ideally one that is both certified to run with Windows Server 2003 and Plug and Play–compatible. It is wise to have several spare NICs; they are not terribly expensive (see "Network Interface Cards" in Module 7), and switching out a suspected bad one can quickly solve problems.

CRITICAL SKILL
8.2 Install Network Functions and Configure Protocols

Installing and checking out the NIC is half of the equation; the other half has to do with setting up the networking functions within Windows Server 2003 as well as identifying and configuring the networking standards or protocols that will be used.

Install Network Functions

Networking functions provide the software for a computer to access other computers and, separately, for other computers to access the computer you are working on. In other words, the two primary functions allow the computer to be a client (it accesses other computers) and to be a server (other computers access it). Make sure that these two services are installed by following these steps:

1. Open Start | Control Panel | Network Connections | Local Area Connection. The Local Area Connection Status dialog box opens, as shown next. In the particular case shown here, the computer thinks it is connected to the network and is sending and receiving information.

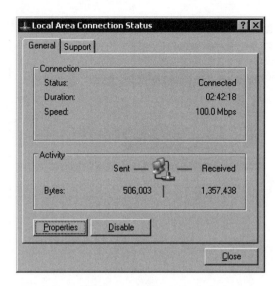

2. Click Properties. The Local Area Connection Properties dialog box, shown in Figure 8-1, opens and displays the services and protocols that have automatically been installed. Under the default circumstances, this includes two services—Client For Microsoft Networks, and File And Printer Sharing For Microsoft Networks—and one protocol—Internet Protocol (TCP/IP). If you have the two services installed, you have achieved the objective of this section, but in any case, continue and explore the alternatives.

3. Click Install. The Select Network Component Type dialog box opens, in which you can add clients, services, and protocols.

4. Double-click Client. If you already have Client For Microsoft Networks installed, you will only have Client Service For NetWare (or Gateway [and Client] Services For NetWare in a domain server) in the list.

5. If Client For Microsoft Networks is not installed, select it and click OK. If you also need to access a NetWare server, select Client Service For NetWare and click OK.

6. Back in the Select Network Component Type dialog box, double-click Service. If you did a default installation, you already have File And Printer Sharing For Microsoft Networks and Network Load Balancing installed, and you will have QoS (quality of service) Packet Scheduler and Service Advertising Protocol available to be installed.

7. If File And Printer Sharing For Microsoft Networks is not installed, select it and click OK. If you need one of the other services, select the one(s) you need, and click OK.

This should assure that you have the two primary services installed.

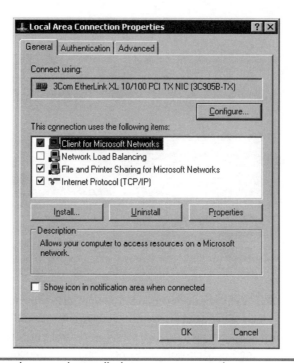

Figure 8-1 Services and protocols installed to support networking

Choose and Configure a Networking Protocol

As you read in Module 7, networking protocols are a set of standards used to package and transmit information over a network. The protocol determines how the information is divided into packets, how it is addressed, and what is done to assure it is reliably transferred. The protocol is therefore very important to the success of networking, and its choice is a major one. Windows Server 2003 offers four protocols:

● **AppleTalk** For use with earlier Apple computers.

● **Internetwork Packet Exchange/Sequenced Packet Exchange (IPX/SPX)** For use with networks running Novell NetWare.

● **TCP/IP** For use with the Internet and most newer systems. Windows Server 2003 provides the original TCP/IP, which is installed by default, and the new TCP/IP version 6, which is generally not needed at the moment but someday will provide addressing for every toaster, refrigerator, and microwave in the world.

- **Reliable Multicast Protocol** For use with the transmission of very large files, such as multimedia, especially video files. IP by itself is not reliable and requires TCP to confirm that data has been correctly received. This adds overhead, slowing down the transmission. Reliable Multicast Protocol provides the confirmation information with a much lower overhead, speeding up the transmission. Reliable Multicast Protocol is used by Microsoft Message Queuing (MSMQ).

NOTE

IPX/SPX is implemented in Windows Server 2003 with the NWLink IPX/SPX/NetBIOS Compatible Transport Protocol.

AppleTalk is for *earlier* Apple systems. All Apple computers and operating systems produced in the last several years can also use TCP/IP. If the computer you are working on is or will be connected to the Internet, it will require TCP/IP. TCP/IP is a very robust protocol that's suitable for a demanding environment (is there a network environment more demanding than the Internet?) and accepted worldwide. Because of this, it is recommended that TCP/IP be installed as your protocol of choice. If you also need one of the other protocols, because you need to network with an older Apple or a Novell system, then you can additionally install that protocol.

TIP

Each protocol that you install uses CPU, memory, and disk resources and slows startup, so it is important to only install the protocols that are truly needed.

Check and Change Protocols

Use the following instructions to check on and potentially change the protocols that have been installed and the settings that are being used.

NOTE

In the Local Area Connection Properties dialog box, you should see at least one protocol installed, as shown previously in Figure 8-1. In most cases, TCP/IP should already be installed, and possibly NWLink IPX/SPX if that need was identified during setup.

1. With the Select Network Component Type dialog box still open (if it isn't, use the instructions in the last section to do that), double-click Protocol. The Select Network Protocol dialog box opens as shown next. This lists the available protocols. If you want

to install another protocol, do so now by double-clicking that protocol. Otherwise, click OK to close the Select Network Protocol dialog box.

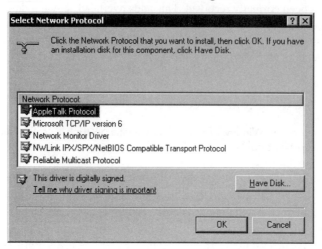

2. Select the TCP/IP protocol in the Local Area Connection Properties dialog box and click Properties. The Internet Protocol (TCP/IP) Properties dialog box opens, shown next, in which you can choose to use either a dynamic IP address automatically assigned by a server running the Dynamic Host Configuration Protocol (DHCP), or a static IP address that you enter in this dialog box.

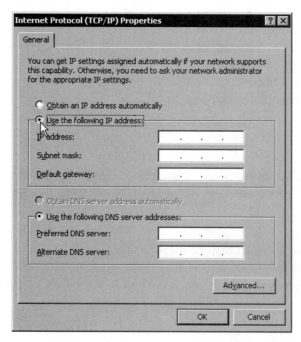

A server that is a DHCP and/or a Domain Name Service (DNS) server must have a static IP address; otherwise, all computers in a network cannot be automatically assigned an IP address from a DHCP server. If the DHCP server is down or nonexistent, Automatic Private IP Addressing (APIPA) assigns an IP address from the block of 65,000 numbers 169.254.0.0 through 169.254.255.255. It also generates a subnet mask of 255.255.0.0. APIPA is limited insofar as a computer using APIPA can talk only to other computers in the same subnet with an address in the same range of numbers. If all computers in a small network are using Windows 98/Me, Windows 2000/XP (which also uses APIPA), or Windows Server 2003 and have Obtain An IP Address Automatically selected, without a DHCP server, they will automatically use the 169.254.0.0 through 169.254.255.255 range of IP numbers.

3. If you are working on a server that will be the DHCP server, the DNS server, or both, or if you know you must assign a static IP address to this computer, then do so by clicking Use The Following IP Address and entering an IP address. The IP address that you use should be from the block of IP addresses that your organization has been assigned by its Internet service provider (ISP) or other authority (see the discussion under "Get Blocks of IP Addresses," later in this module). If your organization is small and doesn't plan to access an outside network, then the static IP address can be from the block of APIPA numbers (but manually entered; refer to the limitations in Step 2) or from several other blocks of private IP addresses (see "Get Blocks of IP Addresses").

4. If you entered a static IP address, you must also enter a subnet mask. This mask tells the IP which part of an IP address to consider a network address and which part to consider a computer or *host* address. If your organization was assigned a block of IP numbers, it was also given a subnet mask. If you used the APIPA range of addresses, then use 255.255.0.0 as the subnet mask.

5. If you don't have a specific reason to use a static IP address, click Obtain An IP Address Automatically, and use the addresses from either a DHCP server on the network or APIPA.

NOTE

In very small networks (three to five workstations), IP addresses can be automatically obtained from a DSL router.

6. Click OK to close the Internet Protocol (TCP/IP) Properties dialog box, click OK to close the Local Area Connection Properties dialog box, and click Close to close the Local Area Connection Status dialog box.

7. Open the Start menu, choose Shut Down, select Restart from the drop-down list that appears, and click OK.

8. When the computer restarts, the Network Connections windows should still be open. Double-click Local Area Connection to open the Local Area Connection Status dialog box. You should see activity on both the Sent and Received sides.

9. If you do not see both send and receive activity, open My Computer and click Search in the toolbar. In the Search Companion pane on the left, click Other Search Options in the bottom of the pane, click Printers, Computers, Or People, click A Computer On The Network, enter a computer name in your same subnet, and then click Search. You should see the computer appear with its location on the right, as shown next. If it does appear, then the computer is networking. If it doesn't work, then you have a problem.

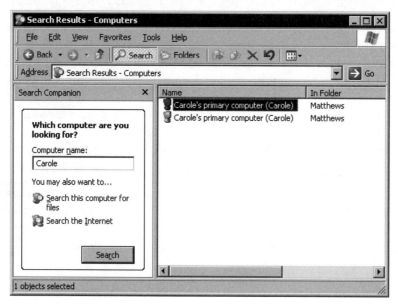

10. If you think you have a problem, double-check all the possible settings previously described. If you are using APIPA, make sure that the computer you are trying to contact is also using that range of numbers either as a static assigned address or with automatic assignment. If all the settings are correct, then check the cabling by making a simple connection of just several computers (if you do a direct UTP connection between two computers, remember that you need a special *crossover* cable with the transmit and receive wires reversed) and, finally, replace the NIC. With a good NIC, good cabling, and the correct settings, you'll be able to network.

CRITICAL SKILL

8.3 Test the Network

There are several command-line utilities that can be used to test a TCP/IP installation. The more useful of these commands are the following:

- **Ipconfig**   Used to determine if a network configuration has been initialized and an IP address assigned. If an IP address and valid subnet mask are returned, then the configuration is initialized and there are no duplicates for the IP address. If a subnet mask of 0.0.0.0 is returned, then the IP address is a duplicate.

- **Hostname**   Used to determine the computer name of the local computer.

- **Ping**   Used to query either the local computer or another computer on the network to see whether they respond. If the local computer responds, you know that TCP/IP is bound to the local NIC and that both are operating correctly. If the other computer responds, you know that TCP/IP and the NICs in both computers are operating correctly and that the connection between the computers is operable.

Use the following steps to test a network setup with these utilities. Figure 8-2 shows the results on my system.

1. Open the Start menu and choose Command Prompt. The Command Prompt window opens.

2. Type **ipconfig** and press ENTER. The IP address and subnet mask of the current computer should be returned. If this did not happen, there is a problem with the current configuration.

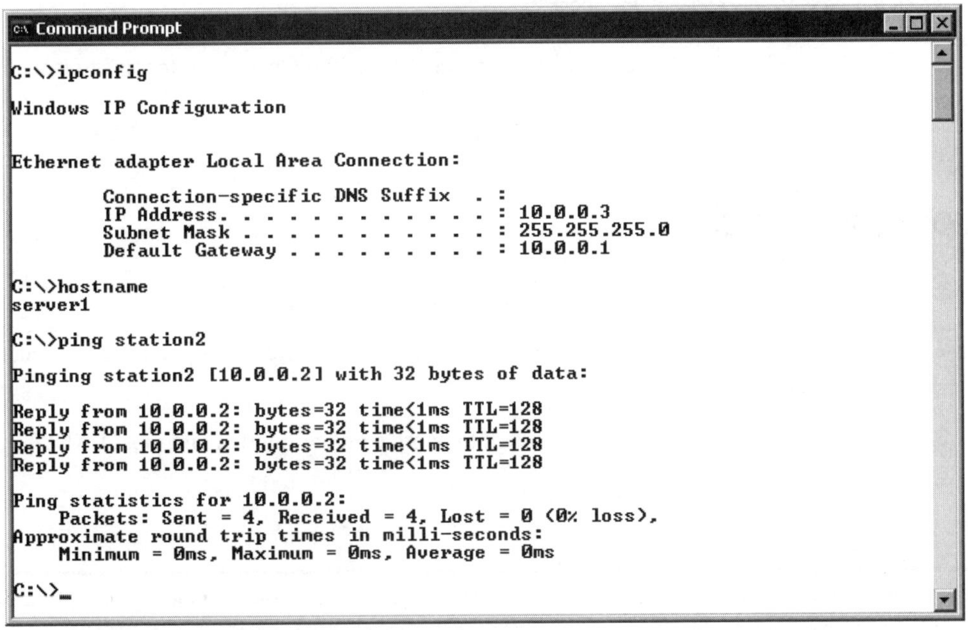

```
cx Command Prompt                                          _ □ X

C:\>ipconfig

Windows IP Configuration


Ethernet adapter Local Area Connection:

        Connection-specific DNS Suffix  . :
        IP Address. . . . . . . . . . . : 10.0.0.3
        Subnet Mask . . . . . . . . . . : 255.255.255.0
        Default Gateway . . . . . . . . : 10.0.0.1

C:\>hostname
server1

C:\>ping station2

Pinging station2 [10.0.0.2] with 32 bytes of data:

Reply from 10.0.0.2: bytes=32 time<1ms TTL=128
Reply from 10.0.0.2: bytes=32 time<1ms TTL=128
Reply from 10.0.0.2: bytes=32 time<1ms TTL=128
Reply from 10.0.0.2: bytes=32 time<1ms TTL=128

Ping statistics for 10.0.0.2:
    Packets: Sent = 4, Received = 4, Lost = 0 (0% loss),
Approximate round trip times in milli-seconds:
    Minimum = 0ms, Maximum = 0ms, Average = 0ms

C:\>_
```

Figure 8-2 Testing a network with TCP/IP utilities

TIP

If you type **ipconfig ?** at the command prompt, you will open Help for ipconfig and be able to see all the options that are available for this powerful command.

3. Type **hostname** and press ENTER. The computer name of the local computer should be returned.

4. Type **ping** *computer name* and press ENTER, where *computer name* is the name of another computer on your network. You should get four replies from the other computer.

5. If Ping did not work with a remote computer, try it on the current computer by typing **ping 127.0.0.1** and pressing ENTER. Again, you should get four replies, this time from the current computer. If you didn't get a reply here, then you have a problem with either the network setup or the NIC. If you did get a reply here, but not in Step 4, then there is a problem either in the other computer or in the line connecting them.

NOTE

The 127.0.0.1 IP address is a special address set aside to refer to the computer on which it is entered, also called "localhost."

If you do find a problem here, use the steps in "Check and Change Protocols" to isolate and fix the problem.

Progress Check

1. What is the ultimate fix if you think your NIC may not be working?

2. What are the two networking services that must be installed for a computer to fully function on a network?

3. What is the protocol that must be installed to operate on the Internet and most LANs?

---

1. Install a spare NIC that you know works. NICs cost about $20, so a spare one should not be difficult.

2. The two services required for networking are Client For Microsoft Networks and File And Printer Sharing For Microsoft Networks.

3. The protocol needed to access the Internet and most LANs is TCP/IP.

CRITICAL SKILL

8.4 Review Server Support and Network Addressing

To set up Windows Server 2003 to support the rest of the network, the following services and facilities must be installed and configured:

- Dynamic Host Configuration Protocol (DHCP)

- Domain Name System (DNS)

- User accounts and group permissions

- Domains and Active Directory

In the process of determining the best settings for all of these elements, you'll also explore the elements themselves in greater depth. While it is not needed for Windows Server 2003, Windows XP, or Windows 2000, you may want to install Windows Internet Name Service (WINS) for connectivity to older Windows systems, so it will also be discussed. Domains and Active Directory are the subject of Module 9, but the remaining elements are discussed here.

Network Addressing

For networking to function, one computer must know how to address another. To do this, every computer has at least two, and probably three, addresses:

- **Physical address**   Address that the manufacturer builds onto each network device or NIC (also called the *hardware address*). In Ethernet cards, this is the media access control (MAC) address.

- **Logical address**   Address assigned to a computer by a network administrator or a server and ultimately by an addressing authority. In TCP/IP, the IP address is the logical address and the Internet Assigned Numbers Authority (IANA) is the addressing authority that assigns a block of addresses, distributed as needed by a server or, less frequently, by an administrator. While the IANA is the ultimate naming authority, most companies and individuals get their IP address(es) from their ISP.

- **Computer name**   Address used in most applications and in My Network Places. In earlier Microsoft Windows networking, this is the *NetBIOS name*. In TCP/IP, this can be a two-part name. The first and required part is for the current computer and is the *host name*; an example is "server1." The second part is the *domain name* for the domain that contains the computer; for example, "matthews.com," making the complete name "server1.matthews.com."

These three addresses operate at different layers of the OSI networking model (see the Module 7 section "The OSI Model"), as shown in Figure 8-3. The physical address operates

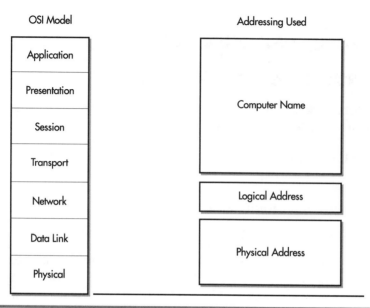

Figure 8-3 Addressing and the OSI model

at the Physical and Data Link layers, the logical address operates at the Network layer, and the computer name is used above the Network layer.

For all three of these addresses to work together, there must be a method of converting one to another. Given a computer name, it must be *resolved* to a logical address, and the logical address must be resolved to a physical address. The task of resolving a computer name into a logical address is the job of DNS or WINS, and resolving a logical address into a physical one is done by the networking protocol (for example, in TCP/IP, this is the Address Resolution Protocol, or ARP). In addition, with an ever-shorter supply of IP addresses, these addresses generally are distributed as needed by a server using DHCP. Choosing and setting up a networking protocol, as well as setting up DNS and DHCP, are major topics in this module, so the many tasks surrounding addressing are a connecting thread throughout the module.

CRITICAL SKILL
8.5 Set Up DHCP, DNS, and WINS

If everything went according to plan, you have DHCP and DNS already installed using the "Configure a Server" section of Module 4. The purpose of this section is to check how that installation went and to correct any problems that may come to light. Also, if you did not install these services earlier, you can do it now.

Set Up the Dynamic Host Configuration Protocol

DHCP, which runs on one or more servers, has the job of assigning and managing IP addresses in a network. A *scope,* or range, of IP addresses is given to DHCP, which in turn *leases* (or assigns for a certain period) an IP address to a client. DHCP removes the possibility of errors inherent in manually assigning and entering IP addresses and also removes the management task of keeping track of who has what IP address. In an environment with very many mobile users, the management task becomes all but impossible, and even in a fairly stable environment, this task is not easy.

For DHCP to perform its function, four steps must be taken:

- A server on which DHCP will be installed must be manually assigned a fixed IP address, as discussed under "Check and Change Protocols" earlier in this module

- DHCP must be enabled and authorized on the server

- DHCP must have a scope of IP addresses and a lease term

- Clients must have Obtain An IP Address Automatically selected in the Internet Protocol (TCP/IP) Properties dialog box, as discussed earlier in "Choose and Configure a Networking Protocol"

How DHCP Works

The first time a client is restarted after Obtain An IP Address Automatically has been selected, it goes through the following process to get an IP address:

1. The client broadcasts on the network a request for a DHCP server and an IP address. It uses 0.0.0.0 as the source address, uses 255.255.255.255 as the destination address, and includes its physical (MAC) address.

2. All DHCP servers that receive the request broadcast a message that includes the MAC address, an offered IP address, a subnet mask, a length of lease, and the server's IP address.

3. The client accepts the first offer that reaches it, and broadcasts that acceptance, including its new IP address and the IP of the server that offered it.

4. This acceptance is acknowledged by the offering server.

Each time the client is started after receiving an IP address, it attempts to use the same IP address from the same server. The server can accept this or not, but during the lease term, it normally is accepted. Halfway through the lease term, the client will automatically ask for the lease to be extended, and under most circumstances, it is extended. If the lease isn't extended, the client will continue to use the IP address and broadcast a request for any other server to renew the current IP address. If this is refused, the client will broadcast a request for any IP address, as it did at the start.

Install DHCP

As a normal part of installing Windows Server 2003, as described in Module 4, DHCP should be installed and properly configured. If you know this to be the case and are comfortable adding and tailoring scopes, then you can skip the rest of this section. Since DHCP is an optional networking component, you'll look at how to install it, and then look at how to add and tailor scopes.

NOTE

There are two ways that you can install DHCP and other components of Windows Server 2003. Module 4 describes how to use Manage Your Server to see what roles have been established for a particular server and, if you want to add a role, to use Configure Your Server Wizard to do so. This was done in the module to add DHCP and DNS. You can also use the Control Panel | Add Or Remove Programs to accomplish the same objective, and in the sections and steps that follow you'll see how that is done.

If DHCP is not installed or you are not sure whether it is, use the following instructions to check and, if necessary, install it:

NOTE

The following instructions also make sure that DNS and optionally WINS are installed.

1. To install DHCP, you need to insert the Windows Server 2003 CD in its drive and click Exit to close the Autorun window that opens.

2. Open the Start menu and choose Control Panel | Add Or Remove Programs. The Add Or Remove Programs dialog box opens.

3. Click Add/Remove Windows Components. The Windows Components Wizard opens.

4. Select Networking Services (click the item, not the check box, which may be grayed) and click Details. The Networking Services dialog box appears, in which you should see Dynamic Host Configuration Protocol (DHCP) on the list, as shown here:

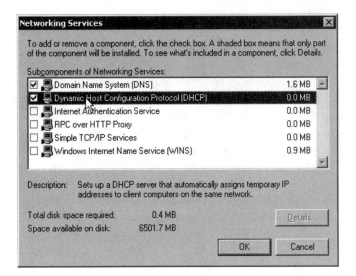

5. If the DHCP check box is not checked, check it. Also if either Domain Name System (DNS) or Windows Internet Name Service (WINS) is not checked (or both are not), check the boxes for both, and then click OK.

6. Back in the Windows Component Wizard, click Next, and then, when it is displayed, click Finish to complete the installation. Click Close to remove the Add Or Remove Programs dialog box.

Configure DHCP

Configuring DHCP is the process of defining IP address scopes, for which you will need the following items:

- A block of IP addresses to use in a scope

- Scope name

- Starting IP address in the scope range

- Ending IP address in the scope range

- Subnet mask to be used with this range of IP addresses

- Starting and ending addresses of the ranges to exclude from the scope

- DHCP client lease duration

- Settings for server, scope, and client options

Get Blocks of IP Addresses   Which block of IP addresses is used in a scope depends on whether the computers to be assigned the addresses will be public or private. If the computers will be interfacing directly with the Internet, they are *public* and thus need a globally unique IP number. If the computers will be operating only on an internal network, where they are separated from the public network by a router, bridge, or firewall, they are *private* and need only organizational uniqueness. IANA has set aside three blocks of IP addresses that can be used by any organization for its private, internal needs without any coordination with any other organization, but these blocks should not be used for connecting to the Internet. These private-use blocks of IP addresses are as follows:

- 10.0.0.0 through 10.255.255.255

- 172.16.0.0 through 172.31.255.255

- 192.168.0.0 through 192.168.255.255

In addition is the APIPA range from 169.254.0.0 through 169.254.255.255, discussed earlier in this module. Remember, though, that APIPA works only with computers within its own subnet and with IP addresses from the same range. In a small network, though, you can mix DHCP and APIPA addressing and always be assured that an IP number will be available independent of DHCP.

If you want a block of public IP addresses, you must request it from one of several organizations, depending on the size of the block that you want. At the local level for a moderate-sized block of IP addresses, your local ISP can assign it to you out of a block they have been assigned. For a larger block, a regional ISP may be able to handle the request. If not, you have to go to one of three international Internet registries:

- American Registry for Internet Numbers (ARIN), at http://www.arin.net/, which covers North and South America, the Caribbean, and sub-Saharan Africa

- Réseaux IP Européens (RIPE), at http://www.ripe.net/, which covers Europe, Middle East, and northern Africa

- Asia Pacific Network Information Center (APNIC), at http://www.apnic.net/, which covers Asia and the Pacific

The coordination of these three organizations is performed by IANA, at http://www .iana.com/. In December 1997, IP addressing authority for the Americas was transferred from Network Solutions, Inc. (InterNIC) to ARIN. ARIN, RIPE, APNIC, and IANA are all nonprofit organizations representing a broad membership of ISPs, communications companies, manufacturers, other organizations, and individuals. The smallest block that ARIN will allocate (to ISPs for reassignment) or assign (to organizations and individuals) is 4,096 addresses, for which they currently charge $2,500 per year. Larger blocks can cost up to $20,000 per year. ISPs will allocate smaller blocks using their own fee structure. The ARIN minimum block size and fee apply to the current Internet Protocol version 4 (IPv4), which has been referred to as "IP addressing" so far in the book. IPv6 is just beginning to be assigned, is a much larger number, and has its own rules for allocation and assignment, but it has a similar current fee structure that ranges from $2,500 to $20,000 per year.

Enable and Define a DHCP Scope   With an IP address range to use, you are ready to enable and define a DHCP scope, using the following instructions:

1. Open the Start menu and choose Administrative Tools | DHCP. The DHCP window will appear like this:

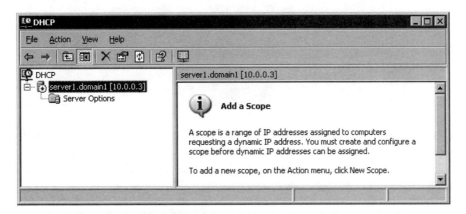

2. Right-click the server for which you want to define a scope and choose New Scope. The New Scope Wizard opens.

3. Click Next. Enter a name and description for the scope, and click Next again.

4. Enter the starting and ending IP addresses for the range to be included in the scope.

5. Enter either a length of the subnet or network portion of the IP addresses being defined or the subnet mask that defines how the new IP addresses are split. A subnet mask divides an IP address into a subnet or network address and a host address. When you are working on a local network, only the host portion is needed, so it speeds up the process if only that portion of the address is searched. An IP address is 32 bits long, so if you say that half of

it (16 bits) is a network address, the local network will only look at the 16-bit host address. The 16-bit subnet mask is 255.255.0.0, as shown here:

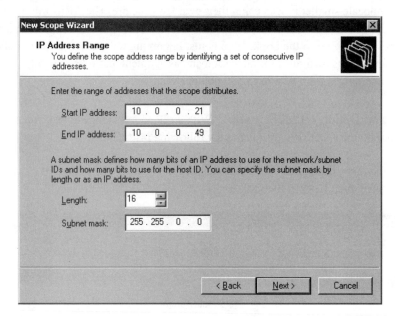

6. Click Next. Enter the IP addresses to exclude from the scope you are working on. These can be either a range, by entering a starting and ending address, or a single address, by entering it in just the Start IP Address position, as shown next. You should enter an exclusion for each static address that has been assigned to a server, workstation, or router.

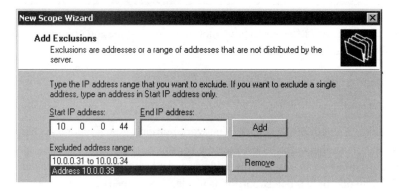

7. Click Add after entering each exclusion address or range. When you have entered all exclusions, click Next.

8. Enter the lease duration, which is the length of time that a client can use an IP address that has been assigned to it. The default is 8 days, but the correct time for your operation could be anywhere from 1 hour for clients mainly jumping on and off a mail server, to 4 days for clients who are mainly traveling mobile computer users, to 90 days for clients in a stable desktop environment.

9. Click Next. Choose Yes to configure DHCP options now, and click Next again. Enter the IP address of each router directly addressed by the network, clicking Add after each.

10. Click Next. If there is a parent domain that you want to use for DNS name resolution, enter that name. Otherwise, enter the server name in the current network that is or will be your DNS server. If you have entered a server name, click Resolve to generate its IP address and then click Add.

11. Click Next. Enter the server name for the WINS NetBIOS name resolution, click Resolve, and click Add.

12. Click Next. Select Yes, you want to activate the scope now, click Next, and then click Finish. Your new scope should appear on the left of the DHCP window.

13. With the server selected in the left pane, open the Action menu and choose Authorize. After a few moments, the window will be redrawn.

14. After the DHCP window is redrawn, click Address Pool, and you should see the details of the scope you defined. Click Address Leases, and you see a list of the clients that are leasing IP addresses from this server.

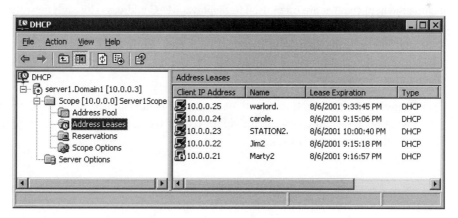

8

Setting Up and Managing a Network

Create DHCP Reservations   Suppose that you want a client to have a particular and permanent IP address. You can configure that by creating a *client reservation* that specifies an IP address to be assigned to the client. In this way, the IP address will not expire until the reservation is removed. To do that, follow these steps:

1. In the scope tree in the DHCP window, select Reservations and click Add Reservations in the toolbar. The New Reservation dialog box opens.

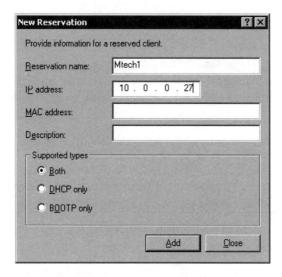

2. Enter a name, an IP address, and the associated MAC physical address (you can get the MAC address from the Unique ID column shown on the list of Address Leases). Do not include the hyphens that are often used to display a MAC address (although they are not shown in the Unique ID column of the list of Address Leases). Enter a Description, if you want one, and leave the Supported Types as the default, Both. Click Add and repeat the process for each reservation you want to make. Close the New Reservation dialog box when you're through.

3. Click Refresh in the toolbar. If Reservations is selected in the left pane of the DHCP window, your new reservation will appear on the right. Also, if you select Address Leases, you'll see the reservation in the list of leases.

NOTE

Another way to get the physical or MAC address needed in Step 2 is to open the Command Prompt window (Start | All Programs | Accessories | Command Prompt) and type **ping *ipaddress***, where *ipaddress* is either the numeric IP address or the computer name of the computer for which you need the MAC address, and press ENTER. Then, at the command prompt, type **arp −a** and press ENTER. The physical address will be displayed, as shown here:

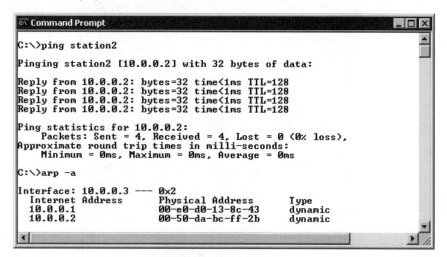

Set DHCP Options   When you went through the steps for the New Scope Wizard in the section entitled "Enable and Define a DHCP Scope," you encountered a group of settings related to the scope's options (Steps 9, 10, and 11). You can add to and change those scope options in the DHCP window, where there are three levels of options that you can set.

- **Server level options**   Apply to all DHCP clients

- **Scope level options**   Apply only to clients who lease an address from the scope

- **Client level options**   Apply to a client with a reservation

Try setting and/or changing the options with the following steps:

1. In the DHCP window, right-click Server Options and choose Configure Options. The Server Options dialog box opens. Here, you can make a number of settings that apply to all DHCP clients. For example, you can keep a list of DNS servers, as shown here:

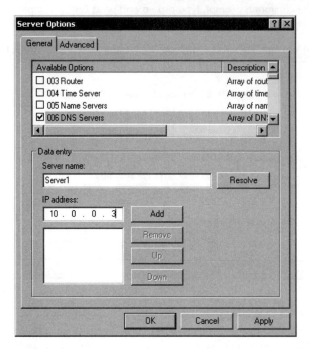

2. Click OK to close the Server Options dialog box, right-click Scope Options, and choose Configure Options. You'll see a similar dialog box, called Scope Options, with a similar list of available options.

3. Click OK to close the Scope Options dialog box. If you previously created a reservation, open the Reservation object in the scope tree, right-click your reservation in either the left or the right pane of the window, and choose Configure Options, to get a third similar list of options.

4. Click OK to close the Reservation Options dialog box. Your DHCP window now looks much different than it did initially.

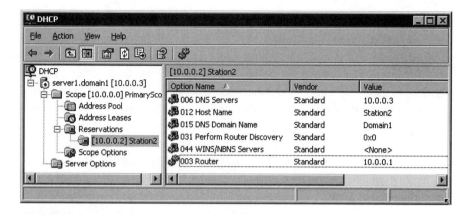

5. Close the DHCP window.

Set Up the Domain Name System

DNS has the job of resolving or converting an easy-to-remember user-friendly name into an IP address. It does this by maintaining a database of name–IP address pairs. DNS is an application in the TCP/IP protocol suite that was developed to handle the name resolution needed on the Internet. As a result, it uses a hierarchical *domain name space* that you use on the Internet. For example, the name server1.editorial.osborne.com has the following structure:

Root domain	.
Top-level domain	Com
Second-level domain	Osborne
Third-level domain	Editorial
Host name	server1

A host name is always the leftmost portion of a name and refers to a specific computer. Within a specific domain, you need only to use the host name. It is only as you move outside of a domain that you need to use the domain names.

TIP

When creating a domain name space, keep it simple. Use short, simple, unique names and keep the number of levels to a minimum.

To make a domain name space easier to manage, it can be broken into *zones,* or discrete segments. A separate name database is kept for each zone, giving a network administrator a more manageable task. A DNS server, or a *name server,* can contain one or more zones, and multiple servers may contain the database for the same zone. In the latter case, one server is designated as the *primary server,* and the other name servers within that zone periodically query the primary server for a *zone transfer* to update the database. As a result, all zone maintenance must be performed on the primary server.

DNS can resolve a name to an IP address, in what is called a *forward lookup,* as well as resolve an IP address into a name, in what is called a *reverse lookup.* In the process of name resolution, if a local name server cannot resolve a name, it passes it on to the other name servers the local server knows about, including accessing the Internet to query name servers there. As a name server queries for a name, it caches the results, so that it does not have to do the query again in the near future. This caching is done for a finite period of time, called the *time to live (TTL),* which you can set; the default time is 60 minutes.

Set Up DNS

Setting up DNS assumes that DNS has been installed on the server from which you want it to run. As a part of installing the server in Module 4, DNS should have been installed, and if it wasn't, it should have been installed earlier in this module, under "Install DHCP." Use the following instructions to set up DNS:

1. Open the Start menu and choose Administrative Tools | DNS. The DNS window opens.

2. Open the DNS Server if it isn't already, open Forward Lookup Zones, and then open one of the zones within it, so you see the host names that are contained there, as shown here (yours may only show the server):

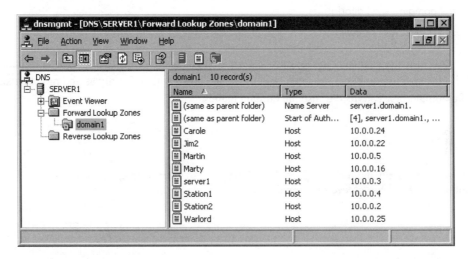

3. Add a host name to the open zone by right-clicking the zone and choosing New Host. The New Host dialog box opens.

4. Enter the host name and IP address, click Add Host, and then click OK when told that the host record was successfully created. Repeat this for as many hosts as you want to enter. When you are finished adding hosts, click Done.

5. Add a zone to the current name server by selecting the server and opening the Action menu and choosing New Zone. The New Zone Wizard opens. Click Next. Leave the default of Primary Zone to create a copy of the zone that can be directly updated. Module 9 will explore storing the zone in Active Directory.

6. Click Next. Again, accept the default of All Domain Controllers In The Active Directory Domain, and once more click Next. You'll be asked if this is either a forward or reverse lookup zone. Accept the default of a forward zone, and click Next.

7. Enter a name for the zone. Click Next. Accept the default of Allow Only Secure Dynamic Updates, click Next, and then click Finish.

8. Add new host names to this zone, as you did in Step 3. When you are finished adding hosts, click Done to close the New Host dialog box.

Set Up Reverse Lookup Zones

Reverse lookup zones, which allow the resolution of an IP number into a name, are only used in problem solving and by Internet Information Services (IIS) to add a name instead of an IP address in log files. To implement a reverse lookup capability, a special domain named In-addr.arpa is automatically created when DNS is set up. Within this domain, subdomains are defined for each *octet* or portion of an IP address between periods for the network portion of the address, and then *pointer* records are created for the final host portion of the address giving the host name and IP address. See how a reverse lookup zone is set up with these steps:

1. Right-click Reverse Lookup Zones and choose New Zone. The New Zone Wizard appears. Click Next.

2. Accept the default of Primary Zone and click Next. Accept the default All Domain Controllers In The Active Directory Domain and once more click Next.

3. In the Network ID, enter the network portion of your IP address. For example, if your IP address range is 10.0.0.1 through 10.0.0.99 with a subnet mask of 255.255.255.0, then your network ID is 10.0.0.

4. Click Next. Accept the default of Allow Only Secure Dynamic Updates, click Next, and then click Finish.

5. Right-click the new zone that was just created and choose New Pointer. The New Resource Record dialog box opens.

6. Enter the host portion of an IP number and the host name that corresponds with this.

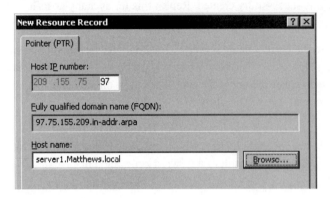

7. Click OK. Repeat Steps 5 and 6 as necessary to add additional pointers.

NOTE

You can automatically create pointer records every time you create a new Forward Lookup host record by clicking Create Associated Pointer (PTR) Record in the New Host dialog box.

Set Up Dynamic DNS

The process of adding hosts to a zone, while not terrible, is not something you want to do every time DHCP changes an address assignment. The purpose of dynamic DNS (DDNS) is to automatically update a zone host record every time DHCP makes a change. DDNS ties DHCP and DNS together so that when DHCP makes a change, it sends the information to the appropriate zone in DNS, which then reflects the change. Both DNS and DHCP must be correctly set for this to work. Use the following steps to do that:

1. In the DNS window, right-click the zone to which you want to add DDNS, and choose Properties.

2. In the General tab, opposite Dynamic Updates, open the drop-down list and click Secure Only, if it isn't already selected. (If the DNS server has been integrated with Active Directory, this is the default selection. Module 9 explains how you can choose to allow only secure updates if this isn't already done.)

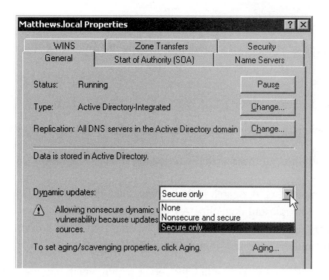

3. Click OK to close the zone's Properties dialog box.

4. Open the Start menu and choose Administrative Tools | DHCP.

5. Right-click the scope that you want to tie to the DNS zone you have been working on, and choose Properties.

6. In the DNS tab, make sure Enable DNS Dynamic Updates is checked and then click Always Dynamically Update DNS A And PTR Records.

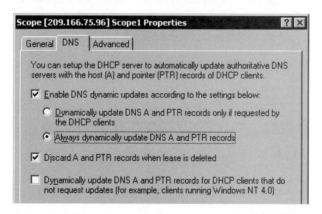

7. Click OK to close the Scope Properties dialog box. Close the DHCP window.

Test DNS

You can test to see whether DNS is working by doing the following:

- Trying to use it

- Using a test facility in DNS

- Using Nslookup in the Command Prompt window, if you created a reverse lookup zone

  Quickly try all three of these with the following steps:

1. Open My Computer, click Search in the toolbar, click Other Search Options, click Printers, Computers, Or People and then click A Computer On The Network, enter a computer name on the network, and finally click Search. If DNS and DHCP are working, the search should be successful and the computer found. Close My Computer.

2. Reopen the DNS window, right-click the server within which you created a zone, and choose Properties. Open the Monitoring tab, select both A Simple Query and A Recursive Query, and click Test Now. You should get test results at the bottom of the dialog box stating that both tests were passed. Close the server's Properties dialog box and the DNS window.

3. Open the Start menu, click Command Prompt, type **nslookup**, and press ENTER. If you created a reverse lookup zone that included the server, you get the name of the server and its IP address. Type a host name, press ENTER, and you get the full host name with its domain and its IP address. Type an IP address, and you get the full host name with its domain. After typing these three items, your Command Prompt window should look similar to this:

4. Type **Exit** to get out of Nslookup, and type **Exit** again to close the Command Prompt window.

NOTE

Nslookup requires that you have a reverse lookup zone, which is one of the reasons for creating one.

Set Up Windows Internet Name Service

WINS has the same job as DNS: resolving or converting an easy-to-remember user-friendly name into an IP address. WINS utilizes the NetBIOS naming convention developed by IBM and Microsoft as part of an early networking scheme. NetBIOS, which operates at the Session (fifth) layer of the OSI networking model, normally interacts with NetBEUI at the Transport and Network layers of the OSI model (see Figure 8-4) and does so by converting a user-friendly name directly to a physical (MAC) address. WINS, which like DNS is an application, maintains a database of NetBIOS names and their IP address equivalents. NetBIOS names using NetBIOS over TCP/IP, which calls on WINS, can then be used with TCP/IP in place of NetBEUI.

NOTE

Support for the NetBEUI protocol, which was used in communicating with earlier Microsoft networking systems, has been removed from Windows Server 2003.

WINS requires very little maintenance, initially building itself, and maintaining itself as changes occur. You only need to turn it on and specify the server IP address in the clients.

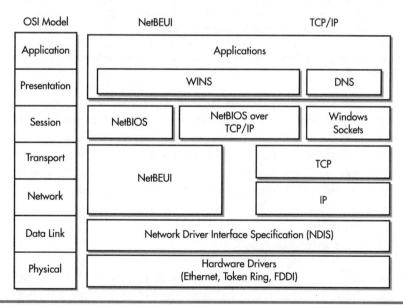

Figure 8-4 WINS, NetBIOS, TCP/IP, and the OSI model

WINS, while still available in Windows Server 2003, has had its function largely usurped by DDNS, because DDNS is integrated into Active Directory, and because DNS offers security features that are not available in WINS. If your network has only Windows Server 2003 or Windows 2000 servers and Windows XP and 2000 clients, you do not need WINS, because NetBIOS names are not used. If you have computers with earlier Windows operating systems (Windows 95, 98, Me, or NT) in your network, then WINS may be beneficial.

WINS can safely coexist with DNS, *if* you don't have security concerns about the WINS database being automatically created and updated, and if the integration with Active Directory is not important to you. In a shared environment, WINS handles the 16-character-maximum (the user can enter 15) single-part NetBIOS name used in all Microsoft operating systems up through Windows 98 and NT 4, while DNS handles the multipart, 255-character-maximum domain name used in Windows Server 2003, Windows XP, and Windows 2000.

NOTE

In smaller networks (having a practical maximum in the range of 35 to 50 computers, and an absolute maximum of about 70), you do not need to use either WINS or DNS. Each computer in the network periodically broadcasts to the other computers in the network for their NetBIOS names and their IP addresses and then stores this information in a working file on the computer making the initial request. This generates a lot of network traffic, and as the network grows, that traffic can be overpowering. You can reduce this traffic by manually creating and maintaining a static text file named Lmhosts (LM for LAN Manager, the original Microsoft networking system) that is checked before broadcasting on the network (search for Lmhosts.sam [it is probably in C:\Windows\ System32\Drivers\Etc\], open it with Notepad, and follow the instructions at the beginning of the file to create it). Maintaining this file on a number of computers becomes a major chore and is the reason that WINS was developed. A similar static file, Hosts, can be used with DNS, but both of these text files are practical for only the smallest networks.

WINS, like DNS, resides on a server. To use it, a client queries the server with a NetBIOS name, and the server replies with an IP number for that name. When you set up a WINS server and start a client by giving it the server's address, the client automatically registers its name and IP address with the server. The server responds with the TTL, the amount of time it will maintain the registration. From then on, each time the client starts it will repeat this process, or if it is on for half of its TTL, it will automatically re-register its name.

Set Up WINS on a Server

Set up WINS on the server with these steps:

1. Open the Start menu, choose Control Panel | Network Connections | Local Area Connection, and choose Properties. The Local Area Connection Properties dialog box opens.

2. Select Internet Protocol (TCP/IP) and click Properties. The Internet Protocol (TCP/IP) Properties dialog box opens.

3. Click Advanced, select the WINS tab, and click Add. Enter the IP address of the WINS primary server and click Add. If you have a secondary (or more) WINS server, enter it in the same way.

4. When you are done entering WINS servers, click OK twice and click Close twice to close all the open dialog boxes.

5. Open the Start menu and choose Administrative Tools | WINS. The WINS window should open with your WINS server listed.

6. Open the server, right-click Active Registrations, choose Display Records, and then click Find Now at the bottom of the dialog box that opens. A list of NetBIOS names and IP addresses should be displayed, as shown here:

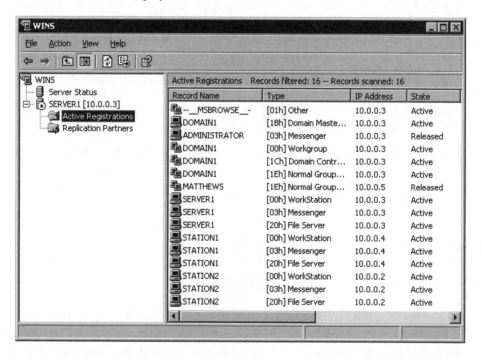

7. If you have non-WINS clients, you can add static registrations for them by right-clicking Active Registrations and choosing New Static Mapping. The New Static Mapping dialog box opens.

8. Enter the computer name and the NetBIOS scope, if desired (the scope is an extension to the name used to group computers). Then, choose a type (see Table 8-1) and enter one or more IP addresses, as needed. When done, click OK to close the dialog box, and then close the WINS window.

Type	Explanation
Unique	A single computer with a single IP address
Group	A group name with only one IP address for the group
Domain Name	A domain name with up to 25 IP addresses for its members
Internet Group	A group name with up to 25 IP addresses for its members
Multihomed	A computer with up to 25 IP addresses for multiple NICs

Table 8-1 Types of Static WINS Registrations

Set Up WINS on Clients

Setting up a WINS client often is done on computers running something other than Windows Server 2003, Windows XP, or Windows 2000. The steps for doing that in Windows 98 are as follows:

1. Open the Start menu, choose Settings | Control Panel, and double-click Network. The Network Properties dialog box opens.

2. Select TCP/IP for the NIC and click Properties. The TCP/IP Properties dialog box opens.

3. Click the WINS Configuration tab and click Enable WINS Resolution. Enter the WINS server IP address and click Add.

4. When you are done entering WINS servers, click OK twice to close all the open dialog boxes. Click Yes to restart your computer.

5. Repeat Steps 1–4 for each client on the network.

CRITICAL SKILL
8.6

Set Up User Accounts and Group Permissions

To gain access to another computer or to other resources (such as a printer) on the network, a user must have been given permission to do so. Such permission begins with the user being a known entity, by having a user account. You can have *local user* accounts, which provide access to one computer, and *domain user* accounts, which provide access to all the resources in the domain. Domain user accounts, as implemented by Active Directory, which can be very valuable and can provide the way to structure a network in many cases, are discussed in Modules 9 and 17.

Instead of assigning permissions to individuals, you assign individuals to groups that have certain permissions. This section looks at setting up local user accounts, setting up groups, and assigning users to groups.

User accounts, groups, and permissions are an important part of network security, and the security aspects of these elements, such as password strategies, are discussed in Module 17. This section focuses on setting up the elements, not on how they should be used for security purposes.

NOTE

If you are using or are going to use a domain, it is important to set up domain user accounts rather than local user accounts on computers within the domain. Local user accounts are not recognized by the domain, so a local user cannot use domain resources and a domain administrator cannot administer the local accounts.

Plan for Usernames and Passwords

Before setting up either domain or local user accounts, your organization should have a plan for the usernames and passwords that the company will use. The objectives are to be consistent and to use prudent practices. Here are some considerations:

- Are you going to use first name and last initial, first initial and last name, or full first and last names?

- How, if at all, are you going to separate the first and last names? Many organizations don't use any separation, whereas others use either periods or the underscore.

- How are you going to handle two people with the same first and last names? Adding a number after the name is a common answer; using the middle initial is another.

- Do you need a special class of names for, for example, subcontractors in your organization? If so, how, if at all, do you want to differentiate them from other users? One method is to precede their names with one or more characters to indicate their position, such as "SC" for subcontractor.

- Names must be unique, cannot be over 20 characters long (or 20 bytes long if a character takes over one byte), are not case-sensitive, cannot contain the @ character, and cannot consist solely of periods and/or spaces. Leading or trailing periods or spaces are ignored.

- Passwords must be unique; cannot be over 127 characters; can use both upper- and lowercase letters; should use a mixture of letters, numbers, and symbols; and should be at least 7 characters long.

NOTE

If your password is over 14 characters, you will not be able to log on to the network from a Windows 95/98/Me computer.

Set Up Local User Accounts

Windows Server 2003 and Windows XP Professional create several user accounts when installed, among which are two that initially are named Administrator and Guest. You can change the name and password for each of these accounts, but you cannot delete them. When you go through the installation of Windows Server 2003, as described in Modules 3 and 4, you establish the initial password for the Administrator account, but all other account creation and maintenance is done outside Setup.

 NOTE

If your server is a domain controller, you'll only be able to set up domain user accounts. Local user accounts can be created only on servers that are not DCs or on clients.

Follow these steps to see how local user accounts are set up (remember, if the server you are looking at is a domain controller, you will not be able to find the Local Users and Groups discussed in these steps):

1. Open the Start menu and choose Administrative Tools | Computer Management. The Computer Management window opens.

2. Open System Tools and then open Local Users And Groups. Right-click Users and choose New User. The New User dialog box opens.

3. Enter a User Name, Full Name, Description, and Password, as shown next. Select how you want to handle passwords, and click Create.

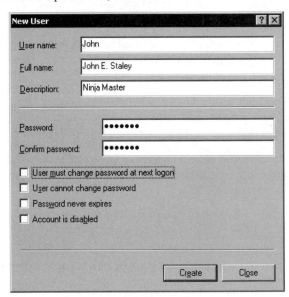

4. Repeat Step 3 for as many local users as you have.

Set Up Groups and Their Members

Groups allow you to define what a particular type of user is allowed to do on the computer. Once you have done that, the users you have defined can be made members of these groups and will then have the same permissions as the groups to which they belong. Windows Server 2003 comes with a number of groups already defined, so the first step is to understand what those are. Then, you can add one or more of your own groups.

1. In the Computer Management window, open Groups in the System Tools | Local Users And Groups tree. The list of currently defined groups appears, as shown here:

The standard set of groups provides a good spectrum of permissions, as you can see by reading the Description column in the Computer Management window.

2. Create a new group by right-clicking Groups in the left pane and choosing New Group. The New Group dialog box opens.

3. Enter the group name and a description, which should list the permissions the group has.

4. Click Add, and the Select Users dialog box opens. Either type the users you want to add in the lower text box, clicking Check Names after each entry, or click Advanced, click Find Now, select a name from the list, and click OK to transfer it to the list of names.

5. When you are done, click OK, click Create to create the new group, and click Close to close the New Group dialog box.

NOTE

If you are wondering how permissions get assigned, it is done through objects such as disk drives and printers. Module 17 discusses in detail how to set permissions.

Add Users to Groups

Although you can add users to groups when you create the groups, you most often will add users to groups independently of creating groups, as follows (you should still have the Computer Management window open):

1. Open Users by clicking it in the left pane, locate and right-click a user whose group memberships you want to change in the right pane, and choose Properties. The user's Properties dialog box opens.

2. Click the Member Of tab, and click Add. The Select Groups dialog box opens, as shown here:

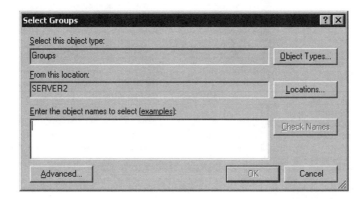

3. Either type the groups you want to add in the lower text box, clicking Check Names after each entry, or click Advanced, click Find Now, select a name from the list, and click OK to transfer it to the list of names. When you have selected all the groups you want, click OK.

4. When you are done with the user account, click OK to close the Properties dialog box, and then click Close to close the Computer Management window.

The user's Properties dialog box contains several tabs not previously mentioned. These will be discussed in future modules. Profile, for example, allows you to define a profile for a user so that when that user logs in to a computer, the profile automatically sets up the desktop, menus, and other features for that user. It is discussed in Module 16. Another example is Dial-In, which sets up how a user will work with remote access and virtual private networking; it is the subject of Module 13.

Remember that local user accounts are limited to a single computer and cannot be centrally managed. The broader and more easily managed way to implement user accounts is with domains, which are discussed in Module 9.

Progress Check

1. What do you need to set up so that Windows Server 2003 can support the rest of the network?

2. How can IP addresses be automatically distributed to computers in a network?

3. What is a DHCP scope and how is it used?

Project 8   Make Sure Networking Is Properly Set Up

This exercise will quickly go through the steps to make sure networking is properly installed and working, including determining if

- You have a network connection

- Your computer recognizes your NIC

- The correct driver is installed for your NIC

- The appropriate networking services are installed

- The correct protocol is installed and properly configured

- Your computer can talk to itself and the rest of the network

If the sum of these items says that networking is not working properly, then you need to return to the first section, "Set Up Network Interface Cards," and follow the instructions in that and the section following it.

(continued)

---

1. To set up Windows Server 2003 to support the rest of the network, DHCP, DNS, and user accounts and group permissions must be installed and configured. Additionally, you may want to install a domain and Active Directory. If you have older operating systems (Windows 95 and before or Windows NT 3.1) on the network, you may also need to install WINS.

2. IP addresses are automatically distributed to computers in a network as needed by a server using DHCP.

3. A DHCP scope is a range of IP addresses that DHCP in turn leases (or assigns for a certain period) to a client on the network served by the DHCP server.

Step by Step

1. Open the Start menu and choose Control Panel | Network Connections. If the flyout menu shows Local Area Connection, you have a network connection. If not, you need to return to the first section, "Set Up Network Interface Cards," and follow the instructions in that and the section following it.

2. Click Local Area Connection to open the Local Area Connection Status dialog box. If this shows you are connected and that bytes are being both sent and received, then your connection is operating properly and you can skip to Step 7.

3. Click Properties. In the Local Area Connection Properties dialog box that opens, you should see your NIC listed. If so, your computer recognizes your NIC; if not, you need to return to the first section "Set Up Network Interface Cards" and follow the instructions in that and the section following it.

4. Click Configure. In your NIC's Properties dialog box, you should see under Device Status "This Device Is Working Properly." If so, the correct driver is installed for your NIC and you can skip to Step 6.

5. Click the Driver tab, click Update Driver, and follow the directions in the Hardware Update Wizard. When the Wizard is finished, click the Resources tab and make sure that the box under Conflicting Device List reads "No Conflicts." If not, you need to return to the first section, "Set Up Network Interface Cards," and follow the instructions in that and the section following it.

6. Close the NIC's Properties dialog box and reopen the Local Area Connection's Properties dialog box by clicking Properties in the Local Area Connection Status dialog box. In the list of items in the middle, you should see at least the following two services and one protocol

   Client For Microsoft Networks
   File And Printer Sharing For Microsoft Networks
   Internet Protocol (TCP/IP)

   If so, the appropriate networking services and protocol are installed. If not, you need to return to the section "Set Up Network Interface Cards." Close the Local Area Connection Properties dialog box and close the Local Area Connection Status dialog box.

7. Open the Start menu and choose Command Prompt. Type **ipconfig** and press ENTER. If you get a response with an IP address and a subnet mask, then your network components can talk to themselves. Type **ping *computername***, where *computername* is the name of another computer on your network. If you get a response, then your network components can talk to the rest of the network. If you do not get a response, you need to return to the section "Set Up Network Interface Cards."

Project Summary

For an organization of any size, networking is extremely important because it allows that organization to share information, communicate, and share resources. Therefore, to make sure that the network is set up and running properly is equally important. If the information in this module is not sufficient, check out Tom Sheldon's *Encyclopedia of Networking & Telecommunications* (McGraw-Hill/Osborne, 2001).

✔ Module 8 Mastery Check

1. If a NIC is properly plugged into a computer, what are three things that could be causing it to not operate?

2. What is the primary protocol used in Windows networking, and what do its components do?

3. What are three things to check if you think networking is not working properly?

4. What are two different ways to test and determine if a network connection is working?

5. What are the three types of network addressing?

6. How are the three types of network addressing used together? In other words, how is one type of address translated or resolved into another type of address?

7. What are the four tasks that must be performed for DHCP to perform its function?

8. Where can you get a block of IP addresses to use in a DHCP scope?

9. How can you get the physical or MAC network address?

10. What does DNS do and how does it do it?

Module 9

Using Active Directory and Domains

Probably the single biggest change in Windows 2000 over Windows NT was the addition of Active Directory (AD). In Windows Server 2003 AD has been enhanced, making it an even more important part of the operating system. *Active Directory* provides a single reference, called a *directory service,* to all the objects in a network, including users, groups, computers, printers, policies, and permissions. For a user or an administrator, AD provides a single hierarchical view from which to access and manage all of the network's resources. AD utilizes Internet protocols and standards, including Kerberos, Secure Sockets Layer (SSL), and Transport Layer Security (TLS) authentication; the Lightweight Directory Access Protocol (LDAP); and the Domain Name System (DNS). AD requires one or more domains in which to operate.

A *domain,* as used within Windows NT, 2000 and Windows Server 2003, is a collection of computers that share a common set of policies, a name, and a database of their members. A domain must have one or more servers that serve as *domain controllers* and store the database, maintain the policies, and provide the authentication of domain logons. A *domain,* as used within the Internet, is the highest segment of an Internet domain name and identifies the type of organization; for example, .gov for government agencies, and .net for Internet service providers (ISPs). A *domain name* is the full Internet address used to reach one entity registered on the Internet. For example, www.osborne.com or www.mit.edu.

Review the Active Directory Environment

AD plays two basic functions within a network: that of a directory service containing a hierarchical listing of all the objects within the network, and that of an authentication and security service that controls and provides access to network resources. These two roles are very different in nature and focus, but they combine together to provide increased user capabilities while decreasing administrative overhead. At its core, Windows Server 2003 AD is a directory service that is integrated into DNS, plus a user authentication service for the Windows Server 2003 operating system. This explanation, however, introduces a few new terms and involves a number of complex concepts.

While AD is both a directory and a directory service, the terms are not interchangeable. In Windows Server 2003 networking, a *directory* is a listing of the objects within a network. A hierarchical directory has a structure with a top-to-bottom configuration that allows for the logical grouping of objects, such that lower-level objects are logically grouped and contained in higher-level objects for as many levels as you want. This grouping can be based on a number of different criteria, but the criteria should be logical and consistent throughout the directory structure.

Two of the more common directory structures in use within networks are based on object function (such as printers, servers, and storage devices) and organizational responsibility (such as marketing, accounting, and manufacturing). The organizational model allows you to store objects in groups, or *containers,* based on where they are in an organization, which might have its own structure, such as departments within divisions. A particular department would be the first organizational point within an organization. A container holding all the objects in a department is called an *organizational unit (OU)* and is itself grouped into higher-level OUs based on the logical structure.

After you create a group of OUs, you may find that the structure causes your directory to be cluttered and/or awkward to navigate. As a result, you may need to change your network to have more high-level OUs or more low-level OUs. At the top of all directories is the master OU that contains all the other OUs. This directory is referred to as the *root* and is normally designated by a single period. Such a hierarchical structure might look like this:

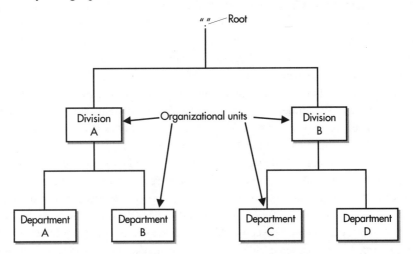

AD is just as basic as the organization just displayed. However, much of AD's core structure has already been mapped out by Microsoft and is consistent throughout all Windows Server 2003 implementations. For this reason, some of the containers, which are just OUs, have been assigned specific names and roles within AD. As this preconfigured directory structure is explained in the rest of the module, don't let the terms and names confuse you. Everything is still simply a collection of objects within OUs.

The "service" in "directory service" adds to a server features that are not otherwise available. Primarily, a directory service provides access to the directory of information, as well as to services that provide information about the location, access methods, and access rights for the objects within the directory service tree. This means that users can access a single directory and then be directly connected to a variety of other servers and services that appear to all be coming from the original directory. Much of this module discusses the different kinds of objects and methods of access that AD can provide to both users and administrators.

NOTE

AD, Microsoft Exchange, and Novell Directory Services (NDS) are all based on the X.500 standard, which is an internationally recognized standard used to create a directory structure. Specifically, AD is based on the newer X.509 version of the X.500 family.

Integration with DNS

Much of AD's structure and services, as well as the namespace that it uses, is based on DNS. (*Namespace* is the addressing scheme that is used to locate objects on the network. Both AD and the Internet use a hierarchical namespace separated by periods, as described earlier in this module.) How AD uses DNS will be discussed in a moment, but it is necessary to first look at the structure and workings of DNS and how it is used to build the AD foundation.

All servers and services on the Internet are given an Internet Protocol (IP) numerical address, and all Internet traffic uses this IP number to reach its destination. IP numbers change, and may host multiple services at the same time. In addition, most people have a hard time remembering large arbitrary numbers such as IP addresses. IP addresses are decimal-based descriptions of binary numbers without a discernable pattern. DNS services were created to solve these problems by allowing servers and other objects on the network to be given a user-friendly name, which DNS translates to an IP number. For example, a user-friendly name such as mail.osborne.com might be translated, or *resolved,* in a DNS server to an IP address such as 168.143.56.34, which the network can then use to locate the desired resource.

DNS servers use hierarchical directory structures, just like the example described at the beginning of the module. At the core of DNS servers are root domains with a root directory, which is described by a single period. The first groups of OUs below the root are the various types of domains that can exist, for example, COM, NET, ORG, US, GOV, and EDU. Over 250 of these top-level domains are controlled within the United States by InterNIC, an arm of the U.S. Department of Commerce and run by a private, nonprofit corporation named the Internet Corporation for Assigned Names and Numbers (ICANN), which controls a number of root servers that contain a listing of all the entries within each subdomain.

The next group of OUs following the ".COMs" consists of domain names, such as coke.com, microsoft.com, and osborne.com. These domains are registered and administered by the organizations or individuals who own them. A number of companies have contracted with InterNIC/ICANN to register new domain names added to the Internet; you can see an alphabetical list of those companies at http://www.internic.com/alpha.html.

A domain name, such as osborne.com, can contain both additional OUs, called *subdomains,* and actual server objects. In the example previously given, mail.osborne.com, the mail server is an object in the osborne.com domain. A server name such as mail.osborne.com that contains all OUs between itself and the root is called a fully qualified domain name (FQDN). Figure 9-1 shows the actual name resolution process required when a client such as the one in the lower left of Figure 9-1 requests a DNS server to resolve an FQDN to an IP address by going up and back down the chain of DNS servers.

Active Directory and Domains

AD and DNS share the same central OU, called a *domain.* For those familiar with Windows NT 4 or Windows 2000, the domain concept should be a familiar one. A domain is a central authentication and directory service that contains all the information for a group of computers.

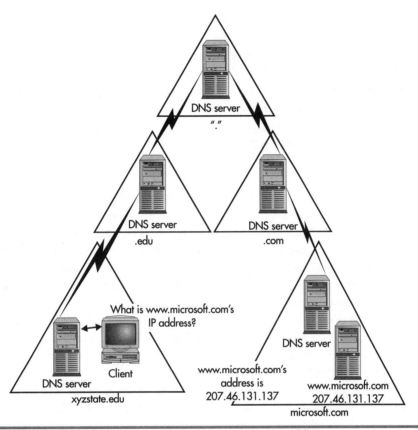

Figure 9-1 The process of resolving a domain name to an IP address

NT 4 had a number of significant limitations in the utilization of domains. Primarily, domains were not actual directory servers, because they contained only users, groups, and computers in a nonhierarchical structure. Although all computers were able to use the central repository of information for authentication issues, the directory was not available for object location or resource management. In AD, the core features and look of legacy NT domains are still present, but they have been greatly extended. Among the many enhancements, which will be discussed over the course of this module, is the ability of AD domains to scale to virtually any size, as opposed to the 40,000-object limit placed on NT domain structures. Another enhancement is AD's ability to form transitive two-way trusts with other domains in the network (this will be discussed further, later in the module).

The close integration between AD and DNS can, at first, be a little confusing. Looking at AD and DNS, it is easy to think they are actually the same thing, because they use the same names and naming scheme. However, this is not true. In actuality, DNS and AD are separate directory services that are using the same names for different namespaces. Each directory contains different objects, and different information about the objects in its own database. However, those object names, as well as the directory structure, often are identical.

Every Windows Server 2003 computer has an FQDN. This is a combination of its own computer name and the domain name of the domain in which it currently resides. For example, Windows Server 2003 computers in the Osborne domain may very well have a computer name equal to *computername*.osborne.com. However, that same computer may in fact be a member of the subdomain of editorial.osborne.com. In this case, the computer's FQDN would actually be *computername*.editorial.osborne.com.

DNS Directories

A DNS directory doesn't really store objects in its database. Rather, DNS stores domains, the access information for each domain, and the access information for the objects (such as servers and printers) within the domain. The access information is normally just the FQDN and the related IP address. All queries for an object's IP address will match the FQDN in the request to the FQDN index in the DNS directory and return (*resolve to*) the IP address. In some cases, the access information (or *resource reference*) simply points to another object (or *resource*) within the same or a different DNS domain.

A standard DNS domain is not capable of reversing this process by returning an FQDN when provided with an IP address. To make this kind of resolution possible, a reverse lookup zone is required, as discussed in Module 8. These domains are referenced as "in-addr-arpa" domains within the DNS hierarchy.

Among the other special functions of DNS that add features to a network is the Mail Exchanger reference that can be added to a DNS domain name. A Mail Exchanger reference (referred to as MX) enables mail servers to locate the mail servers of other domains to allow for the transferring of e-mail across the Internet.

Active Directory Services

AD services contain a lot more information than what is available in DNS directories, even though the names and structure are nearly identical. AD resolves all information requests for objects within its database using LDAP queries. The AD server is able to provide a varied amount of information about each object within its database. The information that AD can provide includes, but isn't limited to, the following:

- Username

- Contact information, such as physical address, phone numbers, and e-mail address

- Administrative contacts

- Access permissions

- Ownerships

- Object attributes, such as object name features; for example, Color Laser Jet Printer, 20 sheets per minute, duplex printing

Although DNS does not require AD, AD requires a DNS server to be in place and functioning correctly on the network before a user will be able to find the AD server. With Windows Server 2003 moving entirely to Internet standards for its network operating system, a method of locating network services had to be found other than using the NetBIOS broadcasts used in Windows NT. This was done through the use of a new DNS domain type known as *dynamic DNS (DDNS)* domains. A DDNS domain, which is integrated into AD, allows all domain controllers to use the same database, which is automatically updated as new Windows Server 2003 computers are added and removed from the network. The DDNS domain also allows DNS to function with networks based on DHCP (Dynamic Host Configuration Protocol), where the IP addresses of the network objects are constantly changing. Besides providing the name resolution for the network, the DDNS domains also contain a listing of all the domains and domain controllers throughout the network. This means that as new Windows Server 2003 systems are added to a network, they will query the DDNS servers to get the name and connection information, including IP address, of the domain controllers they are closest to.

NOTE

In Windows NT installations, Windows Internet Naming Service (WINS) servers provided new workstations with the location of the domain controllers. To allow for compatibility with Windows 3.11, Windows 95, and Windows 98 workstations not running the AD client, WINS servers are still required on the network. Both Windows Server 2003 and Windows 2000 servers as well as legacy NT servers have the ability to host WINS services and integrate them with DNS.

Active Directory and the Global DNS Namespace

AD domains are designed and intended to exist within the naming scheme of the global DNS domain operated through the Internet. This means that, by design, the DNS domain of your network would also match the AD domain-naming scheme. In some organizations, migration from a legacy NT local area network (LAN) is difficult, because independent LAN and Internet domains are already in place and entrenched. In this case, DDNS servers can be used for the LAN AD domain and hosted on internal DNS servers. The external servers providing Internet web hosting services, such as the Simple Mail Transfer Protocol (SMTP) and the Hypertext

Transfer Protocol (HTTP), would still use the Internet DNS structure and provide the necessary resource mapping in each domain to allow for coexistence, as shown here:

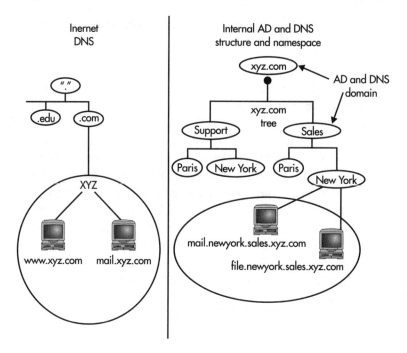

 NOTE

The functions provided by the DDNS domain that are required for AD are the listing of the domain information and the location of the domain servers. These functions are provided by a resource object called a Service Location Resource (SRV). SRVs are not unique to Windows DDNS domains, and therefore some third-party DNS server products work with AD. However, configuring these third-party DNS servers to integrate with AD can be a significant undertaking.

CRITICAL SKILL
9.2 Install Active Directory

There are two ways to install AD: into an existing domain, or to form a new domain. (For those a little more familiar with AD, some issues regarding forests and trees are affected here, as well, but those will be discussed later in the module.) Installing AD on a server turns the server into a *domain controller,* a server that hosts a central database of all users and groups within the domain and manages all domain-related functions, such as user logon authentication and trust relationships. This process can be done on existing NT servers or on newly installed Windows Server 2003 or Windows 2000 AD servers. Windows 2000 was the first Windows platform that allowed for the promotion of member servers to domain controllers. If a domain contains multiple AD servers, then the AD services can be removed from a domain controller and the server can be returned to a standard member server within the domain.

When installing AD into an existing legacy NT-based domain, the primary domain controller (PDC) of the domain has to be a Windows Server 2003 or Windows 2000 server running AD. This is obviously only an issue in cases in which both Windows Server 2003 or Windows 2000 and legacy NT domain controllers exist in the domain (called a mixed-mode network). In cases where you are installing the first AD server in an existing legacy domain, the existing PDC will have to be upgraded to Windows Server 2003 or Windows 2000, and then AD can be added. A Windows Server 2003 or Windows 2000 server can exist without AD in an NT legacy domain, but before AD can be added, the PDC has to be upgraded to Windows Server 2003 or Windows 2000.

TIP

In some cases, adding a new domain controller with no services other than the NT domain functions is advisable to make the upgrade as smooth as possible. This domain controller can then be upgraded to assume the role of PDC in the legacy domain. With this migration complete, the existing servers can be migrated in any manner, including reformatting and reloading the hard drive, that is advisable. Some companies, such as Hewlett-Packard, Compaq, and IBM, have automated Windows 2000 (and probably Windows Server 2003 shortly) installation CDs for many of their servers, which will automatically load the correct drivers for their system's hardware. The extra domain controller can be removed from the network at a later time or can be used to replace one of the exiting domain controllers.

To install AD on Windows Server 2003, use the AD Installation Wizard, which appears automatically if you are upgrading a domain controller, or it can be started in the Manage Your Server Wizard (see "Set Up a Domain Controller" in Module 4) when you choose to make the server a domain controller and install AD. In the AD Installation Wizard, you are asked if you want to create a new domain or add a domain controller to an existing domain, as shown in Figure 9-2.

CAUTION

As you can read in Figure 9-2, if you are up grading a computer as a domain controller in an existing domain, all existing local accounts, including all cryptographic keys, will be deleted. All cryptographic keys should be exported to another computer, and all encrypted files and e-mail should be decrypted before going ahead with the installation of AD. Also, note that computers running Windows 95 or Windows NT 4 SP3 and earlier will no longer be able to log on to a Windows Server 2003 domain controller or access domain resources unless you install the Active Directory client for those systems.

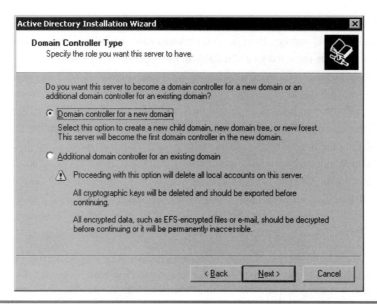

Figure 9-2 Choosing between creating a new domain and adding a domain controller to an existing one

NOTE

Active Directory clients for Windows 95, Windows 98, and early versions on Windows NT 4 are available for download on the Microsoft web site on pages for the various operating systems.

When installing into an existing domain, your administrative rights on the domain will be checked. It is possible to have administrative rights on the server being upgraded but to not have sufficient rights on the domain and domain controllers to do the installation. After you install the AD service, you do the remaining configuration through the AD Domains And Trusts, AD Sites And Services, and AD Users And Computers windows, which Microsoft calls "snap-ins for the Microsoft Management Console (MMC)," as shown in Figure 9-3.

Replace Existing Domain Controllers

Windows Server 2003 servers functioning in native domains (domains that contain only Windows Server 2003 domain controllers) act as peers with all members containing the AD services database with equal read/write privileges. In legacy NT domains, only the PDC contains the master, read/write copy of the domain's directory store. All the other domain controllers in NT domains, referred to as *backup domain controllers (BDCs),* contain read-only copies of the domain directory information store. BDCs are able to authenticate users and provide domain information, but all additions and modifications to the existing data have to be made to the PDC. When installed in

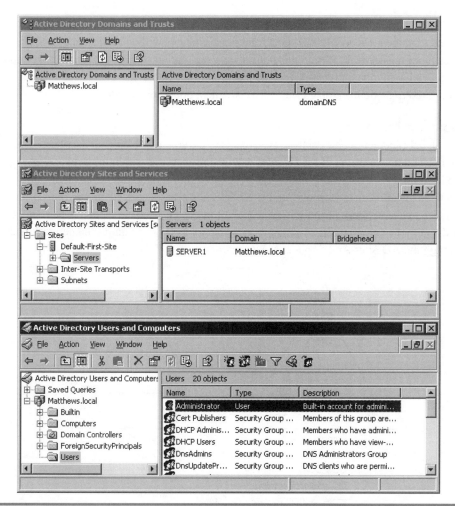

Figure 9-3 Configuring AD in one of three MMC snap-ins

mixed mode, an AD server will still respond to remote procedure calls (RPCs) as if it were a PDC and then replicate directory changes to the legacy BDCs. This means that all remaining legacy domain controllers do not recognize that there has been any major modifications to the network. In Windows 2000 domains, all domain controllers act as peers with all members containing the AD services database with equal read/write privileges similar to Windows Server 2003, but if you mix Windows 2000 and Windows Server 2003 domain controllers in the same forest, they will operate as if they are all Windows 2000 domain controllers and several of the AD replication improvements in Windows Server 2003 will not be available. When all Windows 2000 domain controllers have been upgraded to Windows Server 2003, the functionality level can be advanced to Windows Server 2003, providing access to all the new features.

The method of operation used by AD is that of *multimaster replication,* which means that changes can be made to any AD server and those changes will be replicated to other servers throughout the network. Within this multimaster replication scheme are a couple of important concepts that involve the first AD server installed in the domain, which is automatically configured to be both a global catalog server and an operations master.

Global Catalog Server

The global catalog is a new database type that is at the core of the directory services. The *global catalog* contains a listing of the services that can be accessed within the network, and not just the local domain. The global catalog can be kept on multiple domain controllers, but it always has to be installed on at least one, and by default it is always created on the firstAD server installed in a new forest. (The forest concept is explained later in the module.) The configuration of the global catalog and its placement on various servers throughout the network is done through the AD Sites And Services MMC snap-in.

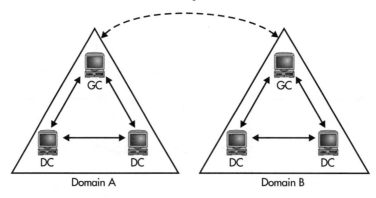

Domain A   Domain B

DC = Domain controller
GC = Global catalog
—— = Domain directory replication
– – = Global catalog replication

TIP

When operating in mixed mode, all domain controllers can perform user logins independently. However, when operating in native mode, a query to a global catalog server is required (because it determines a user's global group memberships). Therefore, the rules for installing multiple global catalogs within a network are very similar to those for installing additional BDCs to an NT 4 domain. When installing multiple distant sites, having a global catalog server in each site will decrease the network load on WAN links otherwise used to provide user authentication. Additionally, having multiple global catalog servers to distribute the network load of authentication traffic evenly across multiple servers, instead of stacking this load onto a single server to handle, is much more efficient. Of course, the need for additional global catalog servers increases the network bandwidth consumed for directory synchronization.

In general, the global catalog servers within a network provide two main features: logon and querying. When operating a domain in native mode, universal groups are allowed to exist within the forest. Because universal groups can contain users and groups from multiple domains, the universal group cannot exist within an individual domain. Therefore, the global catalog maintains the universal groups within the network as well as each group's memberships. In Windows 2000 domains, this means that whenever operating a network in native mode, the AD server logging a user into the network has to query a global catalog server to determine the universal group memberships that the user may be a part of. In cases in which a user logs in and a global catalog server is not available, the user will be granted access only to the local computer. This avoids any potential security issues in which a global group based in the domain granted a user access to a resource that the universal group excluded the user from gaining access to. In case of an emergency, however, any user account that is a member of the local domain's Domain Admin group will be allowed to log in to the network. In Windows Server 2003, domain controllers can cache universal group memberships that they have looked up on a global catalog server during user logon, so the next time a universal group member logs through a particular domain controller, the membership can be confirmed locally. This both reduces network traffic and provides confirmation when the global catalog server is down.

The second major feature provided by the global catalog, querying, is a little more obvious. A large network may have numerous domains that all exist together. In this case, the global catalog provides a single place for all of the network's users to reference whenever searching for specific resources. The alternative to the global catalog in this instance would be the requirement for each user either to know the exact location of the resources the user wants to use, or to search each domain independently. The querying feature of AD provides another main reason to have multiple global catalog servers throughout a network.

Operations Master

The second main service added to the first AD server within a network is the operations master. Within Windows Server 2003 domains, there is a need to centralize some changes to the directory services. Even though AD is based on the multimaster replication model, and all domain controllers are peers within Windows Server 2003, there are still some changes that can cause too many issues if configured from multiple locations. For this reason, only one Windows Server 2003 domain controller within any forest and within any domain is assigned to become the operations master for that domain or forest. For domain operations, three roles are assigned to the domain's operations master:

- **PDC emulator**   Looks like a PDC to legacy network members in a mixed-mode network

- **Relative ID master**   Assigns blocks of security IDs to the other domain controllers in a network

- **Infrastructure master**   Updates the other domain controllers for changes in usernames and group-to-user references

Ask the Expert

Q: Does every network need the infrastructure master role?

A: No, the infrastructure master role is not needed in all networks. In cases in which all domain controllers in the network contain a copy of the global catalog (especially in cases in which only one server is in the network), the infrastructure master service is not needed. If the infrastructure master service is installed on a server with the global catalog, it will not function.

A forest has only two roles that are assigned to the forest's operations master:

- **Domain naming master**   Adds and removes domains in a forest
- **Schema master**   Updates the directory schema and replicates that to the other domain controllers in a forest

Progress Check

1. What is Active Directory?

2. What is a Windows Server 2003 directory and in particular a hierarchical directory?

3. Can computers running Windows 95 or Windows NT 4 SP3 or earlier log on to a Windows Server 2003 domain controller?

---

1. Active Directory provides a single reference, called a directory service, to all the objects in a network, including users, groups, computers, printers, policies, and permissions. AD also provides a single hierarchical view from which to access and manage all of the network's resources. AD utilizes Internet protocols and standards and requires one or more domains in which to operate.

2. In Windows Server 2003 networking, a directory is a listing of the objects within a network. A hierarchical directory has a structure with a top-to-bottom configuration that allows for the logical grouping of objects, such that lower-level objects are logically grouped and contained in higher-level objects for as many levels as you want.

3. Computers running Windows 95 or Windows NT 4 SP3 or earlier will no longer be able to log on to a Windows Server 2003 domain controller or access domain resources unless you install the Active Directory client for those operating systems.

CRITICAL SKILL
9.3 Understand Active Directory Structure and Configuration

An AD network contains a number of objects in a fairly complex structure and can be configured in several ways. This section focuses on some of the main objects in Active Directory, as well as some of the basic configuration involved with each of these objects as follows:

● AD objects and what they do

● Domains, trees, forests, and the other OUs within AD

● Sites and site-based replication

Active Directory Objects

An *object* within AD is a set of attributes (name, address, and ID) that represents something concrete, such as a user, printer, or application. Like DNS, AD groups and lists these objects in OUs, which are then grouped into other OUs until you reach the root. Also, like DNS, AD then provides access to and information about each of these different objects. As a directory service, AD maintains a list of all objects within the domain and provides access to these objects either directly or through redirection. The focus of this section is the foundation and structure of the objects in AD. By recalling the differences between AD and DNS and the objects that they contain, you can appreciate the wide variety of objects allowed in directory services. In the case of AD and the other X.500-based directory services, the creation and use of this variety of objects is governed by the schema used in the directory.

Schema

The *schema* defines the information stored and subsequently provided by AD for each of its objects. Whenever an object is created in AD, the object is assigned a globally unique identifier, or GUID, which is a hexadecimal number unique to the object. A GUID allows an object's name to be changed without affecting the security and permissions assigned to the object, because the GUID is still the same. Once the object is created, AD uses the schema to create the fields defined for the object, such as phone number, owner, address, description, and so forth. The information for each of these fields is supplied by the administrator or a third-party application pulling the information from a database or preexisting directory structure, such as Microsoft Exchange.

NOTE

For reverse-compatibility reasons, support for security identifiers (SIDs), NT 4's version of GUIDs, is also maintained within AD.

Add to the Base Schema

Because the schema provides the rules for all objects within AD, you'll eventually need to extend the default object classes that come standard within AD. One of the first times this will happen is when a mail server is added to the network, which will require that mail-specific attributes be added to the AD schema. This addition may also require that new object classes be created. The process of adding classes and attributes is done by modifying or adding to the AD schema. The modification of the schema takes place using an automated installation function that affects the schema for the entire network. Schema updates cannot be reversed, so always exercise caution when updating the schema.

TIP

It is possible to modify the schema through the Active Directory Service Interface (ADSI) and by using the LDAP Data Interchange Format utility. It is also possible to modify the schema directly by using the AD Schema tool. These programs should be used only by AD experts and should always be tested in a lab environment before being implemented on production servers.

Publish Items to the Directory

At face value, Windows Server 2003 functions very much like legacy NT-based products, especially in its sharing and security functions. When an item is shared or a new resource is added to Windows Server 2003, such as a printer, the object is shared and secured using nearly the same process as with legacy NT servers. Additionally, not all Windows NT–based servers may become AD servers. With these two facts in mind, some method is needed to distribute information about objects hosted on Windows Server 2003 servers throughout the network into AD. This process is called *publishing*. When an object is published in AD, information about the resource is added to AD, and users are then able to access that resource through AD. The main benefit provided by publishing is that it allows large networks with resources hosted by servers throughout their various sites to all share their information from a central point on the network. Users within the network can access the AD servers and search for, locate, and access the resources they need through the single entry point of AD.

Some objects are added to AD automatically, such as user, group, and server objects. However, some objects have to be published in AD by an administrator. The two most common items that most administrators will find themselves adding to AD are directories and printers.

Directory Publishing   To add a directory to AD, the directory or folder must first be created in Windows Explorer or My Computer and secured using the Sharing and Security tabs in the directory's properties dialog box, as shown next. This security has to include both share-level security and the NTFS permissions associated with the directory and all of the files and subdirectories within that share.

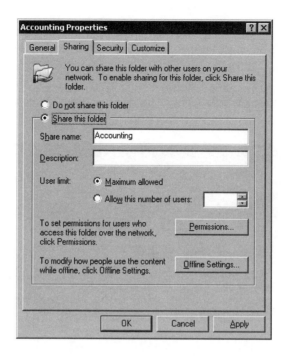

TIP

With the advent of AD, new methods of organizing and providing access to network resources have been added to the network administrator's tools. However, the methods for administering network security that were used with Windows NT are still very much in effect.

Printer Publishing   Publishing a printer in AD is a simple process that provides several new features that were not available with previous versions of NT. Primarily, when a number of printers exist within an AD network, users within that network can search for printers according to specific features, such as color, resolution, or duplexing.

To publish a printer in AD, the printer must first be installed and configured to function on the print server in question. (The print server in this case can be any Windows Server 2003 or Windows 2000 Server or any Windows XP or 2000 Professional computer to which a printer is attached.) After a printer is configured, is shared, and has the proper security set (see Module 15 for details on how to do this), it is ready to be published in AD. In fact, the default action taken by a Windows Server 2003/2000/XP print server is to publish any printer automatically after it has been installed and shared. Once published, the printer can then be managed and accessed through all AD servers within the domain, and it is automatically included in the global catalog for the other domains within the forest.

In some cases, especially domains still running in mixed mode, non–Windows Server 2003/2000/XP print servers may be hosting printers that are of significant importance to the domain. In this case, an object can be added to the AD domain by using the URL of the printer share. This can be accomplished using the AD Users And Computers snap-in, selecting the domain, and choosing Action | New | Printer (shown next), or through the use of a Visual Basic script (Pubprn.vbs) included with Windows Server 2003 and located in the System32 folder. Although a little more difficult to set up, using Pubprn.vbs enables you to add numerous printers to AD at one time.

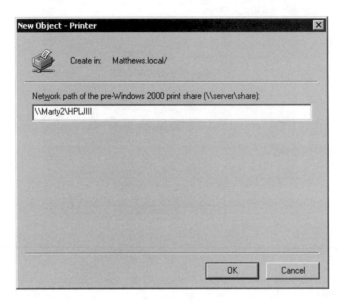

NOTE

Resources shared on the network should not always be published in AD. Only objects used by a large part of the network or that need to be available for possible searches should be published. Publishing objects in AD increases the domain's replication traffic that is necessary to ensure all AD servers have the most recent information. In large networks with multiple domains, the replication traffic to synchronize the global catalog servers for each domain can be overwhelming if poorly planned.

The Structure of Active Directory

There are various OUs within AD that have very specific roles within the network. These roles are established via the schema. To administer and configure an AD network, you need to understand what each of these OUs are, and the role that each plays within the network.

Active Directories are made up of one or more domains. When the first AD server is installed, the initial domain is created. All AD domains map themselves to DNS domains, and DNS servers play a crucial role within any AD domain.

Domains

Domains are at the core of all Windows NT/2000/Windows Server 2003–based network operating systems. This section looks at the structure of domains within AD, as well as the various factors involved in creating multiple domains within a network.

Domains in AD delineate a partition within the AD network. The primary reason for creating multiple domains is the need to partition network information. Smaller networks have very little need for more than one domain, even with a network spread across multiple physical sites, since domains can span multiple Windows Server 2003 sites. (The site concept is covered in more detail later in this module.) However, there are still reasons to use multiple domains within a network:

- **Provide network structure**   Unlike in legacy NT domains, there is no real limit to the number of objects that can be added to an AD domain running in native mode. For this reason, most networks do not need to establish separate domains for each business unit. However, in some very large networks, various political factors may necessitate multiple domains. For example, one company may own several subsidiary companies that are completely autonomous from the parent company. A central AD shared between the companies provides numerous benefits; a shared domain may not make as much sense. In this case, a separate domain can be set up for each company.

- **Replication**   AD servers contain information only about their own domain. Global catalog servers are required to publish information between domains for user access. This means that all objects within a domain are replicated to all the other domain controllers, but external resources are replicated only between global catalog servers. In large networks spread across multiple WAN links, each physical site should be its own domain, to ensure that unnecessary replication traffic does not consume the limited bandwidth of the WAN links.

- **Security and administration**   Although AD provides the appearance of a central network infrastructure to the users of the network, administrative abilities and user permissions will not cross domain partitions. This limitation is overcome through the use of global and universal groups and trust relationships, but domains are truly separate administrative groups that may or may not be linked together.

- **Delegation of administration**   Although the delegation of administrative authority throughout the network makes multiple domains easy to handle, and Windows Server 2003 provides a number of administrative tools, there still may be benefits for some networks in splitting domains along the lines of administrative authority and responsibility.

Forests

Besides domains, AD is composed of forests, trees, and other custom OUs. Each of these OUs exists on a specific level of AD's hierarchy, beginning with the uppermost container, forests. A *forest* is the highest OU within the network and can contain any number of trees and domains. All domains within a forest share the same schema and global catalog. In essence, forests are similar to DNS's root container. A vast majority of organizations implementing AD will have only one forest; in fact, smaller organizations that have only one domain may not even realize the existence of the forest, because all functions appear to exist on the domain level only. In effect, the forest is used as the main directory for the entire network. The forest encompasses all the trees, domains, and other OUs, as well as all the published information for all the objects in the forest, as you can see here:

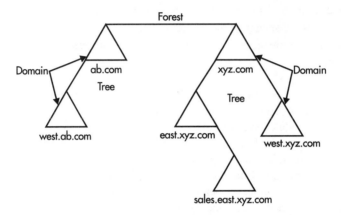

Domains within a forest are automatically configured with two-way transitive trusts. A *trust relationship* allows two domains to share user and group resources so that users authenticated by a "trusted" domain can access resources on the "trusting" domain. *Transitive trusts,* shown in Figure 9-4, allow user accounts within a domain to use a second domain's trust relationships to access resources in a third domain. Legacy NT domains did not support transitive trust relationships. In Figure 9-4, a user account from Domain A is able to access resources in Domain C because both Domain A and Domain C have established transitive trust relationships with Domain B. If Figure 9-4 were illustrating a legacy NT domain, a trust relationship would have to be directly established between Domains A and C before the resources could be accessed.

Creating additional forests in a network should be undertaken with great care. The additional forests can cause a tremendous amount of administrative overhead, especially when adding AD-aware messaging platforms, such as Exchange. Other than the obvious political issues, there are very few reasons for any one network to have multiple forests.

Trees

Within AD, trees are used more for administrative grouping and namespace issues than anything else. Basically, a *tree* is a collection of domains that share a contiguous namespace and form a hierarchical environment. For example, it is possible for an organization such as Microsoft to split its DNS structure so that the Microsoft.com domain name is not the primary name used in e-mails and resource references. For example, assume that Microsoft is split geographically first, so that there is a West Coast OU and an East Coast OU within the Microsoft domain, and that

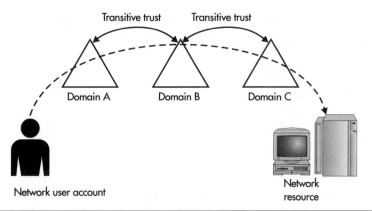

Figure 9-4 Transitive trust relationships allow Domain A to access resources in Domain C.

these OUs (or child domains) each contain a tree of further divisions, such as Sales and Tech Support, which could be further split into Operating Systems and Applications. In this example, so far, Microsoft would have two trees within its DNS structure, West Coast and East Coast. Both of these domains are then split further still, creating a potential FQDN of a server within the technical support department as follows:

```
ServerName.OperatingSystems.TechSupport.WestCoast.Microsoft.Com
```

The entire discussion of trees within AD so far has focused entirely on DNS, since AD has to match the DNS domain structure in the network, although the directory services contained by the two services are independent. In cases in which an organization has decided to implement multiple domains, and those multiple domains exist within a contiguous DNS naming scheme, as previously outlined, the network will have formed a tree connecting the multiple domains. Because the DNS requirements to host such a domain are very large, most organizations implementing trees host the DNS services for the tree internal to the network only, and maintain a separate DNS substructure for Internet hosting services.

All domains within a tree are linked by two-way transitive trust relationships, although the domains are independent. Domains within a tree, just like domains within a forest, share a trust relationship and a namespace (in the case of a tree, it's a contiguous namespace), but the independence and the integrity of each domain remain unchanged. Administration of each domain, as well as directory replication of each domain, is conducted independently, and all information shared between the domains is done through the trust relationships and the global catalog.

When there are multiple trees within a forest, it is possible for each tree to maintain its own independent naming scheme. Looking at the Microsoft example, if you move up the DNS hierarchy, the Microsoft forest may very well include both MSN.com and Microsoft.com. In this case, there is no clear upper layer to the AD domain structure.

The first domain created in the forest is called the *forest root domain.* Two default groups exist within the entire forest, and they exist within the forest root domain:

- Enterprise Administrators
- Schema Administrators

Additionally, the root domain for each tree automatically establishes a transitive trust relationship with the forest's root domain. This relationship is highlighted in Figure 9-5, which is based on the hypothetical Microsoft AD structure. In this example, a third domain is added, MSNBC.com, to further highlight the transitive trusts that are formed throughout the network. Microsoft.com is the forest root domain in this example.

TIP

Domains cannot be moved between forests and cannot be removed if they contain child domains underneath them. Therefore, it is best to plan the entire AD network from top to bottom, before the first AD is installed. A little time spent planning can save a lot of time improvising.

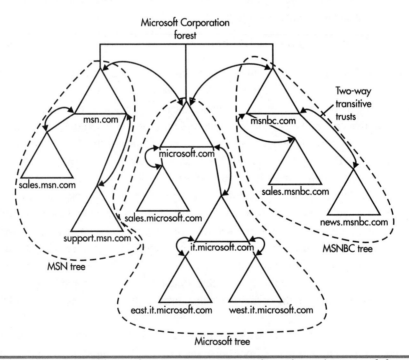

Figure 9-5 Transitive trust relationships among trees in a hypothetical Microsoft forest

Shortcut Trusts

The transitive trust relationships that exist between domains in AD forests can be a very tricky subject. Specifically, the overhead and time involved using the transitive trust relationships to pass all authentication requests throughout a network can sometimes be tremendous. Looking back to the Microsoft example and Figure 9-5, assume that the users who exist in the Microsoft IT group are always logging in to the News.MSNBC.com domain to fix some problems. This means that all login traffic is first passed up the MSNBC.com tree, and then down the Microsoft.com tree, before being authenticated by the IT domain. In cases like these, a *shortcut trust* can be created to pass the information directly between the two domains in question. Shortcut trusts are one-way transitive trusts that are used for authentication in large networks with diverse tree structures. A modified version of the forest from Figure 9-5 is shown in Figure 9-6, with the necessary shortcut trust added.

Other OUs

OUs are simply containers in which multiple objects and additional OUs can be stored. Within AD, some of these OUs are predefined and serve specific roles within the network, such as creating domains. Other OUs revolve around the needs and interests of the administrator, and not those of AD. Within AD, administrators have the ability to create their own AD structure below the OUs that are predefined or serve a specific role. These other OUs can be used to group users, printers, or servers together for ease of administration.

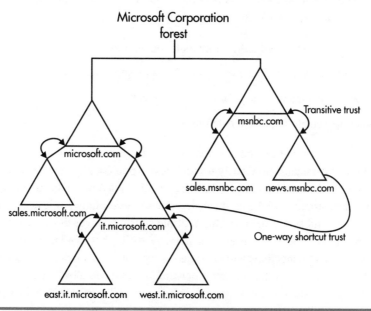

Figure 9-6 A shortcut trust short-circuits trust relationships between domains.

There aren't a lot of rules on the creation of OUs within AD, so instead you must rely on general guidelines and practical uses. Initially, recall that users have the ability to search AD for the resources they need to use. This searching function allows users to specify the specific resource or the type of resource they want to locate, so this should be considered the primary means by which most users will operate with AD. Therefore, administrative needs rather than user needs can determine the creation of OUs. Group policies can be set in OUs that allow the administrator to customize the desktop and permissions of the users and resources within that container. Likewise, giving permission to an entire OU allows an administrator to easily delegate to others administrative rights to specific objects within the domain without compromising the security of the overall network.

Sites

Domains are at the root of the directory services in Windows Server 2003. Everything within AD is simply a collection of one or more domains. Even with the fundamental role of domains defined, many issues still need to be addressed. For example, how is interdomain synchronization handled within small and large domains? How does a large domain span multiple physical networks? How is interdomain replication traffic controlled? For the answers to all of these questions, a new concept needs to be introduced. Windows Server 2003 domains can be divided into units called *sites*. Sites can be used to regulate replication traffic across slower WAN links, and can use various connection methods and replication schedules to ensure a minimal network overhead bandwidth. In general, sites provide a number of basic services for Windows Server 2003 networks, including:

● Minimizing the bandwidth used for intersite replication

● Directing clients to domain controllers in the same site, where possible

● Minimizing replication latency for intrasite replication

● Allowing the scheduling of intersite replication

In general, sites are not related to domains, even though they provide a solution to many of the issues faced by domains previously listed. Sites map to the physical layout of the network, such as offices, floors, and buildings, whereas a domain's layout can be affected by everything from the physical structure to the political structure to the administrative needs of a network. Organizations should split a domain into multiple sites whenever the network will span a connection that is less than LAN speed, which has been 10 Mbps, but increasingly is 100 Mbps. Because most WAN connections will be routed, a separate IP subnet should exist on both sides of the WAN connection. For this reason, Microsoft has mapped most site discrimination to IP subnets. Officially, a site is a collection of "well-connected" (meaning LAN speed or better) Windows Server 2003 systems on the same IP subnet. Sites are managed and created using the AD Sites And Services console.

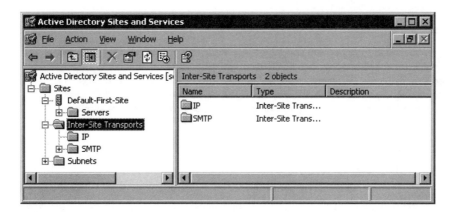

CRITICAL SKILL
9.4 Replicate Active Directory among Sites

In AD, *replication* means the copying of directory information among domain controllers so that they all have the same information and any of the domain controllers can be queried with the same results. Within an AD domain, four main categories of information require replication: configuration, schema, domain, and global catalog information. Each of these categories is stored in separate directory partitions. These partitions are what each AD server replicates and are used by different servers throughout the forest depending on their role within the network. The following three partitions are held by all the AD servers in a forest:

● **Configuration data partition**   Holds information stored and used by AD-aware applications and is replicated across all domains in the forest.

● **Schema data partition**   Holds the definitions of the different types of objects, as well as their allowable attributes, and is replicated across all domains in the forest.

● **Domain data partition**   Holds information unique to the domain in which the server resides. It contains all the objects in the directory for the domain and is replicated only within the domain. The data in this partition is not replicated between domains and will differ greatly from domain to domain.

The fourth type of partition is used by global catalog servers to allow directory information to be shared between domains:

● **Global domain data partition**   Holds information about all the objects in the global catalog but includes details on only a few of the objects' attributes, to allow quick searches for and access to resources in external domains, and to reduce the bandwidth used in replications. This information is replicated to all the other global catalog servers within the network. When a client in a foreign domain actually needs access to the resources or the nonreplicated attributes of a resource, the client is directed to that resource's native domain.

NOTE

Most replication among domain controllers is done over the network. This can be a problem if it is a low-bandwidth network or if a number of domain controllers are added rapidly. A new feature in Windows Server 2003 allows the Active Directory database files to be backed up to tape, CD, DVD, or a removable hard disk and used as the source of an initial replication on a new domain controller or global catalog server.

Internal Site Replication

There will always be at least one site within every AD implementation. When the first Windows Server 2003 domain controller is installed, it creates a site called the Default-First-Site-Name. The new domain controller then adds itself to that site. Whenever new domain controllers are added to the network, they are automatically added to this new site first; they can be moved at a later time. There is, however, an exception to this statement. When a new site is created, one or more IP subnets are assigned to that site. After there are two or more sites, all new domain controllers added to the forest will have their IP addresses checked and will be added to the site with a matching IP address.

Directory information within a site is replicated automatically to ensure all domain controllers within the site have the same information. Additionally, all intersite replication occurs in an uncompressed format, which consumes more network traffic but less system resources. For these reasons, a site should always be a LAN network of high-speed connections (10MB or higher). When multiple domains exist within a single site, replication occurs only among domain controllers in a given domain. However, replication traffic between global catalog servers occurs across the site on an as-needed/uncompressed basis, as well. Figure 9-7 shows the single-site replication traffic between two domains.

Site-to-Site Replication

When deciding to split a network into multiple sites, a number of new issues arise. These issues, and the configuration needed to make multiple sites work, are the subject of the remainder of this section.

Two main rules should be adhered to whenever planning a multisite design, to minimize the potential problems:

- Sites always should be split by geographic regions. When two or more LANs are connected by WAN links, each LAN should represent its own site.

- Whenever possible, each site should have its own AD and global catalog server. In some smaller networks, this server may be the only server in the site, in which case it should also serve as the DNS and DHCP server. This will increase fault tolerance as well as client performance, while decreasing WAN bandwidth utilization.

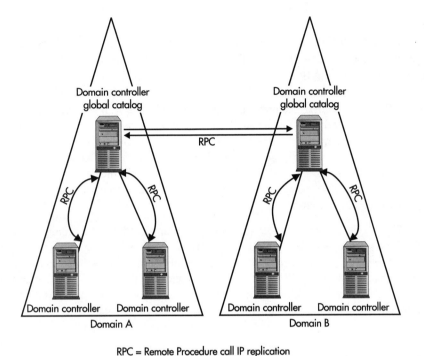

Figure 9-7 Replication traffic between two domains within the same site

Site Connectivity

Sites are connected using *site links,* which are domain controllers configured to serve as
a connection to a particular site. Site links have to be manually configured using the AD
Sites And Services console. When creating a site link, the administrator has a number of
configuration options.

The first of these configuration options is the replication schedule. An administrator can
determine when replication should occur across a particular site link. When setting the replication
schedule, an administrator will set the replication cost, replication availability, and replication
frequency associated with the site link. When the site link is created and configured, AD
automatically creates a connection object, which will use the information provided by the site
link to actually transfer the information between the domains.

By default and design, all site links are transitive, which allows sites to be used in the
same manner transitive trusts are used. This means that a site can replicate its changes to
another site, via a site connector to a third site, as long as the third site has a valid connection
to both sites. In some organizations in which multiple field offices all connect to central
corporate offices, this kind of replication allows for the greatest efficiency. All sites replicate
their information to the central office site, which in turn replicates the information back out
to the other field offices.

Protocols

There are two protocol options within any network for connecting sites together. Both options, though, are protocols within the TCP/IP protocol stack. There is no way to connect two sites using anything other than IP.

- **RPC (IP replication)**   Remote Procedure Call (RPC) is an IP-based, connection-oriented protocol that is at the base of legacy Exchange installations. RPC is fast and reliable when used on connection-friendly networks (networks that allow packets to travel the same path and arrive in sequence at the destination). However, RPC is less than reliable in large mesh networks, such as the Internet. RPC communication is still the default replication method for servers within the same site as well as intrasite communication for other Microsoft services such as Exchange.

- **SMTP**   A feature that was introduced with Windows 2000 and Exchange 2000 is the ability to connect sites using SMTP connectors. SMTP is just beginning to be used and cannot be used for replication between servers in the same site (although it is the default for Exchange 2000). SMTP is not capable of replicating the domain partition, and therefore it is suitable only for linking two sites that are also separate domains. SMTP can pass the schema, configuration, and global catalog partitions very efficiently.

NOTE

SMTP is, by nature, very insecure. All SMTP messages are sent in formats that can be easily interpreted by the most basic of sniffing tools. For this reason, using the SMTP protocol to connect two sites requires that an enterprise certification authority be installed and configured on the network. This allows for all SMTP traffic generated by AD to be encrypted using at least 56-bit encryption.

Collision Detecting and Resolution

What happens when the same object is modified from two different spots in the network at the same time, or two objects with the same name are created at the same time within the network? Even in the most basic networks, if two domain controllers exist, the two directories that exist on each domain controller will not be exactly the same at all times, because replication takes time. Legacy versions of NT dealt with this issue by allowing only one read/write copy of the directory to exist on the network at any one time. This meant that all changes could be made only by one server, and those changes were then propagated to the read-only copies of the directories that the remaining domain controllers maintained.

When a change to an object occurs before a previous change to that object has been completely replicated, a replication *collision* occurs. AD can track the versions of objects by looking at each object's version number. When an object is changed, its version number is increased, so that when a server receives an update, it can compare the version number of the incoming object with the version number of the existing object. When the existing object's version number is less than the version number coming in, the replication continues and all is considered well. A collision occurs when the version number of the existing item is equal to or greater than the version number of the incoming item. In this case, AD compares the timestamp of the incoming object to the timestamp of the existing object to determine which one it's going to keep. This is the only instance in which time is used in replication. If the timestamps don't settle the issue, the item with the highest GUID is kept. In situations in which the incoming version number is actually lower than the existing version number, the replication object is considered to be stale and is discarded.

Active Directory Summary

Active Directory is one of most important features of Windows Server 2003. AD is a directory service based on the X.500 directory scheme that contains a variety of predefined and preconfigured objects and OUs. A large part of any Windows Server 2003 administrator's job will be the administration and configuration of the special objects and OUs within the AD forest. Additionally, the namespace of AD has to match that of a DNS domain, and in cases in which the AD domain and the Internet DNS domain for the company don't match, separate DNS domains have to be maintained, because AD requires DNS to allow for client connectivity.

If used correctly, AD can add tremendous value and reliability to a network, as well as decrease the administrative overhead involved in the network's daily maintenance. However, if configured incorrectly or if ill-planned, AD can drastically increase the administrator's workload, and decrease the network customer's satisfaction. When dealing with AD, a little bit of forethought and planning can save a huge amount of work and heartache.

Progress Check

1. What is an object within AD?

2. What are GUIDs and SIDs and how are they used in AD?

3. After a printer is configured, shared, and has the proper security set, what action must be taken to publish it in AD?

---

1. An object within AD is a set of attributes (name, address, and ID) that represents something concrete, such as a user, printer, or application. Like DNS, AD groups and lists these objects in OUs, which are then grouped into other OUs until you reach the root.

2. A GUID is a globally unique identifier, and a SID is a security identifier. A GUID is given to each AD object to identify it independent of the object's name, so the name can be changed. For reverse-compatibility reasons, support for SIDs, NT 4's version of GUIDs, is also maintained within AD.

3. None; after a printer is configured, shared, and has the proper security set, the default action taken by a Windows Server 2003/2000/XP print server is to publish any printer automatically.

Project 9 Plan an Active Directory Implementation

Active Directory is a very powerful and important feature in Windows Server 2003, but it is also reasonably complex with many nuances that require some consideration before it is implemented. This project will help plan an AD implementation.

Step by Step

1. Review the current or planned network to which AD will be added and determine the answers to the following questions:

   a. Will there be more than one forest? If so, determine

   i. What will constitute the forest boundaries?

   ii. How many forests will that make?

   iii. What will the forests be named?

   iv. How will the forests be managed?

   b. Will there be more than one tree in each forest? If so, determine

   i. What will constitute the tree boundaries?

   ii. How many trees will that make?

   iii. What will the trees be named?

   iv. How will the trees be managed?

   c. Will there be more than one domain in each tree? If so, determine

   i. What will constitute the domain boundaries?

   ii. How many domains will that make?

   iii. What will the domains be named?

   iv. How will the domains be managed?

   d. Will there be more than one OU in each domain? If so, determine

   i. What will constitute the OU boundaries?

   ii. How many OUs will that make?

   iii. What will the OUs be named?

   iv. How will the OUs be managed?

   e. Will there be subsidiary OUs in each OU? If so, determine

   i. What will constitute the subsidiary OU boundaries?

   ii. How many subsidiary OUs will that make?

      iii. What will the subsidiary OUs be named?

      iv. How will the subsidiary OUs be managed?

   f. Repeat Step e for each additional level of OU in the organization.

2. In each of the bottom level OUs, determine

   a. The number of servers

      i. What is the function of each server?

      ii. What is the name of each server?

      iii. Who is responsible for each server?

   b. The number of storage devices

      i. What is the name of each storage device?

      ii. Who is responsible for each storage device?

   c. The number of printers

      i. What is the name of each printer?

      ii. Who is responsible for each printer?

   d. The number of workstations

      i. What is the name of each workstation (if known)?

      ii. Who is responsible for each workstation?

3. For the network structure you have just laid out, determine the answers to the following questions:

   a. How well will network traffic be handled?

   b. Where will the global catalog reside?

   c. How will the network structure map to physical sites?

   d. Are any one-way shortcut trusts required, and if so, where?

   e. What is the replication plan throughout the network?

   f. Are any changes necessary in the decisions you made in earlier steps?

Project Summary

If you have a very simple network, the preceding steps all but answer themselves. With a large, complex network it will be a significant task to answer all the questions. The importance of answering the questions is almost directly proportional to the difficulty of doing that. Planning out your AD lays the foundation of your network. If it is done well, you will reap the benefits for some time.

Project 9

Plan an Active Directory Implementation

Module 9 Mastery Check

1. What is a domain?

2. What is the directory structure used within Windows Server 2003, and how is it used?

3. What is an FQDN, and how is it used in Windows Server 2003?

4. What kind of structure does DNS use to relate computer names to IP addresses?

5. What is the information that AD stores for a particular directory entry?

6. Is there a PDC in AD and how are the functions of a PDC handled?

7. What is a schema, and how is it used in AD? What part does a GUID play in the AD schema?

8. How are multiple domains in AD helpful?

9. What is a forest, and how is used in AD?

10. In working with domains, what is a trust relationship, and in particular, what is a transitive trust?

11. What is meant by AD replication, and how is it used?

Part IV

Communications and the Internet

Module 10

Communications and Internet Services

Networking today definitely extends beyond the local area network (LAN) to include the Internet itself, as well as using the Internet and other forms of communication to access your LAN or other computers. This part of the book covers the ways that you and your organization can reach out from your LAN to connect to others, or allow others to connect to you. This module provides an overview of communications and how to set up the various Windows Server 2003 communications features. It then discusses establishing a dial-up connection and using it with the Remote Access Service (RAS). This module concludes by explaining how to set up and use an Internet connection with Internet Explorer and Outlook Express for accessing the Web and exchanging e-mail, respectively. Module 11 looks at Internet Information Services (IIS), how it's set up, and how it's managed. Module 12 describes virtual private networking (VPN), using the Internet to connect to a remote LAN with a high degree of security, and Module 13 discusses terminal and application services, which is the modernization of the decades-old method of accessing a time-sharing mainframe with a dumb terminal.

Communication may include a modem or other device to connect a single computer to a method of transmission, or it may use a router or other device to connect a network to the method of transmission. Communications can be over copper wires, fiber-optic cable, microwave, ground or cell wireless, or satellite transmission.

Windows Server 2003 includes a number of programs that control or utilize communications, among which are Internet Explorer, for web browsing; Outlook Express, for e-mail; HyperTerminal, for computer-to-computer communications; NetMeeting, for multimedia communications; the New Connection Wizard, for the Internet and other connections; and the Phone And Modem Options dialog boxes to establish and maintain connections. In addition, Windows Server 2003 includes programs to set up and manage RAS networking over communications lines. HyperTerminal and NetMeeting are aimed at the client user and are left to a book on that subject (see my book *Windows XP Professional, A Beginner's Guide* [McGraw-Hill/Osborne, 2002]). The remaining programs are discussed here.

Communications can be broken into three areas:

- Direct connections between computers other than a LAN

- Telephony connections between computers other than the Internet

- Connections to and through the Internet

Connect Directly Between Two Computers

If you want to transfer information between two computers, at least one of which is not connected to your LAN, you can do so by using a direct connection between the computers. Such a connection can connect to a network if the other computer is connected to it, and it can be used to connect a handheld Windows CE computer. Two computers can be directly connected in either of two ways:

- By a special parallel or serial cable
- By an infrared port

Use a Parallel or Serial Cable

The most common way to directly connect two computers, other than through a LAN, is by using a cable, either a special serial cable, called a *null modem cable,* or a special parallel cable, both of which are made just for PC-to-PC file transfer. These cables are sometimes called *LapLink* cables, after an early program of that name that was used to transfer information between laptop and desktop computers. The cables have the same connectors on both ends (DB9 female connectors on the serial cable, and DB25 male connectors on the parallel cable), but the wires are crossed in the cable so that the wire connected to the transmit pin on one end is connected to the receive pin on the other end.

To set up a physical direct connection between two computers, you need to do the following:

- Purchase and install a parallel or serial PC-to-PC direct connect cable
- Set up a computer to be the host in a direct connection
- Set up another computer to be the guest in a direct connection

Purchase and Install a Cable

You can purchase a direct connect serial or parallel cable at most computer stores (including catalogs and Internet sites). Be sure you order a PC-to-PC file transfer cable, also called a *direct cable connection* cable, a LapLink cable, or a *null modem* cable. Both ends should be the same, and the wires need to be "crossed over," not "straight through." Belkin, a brand of

Ask the Expert

Q: On my computer the nine-pin serial port is used by a mouse, and the parallel port is used by a printer. How am I going to use a direct cable?

A: The mouse normally is more important than the printer when using Windows, and parallel ports are faster than the serial ports, because you are sending eight bits at a time instead of one bit. Therefore, unplug the printer and use a parallel cable.

cables carried by many stores, has a serial PC-to-PC file transfer cable, part number F3B207, and a similar parallel cable, part number F3D508. Several catalogs and web sites have these cables, namely PCZone (http://www.zones.com), MicroWarehouse (http://www.warehouse.com), CDW (http://www.cdw.com), and PC Connection (http://www.pcconnection.com).

NOTE

Parallel and serial extension and switchbox cables will not work for PC-to-PC file transfer, because the wires are straight through and often the ends are different genders.

To install the cables, simply locate the parallel or serial connectors on the back of the computers that are opposite in gender to the cables (the parallel connection on the computer would be a 25-pin female connector and the serial connection would be a 9-pin male connector). Insert the cables and screw them down tightly.

Set Up the Host Computer

To set up the host computer, which can be running either Windows Server 2003 or Windows XP Professional, you should be signed on as the Administrator or a member of the Administrators group and then use the following steps:

NOTE

If the host computer to which you want a direct connection is a domain controller and you have Routing and Remote Access enabled, you must follow a different procedure. See the next section, "Use a Domain Controller to Host a Direct Connection."

1. Open the Start menu, choose Control Panel | Network Connections | New Connection Wizard. The New Connection Wizard will open. (On Windows XP Professional you need to open the Start menu, choose Control Panel, and then in Classic view double-click Network Connections. In the Network Connections window click Create A New Connection. The New Connection Wizard will open.)

2. Click Next. Under Network Connection Type, select Set Up An Advanced Connection, as shown here, and then click Next.

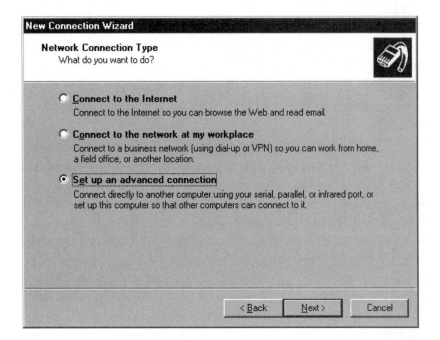

3. Choose Accept Incoming Connections, and click Next. (If you are on a domain controller and have Routing and Remote Access enabled, you will get a message that you need to switch to the Routing and Remote Access system console, and asking if you want to do that now. Click No.)

4. The Devices For Incoming Connections dialog box opens, enabling you to choose from the modem(s), parallel (Direct Parallel), serial (Communications Port), and infrared ports that the computer has available.

5. Choose the connection device that you want to use. If that device is a serial port and has not been used for this purpose in the past, you will be told that the port is not enabled for a direct connection and that the Network Connection Wizard will do that for you. Then, after the connection is established, you can right-click the connection icon in the Network Connection dialog box and set the properties, such as speed, for this port.

6. Click Next. Choose whether to allow virtual private networking through the port you are establishing. Direct cable connections don't need VPN, so, if it isn't already selected, select Do Not Allow Virtual Private Connections and click Next.

7. Select the users that you want to be allowed to use this connection. If you are the administrator, this should include you. If you want others to be able to use the port, then select Guest. If you want to add a new user, click Add; enter the username, full name, and password; confirm the password; and then click OK.

8. Select Administrator and click Properties. In the user's Properties dialog box's General tab, you can add or change the same information that you could add for a new user. The Callback tab is not meaningful for a direct cable connection and will be discussed later in this module.

9. Change any other user properties that need to be changed, and then click Next. Select the networking software that you want to use with your full range of connections. If you wish to install additional software (you probably don't for direct connections) click Install; choose if you want to install an additional client, service, or protocol as discussed in Module 8; click Add; select the software component; and click OK. Close the Select Network Component Type dialog box, and click Next.

10. You will be told that the name of the connection you are creating is Incoming Connections. Accept that and click Finish. A new icon will appear in your Start | Control Panel | Network Connections flyout menu or in the Network Connections window.

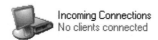

Incoming Connections
No clients connected

11. Check that the users you want to grant access over this new connection have the necessary permissions. Do this by opening Start and choosing Administrative Tools | Computer Management. (If this computer is a domain controller, see the next section.) In the left pane, open System Tools | Local Users And Groups | Users. In the right pane, right-click each user to whom you want to give access, choose Properties, click the Dial-In tab, click Allow Access in the Remote Access Permission area, and click OK. Close Computer Management when you have handled all necessary users.

NOTE

You can create several direct connections for different ports and computers by copying the first direct connection, renaming the copy, and changing the settings.

Use a Domain Controller to Host a Direct Connection

If you are setting up a direct connection host site on a domain controller, you must use Routing and Remote Access to be the incoming host. Do that by turning to the "Setting Up Remote

Access Service" section later in this module. Once you have set up the RAS server, you need to perform an extra step of enabling incoming connections:

1. Open the Start menu and choose Administrative Tools | Routing and Remote Access. The Routing and Remote Access console will appear.

2. Open the local server, right-click Ports, and choose Properties. In the Ports Properties dialog box, select Direct Parallel and click Configure.

3. Select Remote Access Connections (Inbound Only), and click OK. The top portion of your Ports Properties dialog box should look similar to this:

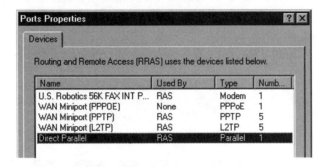

4. Click OK to close the dialog box. The Direct Parallel port should appear in the list of ports on the right of the Routing and Remote Access console.

5. Check that the users you want to grant access over this new connection have the needed permissions. Do this by opening Start and choosing Administrative Tools | Active Directory Users And Computers. (If this computer is not a domain controller, see the preceding section.) In the left pane, open the local domain | Users. In the right pane, right-click each user to whom you want to give access, choose Properties, click the Dial-In tab, click Allow Access in the Remote Access Permission area, and click OK. Close Active Directory Users And Computers when you have handled all necessary users.

Set Up the Guest Computer

The guest computer can be either a server or a workstation, but it is most likely a workstation. You do not have to be signed on as an administrator, but if you want to use a serial port that is not currently configured for a direct connection (a null modem), you need an administrator to do that. Here are the steps for setting up a Windows XP Professional guest computer with a direct cable connection:

1. Open the Start menu, choose Control Panel, in Classic view double-click Network Connections, and then click Create A New Connection. The New Connection Wizard will open.

2. Click Next. In the Network Connection Type dialog box, select Set Up An Advanced Connection, and then click Next.

3. Choose Connect Directly To Another Computer, and click Next. Choose the role of Guest and once more click Next.

4. Enter the name of the other computer you want to connect to. This will be the name of the connection. Click Next. The Select A Device dialog box opens, enabling you to choose the type of connection.

5. Choose your connection device and click Next. You will be told that the name of the connection you are creating is the name of the computer you are connecting to and that it will be shared with other users of this computer. Accept that and click Finish. A new icon will appear in your Network Connections window and a Connect dialog box will open, as you can see in Figure 10-1.

Server1
Disconnected
Direct Parallel

Figure 10-1 Connecting a guest to a host

Transfer Information over a Direct Connection

Once you have set up a direct cable connection, you can use it in Windows XP Professional with these steps (if you have come directly from the immediately preceding steps and the Connect dialog box is open, you can skip to Step 2):

1. Open the Start menu and choose Connect To | the direct connection you just created. The Connect dialog box will open.

2. Enter the appropriate username and password and click Connect. You will see messages stating that the connection is being made, that the username and password are being checked, that the computer is being registered on the network, and then that the connection is complete. Click OK. The connection icon will appear on the right of the taskbar, and the icon in Network Connections will change to "Connected".

NOTE

If you are unable to make a connection, there are a number of possible reasons. Is the serial or parallel cable properly installed? Have all the preceding steps for setting up the host, in a domain controller or otherwise, and a guest been properly carried out? Have the same networking protocols been set up on both the host and the guest? Is there an active DHCP server on the network? Is the host computer a member of the RAS And IAS Servers group? Do the users have Allow Access selected under Remote Access Permission in the Dial-In tab of the user's properties dialog box?

3. Utilize the connection by opening Windows Explorer, My Network Places | Entire Network | Microsoft Windows Network, and finally the domains or workgroups, computers, and shares that you want to access.

4. Transfer information across the direct cable connection in the same way as you transfer any information in Windows Explorer, by locating the destination folder in the left pane, selecting the files or folders to be transferred in the right pane, and then dragging the information from the right pane to the folder in the left pane.

5. When you are done using the direct cable connection, you can terminate it by double-clicking the connection icon in the taskbar or the Direct Connection icon in the Network Connections window, and then clicking Disconnect in the dialog box that opens.

NOTE

If the host in a direct cable connection is itself connected to a LAN, the guest in the direct cable connection can get on the LAN through the host and use the LAN as if the guest were connected to it.

While a direct cable connection is operational, the host can look at the status of the connection, see who is connected to it, see how much information has been transferred, and disconnect them if desired. This is done in two slightly different ways, depending on whether or not the host is using the RAS server.

Host Status on a RAS Server   If RAS is being used to provide incoming services for a direct cable connection, status and control of the connection can be obtained with these steps:

1. Open the Start menu and choose Administrative Tools | Routing and Remote Access.

2. Open the local server and select Ports. The right pane should show a list of ports, including a direct connection, either parallel or serial.

3. Right-click the direct connection port and choose Status. The Port Status dialog box will open, as shown in Figure 10-2.

4. If you wish to disconnect the guest, click Disconnect; in any case, when you are done, click Close and then close the Routing and Remote Access console.

Host Status on Incoming Connections   If Network Connections is being used to provide an incoming connection, status and control of the connection can be obtained with these steps:

1. Open the Start menu and choose Control Panel | Network Connections on Windows Server 2003 or open the Start menu, choose Connect To, and click Show All Connections on Windows XP Professional computers. You will see that the Incoming Connections icon is shown as active and has been retitled with either the name of the user or Unauthenticated User.

2. Right-click the connection icon and choose Status. The connection's Status dialog box will open.

3. If you wish to disconnect the guest, click Disconnect; in any case, when you are done, click Close and then close the Network Connections window.

Using an Infrared Port

If you have two infrared ports, such as one on your laptop and one on your desktop, you may create a direct connection between the computers by following the preceding steps for a

Figure 10-2 Checking the status of a direct cable connection

parallel or serial cable, but instead selecting the infrared port in place of a parallel or serial port.

Depending on your computer and its BIOS (basic input/output system), you may have to do other unique steps to enable an Infrared port. See the documentation for your computer. Also, an infrared port can be a pain in a meeting full of other computers with infrared ports because they may be constantly trying to connect with one another and asking you if you want to do that. You may want to disable your infrared port in those circumstances or at least block your infrared transmitter/receiver with some object, like a cup.

CRITICAL SKILL
10.2 Set Up and Use Telephony Connections

Telephony (telephone lines, their switches, and their terminations) has been used to connect computers for some time. The most common approach is to use a *modem* (short for "modulator-demodulator") to convert a digital signal (patterns of ones and zeros) in a computer to an analog signal (current fluctuations) in a phone line and then use a second modem on the other end to convert the analog signal back to digital for use in the connecting computer. Modems can be internal (inside the computer), in which case the phone line connects to the computer, or external, whereby the phone line plugs in to the modem and the modem plugs in to a serial port in the computer. The fastest modems today receive data at up to 56 Kbps (thousand bits per second) and send data at up to 33.6 Kbps.

In recent years, telephone companies have started to offer several forms of digital signals over phone lines, so that a modem (as just described) isn't necessary—all you need is a connection between the digital line and the computer. Two common forms of digital telephone service are ISDN (Integrated Services Digital Network) and DSL (digital subscriber line). ISDN was the first digital service and is both expensive and relatively slow (a maximum speed of up to 128 Kbps) when compared to DSL. There are several forms of DSL, the most common of which is ADSL (asymmetric digital subscriber line), over which data is received at up to 1.5 Mbps and sent at up to 512 Kbps. Most often, an ISDN or DSL line is terminated in a router that directly connects to your network and not to a computer. Later in this module, though, you'll see how a computer with Windows Server 2003 can act as a router for lines terminated in it through an ISDN or DSL adapter.

NOTE

Sometimes an ISDN or DSL adapter is called a "modem," but it is not an analog to digital converter, which is the major point of a modem. Therefore in this book they are not included in discussions on modems.

Install a Modem

There are several ways to install modem support within Windows XP or Windows Server 2003. During installation of the operating system or the first time you attempt to connect to the Internet, support for a modem will be installed for you if you have a Plug and Play modem. If you set up a dial-up connection and you don't have modem support installed, it will be installed for you, again with a Plug and Play modem. Here, though, we'll look at installing a modem by itself, which you will need to do if it has not been automatically installed. Later, we'll also look at installing it with an Internet connection.

To install a modem, of course, you must have one plugged in or attached to your computer. An *internal* modem is a card that plugs in to an expansion slot on the main or "mother" board inside your computer. An *external* modem is a small box that plugs in to a serial or communications (COM) port on the outside of your computer. Also, both external and internal modems may have switches or jumpers that need to be set, or they may be *Plug and Play,* which means that they do not have switches or jumpers—software sets them up. Whichever kind of modem you have, the instructions that came with it tell you whether it is internal or external, how to plug it in, and how to set it up.

With a modem physically attached to your computer (and, if external, turned on), use the following instructions to install it in Windows XP or Windows Server 2003:

1. In Windows XP Professional, open the Start menu, choose Control Panel, and in Classic view double-click Phone And Modem Options. In Windows Server 2003, open the Start menu, choose Control Panel | Phone And Modem Options. The Phone And Modem Options dialog box will open.

2. Open the Modems tab. If it shows Unknown Modem, select that and click Remove. If it shows a likely modem, such as what is shown next, you already have a modem installed and you can skip to the next section.

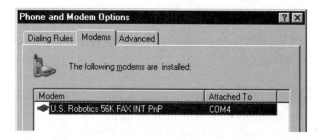

3. Click Add. You are told that Windows will try to detect your modem, and are reminded to turn on the modem and to quit any programs that may be using it. Click Next. A list of possible modems may be shown to you. If only the correct modem is displayed, skip the next step. If several modems are shown and one is correct and the rest are not, uncheck the incorrect ones and skip the next step. If an incorrect modem or Unknown Modem is shown, select it and click Change. If no modem is found, click Next.

4. Select the correct manufacturer from the list on the left and the correct model from the list on the right and click Next. If your modem is not on the list but you have a disk, click Have Disk, insert the disk, select the drive, click OK, select the manufacturer and model, and click OK.

5. Select the COM port to which the modem is connected and click Next. Windows starts to install your modem. If you are using an older modem, you may be told that the driver does not have a digital signature. If so, click Yes to continue. Finally, you are told that your modem has been installed successfully. Click Finish.

6. Back in the Phone And Modem Options dialog box, select your newly installed modem, and click Properties. In the Properties dialog box, click the Diagnostics tab, and then click Query Modem. You will be told that the query process will take several seconds.

If your modem is properly installed, you'll see a set of commands and responses, as shown in Figure 10-3. Not all of the responses have to be positive. The point is that Windows XP or Windows Server 2003 is talking to the modem. If you do not get the set of commands and responses, you will probably get some sort of error message, such as Modem Not Found, which has three possible causes: the modem is not operating correctly, the wrong driver is installed, or the wrong COM port is being used. You generally can tell whether the COM port is correct by looking at what Windows detected. It may not detect the type of modem correctly, but it generally detects the port that has a modem attached to it. To find the correct manufacturer and model for the driver, you may need to look at the actual modem by physically opening the computer. To get a driver that is not in the Windows driver database, use another computer to connect to the Internet, browse to the modem manufacturer's web site, and download the correct driver. Put that driver on a floppy disk and take it to the computer you arc installing. If you are certain that both the port and driver are correct, then the modem may be malfunctioning.

7. Click OK to close the Properties dialog box, and then click OK to close the Phone And Modem Options dialog box.

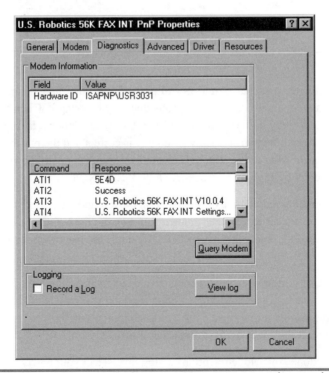

Figure 10-3 Commands and responses showing communication with a modem

Establish a Dial-up Connection

Establishing a dial-up connection, which can be done on either Windows Server 2003 or Windows XP Professional, identifies a particular destination to which you want to dial—a phone number that is dialed and a connection that is made to your modem. The following steps, which assume that a modem has already been set up (as done in the preceding section), show how to establish a dial-up connection (if you are working on a domain controller, you may either create a dial-up connection in this section and or create a remote access service in the next section, "Set Up Remote Access Service":

1. Open the Start menu, choose Control Panel | Network Connections | New Connection Wizard in Windows Server 2003 or open the Start menu, choose Control Panel, in Classic view double-click Network Connections, and click Create A New Connection in Windows XP Professional. The New Connection Wizard will open. Click Next.

2. Select Connect To The Network At My Workplace and click Next. If it isn't already selected, select Dial-Up Connection, and once more click Next. If you have more than one modem, choose the one you want to use and again click Next. Enter the name for the connection you are creating and click Next.

3. Enter the phone number that will be the destination of the connection. If you want to use area/city/country codes, enter them. Click Next when the phone number has been entered.

4. In Windows Server 2003, choose whether you want to create this connection for anyone's use or just for your use and click Next. In either Windows Server 2003 or Windows XP, you are told you have successfully completed the steps necessary for a dial-up connection. Click Finish to create the connection. An icon will appear in the Network Connections window or on the Network Connections flyout menu, and the Connect dialog box will open.

Server1 (Dial-up)
Connected
3Com Megahertz LAN+56K PC...

5. To dial the connection, enter a username and password required for the connection and click Dial. When the Connect dialog isn't open, you can open the Network Connections flyout menu or window and click or double-click the dial-up connection's icon. You should hear the modem dialing, the ring at the other end, and the answering tone.

   A dial-up connection can be used with RAS, discussed next.

Set Up Remote Access Service

RAS provides access to a LAN from a dial-up line, a leased line, or a direct connection. RAS acts as a host or server to a dial-up or direct connection guest or client. RAS commonly is used by travelers whose laptops have a dial-up connection that can be used from a remote location to connect through RAS to the home office LAN. The next set of steps shows how RAS is set up and then used in Windows Server 2003:

1. Open the Start menu and choose Administrative Tools | Routing And Remote Access. The Routing And Remote Access console will open.

2. Select the local server (the computer you are working on), open the Action menu, and choose Configure And Enable Routing And Remote Access. The Routing And Remote Access Server Setup Wizard will open. Click Next.

3. Select Remote Access (Dial-Up Or VPN), as shown in Figure 10-4, and click Next. You are asked if you want RAS to use VPN and/or Dial-up; click Dial-up and then click Next. You are asked how you want addresses assigned; leave the default Automatically and click Next.

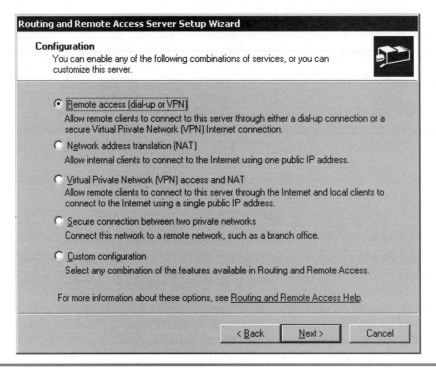

Figure 10-4 Setting up a remote access server

4. When asked if you want to Use Routing And Remote Access To Authenticate Connection Requests or use a RADIUS Server, leave the default of Use Routing And Remote Access and click Next. When you are shown the summary of your settings, click Finish.

5. Choose whether you want to see the Help pages on managing a remote access server, and then click Finish.

NOTE

If you are setting up RAS on a server in Active Directory that is not the primary domain controller and you are not a domain administrator, a domain administrator must add the server on which you are working to the RAS and IAS Servers group in the Computers folder of the Active Directory Users And Computers console and to the list of servers in Routing and Remote Access on the primary domain controller. To support the relaying of DHCP messages from remote access clients, the domain administrator must configure the properties of the DHCP Relay Agent with the IP address of your DHCP server.

Use Remote Access Service

With a dial-up connection set up on the guest or client computer (for this example, a laptop in a remote city running Windows XP Professional) and a remote access server set up and enabled on the host computer (for this example, a server in the home office running Windows Server 2003), you can use RAS with these steps:

1. Log on to the dial-up client (here the laptop with XP) with a username and password that can be authenticated by the RAS. Then, on the client, open the Start menu, choose Connect To, and select the dial-up connection you want to use. The Connect dialog box opens.

2. Enter the appropriate username and password and click Dial. You will see messages stating that the number you entered is being dialed, that the username and password are being checked, that the computer is being registered on the network, and then that the connection is complete. Click OK. The connection icon will appear on the right of the taskbar.

3. Utilize the connection by opening Windows Explorer, My Network Places | Entire Network | Microsoft Windows Network, and finally the domains or workgroups, computers, and shares that you want to access.

4. Transfer information across the dial-up connection in the same way as you transfer any information in Windows Explorer, by locating the destination folder in the left pane, selecting the files or folders to be transferred in the right pane, and then dragging the information from the right pane to the folder in the left pane, as shown previously for a direct cable connection.

5. When you are done using the RAS connection, you can terminate it by double-clicking the connection icon in the taskbar or the dial-up connection icon in the Network Connections window, and then clicking Disconnect in the dialog box that opens.

While a dial-up connection is operational, you can see the connection in the Routing And Remote Access window on the server and see who it is by opening the server and clicking Remote Access Clients in the left pane, as shown in Figure 10-5. If you right-click the user in the right pane and choose Status, you can see how much information has been transferred, and disconnect the user, if desired.

Progress Check

1. How can two computers directly connect other than using a LAN?

2. Can you use a parallel or serial extension cable for a direct cable connection?

3. What is a dial-up connection and how is it used?

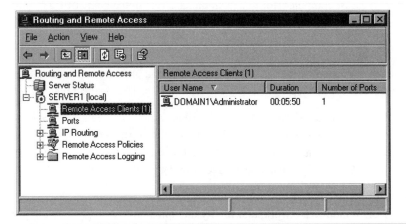

Figure 10-5 Looking at an RAS user in the server

---

1. Two computers can be directly connected using either a special parallel or serial cable or an infrared port.

2. Parallel and serial extension and switchbox cables will not work for PC-to-PC file transfer because the wires are straight through and often the ends are different genders.

3. A dial-up connection identifies a particular destination to which you want to dial, a phone number that is dialed, and a connection that is made with your modem. Such a connection can then be used to transfer information between the two computers at each end of the connection.

CRITICAL SKILL

Set Up and Maintain the Windows Server 2003 Router

Routers are network devices that are used to join two separate, independent networks, such as a LAN and the Internet. Routers operate at the Network (third) layer of the OSI (Open Systems Interconnection) networking model and therefore use the full IP address, consisting of both network and host components (see Module 7 sections "The OSI Model" and "Routers"). A router looks at all the traffic on both networks but transfers only those packets that are specifically addressed to the other network. Routers also provide a network address translation (NAT) function. NAT allows your LAN to use a set of non-Internet-usable IP addresses, such as 10.0.0.9, but when the LAN users access the Internet, they are assigned an Internet-usable IP address, with the router translating between the two. Finally a router can be used to connect two networks that use two different protocols, such as TCP/IP (Transmission Control Protocol/Internet Protocol) and IPX (Internetwork Packet Exchange).

Normally, a router is a stand-alone electronic device (or "box") separate from a computer, to which two networks are connected. One of the network connections may be a phone connection (DSL, ISDN, or T1 line) and the other may be a standard 10/100BaseT Ethernet connection, or both may be Ethernet connections, or some other combination. Windows Server 2003 can provide some of a router's capabilities, the most important of which are the functions of connecting a LAN to the Internet or WAN (wide area network), NAT, and connecting two networks with dissimilar protocols. To function, the Windows Server 2003 must be connected to both networks, for example the Internet and the LAN. The LAN connection is just the standard network interface card (NIC), while the Internet or WAN connection is some sort of telephone line termination in or directly connected to the computer, such as a modem, an ISDN adapter, or a DSL termination.

Set Up the Windows Server 2003 Router

If you want to set up a server connection to the Internet that can be used by the entire network, then the server that you want to be the router must have both LAN and communications connections. Also, you must be an administrator or have Administrator privileges. You can then set up this router function through the Routing And Remote Access console and the following steps:

NOTE

If you are not using DHCP, you need to set up Internet connection sharing from Network Connections. See the following section.

1. Open the Start menu and choose Administrative Tools | Routing And Remote Access. The Routing And Remote Access console will open.

NOTE

If you have set up RAS earlier in this module and it is currently running, you must disable it to install the Internet Connection Server. To do that, in the Routing And Remote Access window, select the local server, open the Action menu, choose Disable Routing And Remote Access, and click Yes when asked if you want to continue. Finally, continue on with Step 2.

2. Select the local server (the computer you are working on), open the Action menu, and choose Configure And Enable Routing And Remote Access. The Routing And Remote Access Server Setup Wizard will open. Click Next.

3. Select Network Address Translation and click Next. If you want to use an existing Internet connection, choose Use This Public Interface To Connect To The Internet (if your Internet connection has its own routing, as is the case with DSL, this option will be grayed), select the connection you want to use, and click Next.

4. If you want to create a new dial-up Internet connection, such as might be used with a modem, select Create a New Demand-Dial Interface To The Internet and click Next twice to open the Demand Dial Interface Wizard, where you need to click Next again.

5. Accept the default name of Remote Router or enter the name you want to use for the interface, and click Next. Choose Connect Using A Modem, ISDN Adapter, Or Other Physical Device and click Next. Choose the specific modem or adapter to use, and click Next. Enter the phone number and click Next.

6. Select the options that you want to use. In most cases, the default Route IP Packets is all you need. After selecting the needed options, click Next. Enter the username, domain name, and password; confirm the password; and click Next. Click Finish twice.

Set Up Internet Connection Sharing

Internet connection sharing is a small system alternative to server routing. Internet connection sharing allows a small network of computers to all connect to the Internet through one computer, which can be running either Windows Server 2003 or Windows XP Professional, that is physically connected to the Internet using phone lines, a cable modem, or some other means. You first set up the connection to the Internet as explained elsewhere in this module, then use the following steps to share that connection.

NOTE

You must have at least two networking or communications connections, one through which the computer is connected to the Internet and another through which the computer is connected to the other computers.

1. In Windows Server 2003, open the Start menu and choose Control Panel | Network Connections. In Windows XP open the Start menu, choose Control Panel, and double-click Network Connections.

2. Click (in Windows Server 2003) or right-click the connection that you want to share and choose Properties. In the Properties dialog box that opens, click the Advanced tab.

3. Under Internet Connection Sharing, click Allow Other Network Users To Connect Through This Computer's Internet Connection, as shown in Figure 10-6 for Windows XP Professional (the Windows Server 2003 dialog box does not have the third option to Allow Other Network Users To Control).

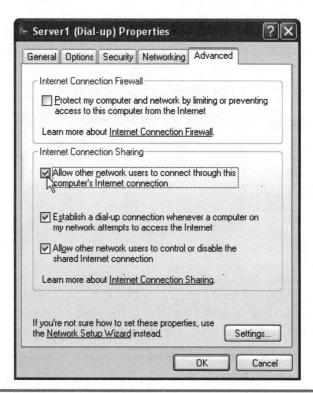

Figure 10-6 Sharing an Internet connection

Communications and Internet Services

4. Select Establish A Dial-Up Connection Whenever A Computer On My Network Attempts To Access The Internet and (if you are doing this under Windows XP) Allow Other Network Users To Control Or Disable The Shared Internet Connection if you want those options. In most cases, the first option is desirable, but often the second is not.

5. Click OK to close the Properties dialog box, and, if needed, click Close to close the Network Connections dialog box.

Maintain a Windows Server 2003 Router

You can see, test, and maintain the router you have just installed in the Routing And Remote Access console. In the next set of steps, you locate the new router, connect it to its destination, and see how to set up IP filters and the hours the router can be used:

1. In the Routing And Remote Access console, which should be open from the last exercise, open the local server and select Network Interfaces. In the right pane, you should see your demand-dial interface, similar to mine (Remote Router) shown here:

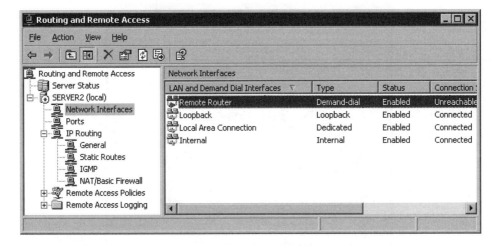

2. Right-click your demand-dial object and choose Set Credentials. Here, you can change the username, domain, and password that are used to connect to the ISP. When you open this dialog box, the password is cleared and must be reentered. Also, you may not need to enter a domain. Click OK after you have completed the entry.

3. Right-click the demand-dial interface and choose Connect. You should hear the modem dialing and see a message with the status of "Connecting." When the actual connection is made, the Connection State in the Routing And Remote Access dialog box will change to Connected.

4. Right-click the demand-dial interface and choose Set IP Demand-Dial Filters. This enables you to specify either IP addresses that will be the only ones allowed into the network or, conversely, IP addresses that are not allowed into the network. Click New to add the IP addresses, which can be within the LAN or in the remote network. After you have set the filters you want, click OK.

5. Right-click the demand-dial interface and choose Dial-Out Hours. Here, you can specify the hours that the demand-dial connection will not be available by selecting a particular hour and clicking Denied. For example, if you want from 11:00 P.M. Saturday through 3:00 A.M. Sunday to be blocked out, the dialog box will look like the next image after you have selected times. After you have set the times you want, click OK.

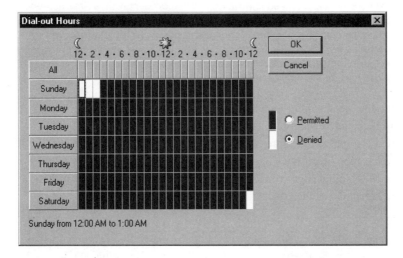

6. Right-click the demand-dial interface and choose Properties. This allows you to set the properties of the connection, including the phone number, the type of connection, several security options, and network properties. When you are done, click OK and then close the Routing And Remote Access console.

To use the router, you need to install an Internet connection in the client that connects through a LAN. See the next section, "Set Up an Internet Connection."

CRITICAL SKILL
10.4 Set Up an Internet Connection

An Internet connection is one of the major reasons (and sometimes the only reason) to own a computer. In businesses, more and more work is being done through business-to-business transactions over the Internet. Making the most of the Internet connection is therefore of significant importance.

If a computer can connect to the Internet over the LAN, Windows Server 2003 Setup will automatically connect that computer to the Internet and no further work needs to be done to accomplish it. The problem is that it is not obvious whether you are connected or not. The only way to tell is to try to use the Internet and see what happens. Try that now with the next set of steps. These steps assume that neither a modem nor a dial-up connection has been previously set up, although they do assume that the phone line is connected to a modem and that the modem is installed in or connected to the computer being set up.

NOTE

To connect to the Internet, you need to have an existing account with an Internet service provider (ISP), and you need to know the phone number for your modem to dial (the ISP's modem phone number), and the username and password for your account. If you want to use Internet mail, you need to know your e-mail address, the type of mail server (POP3, IMAP, or HTTP), the names of the incoming and outgoing mail servers, and the name and password for the mail account.

Internet
Explorer

1. Open the Internet Explorer icon by double-clicking its icon if on the desktop, by opening the Start menu and clicking its icon if there, or by opening Start | All Programs | Internet Explorer. The Internet Explorer will open and tell you about Internet security. In the Address bar type **http://www.msn.com** and press ENTER. If the Internet Explorer opens with the MSN initial page, you know you already have an Internet connection and you can skip the remainder of these steps.

If the New Connection Wizard opens, you know you need to create an Internet connection. In that case, the Location Information dialog box may open where you will need to enter your country or region, area or city code, and other information. Do that, and click OK twice to return to the New Connection Wizard.

NOTE

If Internet Explorer did not find the Internet and the New Connection Wizard did not open, you can start the New Connection Wizard by opening Start and choosing All Programs | Accessories | New Connection Wizard. The choices and wording are slightly different than using the approach described in the next steps, but you can accomplish the same objective. Follow the dialog boxes and not these steps.

2. Click Next, you are asked how you want to connect to the Internet. If you do not have an existing account with an ISP and are going to use a modem, leave the default choice of the first option, Create A New Internet Account. If you have an existing Internet account but do not know the settings to use, select the second choice; otherwise, select the third choice. In any case, once you have made the choice you want, click Next.

3. If you chose either of the first two choices, the Internet Connection Wizard will try to dial a phone number that will connect to a Microsoft site that will help you locate an ISP, either a new one or one you already have an account with, and help you set up your computer to use that ISP. Skip to Step 5.

4. If you made the third choice in Step 2, choose whether to connect through a phone line and a modem or through the LAN and then click Next. If you don't have a modem installed, you will be asked to do that and led through several additional dialog boxes. If you are connecting through a phone line and modem, enter the telephone number, click Next, and enter your username and password.

5. Enter the name of your Internet service provider, which will be the name of this connection, and click Next. You may be asked if you want to set up an Internet mail account. If so, click Yes and Next and then enter your display name, your e-mail address, your incoming and outgoing mail servers, and your account name and password, clicking next after each.

6. You are shown a summary of the connection that you want to make. If it is not correct, click Back and make the necessary corrections. When it is correct, click Finish.

7. Once more, double-click the Internet Explorer icon and, if asked, click Connect. If you still do not connect to the Internet, you may need to reinstall your modem, in which case you should go to "Install a Modem" earlier in this module and then return here; otherwise, go to the next step.

TIP

If you think you have a modem set up and you are not getting connected when you open Internet Explorer, look at the Internet Options in Internet Explorer by opening the Tools menu, choosing Internet Options, and clicking the Connections tab. See if you have a connection specified and that it dials the connection. If not, make the necessary corrections.

8. When you have successfully installed your Internet connection and attempted to open Internet Explorer with a modem, the Dial-up Connection dialog box will appear. Click Connect. Your modem dials the number, you will be connected, and a connection icon will appear in the tray on the right of the taskbar. By default, you will be shown an information screen on security. In the Address bar, type **http://www.msn.com** and press ENTER. You will be connected to MSN's home page, similar to the one shown in Figure 10-7. The next section shows you how to change this default.

9. If you were not asked if you want to set up an Internet mail account in Step 5 and you do, go to Step 10; otherwise, go to Step 12.

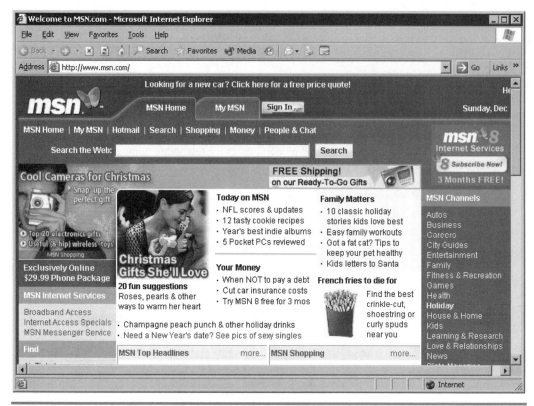

Figure 10-7 Connecting to MSN

10. Open the Start menu and choose All Programs | Outlook Express. The Internet Connection Wizard will open and ask you to enter the name you want to be displayed when your account is referenced. Do that and click Next.

11. Enter your e-mail address, and click Next. Select the type of mail service that you have (POP3 is the most common and the default), enter the name of the incoming and outgoing mail servers, and click Next. Enter the mail account's name and password, choose whether you want Windows to remember the password, choose whether you need to use Secure Password Authentication, click Next, and then click Finish. Outlook Express will open and connect you to your mail account. In the future when you open Outlook Express and you are not connected to the Internet, you will be.

12. When you are done using the Internet connection, you can disconnect by right-clicking the connection icon in the tray of the taskbar and choosing Disconnect.

CRITICAL SKILL
10.5 Find Information on the Internet

Once you are connected to the Internet with Internet Explorer open, you most probably will want to go to pages other than the MSN home page. There are a number of ways to do that, including the following:

- Navigating within a web site

- Going directly to a web site

- Searching for a web site

- Setting up a different default home page

Navigate Within a Web Site

A good web site gives you many ways to navigate within it. As you look at the MSN home page in Figure 10-7, you see a number of terms or phrases that become underlined when you move the mouse pointer over them. These are *links* that, when clicked, take you to another part of the web site. The home page is almost all links of several kinds. It has horizontal menus (MSN Home, My MSN, Hotmail, and so forth), vertical menus (Autos, Business, and so on), block menus (Broadband Access, Air Tickets, Auctions, and so forth), headings, terms by themselves (More), and article lists. Also, there is normally a Search capability, similar to the one at the top of the MSN home page. Here, you can enter a term or a phrase and click Search.

TIP

Often, if you enter a phrase in a text search, the search will be done on each word, not on the complete phrase. To fix that, in many text searches, you can enclose the phrase in quotation marks and the search will be done on the entire phrase.

Internet Explorer also provides tools to navigate within a site: the Back and Forward arrows on the toolbar take you to the preceding and next pages, respectively. Also, the down arrows on the right of the Back and Forward arrows will list the last several pages you have viewed in each direction.

Go Directly to a Web Site

To go directly to a site, you must know the address, or URL (Uniform Resource Locator), for that site. With increasing frequency in publications, letterheads, and advertising, you will find an organization's URL. When you have a site's URL, you can enter it into the Address box under the toolbar in Internet Explorer, as shown next, and then press ENTER, click the right-pointing arrow, or click Go, which takes you directly to the site. URLs that you frequently use can be stored in the Favorites folder, on the desktop, and in the Links folder on the Address bar of Internet Explorer. If you select one of these addresses and you are not already connected to the Internet, you will be connected automatically (or you might have to click Dial in a connection dialog box), Internet Explorer will open, and the addressed site will be displayed.

Place a URL in Favorites   You can store a URL in the Favorites folder by entering it or otherwise displaying it in the Address box of Internet Explorer, opening the Favorites menu, and choosing Add To Favorites. The Add Favorite dialog box will open, show you the name the site will have in the Favorites folder, and allow you to place the URL in a subfolder with the Create In option.

NOTE

The Favorites folder is in each user's area of the hard disk. By default, this is C:\Documents and Settings*user*\Favorites. This should be backed up from time to time.

Place a URL on the Desktop   You can place a URL on the desktop or in the Quick Launch toolbar by dragging the icon in the Address box of Internet Explorer to the desktop or Quick Launch toolbar. This creates a shortcut that, when double-clicked or clicked, connects to the Internet, opens Internet Explorer, and displays the site.

Place a URL in the Links Folder   The Links folder is a subfolder of Favorites and is displayed on the right of the Address bar in the upper part of Internet Explorer windows. Open the View menu and choose Toolbars | Lock The Toolbars to unlock the Links bar and then drag the Links bar to the left to display more of it. You can add a URL to the Links folder and bar by dragging the icon in the Address box to the Links bar on the right. You can place it within the Links bar in the location you want. You can remove any unwanted links by right-clicking them and choosing Delete.

Search for a Web Site

If you don't know a web site's URL, you can search for it in either of two ways. If it is a web site that you have been to recently, you likely can find it in your web site history. If you have not been to the site recently, you can do a full search of the Internet to find it.

Check History   To check the history of your web site visits, click History in the Internet Explorer toolbar. A History pane will open and show you the sites you have visited by day for the current week, and then by week for the last several weeks. By opening a day or week, you can see and select a URL that you have previously visited and have it quickly displayed.

You can determine how many days to keep History and clear History by opening the Tools menu and choosing Internet Options. In the General tab of the dialog box that opens, in the bottom panel, you can set the Days To Keep Pages In History and Clear History.

Search the Internet   You can search for a web site on the Internet at three levels:

- Type in the Address box what you believe is part of the URL, and Internet Explorer will search for a site that has in its URL the text you entered. If what you enter has been indexed to a site, for example "3com" or "united" (for United Airlines), you will be taken directly to the site, even though the actual URL may not contain what you typed (United's URL is http://www.ual.com). In other cases, such as "Osborne" a Search site appears displaying a list of possible URLs, as you can see in Figure 10-8, even though a site exists with what you typed in it (Osborne's URL is http://www.osborne.com). In still other cases, for example "martymatthews," you get "Sorry, no results were found" even though a site exists with that name (my URL is http://www.martymatthews.com). It all depends on how well the site has been indexed.

TIP

You can change how Internet Explorer responds to Address box search (typing less than a full URL) by opening the Tools menu, choosing Internet Options, clicking the Advanced tab, and scrolling down to Search From The Address Bar.

- Click Search in the toolbar, and the Search Companion pane will open on the left of Internet Explorer. Here, you can enter a word or phrase and click Search. A list of web sites containing that word or phrase will be displayed. You can then click a site in the list and it will be displayed. As described earlier in the tip under "Navigate Within a Web Site," if you want to search for a complete phrase, you need to place the phrase within quotation marks.

- Use another search site such as Google, Yahoo, Excite, Go, Lycos, or AltaVista by typing the name in the Address bar (see Figure 10-9 for Excite's home page). Internet Explorer 6.0 (IE) in Windows Server 2003 depends entirely on the MSN search engine and does not give you direct links to other search engines that were available in IE 5.0. These other search sites provide different results for the same searches, and so it is often worthwhile to check several sites. You can do this not only when searching for web pages, but also when searching for a person's mailing address or e-mail address, finding a business, locating a map, looking up a word, finding a picture, finding a reference in a newsgroup, and searching your previous searches.

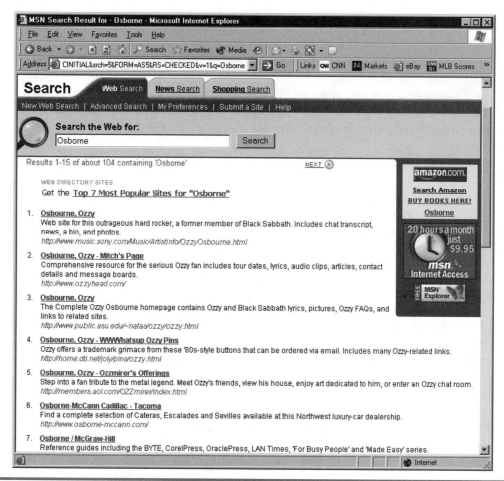

Figure 10-8 Searching for "Osborne"

Set Up a Different Default Home Page

The page that opens when you first start Internet Explorer or click the house icon in Internet Explorer's toolbar is called Home, your home page. By default, when you first install Windows Server 2003 with Internet Explorer, this page is the MSN (Microsoft Network) home page. If you want to change that to, say, the CNN home page, you can do so with these steps:

1. Open Internet Explorer and display the page that you want to be your home page, which is the CNN home page in this example.

2. Open the Tools menu and choose Internet Options.

3. In the General tab, Home Page section, click Use Current.

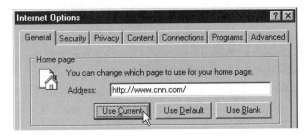

If you ever want to return to using MSN as your home page, reopen Internet Options and click Use Default.

TIP

If you don't have a particular site you want to go to every time you open Internet Explorer, and you don't want to wait while one displays, click Use Blank.

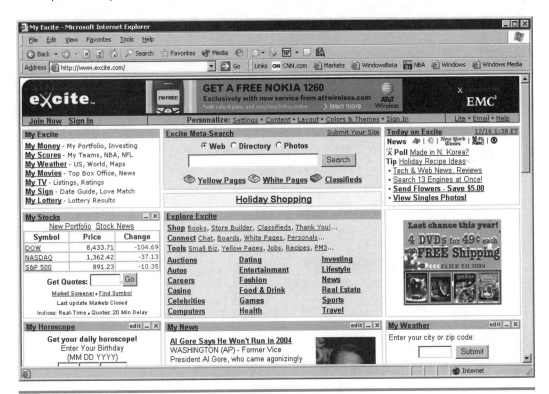

Figure 10-9 The Excite search site

10.6 Send and Receive Internet Mail

It is arguable which is the more important aspect of the Internet, the World Wide Web or Internet e-mail. E-mail provides one-on-one communications, which is vital to carrying out business functions as well as building and maintaining relationships. With Windows Server 2003, e-mail is handled with Outlook Express, which enables you to do the following:

● Send, receive, and store e-mail

● Participate in newsgroups

● Maintain and use an address book

Opening the Start menu and choosing All Programs | Outlook Express starts Outlook Express, which is shown in Figure 10-10.

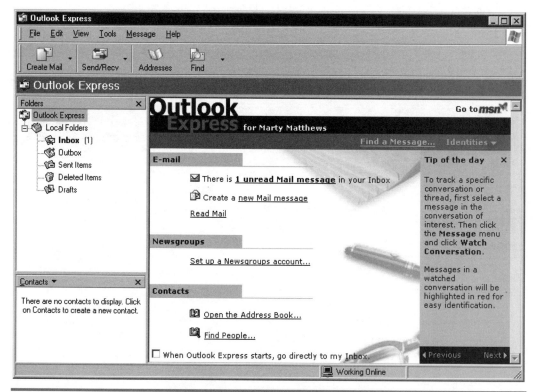

Figure 10-10 Outlook Express provides e-mail and newsgroup services.

Outlook
Express

If you use Outlook Express often, you can make it easier to start by placing its icon on the desktop and in the Quick Launch toolbar. Do that with the following steps:

1. Open My Computer or Windows Explorer and navigate to the C:\Program Files\Outlook Express folder as shown in Figure 10-11.

2. Drag the Msimn.exe file in the Outlook folder (shaded in Figure 10-11) to the desktop to create a shortcut to that program.

3. Drag the Msimn.exe file to the Quick Launch toolbar to create a shortcut there.

NOTE

If you upgraded from Windows 2000 to Windows Server 2003, there will already be Outlook Express shortcuts on the desktop and in the Quick Launch toolbar.

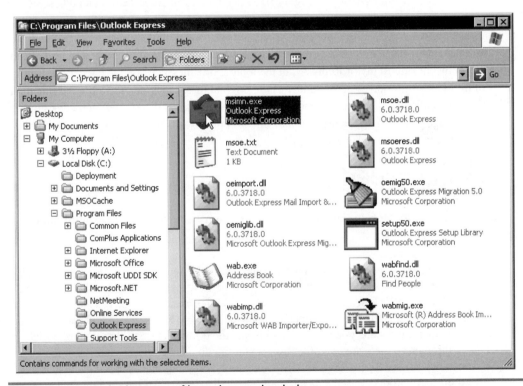

Figure 10-11 Outlook Express file to drag to the desktop

Send, Receive, and Store E-Mail

When you first open Outlook Express, it automatically connects to the Internet and retrieves any mail that your ISP is holding for you. Then, as long as Outlook Express is loaded, it will periodically try to get your e-mail, by reconnecting to the Internet as necessary. You can change if and how often your mail is checked by opening the Tools menu, choosing Options, and looking under Send/Receive Messages in the General tab. You can also manually retrieve your mail by clicking Send/Recv in the toolbar, or by clicking the down arrow on the right of Send/Recv to choose to either send or receive, and select the account to send to or receive from. By opening Local Folders and clicking Inbox in the left pane of the Outlook Express window, you will see in the upper-right pane a list of the messages you have received. If you click a message, some of the content of the message appears in the bottom-right pane. If you double-click a message, the message opens in its own window. Finally, if you do not delete the message, it stays in the Inbox for as long as you want.

You can create a new message to send by clicking Create Mail in the toolbar. This opens a New Message window, shown in Figure 10-12, in which you enter the e-mail address(es) of the recipients (separated by semicolons), a subject, which is helpful for identifying and locating messages, and the body of the message. When you are done with the message, click Send, and it will be sent. You can also get a New Message window with the recipient(s) and subject already filled in by clicking Reply or Reply All in the toolbar of a message you have received. Reply will fill in only the address of the sender of the original message, whereas Reply All fills in the addresses of all the people, sender and recipients, in the original message. If you click Forward on a message you receive, the original message is copied to a New Message window, but the address fields are left blank for you to fill in.

Ask the Expert

Q: Are there any tools in Outlook Express for suppressing the many pieces of junk e-mail I get?

A: Yes, there are. You can block all mail from a particular sender or domain by selecting a message from the sender or domain you want to block, then opening the Message menu and choosing Block Sender. You can also set up rules to automatically delete certain messages by opening the Tools menu, choosing Message Rules | Mail, and selecting the conditions and actions you want take with specific e-mail. This still lets a lot of e-mail slip through, so there are two other things you can do. One is to ask your ISP if they can block certain types of e-mail; most have tools for doing this. The second is to get a third-party product to reduce junk mail (also called "spam"). One such product is MailWasher at http://www.mailwasher.net/; there are others—search on "Spam elimination."

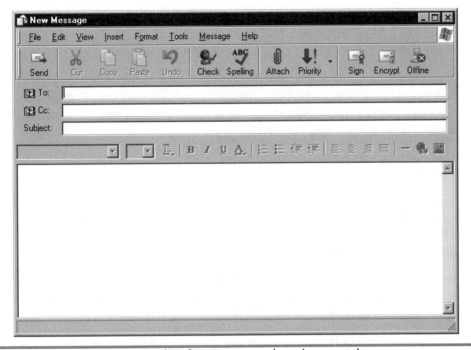

Figure 10-12 New Message window for creating and sending e-mail

You can attach one or more computer files to an e-mail message either by dragging the file from Windows Explorer or the desktop to the New Message window, or by clicking Attach in the toolbar of a New Message window and entering the file path and name or browsing for the attachment.

Participate in Newsgroups

Newsgroups are an organized chain of messages on a particular subject. Newsgroups are sponsored by some organization, such as a company, university, or club, and allow people to enter new messages and respond to previous ones. To access a newsgroup, you need to set up a new account for the newsgroup, similar to the account you set up for your e-mail. To set up and use a newsgroup account, you need the name of the news server and possibly an account name and password. Then, use the following steps:

1. In the Outlook Express window, open the Tools menu and choose Accounts. The Internet Accounts dialog box will open.

2. Click Add | News. Enter the name you want displayed, and click Next. Enter your e-mail address if not already displayed so that people can directly reply to you, and click Next.

3. Enter the name of your news server. Your ISP or another sponsoring organization will give this to you. If you do not need to enter an account name and password, your ISP or sponsoring organization will tell you this, in which case you can skip to Step 5.

4. If you need to enter an account name and password, click My News Server Requires Me To Log On, and click Next. Enter your account name and password, click Remember Password (if desired), and then, if necessary (your ISP or sponsor will tell you), click Log On Using Secure Password Authentication (SPA).

5. Click Next, click Finish, and then click Close. A new folder will appear in the Folders pane of Outlook Express.

6. You will see a message asking whether you want to download the newsgroups from the news account you just set up. Click Yes. If necessary, click Connect to connect to the Internet. If all of your entries are okay, you will be connected. If your account name and password are in error, you are told so and given a chance to fix them.

7. A list of newsgroups will be displayed. Double-click the ones to which you want to subscribe (meaning read and reply to messages it contains). After you have selected the newsgroups, click OK. You are returned to Outlook Express.

8. In the Folders pane on the left, click a newsgroup you want to open. A list of messages will be displayed. Click one to have it shown in the bottom pane, or double-click to have a message opened in its own window.

You can treat a newsgroup message like an e-mail message, but with two differences. You can choose to reply to the newsgroup or to the individual, and a new message is called a New Post. In newsgroups, a new message is "posted" as one would be on a bulletin board. If someone replies to this message, it gets added to the end of the original message, thereby creating a chain, or *thread,* of messages on a given subject. For example, Figure 10-13 shows a thread on the topic of Jaguar automobile speakers, in a newsgroup on that car.

Maintain and Use an Address Book

Outlook Express maintains an address book to help you keep track of your e-mail and snail-mail addresses and phone numbers. When you reply to a message that you have received, the addresses automatically go into the address book. When you create a new message, as you start typing a name, it will be looked up in the address book and completed for you, if it's already in the address book. You can also manually add a name to the address book, manually look up an address, and create a group of addresses that can be referred to by the group name and added to a message all at once.

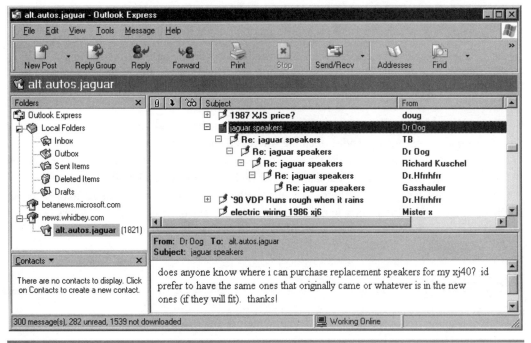

Figure 10-13 A newsgroup thread

Add a Name to the Address Book   The following are a few ways to add names to the address book:

- From the Outlook Express window, click Addresses in the toolbar to open the Address Book window, click New in its toolbar, select New Contact, and fill in the dialog box that opens.

- From a New Message window, click the address book icon next to the "To" and "Cc" blocks to open the Select Recipients dialog box, click New Contact, and fill in the dialog box that opens.

- From an existing message, right-click an address anywhere in the message and choose Add (Sender) To Address Book.

Look Up an Address   You look up addresses in much the same way as you add them to the address book:

- From the Outlook Express window, click Addresses in the toolbar to open the Address Book window. Use the scroll bar or begin typing a name to locate it. When it is found, the e-mail address is shown in the Address Book window. If you want the postal address or other information not shown in the window, double-click the name to open the Properties dialog box, which shows all of the information on that individual.

● From a New Message window, click the address book icon next to the "To" and "Cc" blocks to open the Select Recipients dialog box. Double-click all the entries you want to receive the message, and then click OK.

Create and Use a Group To create a group of addresses that you can repeatedly use to send e-mail to a group of people, open the Address Book window, open the File menu, and choose New Group. Enter a name for the group, and click Select Members. Either type a name or use the scroll bar to find it, and then double-click the name to add it to the list of members. When you are done, click OK twice. An entry with a distinctive icon will appear in the address book. You use the group entry in the same way you use any other entry in the address book, but when you choose a group entry, all of the members are added to the list of recipients.

Progress Check

1. For a server to act as a router between the Internet and a LAN, what sort of connections must it have?

2. What is the simplest way to determine if you have an operating Internet connection?

3. If there are multiple users on a computer, does each user have his or her own folder of favorite web sites?

Project 10 Plan the Use of Communications and the Internet

There are many potential uses for communications and the Internet. This project will help you look at which aspects of those items that you want use and how to implement them.

---

1. For a server to act as a router between the Internet and a LAN, the server must have both LAN and communications connections.

2. The simplest way to determine if you have an operating Internet connection is to try it by opening Internet Explorer.

3. Yes, a Favorites folder is in each user's area of the hard disk. By default, this is C:\Documents and Settings*user*\Favorites.

Step by Step

1. Determine if you want to directly connect two computers other than through a LAN through

   a. A direct cable connection with a

      i. Serial cable

      ii. Parallel cable

   b. Infrared ports

   c. Select the host computer as a

      i. Domain Controller set up through RAS

      ii. Windows Server 2003 or XP Professional set up through Network Connections

   d. Select the client or guest computer set up through Network Connections

   e. Establish and manage the connection using

      i. A RAS server

      ii. An incoming connection

2. Determine if you want to connect a computer or a network to other computers or networks by:

   a. Installing and using a modem

   b. Establishing a dial-up connection

   c. Setting up and using RAS

   d. Setting up and using Windows Server 2003 as a router

   e. Setting up Internet connection sharing

3. Determine if you want to set up a connection to the Internet for:

   a. Gathering information on the Internet

   b. Sending and receiving Internet mail

   c. Participating in newsgroups

   d. Conducting business on the Internet

   e. Shopping on the Internet

Project Summary

There is one other way you can use the Internet not discussed in this module, and that is to supply information to the Internet. That is the subject of the next module, which discusses Internet Information Services (IIS).

Module 10 Mastery Check

1. What is a direct cable connection, and how is it accomplished?

2. What are some of the reasons that a direct cable connection might not work?

3. What is a modem, and how is it used?

4. How can you check if a modem is working other than trying to use it?

5. What is Remote Access Service (RAS), and how is it used?

6. What is a router, and how is it used?

7. What do you need to know to connect to the Internet?

8. What are some of the ways you can locate information on the Internet?

9. What are the three major ways you can search for a web site?

10. What does Outlook Express enable you to do?

Module 11

Internet Information Services Version 6

This module introduces you to Internet Information Services Version 6 (IIS 6) and the role that IIS plays within Windows Server 2003. In addition, this module discusses the major changes from IIS 4 to IIS 6. The Windows Server 2003 operating system (OS) is designed to integrate with IIS, and future Microsoft server products will be built directly into the core protocol support provided to Windows Server 2003 by IIS. This module looks at some of the new features included in IIS 6 as well as how to install, customize, and migrate IIS installations to meet various business and networking goals.

CRITICAL SKILL

11.1 Explore the IIS 6 Environment

IIS is a collection of web-enabled services and protocols configured to run with and on the Windows server-based operating systems. IIS 6, the latest in the line, is completely integrated into Windows Server 2003. While IIS is primarily known for hosting web services, within Windows Server 2003 IIS also provides a number of services and protocols fundamental to a Windows Server 2003–based organization.

NOTE

Windows XP Professional includes a limited version of IIS named IIS 5.1, just as IIS 5 is available in a limited version in Windows 2000 Professional. The version on Windows XP Professional is designed for people developing web sites and for small businesses to bring up a limited intranet site within the business. The limitation in the Professional version is that IIS can service only ten client connections at a time and some of the IIS features are not as capable as they are in the server version. This book will discuss only the server version of IIS 6.

Based on the Transmission Control Protocol/Internet Protocol (TCP/IP) and common Internet and industry standards, mainstream IIS first appeared with IIS 2, which is an installation option of NT Server 4. Initially, IIS offered services based on the Hypertext Transfer Protocol (HTTP), File Transfer Protocol (FTP), Gopher, and Simple Mail Transfer Protocol (SMTP). IIS 3 and 4 were available via Service Pack upgrades to the NT platform and introduced a number of new services, most notably Active Server Pages (ASP). With the advent of IIS 4, Microsoft dropped support of the Gopher web service but continued to add support for emerging web technologies, such as the Web Distributed Authoring and Versioning (WebDAV) protocol and the Extensible Markup Language (XML).

IIS has always been primarily a web server hosting web services, such as Hypertext Markup Language (HTML) web pages for use by external clients, normally via web browsers and HTTP connections, although IIS is a lot more than this. As previously mentioned, IIS can also host FTP and SMTP services.

Whenever you use a web browser to connect to a web site, such as www.microsoft.com, you connect to a web server; download the text, media, and images found there; and then look at this information on your local computer. Obviously, the quality and complexity of each web site varies tremendously, as does the quality and stability of web servers. This module will spend some time talking about the unique features and functions offered by both IIS 5 and IIS 6 that support both higher quality web sites and improved server stability.

While it is easy to pigeonhole IIS for web use only, IIS is actually used in a variety of non-web-related areas. The following are some of the areas that represent the diversity of functions offered by IIS:

- **FTP**   An industry-standard file-exchange protocol that allows different systems to exchange files. A large number of organizations running both NT- and UNIX-based platforms are using FTP to exchange files. This is even possible with larger systems, such as IBM and SUN. FTP allows systems to exchange files across the Internet in a quick and efficient manner. With FTP, data that's input and processed within a mainframe environment can be FTP'd to a Windows server and automatically input into a SQL database with no user interaction, through the use of a few simple scripts running on each end.

- **SMTP**   A TCP/IP-based protocol that allows for the formation and transfer of text messages between systems. In short, SMTP is e-mail. If you've ever used e-mail over the Internet, you've used SMTP. Within Windows Server 2003, SMTP is now a part of Active Directory and can be used to link Active Directory sites together across the Internet. With SMTP, Windows Server 2003 organizations can be integrated through the Internet using nothing but standard Internet technologies.

NOTE

Windows Server 2003 uses the IIS certificate server to keep the information exchanged between the two Active Directory sites encrypted and secure from prying eyes.

IIS 5 Enhancements

IIS 5 ships with Windows 2000 and represents a very major upgrade to IIS 4. All of the features in IIS 5 are also in IIS 6. Because of its strong integration with the OS, IIS 5 makes it easier to share documents and information across a company intranet or the Internet. With IIS 5, you can also deploy scalable and reliable web-based applications. In addition, bringing existing data and applications to the Web using Active Directory is much easier and provides a higher level of security and control. Technically, IIS 5 offers a variety of new features that focus on the data collaboration and sharing that is at the core of the Windows Server 2003 product family. IIS 5's integration into the Windows 2000 OS leads to a number of other advantages, including increased reliability and stability, compared to earlier IIS/OS combinations. Besides integration with the OS, IIS 5 also provides a higher degree of integration with the other Microsoft products, such as Exchange and SQL. Many of these new features are based around the WebDAV protocol and XML technologies, which allow for a higher degree of data sharing between dissimilar applications and are at the heart of what is meant by .NET.

Reliability and Performance

IIS 4 installations within many organizations had some reliability and performance issues. While no application is perfect, IIS 4 occasionally suffered from memory leaks (system resources that are not returned to the system's control when an application or script ends). Although these issues were rare, they would occasionally cause a server to consistently have to be rebooted before the lost system resources would be returned to the system for use by other services or applications. These and other issues did not stop e-commerce-based companies from developing e-commerce sites on the IIS 4 platform, but they still caused extra network administration in already hectic situations.

One of the main technologies that IIS 4 did add is an HTML alternative called *Active Server Pages (ASP)*. Originally introduced with IIS 3, ASP became native and stable within the IIS 4 platform. ASP is the cornerstone of a lot of very successful IIS deployments, including www.microsoft.com. Because of the success IIS 4 has achieved, Microsoft has been able to focus primarily on the reliability and performance of IIS 5 instead of on the addition of new features. In fact, in some instances, IIS 5 has increased performance up to 40 percent over like-configured IIS 4 installations, a number that can translate into millions of dollars in hardware to large e-commerce sights. In addition to the general integration changes made to IIS 5, the following specific changes have been made:

- **Reliable restart feature** Allows an administrator to restart web services without rebooting the computer.

- **Application protection** Allows applications to run in their own environments separate from the memory space of the web services and other applications running on the server. If an application environment fails, the OS will not fail and will not need to be restarted. Only the process that fails needs to be restarted, which the OS can do automatically.

- **CPU throttling and socket pooling** Protect the OS and other users by placing limits on the resources any one user can consume.

- **Development tools** Provide features that benefit the web site developer by improving the ease and reliability in the development process. Among these features are the following:
  - Scriptless Microsoft ASP processing
  - ASP self-tuning
  - Performance-enhanced ASP objects

Features New to IIS 5

Many of the features that were new to IIS 5 are just new versions of, or enhancements to, existing services available in IIS 4. These features make the product very easy to learn for those administrators already familiar with previous versions of IIS. The following sections describe a number of the more significant new features and enhancements within the IIS 5 product, separated by the subcategories to which they best relate.

Security   In keeping with the increased emphasis on security in the rest of Windows 2000, a number of new or enhanced security features were added to IIS 5. These include the following:

- **Digest authentication**   Adds user authentication across proxy servers and firewalls, which was not available in NT 4–based systems due to their inability to securely pass authentication credentials between servers. With the advent of Kerberos (which is explained later on in this module), a user can now authenticate to a single "front-end server" and then access network resources behind that server securely and without having to continually log in to each server. With digest authentication, the server negotiates a kind of certificate exchange utilizing encryption in a way that the server and client can be sure of reliable authentication.

- **Server-Gated Cryptography (SGC)**   Allows 128-bit encryption between client and server using Secure Sockets Layer (SSL) and a special SGC type of certificate, assuming the client's browser supports 128-bit encryption.

- **Security wizards**   Make it easier to set up the more complicated encryption components, including the following:

  - **Web Server Certificate Wizard**   Assists in administering certificates
  - **Permissions Wizard**   Assists in setting up access permissions to virtual directories
  - **CTL Wizard**   Assists in setting up a list of certified authorities, also called and named after a certificate trust list (CTL), with Kerberos v5 compliance

- **Kerberos**   Provides Internet standards–based authentication for accessing Active Directory–managed objects. Kerberos lets a user request an encrypted "ticket" that is used for authentication so that the user's credentials, such as username and password, are no longer needed. Kerberos is based on public key/private key technologies (see the discussion of this in Module 17) and cannot be used by others to access secure network resources. Since Kerberos is an industry standard, Windows 2000 and Windows Server 2003 users can use it to interact with third-party products, as well as other OSs.

- **CryptoAPI**   Provides a single certificate management system for both IIS and Windows Server 2003 that allows you to store, back up, and configure server certificates.

- **Fortezza**   Allows use of a U.S. government security standard in IIS 5. This standard satisfies the Defense Message System security architecture with a family of cryptographic products, including smart cards, modems, and Ethernet cards that provide message confidentiality, integrity, authentication, nonrepudiation, and access control to messages, components, and systems.

11

Internet Information Services Version 6

Administration   Being able to control the web sites that are being hosted by an IIS server is extremely important. Windows 2000 added the following very important administrative tools to IIS 5:

- **Reliable restarts**   Allows you to stop and restart all of your Internet services from within IIS, making it unnecessary to restart your computer when applications misbehave or become unavailable.

- **Process accounting**   Adds fields to the World Wide Web Consortium (W3C) extended log file to record information about how web sites use CPU resources on the server. With this information, CPU utilization can be analyzed in relation to IIS performance and possible billing schemes worked out.

- **Process throttling**   Limits how much processor time a web site's out-of-process applications are permitted to utilize. This ensures that processor time is available to other web sites and non-web applications.

Programmability   Web sites are becoming increasingly sophisticated, and that sophistication is coming from programming. IIS 5 added the following features in support of programming:

- **Application environment**   Expands the web server's application development environment by building on new technologies included in Windows 2000 Server. These include Active Directory and the expanded Component Object Model (COM+). In addition, enhancements to IIS ASP, such as scriptless ASP processing, as well as improved flow control and error handling, let developers write more efficient web-centric applications.

- **New ASP features**   Includes the following new improvements, which significantly reduce the time spent in troubleshooting web page problems:
  - New flow-control capabilities
  - Error handling
  - Scriptless ASP
  - Performance-enhanced objects
  - XML integration
  - Windows script components
  - ASP self-tuning

Application Protection   In IIS 4, applications can be set to run in the same process (memory space and virtual machine) as web services or in a process separate from web services. IIS 5 offers a third option in which multiple applications can be run in a pooled process together, but still separate from the main IIS process and other applications. Other features in IIS 5 that provide application protection include the following:

- **ADSI 2 support**   Gives administrators and application developers the ability to add custom objects, properties, and methods to the existing Active Directory Service Interface (ADSI) provider, offering more flexibility in creating a site, as well as isolation from the actual data store and protocol being used.

- **Web Distributed Authoring and Versioning (WebDAV)**   Extends the HTTP/1.1 protocol to allow clients to publish, lock, and manage resources on the Web. Most of the features supported by WebDAV are supported only by browsers that have fully adopted and integrated the HTTP/1.1 protocol standard. Currently, only Internet Explorer Version 5 or later fully supports IIS 5's WebDAV features, but other supporting browser technologies may have been released by the time you read this. Integrated into IIS 5, WebDAV allows clients to do the following:

  - Manipulate resources
  - Modify properties
  - Lock and unlock resources
  - Search

- **FTP restart**   Resumes an FTP download if an Internet connection is lost. This feature resumes the download at the same spot it was interrupted.

- **HTTP compression**   Compresses web pages for download to a supporting browser. This feature should be balanced between processor utilization and network bandwidth consumption. Increasing compression decreases the bandwidth consumed by the request but increases processor load during the compression.

NOTE

IIS 4 is the latest product available for use on NT 4, because IIS 5 is supported only by Windows 2000 and IIS 6 is supported only by Windows Server 2003 due to their high degree of integration with the OS. However, in organizations not ready to switch to Windows 2000 or Windows Server 2003 completely, a new server running either of the newer OS and IIS 5 or IIS 6 can be integrated into the security domains provided by NT 4 with very little configuration and effort.

IIS 6 Enhancements

IIS 6 has a number of significant enhancements over IIS 5 to the point where it is difficult to determine which has more. Many of the features of IIS 5 have been enhanced in IIS 6, and there are a number of new features, most importantly in the areas of security, reliability, administration, and scalability.

Security

Microsoft has a major effort underway to improve the security of IIS, including many small code changes to plug suspected vulnerable areas. In addition, IIS 6 has included a number of new features, including advanced digest authentication, selectable Cryptographic Service Provider, configuring worker process identity, and disabling unknown extensions.

- **Advanced digest authentication**   Enhances digest authentication by storing and transmitting security credentials, such as passwords, in a particularly difficult-to-break encryption technique called MD5 hash.

- **Selectable Cryptographic Service Provider (CSP)**   Allows an administrator to switch between using basic computer hardware (CPU, RAM, and hard disk) and software (Windows and the Registry) to perform the functions of calculating and storing private and public keys used in encryption, and handling some or all of those functions on a smart card or a cryptographic accelerator card.

- **Configuring worker process identity**   Allows the configuration of application pools, where server-based web processes are run, to have a particularly limited set of privileges in order to block hackers.

- **Disabling unknown extensions**   Allows configuring IIS so that it will pass on only known file extensions and block unknown ones with an "access denied" error message.

Reliability

Reliability can be broken into two main areas: preventing applications from crashing (undesired termination), and containing such a crash so that it doesn't bring down IIS or the OS. Preventing third-party applications from crashing is a finger-pointing contest between Microsoft and the application developers, so the focus in improving IIS reliability is to better contain applications so that they cannot affect the rest of the system. Microsoft has made a number of changes in IIS to accomplish this, including establishing a dedicated operation mode, isolating applications through worker processes and application pools, limiting queued requests for an application, establishing a separate Web Administration Service (WAS), and monitoring the health of worker processes.

- **Dedicated operation mode**   Allows applications to run in an isolated environment in contrast to standard application mode used in IIS 5 where applications run as a part of the web service. Many of the other reliability enhancements depend on using dedicated operation mode.

- **Application pools and worker processes**   Provide for the isolation of applications by assigning them to particular application pools that are run with specific worker processes. Application pools can be configured with a set of time and space limits and to use a given set of resources, including a particular processor in a multiprocessor server. Application pools and worker resources require dedicated application mode.

- **Limiting queued requests**   Allow the setting of limits with dedicated application mode on the number of requests that can be queued for a particular application pool. This limits the amount of system resources that any one application pool can utilize.

- **Web Administration Service (WAS)**   Provides a web management space that is separate from application processes to keep management functions isolated from any problems in web applications. WAS is used to configure application pools, to determine their health (whether or not they are running), and to restart them.

- **Health monitoring**   Allows in dedicated application mode the determination of how an application pool is running and, under prescribed circumstances, terminating and optionally restarting it. If the application pool has crashed, it can be terminated and immediately restarted; if the application pool is idle, it can be terminated and restarted on demand; if it has repeatedly failed, it can be disabled and not allowed to restart; and if a detectable part of a pool has failed, it can be separated from the process and restarted as another process.

Administration

IIS administration in IIS 4 is through an HTML-based Internet Services Manager (ISM). In IIS 5, administration is handled directly with the Internet Information Services Snap-In to the Microsoft Management Console (MMC) (called the "IIS console" here) or remotely with the HTML-based ISM. In both IIS 4 and IIS 5, configuration information is stored in an uneditable binary file called the metabase. IIS 6 still uses the IIS console, but it has replaced the HTML-based ISM with both a Terminal Services capability to remotely access the IIS console (called the "remote console") and Remote Administration (HTML), a capability for performing some management functions over either an intranet or the Internet connection. Also IIS 6 replaces the binary metabase with an editable XML-based metabase stored in two easily accessible files. Many of the administrative enhancements in IIS 6 involve the new XML metabase, such as the ability to import and export web site configurations, using command-line scripts to manage web and FTP sites, and including an IIS provider in the Windows Management Instrumentation (WMI).

- **Metabase enhancements**   Allows the direct reading and editing of the IIS configuration and schema information even while IIS is running, the easy rollback to a previous version of the configuration and schema information if it gets corrupted, and the backing up and restoring of the information with a password.

- **Import/export web site configurations**   Provides the means to export from one node to an entire tree of a web site's configuration information to a readable XML file that can be imported into another server.

- **Command-line scripts**   Allows the direct or indirect administration of web sites, FTP sites, virtual directories, web applications, and configuration information using command-line scripts.

- **IIS provider in WMI**   Allows the management and configuration of IIS programmatically using the Windows Management Instrumentation (WMI) program interfaces to query and configure the metabase.

Scalability

As a web site or web hosting service grows, it needs to do so with as little disruption to the customer as possible. IIS 6 has added a number of features to improve this ability to smoothly grow, called scalability, including a 64-bit version of IIS, use of full Windows clustering, multiple worker processes, caching of ASP templates, using tracing for capacity planning, and better bandwidth management.

- **A 64-bit version of IIS**   Allows running IIS and its web applications on the Intel Itanium 64-bit processor with the capability to handle large loads.

- **Use of Windows clustering**   Allows using the operating system's built-in capability for clustering, the connecting of multiple computers with potentially shared resources, and the capability to balance the load among the computers. Upon failure of one computer in a cluster, the load is automatically switched to another computer. IIS 5 has limited clustering capability within itself, but it could not use Windows 2000 clustering. IIS 6 no longer tries to do its own clustering but makes full use of Windows Server 2003's clustering capability.

- **Multiple worker processes**   Allows running multiple web applications simultaneously, each in its own protected environment. In multiple processor computers, a given worker process can be run on a dedicated processor. In IIS 5 and in the standard application mode of IIS 6, all applications have to be run through a single worker process, whereas the dedicated application mode of IIS 6 provides for multiple worker processes, each running one or more applications.

- **ASP template caching**   Provides for caching (holding in active memory, which can be either RAM or hard disk) common pieces of Active Server Pages (ASP) script, called "templates," so that when those templates are reused, they are made usable very rapidly, because they are immediately available and do not need to be recompiled.

- **Tracing for capacity planning**   Allows the analysis of how various workloads are handled with different hardware configurations to plan the hardware needed as the workload grows.

- **Bandwidth management**   Provides for the control of the level and quality of user service through bandwidth throttling, application pool queue limits, process accounting, and connection limits and timeouts.

Internet Services in IIS 6

IIS 6 publishes information using standard Internet services and protocols, including the World Wide Web (WWW), FTP, SMTP, and Network News Transfer Protocol (NNTP).

- **WWW services** Uses HTTP to allow users to publish content to the Web using HTML. Files are placed in folders or subdirectories connected to a web site. These documents can be viewed by using an Internet browser, such as Netscape Navigator or Internet Explorer. Because of the graphical nature of HTML, businesses can use this format to display and explain products and services, as well as create e-commerce applications to purchase these products and services.

- **FTP services** Used to transmit files over the Internet. This is an older protocol that provides a reliable and speedy transfer of files. FTP can be used with a web browser via web-FTP, to speed up downloading large files from normal web sites, as well as with an independent legacy FTP client connected to the FTP server, which can provide access to files that are independent of HTTP protocols. FTP.Microsoft.com is an example of an open FTP server. While some web browsers can be used to access FTP servers, separate FTP clients are normally used. Although all Microsoft clients contain an FTP client as part of the TCP/IP stack, this client is DOS and command-line driven (type **FTP** at the command prompt). Many third-party 32-bit FTP clients are available that can run within the Microsoft OS and that provide numerous additional features not provided by the built-in FTP clients. The classic example is WS_FTP, which is available from http://www.ipswitch.com/products/ws_ftp/. Many other FTP clients are available.

- **SMTP services** Used for Internet e-mail, SMTP is dependent on TCP/IP protocols and uses the Domain Name System (DNS) servers on the Internet to translate an e-mail name such as billg@microsoft.com to an IP address like 207.46.230.219.

- **NNTP services** Allows a web site to host its own newsgroups, which provide for the exchange of threaded messages connected to a single topic. Messages are sent to the news server, which posts them to the appropriate newsgroup. A *newsgroup* is a community of people interested in a specific subject. The people in this community log on to the newsgroup to read and reply to messages on the subject of the newsgroup.

WWW services are installed with IIS by default in all cases. By utilizing the WWW services, graphical HTTP sites can be hosted. FTP, SMTP, and NNTP services augment IIS and can be optionally installed with it. These services allow multiple communication options. Using FTP services, files can be distributed quickly across the Internet. Both WWW and FTP services allow multiple sites to be set up on one IIS server, such that the one web server can appear to be multiple WWW and/or FTP sites to a user on the Internet. SMTP allows e-mail communication with users of the Internet, as well as an additional method of communication between servers. NNTP allows the hosting of newsgroups, which can provide feedback and communication between an organization and people associated with it, such as customers, suppliers, users of services, and employees.

CRITICAL SKILL
11.2 Install IIS 6

When setting up IIS for web-hosting purposes, you need to create one or more dedicated web servers. In some larger organizations, the potential load on the web servers can be dramatic. In smaller organizations, however, a single-server installation is adequate. The design of any two networks is rarely going to be exactly the same, because various political and geographical factors affect even the most basic of network installations.

When designing and eventually installing a web server based on IIS 6 and Windows Server 2003, you need to consider a variety of factors, primarily what services the web site will host and what connection security the site will implement. For web sites hosting information that is free and available for everyone to see, anonymous access can be used where all users connecting to the web server will automatically be granted access to the server based on the Guest account and will not be prompted for a username or password. This situation then allows the user to pass secure information to the server (such as credit card data, to place an order) via technology such as SSL (discussed in Module 17). When data is being hosted on the server that needs to be secure from unauthorized access, some form of authentication is required, such as Windows Authentication or Kerberos.

Install IIS from Scratch

No single method of installing IIS applies in every case. In a new or "clean" installation, Windows Server 2003 Standard or Enterprise Edition Setup does not by default install IIS, whereas Windows Server 2003 Web Edition Setup does. In the cases where IIS is not installed by default, it can be installed with either Manage Your Server (recommended) or Add Or Remove Programs, as explained later in this module. Using the default installation of IIS from Manage Your Server or Add Or Remove Programs, different features and settings are installed with each method, and Web Edition Setup installs a third set of defaults. A comparison of the default and optional services that are installed with the three different methods is shown in Table 11-1 (Manage Your Server and Add Or Remove Programs are available with either Windows Server 2003 Standard or Enterprise Edition).

Install IIS from Manage Your Server

The surest and possibly easiest way to install IIS 6 is with the Manage Your Server. When you do a new installation of Windows Server 2003, Manage Your Server automatically opens at

Service Installed by Default?	Manage Your Server	Add or Remove Programs	Web Edition
BITS Server Extensions	No	No	No
Common files	Yes	Yes	Yes
FTP service	No	No	No
FrontPage Server 2002 Extensions*	Yes	No	No
Internet Information Services Manager	Yes	Yes	Yes
Internet Printing	No	No	No
NNTP service	No	No	No
SMTP service	No	No	Yes
World Wide Web service	Yes	Yes	Yes
Active Server Pages	No	No	Yes
Internet Data Connector	No	No	No
Remote Administration (HTML)	No	No	Yes
Remote Desktop Web Connection	No	No	No
Server Side Includes	No	No	No
WebDAV Publishing	No	No	No

*With Office 2003 FPSE is being replaced with Microsoft SharePoint Services.

Table 11-1 Default Services Installed with IIS 6 in Windows Server 2003s

the completion of Setup. At any time, you can open Manage Your Server and install IIS 6 using these steps:

1. If Manage Your Server is not automatically open on your desktop, open the Start menu and choose Manage Your Server. The Manage Your Server window will open.

2. Click Add Or Remove a role, click Next after reading the Preliminary Steps, and a list of server roles will appear in Configure Your Server Wizard. Click Application Server (IIS, ASP.NET) and click Next. Choose if you want to install the FrontPage Server Extensions and Enable ASP.NET, and click Next.

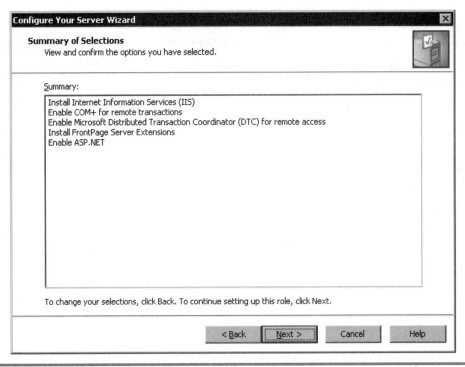

Figure 11-1 Selected items to install IIS 6 with the Configure Your Server Wizard

3. Review the Summary Of Selections that appears (mine is shown in Figure 11-1). If you want to change anything, click Back and make the change. When you are comfortable with the selection, click Next. IIS will be installed and configured by the Windows Components Wizard (you may need to insert the Windows Server 2003 CD).

4. When installation is complete, you are told that the server is now an application server. Click Finish to complete the installation.

Install IIS from Add Or Remove Programs

Using Add Or Remove Programs gives you the advantage of being able to choose the specific set of options that you want to install. One that you may want later in this module that isn't normally installed is Remote Administration (HTML). Install IIS 6 from Add Or Remove Programs in the Control Panel with the following steps:

1. Open the Start menu, choose Control Panel | Add Or Remove Programs. Click Add/Remove Windows Components to open the Windows Components Wizard.

2. Select Application Server, click Details, select Internet Information Services (IIS), and click Details again. This allows you to select the subcomponents within IIS, as shown next. The optional File Transfer Protocol (FTP) Service is often desired. Select World Wide Web Service and click Details one more time. Here you can choose many of the newest IIS components.

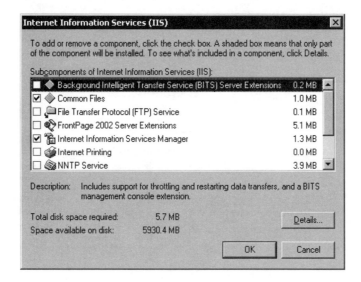

3. Select the components that you want to install, click OK three times, and click Next. You may need to insert your Windows Server 2003 CD or point to the correct files on your network. The necessary files will be copied to the hard drive, and the desired services will be configured. Click Finish when you are told that you have successfully completed the Windows Components Wizard and, if necessary, close Add Or Remove Programs and the Control Panel.

CRITICAL SKILL
11.3 Migrate to IIS 6

The migration or upgrading process is dependent on the type of web server being upgraded:

● **Current users of IIS**   Will be upgraded to version 6 by Windows Server 2003 Setup. Once installation is complete, you can see that IIS is installed in the Manage Your Server window, as shown in Figure 11-2. Setup and configuration are for the most part automatic, and current users of IIS will have few problems making the transition to IIS 6.

● **Users of other web servers**   Will need to transfer configuration settings and content, as well as web applications, to the IIS environment from such web servers as Netscape Enterprise Server or Apache HTTP Server.

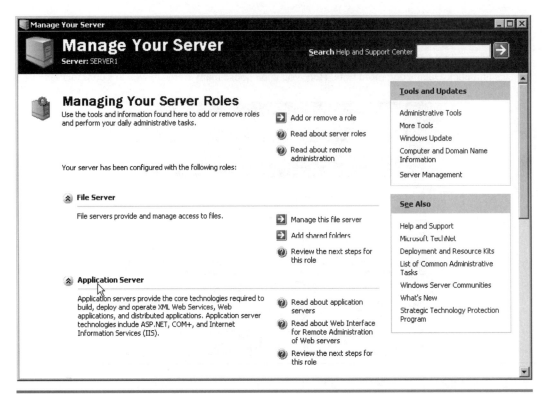

Figure 11-2 IIS 6 migration from a prior version is in part automatic.

NOTE

If you are upgrading from NT 4 or Windows 2000 and you have removed IIS before doing the upgrade using Add Or Remove Programs, Setup will still install IIS 6.

Plan the Migration

When an organization has a current Internet and/or intranet site or sites, planning is an essential part of any migration, to maintain that site's presence. In choosing a migration path, the primary considerations are as follows:

- Risk to the current system and total downtime acceptable

- Existing hardware role in the new installation

- Content changes expected to web data (are new web pages expected with the new servers?)

- Potential network load and available network resources

- Additional services that the organization is planning on adding

TIP

In some organizations, a certain amount of downtime is acceptable and expected; however, in other organizations, such as e-commerce businesses, a web site is supposed to be always available. In-place migrations, with zero downtime, are possible, but very expensive and tricky to plan. Most managers, when asked to define acceptable system downtime, set a very low number. However, when those same managers are presented with the support costs to maintain that number, they normally set a more realistic goal. In general, you can expect to find an exponential relationship between downtime allowed and planning/resources needed for the migration to take place.

Migration Methods

There are at least three ways to carry out a migration to IIS 6, as described in the next several sections.

NOTE

When upgrading existing Windows NT 4 or Windows 2000 servers, the installation options are automatically chosen for Windows Server 2003 and match those of the system being upgraded. This means that IIS itself will install only if it is currently on an existing NT 4 or Windows 2000 server (most do contain some form of IIS) or if you removed it with Add Or Remove Programs.

Migrate to a Clean Windows Server 2003 Installation

Perform a clean installation of Windows Server 2003 and then use Manage Your Server to install IIS 6 on a computer other than the production web server, called a "staging" server. Migrate settings, content, and applications from the production web server to the new IIS 6 server. Test and debug the new server before it is deployed. Although this is the ideal solution, in many cases it may not be practical, due to software, hardware, and cost factors.

Hardware Needed	Pros	Cons
A second computer is required, in addition to the existing production web server.	Minimum downtime. You can put new, updated hardware in place at the same time you perform the migration. You also avoid taking your production web server offline until the new server is tested and deployed. Following deployment, if problems arise with the new server that didn't appear during testing, you can use the original server as a backup.	High cost. You might need new hardware. However, the cost will be offset at least partly by the time saved conducting the migration as well as troubleshooting any problems that occur during the migration. If you are running an e-commerce site, the added revenue of leaving the site up may cover some or all of the cost of new equipment.

Migrate to a Mirror of the Existing Web Server

If you are migrating from a computer running Microsoft Windows NT or Windows 2000, you can use this approach. On a second computer that is a hardware duplicate of the one you want to migrate, copy the hard disk that exists on the production web server using a product such as Symantec's Ghost, and then use the Windows Server 2003 Setup to upgrade to Windows Server 2003 and IIS 6. The web configuration settings, content, and applications would be on the new web server as a part of creating the mirror. Test and debug the new server before deploying it. This option allows for the testing of third-party applications to be installed on the new, mirrored server, to test for compatibility with Windows Server 2003 and IIS 6.

Hardware Needed	Pros	Cons
A second computer is required that is a duplicate of the existing production web server. You also need a program such as Symantec's Ghost.	Minimum downtime. You can put new, updated hardware in place at the same time you perform the migration. You also avoid taking your production web server offline until the new server is tested and deployed. Following deployment, if problems arise with the new server that didn't appear during testing, you can use the original server as a backup.	High cost. You might need new hardware. However, the cost will be offset at least partly by the time saved conducting the migration as well as troubleshooting any problems that occur during the migration. If you are running an e-commerce site, the added revenue of leaving the site up may cover some or all of the cost of new equipment.

Upgrade the Production Web Server

If your circumstances allow, you can take your production web server currently running Windows NT or 2000 Server and IIS 4 or 5 offline long enough to upgrade it and get Windows Server 2003 and IIS 6 installed. The majority of your web configuration settings, content, and applications should fully migrate to IIS 6 "in place" on the production web server. Nevertheless, you'll need to thoroughly test and debug the server before deploying it.

Hardware Needed	Pros	Cons
No new hardware is required unless it is needed to run Windows Server 2003, such as memory.	There is no hardware cost.	Downtime. If the server installation does not go as planned, this could be one of those really long weekends that all administrators dread. However, in most IT shops where cost is a factor, this may be the only option where you do not need a second server.

Preinstallation Requirements

IIS requires or can benefit by the following software and protocols, which must be installed on the computer prior to installing IIS:

- **Windows TCP/IP protocol**   Provides the means to convert information into packets and the transmission and control of those packets over a network, which could be the Internet. TCP/IP, which is required by IIS, in turn requires an IP address and subnet mask, which are supplied by your Internet service provider (see Figure 11-3), as well as your default gateway's IP address (the default gateway is your ISP's address through which your computer routes all Internet traffic).

- **DNS service**   Provides a central index of friendly computer names to their IP addresses. DNS is by default set up on a server.

- **NT File System (NTFS)**   Provides improved security, the use of Active Directory, and many other functions and features.

- **FrontPage**   Allows the creation and editing of HTML pages for generating web sites using a WYSIWYG (what you see is what you get) editor that provides a friendly, graphical interface for tasks such as inserting tables, graphics, and scripts.

- **FrontPage Server Extensions (FPSE)**   Provides the server enhancements that allow a web site to be automated, such as interactive forms, discussion groups, and search components.

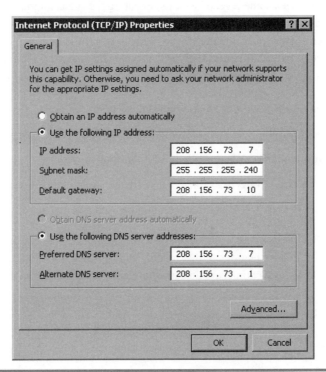

Figure 11-3 IP address information used with the TCP/IP protocol

Internet Information Services Version 6

11

Implement Security

IIS 6 starts "locked down" unlike previous versions that started unlocked. You may need to install IIS and must enable IIS to allow certain processes to run. The elements of this locked-down stance include:

- Not installing IIS by default on all Windows Server 2003 editions except the Web Server Edition.

- Not enabling any dynamic web content or web automation features including ASP, ASP.NET, FrontPage Server Extensions, Server Side Includes, and WebDAV and allowing only static pages to be delivered by IIS. (The Web Edition of Windows Server 2003 by default has ASP and ASP.NET enabled.)

- Not allowing any applications to run that have not been mapped or registered in IIS.

- Not allowing direct editing of the IIS metabase configuration file.

Nevertheless, IIS 6 does by default in all editions enable anonymous access to all but administrative web sites. This means that once the web server is running, security should be addressed. All sites need some level of security. Securing the site is important regardless of the size of the company or who will be using the site, and it is important to consider both internal and external users. Statistically, the users most likely to require security policies are those in your own organization. Laxity about internal security is where the majority of problems pop up. In setting up security, you should develop and implement policies for handling the following issues:

- **Installing IIS**   On what servers do you want IIS running?

- **Dynamic web content**   What types of dynamic web content do you want enabled?

- **Running applications**   What application extensions do you want mapped in IIS?

- **Setting NTFS and IIS permissions**   What are the assignments to various groups?

- **Security certificates**   How are they going to be used and managed?

Installing IIS is discussed earlier in this module, and setting permissions and using certificates are discussed a bit in later sections of this module and in Module 17. Enabling dynamic web content and enabling applications are discussed in the next two sections.

Enable Dynamic Web Content

Dynamic web content provides for the running of certain types of programs on the server while a web page is being viewed. The particular types of programs included are:

- **Active Server Pages (ASP)** Used to create web pages "on-the-fly" by running a script at the time a page is requested.

- **ASP.NET** Used for the same end purpose as ASP, but includes improved manageability, security, performance, and scalability.

- **Internet Data Connector** Used to attach to an Access or SQL database and supply content from the database to a web page as the page is being displayed.

- **Server Side Includes (SSI)** Used to insert content into a web page at the time a page is requested.

- **Web Distributed Authoring and Versioning (WebDAV)** Used to publish, lock, and manage web resources, for example the copying and moving of a file, modifying a file's properties, locking resources so that only one person can modify a file, and searching file contents.

- **FrontPage Server Extensions (FPSE)** Used to add features to web sites created with FrontPage such as forms, search tools, and usage analysis, as well as to improve the manageability and security of web pages and track server errors.

NOTE

The use of ASP, ASP.NET, SSI, WebDAV, and FPSE are discussed in _FrontPage 2002: The Complete Reference,_ by Martin Matthews and Erik Poulsen (McGraw-Hill/Osborne, 2001). A new edition is due out in 2003.

The enabling of the dynamic content is fairly straightforward, as you can see with these steps (you must be a member of the Administrator's group on the local server):

1. Open the Start menu and choose Administrative Tools | Internet Information Services (IIS) Manager.

2. Open the local server and click Web Service Extensions. The Web Service Extensions pane will open as shown in Figure 11-4.

3. In the Web Service Extensions pane, click the web service extension that you want to enable, for example Active Server Pages, and click Allow.

4. To add and enable a web service extension not shown in the default page, click Add A New Web Service Extension, enter the extension name, click Add, enter the path or browse to the files required to support the extension, click OK, click Set Extension Status To Allowed, and click OK again.

5. Close the IIS Manager.

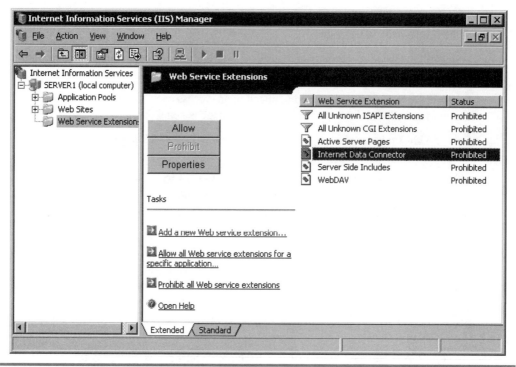

Figure 11-4 Enabling dynamic web content

Enable Running Server Applications

In addition to the programs that are specifically discussed in the preceding section, on dynamic web content, there are other programming and scripting languages that you can use to develop server applications. For IIS to know which Internet Server Application Programming Interface (ISAPI) or Common Gateway Interface (CGI) routine to use for a particular server application, you must associate the application's filename extension with an ISAPI or CGI routine, called *application mapping.* If you are a member of the Administrator's group, you can do application mapping with these steps:

1. Open the Start menu and choose Administrative Tools | Internet Information Services (IIS) Manager.

2. Open the local server, open Web Sites, right-click the web site with which the application will be used, and click Properties.

3. Click the Home Directory tab and click Configuration in the Application Settings area. In the Application Configuration dialog box that opens, the Mappings tab should be displayed, as you can see next. If not, click that tab and then click Add.

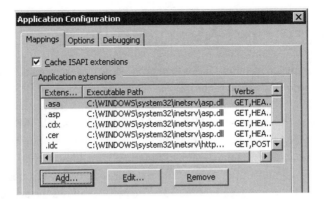

4. Enter the ISAPI or CGI routine that will be used to run files with the extension that is next entered. Keep the default All Verbs, as well as the default selections of Script Engine (which allows the running of scripts) and Verify That File Exists. Click OK.

5. When you are done adding all the extensions you want, click OK in the Application Configuration dialog box, click OK again in the Web Site Properties dialog box, and close the IIS Manager.

Progress Check

1. Is the IIS in Windows XP the same as IIS 6 in Windows Server 2003?

2. What is meant by "the Web"?

3. What is FTP?

4. How is dynamic web content provided?

---

1. No, Windows XP Professional includes a limited version of IIS named IIS 5.1. The version in Windows XP Professional is designed for people developing web sites and for small businesses to bring up a limited intranet site within the business. The limitation in the Professional version is that IIS can service only ten client connections at a time and some of the IIS features are not as capable as they are in the server version.

2. "The Web" is short for the World Wide Web or WWW, which uses HTTP to allow users to publish content to the Web using HTML. Files are placed in folders or subdirectories connected to a web site. These documents can be viewed by using an Internet browser, such as Netscape Navigator or Internet Explorer.

3. FTP services are used to transmit files over the Internet. This is an older protocol that provides a reliable and speedy transfer of files. FTP can be used with a web browser via web-FTP, to speed up downloading large files from normal web sites, as well as using an independent legacy FTP client connected to an FTP server.

4. Dynamic web content is provided through: Active Server Pages (ASP), ASP.NET, Internet Data Connector, Server Side Includes (SSI), Web Distributed Authoring and Versioning (WebDAV), and FrontPage Server Extensions (FPSE).

CRITICAL SKILL
11.4 Customize and Maintain IIS 6

After you have completed installing IIS, it then needs to be customized and maintained. In IIS 4, the tool for managing IIS is called Internet Service Manager (ISM). In IIS 5, the remote web service is still called ISM, but the non-web version of this management service is called Internet Information Services console for the Microsoft Management Console (MMC) (see Module 16 for a discussion of the MMC). In IIS 6, ISM has been renamed Remote Administration (HTML) and can handle the majority of management functions. In addition, the IIS console can be configured to allow administration locally at the server or remotely through an administrator's console or Terminal Services (see Module 13). The console allows the administration of the IIS server components and services, through either the Computer Management console or a separate IIS console, both of which are shown in Figure 11-5.

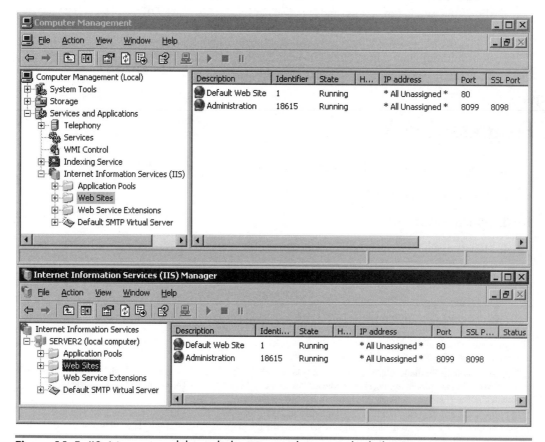

Figure 11-5 IIS 6 is managed through the IIS console seen in both the Computer Management console and its own console.

Start by looking at IIS in the Computer Management console and then in its own console with the following steps:

1. Open the Start menu and choose Administrative Tools | Computer Management. In the left pane, open Services And Applications so that you can see Internet Information Services.

TIP

You can also open Computer Management by right-clicking My Computer and choosing Manage.

2. Once again open the Start menu, and choose Administrative Tools | Internet Information Services (IIS) Manager.

TIP

To easily open IIS in the future, right-drag the IIS icon from the Administrative Tools menu to the desktop or Quick Launch toolbar and choose Copy Here.

3. In either the Computer Management or Internet Information Services console, click Internet Information Services (in the IIS console also click the local server). This gives you access to the IIS components, which vary depending on what was installed, but most importantly include the web sites being hosted. These can be opened for management purposes, as shown in Figure 11-5 (depending on the method of and choices made during installation, the services, such as FTP and SMTP, may or may not appear).

Administer Sites Remotely

Because it may not always be convenient to perform administration tasks on the computer running IIS, several remote administration options are available: Remote Desktop, which is used with Terminal Services, Remote Console, which is used within a LAN, and Remote Administration (HTML), which is used over an intranet or the Internet.

Remote Desktop

You can remotely open the desktop of any computer for which you have permission using Windows Server 2003 Terminal Services, as explained in Module 13, and from that desktop you can open the IIS console on the remote server.

Remote Console

Within the local area network, you can open the IIS console and with the appropriate permissions open the console for any IIS server on the network. Here's how:

1. Open the Start menu and choose Administrative Tools | Internet Information Services (IIS) Manager.

2. Click Add A Computer To The List in the toolbar, enter the computer name, if necessary click Connect As, enter a username and password, and in all cases click OK. The new server will appear in the console.

3. Open the new server and then the folders beneath it as shown in Figure 11-6. When you are done looking at the remote server, close the IIS console.

Remote Administration (HTML)

If you are connecting to your server over the Internet or through a proxy server, you can use the browser-based Remote Administration (HTML) to change properties on your site. If you are on an intranet, you can use either Remote Administration (HTML) or the IIS console in the MMC. Remote Administration (HTML) offers many of the same features as the snap-in, such as starting, stopping, and pausing services, as well as adjusting permissions. Remote Administration (HTML) can't be used to create new web and FTP sites, or to make property changes that require coordination with Windows utilities, such as certificate mapping.

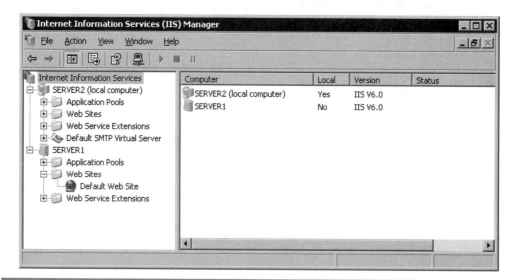

Figure 11-6 Remotely administering an IIS server

NOTE

Remote Administration (HTML) is not installed by default except in the Web Server Edition of Windows Server 2003. To use it with the other editions, you must use the Control Panel's Add Or Remove Programs to install it (see "Install IIS from Add Or Remove Programs" earlier in this module).

Remote Administration (HTML) uses the Administration Web Site to access IIS properties. When IIS is installed, port number 8099 is assigned to this web site for nonsecure access, and port 8098 is assigned for secure access. The site responds to web browser requests for all host, server, or domain names for the computer, provided the port number is appended to the address. For example, you could use any of the following names if they were all assigned to the computer you want to access: http://localhost:8099 (for access from the computer itself), http://_myserver_:8099 (for access from the LAN), or http://www._mydomain_.com:8099 (for access from the Internet).

Remote Administration (HTML) in IIS 6 requires secure access using Secure Sockets Layer (SSL) security. Therefore, to access Remote Administration (HTML), you must enter in the browser Address box **https://localhost:8098** (from the computer itself), **https://_myserver_:8098** (from the LAN), or **https://www._mydomain_.com:8098** (from the Internet). (Note the "s" in "https" to indicate the use of SSL.) If Basic authentication is used, the administrator will be asked for a username and password when the site is reached. Only members of the Windows Administrators group can use the Administration Web Site.

To enable the browser-based Remote Administration (HTML), follow these steps:

1. Open the Start menu, choose Administrative Tools | Computer Management, open Services And Applications | IIS | Web Sites, right-click Administration, and choose Properties. Start the site if it is stopped and note the TCP port number on the Web Site tab, as shown in Figure 11-7.

2. In the Directory Security tab, click Edit under IP Address And Domain Name Restrictions to set permissions for computers that will be used to administer IIS remotely, like this:

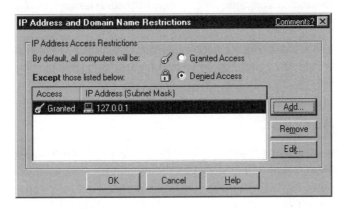

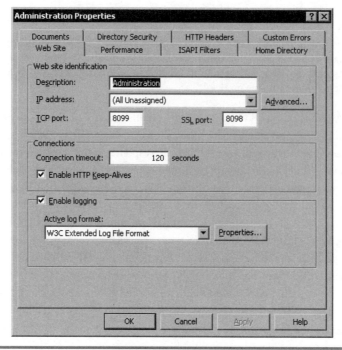

Figure 11-7 The TCP port numbers 8099 and 8098 used with Remote Administration

3. After you make the settings you want, click OK twice to close the two dialog boxes.

4. To start Remote Administration (HTML), open Internet Explorer and in the Address box type **https://**, the name of the server or the domain name, and the assigned SSL port number for the Administration Web Site, for example, **https://*servername*:*SSL port number*/**, and press ENTER or click Go.

5. Click OK to view pages over a secure connection. Enter the username and password for an administrator, and again click OK. Remote Administration (HTML) will open, as you can see in Figure 11-8.

Create Web Sites

Once the server is set up, web sites can be created using web authoring packages, such as Microsoft FrontPage. IIS 6 can manage one site or multiple sites. Each site can appear as a separate location to Internet web surfers. When you install IIS 6, a default web site is set up for you. You can publish your content in the default web site immediately. Most organizations,

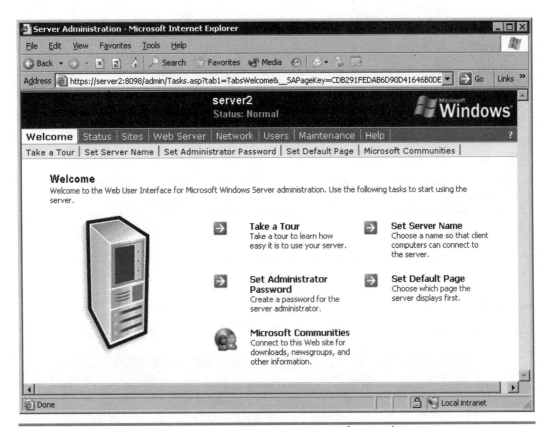

Figure 11-8 Browser-based Remote Administration (HTML) for a web server

though, start with a new site, so that the site can be customized to the needs of the organization. You can add new sites to a computer by launching the Web Site Creation Wizard with the following instructions:

NOTE

The following steps work in either the IIS console, as described here, or the IIS folder in Computer Management.

1. In the IIS console (opened through Start | Administrative Tools | Internet Information Services (IIS) Manager), open the local server, and select the Web Sites folder.

2. Open the Action menu and choose New | Web Site. The Web Site Creation Wizard will open. Click Next.

3. Enter a description for the site and click Next. Enter the IP address to use for the site, or open the drop-down box and select the IP address for the server. Accept the default port address of 80 and leave the Host Header blank. Click Next.

NOTE

Each site must have at least one of the three address components (IP address, TCP port, or host header) unique; otherwise, the site will not be started and you will get an error message telling you about the problem when you try to start it. See "Host Multiple Sites," next in this module.

4. Enter or browse for the path on the server with the home directory containing the HTML files to be displayed when the web site is accessed. Click Next.

5. Enter the permissions that you want to assign. Click Next and then click Finish.

When you are done, the new site will appear on the IIS console like this:

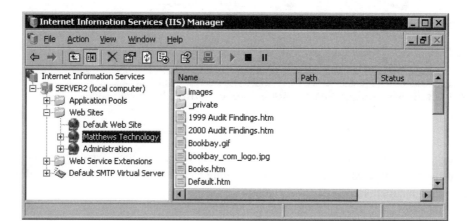

Host Multiple Sites

Multiple web or FTP sites can be hosted simultaneously on a single computer running IIS. This gives the appearance of separate and distinct sites to the web surfer. Each IIS server has the capability to host one or more domain names. For this reason, sites are sometimes referred to as *virtual servers.*

A web site has three identifiers it uses to identify itself on the Internet or an intranet. When queried, it must be able to respond with each of these settings:

- A port number

- An IP address

- A host header name

By changing one of these three identifiers, you can host multiple sites on a single computer:

- **Port numbers**   By using appended port numbers, your site needs only one IP address to host many sites. To reach your site, clients would need to attach a port number (unless using the default port number, 80) at the end of the static IP address. Using this method of hosting multiple sites requires clients to type the actual numerical IP address followed by a port number. Host names or "friendly names" cannot be used.

- **Multiple IP addresses**   To use multiple IP addresses, you must add the host name and its corresponding IP address to your name resolution system, which is DNS in Windows Server 2003. Then, clients need only type the text name in a browser to reach your web site. Multiple IP addresses can be hosted on the same network card.

NOTE

If you are using the multiple IP addresses method of hosting multiple sites on the Internet, you will also need to register the text names with an InterNIC accredited registrar. You can find a list of InterNIC accredited registrars at http://www.internic.net/.

- **Host header names**   Sites can also use host header names with a single static IP address to host multiple sites. As with the preceding method, you would still add the host name to your name resolution system. The difference is that once a request reaches the computer, IIS uses the host name passed in the HTTP header to determine which site a client is requesting. If you are using this method of hosting multiple sites on the Internet, you will also need to register the host header names with InterNIC.

NOTE

Sites cannot use host headers when using SSL. Host headers are part of the encrypted request and cannot be interpreted and routed to the correct site. Be aware that older browsers do not support host header names.

The majority of multiple web site hosting is done with multiple IP addresses.

Web Site Management

Whether your site is on an intranet or the Internet, the principles of publishing information are the same. Here are the steps:

1. Web files are placed in directories on the server.

2. The directories are identified to IIS as belonging to a web site.

3. When a user establishes an HTTP connection to that site, IIS sends requested files to the user's browser.

While the process to store the files is simple, part of the web site manager's job must be to determine how the site is deployed, and how it and the storage will evolve. Most successful web administrators are kept busy accommodating ever-changing web content. Step back a minute from the content and look at the basics of managing a web site's infrastructure, from redirecting requests to dynamically altering web pages.

Define Home Directories

Each web or FTP site must have a home directory, which is where the root site information is stored. As a user logs in to a specific site, IIS knows the home directory and the default first document that all users see when connecting, and it provides that document to the requesting user's browser for translation and display. For example, if your site's Internet domain name is www.mycompany.com, your home directory is C:\website\mysite\, and the default document is Default.htm, then browsers use the URL http://www.mycompany.com, which causes IIS to access your home directory C:\website\mysite\ and transmit the file Default.htm.

On an intranet, if your server name is Marketing, then browsers use the URL http://marketing to access files in your home directory. A default home directory is created when IIS is installed or when a new web site is created. The web site properties determine the location of the files.

Change the Home Directory

When setting up both a web site and an FTP site on the same computer, a different home directory is specified for each service (WWW and FTP). The default home directory for the WWW service is C:\inetpub\wwwroot\. The default home directory for the FTP service is C:\inetpub\ftproot\. The home directory can be changed to any location on the network and can be listed as a URL or a path statement. Here is how to change the home directory:

1. In the IIS console, open the local server and the Web Sites folder, right-click Default Web Site, and open its Properties dialog box.

2. Click the Home Directory tab, and then specify the local path where your home directory is located. You can select:

- A directory located on a hard disk on your computer

- A shared directory located on another computer

- A redirection to a URL (although an FTP directory cannot be redirected this way)

3. In the Local Path text box, type in the path name, share name, or URL (WWW only) of your directory, as shown in Figure 11-9 for the default web site.

Virtual Directories

Virtual directories allow access to files located on a directory not within the home directory. This is a big advantage when trying to access information to be published on an intranet that is located in multiple locations across the network. Using virtual directories is one way to link that information more easily. For the browser, everything seems to be in one location. For the administrator who has to collect everything, it can be easier to store each person's data in a separate virtual directory.

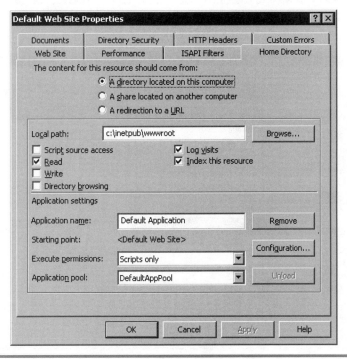

Figure 11-9 Modifying the home directory of a web site

A virtual directory has an alias that the web browser uses to access that directory. As added benefits, using an alias often is more convenient than typing a long path and filename, and the URL for a site does not have to change when the directory changes; only the mapping between the alias and the physical location needs to change.

Create Virtual Directories   Create virtual directories to include those files in your web site located in directories other than the home directory. To use a directory on another computer, specify the directory's Universal Naming Convention (UNC) name in the form *\\servername\drive:\path\filename,* and provide a username and password to use for access permission. Use the following steps to create a virtual directory:

1. In the IIS console, select the web site or FTP site to which you want to add a virtual directory.

2. Open the Action menu (or right-click the site) and choose New | Virtual Directory, as shown in Figure 11-10. The Virtual Directory Creation Wizard will open. Click Next.

3. Enter the alias you want to use, and click Next. Enter or browse to the path that contains the desired files. Click Next.

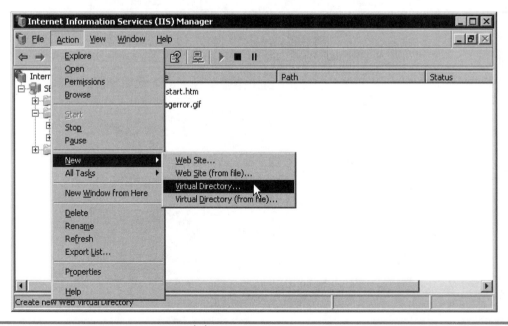

Figure 11-10 Creating a new virtual directory

4. Enter the permissions that you want to give to the people who access these files. Click Next and then click Finish. The virtual directory will appear in the IIS console like this:

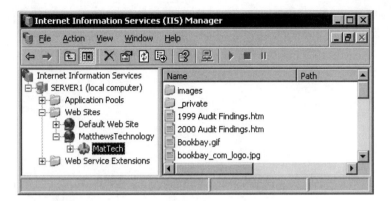

TIP

If you are using NTFS, you can also directly create a virtual directory: right-click a directory in Windows Explorer, choose Sharing and Security, select the Web Sharing tab, select the web site it is to be shared on, click Add, enter the alias name, select the permissions, and click OK twice.

Delete Virtual Directories   To delete a virtual directory, use the following steps:

1. In the IIS console, select the virtual directory you want to delete.

2. Click the Action menu (or right-click the site), select Delete, and click Yes when asked if you are sure you want to delete the item.

NOTE

Deleting a virtual directory does not delete the corresponding physical directory or files.

Troubleshoot IIS

A lot of issues affect the performance of IIS. Problems have three main causes: hardware issues, software issues, and site activity issues. Each of these causes is discussed in the following sections.

When troubleshooting IIS, it is important to have a baseline to compare problems against. To create a baseline for your IIS server, apply a typical network load to the server and log all of the server's performance characteristics using the Performance Monitor (Start | Administrative

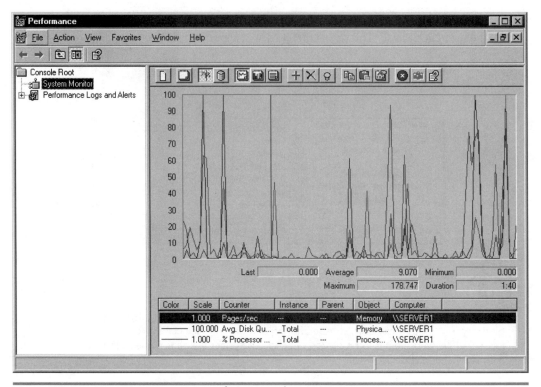

Figure 11-11 Capturing a server's performance characteristics

Tools | Performance), as you see in Figure 11-11. This provides a picture of how the server looks with respect to CPU, memory, hard drive performance, and other measures. Then, when performance is questionable, you can compare the baseline to the current situation to determine where the possible bottleneck is occurring. The issues in the following sections should be analyzed when baselining and later troubleshooting an IIS server.

Memory Allocation

On Windows Server 2003 running IIS, memory allocation must be balanced with all applications and other processes running on the server. Allocating too much memory to any one process or application may have consequences to overall system performance. There are a number of Performance Monitor measures or *counters* that deal with memory issues. To look at these and select the ones you want to use, open the Performance Monitor, right-click in the right pane, and choose Add Counters. In the Performance Object drop-down list, choose Memory. Select the counters listed next one at a time and click Add, as shown in Figure 11-12. You can get more information about each counter by selecting the counter and clicking Explain. The recommended

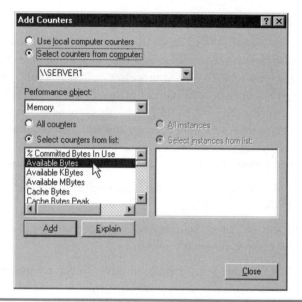

Figure 11-12 Adding counters to the Performance Monitor

counters to monitor and troubleshoot memory allocation issues are as follows (each of these should have a baseline established for it):

● **Memory: Available Bytes**   Measures the total physical memory available to the OS. Available bytes should be tracked over several days to cover several periods of peak activity. You should always have at least 4MB or 5 percent available memory.

● **Memory: Page Faults/sec**   Measures page faults that occur when an application attempts to read from a virtual memory location that is marked "not present." Zero is the optimum measurement. Any measurement higher than zero delays response time. This counter measures both *hard page faults,* which occur when a file has to be retrieved from a hard disk rather than virtual memory, and *soft page faults,* which occur when a resolved page fault, found elsewhere in physical memory, interrupts the processor; soft page faults have much less effect on performance than hard page faults.

NOTE

When describing Performance Monitor's counters, they are normally subdivided into three segments. The first segment lists the performance object (specified in the drop-down list of that name), followed by the counter name, and the instance. Documentation may separate Performance Monitor's sections with colons, for example: Process:Thread Count:Inetinfo, or with forward slashes: Process/Thread Count/Inetinfo.

Processor Threads

If you have web sites that use ASP or ISAPI applications, you will want to baseline and monitor the processor threads used by these applications. IIS 6 sets the default value of ASP worker threads per processor at 25. A quad-processor computer would, therefore, have 100 threads. In IIS 4, you had to change the number of threads per processor value by changing ProcessorThreadMax in the Registry. In IIS 5 and 6, this is handled automatically.

Here are some Performance Monitor counters that will help you monitor threads:

- **Process: Thread Count: Total**   Counts the number of threads currently active.

- **Process: Thread Count: Inetinfo**   Counts the number of threads created by IIS. Compare this to the total count.

- **Thread: % Processor Time: Inetinfo**(thread#)   Measures the percentage of processor time each thread of the Inetinfo process is using.

- **Thread: Context Switches/sec: Inetinfo**(thread#)   Measures the rate of switching from one thread to another. You should monitor this counter to make sure you are not creating so many context switches that the memory being lost to context switching supercedes the benefit of added threads, at which point your performance will decrease rather than improve.

CRITICAL SKILL
11.5 Understand and Manage Windows Media Services

Windows Media Services enables streaming of multimedia content over all types of networks. These networks can range from low-bandwidth, dial-up Internet connections to high-bandwidth local area networks. Windows Media Services is installed from the Add Or Remove Programs control panel in Windows Components Wizard, as previously described in "Install IIS 6." The complete installation includes Multicast And Advertisement Logging Agent, Windows Media Services, Windows Media Services Snap-In, and Windows Media Services Administrator For The Web. The default installation includes only Windows Media Services and Windows Media Services Snap-In, but this discussion assumes that both the Snap-In and the Administrator For The Web are installed to allow management on the local machine, across the network with Terminal Services, and across the Internet.

TIP

Windows Media Services Administrator For The Web requires that IIS 6 be installed and that ASP and SSI be enabled.

NOTE

Streaming audio and video allows the media to be played on the receiving computer as it is being downloaded, instead of waiting for it to completely download before playing it. The Microsoft Windows Media Player, included in Windows 2000/XP/2003, can be used to play streaming audio and video.

Understand Windows Media Services

Utilizing Windows Media Services, a media server can stream audio and video content over the Web. To understand why this is significant, it helps to understand the way a typical HTTP session works. First, a web browser logs on to the web server. The web server recognizes the URL and downloads the appropriate information to the browser. Once the web pages are downloaded from the site, the browser displays them. When the user clicks another link, the browser requests another download. This works great for small file sizes, such as a web page, but video and audio files are so large that waiting for files to download in this way is like waiting for paint to dry. Windows Media Services uses streaming technology to enable you to load and play the audio or video while it is still downloading. This greatly increases the satisfaction of the user who is downloading the file.

Stream Methods

There are two ways to stream audio and video. One uses a web server alone; the other separates the web tasks from the streaming media tasks. The second method utilizes a media server to stream audio or video, in conjunction with a web server used to download the rest of the web information.

Stream with a Web Server   The server sends the audio and video files in the same fashion as it would send any type of file. The streaming client stores, or *buffers,* a small amount of the audio or video stream and then starts playing it while continuing the download. Buffering theoretically allows the media to continue playing uninterruptedly during periods of network congestion. In fact, it is normal for it to get interrupted on a 56 Kbps connection. The client retrieves data as fast as the web server, network, and client connection allow.

Stream with a Media Server   With a media server, the first step is to compress the media file and copy it to a specialized streaming media server (such as Microsoft Windows Media Services). Next, a reference is made on the web page so that IIS knows when and where to retrieve the streaming data for the page. Then, data is sent to the client such that the content is delivered at the same rate as the compressed audio and video streams. The server and the client stay in close touch during the delivery process, and the streaming media server can respond to any feedback from the client.

Ask the Expert

Q: If I can stream media from a normal web server such as IIS, why do I need a streaming media server such as a Windows Media server?

A: A lot depends on what you want to do and what kind of files you have. Only certain media file formats support the type of progressive playback used by a normal web server. Microsoft's Advanced Streaming Format (ASF) is one of them. Also, with a normal web server and a normal web browser the receiving of the file has to perfectly keep up with the sending of the file except for the small buffering that is done. Whenever the sending gets ahead of the receiving, which happens quite often, some of the media will be lost. A streaming media server does a much better job of managing this.

Stream with Windows Media Services   Designed specifically for the task of delivering live or on-demand streaming media rather than many small HTML and image files, a Windows Media Services server offers many advantages over standard web servers:

- More efficient network throughput
- Better audio and video quality to the user
- Support for advanced features
- Cost-effective scalability to a large number of users
- Protection of content copyright
- Multiple delivery options

Windows Media Services, diagrammatically shown in Figure 11-13, automatically switches to the appropriate protocol, so no client-side configuration is necessary.

Manage Windows Media Services

Once Windows Media Services is installed, you can configure and manage it on an ongoing basis directly through the Windows Media Services administration console or through the web administration. Look at Windows Media administration console by opening the Start menu and choosing Administrative Tools | Windows Media Services. The Windows Media Services console will open. Open the local server and click the Getting Started tab to display the windows shown in Figure 11-14. The links open Help files explaining how to accomplish various functions, while the buttons perform specific functions. Start by taking the Windows Media Services tour.

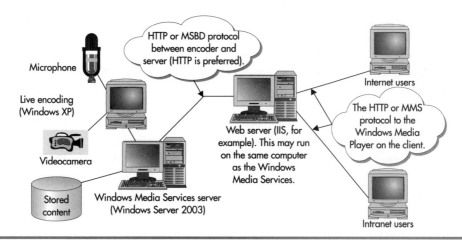

Figure 11-13 Windows Media Services interacts with a web server to provide streaming content to a client's browser.

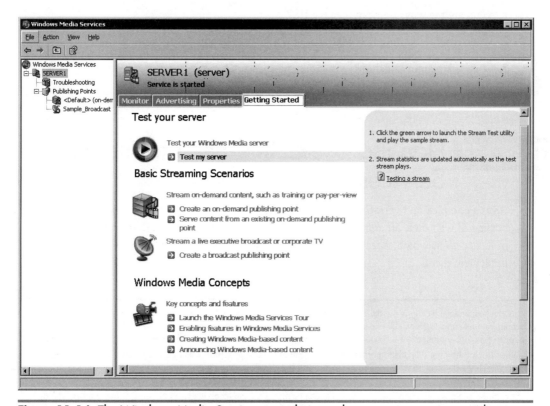

Figure 11-14 The Windows Media Services console is used to manage servers providing streaming audio and video.

This allows you to test your streaming server, to set up streaming on demand, and to learn about the key Windows media concepts, including taking a tour of Windows Media Services. When you are done, close the Windows Media Services console.

In addition to the Windows Media Services console, you can manage Windows Media Services with the Web Administrator, if you have installed it. Do that next by opening the Start menu and choosing Administrative Tools | Windows Media Services (Web). The Windows Media Services Web Administrator will open. You may be told that SSL is not available on your web site. If you wish, at a later time you can learn how to implement SSL by clicking Using Secure Sockets Layer. For now, click Administer The Local Windows Media Server. Here you see a windows very similar to the Windows Media Services console, although the Getting Started is more limited.

Progress Check

1. What are the ways you can manage IIS?

2. When troubleshooting IIS, what is it important to already have?

3. What is streaming media?

Project 11 Plan the Use of Internet Information Services

IIS is a complex and versatile capability within Windows Server 2003 that provides for the hosting of web sites, among other services. This project will help you look at which aspects of it, as well as which aspects of Windows Media Services, you want to use and how to implement them.

---

1. IIS can be managed locally using the Internet Information Services console, which you can open directly or through Computer Management. IIS can be managed remotely using Remote Administration (HTML), using the IIS console, which can open a remote administrator's console, or using Terminal Services to open the IIS console on a remote computer.

2. When troubleshooting IIS, it is important to have a baseline to compare problems against. To create a baseline for your IIS server, apply a typical network load to the server and log all of the server's performance characteristics using the Performance Monitor.

3. Streaming media is audio and video content that can be played on the receiving computer as it is being downloaded, instead of waiting for it to completely download before playing.

Step by Step

1. Determine which information delivery services provided by IIS will be used:

   a. World Wide Web (WWW) service using the Hypertext Transfer Protocol (HTTP) to publish web content

   b. File Transfer Protocol (FTP) service to transfer files

   c. Simple Mail Transfer Protocol (SMTP) service to handle e-mail

   d. Network News Transfer Protocol (NNTP) service to host newsgroups

2. Determine which means will be used to manage IIS:

   a. Locally, using IIS Manager via the IIS console

   b. Locally, using IIS Manager via the Computer Management console

   c. Remotely, using the local IIS console with a remote server

   d. Remotely, using Terminal Services and a remote IIS console

   e. Locally, or remotely using Remote Administration (HTML)

3. Determine which of the web support services will be used:

   a. Background Intelligent Transfer Service (BITS) to handle throttling and restarting data transfers; add a BITS management console

   b. FrontPage Server Extensions (FPSE) to support the use of FrontPage web authoring

   c. Internet printing to support using a printer over the Internet

4. Determine which means of content creation and automation will be used:

   a. Hypertext Markup Language (HTML) for basic web creation

   b. Extensible Markup Language (XML) for web creation and integration

   c. Active Server Pages (ASP) and ASP.NET for dynamic web content

   d. Web Distributed Authoring and Versioning (WebDAV) to manage the creation and maintenance of web sites

   e. Server Side Includes (SSI) for dynamic web content

   f. Internet Data Connector (IDC) to connect to and use databases

5. Determine if IIS will be installed by using:

   a. Manage Your Server

   b. Add Or Remove Programs

(continued)

11

Internet Information Services Version 6

Project 11

Plan the Use of Internet Information Services

6. Determine how existing hosted web sites will migrate to IIS 6:

   a. Migrate to a clean Windows Server 2003 installation

   b. Migrate to a mirror of an existing web server

   c. Upgrade an existing web server

7. Determine if Windows Server 2003 has been set up for IIS:

   a. TCP/IP has been installed and properly configured

   b. DNS has been installed and properly configured

   c. NTFS is being used as the server's file system

8. Determine which of IIS's security precautions to enable:

   a. Which of the dynamic web content options will be used:

      i. ASP and ASP.NET

      ii. FrontPage Server Extensions

      iii. Server Side Includes

      iv. WebDAV services

      v. Internet Data Connector

   b. Mapping application extensions that will be allowed to run

   c. Allowing direct editing of the IIS metabase configuration file

9. Determine how multiple web sites will be uniquely identified using:

   a. A port number

   b. An IP address

   c. A host header name

10. Determine for each web site hosted:

   a. The name of the site

   b. The unique IP address, port number, or host header

   c. The path to the home directory

   d. Whether to allow anonymous access to the site

   e. The permissions to allow users of the site

   f. Any virtual directories to attach to the site

11. Determine the baseline performance of the IIS server by logging, while under reasonable load, the following performance counters:

a. Memory: Available Bytes

b. Memory: Page Faults/sec

c. Process: Thread Count: Total

d. Process: Thread Count: Inetinfo

e. Thread: %Processor Time: Inetinfo(thread#)

f. Thread: Context Switches/sec: Inetinfo(thread#)

12. Determine how streaming media will be delivered:

a. With a normal web server

b. With a media server

c. With Windows Media Server

Project Summary

IIS is an extremely capable web server that provides a number of services and several ways to manage them. To use it well requires more than a little study and a bit of finesse.

Module 11 Mastery Check

1. What are some of the services that IIS 6 can provide?

2. What is the primary function of IIS, and what language and protocol is that function based upon?

3. What is Kerberos?

4. How is IIS managed?

5. What are the ways that IIS can be installed with Windows Server 2003?

6. What are the primary considerations in choosing a migration path?

7. What is IIS 6's default security posture, and what elements are enabled and what are disabled?

8. How do you differentiate among the sites when hosting several of them?

9. What are the home and virtual directories for a web site, and how do they differ?

10. What are some of the advantages that Windows Media Services server offers over standard web servers?

Module 12

Virtual Private Networking

12.1 Understand VPN

Virtual private networking (VPN) uses an insecure public network to handle secure private networking. Most commonly today, that means connecting to or extending a LAN using the Internet, which replaces leased lines and/or dedicated value added networks (VANs) at a considerable savings. VPN allows a traveling worker to connect to and utilize an organization's LAN by first connecting to and utilizing the Internet. The key ingredient in VPN is security. VPN allows one to use a public network with a high degree of certainty that the data sent across it will be secure. You can think of VPN as a secure pipe through the Internet connecting computers on either end, as you can see in Figure 12-1. Information is able to travel through the pipe securely and without regard to the fact that it is part of the Internet. This concept of a pipe though the Internet is called *tunneling*. The secure "tunnel" is achieved by first encrypting the data, including all its addressing and sequencing information (where the individual piece of data, called a "datagram," fits in a longer message), and then encapsulating or wrapping

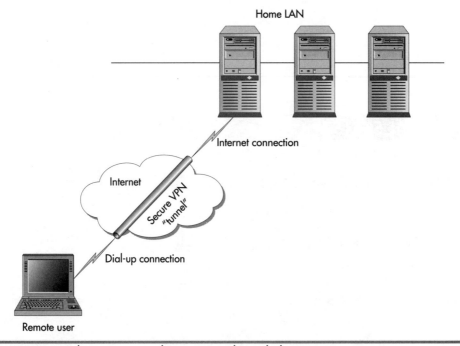

Figure 12-1 Virtual private networking, a pipe through the Internet

that data in a new Internet Protocol (IP) header with routing and addressing information, as shown next. The outer package can then weave its way through the servers and routers of the Internet without the inner datagram ever being exposed.

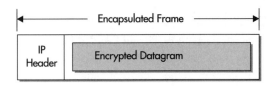

VPN replaces both leased lines between facilities and the need for long-distance dial-up connections. For example, before VPN a company needed a leased line between the headquarters and a branch office in another city. With VPN, each office just needs a local, probably high-speed, connection to the Internet, which is then used with VPN to transmit information between the offices. In another example, before VPN a traveling worker would make a long-distance call into a remote access server to connect to the company's LAN, incurring a long-distance charge. With VPN, the worker places a local call to an Internet service provider (ISP) to connect to the Internet, which is then used with VPN to connect to the company's LAN. In both cases, significant cost savings are achieved.

VPN establishes a secure pathway across the Internet from a client connected to the Internet on one end to a server connected to the Internet on the other. This is called a *point-to-point* connection. Once the connection is made between the two points, it conveys information as though a private line were being used, without regard to the many servers and routers in the path and with a high degree of security. This is done in Windows Server 2003 and Windows XP with one of two protocols:

- Point-to-Point Tunneling Protocol (PPTP)
- Layer Two Tunneling Protocol (L2TP)

CRITICAL SKILL
12.2 Use the Point-to-Point Tunneling Protocol

PPTP was originally developed by Microsoft to do VPN with Windows NT 4 and Windows 9*x*/Me. PPTP incorporates and extends the Point-to-Point Protocol (PPP) and the Microsoft Point-to-Point Encryption (MPPE), is the simpler to install of the two VPN protocols, and is an industry standard (RFC 2637). See Module 7, under "Implement Networking Protocols" for a discussion of networking standards documents called Requests for Comments (or RFCs).

NOTE

If you want to use VPN with Windows NT 4 or Windows 9x/Me, you have to use PPTP.

The Point-to-Point Protocol

PPP, the foundation protocol for both PPTP and L2TP, which is used in many areas of the Internet, including many e-mail connections, is an industry standard defined in several RFCs, but primarily 1661. PPP operates at the second or Data Link layer of the Open Systems Interconnection (OSI) model (see Module 7, under "The OSI Model") and provides the functions of compressing and encapsulating the information, as well as authenticating the client and the server. PPP is built upon two other protocols, the Link Control Protocol (LCP) for handling the connections and authentication, and the Network Control Protocol (NCP) for handling the compression and encapsulation. The networking protocol being used (TCP/IP, IPX/SPX, or AppleTalk) determines the properties of NCP and how it does its job.

PPP defines the building of a *frame* that takes the datagram built at the third or Networking layer of the OSI model (see Module 7, "IP" under "Implement Networking Protocols"), compresses and encapsulates it, and adds address and control information, so it looks like this:

Starting delimiter 1 byte	Address 1 byte	Frame control 1 byte	Network protocol 1 byte	Data variable	FCS 2 bytes	Ending delimiter 1 byte

The PPP frame

- **Starting and ending delimiters** mark the start and end of the frame.

- **Address** is the destination address.

- **Frame control** is a sequence number to maintain the proper order.

- **Network protocol** is the protocol (IP, IPX, or AppleTalk) being used.

- **Data** is the actual datagram being transferred.

- **FCS** is the frame check sequence used for error checking.

In PPP, LCP establishes the connection between the server and the client and then negotiates between the two computers to determine the type of authentication to be used, as well as several of the link parameters, such as the maximum frame length. NCP is used to determine the networking protocol to be used and then, based on that, how the datagram will be compressed and encapsulated.

Although PPP has a prominent role in authentication, it doesn't actually carry out the authentication; that function is performed by one of several authentication protocols. VPN and Windows Server 2003 use two authentication protocols, each with several variants. These are:

- Challenge Handshake Authentication Protocol (CHAP)

- Extensible Authentication Protocol (EXP)

Challenge Handshake Authentication Protocol

CHAP, the most common and widely supported of the two primary authentication methods, depends on using a password known to both the client and the server in the authentication. (CHAP is defined in several RFCs, primarily 1994.) Unlike in earlier authentication methods, though, the password is not transmitted during authentication. Instead, the server sends out a unique string of characters called the "challenge string." The client uses its password and the challenge string to compute a Message Digest hash and send it back to the server. The server also computes the hash according to its knowledge of the password and the string it sent and compares that hash to the one sent by the client. If the two hashes are the same, the client is authenticated. A *hash* is an algorithm or function that is very easy to calculate if you know the originating data, but it is very difficult if not impossible to compute the data from the hash.

Microsoft has developed two variants of CHAP: MS-CHAP and MS-CHAP v2, which are designed to work with Windows 9*x*, Me, 2000, and XP, as well as with Windows Server 2003, and are what is used with VPN. MS-CHAP primarily differs from CHAP by using a different Message Digest hash algorithm, by encrypting the challenge and the response, and by not requiring that the password be stored in a reversibly encrypted form. MS-CHAP v2 primarily differs from MS-CHAP by being more secure with stronger encryption keys, by authenticating both the client to the server (as in CHAP and MS-CHAP) and the server to the client, and by providing separate encryption keys for sending and receiving information.

Extensible Authentication Protocol

If in place of a password a smart card or other device is used for identification, then EAP is used for authentication. EAP, which is a networking standard defined in RFC 2284, is a general framework that allows an arbitrary authentication method to be negotiated and used. With Windows Server 2003, VPN, and smart cards, EAP-TLS (Transport Layer Security) is the protocol of choice. EAP-TLS causes certificates stored both on the server and on a smart card at the client to be exchanged, and, if the certificates are accepted, to authenticate both the client and the server. In the process, shared encryption keys can be exchanged, as well as other information. EAP-TLS provides a very high level of mutual authentication.

Microsoft Point-to-Point Encryption

Once a PPTP connection has been made, the end points authenticated, and the details of the transmission negotiated—all the functions of PPP—the data to be transmitted must be encrypted so that it is secure on the Internet. That is the function of MPPE. MPPE can provide three levels of encryption using a 40-bit, 56-bit, or 128-bit private key (see Module 17 for a description of private and public keys and how they are used in encryption). The keys are generated as part of the authentication process in MS-CHAP, MS-CHAP v2, or EAP-TLS, so one of these authentication methods must be used.

CRITICAL SKILL
12.3 Use the Layer Two Tunneling Protocol

While Microsoft was developing PPTP, Cisco was developing a protocol called Layer Two Forwarding (L2F) to do VPN. This has been combined with PPTP to come up with the second protocol supported by Microsoft in Windows 2000/XP/Server 2003, L2TP. L2TP has become a recent industry standard, primarily defined in RFC 2661, and although it is the more secure and robust of the two VPN protocols, it has many similarities with PPTP, primarily that it makes full use of and extends PPP for authentication, compression, and encapsulation. Unlike PPTP, though, L2TP, as it has been implemented in the latest versions of Windows, uses Internet Protocol Security (IPSec) to handle encryption in place of MPPE (see RFC 2888). This is what makes L2TP more robust and secure.

NOTE

In Windows Server 2003, L2TP is designed to run over IP networks such as the Internet and does not directly support running over X.25, Frame Relay, or ATM networks.

Internet Protocol Security

IPSec is actually a set of authentication and security protocols that can operate without interference and in addition to other protocols being used. Thus L2TP can use the authentication services in PPP and then additionally use the authentication that is part of IPSec. As a result of this, IPSec can provide unbroken security over several segments of a network that, for example, begins on a private network, goes out over a public network, and then returns to a private network, so long as all the networks are using IP. IPSec accomplishes this by doing its authentication and encryption at the third or Network layer of the OSI model, ahead of PPP, which operates at the second or Data Link layer, as shown in Figure 12-2. IPSec can use either a 56-bit Data Encryption Standard (DES) key or Triple DES (3DES), which uses three 56-bit DES keys for the very highest security.

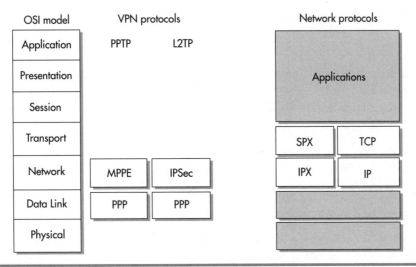

Figure 12-2 The OSI model, VPN protocols, and network protocols

CRITICAL SKILL

12.4 Prepare for VPN

To set up VPN, you need to have both networking and Remote Access Service (RAS) set up and running. With that done, setting up VPN is just an enabling and configuration task. Setting up networking is described in Module 8, and Module 10 discusses setting up RAS. Here these topics will be briefly reviewed, but you should refer to the primary modules if you have questions about these topics.

NOTE

It is very important that you know RAS is operating correctly before setting up VPN. Too often, a problem in RAS is the cause for VPN to not operate correctly.

Check Networking and RAS Hardware

Networking and RAS hardware includes at a minimum a network interface card (NIC) and probably also a communications interface device, such as a modem; an ISDN (Integrated Services Digital Network) or DSL (digital subscriber line) adapter; or a router on the network with a connection to a DSL, T-1, or frame-relay communications line. Assuming that this hardware has been installed in accordance with the manufacturer's instructions, then it was most likely automatically set up in Windows Server 2003 either when the operating system (OS) was installed or when the hardware was installed and detected by the OS. Here, you should only need to make sure that the correct driver has been installed and that the device is operating properly. You can do both of these through the Device Manager and these instructions:

1. Open the Start menu, choose Control Panel | System, click the Hardware tab, and click Device Manager.

2. Open the local computer and Network Adapters, and double-click the NIC that you want to check. The Properties dialog box for that device will open as shown in Figure 12-3.

3. If the device is operating properly, you should see a statement to that effect, as you can see in Figure 12-3, in which case, click OK to close the Properties dialog box.

4. If the NIC is not operating properly, you may be given some indication as to what is the problem. If you are told there is a driver problem, open the Driver tab and click Update Driver. If there is a resource-sharing problem, open the Resources tab and see if it indicates

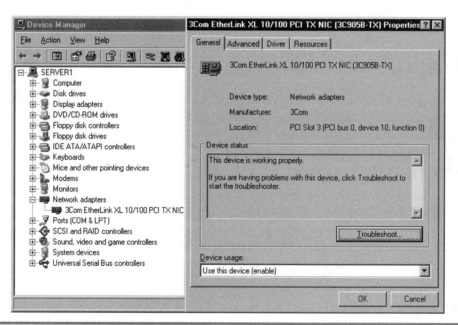

Figure 12-3 Checking to see if a NIC is operating properly

where the problem is; if so, click Change Setting and make the necessary change. If there is some other problem or if you were not able to cure a driver or resource problem, go back to the General tab, click Troubleshoot, and follow the instructions. Module 8 has more detail on setting up a NIC.

5. When you have the NIC properly installed, close its Properties dialog box and, if present, open the Properties dialog box for the communications device in the computer. Again you should see a summary device status. If the device is a modem, open the Diagnostics tab and click Query Modem. After waiting a few moments, you should see a list of commands and responses. It does not matter if you get "Command Not Supported" so long as you get other normal-looking responses, such as you see here (Module 11 has more detail on setting up a modem):

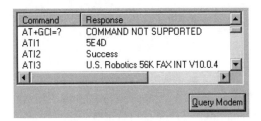

6. If the device is operating properly, click OK to close the Properties dialog box. Otherwise, use a procedure similar to Step 4 to isolate and correct the problem(s). When you are done, close the Properties dialog box, the Device Manager window, and the System Properties dialog box.

Although you may think that hardware is not a problem, it is wise to check it out and eliminate it as a possible reason VPN is not working.

Configure Networking

When Plug and Play networking hardware is installed or when Windows Server 2003 is installed and detects Plug and Play networking hardware, the networking components of Windows Server 2003 are automatically installed. Since you have already detected that your hardware is installed and operating, it is highly likely that networking is as well. Check that here:

1. Open the Start menu, choose Control Panel | Network Connections, and observe if you have a Local Area Connection. If so, networking has been set up on the server you are looking at.

2. Click Local Area Connection. The Status dialog box should open and show Connected with a significant activity of bytes sent and received, like this:

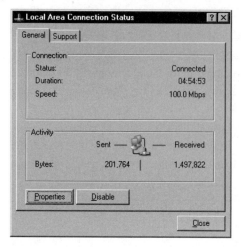

3. Click Properties. The Properties dialog box should open and show the components set up for the connection. These should include, as a minimum, File And Printer Sharing For Microsoft Networks and Internet Protocol (TCP/IP), and probably Client For Microsoft Networks, as you can see in Figure 12-4.

4. Double-click Internet Protocol (TCP/IP) to open its Properties dialog box. What you see here will depend on the role of this computer in the network. At least one server must have a fixed or static IP address (with Use The Following IP Address selected) and be the DHCP (Dynamic Host Configuration Protocol) and DNS (Domain Name System) server.

5. Close Internet Protocol (TCP/IP) Properties, Local Area Connection Properties, and Local Area Connection Status.

6. If you found in Step 4 that this server did have a fixed IP address, then check DHCP by opening the Start menu, choosing Administrative Tools | DHCP, and opening the local server. You should see that the server listing includes an upward-pointing green arrow (saying the service is enabled) and at least one scope, like this:

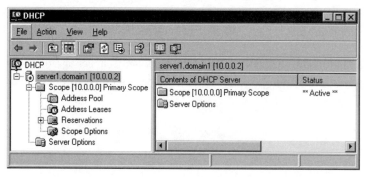

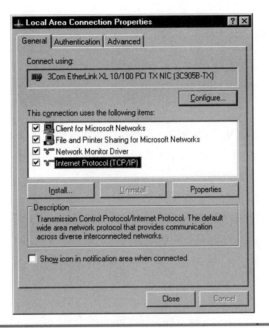

Figure 12-4 Checking the network connection properties

7. Close the DHCP window. If any of the preceding steps did not produce the expected results or some problem was observed, go back to Module 8 and review setting up a network.

8. If you are using Active Directory, open Start | Administrative Tools | Active Directory Users And Computers, open the local domain, and then open Users. Double-click the user you want to allow to dial in (or create a new user if needed—see Module 9), click the Dial-In tab, click Allow Access, and click OK. Close the Active Directory Users And Computers window.

NOTE

For RAS and especially for VPN, you need to have a static IP address assigned by an Internet authority. In other words, you need an IP address that is acceptable across the Internet, not one, such as 10.0.0.2, that you assigned yourself.

Set Up Remote Access Service

RAS is installed by default as a part of installing Windows Server 2003, but it is not enabled. So setting up RAS is simply enabling and configuring it. To do this, you must have administrative privileges and use these steps:

1. Open the Start menu and choose Administrative Tools | Routing And Remote Access to open the Routing And Remote Access console or window. The local server should have a downward-pointing red arrow if it is not enabled, or an upward-pointing green arrow if it is.

2. Select the local server (the computer you are working on), open the Action menu, and choose Configure And Enable Routing And Remote Access. The Routing And Remote Access Server Setup Wizard will open. Click Next.

3. Select Remote Access (Dial-Up Or VPN) and click Next. Choose Dial-Up (make sure it works before choosing VPN) and click Next. Select Automatically Assign IP Addresses, since you do have a DHCP server.

4. Click Next. Choose whether to use Remote Authentication Dial-In User Service (RADIUS) authentication for several RASs. It provides another level of authentication that you may or may not need. Click Next.

5. Choose whether you want to see the Help pages on managing a remote access server, and then click Finish. You are told that to support the relaying of client DHCP messages, the DHCP Relay Agent must be configured. Click OK. If your DHCP server is on the same subnet as the RAS server, which is normally the case, you do not need a DHCP Relay Agent.

When RAS has been enabled and configured as is done with the preceding steps, your console should look like this:

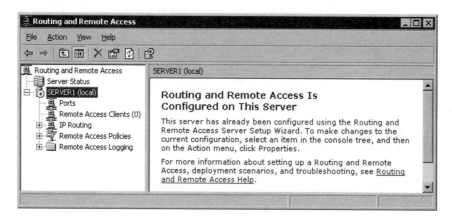

Test RAS

It is very tempting at this point to jump ahead and set up VPN; after all, that is the objective here. But it is prudent to make sure RAS is working properly before going ahead. To test RAS, you must have a dial-up connection on a client. It is assumed that the client is running Windows XP Professional, that the server is Windows Server 2003, and that both have a communications connection that is already installed and running possibly using the modem (Module 11 has instructions for installing a modem).

Set Up a Dial-Up Connection

Quickly set a dial-up connection on a client with these steps:

 NOTE

Your client's user interface may be different if it uses the Classic or other look available in Windows XP Professional.

1. On the client computer, open the Start menu. If you have an existing network or Internet connection, choose Connect To | Show All Connections. If you don't have an existing connection, click Control Panel and double-click Network Connections. In the Network Connections dialog box that opens, click Create A New Connection in the Network Tasks panel to open the New Connection Wizard. Click Next.

2. Click Connect To The Network At My Workplace and then click Next. Select Dial-Up Connection and click Next. Enter a name for the connection and once more click Next.

3. Enter the phone number of the server including, if necessary, "1" and the area code, then click Next. If you have multiple profiles on the client, determine if you want the connection for Anyone's Use or for My Use Only and click Next. If you want a shortcut to this connection on the desktop, select that option and then click Finish. A Connect dialog box will open and a new connection icon will appear in the Network Connections window. Also, if you chose it, a new connection icon will appear on the desktop, as shown on the left.

Server1

Use RAS

With a dial-up connection set up on the client and a remote access server set up and enabled on the server, you can use RAS with these steps:

1. If the Connect dialog box is still open from the last step, skip to Step 2; otherwise, log on to the dial-up client with a username and password that can be authenticated by RAS.

Then, on the client, open the Start menu, choose Connect To, and select the dial-up connection you want to use. The Connect dialog box opens.

2. Enter the appropriate username, the password, and possibly the domain, and click Dial. You will see messages stating that the number you entered is being dialed, that the username and password are being checked, that the computer is being registered on the network, and then that the connection is complete. Click OK. The connection icon will appear on the right of the taskbar.

3. Test the connection in the client by opening Windows Explorer; My Network Places | Entire Network | Microsoft Windows Network; and finally the domains or workgroups, computers, and shares that you want to access. If you can see these shares, the remote access connection is working.

4. Test the connection in the server by opening the Start menu and choosing Administrative Tools | Routing And Remote Access. In the Routing And Remote Access console, open the local server and click Remote Access Clients. You should see that at least one client is connected, like this:

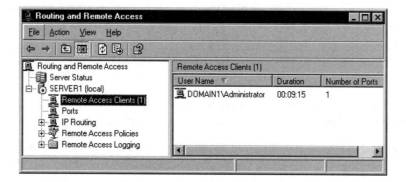

5. When you are done testing the RAS connection, you can terminate it by double-clicking the connection icon in the taskbar of the client and then clicking Disconnect in the dialog box that opens.

With RAS fully accessible from a remote dial-up client, you know that all but the unique VPN components are fully operational on the two computers that you tested. If your dial-up RAS connection did not work, look back at Module 10, which discusses this in more detail.

Ask the Expert

Q: RAS works rather well for me, why get mixed up in the complexities of VPN?

A: There are two reasons: reduced cost and improved security. Under many circumstances, RAS requires either leased telephone lines or long-distance charges. VPN, on the other hand, uses the Internet, which in most circumstances has no additional cost for its use. RAS generally uses no security and yet often uses public phone lines and switches. VPN uses very sophisticated security techniques that make it very hard for an intruder to misuse the information being transmitted. You, of course, are the only one who can determine the actual cost and value of the security.

Progress Check

1. What are the two protocols used by VPN?

2. What is the primary difference between the two VPN protocols?

3. What other two services do you need to have installed in order to set up VPN?

CRITICAL SKILL
12.5 Set Up a VPN Server

VPN, like RAS, has both client and server components. The most common setup, and the one described here, is for the client (assumed to be running Windows XP Professional) to have a dial-up connection to an ISP, and for traffic to travel across the Internet to the server (assumed to be running Windows Server 2003), where a VPN termination is active and allows access to the LAN. See how this is done, first in terms of configuring the server and then the setup that is needed on the client.

---

1. The two protocols used by VPN are Point-to-Point Tunneling Protocol (PPTP) and Layer Two Tunneling Protocol (L2TP).

2. Both PPTP and L2TP use PPP to do the encapsulating and transmitting of data over a network at the second layer of the OSI model. But, unlike PPTP, L2TP uses Internet Protocol Security (IPSec) to handle encryption in place of MPPE at the third layer of the OSI model. This is what makes L2TP more robust and secure.

3. To set up VPN, you need to have both networking and Remote Access Service (RAS) set up and running.

Reconfigure RAS

VPN requires that you have RAS configured for VPN, so the following instructions assume that you have gone through the steps in the previous sections and must reconfigure RAS:

1. Open the Start menu and choose Administrative Tools | Routing And Remote Access. Right-click the local server and choose Disable Routing And Remote Access. Answer Yes, you really want to delete the RAS server.

2. With the local server still selected, open the Action menu and choose Configure And Enable Routing And Remote Access. The Routing And Remote Access Server Setup Wizard will open. Click Next.

3. If you have two NICs in your server (one for VPN and one for the LAN), choose Remote Access (Dial-Up Or VPN), as shown in Figure 12-5; otherwise, choose Custom Configuration. Then click Next. Select VPN Access and click Next. If it appears, accept the default of automatically assigning IP addresses using your DHCP server. Then click Next.

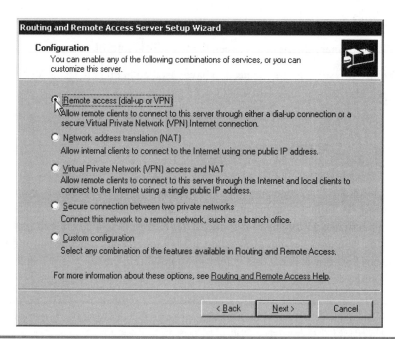

Figure 12-5 Setting up RAS for VPN

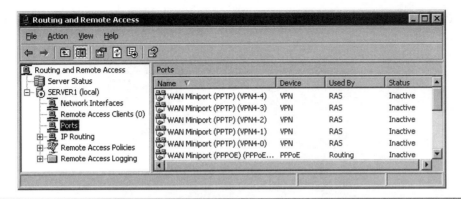

Figure 12-6 RAS set up with VPN ports

12

Virtual Private Networking

4. If offered the choice, decide if you want to use Remote Authentication Dial-In User Service (RADIUS) to manage the authentication of several RAS servers. If you have only one RAS server, the answer is obvious; if you have several, then RADIUS would be worthwhile. Click Next.

5. You are told that you have successfully completed the Routing And Remote Access Server Setup Wizard. Click Finish. You may be told that to support the relaying of client DHCP messages, the DHCP Relay Agent must be configured. If so, click OK. If your DHCP server is on the same subnet as your VPN server, you do not need a DHCP Relay Agent. RAS will be configured for VPN. You are asked if you want to start the service. Click Yes.

6. In the Routing And Remote Access console, open the local server and click Ports. Here there are initially 128 PPTP and 128 L2TP ports set up for VPN, some of which are shown in Figure 12-6.

At this point, you need to choose which of the two VPN protocols you want to use and then configure that protocol.

Configure a PPTP Server

PPTP is the easier of the two VPN protocols to set up and can be used with a wide range of clients, including Windows 95 (with upgrade 1.3 to Dial-Up Networking), Windows 98, Windows Me, Windows NT 4, Windows 2000, and Windows XP, but it provides a lower level of security. You can configure PPTP and adjust the number of its ports with these steps:

1. Right-click Ports in the left pane of the Routing And Remote Access console and click Properties. The Ports Properties dialog box will open.

2. Click WAN Miniport (PPTP) and then click Configure. Configure Device – WAN Miniport (PPTP) opens, like this:

3. Given that you are using VPN over the Internet and you don't want the client to dial and come in through the server's modem, uncheck the Demand-Dial Routing Connections (Inbound And Outbound) check box. Set a reasonable number of PPTP ports that you will be using and click OK. Click Yes, you want to reduce the number of ports (if you do), click OK to close Ports Properties, and close the Routing And Remote Access console.

TIP

At this point, it is generally a good idea to jump down to "Set Up a VPN Client," set up the client, and try out the PPTP connection as described there. When PPTP is working, you can come back and try L2TP, which causes most people (including me) more problems.

Configure a L2TP Server

L2TP can be used only with Windows 2000, Windows XP, and Windows Server 2003, but it provides a higher degree of data integrity, data authentication, and data confidentiality. It also is more difficult to set up because of the need to configure the additional security and authentication infrastructure. Because L2TP uses IPSec and the most common form of IPSec uses computer certificates for authentication, you must have a certification authority active on the network and have it set up to automatically issue certificates to VPN computers. The first steps, then, are to install or confirm the presence of a certificate authority and to assure that it is properly set up. Then the filters that are an integral part of IPSec can be configured, and finally L2TP over IPSec can be selected and its ports set up.

Install and Configure a Certificate Authority

If you are not sure if a configuration authority is installed on your LAN or if you know it is not, follow these instructions to check out or install and configure it (you must be logged on as an administrator or domain administrator):

1. Open the Start menu, choose Control Panel | Add Or Remove Programs, and select Add/Remove Windows Components.

2. Select Certificate Services if it isn't already checked (if it is, Certificate Services is already installed on this computer and you can jump to the next section). Click Yes when you are told that if you install Certificate Services, you will not be able to rename the computer, and then click Next.

3. Select the type of certificate authority (CA) to be installed, as shown in Figure 12-7. Choose:

   - **Enterprise Root CA** if you are using Active Directory (AD) and this is the first CA in the network

   - **Stand-Alone Root CA** if you are not using AD and it is the first CA in the network

   - **Enterprise Subordinate CA** if you are using Active Directory (AD) and this is not the first CA in the network

   - **Stand-Alone Subordinate CA** if you are not using AD and it is not the first CA in the network

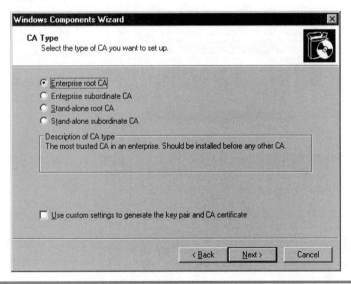

Figure 12-7 Choosing the type of certificate authority

4. Select Use Custom Settings to consider changing the settings for the generation of key pairs and CA certificates and click Next.

The custom settings allow you to select the cryptographic service provider (CSP) that you want to use, the hash algorithm (explained under Challenge Handshake Authentication Protocol earlier in this module), the key length, and whether you want to use an existing key. Under most circumstances, except if you are using smart cards, you want to leave the defaults shown in Figure 12-8. If you are using smart cards, you may need to select a CSP that is used by the smart card.

5. Click Next, enter the name for the CA, and click Next again. You are shown where the certificate database and log will be stored. Once more click Next, and click Yes to temporarily stop Internet Information Services (IIS) (you may need to insert your Windows Server 2003 CD and click Exit to close the automatic Welcome message).

6. Click Finish when you are told that you have successfully completed installation. Close Add Or Remove Programs.

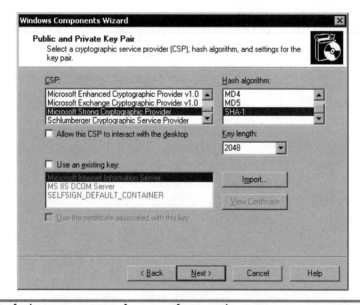

Figure 12-8 Default custom settings for a certificate authority

Administer a Certificate Authority

Once a CA is installed, it can be administered through the Certification Authority console. Here's how:

1. Open the Start menu and choose Administrative Tools | Certification Authority (if you just installed it, Certification Authority may be out of alphabetical sequence in the menu).

2. In the left pane, open the local server and select Issued Certificates. You should see at least the certificate issued to the server, like this (if you don't see the certificate, reboot the server and the certificate should appear):

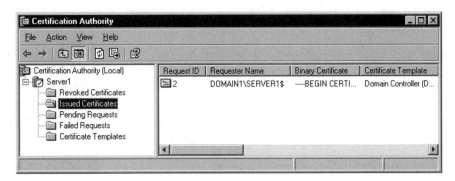

3. Right-click the certificate in the right pane and click Open. Here you can look at the details of a certificate, including who issued it, the date it was issued, and the date it expires. Also, if you choose All Tasks in place of Open, you can revoke the certificate. Click OK to close the certificate.

4. Right-click the local server in the left pane and select All Tasks. In the submenu, you can stop the issuing of certificates and back up and restore the CA. Back in the context menu with All Tasks, click Properties. In the Properties dialog box that opens, select the Policy Module tab and click Properties. In the Request Handling tab, you can choose manual or automatic issuing of certificates, as you can see here:

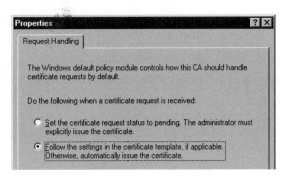

5. Close the two Properties dialog boxes. Back in the Certification Authority console, you'll see a Pending Requests folder. If you select manual certificate issuing, then all certificate requests will go into this folder. When you are done looking at the Certification Authority console, close it.

Starting and Configure IPSec

IPSec is controlled by group policies, which can be set at various levels, the primary of which is the domain. Start and configure IPSec at the domain level with these steps:

1. Open the Start menu and choose Administrative Tools | Active Directory Users And Computers.

2. Right-click the domain, choose Properties, and click the Group Policy tab. Select the Default Domain Policy and click Edit.

3. In the left pane, open Computer Configuration | Windows Settings | Security Settings | IP Security Policies On Active Directory. Open the Action menu and choose Create IP Security Policy. The IP Security Policy Wizard opens. Click Next.

4. Enter the name and a description of the policy and click Next. Accept the automatic activation of the default response rule, which automatically responds to remote computers that request security. Click Next.

5. Accept the default Active Directory authentication using the Kerberos V5 protocol and click Next. Leave Edit Properties checked and click Finish. The Properties dialog box for your new policy will open with a single IP filter. Click Add. The Security Rule Wizard will open. Click Next.

6. Select The Tunnel Endpoint Is Specified By The Following IP Address, enter the IP address of the computer to which the server will be connecting, and click Next. Select Remote Access and click Next.

7. Click All IP Traffic for the IP filter to use, and click Next. Click Permit, again click Next, and then click Finish. Close your policy's Properties dialog box.

8. Back in the Group Policy window, right-click your new IPSec policy in the right pane and click Assign. Leave Security Settings in the Group Policy window open.

Start to Issue Certificates

Certificates like IPSec are controlled by group policies at various levels. Start issuing domain-level certificates by connecting the computers that need them to the LAN and use these steps:

1. In the left pane of the Group Policy windows under Security Settings, select and then open Public Key Policies. In the right pane, right-click Automatic Certificate Request Settings and choose New | Automatic Certificate Request. The Automatic Certificate Request Setup Wizard will open.

2. Click Next. Select Computer as the certificate template to use (see Figure 12-9) and click Next.

3. Review the template and the authority that you want to use; if they are not correct, click Back and make the necessary changes. When they are correct, click Finish. With Public Key Policies | Automatic Certificate Request Settings open in the left pane of the Group Policy window, the right pane should show Computer and its icon.

4. Right-click Computer and choose Properties. You should see a certificate type of Computer and the certificate authority you set up earlier and chose in Step 3. Close the Computer Properties dialog box, the Group Policy window, the domain Properties dialog box, and the Active Directory Users And Computers console.

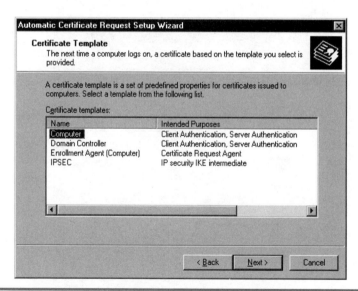

Figure 12-9 Selecting the template to use in issuing certificates

Select and Configure L2TP over IPSec

The final step in setting up L2TP for use with VPN is to select L2TP over IPSec and configure the L2TP ports.

1. Open the Start menu and choose Administrative Tools | Routing And Remote Access. In the left pane, open both the local server and IP Routing, and select General. In the right pane, note the IP Address of the LAN and then right-click Local Area Connection and choose Properties.

2. Click Inbound Filters and click New. In the Add IP Filter dialog box, select Destination Network and enter the IP address for the LAN and a subnet mask of 255.255.255.255. For the Protocol, select UDP and then in both the Source Port and Destination Port, enter **500** (given that this is your first IPSec input filter), as you can see in Figure 12-10, and then click OK.

3. You are returned to the Inbound Filters dialog box, where you should select Drop All Packets Except Those That Meet The Criteria Below. Click OK.

4. Back in the Local Area Connection Properties dialog box, click Outbound Filters and click New. In the Add IP Filter dialog box, select Source Network and enter the IP address for the LAN and a subnet mask of 255.255.255.255. For the Protocol, select UDP and then in both the Source Port and the Destination Port, enter **500** (given that this is your first IPSec output filter), and then click OK.

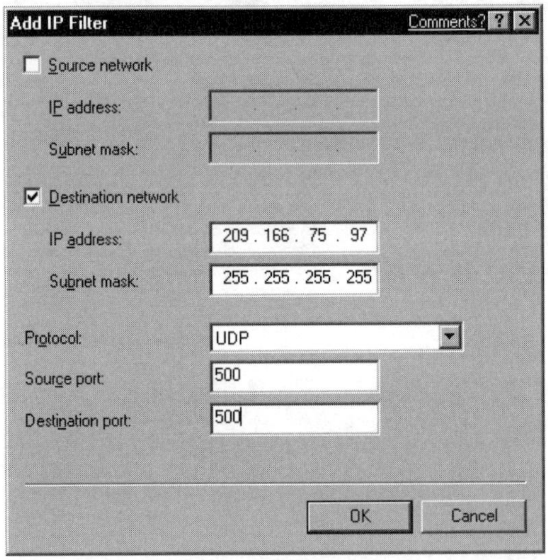

Figure 12-10 Adding an IP filter for L2TP over IPSec

5. In the Outbound Filters dialog box, select Drop All Packets Except Those That Meet The Criteria Below. Click OK. Click OK again to close the Local Area Connection Properties dialog box and return to the Routing And Remote Access console.

6. Right-click Ports in the left pane of the Routing And Remote Access console and click Properties. The Ports Properties dialog box will open.

7. Click WAN Miniport (L2TP) and then click Configure. Configure Device – WAN Miniport (L2TP) opens similar to what you saw under "Configure a PPTP Server."

8. Uncheck the Demand-Dial Routing Connections (Inbound And Outbound) check box. Set a reasonable number of L2TP ports that you will be using and click OK. Click Yes, you want to reduce the number of ports, click OK to close Ports Properties, and close the Routing And Remote Access console.

CRITICAL SKILL
12.6 Set Up a VPN Client

Setting up a VPN client is a relatively simple task. You need to set up a dial-up connection for the client to connect to the Internet and then a connection between the client and the VPN server. In Windows 2000, XP, and Server 2003, there is an integrated and automated approach to these two tasks, whereas in Windows 9*x*/Me and NT, you have to separately set up the dial-up connection to the Internet and then without the help of a wizard create the VPN connection.

Set Up a Windows XP VPN Connection

Although the Windows XP VPN connection is integrated and automated, it is still done in two steps, connecting to the Internet and connecting to the VPN server.

Establish a Windows XP Dial-Up Connection

This is the standard dial-up connection done elsewhere in the book, so if you have a dial-up connection already that you know works, you can skip this.

1. Open the Start menu, choose Control Panel, and double-click Network Connections. Click Create A New Connection to start the New Connection Wizard. Click Next.

2. Click Connect To The Internet and click Next. Choose Set Up My Connection Manually as the method you want to use to connect to the Internet, click Next, choose Connect Using A Dial-Up Modem as the way to connect, click Next, enter the name of the ISP, click Next, enter the phone number of the ISP, and click Next.

3. If you have multiple profiles on the client, you will get the Connection Availability dialog box. Determine if you want the connection for Anyone's Use or for My Use Only and click Next.

4. Enter the username and password needed for the Internet connection, confirm the password, determine if the username and password can be used by anyone using this computer, accept that this will be the default Internet connection, turn off the default firewall, click Next, and then click Finish.

5. In the Connect dialog box, click Dial to try out the connection. If all your settings are correct, you should connect. If not, go back over the preceding three steps and make the necessary corrections.

Connect to a VPN Server

The VPN connection is just another network connection.

1. If your Network Connections window is not already open, open the Start menu, choose Control Panel, and double-click Network Connections. In the Network Connections window, click Create A New Connection to start the New Connection Wizard. Click Next.

2. Select Connect To The Network At My Workplace and click Next. Choose Virtual Private Network Connection, click Next, enter the name of the company or connection, click Next, choose whether to automatically dial a connection using the dial-up connection established in the preceding series of steps (assumed in these steps) or to use an existing connection, and click Next.

3. Enter a registered host name (such as osborne.com) or an IP address like 123.10.78.100 and click Next. If you have multiple profiles on the client, you will get the Connection Availability dialog box again. Determine if you want the connection for Anyone's Use or for My Use Only and click Next and then Finish.

4. Answer Yes, you want to connect through your dial-up connection; the Connect dialog box will open. Enter the username and password required by the dial-up connection, choose whether to save the username and password for yourself personally or for anyone using this computer, and click Dial. The Connect dialog will reopen.

5. Enter the username and password required by the VPN server, choose whether to save the username and password for yourself personally or for anyone using this computer, and click Properties. In the General tab, you will see the settings you have already made.

6. In the Options tab, select both Include Windows Logon Domain and Redial If Line Is Dropped. In the Security tab, use Typical settings and check Automatically Use My Windows Logon And Password.

7. In the Networking tab, select PPTP VPN as the Type Of VPN (after you get PPTP to work, you can come back and try L2TP IPSec VPN), clear File And Printer Sharing For Microsoft Networks, and click OK. Click Connect. You should be connected to the VPN server and be able to browse the portions of the network for which you have permission. Two connection

Figure 12-11 Both a dial-up connection and a VPN connection are visible in Network Connections.

icons should appear in the tray on the right of the taskbar, and your Network Connections window should look something like Figure 12-11.

8. In the VPN server, you should be able to see the connection in the Routing And Remote Access console by opening the local server and Remote Access Clients, like this:

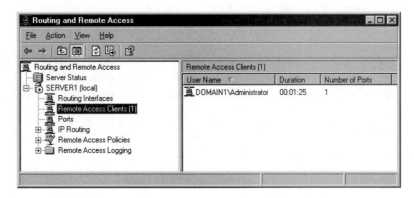

9. If you opened the Routing And Remote Access console, close it. In the client, double-click each of the connection icons in the taskbar and click Disconnect.

If you did not connect, take heart, I didn't either the first time. There are a number of reasons that may not happen. If RAS worked, that eliminates many of the potential reasons. First try connecting with PPTP, then try L2TP, which is much harder. If you set up both PPTP and L2TP before trying the connection, go back to "Reconfigure RAS," use the instructions there and in the following sections to disable RAS, reestablish it just for PPTP, and then try the connection. If it still doesn't work, carefully go over all the steps to set up the service you want to use and look for what you did differently.

Set Up a Windows 9x/Me/NT VPN Connection

Depending on the version of Windows you are running, you may need to download and install additional files. You should install the download before setting up VPN. Windows Me, Windows 98 Second Edition, and Windows NT 4.0 with Service Pack 4 and later all have a VPN client that is compatible with either a Windows 2000 or Windows Server 2003 PPTP VPN server, and so no download is required. Windows 98 original or Service Pack 1 require that you download Microsoft Virtual Private Networking, which is available at http://www .microsoft.com/windows98/downloads/corporate.asp. Windows 95 and Windows 95 OEM Service Release 2 (OSR 2) require that you first download and install Dial-Up Networking 1.3 Performance & Security Update, and then that you download and install Microsoft Virtual Private Networking. Both of these are available at http://www.microsoft.com/windows95/ downloads/, about halfway down the page under Networking. You can tell which version of Windows you have by opening the Start menu and choosing Control Panel | System. The General tab of the System Properties dialog box will show the version.

Setting up VPN on a Windows 9x/Me/NT machine requires that VPN be installed, that a dial-up connection be made, and finally that a VPN connection be made. Do all three of those steps plus test out the connection by inserting the Windows distribution disk and then using the following instructions (there are some differences between various versions of Windows; the instructions here reference Windows 98 SE):

1. Open the Start menu, choose Settings | Control Panel, and double-click Add/Remove Programs. Open the Windows Setup tab, select Communications, click Details, scroll to the bottom of the list of components, click Virtual Private Networking, and click OK twice. The necessary files will be installed. When installation is complete, restart the computer as requested.

2. Open My Computer and double-click Dial-Up Networking. If you already have a dial-up connection, skip to Step 4; otherwise, double-click Make New Connection. The Make New Connection wizard opens.

3. Enter a name for the dial-up connection, select the modem through which the connection will be made, and click Next. Enter the area code and phone number, select the country or region, click Next, and then click Finish.

4. In the Dial-Up Networking window, double-click Make New Connection. Enter a name for the VPN connection, select Microsoft VPN Adapter for the device, and click Next.

5. Enter the IP address of the VPN server, such as 123.10.78.100, click Next, and click Finish. Right-click the VPN connection and choose Properties.

6. Open the Server Types tab and select Require Encrypted Password, select Require Data Encryption, and uncheck NetBEUI and IPX/SPX, as shown here:

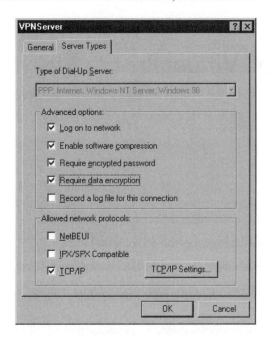

7. Click OK. In the Dial-Up Networking window, double-click your dial-up connection to the Internet, enter the password, if necessary, and click Connect.

8. When you have successfully connected to the Internet, double-click the VPN connection. Enter your username and password, if desired select Save Password, and click Connect. You should see a connection message, and a second connection icon should appear in the tray on the right of the taskbar.

9. Use the Windows Explorer to look at the network to which you are now connected. When you are done, double-click the VPN connection in the taskbar and click Disconnect. Finally, do the same thing with the dial-up connection.

VPN is a very handy tool for mobile workers and is really worth all the trouble it takes to set it up (well, maybe all the trouble PPTP takes—I'm not so sure L2TP is worth its extra trouble!).

Progress Check

1. How must RAS be set up for VPN?

2. Windows 95/98/Me and Windows NT 4 can only use which of the two VPN protocols?

3. What do you need to do to set up a VPN client?

Project 12 Install Virtual Private Networking

VPN has great benefits and cost savings for organizational communications. At the same time, it is one of the more complex features to set up with Windows Server 2003. Use this project as a check list to install VPN using PPTP.

Step by Step

1. Determine if networking is set up and running on the server:

   a. Is at least one NIC installed on the server?

   b. Does the NIC have the appropriate driver installed?

   c. Does the Device Manager say that the NIC is working properly?

   d. Does the Local Area Connection Status dialog box indicate that networking is operating properly?

   e. Does the Network Properties dialog box indicate that TCP/IP is being used?

   f. Does the TCP/IP Properties dialog box indicate that there is a static IP address?

   g. Does Administrative Tools | DHCP and Administrative Tools | DNS indicate that DHCP and DNS are installed, started or authorized, and running?

---

1. VPN requires that you have RAS configured for VPN, so if you have RAS set up for use of RAS by itself, you must reconfigure RAS for VPN.

2. Windows 95/98/Me and Windows NT 4 can use only the PPTP VPN protocol.

3. To set up a VPN client, you need to set up a dial-up connection for the client to connect to the Internet and then a connection between the client and the VPN server.

2. Determine if the communications connection—possibly a modem—is set up and running on the server and the client:

   a. Is there a connection installed on both the server and the client?

   b. Does the connection have the appropriate driver installed?

   c. Does the Diagnostics tab Query Modem option indicate that the modem is operating appropriately?

3. Set up RAS on the server:

   a. Open Start | Administrative Tools | Routing and Remote Access.

   b. Select the local server, open the Action menu, choose Configure And Enable Routing and Remote Access.

   c. Select Dial-Up, Automatically Assign IP addresses, and complete the Routing and Remote Access Server Setup Wizard.

4. Set up RAS on the client and test it (assumed to be running Windows XP Professional):

   a. Open Start | Control Panel and double-click Network Connections.

   b. Click Create A New Connection, choose Connect To The Network At My Workplace, select Dial-Up Connection, and complete the New Connection Wizard for connecting to the RAS server.

   c. On the client, open Start | Connect To | your new dial-up connection.

   d. Enter the appropriate username and password for the server and click Dial.

   e. Click OK to complete the connection and test it with Windows Explorer.

   f. On the server, open the Routing And Remote Access console | local server | Remote Access Clients and observe the client connection.

5. Set up the VPN server:

   a. From the Routing And Remote Access console local server, open the Action menu and choose Disable Routing And Remote Access.

   b. Again open the Action menu and choose Enable Routing And Remote Access.

   c. Choose Custom Configuration, select VPN, and complete the Wizard.

   d. In the Routing And Remote Access console, right-click Ports, click Properties, click WAN Miniport (PPTP), and click Configure.

   e. Uncheck Demand-Dial Routing Connections and set the number of ports.

6. Set up the VPN client and test it (assumed to be running Windows XP Professional):

   a. Open Start | Control Panel and double-click Network Connections.

(continued)

12

Virtual Private Networking

Project 12

Install Virtual Private Networking

b. Click Create A New Connection, choose Connect To The Internet, choose Set Up My Connection Manually, choose Connect Using A Dial-Up Modem, and complete the New Connection Wizard for connecting to the Internet service provider.

c. In Network Connections, again click Create A New Connection, choose Connect To The Network At My Workplace, choose Virtual Private Network Connection, and complete the New Connection Wizard for connecting to the VPN server.

d. On the client, open Start | Connect To | your new dial-up connection, enter the appropriate username and password for the ISP, and click Dial.

e. In the reopened Connect dialog box, enter the appropriate username and password for the VPN server and click Properties.

f. In the Networking tab, select PPTP VPN, clear File And Printer Sharing, For Microsoft Networks, and click OK.

g. Click Connect to complete the connection, and test it with Windows Explorer.

h. On the server, open the Routing And Remote Access console | local server | Remote Access Clients and observe the client connection.

Project Summary

If you or your organization does much work remotely, VPN is almost always worth the time to set it up and the patience needed to get it to work. Stick to it, and you will be pleased you did.

Module 12 Mastery Check

1. What is VPN?

2. Why is VPN considered "tunneling"?

3. What are the hardware and software requirements for RAS and VPN?

4. What is a basic networking requirement to use either RAS or VPN?

5. What is IPSec, and how does it function?

6. What is the most common setup for VPN?

7. Why is L2TP harder to set up than PPTP?

8. What must you do to set up a VPN client?

9. What are some of the reasons that VPN may not work?

10. What do you need to do to install VPN on Windows 95/98/Me and Windows NT 4?

Module 13

Terminal Services and Remote Desktop

CRITICAL SKILL

13.1 Understand Terminal Services

Terminal Services allows a minimal computer called a *thin client* or a *terminal* to connect to a Windows server, display a Windows desktop, and use Windows remotely, with Windows and its applications running on the server. The thin client (called simply "client" in much of this module) can run Windows 95/98/Me, Windows NT 4.0/2000/XP, or, with third-party software, MS-DOS, UNIX, Linux, Mac OS, or Windows for Workgroups 3.11. It can even access the server over the Internet. Only the user interface runs on the client, which returns keystrokes and mouse clicks to the server. The client computer can have a slow processor like a Pentium 100, a small amount of memory, say, 8MB, and a small hard disk or even no hard disk. To the application running on the server, the user appears to be on that machine. Multiple terminal sessions can be running on the server, but each client sees only its own session, and to clients, the application appears to be running on their machines, given a reasonable network speed. A good use of thin clients with Terminal Services is one where the client is used for a single purpose, such as order entry, ticketing, or inventory tracking, where it is beneficial for the application and its related database to be on a server.

There are a number of reasons to use Terminal Services, among which are:

- To use legacy hardware and older operating systems (OSs) that can't directly run the latest Windows

- To allow multiple people to use the same application, possibly with a common database, especially "line of business" applications and applications that are frequently updated or seldom used (applications heavy with graphics and multimedia are not good candidates for Terminal Services)

- To centralize the focus of application deployment, administration, and maintenance on a centralized server

- To control applications that are available to users and how they are configured

- To access a computer remotely, say, one at work from one at home or one on the road

- To manage several to many servers remotely with remote administration

Terminal Services is an integral part of Windows Server 2003, as it was in Windows 2000. In Windows NT 4, you had to purchase a separate Terminal Server Edition (TSE). The original Windows terminal service was developed by a separate company, Citrix Systems, Inc., in a product they called Winframe, a variant of which, called MultiWin, was licensed by Microsoft. Citrix has gone on to provide an advanced applications server package called MetaFrame that runs on Windows 2000 and 2003 servers. You can reach Citrix at http://www.citrix.com.

Terminal Services works with the Transmission Control Protocol/Internet Protocol (TCP/IP), common to Windows Server 2003 networking and the Internet, and uses the Remote Desktop Protocol (RDP). RDP is a broad protocol facilitating the simultaneous transmission of a wide range of data, including user, application, licensing, and encryption information. RDP also has the capability to transmit audio and video information.

CRITICAL SKILL
13.2 Set Up Terminal Services

Terminal Services has two distinct modes of operation and several components. The two modes are:

- **Applications Server Mode**, which allows a client computer to display a Windows desktop and run applications remotely from a server

- **Remote Administration Mode**, which provides the means to remotely administer a computer running Windows Server 2003 including Internet Information Services (IIS). Microsoft now calls this *Remote Desktop for Administration.*

There is also a derivative of Remote Administration Mode called *Remote Desktop* that allows you to remotely use a computer, for example to remotely use your computer at work from your computer at home.

The components of Terminal Services in Windows Server 2003 are

- **Terminal Server**, which runs on the Standard, Enterprise, Datacenter Editions of Windows Server 2003 and provides the central component that allows multitasking on a server

- **Terminal Services Configuration**, which allows you to determine the Terminal Services connections that are on the computer and their properties, as well as the server settings

- **Terminal Services Manager**, which provides the administrative functions for Terminal Services

- **Terminal Services Licensing**, which provides for client licensing of Windows Terminal Services

- **Remote Desktop Connection** (previously Terminal Services Client), which is preinstalled software on Windows Server 2003, Windows XP Professional, and Windows XP Home that allows the client to connect to and use a Terminal Server

- **Remote Desktop Web Connection** (previously Terminal Services Web Connection), which allows hosting Remote Desktop Connections over the Web

- **32-bit Terminal Services Client**, which is additional client software that can be installed on older versions of Windows

In this section ("Set Up Terminal Services"), we'll talk about setting up Terminal Server and using Terminal Services Manager. In the later section "Use Applications Server Mode," we'll talk about Remote Desktop Connection (formerly the Terminal Services Client), and Terminal Services Licensing. In the final two major sections, we'll talk about implementing and using Remote Desktop for Administration and Remote Desktop, where a client is used to manage one or more servers in the first case, or is used to access and use another Windows computer.

NOTE

Microsoft in its infinite wisdom has renamed components of Terminal Services. What used to be called Terminal Services Client is now called Remote Desktop Connection. What used to be called Terminal Services Remote Administration Mode is now called Remote Desktop for Administration, and what used to be called Terminal Services Web Connection is now called Remote Desktop Web Connection. This can make for a lot of confusion. Throughout this module, I and several editors will try to make sure we are using the new terms. Periodically, though, I will parenthetically mention the old term to make sure it is clear what we are talking about.

Set Up Terminal Server

Terminal Server is not installed by default when Windows Server 2003 is set up. The easiest way to set it up is to use the Configure Your Server Wizard. This wizard is started either directly or through the Manage Your Server window. When you first install Windows Server 2003, the Manage Your Server window automatically appears. Unless you change the default, this window automatically reappears when you next start or restart Windows Server 2003 until you tell it otherwise. You can open it by opening the Start menu and clicking Manage Your Server. In the Manage Your Server window, you start the Configure Your Server Wizard by clicking Add Or Remove A Role.

Ask the Expert

Q: Okay, I understand that Microsoft has renamed several items that used to start with "Terminal Services" so that they now start with "Remote Desktop." Does that mean "Terminal Services" is synonymous with "Remote Desktop"?

A: Well, almost. In all the examples mentioned in the preceding note, the two are in fact synonymous. The hitch is that there is now something Microsoft calls "Remote Desktop" that is not the same as Terminal Services, as explained later in this module.

You can directly start the Configure Your Server Wizard by opening the Start menu, choosing Administrative Tools, and clicking Configure Your Server Wizard. With this method, you will get a Welcome message not seen if you start through the Manage Your Server window. If you see the Welcome message, click Next and then use the following steps to set up Terminal Server:

1. Verify that the necessary preliminary steps listed in the Configure Your Server Wizard have been completed and then click Next. Your network is checked and then a series of server roles is displayed.

2. Select Terminal Server, as shown in Figure 13-1, and click Next. You are told you have selected Install Terminal Server. Click Next again. You are told that your server will be restarted and you should close any open program. Do that by right-clicking the program on the taskbar and choosing Close.

3. When you have closed all open programs except Configure Your Server, click OK. The Windows Components Wizard will open, and you may be asked to insert the Windows

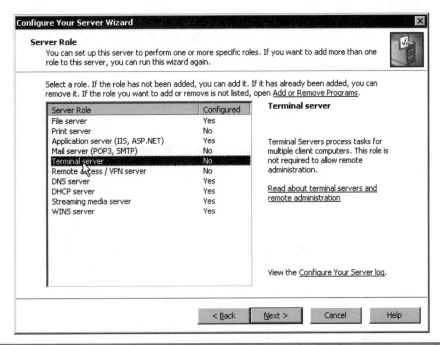

Figure 13-1 Choosing to install Terminal Server

Server 2003 CD. If so, insert the CD and click OK. When the copying and configuration is complete, Windows will be restarted.

4. When Configure Your Server Wizard reappears and you are told Terminal Server has been successfully set up, click Finish.

NOTE

Remote Desktop Connection is installed by default on Windows XP and Server 2003 and so is not discussed here. See "Use Applications Server Mode" later in this module.

Set Up Remote Desktop Web Connection

The Remote Desktop Web Connection is a web-based terminal server connection that allows a client to connect over the Web to the server. This requires that Internet Information Services (IIS) be already installed (if not, see Module 11). The Remote Desktop Web Connection is a subcomponent of the World Wide Web service (WWW) in IIS. The following steps install the Remote Desktop Web Connection:

1. Open the Start menu | Control Panel | Add Or Remove Programs, and select Add/Remove Windows Components. Click Application Server and click Details.

2. Click Internet Information Services (IIS), click Details, scroll down and select World Wide Web Service, and again click Details. If it isn't already selected, click Remote Desktop Web Connection, as shown in Figure 13-2, click OK three times, and click Next.

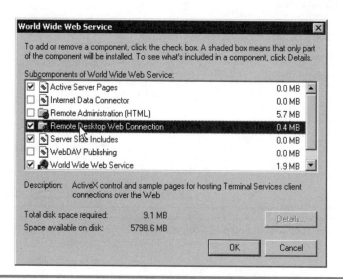

Figure 13-2 Installing the Remote Desktop Web Connection

3. Insert your Windows Server 2003 CD when requested, click OK, and close the Setup Welcome window if it opens. When IIS installation is complete, click Finish, close Add Or Remove Programs, and remove the CD.

This adds a folder named TSWeb containing a set of files to C:\Windows\Web\. To be able to easily use this folder, which you need to do to access the terminal server from the Web, you need to copy this folder or its parent folder, Web, to C:\Inetpub\Wwwroot, which is the default folder opened by IIS. As a final step, copy the parent folder Web to C:\Inetpub\Wwwroot.

4. Open Start | Windows Explorer; in the folders pane, open My Computer | Local Disk (C:) | Windows. Click the Windows folder so that it is displayed in the right pane. In the left pane, open Inetpub so that you can see Wwwroot. Scroll the right pane until you can see the Web folder. Point to the Web folder, press and hold the right mouse button while dragging the folder to C:\Inetpub\Wwwroot, release the right mouse button, and choose Copy Here.

CRITICAL SKILL
13.3 Manage Terminal Services

There are three separate tools for managing Terminal Services: Terminal Services Configuration and Terminal Services Manager, which will be discussed here, and Terminal Server Licensing, which will be discussed under "Understand User Licensing."

Terminal Services Configuration

Terminal Services Configuration allows you to determine the Terminal Services connections that are on the computer and their properties, as well as the server settings. There can be only one connection for each network interface card (NIC) in the computer, and all connections use RDP with TCP/IP. Therefore, if you have only one NIC, the default connection is all that you need. There are, though, some important settings in the connection's Properties dialog box. Look at both the connection's settings and the server settings that are available in Terminal Services Configuration with these steps:

NOTE

Most of the settings that can be made in the Terminal Services Configuration window can also be made using Group Policies, which will override the settings in the Terminal Services Configuration window. For this reason, the best practice is to use Group Policies for these settings. Group Policies are discussed in Module 17.

1. Open Terminal Services Configuration by opening the Start menu and choosing Administrative Tools | Terminal Services Configuration. The Terminal Services Configuration/Connections (TSCC) window will open.

2. If the server has more than one NIC, you can add additional connections by right-clicking the Connections folder and choosing Create New Connection. The Terminal Services Connection Wizard will open. Click Next and answer the questions that are asked, click Next as needed, and click Finish at the end.

3. To change the properties of an existing connection, click Connections, right-click the default RDP-TCP connection or custom connection, and choose Properties. The RDP-TCP Properties dialog box will open as shown in Figure 13-3.

4. Go through each of the tabs. The settings you can change are as follows:

- **General**   Add a comment to the connection's description and switch to High encryption.

- **Logon Settings**   Provide automatic logon by specifying the logon information to always use and whether a password will be requested.

- **Sessions**   Determine when to end a terminal session and how to reconnect if disconnected.

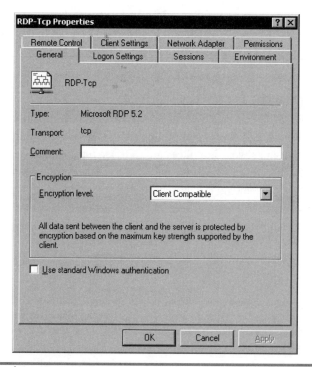

Figure 13-3 Terminal Services connection properties

- **Environment**   Specify which, if any, program should be started when the user logs on, and what folder it should point to.

- **Remote Control**   Determine whether to allow the remote control or observation of a user's terminal session and set the conditions under which it is allowed.

- **Client Settings**   Specify which of the client devices and capabilities will be available during a terminal session.

- **Network Adapter**   Specify the NIC that will be used for this connection and the maximum number of connections to be allowed.

- **Permissions**   Determine the permissions to be allowed for a particular group or user and add groups and users as desired.

5. When you have completed any changes you want to make, click OK to close the connection's Properties dialog box and return to the Terminal Services Configuration window.

6. Click Server Settings. The settings will appear on the right of the windows as shown next. These settings are self-explanatory. The setting is changed by right-clicking it; either select the opposite attribute or click Properties and choose the desired value.

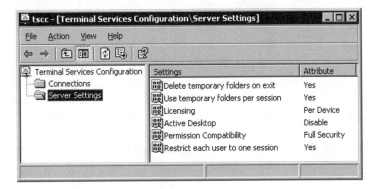

7. When you have completed making any needed changes to Server Settings, close the Terminal Services Configuration window.

Terminal Services Manager

Terminal Services Manager allows you look at and manage the terminal servers within your trusted domains, including the users, processes, and sessions that are currently active on each server. Start Terminal Services Manager and see what you can do with it using the next set of steps.

NOTE

When you first start Terminal Services Manager, you get a message that certain features, such as Remote Control And Connect, work only in a client session and are disabled in a console or server session. In other words, you must access the server and run Terminal Services Manager from a client in order to use Remote Control and Connect.

1. Open Terminal Services Manager by opening the Start menu and choosing Administrative Tools | Terminal Services Manager. The Terminal Services Manager window for the local server will open. Click OK to close the message about Remote Control And Connect.

2. Click the Sessions tab in the right pane and your window will look something like this if you have only the administrator as a user:

3. If you right-click a client session in the right pane and open its context menu, you can disconnect it, reconnect if disconnected, send a message to the client, take control of the client if the client allows you, reset the client, and display the status of the session, which shows the incoming and outgoing bytes, frames, and errors.

NOTE

The context menu actions just described are also available in the toolbar and in the Action menu.

4. If you click a client session in the left pane and select the Information tab, you will see all the pertinent information about the client, as shown in Figure 13-4.

5. Clicking the Processes tab shows the programs that are currently running in the remote session.

6. When you are done looking at the Terminal Services Manager, close it.

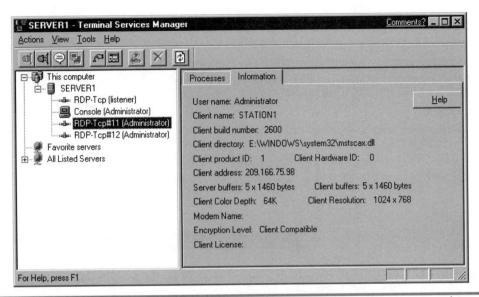

Figure 13-4 Terminal Services Manager can provide full information about a terminal session.

CRITICAL SKILL
13.4 Use Applications Server Mode

Terminal Services Applications Server Mode is a true multiuser environment similar to the mainframe timesharing systems that were popular in the 1970s prior to the advent of the PC. Each applications server user has an independent slice of the server and its resources. That means that the server can get overloaded. Applications servers with any significant number of simultaneous users (over ten) require a more powerful computer with a substantial amount of memory (1GB or more). The client, on the other hand, as described earlier, does not require much power to display the user interface, collect keystrokes and mouse events, and transmit the information to the server. Most of the processing is at the server.

Set Up Remote Desktop Connection

Setting up Remote Desktop Connection (previously Terminal Services Client) depends on what OS is installed on the computer used for the client. Here we'll look at computers running Windows XP Home Edition and Windows 98 Second Edition as examples of the two types of setup that are used with the Remote Desktop Connection. You'll see how most other Windows-based computers fall into one of these two types of setup.

Set Up Windows XP Home Edition as a Client

In Windows XP Home and Professional Editions and in Windows Server 2003, the Remote Desktop Connection is normally installed as a part of the default installation. You should check on it and, if it is not installed, do so with these steps:

1. Open the Start menu, click All Programs | Accessories | Communications. You should see Remote Desktop Connection, like this:

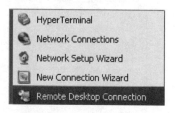

2. If you do see Remote Desktop Connection, skip to the next section, "Understand User Licensing."

3. If you do not see Remote Desktop Connection, insert the Windows XP installation CD in its drive. In the Welcome window, click Perform Additional Tasks, and then click Set Up Remote Desktop Connection. The Remote Desktop Connection – InstallShield Wizard opens.

4. Click Next, click I Accept The Terms In The License Agreement, and click Next. The current User Name and Organization are displayed, as is the default Anyone Who Uses This Computer Can Use Remote Desktop Connection. Accept or change these as needed, click Next, and then click Install.

5. When the installation is complete, click Finish, close Setup's Welcome window, and remove the CD.

Set Up Windows 98 Second Edition as a Client

Windows 95/98/Me and Windows NT 4/2000 Server and Workstation/Professional require that you install the 32-bit Terminal Services Client that comes with Windows Server 2003. When you are done, you will see that you have the Remote Desktop Connection running on these earlier versions of Windows. You can install this client by first sharing the folder on the server containing the client and then running Setup in that folder. Do that with the following instructions:

1. On the server, open Start | Windows Explorer. In Windows Explorer, browse to and right-click C:\Windows\System32\Clients\Tsclient\Win32, as shown next. Choose Sharing And Security, click Share This Folder, and click OK.

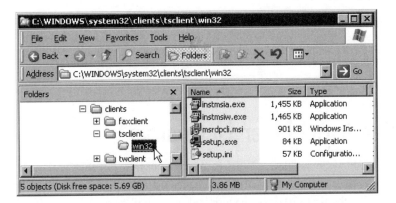

2. On the client desktop, double-click Network Neighborhood, browse to and open C:\Windows\System32\Clients\Tsclient\Win32 on the server. Double-click Setup. The Remote Desktop Connection – InstallShield Wizard opens and installs itself. Click Restart System when the corresponding message appears. After restarting, the Remote Desktop Connection – InstallShield Wizard opens again with a welcome message.

3. Click Next, click I Accept The Terms In The License Agreement, and click Next. The current User Name and Organization are displayed. Accept or change these as needed, click Next, and then click Install.

4. When the installation is complete, click Finish, and close Setup's Welcome window.

NOTE

Remote Desktop Connections (Terminal Services Clients) for other operating systems, including UNIX, Linux, Macintosh, and OS/2, as well as a more robust Terminal Services server are available from Citrix Systems, Inc., at http://www.citrix.com.

Progress Check

1. What is Terminal Services?

2. What are the two modes in which Terminal Services can operate?

3. What are three sources of Remote Desktop Connection (Terminal Services Client) software?

CRITICAL SKILL

13.5 Understand User Licensing

A Remote Desktop Connection is in effect able to use Microsoft Windows without having Windows installed. As a result, Microsoft believes that it has a right to collect license fees for this service. For the first 120 days, the terminal server will automatically issue free temporary licenses to any client addressing the server. The terminal server will stop issuing temporary licenses to clients 120 days after it receives the first connection, and the clients will no longer be able to connect.

Terminal Server Licenses

Terminal server licenses are different from the workstation licenses required to connect to and use Windows Server 2003. To use terminal server licensing, a Terminal Server License Server must be activated on the network and the terminal server and client access licenses must be installed using the Terminal Server License Server Activation Wizard. The Terminal Server License Server can be any server on the network running Windows Server 2003, and because of the traffic it will generate, you may *not* want the license server to also be a terminal server. The license server stores all of the licenses that have been installed for a network, and all of the terminal servers on the network must be able to quickly access the license server before clients are allowed to connect to the terminal server.

---

1. Terminal Services allows a minimal computer called a thin client or a terminal to connect to a Windows server, display a Windows desktop, and use Windows remotely with Windows and its applications running on the server.

2. Terminal Services has two modes of operation: Applications Server Mode, which allows a client computer to display a Windows desktop and run applications remotely from a server, and Remote Administration Mode, which provides the means for remotely administering a Windows Server 2003, now called Remote Desktop for Administration.

3. Remote Desktop Connection, which was formerly called Terminal Services Client, is available already installed in both editions of Windows XP and in all editions of Windows Server 2003. The 32-bit Terminal Services Client is available on the server for use in Windows 95 through Windows 2000 clients. Finally, clients for other computers are available from third-party sources such as Citrix Systems, Inc.

NOTE

You do not need to have licenses or a license server to use Remote Desktop for Administration (formerly Terminal Services Administration Mode) or Remote Desktop.

Terminal server licenses can be generated in two ways, by a domain license server or by an enterprise license server, the latter of which is the default. An enterprise license server can handle the terminal servers in several domains so long as the domains use Windows 2000 or Windows Server 2003 Active Directory. Enterprise license servers are polled by terminal servers every 60 minutes, even after they are located. A domain license server can handle only the terminal servers in the same domain the license server is in, but that domain can contain workgroups and be a Windows NT 4 domain. Domain license servers are polled by terminal servers every 15 minutes until they are found, and then they are polled every two hours.

Install a Terminal Server License Server

Bearing in mind that you must decide between enterprise licensing and domain licensing, use these steps to install a Terminal Server License Server:

1. Open the Start menu and choose Control Panel | Add Or Remove Programs, and click Add/Remove Windows Components. The Windows Components Wizard will open.

2. Scroll down to and select Terminal Server Licensing, as shown in Figure 13-5, and click Next. Choose whether you want enterprise or domain licensing, accept the default location for the licensing database, and click Next. The installation and configuration will begin.

3. If you are asked to insert the Windows Server 2003 CD, do so, click Exit to close Setup's Welcome window, and when you are told you have successfully completed the installation, click Finish.

Activate a License Server and Install Client Licenses

To activate a license server, the Microsoft Clearinghouse must be contacted either over the Internet or through your local Microsoft Customer Support Center. This can be done in three ways:

● Automatically by the licensing server directly connecting to the Microsoft Clearinghouse over the Internet, meaning that the licensing server must have an Internet connection.

● Manually by an administrator in front of a browser on any computer connecting over the Internet to the Microsoft Terminal Services web site.

● Manually by an administrator calling the local Microsoft Customer Support Center.

Terminal Services and Remote Desktop

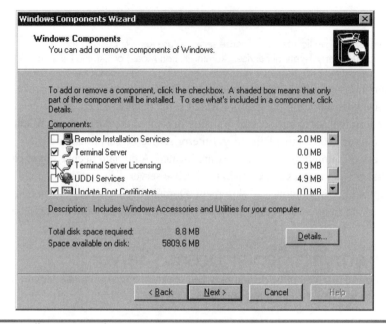

Figure 13-5 Installing Terminal Server License Server

With a decision in mind on how the Microsoft Clearinghouse will be contacted, use the following steps to activate a Terminal Server License Server:

1. Open the Start menu and choose Administrative Tools | Terminal Server Licensing. The Terminal Server Licensing window will open showing the server you installed in the preceding series of steps with a Not Activated status, like this:

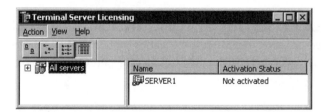

2. Open All Servers so that you can see your new server in the left pane console tree, right-click the new server, and choose Activate Server. The Terminal Server License Server Activation Wizard will open. Click Next.

3. Select the activation method you want to use (Automatic, Web Browser, or Telephone) and click Next. Assuming the Automatic method, enter your name, company, and country or region and click Next. Enter your e-mail address, organizational unit, and street address and click Next.

4. You are told your license server has been successfully activated. Leave the check box checked and click Next to install client licenses (assumed here). Alternatively, uncheck the check box and click Finish to delay installing client licenses. The Terminal Server Client Access License (CAL) Installation Wizard will open, as shown in Figure 13-6.

5. You are told that to install client licenses, you will need information about the type of licensing your server was purchased with. The settings that the system believes were used are displayed. Click Next to change the license program.

6. Change the license program, verify your license code looks like the sample shown, and click Next. Enter the license code(s), click Add for each, and when you are done, click Next. Click Finish when you are told that needed licenses are installed.

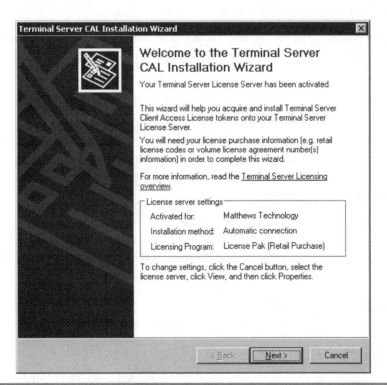

Figure 13-6 Installing terminal server client licenses

NOTE

If you want to install licenses at another time, you can do so in the Terminal Server Licensing window by right-clicking the server in either pane and choosing Install Licenses. The Terminal Server CAL Installation Wizard will open as you saw in the preceding steps.

Set Up and Enable Users

Once licensing has been handled, you need to set up and enable users. For you to do that, the server or the domain must have user accounts that are established for that purpose (meaning that the users are members of the Remote Desktop Users group), the user account must have a password, and the accounts must be enabled for terminal services or remote connections. Here is how this is done:

1. Open the Start menu and choose Administrative Tools | Active Directory Users And Computers. Open the local domain, right-click Users, and choose New | User. The New Object – User dialog box will open.

2. Enter the full name and the logon name and click Next. Enter and confirm the password to be used, decide how that password can be changed, click Next, and then click Finish. Use these steps to enter as many new users as desired.

3. In the right pane of Active Directory Users And Computers, double-click one of the new users you just created to open the user's Properties dialog box.

4. Click the Member Of tab and click Add. In the Select Groups dialog box, click Advanced and then click Find Now to search for groups. Scroll down and select Remote Desktop Users, and click OK three times. Repeat this process for all the users who will use Terminal Services or Remote Desktop.

5. Close Active Directory Users And Computers, open Start, choose Control Panel | System, and click the Remote tab. In the Remote Desktop portion of the dialog box, click Allow Users To Connect Remotely To Your Computer, as shown in Figure 13-7, and then click OK.

Use Terminal Server

A terminal server can be used either across a LAN or across the Web.

Access a Terminal Server Across a LAN

Sitting at a local client computer and with a LAN connected to both you and the terminal server, use the following steps to connect to the server:

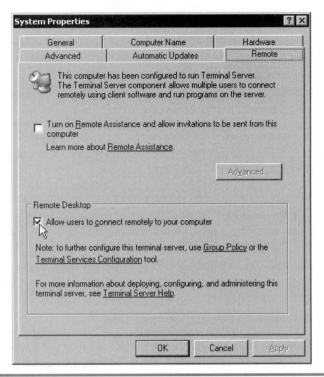

Figure 13-7 Enabling remote connections to the server

1. On the client, open the Start menu, click All Programs or Programs | Accessories | Communications.

2. Click Remote Desktop Connection. The Remote Desktop Connection dialog box opens like this:

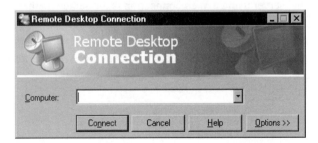

3. Enter the name or IP address of the computer to which you want to connect. If you are not sure of the computer name, click Browse For More in the Computer drop-down list box.

This lists the computers in your immediate domain or workgroup. If you want to connect to a computer outside your local domain or workgroup, you may be able to find the name by opening My Network Places | Entire Network | Microsoft Windows Network, which will show you the domains and workgroups that are available to you and within each of those, the computers. If that doesn't work, see the discussion of using an IP address in the next section, "Access a Terminal Server Across the Web."

4. When you have found or entered the computer name, click Connect. The Remote Desktop toolbar appears in the top center of the screen. Enter the username and password for the terminal server and click OK.

At this point, the terminal server desktop appears just at it would on the server itself if the current remote user were sitting in front of the server. The remote user can run any programs or do any task that can be done at the server provided that he or she has permisssion. The screen looks the same except for the Remote Desktop toolbar (called the *connection bar*) that appears at the top center of the screen. The "push-pin" icon on the left of the toolbar allows you to hide the connection bar until you move the mouse pointer to the upper center of the screen. The icons on the right are the standard icons in every window that allow you to minimize, maximize, and close the window.

5. Click the push-pin icon and move the mouse pointer down on the screen. The connection bar will disappear. Move the mouse pointer back to the upper middle of the screen and the connection bar will reappear.

6. Click the Close icon in the connection bar to close the terminal server window.

See the discussion near the end of this module under "Put Remote Desktop to Work" that talks more about how to use the terminal server window.

Access a Terminal Server Across the Web

Accessing a terminal server using a Web connection is the same whether you are going a great distance across the Internet or a short distance across an intranet. The major difference is in the security desired. For an Internet connection, you will probably want to use VPN, which was discussed in Module 12. Here we'll look at a simpler and less secure approach that would be used with an intranet:

NOTE

The client must have a TCP/IP connection to the Web and must be using Internet Explorer 5 or later. Also, Internet Information Services (IIS) must be installed and running on the server.

1. Open the Start menu, click Internet Explorer, and enter the Uniform Resource Locator (URL) for the terminal server and the name of the program to use, Tsweb.

   The form of the URL is http://*hostname/path*/tsweb; the "http://" is frequently not required. The *hostname* is the name of the terminal server, such as "Server1," or the Internet Protocol (IP) address (see following note) of the server if you are coming in over the Internet. The *path* is the directory path to the Tsweb folder. If you followed the instructions in the section "Set Up Remote Desktop Web Connection" earlier in this module, then with a terminal server named "Server1," the URL and path should be http://Server1/Web/Tsweb.

TIP

As described in detail in Module 7, the Internet Protocol (IP) address is either temporarily or permanently assigned to every computer on the Internet and every computer on a LAN that uses the TCP/IP protocol. On a LAN, you can use the computer name, but when you are outside of the LAN, for example at home, you will probably have to use the computer's IP address. You can find out a computer's IP address by opening the Start menu and choosing Control Panel | Network Connections. Right-click the LAN connection and choose Status. In the LAN Status dialog box, click the Support tab. You will see the IP address of the computer you are on, like this:

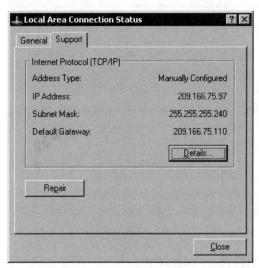

2. After entering your URL and pressing ENTER, you will be asked if you want to install and run Remote Desktop ActiveX Control. Click Yes and the Remote Desktop Web Connection page will open, as shown in Figure 13-8.

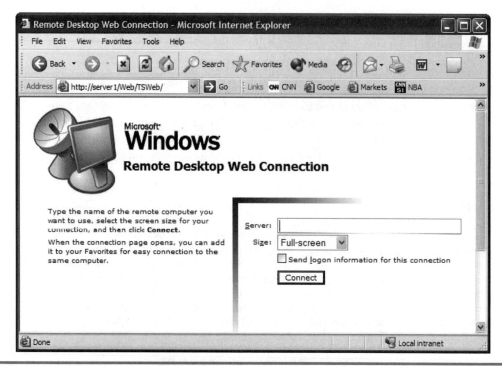

Figure 13-8 Connecting to a terminal server using a Web connection

3. Enter the terminal server's computer name or IP address, select the screen size to use, and click Connect. Enter your User Name and Password and click OK. You will be logged on as you were in the LAN-based technique, and you can do anything here that you could do with the LAN-based technique.

The Web-based connection can also be used with VPN or a dial-up RAS access. As mentioned at the end of the last section, see the discussion near the end of this module under "Put Remote Desktop to Work" that talks more about how to use the terminal server window.

CRITICAL SKILL
13.6 Use Remote Desktop for Administration

Remote Desktop for Administration uses the Terminal Services environment much as Applications Server Mode does, but it is limited to a maximum of two users, who must be members of the administrator group, so it does not demand much from the server, does not require licensing, and can be easily used to manage a server without a significant impact on the other processes going on in the server. To do that, it does not include the multiuser and process scheduling components that are present in full Terminal Services.

Enable Remote Desktop for Administration

Windows Server 2003 has Remote Desktop for Administration installed by default so that nothing further needs to be done to have the programs available to use. *But,* Windows Server 2003 by default has Remote Desktop for Administration disabled, and to use it, you must enable it. You can do that very simply with these steps:

1. Open the Start menu, choose Control Panel | System, and click the Remote tab to open the System Properties dialog box tab dealing with Remote Assistance and Remote Desktop shown earlier in this module in Figure 13-7.

2. In the Remote Desktop section in the lower part of the tab, click Allow Users To Connect Remotely To Your Computer.

3. Click OK to close the dialog box.

Clients for Remote Desktop for Administration

Remote Desktop for Administration uses the same Remote Desktop Connections that were discussed earlier in the module and is installed in exactly the same way. The only difference is that you must log on as an administrator and you then have full administrative privileges.

Managing Through Remote Desktop for Administration

Using Remote Desktop for Administration, you can perform virtually any administrative function you can do sitting in front of the computer, and you can do it over a LAN, over a remote access (RAS) connection (see Module 10), or over the Internet using VPN (see Module 12). You can use the full Control Panel and Administrative Tools including Active Directory, Computer Management, DHCP, DNS, Licensing, Manage Your Server, Remote Desktops, and Terminal Services Manager.

Since the person sitting remotely has all but complete control of the server, it is mandatory that security for this person be kept very tight. Some of the security elements to consider include:

● Implementing a firewall in front of the server

● Using VPN for access across the Internet

● Using strong passwords for all administrators

- Carefully limiting the individuals or groups that have remote administrative access
- Carefully reviewing the policies that affect remote administration

Beside Terminal Services, there are several other ways of remotely managing one or more servers. Among these are: Microsoft Management Console (MMC), Active Directory Service Interface (ADSI), and Windows Management Instrumentation (WMI). The MMC and WMI are discussed in Module 16, and ADSI is discussed in Module 9.

CRITICAL SKILL
13.7 # Use Remote Desktop

Remote Desktop is just a special case of Remote Desktop for Administration that does not require a server for one end of the connection. For example, you can have Windows XP Professional on one computer running at your office and Windows XP Home Edition at home, and from the home computer with the appropriate permissions, you can access the office computer using either RAS or VPN and do almost anything on the office computer you could do if you were sitting in front of it. Since the office computer is not truly a server, it is called a "host." The home computer is the client. The host must be Windows XP Professional, but the client can be any computer that can run Remote Desktop Connection (see "Set Up Remote Desktop Connection" earlier in the module). In Windows XP, the client is installed and enabled by default, but host must be enabled as described in "Enable Remote Desktop for Administration."

The user of Remote Desktop must be a member of the Remote Desktop Users group on the host computer but does not have to be an administrator. With Remote Desktop, only one user can be using the host at any one time, although several user sessions can be active. When the remote client logs on to the host, the host is "locked" so that another user cannot access it, although programs that are running can continue to run and you can use user switching to move to another user session. User switching can also be used on the client to switch from the person who is using the Remote Desktop on the host, to another user, and then switch back.

Put Remote Desktop to Work

Once you are connected to either a Remote Desktop host or a Terminal Services server, you can do almost everything that you could do if you were sitting in front of the host. You can run programs, access data, and perform most management and other functions you could otherwise perform. In addition, the Remote Desktop toolbar, or "connection bar," allows you to close the Remote Desktop window without logging out, so your programs will keep running, to minimize the window, so you can see the actual machine you are sitting at, and to maximize the window. Also, there is a push-pin icon that determines whether or not the connection bar is always on the desktop or there only when you move the mouse to the top center of the screen.

Set Connection Options

Remote Desktop also gives you the capability of transferring information between the host computer and the local client computer you are using. This means that you can print to a local printer connected to the client (the default), work with files on both the remote host and the local client in the same window (not the default), and cut and paste between both computers and documents on either one (also not the default). The local client resources that are available in a Remote Desktop session are controlled by the Remote Desktop Connection dialog box options. Use the following steps to explore what you can do with these settings:

1. On a Windows XP Professional computer, open the Start menu and choose All Programs | Accessories | Communications | Remote Desktop Connection. The Remote Desktop Connection dialog box opens. Click Options and the box expands to give you a number of controls for Remote Desktop in four additional tabs, as shown in Figure 13-9.

2. Click the Display tab. The default for a LAN is to use Full Screen and up to True Color (24 bit) if your computer can handle it, and to display the connection bar. If your LAN has particularly heavy traffic and is slow, you might want to lower the screen size and colors.

Figure 13-9 Expanded Remote Desktop Connection provides controls.

3. Click the Local Resources tab. As you can see in Figure 13-10, here you can determine if you want sound brought to the client and the ability to use shortcut keys. Again, if you have a slow network, you might not want to do either of these. If you want to transfer information, even cut and paste, between the two computers, select Disk Drives; if you want to print on the printer attached to the local client, leave the default Printers selection; and if you intend to use a modem or other serial device on the local client, choose Serial Ports.

NOTE

To cut or copy and paste, you must have the local client's disk drives available and therefore they must be selected in the Remote Desktop Connection dialog box Local Resources tab.

4. If you want to start a program when you open the Remote Desktop Connection, open the Programs tab, click the check box, and enter the path and filename of the program and the starting folder to use.

5. Click the Experience tab and select the connection speed you are using. This will determine which of the items below the drop-down list box are checked. You can change the individual items if you want.

Figure 13-10 Controlling the resources that are available

6. Click the General tab. If you will use several settings, save the ones you just made by clicking Save As, entering a name, and clicking Save.

7. Finally, enter your password and click Connect. If you have said that you want the local disk drives available, you will get a message saying that you should proceed only if you trust the computer you are connecting to. Click OK or Cancel.

8. When you are done using Remote Desktop, leave it by

- Clicking the Close button in the connection bar. This leaves you logged on, and any programs you have running will remain that way. If you restart Remote Desktop Connection with the host computer and no one else has logged on locally, you will return to the same session you left.

- Clicking Start | Log Off. This terminates your Remote Desktop session, and all programs are stopped. If you restart Remote Desktop Connection with the host computer, you will begin a new session.

Use Remote Desktop/Terminal Server

Most of what you can do in the Remote Desktop or Terminal Server window is obvious; it is the same as directly using Windows. There are two functions, though, that are unique to this environment. An example will show how they work.

Saving to a Local Disk   With the default settings, all files and folders referenced during a Remote Desktop or Terminal Services session are on the host or server computer. If you reference a folder on disk C:, it is by default disk C: on the host or server. If you specified that you wanted the local disk drives available in the Remote Desktop Connection dialog box (see earlier Figure 13-10), then you can use either the disks on the host/server or those on the local computer. For example, if after turning on the local disk drives when you connected, you are working in Microsoft Word on the host/server and open Save As, the upper-left corner of the dialog box will look something like this:

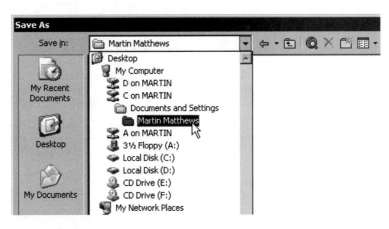

You do have to be careful about the terminology. Here "C on Martin" is the local drive (Martin is the name of the laptop I have connected to the terminal server) and "Local Disk (C:)" is on the server. You can see how easy it is to use either drive.

Printing to a Local Printer   Using the default settings, all printing is directed to the default printer on the local computer. For example, if you open the Print dialog box from Microsoft Word you will get the local default printer like this:

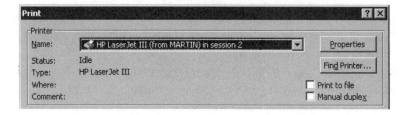

If you want to use a different printer, you have three alternatives:

- Install another printer in Windows during the Remote Desktop or Terminal Services session using, if in Windows XP, Start | Printers And Faxes.

- Select a different printer as the default printer in the local computer before starting the Remote Desktop or Terminal Services session.

- Turn off the use of the local printer in the Remote Desktop Connection dialog box as you are logging on. This will then allow you to use the default printer on the host/server.

Progress Check

1. What are the three ways you can access a remote desktop?

2. Can you use Windows XP Home Edition with Remote Desktop?

3. What essential element must a user account have to use Remote Desktop?

---

1. You can access a remote desktop over a LAN, through the Internet or an intranet, or with a dial-up RAS connection.

2. Windows XP Home Edition can be a Remote Desktop client, but not a host.

3. To use Remote Desktop, the user account must have a password.

Project 13 Plan the Use of Terminal Services and Remote Desktop

Terminal Services and Remote Desktop are two related components of Windows Server 2003 that may not be needed by everybody, but if needed they are very powerful. This project will help you determine if you want to use any of the Terminal Services and if so what aspects of it you need to set up.

Step by Step

1. Determine which needs you have for Terminal Services and Remote Desktop:

   a. Use recent Windows applications with older hardware and OSs.

   b. Allow multiple users to use common applications and databases.

   c. Centralize the deployment, administration, and configuration of applications.

   d. Manage several to many servers remotely.

   e. Access a computer remotely, like the office from home.

   (Choices a, b, and c require Terminal Services Applications Server, d requires Remote Desktop for Administration, and e requires Remote Desktop.)

2. Determine the Terminal Services Components that you need:

   a. For Terminal Services Applications Server:

      i. Terminal Server

      ii. Terminal Services Configuration

      iii. Terminal Services Manager

      iv. Terminal Services Licensing

      v. Remote Desktop Connection

      vi. Remote Desktop Web Connection

      vii. 32-bit Terminal Services Client

   b. Remote Desktop for Administration:

      i. Terminal Server

      ii. Remote Desktop Connection

      iii. Remote Desktop Web Connection

      iv. 32-bit Terminal Services Client

(continued)

    c. Remote Desktop:

        i. Remote Desktop Connection

        ii. Remote Desktop Web Connection

        iii. 32-bit Terminal Services Client

3. Determine how you want Terminal Services configured:

    a. Use automatic logon?

    b. When to end a Terminal Services session?

    c. How to reconnect if disconnected?

    d. What program(s) should be started and what folder opened?

    e. Allow remote control and/or observation of a terminal session?

    f. Which of the client's devices (disks, printers) will be available?

    g. What permissions will be allowed for what users and groups?

4. Determine the Remote Desktop Connection (Terminal Services Client) needs:

    a. Client uses Windows XP or Windows Server 2003?
       (If so, Remote Desktop Connection is already installed.)

    b. Client uses Windows 95/98/Me, Windows NT 4/2000?
       (If so, 32-bit Terminal Services Client must be installed.)

    c. Client uses some other operating system?
       (If so, install a third-party Terminal Services Client, e.g., Citrix Systems.)

    d. Client will connect over the Internet or an intranet?
       (If so, install Remote Desktop Web Connection in the server.)

5. Determine your Terminal Server Licensing needs (needed only for Applications Server):

    a. Determine the server to be the Terminal Server License Server.

    b. Generate licenses with a domain license server.

    c. Generate licenses with an enterprise license server (the default).

    d. Activate the Terminal Server License Server:

        i. Automatically over the Internet

        ii. Manually, using a browser connected to the Internet

        iii. Manually, using a telephone

    e. Install client licenses with the Terminal Server CAL Installation Wizard.

6. Determine the users with Terminal Services access:

   a. Add users as necessary to Active Directory Users And Computers.

   b. Add users to the Remote Desktop Users group.

   c. Enable Allow Users To Connect Remotely To Your Computer.

7. Determine the security needs of Terminal Services:

   a. Implement a firewall in front of the server.

   b. Use VPN for access across the Internet.

   c. Use strong passwords by all users.

   d. Carefully limit the individuals who have access.

   e. Carefully review the policies that affect Terminal Services.

Project Summary

If your organization has needs that can be fulfilled by Terminal Services and/or Remote Desktop, Windows Server 2003 provides the means to excellently handle those needs. It will be worth the time and effort to set them up and master them.

✓ Module 13 Mastery Check

1. What are some of the characteristics of a thin client?

2. What are some of the reasons to use Terminal Services?

3. What are the components of Terminal Services in Windows Server 2003?

4. Which Terminal Services components—Terminal Server, Remote Desktop Connection, or Remote Desktop—require installation, and what is the final step that both forms of Terminal Services as well as Remote Desktop require to be operational?

5. What are the ways that you can connect to a terminal server, and what do you need to do for each?

6. What are the two different ways that terminal server licenses can be generated, and how do they differ?

7. How can you find out what the IP address is for a computer?

8. What are the differences between Remote Desktop for Administration and Terminal Services Applications Server?

9. In a default installation of Remote Desktop, can you cut and paste between the remote host and the local client?

10. What is the difference between clicking Close in the connections bar and logging off a Remote Desktop connection?

Part V

Administering Windows Server 2003

Module 14

Managing Storage and File Systems

The foundation task of a server is to store, retrieve, and manage files. If that is not done easily and efficiently, there is not a lot of reason for the server. This module looks at how Windows Server 2003 handles this function. In the process, the module discusses the structure and systems used for file storage, and the management features that Windows Server 2003 makes available in this area.

Understand Storage and File Systems

Windows Server 2003 is meant to work in a wide range of computing environments and with several other operating systems. As a result, the structure of its file storage has to be flexible. This is manifest in the types of storage that are available, and in the file systems that Windows Server 2003 can utilize.

Types of Storage

Prior to Windows 2000, there was only one type of storage, called *basic storage,* which allowed a drive to be divided into partitions. Windows Server 2000 added *dynamic storage,* which allows the dynamic creation of partitions or volumes. On a disk-by-disk basis, you must choose which type of storage you want to use, because you can use only one type on a drive. You can have both types in a computer that has two or more drives.

Basic Storage

Basic storage, which provides for the partitioning of a hard disk, is the default type of storage in Windows Server 2003 and is the type of storage used in versions of Windows prior to Windows 2000, including Windows NT and MS-DOS. Partitioning uses software to divide a single disk drive into *partitions* that act as if they were separate disk drives. There are primary partitions and extended partitions. (Partitions are the same as simple volumes which are discussed under "Dynamic Storage.")

Primary partitions are given a drive letter, are separately formatted, and are used to boot or start the computer. There can be up to four primary partitions on a single drive. One partition at a time is made the *active* partition that is used to start the computer. You can put different operating systems on different partitions and start them independently (called dual-booting). Since each partition is formatted separately, another use of partitions is to put data on one partition and the programs and operating system on another partition, allowing you to reformat the applications/OS partition without disturbing the data.

NOTE

There are some limitations and/or downsides to dual-booting. See "Decide Whether to Dual-Boot" in Module 3.

One partition on a disk drive can be an *extended* partition in place of a primary partition, so there can be only three primary partitions if there is an extended partition. An extended partition does not have a drive letter and is not formatted; rather, you divide an extended partition into *logical drives,* each of which is given a drive letter and separately formatted. An extended partition with logical drives allows you to divide a disk into more than four segments. You do not need to have a primary partition to create an extended partition, but in that case, you must start the computer from another drive.

Partitions are usually created and changed while you are doing a clean install of an OS. In Windows Server 2003, though, you can use the Disk Management pane (see "Use Disk Management," later in this module) to create a new partition if there is enough unpartitioned space, or you can delete a partition to create more unpartitioned space. If you delete a partition, you lose all of its contents and must reformat any new partition that is created.

Dynamic Storage

Dynamic storage uses a single partition spanning an entire disk that has been upgraded from basic storage. This single partition can be divided into volumes. *Volumes,* which in their simplest form are the same as partitions, may also have additional features. The following are the five different types of volumes:

- **Simple volumes**   Identify disk space on a single drive, and are the same as partitions.

- **Spanned volumes**   Identify disk space on 2 to 32 disk drives. The space is used sequentially, as it is on a single drive. When the first drive is filled, the second drive is used, and so on. If any disk in a spanned volume fails, the entire volume fails.

- **Mirrored volumes**   A pair of simple volumes on two separate disk drives on which the exact same information is written simultaneously. If one disk fails, the other can be used.

- **Striped volumes**   Identify disk space from 2 to 32 disk drives, where a portion of the data is written on each drive at the same time. This makes for very fast reading and writing, but if any disk fails, the entire volume fails.

- **RAID-5 volumes**   Striped volumes on at least three disks where error-correction information has been added such that if any disk fails, the information can be reconstructed. (RAID stands for *redundant array of independent disks* or, alternatively, *redundant array of inexpensive disks.*)

NOTE

Mirroring and striping are actually two of the three RAID levels that Windows Server 2003 supports, RAID-5 being the third. Mirroring is Level 1, and striping is Level 0. Special hardware disk controllers are needed for mirrored, striped, and RAID-5 volumes.

Unlike basic storage, dynamic storage can be changed in real time without rebooting the computer. Using Dynamic Volume Management (discussed later in the module), you can upgrade basic storage to dynamic storage and add, delete, and change the size of volumes, all without rebooting (although you must reboot after the initial conversion to dynamic storage). You cannot upgrade to dynamic storage either in portable computers or on removable storage.

File Systems

File systems determine the way data is stored on a disk, and are the data structure or format of the data. When you format a disk, you must specify the file system that will be used. In Windows Server 2003, you have a choice of three file systems: FAT (file allocation table), FAT32, and NTFS (new technology file system).

FAT and FAT32 File Systems

FAT was the original file system used in MS-DOS and early versions of Windows through Windows 3.*x* and Windows for Workgroups. The initial releases of Windows 95 used VFAT (virtual FAT), and Windows 95 OSR2 (original equipment manufacturers, or OEMs, service release 2) and Windows 98 used FAT32. FAT is a 16-bit file system with a maximum disk partition size of 512MB; it uses a maximum eight-character filename with a three-character extension. VFAT is also a 16-bit file system, but it supports disk partitions up to 2GB and allows long filenames of up to 255 characters. FAT32 is a 32-bit file system, allows disk partitions of over 2TB (terabytes or trillion bytes), and allows long filenames. In Windows NT, 2000, and 2003, FAT partitions can go up to 4GB.

FAT, VFAT, and FAT32 store information using a fixed-sized increment of the disk, called a *cluster*. Clusters range in size from 512 bytes to 32KB, depending on the size of the disk partition, as shown in Table 14-1. Therefore, as the size of the partition increases, the minimum cluster size increases. A large cluster size can be very inefficient if you are storing a lot of small files. FAT32 made a big improvement in the minimum cluster size and is therefore a major benefit with today's large disks.

Since most files are substantially larger than the cluster size, a number of clusters are necessary to store a single file. The FAT has an entry for each file, containing the filename, the creation date, the total size, and the address on the disk of the first cluster used by the file. Each cluster has the address of the cluster after it, as well as the address of the preceding cluster. One cluster getting corrupted can break cluster chains, often making the file unreadable. Some

Disk Partition	FAT and VFAT Cluster	FAT32 Cluster
0–31MB	512 bytes	512 bytes
32–63MB	1KB	512 bytes
64–127MB	2KB	512 bytes
128–255MB	4KB	512 bytes
256–511MB	8KB	4KB
512–1023MB	16KB	4KB
1024–2047MB	32KB	4KB
2–4GB	64KB	4KB
4–8GB		4KB
8–16GB		8KB
16–32GB		16KB
33GB and above		32KB

Table 14-1 Cluster Sizes Resulting from Various Partition Sizes

utilities occasionally can restore the file by several techniques, including reading backward down the cluster chain. The common end result is orphaned clusters, which can only be deleted.

Clusters can be written anywhere on a disk. If there is room, they are written sequentially, but if there isn't room, they can be spread all over the disk. This is called *fragmentation,* which can cause the load time for a file to be quite lengthy. Utilities are available, including one in Windows Server 2003, to defragment a partition by rearranging the clusters so that all the clusters for a file are contiguous (see "Drive Defragmentation," later in this module).

NTFS File System

NTFS was developed for Windows NT and contains features making it much more secure and less susceptible to disk errors than FAT or FAT32. NTFS is a 32-bit file system that can utilize very large (in excess of 2TB) volumes or partitions and can use filenames of up to 255 characters, including spaces and the preservation of case. Most importantly, NTFS is the only file system that fully utilizes all the features of Windows Server 2003, such as domains and Active Directory.

NOTE

NTFS can also be used in Windows 2000, both Server and Professional, and Windows XP, both Professional and Home Editions.

Managing Storage and File Systems

14

One of the most important features of NTFS is that it provides file- and folder-level security, whereas FAT and FAT32 do not. This means that with FAT or FAT32, if someone gets access to a disk, every file and folder is immediately available. With NTFS, each file and folder has an *access control list (ACL),* which contains the *security identifiers (SIDs)* of the users and groups that are permitted to access the file.

Other features that are available under NTFS and not under FAT or FAT32 are the following:

● File encryption

● Disk compression

● Remote storage management (in Windows 2000 Server and Windows Server 2003 only)

● Disk quotas

● Improved performance with large drives

The first four items are discussed further later in this module. The improved performance with large drives occurs because NTFS does not have the problem of increasing cluster size as the disk size increases.

The sum of all this is that NTFS is strongly recommended. The only situation in which you would not want to use NTFS is if you want to dual-boot with another operating system that cannot read NTFS.

Convert a FAT or FAT32 Drive to NTFS

Normally, you would convert a drive from FAT or FAT32 to NTFS while you are installing Windows Server 2003. Modules 4 and 5 have instructions to do that. You can also convert a FAT or FAT32 partition, volume, or drive at any other time in either of two ways:

● By formatting the partition, volume, or drive

● By running the program Convert.exe

"Use Disk Management," upcoming in this module, discusses formatting, which of course deletes everything on the partition, volume, or drive. Using Convert.exe preserves the partition, volume, or drive. Use the following instructions to use Convert.exe:

NOTE

Many of the steps in this module require that you be logged on either as the Administrator or as someone with Administrator permissions.

1. Open the Start menu and choose Command Prompt if it is available, or All Programs | Accessories | Command Prompt if not directly available on the Start menu. The Command Prompt window opens.

2. At the command prompt, type **convert** *drive:* **/fs:ntfs** and press ENTER, where *drive* is the drive letter of the partition, volume, or physical drive that you want converted. If you would like to see a list of the files that are being converted, you can add /v after /fs:ntfs and a space. The partition, volume, or drive will be converted.

3. When you see Conversion Complete, at the command prompt, type **Exit** and press ENTER.

   Convert.exe has five switches:

- **/fs:ntfs**   Specifies a file system conversion to NTFS

- **/v**   Specifies verbose mode, which displays all the files being converted

- **/cvtarea:***filename*   Uses a file named *filename* that is created outside of Convert (you can use Fsutil File Createnew at the command prompt to create the file) and is in the root directory of the drive to be converted. Convert will use this file to store NTFS metadata files such as the Master File Table (MFT) that will increase the efficiency of Convert and reduce the amount of fragmentation of the resulting NTFS volume.

- **/nosecurity**   Specifies that the security settings of the converted files and folders will be set such that anybody has access.

- **/x**   Specifies that the volume will be dismounted, so any open connection with the volume will be disconnected

   The only way to return a partition, volume, or drive to FAT or FAT32 after converting it to NTFS is to reformat it.

File System Management

The Windows Server 2003 file system extends well beyond a single drive, or even all the drives in a single machine, to all the drives in a network and even includes volumes stored offline on tape or disk. The management of this system is significant, and Windows Server 2003 has a very significant set of tools to handle it. Among these are the following:

- Disk Management

- Dynamic Volume Management

- Distributed File System

- Removable Storage Manager

- Remote Storage Service

- Disk Backup and Restore

CRITICAL SKILL
14.2
Use Disk Management

Disk Management provides a means for managing both local and remote network drives, which includes partitioning, disk compression, disk defragmentation, and disk quotas. Disk management is handled by the Disk Management pane of the Computer Management window. Use the following steps to open Disk Management:

1. Open the Start menu and choose Administrative Tools | Computer Management. The Computer Management window opens.

2. Open Storage in the left pane and click Disk Management. The Disk Management pane appears, as shown in Figure 14-1.

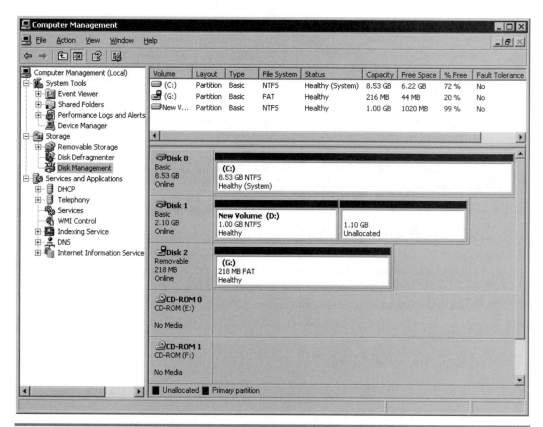

Figure 14-1 Storage management with the Disk Management pane

Disk Management Pane

The Disk Management pane has two main sections: a character-based listing of partitions, volumes, and drives at the top, and a graphic display of the same objects at the bottom. Explore the Disk Management pane with the next set of steps:

1. Right-click an object in the Volume column of the character-based listing to open its context menu. From this menu, you can look at the contents in Windows Explorer; mark the partition or volume as active, if it isn't already so; change the drive letter and path; format or delete the partition or volume if it isn't the active or system partition or volume; open the partition's or volume's Properties dialog box; and get help.

2. Right-click a partition or volume on the right of the graphic display at the bottom of the pane. You'll see a menu similar to that in Step 1 (depending on the type of partition, you may see some differences).

3. Right-click a drive on the left of the graphic display. You will see a drive menu that allows you to convert to a dynamic disk, if you click a basic disk that is not removable and you are in a desktop computer, not a laptop. This menu also allows you to open the drive's Properties dialog box and open Help.

4. Click the Action menu to open it. Here, you can quickly refresh the current status of the storage objects; rescan all drives, which is usually done only when the computer is restarted, and is used to display a drive that has been added or removed without restarting the computer *(hot swapping)*; restore a previous drive configuration; display the menu for the partition, volume, or drive that is currently selected (All Tasks); and access Help.

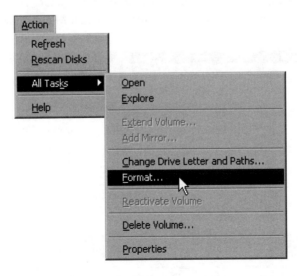

Customize the Disk Management Pane

The Disk Management pane can be significantly customized through both the toolbar and the View menu. Disk Management is an important tool, so you should take the time to customize it by using these steps:

1. In the Computer Management window, open the View menu. The first two options let you determine what is in the top and bottom sections of the pane. The default is a list of partitions or volumes at the top and the graphical view at the bottom. The third alternative for either the top or bottom view is a list of disk drives, which is the same information that is presented in the graphical view.

2. Try several changes to see if any suit you more than the default. Figure 14-2 shows a compact alternative with the Disk list on top and the Volume list on the bottom. Keep the layout you like best.

3. Either click the Settings button on the right of the toolbar or reopen the View menu and choose Settings. The Settings dialog box opens. In the Appearance tab, you can choose the colors and patterns used to represent the various types of partitions and volumes.

4. Select the colors you want to use, and click the Scaling tab. Here, you can choose the way that disks and disk regions (partitions and volumes) are graphically displayed relative to each other. To show capacity logarithmically is probably the best choice if you have drives and regions of substantially different sizes.

5. Make the choices that are correct for you and click OK. Reopen the View menu and choose Customize. The Customize View dialog box opens. Here, you can customize the Computer Management window (called MMC in the dialog box, for Microsoft Management Console).

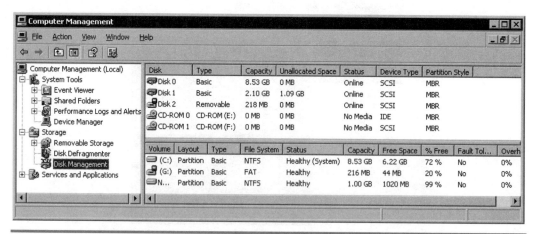

Figure 14-2 An alternative layout for the Disk Management pane

6. Try several changes to see if you like them, and configure the window the way that is best for you. When you are finished, click OK to close the Customize View dialog box.

NOTE

The Drive Paths option of the View menu will be discussed in "Use Dynamic Volume Management," later in this module.

Drive and Partition Properties

There are separate Properties dialog boxes for drives and for partitions. What many people have thought of as the drive properties are really the partition or volume properties. See this for yourself next:

1. Right-click a drive on the left side of the graphic view and choose Properties. The Disk Properties dialog box, similar to Figure 14-3, opens. This is primarily an information dialog box, although you can troubleshoot the drive, set write-caching policies, open the Properties dialog box for a partition or volume, and update or change the driver for the drive.

Figure 14-3 Disk Properties dialog box for a drive

2. Click the Volumes tab, click a partition or volume in the lower part of the Disk Properties dialog box, and click Properties. The Properties dialog box for the partition or volume opens, as you can see in Figure 14-4. This dialog box also provides some information, but unlike the Disk Properties dialog box, it is primarily a place to perform tasks on partitions and volumes. Many of these functions are discussed elsewhere in this module, although sharing and security are discussed in Module 17.

3. Click Disk Cleanup. You'll see a message telling you that Disk Cleanup is calculating how much space will be freed up by eliminating various types of files. When this is finished, the Disk Cleanup dialog box opens with a list of file types that can be deleted. When you click a file type in the list, the Description describes the files; in most cases, you can click View Files to see a list of the files that will be deleted.

4. Review the file types and select those to be deleted. Do not compress old files. That is discussed under "Data Compression," later in this module. When you have selected all the files to be deleted, click OK, and answer Yes, you are sure you want to delete files. You will be told what is happening. When Disk Cleanup is done, the Used Space value in the Properties dialog box for the partition or volume will decrease by the amount you recovered.

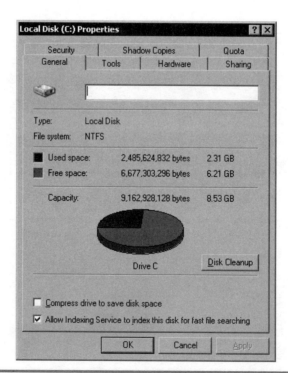

Figure 14-4 Volume or partition Properties dialog box where settings can be changed

5. Click each of the tabs of the Properties dialog box to see the many features and tools that are available. Two features that are not discussed elsewhere are Error-Checking in the Tools tab and the Hardware tab.

6. Open the Tools tab and click Check Now in the Error-Checking section. The Check Disk dialog box opens and explains that you can, at your option, automatically fix file system errors, such as lost clusters, and look for and attempt to recover data that is in a bad sector on the disk.

7. Select what disk checking you want to do, and click Start. If you are on an active server, you are told that exclusive access is not available and thus disk checking could not be done; you are asked whether you want to do the checking the next time you restart the computer. Choose what you want to do, by clicking Yes or No.

8. Open the Hardware tab. Here, you see a list of the drives in the computer. If you select a drive and click Properties, you'll see yet another drive Properties dialog box (the same Properties dialog box you opened in Step 1 and shown in Figure 14-3). All other tabs are discussed elsewhere.

9. When you are done looking at the Properties dialog box for the partition or volume, click OK to close it.

NOTE

The Properties dialog box for a partition or volume can be opened by right-clicking a partition or volume and choosing Properties.

Add and Remove a Disk Drive

If you have hardware that allows hot swapping (adding and removing standard, normally not removable disk drives while the computer is running), or you have a removable disk drive that is meant to be removed while the computer is running, Windows Server 2003 has several tools to support this that don't require restarting the computer. Normally, a computer scans its disk drives to determine what is available only when it is started or restarted. Windows Server 2003 makes this scan available while the computer is running, through the Rescan option in the Action menu. Also, if you just remove a disk drive, either hot-swappable or removable, without preparing for it, problems can result, such as losing data or causing your computer to crash. To accommodate this, the Windows Server 2003 Hardware Wizard has an Unplug/Eject option, and you can even put an Unplug/Eject icon on the taskbar for this purpose.

CAUTION

Don't add or remove a disk drive while the computer is running unless you know for sure that the hardware supports hot swapping. Significant damage can occur to both the drive and the computer or to either one of them.

NOTE

Windows Server 2003 is a lot less sensitive than was Windows 2000 to adding and removing drives or media that Windows has identified as "Removable." For example, I have a removable optical drive that you can see in Figure 14-1. If I removed the media in Windows 2000 without first telling Windows about it, I got a nasty error message. In Windows Server 2003, I no longer get that message.

Add a Drive

You can add a new drive or a drive that you have taken out of another computer. After physically adding a new drive—one that has never been used or has been newly formatted prior to installing it—open the Disk Management pane and choose Rescan from the Action menu. After rescanning, the drive should appear in Disk Management, and you can partition and format it as you wish (see the upcoming section "Partition and Format Drives").

If you bring in a disk that has been used on, and contains data from, another computer, use Rescan as just described. After rescanning, the new disk may be marked "Foreign" if Windows Server 2003 detects that the disk is a dynamic disk from another Windows Server 2003 computer (which stores its own configuration data). Right-click the foreign drive, choose Import Foreign Disks, and follow the directions that you see.

Remove a Drive

If you want to remove a drive that is either hot-swappable or removable, it is important to prepare the drive for that event by telling Windows Server 2003 that you are going to remove it, before you actually do so. Knowing this, Windows Server 2003 will prevent further writing to the drive and perform any hardware-specific tasks, such as spinning down the drive and/or ejecting the platter. Depending on your drive and how it has been implemented in Windows Server 2003, you'll have various ways to tell the operating system that you want to remove the drive.

On some devices, such as removable drives (in particular my optical drive), you can right-click the drive on the left of the graphical part of the Disk Management pane and choose Eject. The disk will be prepared and ejected. Other devices have similar commands.

Partition and Format Drives

The first step in preparing a disk for use is to partition it and then format it. Partitioning can be done only when there is unallocated space on the drive—space that is not currently used for an existing partition. If you have no unallocated space, then the only way to create a new partition is to delete an existing one. Therefore, start out looking at deleting partitions, then adding partitions, formatting them, adding logical drives, and changing drive letters.

TIP

Free space is the amount of space available to create logical drives from extended partitions. Unallocated space is space that is not allocated to anything.

CAUTION

Deleting a partition and then formatting it eliminates all information in the partition. Be very sure you want to do this before you execute the commands.

Delete Partitions

To delete a partition, as with the rest of the partitioning and formatting functions, you should have the Disk Management pane open in the Computer Management window. From that point, right-click the partition to be deleted and choose Delete Partition (Delete Volume if it is a dynamic partition). You are warned that all data will be lost. Click Yes if you are sure you want to do that. The partition or volume is deleted.

Add Primary Partitions

Adding a primary partition is a little more complex and has its own wizard. To add a partition:

1. Right-click an unallocated area of a disk and choose New Partition. The New Partition Wizard opens.

2. Click Next. Choose the type of partition you want, either a primary partition or an extended partition. You need to use a primary partition to start an operating system, but you can have only four partitions. If one of the four partitions is an extended partition, you can then divide it into 23 logical drives. After making the decision, click Next.

3. Select the size of the partition. The maximum is the size of the unallocated space; the minimum is 8MB, as you can see in Figure 14-5. When you have selected the size, click Next.

4. Assign a drive letter. The drop-down list shows you the options available, which is the alphabet less the other drives already in the computer. There are two other options: you can make this partition a folder on any other drive that supports drive paths (most do), and you can leave the drive letter unassigned. Make your choice and click Next.

5. Choose how you want the partition formatted (if at all), the label to use, and whether you want to use file and folder compression, as shown in Figure 14-6. Then click Next.

6. Review the options that you have chosen and use Back to correct any that are not what you want.

7. When all the choices are the way you want them, click Finish. The partition will be created and formatted as you instructed.

TIP

One good reason to attach a new partition to an existing drive and folder is to increase the space available in an existing, but empty, shared folder ("a share") on a server, so the users can continue to use an existing path for storing or accessing files.

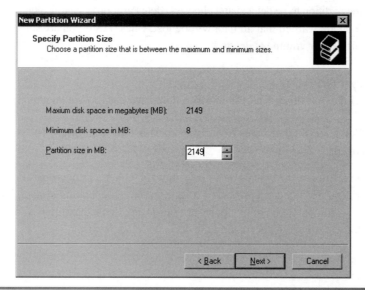

New Partition Wizard

Specify Partition Size
Choose a partition size that is between the maximum and minimum sizes.

Maximum disk space in megabytes (MB): 2149

Minimum disk space in MB: 8

Partition size in MB: 2149

< Back   Next >   Cancel

Figure 14-5 Specifying the partition size

Figure 14-6 Formatting a partition

Format Partitions

Often, you'll format a partition when you create it, as described in the preceding section, but you can also separately format the partition, if either it was not done when the partition was created or you want to replace an existing format. The following steps show you how:

NOTE

If you try to format a partition that contains Windows Server 2003, you'll get a message box that says you can't.

1. Right-click the partition that you want to format, and choose Format. A small Format dialog box opens, asking for the label, the file system, and the allocation unit size.

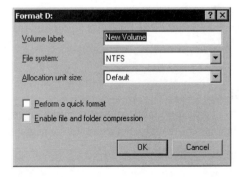

2. Make the choices that are correct for you and click OK. You will be warned that all data on the partition will be erased. Click OK. The drive will be formatted.

Add Logical Drives

To add logical drives, you must first have an extended partition, so do that first. Then add logical drives, as follows:

1. Right-click an unallocated area of a disk and choose New Partition. The New Partition Wizard opens. Click Next.

2. Select Extended Partition and click Next. Specify the partition size and again click Next. Click Finish to actually create the partition. The partition will be created.

3. Right-click the free space in the new partition and choose New Logical Drive. The New Partition Wizard again opens. Click Next. The Select Partition Type dialog box opens, with Logical Drive as your only option.

4. Click Next. Enter the size of the logical drive and again click Next. Assign a drive letter (see the discussion on assigning a drive letter or path in the previous section "Add Primary Partitions") and click Next.

5. Choose the way you want the logical drive formatted, click Next, review the choices you have made, and click Finish. The logical drive will be created as you described it.

6. Repeat Steps 3–5 for as many logical drives (up to 23) as you want.

Change Drive Letters

Changing a drive letter is similar to the previous functions:

1. Right-click the partition or logical drive whose drive letter you want to change, and select Change Drive Letter And Paths. The Change Drive Letter And Paths dialog box opens.

2. You can add additional drive letters and paths on existing drives, edit existing drive letters to change them, and remove (delete) existing drives and/or paths.

3. Click Add, Change, or Remove, fill in the necessary information, click OK (you are reminded that changing drive letters might cause a program that depends on that drive not to run), and click Close.

Data Compression

Data compression allows you to store more information in a given amount of disk space. Different types of files compress differently. For example, some graphics files can be compressed to under 10 percent of their original size, whereas a database file may not get under 90 percent. Compressed files, folders, and partitions or volumes can be used in the same manner as you use uncompressed data. They are uncompressed as they are read, and are recompressed when they are saved again. The negative side of compression is that all file-related actions (reading, writing, copying, and so on) take a little longer.

Data compression in Windows Server 2003 is a lot different from the early compression schemes, in which your only choice was to compress an entire partition. In Windows Server 2003, you can compress a partition or volume, a folder, or a file. You can also automatically compress files that have not been used for a given period of time, as a way to archive them.

NOTE

Data compression in Windows Server 2003 can be done only on or within NTFS-formatted partitions or volumes, and the cluster size must be no larger than 4KB.

Compress Partitions or Volumes

To use compression on a partition or volume, open the Disk Management pane in the Computer Management window, and then follow these steps:

1. Right-click the partition or volume to be compressed and choose Properties. The drive's Properties dialog box opens, as previously shown in Figure 14-4.

2. Click the check box opposite Compress Drive To Save Disk Space and then click OK. You are asked whether you want to compress just the root folder (for example, D:/) or all the subfolders and files in the root folder.

NOTE

A folder can be compressed without its subfolders being compressed, and the subfolders can be compressed without the containing folder being compressed.

3. Make the choice that is correct for you and click OK. You see a message box showing that the compression is taking place. When the message box goes away, the compression is complete.

NOTE

To uncompress data, reverse the steps used to compress it. For a partition, remove the check mark in the Properties dialog box and confirm that you want to uncompress.

Compress Files and Folders

You can compress individual files and folders. This is done from Windows Explorer or My Computer, as follows:

1. Right-click the file or folder and choose Properties. The file's or folder's Properties dialog box opens.

2. Click Advanced. The Advanced Attributes dialog box opens, as you can see in Figure 14-7.

3. Click Compress Contents To Save Disk Space and then click OK twice to close both the Advanced Attributes and the Properties dialog boxes. A Confirm Attributes Changes dialog box opens, giving you a choice between applying the changes to the current folder only or to include the subfolders and files it contains.

4. Make the choice that is correct for you and then click OK. The compression will be done. If the file or folder is large enough for the compression to take a minute or more, you'll see a message telling you the compression is taking place.

   If you reopen the Properties dialog box for the file or folder, you will be shown both the actual size and the size on disk, as shown in Figure 14-8.

NOTE

All files and folders have a Size On Disk value, but for uncompressed files and folders it is usually larger than the actual size due to minimum cluster size taking more space that what is needed for a file or folder.

Figure 14-7 Choosing to compress a folder

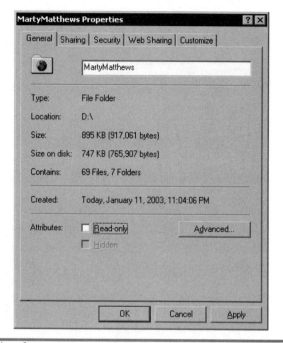

Figure 14-8 The results of compressing a folder of many different files and subfolders

Automatic Archival Compression

Automatic archival compression is a routine that automatically compresses any file that goes unused for a period of time that you set. This gets around the worst problem of compression: if you are regularly using a file, it remains uncompressed and therefore faster to access. If a file is primarily just being stored, it can be compressed without much penalty.

As you read earlier in this module in "Drive and Partition Properties," automatic archival compression can be turned on as a part of Disk Cleanup. See how by following these steps:

1. In the Disk Management pane, right-click a partition or volume where you want to use archival compression, and choose Properties. The partition's Properties dialog box opens, as shown earlier in Figure 14-4.

2. Click Disk Cleanup to open the Disk Cleanup dialog box. In the Disk Cleanup tab, scroll the Files To Delete list until you see Compress Old Files, as you can see in Figure 14-9. This does not delete files but rather compresses them when they have not been accessed for a certain number of days.

3. Select Compress Old Files and click Options. The Compress Old Files dialog box opens and asks you to set the number of days a file must go unused before it is compressed.

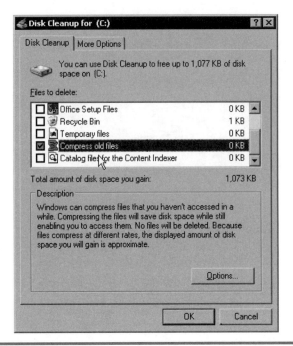

Figure 14-9 Selecting archival compression

4. Enter the shortest number of days that you think is realistic for you. Remember that you can still access the files even if they are compressed—it just takes a moment longer.

5. Click OK twice and answer Yes, you want to delete files (you won't be deleting the compressed files). You will see a message that the disk cleanup is taking place. When it is done, click OK to close the Properties dialog box.

Use NTFS-Compressed Files

If you compress just some of your files and folders, you'll want to know which are compressed and which aren't, and understand how the files behave when they are copied and moved. To know which files and folders are compressed and which aren't, you can change the color in which compressed files and folders (actually their labels) are displayed. To do that, open Windows Explorer's Tools menu, choose Folder Options, and in the View tab of the Folder Options dialog box that opens, scroll the list to the bottom and click Show Encrypted Or Compressed NTFS Files In Color.

When copying and moving compressed files and folders, they are a little slower to process and don't always end up the way they started out. Here are the rules for copying and moving:

- When you copy a compressed file or folder within its original partition or volume or between NTFS partitions or volumes, the file or folder inherits the compression of the folder to which it is copied.

- When you copy a compressed file or folder to a FAT partition or a floppy disk, the file or folder decompresses.

- When you move a compressed file or folder within its original partition or volume, the file or folder retains its original compression.

- When you move a compressed file or folder between NTFS partitions or volumes, the file or folder inherits the compression of the folder to which it is moved.

- When you move a compressed file or folder to a FAT partition or a floppy disk, the file or folder decompresses.

Drive Defragmentation

As explained earlier under "File Systems," files are made up of smaller segments called clusters, and these clusters may not always be stored together in one contiguous region of a disk. The result is the fragmentation of files, causing an increased file-access time. Windows Server 2003 has a utility to defragment the files in a partition or volume, which can be formatted as FAT, FAT32, or NTFS. Defragment a partition or volume with these steps:

1. In the Disk Management pane, right-click the partition or volume to defragment, and choose Properties.

2. In the Properties dialog box, click the Tools tab, and click Defragment Now. The Disk Defragmenter dialog box opens.

3. Select a partition or volume and click Analyze. When the analysis is complete, click View Report and you'll see a numeric analysis of the volume. Click Close and you'll see a display of the fragmented and contiguous files in the partition, similar to that shown in Figure 14-10.

4. Click Defragment. Depending on the amount of information in the partition, this will take some time, but you can watch as the partition slowly becomes defragmented.

5. When the defragmentation is complete, you can see the results. Close the Disk Defragmenter and the partition Properties dialog boxes.

NOTE

The Disk Defragmenter can take a lot of processor resources and significantly slow down disk access. It is therefore important to do the defragmentation when use of the computer is light.

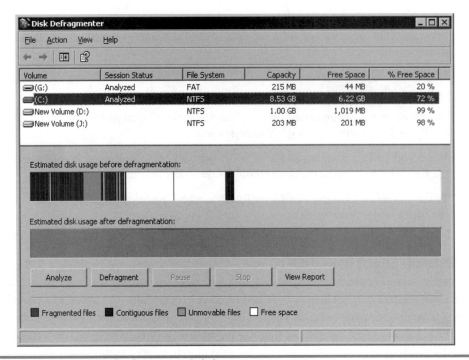

Figure 14-10 Analysis of a fragmented disk partition

Drive Quotas

With NTFS, you can monitor and set policies and limits on the disk space used in a partition or volume, and make sure that one user does not take up more of the disk than is desired. This is particularly important on Internet and intranet file servers. See how to set quotas next:

1. In the Disk Management pane, right-click the partition or volume in which the quotas are to be set, and choose Properties.

2. In the Properties dialog box, click the Quota tab, and then click Enable Quota Management. Set the limits, warnings, and logging that you want to use. Figure 14-11 shows one possible group of settings.

3. When you have the settings that you want, click OK. After you have used the partition for a while, return to the Quota tab in the partition's Properties dialog box and click Quota Entries to open the Quota Entries window. This shows who is using the partition and how that usage relates to the quotas that have been set.

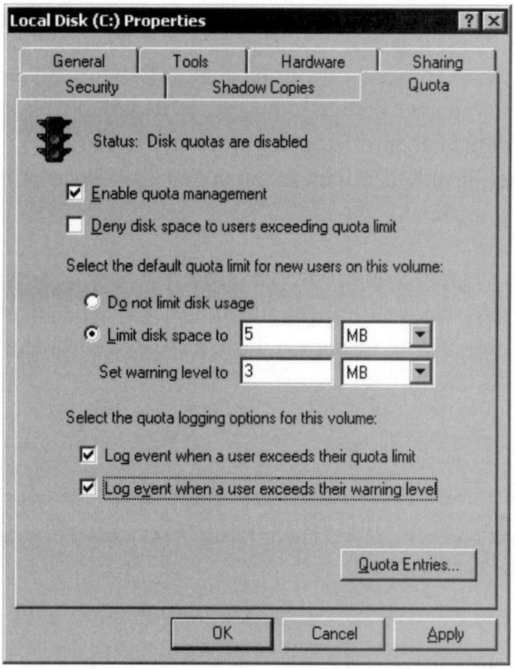

Local Disk (C:) Properties   ? ✕

| General | Tools | Hardware | Sharing |
| Security | Shadow Copies | Quota |

Status: Disk quotas are disabled

☑ **E**nable quota management

☐ **D**eny disk space to users exceeding quota limit

Select the default quota limit for new users on this volume:

○ D**o** not limit disk usage

● **L**imit disk space to   5   MB   ▼

Set warning level to   3   MB   ▼

Select the quota logging options for this volume:

☑ **L**og event when a user exceeds their quota limit

☑ **L**og e**v**ent when a user exceeds their warning level

Quota Entries...

OK   Cancel   **A**pply

Figure 14-11   Quota settings for a drive

NOTE

Disk quotas are allocated by person within a partition or volume. Compression is ignored when calculating quota usage, and the free space reported to a user is the space remaining within their quota.

File and Folder Encryption

Windows Server 2003 NTFS allows the encryption of individual files and folders. With an encrypted file, if someone gets access to the computer, that person still cannot access the file. The person who is logged on when the file is encrypted must be logged on to read the file. Any other person will find the file unreadable, although to all indications, the file is the same. (Module 17 discusses file and folder encryption further.) Here's how to encrypt a file or a folder:

1. In the Windows Explorer, right-click the file or folder to be encrypted and choose Properties. The Properties dialog box opens.

2. Click Advanced. The Advanced Attributes dialog box opens, as shown earlier in Figure 14-7.

3. Click Encrypt Contents To Secure Data and click OK twice. If you chose a file in Step 1, you are warned that you have chosen to encrypt a file without encrypting the folder and as a result the file could become decrypted when it is modified. You are given a choice of encrypting both the file and the folder (recommended) or encrypting only the file. Make your choice and click OK.

If you sign off the computer and someone else signs on, or if someone tries to access the file over the network, they will find the file unreadable. Also, if you look at the file in the Windows Explorer, it will, by default, have a colored entry alerting you to the fact that it is encrypted.

NOTE

You cannot both encrypt and compress a file or folder. If you select one of these attributes, you cannot select the other.

Progress Check

1. What are the two types of storage in Windows Server 2003 and how do they differ?

2. What is partitioning?

3. What are the three RAID levels that Windows Server 2003 supports?

4. What are the three file systems supported in Windows Server 2003?

---

1. The two types of storage in Windows Server 2003 are basic storage, which allows a drive to be divided into partitions or volumes, and dynamic storage, which allows the dynamic creation of partitions or volumes.

2. Partitioning uses software to divide a single disk drive into partitions that act as if they were separate disk drives.

3. Mirroring, striping, and RAID-5 are three RAID levels that Windows Server 2003 supports.

4. In Windows Server 2003, you have a choice of three file systems: FAT (file allocation table), FAT32, and NTFS (new technology file system).

Ask the Expert

Q: How do partitions differ from volumes?

A: In the simplest case, that of simple volumes, there is no difference. Both partitions and simple volumes are areas of a disk that have been identified with a drive letter and separately formatted from the rest of the disk. Both partitions and simple volumes can be on either basic or dynamic disks, but dynamic disks can additionally have striped, spanned, mirrored, and RAID-5 volumes.

CRITICAL SKILL

14.3 Use Dynamic Volume Management

Dynamic Volume Management enables you to create, change, or mirror partitions or volumes without rebooting, by using dynamic storage and disks. A dynamic disk has a single partition within which you can create volumes. Simple volumes are the same as partitions except that they are dynamic (can be changed on the fly), can span disks, and include additional types for advanced hardware (striped, mirrored, and RAID-5).

Convert to Dynamic Storage

Most basic disks can be converted to dynamic disks very easily. The exceptions are disks on portable computers and removable disks. Also, the disk must have 1MB of unallocated space, and Windows Server 2003 can be installed in a dynamic volume only if that volume has been converted from a basic root or boot volume. Here's how to convert:

1. In the Disk Management pane, right-click a disk on the left of the graphical display and select Convert To Dynamic Disk from the pop-up menu.

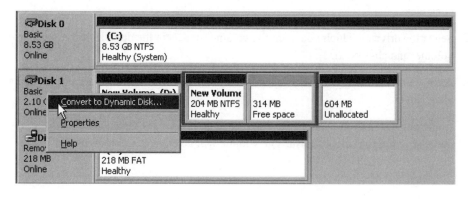

2. Confirm the disk that you want to convert, and click OK. The Disks To Convert dialog box opens showing the disk(s) to be converted. If you click Details, you are shown the volumes that will be automatically created within the disk.

3. Click OK if you opened the Convert Details, and then click Convert. You are warned that you will not be able to boot a previous version of Windows from a dynamic disk, and then you are asked if you really want to continue.

4. If you in fact want to convert, click Yes. You are then told that the file systems on the disk(s) to be upgraded will be dismounted, meaning that any open files will be closed and access to the disk will be prohibited. Again you are asked if you want to continue. If you do, click OK. Conversion will proceed. When it is complete, if you have converted a boot partition or volume, you will be told that the computer will be restarted. Click OK; you will then be told that Windows has finished installing new devices and that you need to restart your computer a second time. Click Yes.

NOTE

The only way to change a dynamic disk back to a basic disk is to delete all dynamic volumes, and therefore all files in those volumes, and then right-click the drive and choose Convert To Basic Disk.

Create Volumes

You can create a new volume within the unallocated space of a dynamic drive. Do that with these steps:

1. Right-click the unallocated space of a dynamic drive and choose New Volume. The New Volume Wizard appears.

2. Click Next. The Select Volume Type dialog box is displayed. Choose Simple Volume and click Next.

3. Select the drive on which you want the volume (or accept the default), enter the size of the volume, and click Next.

4. Assign a drive letter, and click Next. Choose how you want the drive formatted, and again click Next.

5. Confirm the steps you want taken, going back and fixing those that are not correct if necessary, and then click Finish. The volume will be created and formatted.

Extend Volumes

Extended volumes are ones whose size has been increased. Volumes can be extended if they are created on a dynamic disk and are not either a boot disk or one that was created from a basic disk in an earlier version of Windows. Here's how to extend a volume:

1. Right-click a volume you want to extend and choose Extend Volume. The Extend Volume Wizard opens.

2. Click Next. Select the drive on which you want to extend the volume (or accept the default), enter the size of the extended volume, and click Next.

3. Confirm the steps you want to perform, and click Finish.

In the graphical section of Disk Management, this looks like two separate volumes, as shown in Figure 14-12, but they have the same drive letter and appear as one volume in the Volume section.

Create a Spanning Volume

A spanned volume can include disk space on 2 to 32 dynamic disks, and to the user it looks like a single volume. This is a way to get a large volume, but it is also risky, because every disk that is added to the volume increases the chance the entire volume will fail. Create a spanned volume with the following steps:

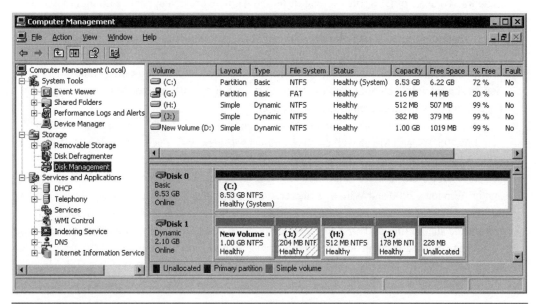

Figure 14-12 An extended volume looks separate, but it isn't.

1. In Disk Management, right-click an area of unallocated space on one of the disks to be included in the volume (all disks must be dynamic disks), and choose New Volume. The New Volume Wizard opens. Click Next.

2. Select Spanned Volume and click Next. Select the disks that you want to include in the spanned volume and the amount of space to use on each disk.

3. Click Next. Assign a drive letter or a folder at which to mount the volume, and again click Next.

4. Specify how you want the folder formatted, and click Next. Confirm the tasks you want performed, and click Finish. The volume will be created and formatted, with the final result displayed in both disks.

NOTE

A spanned volume cannot be striped or mirrored, is not fault-tolerant, and a failure on any one disk is a failure of the entire volume.

CRITICAL SKILL
14.4 Use the Distributed File System

The Distributed File System (DFS) provides for the creation of a directory that spans several file servers and allows users to easily search and locate files or folders distributed over the network. To users of DFS, files spread throughout a network can appear as though they are on a single server, which makes their use much easier than if they appear on their actual servers. Users need to go to only one place on the network to access files located in many different places. DFS also assists in load balancing across several servers, by allowing the distribution of files over those servers without penalizing the end user. DFS can be either stand-alone or domain-based with Active Directory, wherein spreading the information across several domain controllers provides a degree of fault tolerance.

DFS has both server-based and client-based components. The DFS client runs on Windows 95, 98, and Me as well as on Windows NT 4 (Service Pack 3 and above), Windows 2000, Windows XP, and Windows Server 2003. The DFS server-based components, DFS roots and DFS links, run on Windows NT 4 (Service Pack 3 and above) in stand-alone mode, and on Windows 2000 and Windows Server 2003 in both stand-alone and domain-based modes.

The *DFS client* caches referrals for a period of time to DFS roots and DFS links. *DFS roots* store shared files and *DFS links,* which point to other DFS roots, individual shared files, or domain volumes. In a domain-based DFS, the DFS client must be a member of the same domain as the DFS root it is seeking. The stand-alone DFS client is included in Windows 98, Me, NT 4 (with Service Pack 3 and above), Windows 2000, Windows XP, and Windows Server 2003, and is available for download for Windows 95 and domain-based versions at http://www .microsoft.com/NTServer/nts/downloads/winfeatures/NTSDistrFile/download.asp.

There are several important reasons to use domain-based DFS. Domain-based DFS uses Active Directory to store the DFS *topology,* or configuration, providing a common interface for all server-based file handling. Also, by using Active Directory, there is automatic replication to the other domain controllers within the domain.

Create a Distributed File System

The process of creating a Distributed File System includes creating a DFS root and adding DFS links to the DFS root.

Create a DFS Root

A DFS root can be on any server or domain controller in a network, and the server can be formatted with FAT, FAT32, or NTFS, although NTFS offers better security and the use of domains. A server can have only one DFS root. DFS uses its own window to create and manage DFS. Open that first and create a DFS root with these steps:

1. Open the Start menu and choose Administrative Tools | Distributed File System. The Distributed File System window opens.

2. Open the Action menu and choose New Root. The New Root Wizard opens.

3. Click Next. Determine whether you want a domain-based root (recommended) or a stand-alone root and then click Next again.

4. If you choose a domain-based root, enter the domain name or select it from the list of trusting domains and click Next. Enter or browse for the host server and click Next.

5. Enter a unique name for the root, enter any comments, and click Next. Enter or browse for the starting folder or path to share and click Next.

6. Confirm your choices and click Finish. The new DFS root will be created, like this:

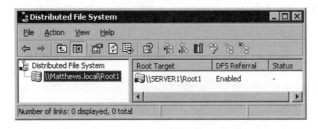

Add a DFS Link

With a DFS root, you can add a DFS link to additional shared folders. See how to do this next (the DFS window should still be open on your screen):

1. With the DFS root selected, open the Action menu and select New Link. The New Link dialog box opens.

2. Enter the link name, the shared folder it will point to, and any comments.

3. When the link is the way you want it, click OK. The DFS link will appear under the DFS root. You can create as many links as you want in this manner. Here are two DFS links under a DFS root:

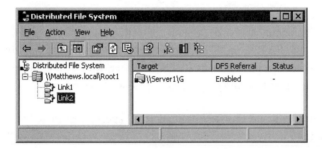

If you open Windows Explorer in the server, you'll see the new DFS links you have added.

Manage a Distributed File System

There are several tools to facilitate managing the Distributed File System. These include replicating the DFS tree, checking whether all the links are still valid, and controlling the display of DFS root.

Replicate the DFS Root

You can assure that the Distributed File System is always available by making sure its structure and links are replicated on several other domain controllers:

1. In the Distributed File System window, right-click the DFS root you want to replicate and choose New Root Target.

2. Enter or browse to the name of the server that will host the replica, and click Next.

3. Confirm your choices and click Finish. The DFS target will be created. The replica will be placed on the new domain controller and appear in the DFS window.

Check DFS Links

You can quickly check the links in a DFS root or DFS link by right-clicking the object you want to check and choosing Check Status. If the check did not find any problems, a green check mark appears next to the object, but if a problem is found, an × appears in a red circle.

When you find a problem, it is often because a share is offline. Depending on how easy that is to check, it might be easier to just remove and re-create the link.

Control the Display of the DFS Root

You can remove the display of the DFS root by right-clicking it and choosing Hide Root. A message tells you what will happen and that client access is not affected. Click Yes to proceed.

If you want to turn the display back on, open the Action menu, choose Show Root, enter or select the domain and the DFS root you want to display, and click OK.

CRITICAL SKILL

14.5 Handle Removable and Remote Storage

Removable Storage provides tracking for media, such as tapes and optical disks, stored both individually and in hardware libraries, such as jukeboxes. Remote Storage monitors disk space and which files have copies in Removable Storage. When free disk space drops below a certain level, the files that are also on remote storage are deleted to provide more room on the hard disk.

Using Removable Storage

Removable Storage manages media, such as tapes and disks, not the data on the media. Removable Storage works with programs such as Backup, which controls the data on the removable media, to organize and track the media that are used for the program. The media are placed into *media pools* in such a way that a media pool provides enough storage space for a given operation, such as a recurring backup. Removable Storage is controlled by the Removable Storage option in the Computer Management window.

Removable Storage Option

Open and look at the Removable Storage option by following these steps:

1. Open the Start menu and choose Administrative Tools | Computer Management. The Computer Management window opens.

2. Under Storage, open Removable Storage and then each of the objects it contains: Media Pools, Physical Locations, and each drive, similar to what is shown in Figure 14-13.

3. Left- and right-click each object under Removable Storage to get an understanding of what is there.

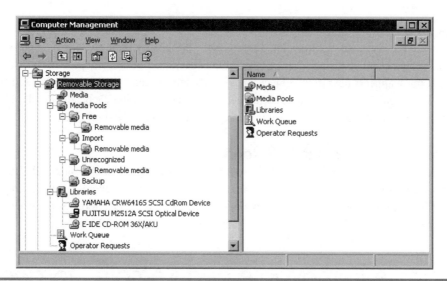

Figure 14-13 Removable Storage tracks the media used on devices that contain it.

You can see that Removable Storage provides a way to control media and the drives that use the media.

Work with Media Pools

The purpose of media pools is to differentiate among both types and uses of media, using the properties that you assign to the media pools available to you. Media pools can hold other media pools or media, but they can't hold both. All media in a given media pool that contains media must be of the same type, such as tape cartridges, optical disks, or rewritable CDs (CD-RWs). A parent media pool can contain subordinate media pools with different media.

There are two classes of media pools: system and application. *System* media pools are created by Windows Server 2003 and are meant to hold media not used by an application. *Application* media pools are obviously created by applications, such as Remote Storage or Backup (both discussed later in this module), or by an administrator and contain media that are currently being used by that application.

The following are the three default system media pools:

- **Free**   Contain media that can be drawn by an application and that do not contain useful information.

- **Import** Contain media that have not been used in the current location but have recognizable data from, for example, a different office. It should be moved to either an application or a free media pool.

- **Unrecognized** Contain new media that do not have recognizable data on them. It should be moved to a free media pool.

The following steps show how to create a parent media pool for backing up, and then how to create two subordinate pools, one each for two different types of media (the Computer Management window should be open with Removable Storage open showing Media Pools in the left pane):

1. Right-click Media Pools and choose Create Media Pool. The Create A New Media Pool Properties dialog box opens.

2. In the General tab, enter a Name and a Description and leave the default Contains Other Media Pools under Media Information. Click the Security tab, set the permissions as you need them, and click OK.

3. Right-click your new media pool, choose Create Media Pool, enter a Name and a Description, and click Contains Media of Type. Open the drop-down list and select the first media type you want to store. Choose the allocation/deallocation policy you want to use, set the permissions you need, and click OK.

4. Repeat Step 3 for the second type of media you want to store. When you are done, you should have a hierarchical structure.

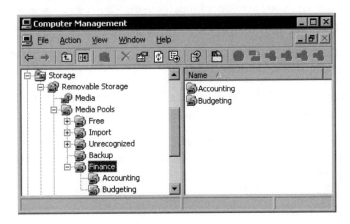

Work with Removable Devices

Under Libraries in the Removable Storage tree on the left of the Computer Management window, you should find all of the removable storage hardware devices on the computer.

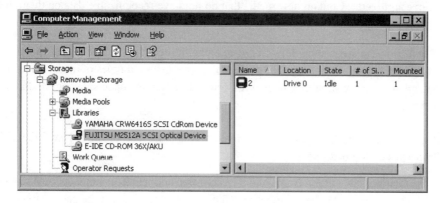

Removable storage devices are of two types: stand-alone devices, such as a tape drive or a rewritable CD-ROM drive, and storage libraries, such as tape and disk jukeboxes. Stand-alone devices have only one piece of media to work with at a time, whereas storage libraries have a number of pieces. There are a number of controls in Windows Server 2003 for libraries, and if you have such a device, you need to look into them; but for this book we'll only talk about stand-alone drives. The following procedure shows you how to enable a device, specify its media, and inject and eject the media:

1. Right-click a device you have under Libraries in the Computer Management window, and choose Properties. The device's Properties dialog box opens, as you can see in Figure 14-14.

2. Enable or disable the drive by selecting or deselecting Enable Drive in the lower part of the dialog box.

3. Look at the other tabs, and in the Security tab, set the permissions you need. When you are finished, click OK to close the Properties dialog box.

4. If the device you just set up has media in it, right-click the device and choose Eject. The media should be ejected. Right-click the device again, and choose Inject. The Media Inject Wizard appears. Click Next.

Figure 14-14 Setting the properties for a removable storage device

5. Place the media in the drive and click Next. You'll see a notice about completing the Media Inject Wizard. Click Finish. With the drive selected, you should see in the right pane the media you just inserted.

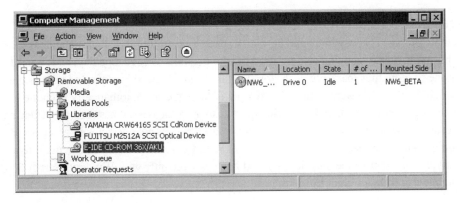

6. Right-click the media entry and choose Properties. The media's Properties dialog box opens. Here, you can enter a name for the media. Note that it has been assigned to the Import media pool. If your media is double-sided, you can enter a name and description for each side. Click OK when you are done with the media's Properties dialog box.

7. Open the media type within the Import media pool and you should again see the media you inserted into the drive. (Notice how the media types that you use have been added to the media pools.) Drag this media from the Import folder to either the Free folder of that media type or an application folder you previously created (it must be the same media type and must be writable) depending on which folder is free (you get a message that all data on the media will be destroyed). Click Yes if that is what you want.

8. Select the removable drive again under Libraries and right-click the media item in the right pane. Choose Eject. The Media Eject Wizard may open or, depending on the drive you have, the media may be automatically ejected. If it isn't, click Next and the media may then be ejected. If not, do it manually, and in any case click Next and click Finish.

The particular piece of media is no longer displayed in the right pane with the drive selected, nor is it in Import, but if you look at where you dragged it, you'll see that it is still there.

The primary means of adding media to media pools is through the drives. The other media-related options that were not demonstrated are

● Prepare, which is used to prepare a piece of media to enter the Free media pool, normally to format the media

● Mount and Dismount, which are applicable only to devices which, separately from loading, place the media online, as you would do in a jukebox device

Understand Remote Storage

Remote Storage is a way to extend hard disk space by monitoring disk usage and, as space gets tight, automatically copying seldom-used files to a remote storage tape device. If a need arises for one or more files that have been stored offline, and that need is requested in the same way it would be if the file were online, the file(s) will be requested automatically from the offline device. Remote Storage uses Removable Storage to track the tapes it has used for offline storage. Backup, on the other hand, is an independent product that does not interact with or replace Remote Storage, nor is it replaced by Remote Storage. With Remote Storage, you can use only certain SCSI tape and removable disk devices, and it is available only with Windows Server 2003 Enterprise and Data Center Editions.

CRITICAL SKILL
14.6 # Use Backup Or Restore

The Backup Or Restore utility is used to blunt the impact of losing information on a volume or partition caused by a hardware failure of a drive or a computer, or the inadvertent erasure of one or more files for whatever reason. You can back up all files in a volume or partition, or just selected files. You can create an Automated System Recovery disk, back up Remote Storage files, and copy the computer's *system state,* the system files such as the Registry and Active Directory. You can back up files on another hard disk, on a tape, on a writable CD, or on a removable disk. Once you have created a backup of whatever data you want, you can restore the data either to the original computer and disk or to others.

Types of Backup

The following are the five types of backup:

- **Normal backup** Copies all the files that have been selected to the backup media and marks the files as having been archived (the Archive bit is cleared).

- **Differential** Copies all the files that are new or changed since the last normal or incremental backup. The Archive bit is not cleared, so the files are continually backed up until the next normal or incremental backup.

- **Incremental** Copies all the files that are new or changed since the last normal or incremental backup. The Archive bit is cleared, so the files are not backed up again.

- **Copy** Copies all the files that have been selected, but does not clear the Archive bit, so it does not affect normal and incremental backups.

- **Daily** Copies all the files that have changed on the day of the backup. The Archive bit is not cleared, so any of the other forms of backup will also copy the files.

If you use a combination of normal and differential backup, your backups will be slower and you will use more media, but restoration will be much faster. If you use a combination of normal and incremental backup, your backups will be faster and you will use less media, but your restoration will take the longest. You need to determine which resources—backup time, restore time, or media—are more important to you. Since you probably back up frequently and restore seldom, optimizing the backup time is often the choice.

Use Backup

Backup can be done manually or on an automatic, scheduled basis. You can use the Backup Or Restore Wizard or the Backup Utility window. Finally, you can back up all the information on the computer and create a system recovery disk or manually select the information you want backed up. Try various combinations of these options next.

Back Up All Information with the Wizard

The simplest and most comprehensive backup is to let the Backup Or Restore Wizard back up all information on a computer and then also create a system recovery disk that will start the computer and restore all the information. Here's how to do that:

1. Open the Start menu and choose All Programs | Accessories | System Tools | Backup. The Backup Or Restore Wizard opens with its Welcome message. In this dialog box, you can turn off the Wizard and go to the Backup Or Restore window, and you can switch to Advanced mode. For now, stay in the Wizard and click Next.

2. Accept the default of backing up and click Next. Again accept the default of backing up all information and creating a system recovery disk and click Next.

3. Open the drop-down list and select the type of backup that is correct for you, specify which piece of media to use, and enter a name for the backup. Also make sure you have a floppy disk ready. Click Next. You are shown a summary of your choices similar to what you can see in Figure 14-15. If you want to change them, click Back.

4. Click Finish to start the backup and create the system recovery disk. Backup will use Removable Storage to try to find the correct media to use and let you know the results, like this:

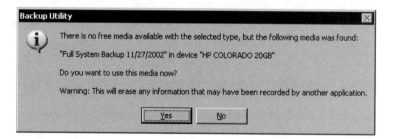

5. Respond to the queries about the backup media, which will depend on the type of media that you are using. Backup will then start and display its progress, as shown in Figure 14-16.

6. When Backup is complete, you are asked to insert a blank, formatted floppy disk. Click OK. When the copying to the floppy is complete, remove it and label it as suggested and click OK. Close the Backup progress dialog box.

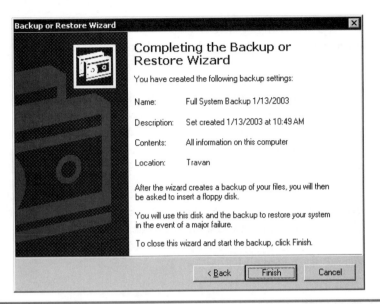

Figure 14-15 Doing a full system backup

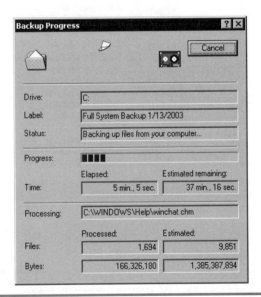

Figure 14-16 Progress of a backup

Manually Back Up from the Window

Manually backing up means to select the files and folders that are to be backed up and then issue the command to do it:

1. Open the Start menu and choose All Programs | Accessories | System Tools | Backup. In the Backup Or Restore Wizard that opens, click Advanced Mode. The Backup Utility window opens and gives you a choice of backing up, restoring, or doing an automated system recovery, all using "advanced" wizards. This is similar to what you saw in the last section, but it offers a few more choices, such as backing up all system files, including the Registry.

2. Here we want to do a manual backup, so click the Backup tab. You can select or open folders on the left pane and see and select subfolders and files in the right pane. Select the folders, subfolders, and files that you want backed up. Selecting a folder selects everything in that folder, but if you want most of a folder, select it and then deselect what you don't want, as you can see in Figure 14-17.

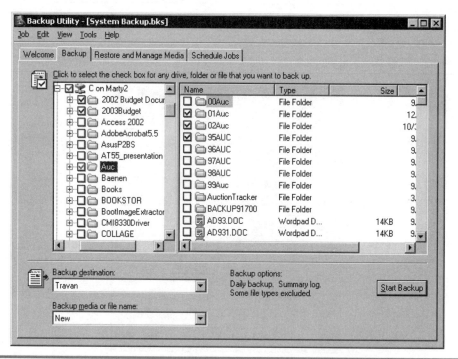

Figure 14-17 Selecting files to be backed up

3. When you have selected all the files and folders you want to back up, select the backup destination, enter a filename for the media you want to use, and click Start Backup. Choose to append this backup to another on the media or to replace the data on the media with this backup and click Start Backup again. The Backup Progress dialog box will open as you saw in the last section in Figure 14-16. If you choose to replace data, you get a Replace Data message box that confirms you want to replace the data. Click Yes if that is what you want to do and the backup will continue. Otherwise, click No, and you will again be asked if you want to append the data. Click Yes if you want to and the backup will proceed. Click No and you will be told the backup was ended. Click OK.

4. When the backup is complete, close the Backup Progress dialog box and the Backup Utility window.

Do Scheduled Backups of System Information

A scheduled backup goes through the same steps as a normal backup, but instead of running it now, you schedule it to be run in the future. This allows you both to run a backup when there is light activity, and to set up a recurring backup. The system information includes all of the system files and the Registry. To see how this is done, use these steps:

1. Open the Start menu and choose All Programs | Accessories | System Tools | Backup. In the Backup Or Restore Wizard that opens, click Advanced Mode. In the Backup Utility window that opens, click Backup Wizard Advanced and then Next.

2. Click Only Back Up The System State Data and click Next. Select the type of backup, select the media to use, if you are using a file to back up to enter a filename, and click Next. In the Completing The Backup Wizard dialog box, click Advanced.

3. Open the Type Of Backup drop-down list and choose Daily, click Next, click Verify Data After Backup, click Next, accept the default of Append This Backup To The Existing Backups, click Next, and accept the default labels unless you are backing up to a file, in which case you won't get this question. If needed, click Next again.

4. In the When To Back Up dialog box, select Later. Click Set Schedule. The Schedule Job dialog box opens. Here, you can enter the schedule you want to use, as shown in Figure 14-18.

5. Click Advanced. In the Advanced Schedule Options dialog box, you can enter a stop date and add variation to the repetition cycle. Enter the schedule you want to use, clicking OK twice to close the Advanced Schedule Options dialog box and then the Schedule Job dialog box.

6. Enter the account name of the person responsible for the backup and enter and confirm that person's password. In the Backup Wizard, enter a job name, click Next, and then click Finish.

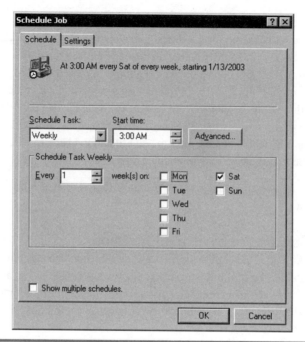

Figure 14-18 Setting a backup schedule

7. In the Backup Utility window, click Schedule Jobs. A monthly calendar opens showing the days on which your scheduled backup will run; in Figure 14-19, the scheduled backups will run on Saturdays. If you move the mouse over the backup icon, you see the job name; if you click the icon, the Scheduled Job Options dialog box opens, in which you can change the characteristics of, or delete, the job.

8. Close the Backup Utility window.

Use Restore

The purpose of backing up is to be able to restore data that, for whatever reason, has been lost. There are many different circumstances in which data is lost, and the loss can affect a single file or folder, up to an entire disk. Therefore, you want to be able to restore data to fit the circumstance. Windows Server 2003 Backup can do that; see how with these steps:

1. Open the Start menu, choose All Programs | Accessories | System Tools | Backup. The Backup Or Restore Wizard opens. Click Next, choose Restore Files And Settings, and click Next again. The What To Restore dialog box appears.

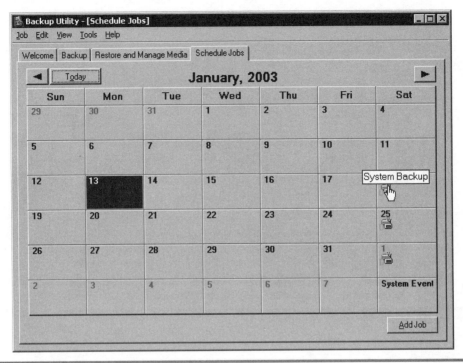

Figure 14-19 Viewing a backup schedule

2. Insert your backup media in its drive and open the hierarchical list in the left pane. If you drill down deep enough, you will see the drives, folders, and files that you backed up, as shown in Figure 14-20.

3. Select the folders and files that you want to restore, and click Next. You are shown the steps that will be taken to perform the restore. If these are all correct, you could click Finish and be done. For the sake of this exercise, look further by clicking Advanced.

4. You are given a choice of restoring to the original location (the default), an alternative location, or a single folder. If you choose anything but the original location, you can enter or select that location or folder. Click Next.

5. You are asked whether and under what circumstances you want to replace existing folders with those that are backed up. Consider this carefully, because you might lose information with an answer that is incorrect for your situation. Click Next.

6. You can then choose to restore several specific storage elements if they exist. These are the original security components, such as permissions; the Removable Storage database; and the folder ("junction point") and the data on a drive mounted to a folder on another drive. When you are done, click Next.

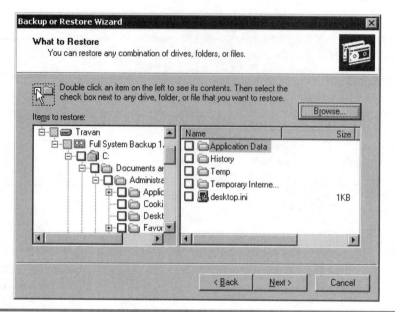

Figure 14-20 Selecting files to restore

7. You are again shown a summary of the steps to be taken in the restore. If they are not correct, use Back to change any of your selections. When you are ready, click Finish.

8. You may be asked to confirm the source files for the restore. Either change it and click OK or simply click OK. The Restore Progress dialog box appears, similar to the Backup Progress dialog box previously shown in Figure 14-16. Finally, you are told the restore is complete.

Prepare for an Emergency

The whole reason for backing up is to prepare for an emergency in which you would otherwise lose information. Besides the normal backup of information, as you have already seen, you can also back up all of the system files in a computer (called the "system state") and you can create a system recovery floppy disk to restart the system when the hard disk fails. Windows Server 2003 Backup Utility has an Automated System Recovery Wizard that will perform both of these functions independent of a normal backup. See how this works by following these steps:

1. Open the Backup Or Restore Wizard (as you previously did), click Advanced Mode, and in the Welcome tab, click Automated System Recovery Wizard. The Automated System Recovery Preparation Wizard will open. Click Next.

2. Select the backup media type and name, and click Next. In the completion dialog box that appears, click Finish. The Backup Progress dialog box will open. Notice in the Status text box that it says that it is preparing to back up using Shadow Copy. The Backup Progress Report will open and begin backing up the system files.

3. When Backup is complete, you are asked to insert a blank, formatted floppy disk. Do that and click OK. When the copying to the floppy is complete, remove it and label it as suggested and click OK. Close the Backup Progress dialog box.

Back Up the System State

In addition to saving the system files as a part of a larger backup, it is possible to back up just the system files, what Backup calls the *system state*. Do that now:

1. In the open Backup Utility window, click the Backup tab. At the bottom of the list of drives on the left, you should see System State, as you can in Figure 14-21.

2. Select System State, select the individual system components if you don't want them all, enter a backup destination, path, and filename, and click Start Backup. The Backup Job Information dialog box opens. You can change the description; choose to append or replace data; and choose to directly start the backup, schedule it, or review advanced options.

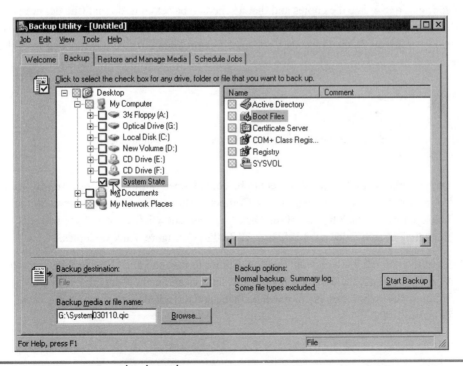

Figure 14-21 Preparing to back up the system state

3. Click Advanced. The Advanced Backup Options dialog box opens. Here, you can choose to back up Remote Storage data, verify what has been backed up, automatically back up system-protected files when you do a System State backup, and choose a type of backup. The key here is the backup of the system-protected files. If that is not selected, do so now and click OK.

4. Click Start Backup. The Backup Progress dialog box appears and the backup of just the system state files progresses as you have already seen.

Use Shadow Copies

Shadow Copies allows you to periodically make a copy of shared folders on a server with Windows Server 2003. This provides the means to quickly retrieve files that are lost or deleted for whatever reason. The client software to view and use these copies is included in Windows Server 2003, is stored on the server, and must be downloaded to the client in order to use it. In client computers, shadow copies are called "previous versions." The minimum amount of disk space that you can use for Shadow Copies is 100MB, and the default is 10 percent of the volume being copied. Shadow Copies will store up to 64 copies, after which the oldest copy will be deleted when a new one is added.

Shadow Copies require that shared folders on a server, of which you want shadow copies, be configured to create the copies and that a schedule be set up to do that (the default is twice a day, every weekday). Then, for the user of the files to see the shadow copies ("previous versions" to the user), the Previous Versions client program must be downloaded from the server and installed on the client. See how to do these tasks with the following steps:

NOTE

Do not use Shadow Copies on dual-booting computers or on volumes that use removable drives.

1. On the server with the shared folders to be copied, open Start and choose Administrative Tools | Computer Management. In the Computer Management window, open Storage | Disk Management. In the left pane of the Disk Management window, open System Tools, right-click Shared Folders, and choose All Tasks | Configure Shadow Copies.

2. Click the volume that you want Shadow Copies to use, and click Enable. You are told that Windows will use the default schedule and settings and make a default copy of the selected volumes now. Click Yes. A copy will be made and the schedule for the next one set as shown in Figure 14-22.

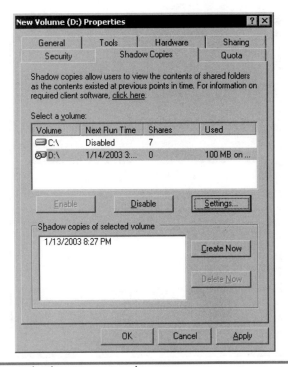

Figure 14-22 Setting up Shadow Copies on the server

3. With the Shadow Copies volume still selected, click Settings. In the Settings dialog box at the top, you can set the drive on which the copies will be stored, as well as the maximum size of the storage area used, and in the bottom, by clicking Schedule, you can select the schedule on which the copies are made in a dialog box that is exactly the same as the one for scheduling backups. Click OK twice when you are ready and close the Computer Management window.

4. On the client, open Windows Explorer and browse to *Server*\C:\Windows\System 32\ Clients\Twclient\X86. Copy (drag) the program file Twcli32.msi to the root directory of the client and then double-click that file to execute it. You are told Previous Versions has been successfully installed.

5. To view a previous version from a client, again in Windows Explorer browse to the original copy in the shared folder on the server of the file for which you want to locate a copy. Right-click the file and choose Properties. In the Properties dialog box, click the Previous Versions tab. Here you will see the previous versions/shadow copies of the file that are available, as shown in Figure 14-23.

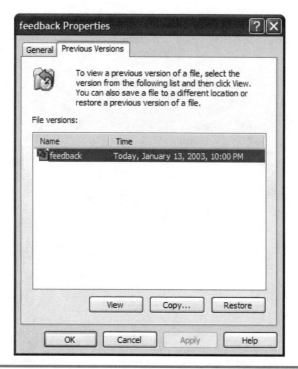

Figure 14-23 Locating previous versions of a file in a shared folder on a server

6. In the Previous Versions tab, you can also copy the selected previous version to a different location and restore the previous version to the original location in the share. When you are done, close the Properties dialog box and Windows Explorer.

TIP

Previous versions are read-only copies and may disappear. If a user wants to change the file or access it in the future, then the user should copy it to another location.

NOTE

The Shadow Copies feature is not a replacement for regular backups. Shadow Copies makes periodic copies that are kept for only a limited period of time and then automatically deleted. Backup copies can be kept for as long as you like and are generally a more complete set of files.

Progress Check

1. What is disk defragmentation?

2. What are disk quotas?

3. How can you change a dynamic disk back to a basic disk?

4. What are extended volumes and how are they used?

Project 14 Plan the Use of Storage and File Systems

Because the file system is such a critical part of a client/server environment, it is very important that it is configured the way you can best use it and that you can make full use of all the file system capabilities available in Windows Server 2003. Use this planning aid to review the Windows Server 2003 file system capabilities and determine how you want to use them.

Step by Step

1. Determine the type of storage to be use:

   a. Basic storage

     i. How many primary partitions (up to 4)?

     ii. Use an extended partition (up to 1, taking away one primary partition)

     iii. How many logical drives (unlimited number)?

(continued)

---

1. Files are made up of clusters that are not always stored together in one contiguous region of a disk, resulting in fragmentation of the files. Windows Server 2003 has a utility to defragment the files in a partition or volume, putting all of the related clusters in one contiguous area of the disk.

2. With disk quotas, you can monitor and set policies and limits on the disk space used in a partition or volume, and make sure that one user does not take up more of the disk than is desired.

3. The only way to change a dynamic disk back to a basic disk is to delete all dynamic volumes, and therefore all files in those volumes, and then right-click the drive and choose Convert To Basic Disk.

4. Extended volumes are ones whose size has been increased. Volumes can be extended if they are created on a dynamic disk and are not either a boot disk or one that was created from a basic disk in an earlier version of Windows.

    b. Dynamic storage

        i. How many of which type of volumes (32 or less recommended)?

- Simple volumes
- Spanned volumes
- Mirrored volumes
- Striped volumes
- RAID-5 volumes

2. Determine the type of file system that will be used:

  a. FAT

  b. FAT32

  c. NTFS (recommended)

  d. Convert drives from FAT or FAT32 to NTFS

3. Determine if you need to use Disk Management to:

  a. Add a disk drive

  b. Remove a disk drive

  c. Delete a partition

  d. Add a primary partition

  e. Add an extended partition

  f. Add logical drives

  g. Format partitions/volumes or drives

  h. Change drive letters

  i. Defragment a drive

  j. Establish drive quotas

  k. Encrypt folders and files

4. Determine if you need to use Dynamic Volume Management to:

  a. Change to dynamic storage

  b. Create volumes

  c. Extend volumes

  d. Create a spanning volume

5. Determine if using the Distributed File System is appropriate

6. Determine if Removable Storage is needed

7. Determine if Remote Storage is appropriate (in Enterprise/Datacenter versions)

8. Determine the type of backup that will be implemented:

    a. Normal backup

    b. Differential backup

    c. Incremental backup

    d. Copy backup

    e. Daily backup

9. Determine if Shadow Copies is appropriate

Project Summary

Storage and file system management is a vital function in Windows Server 2003, and it is well worth any effort you put into it.

Module 14 Mastery Check

1. What are the two types of partitioning in Windows Server 2003, and how do they differ?

2. What are some of the type of volumes, and what are their characteristics?

3. What are some of the more important reasons you should use NTFS rather than FAT and FAT32?

4. How can you convert a FAT or FAT32 partition, volume, or drive to NTFS?

5. What are some of the tools that Windows Server 2003 has to manage storage systems, folders, and files?

6. Where is disk management performed, and what does it include?

7. What is the first step in preparing a disk for use, and what is the major caution to be considered with this step?

8. What is automatic archival compression, and how is it turned on?

9. What is Dynamic Volume Management, and how does it relate to dynamic storage?

10. What is the Distributed File System (DFS), and what are some of its features?

11. What is Removable Storage, and what are some of its features?

12. What are the five types of backup, and how do they compare?

Module 15

Setting Up and Managing Printing and Faxing

CRITICAL SKILLS

15.1 Understand Windows Server 2003 Printing

15.2 Set Up Printing

15.3 Tune a Printer's Configuration

15.4 Control a Printer's Queue

15.5 Manage Fonts

15.6 Set Up and Use Faxing

A lthough talk of a paperless society continues, it does not look like it will occur any time soon. As a result, the ability to transfer computer information to paper or other media is very important and a major function of Windows Server 2003. Both Windows Server 2003 and Windows XP Professional can serve as print servers, and unless otherwise noted, comments in this module apply equally to Windows Server 2003 and Windows XP Professional.

NOTE

Although Windows XP Professional can be used as a print server, it is limited to ten concurrent users and cannot support Macintosh or Novell NetWare users, whereas Windows Server 2003 does not have a user limitation and can support Macintosh and NetWare users.

In this module, you'll look at what constitutes Windows Server 2003 printing, how to set it up, how to manage it, how to manage the fonts that are required for printing, and how to set up and use faxing.

CRITICAL SKILL
15.1
Understand Windows Server 2003 Printing

Windows Server 2003 printing is very similar to printing in Windows 2000, Windows NT 4, and Windows 98, and many of the concepts are the same. Take a moment, though, and make sure you are familiar with the foundation printing concepts and understand the resource requirements.

Printing Concepts

It may seem obvious what a printer is, but when considering the term, you must remember to include "printing" to a file and "printing" to a fax. Also, although "printing" to a network printer does end up using a physical printing device, to the local computer, this form of "printing" is just a network address. So what does "printer" mean to Windows Server 2003?

● **Printer** A name that refers to a set of specifications used for printing, primary among which is a hardware port, such as LPT1 or COM1, a software port, such as FILE or FAX, or a network address.

- **Printer driver**   Software that tells the computer how to accomplish the printing task desired; also part of the printer specifications.

- **Printing device**   The actual piece of hardware that does the printing. *Local printing devices* are connected to a hardware port on the computer requesting the printing; *network printing devices* are connected either to another computer or directly to the network.

- **Print server**   The computer controlling the printing, and to which the printing device is connected.

Printing Requirements

Windows Server 2003 printing has the following requirements that must be satisfied:

- One or more computers on the network must be set up as print servers with one or more local printing devices connected to them.

- The print server must be running either Windows Server 2003 or Windows XP Professional, but if Windows XP Professional is used, there is a limit of ten concurrent users, and neither Macintosh nor NetWare users on the network can use the printer.

- The print server must have enough disk space to handle the expected print load. This varies greatly from organization to organization, so there is no good rule of thumb. Look at the size of documents that your organization normally prints and at the worst-case number of these documents that might be printed at the same time. If ten people in an office are sharing a printer and their largest print jobs are around 2MB, then 20MB is probably enough, but to be conservative, provide 50–100MB.

- Enough memory must be available to handle the printing load. This is a minimum of 128MB, and for a serious print load, 256MB would not be too much. Providing a fair amount of memory will ensure the best performance.

CRITICAL SKILL

15.2 Set Up Printing

Setting up printing is done through the Printers And Faxes window shown next. This window, which is opened by opening the Start menu and choosing Printers And Faxes, contains an Add Printer icon that opens the Add Printer Wizard. This wizard leads you through the process of setting up printers that will be available to the computer on which you are working.

NOTE

In Windows XP, which by default has the tasks pane turned on, the Add Printer icon is replaced by an Add A Printer task in the taskbar. Since this book is primarily about Windows Server 2003, the instructions in this and other modules refer to the Server's default windows and dialog boxes.

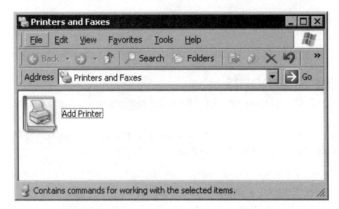

After you double-click the icon (or click the Add A Printer task in a tasks pane) and click Next on the opening dialog box, the very first question asked by the Add Printer Wizard is whether you want to set up a local printer or a network printer:

- **Local printer**   Directly connected to the computer you are sitting at

- **Network printer**   Connected either to another computer on the network or directly to the network, and has been *shared* or set up so that others can use it

Set Up Local Printers

To set up a printer connected to the computer you are at, use these steps (assuming that the Add Printer Wizard is still open as described in the preceding section):

TIP

Before installing a local printer, make sure it is plugged into the correct connector (port) on your computer, is plugged into an electrical outlet, has a fresh ink or toner cartridge (which, along with the print heads, is properly installed), has adequate paper, and is turned on. These simple steps cover most reasons for printers not working!

1. Choose Local Printer Attached To This Computer. If you believe that the printer is Plug and Play–compatible (most printers made since 1997 are), click that check box and then click Next. The Add Printer Wizard will try to detect the printer. If it is successful, the wizard tells you which printer has been found and installs it. You then are asked if you want to test the printer by printing a page. If the printer was not found you are also told that, in which case jump to Step 3.

2. Choose Yes to test the printer, and click Next. The printer name, the port it is connected to, and other bits of information are presented, as shown next. Click Finish. If you chose to print a test page, it will be printed. If the page printed satisfactorily, click OK to that question; otherwise, click Troubleshoot and follow the suggestions you are given.

3. If the local printer you want to set up is not Plug and Play–compatible and you tried to have the wizard detect it, you will be told you need to click Next to manually install it. Do so. Otherwise, choose to install a local printer without trying Plug and Play. In either case, the Select A Printer Port dialog box appears.

4. Select a printer port to which the printer is attached. This is most commonly LPT1, the first parallel port. If it is a serial printer, you might use COM2, because a mouse is often on COM1. After choosing a port, click Next. A list of manufacturers and their printer models is presented.

5. Click the printer manufacturer's name in the left list and then select the printer model in the right list, as shown next. If your printer is not listed but you have a disk with a Windows Server 2003 driver on it, click Have Disk. If your printer is not listed and you don't have a driver, click Windows Update to connect to the Microsoft site over the Internet to see if a recent driver is available for your printer.

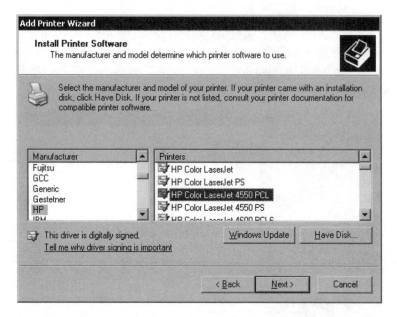

6. When you have selected your printer's manufacturer and model, click Next. Accept the default or enter a printer name, indicate whether you want to use this printer as the default printer, and click Next. Choose whether to share the printer, accept the default or enter the share name, and click Next. If you have chosen to share the printer, enter the printer's location and any comments and click Next. Choose whether to print a test page, and click Next one final time.

7. A final summary of your decisions is displayed, as previously shown with Step 2. If it is all correct, click Finish. If it is not correct, click Back until you get to the dialog box in which you can change the incorrect selection. When the summary is the way you want it, click Finish.

8. If you choose to print a test page, it should be printed now. If it was printed successfully, click OK. Otherwise, click Troubleshoot and follow the suggestions that are presented.

When the last Add Printer Wizard dialog box closes, you should see the printer that you added represented as an icon in the Printers And Faxes window.

TIP

If your printer was automatically installed, but a CD came with your printer and you wonder if you should install using the CD, the general answer is no. Most printer drivers in Windows Server 2003 originally came from the manufacturers and have been tested by Microsoft, so they should work well. Unless the printer came out after the release of Windows Server 2003 (April 2003), the driver in Windows Server 2003 should be newer.

Set Up Network Printers

Setting up network printers refers to setting up a client computer so that it can utilize printers elsewhere on a network. There are two types of network printers:

- Those connected to another computer

- Those directly connected to the network

The processes for setting up each of these are quite different.

Set Up Printers Connected to Other Computers

The process of setting up access to printers connected to other computers (what is normally considered setting up a network printer) is carried out with these steps (assuming that the Add Printer Wizard is still open as described under the previous heading "Set Up Printing"):

1. In the second Add Printer Wizard dialog box, choose A Network Printer and click Next. The Specify A Printer dialog box opens, in which you can search for a printer in the Active Directory, by entering a unique printer name using the Universal Naming Conventions (UNC, for example, \\Server1\HPLJ4550), by searching your local network for a printer, or by entering an Internet URL (Universal Resource Locator) to a printer.

2. If you select Connect To This Printer and then click Next without entering a name, you can browse for a printer, like this:

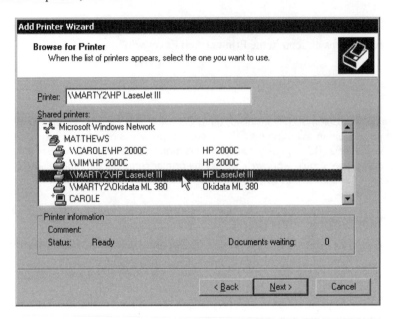

3. When you have selected a printer, click Next. Choose whether the printer you are installing is the default printer for Windows-based programs and click Next. A summary of your printer decisions is presented. If they are correct, click Finish; otherwise, click Back, make the necessary corrections, and then click Finish.

 Again, when you return to the Printers And Faxes window, you will see an icon for the network printer. It will have a cable running beneath it to indicate that it is a network printer.

NOTE

Computers running Windows 98/Me and NT 4 check to see whether they have the latest printer drivers whenever they go to print, and if they don't, they seek a new driver. In Windows Server 2000, a drivers database is installed on each machine. In Windows XP and Windows Server 2003, a drivers database is installed on the print server and then the appropriate driver is downloaded to the client when the client installs the network printer.

Set Up Printers Directly Connected to the Network

A printer directly connected to the network has built in to it a network protocol that it uses to communicate on the network. This protocol, for most recent printers, is TCP/IP. If the printer is using TCP/IP, it may be assigned an IP address by the DHCP server (see Module 8 for a discussion of TCP/IP and DHCP), or an IP address may be directly assigned when the printer is set up. Before beginning the process of setting up this type of printer, you must know the protocol it uses and how it is addressed. Here are the steps to set up a printer directly connected to the network using TCP/IP and a known IP address:

1. From the Printers And Faxes window, double-click Add Printer and click Next on the Welcome message.

2. Select Local Printer, clear the Automatically Detect And Install My Plug And Play Printer check box, and click Next. The Select A Printer Port dialog box opens.

3. Click Create A New Port and select Standard TCP/IP Port from the drop-down list, as shown here:

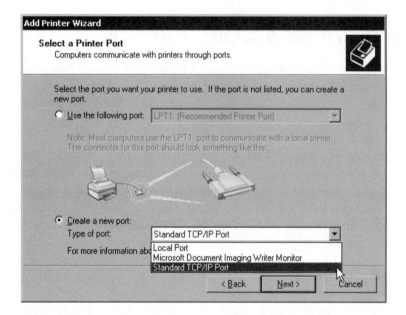

4. Click Next. The Add Standard TCP/IP Printer Port Wizard opens. Make sure the printer is turned on and connected to the network, and then click Next. The Add Port dialog box opens and asks for the Domain Name Service (DNS) name of the printer or its IP address.

5. Enter the name or IP address. As you do so, you see the Port name automatically filled in. Click Next. The Printer Port Wizard will go out and try to identify and set up the printer. If it is successful, you may be told which printer network card was found; otherwise, you are told that the device could not be identified and are asked to select the device type. Click Next.

6. A summary of your responses is displayed. If they are not correct, use Back to correct them. When all are correct, click Finish. You are returned to the Add Printer Wizard, where you must first choose the new TCP/IP port and then identify the manufacturer and model of printer, enter a name, and supply other information, as you did when manually setting up a local printer. Click Finish when the settings are the way you want them.

7. If you printed a test page and it printed satisfactorily, click OK when asked that question; otherwise, click Troubleshoot and follow the suggestions that are presented.

If a printer directly connected to the network uses a networking protocol other than TCP/IP, you must install that protocol by using the steps for installing a networking protocol described in Module 8. With the protocol installed, you will be able to create a new port that uses that protocol. Identifying the printer will vary depending on the protocol.

CRITICAL SKILL
15.3 # Tune a Printer's Configuration

As a general rule, the default configuration for a printer works well in most situations, so unless you have a unique situation, it is recommended that you keep the default settings. That said, it is also wise to know what your alternatives are, so look at the settings you can use to control your printer (these settings vary depending on the printer that you are configuring, so look at your printer[s] during this discussion).

A printer's settings are contained in its Properties dialog box, shown in Figure 15-1. This is accessed by opening the Printers And Faxes window (Start menu | Printers And Faxes), right-clicking the icon of the printer you want to configure, and choosing Properties. For purposes of this discussion, the tabs in the printer Properties dialog box can be grouped into printer configuration, printing configuration, and user configuration.

Configure Printers

Printer configuration has to do with controlling the printer itself. On the General tab (shown in Figure 15-1), you can change the name of the printer, identify its location, and enter a comment about it. You can also set the preferences for layout, paper, and, if available, color, and print a test page. In the Ports tab, you can change the port used by the printer; add, delete, and configure ports; turn on and off bi-directional communication with the printer; and set up printer pooling. In the Device Settings tab, you can set what is loaded in each paper tray, how to handle font substitution, and what printer options are available. Your particular printer may have different or additional options, so review these tabs for your printer. Most of the printer configuration settings are self-explanatory, such as the name and location, and others are rarely changed from their initial setup, such as the port and bi-directional communication, which

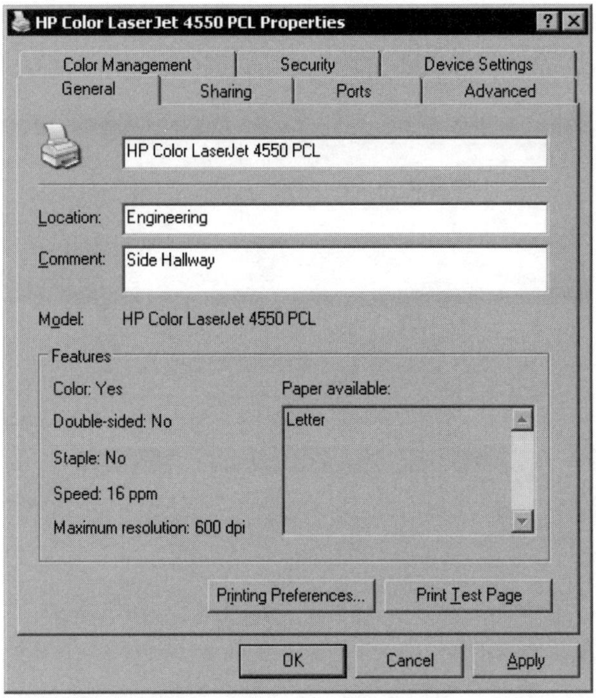

Figure 15-1 A printer is configured in its Properties dialog box.

speeds using the printer. Several items, though, are worthy of further discussion: printer pooling, printer priority, and assigning paper trays.

Printer Pooling

Printer pooling enables you to have two or more physical printing devices assigned to one printer. The printing devices can be local or directly connected to the network, but they must share the same print driver. When print jobs are sent to the printer, Windows determines which of the physical devices is available, and routes the job to that device. This eliminates the need for the user to determine which printing device is available, provides for better load sharing among printing devices, and allows the management of several devices through one printer definition.

You can set up printer pooling with these steps:

1. Install all printers as described previously in "Set Up Printing."

2. In the Printers And Faxes window, right-click the printer to which all work will be directed, and choose Properties. The printer's Properties dialog box opens.

3. Click the Ports tab and click Enable Printer Pooling.

4. Click each of the ports with a printing device that is to be in the pool, as you can see here:

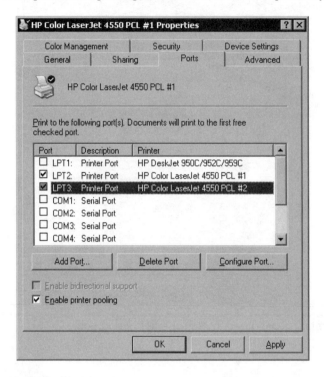

5. When all the ports are selected, click OK to close the Properties dialog box.

6. If the printer that contains the pool isn't already selected as the default printer, right-click the printer and choose Set As Default Printer.

NOTE

The default printer has a check mark above its icon and doesn't have the Set As Default Printer option.

Printer Priority

You can do the opposite of printer pooling by assigning several printers to one printing device. The primary reason that you would want to do this is to have two or more settings used with one device. For example, if you want to have two or more priorities automatically assigned to jobs going to a printing device, you could create two or more printers, all pointing to the same printer port and physical device, but with different priorities. Then, have high-priority print jobs printed to a printer with a priority of 99, and low-priority jobs printed to a printer with a priority of 1.

Create several printers with one print device using the following steps:

1. Install all printers as previously described in "Set Up Printing," except that the printers use the same port. Name each of the printers to indicate its priority. For example, "High Priority Printer" and "Low Priority Printer."

2. In the Printers And Faxes window, right-click the high-priority printer and choose Properties. The printer's Properties dialog box will open.

3. Select the Advanced tab and enter a priority of **99**, as shown Figure 15-2, and click OK.

4. Similarly, right-click the other printers, open their Properties dialog box, select the Advanced tab, enter priorities of **1–98**, and click OK.

Jobs that are printed with the highest priority will print before jobs with a lower priority if they are in the queue at the same time.

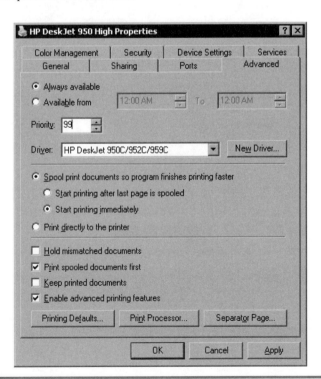

Figure 15-2 Setting one of several priorities for a single printer

Assign Paper Trays

Depending on your printer, it may have more than one paper tray, and as a result, you may want to put different types or sizes of paper in each tray. If you assign types and sizes of paper to trays in the printer's Properties dialog box, and a user requests a type and size of paper when printing, Windows Server 2003 automatically designates the correct paper tray for the print job. Here's how to assign types and sizes of paper to trays:

1. In the Printers And Faxes window, right-click the printer whose trays you want to assign and choose Properties. The printer's Properties dialog box opens.

2. Select the Device Settings tab. Open each tray and select the type and size of paper in that tray, similar to what you see in Figure 15-3.

3. When you have set the paper type and size in each tray, click OK.

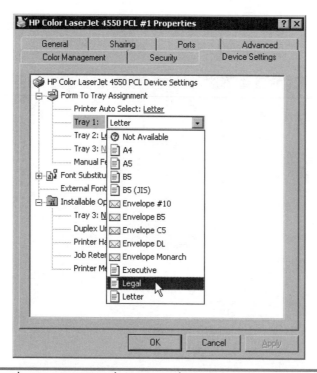

Figure 15-3 Setting the paper type and size in each paper tray

Configure Printing

Printing configuration has to do with controlling the process of printing, not the printer itself or particular print jobs. Printing configuration is handled in the Advanced tab of a printer's Properties dialog box, such as the one shown previously in Figure 15-2. As stated earlier, in most cases, the default settings are appropriate and should be changed only in unique situations. Two exceptions to this are the spooling settings and using separator pages, discussed next.

Configure Spooling

In most instances, the time it takes to print a document is considerably longer than the time it takes to transfer the information from an application to the printer. The information is therefore stored on disk in a special preprint format, and then the OS, as a background task, feeds the printer as much information as it can handle. This temporary storage on disk is called *printer spooling.* Under the majority of cases, you want to use printer spooling and not tie up the application waiting for the printer. However, an alternative pair of settings is available:

- **Start Printing After Last Page Is Spooled**   By waiting to print until the last page is spooled, the application finishes faster and the user gets back to the application faster, but it takes longer to finish printing.

- **Start Printing Immediately**   The printing will be done sooner, but the application will be tied up a little longer.

There is no one correct choice for this. Normally, the default Start Printing Immediately provides a happy medium between getting the printing and getting back to the application. But if you want to get back to the application in the shortest possible time, then choose to wait until the last page is spooled.

Use Separator Pages

If you have a number of different jobs on a printer, it might be worthwhile to have a separator page between them, to more easily identify where one job ends and another begins. You can also use a separator page to switch a printer between PostScript (a printer language) and PCL (Printer Control Language) on Hewlett-Packard (HP) and compatible printers. Four sample SEP separation files come with Windows Server 2003:

- **Pcl.sep**   Prints a separation page before the start of each print job on PCL-compatible printers. If the printer handles both PostScript and PCL, it will be switched to PCL.

- **Pscript.sep**   Does *not* print a separation page, but printers with both PostScript and PCL will be switched to PostScript.

- **Sysprint.sep**   Prints a separation page before the start of each print job on PostScript-compatible printers.

- **Sysprtj.sep**   The same as Sysprint.sep, but in the Japanese language.

NOTE

The separation files work with HP and PostScript or compatible printers. They will not work with all printers.

If you know or have a guide to either the PCL or PostScript language (or both), you can open and modify these files (or copies of them) with any text editor, such as Notepad, to suite your particular purpose.

Configure Users

User configuration has to do with controlling the users of a printer. This is the one area where you may want to change the default, which is to not share the printer and not allow anyone on the network to print on it. User configuration is controlled in the Sharing tab of the printer's Properties dialog box, which turns sharing on and off, and in the Security tab of the same dialog box.

NOTE

Printers, either local or network, on Windows XP computers do not have a Security tab.

If a printer is shared, then the Security tab determines who has permission to use, control, and make changes to the printer, as you can see in Figure 15-4. The four types of permissions and the functions that they allow are as follows:

- **Print**   Allows the user to connect to a printer; print; and cancel, pause, resume, and restart the user's own documents.

- **Manage Documents**   Allows the user to control print job functions for all documents, including canceling, pausing, resuming, and restarting other users' documents.

- **Manage Printers**   Allows the user to control printer properties, including setting permissions, sharing a printer, changing printer properties, deleting a printer, and deleting all documents.

- **Special Permissions**   Indicates that the user has been assigned special permissions using the Advanced button and the Advanced Security Settings dialog box.

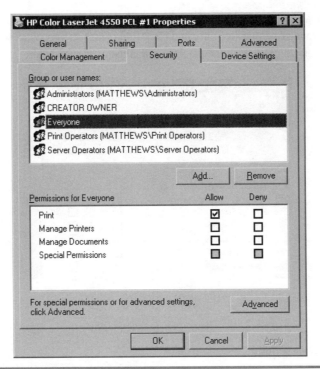

Figure 15-4 Setting permissions to use, control, and make changes to a printer

For each person or group in the Name list, you can select the permissions that you want to give that person or group. The permission can be set in terms of allowing or denying a certain set of functions. Denying takes precedence over allowing, so if a function is denied in one place and allowed in another, it will be denied.

CAUTION

If you deny a set of functions for the Everyone group, then literally everyone will be prevented from performing those functions, even if they have been allowed elsewhere.

If you want a more detailed level of permission, click Advanced at the bottom of the Security tab. Select a particular permission entry and click Edit. This lets you select what the permission applies to, and lets you further refine the permission itself, as shown here:

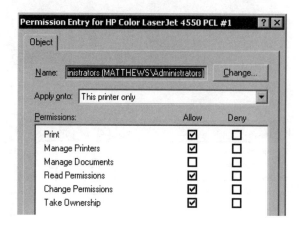

NOTE

Module 17 discusses permissions in more detail.

Progress Check

1. What is a printer?

2. What are the three types of printers?

3. What does the UNC look like for a printer?

4. What do you use to configure a printer?

5. What is printer pooling, and what is its opposite?

---

1. A printer is a name with a set of software specifications and a driver so that Windows can use it.

2. The three types of printers are local devices, network devices, and software devices.

3. The UNC for a printer on your network should look like *servername**printername*.

4. The printer's Properties dialog box is used to configure it.

5. Printer pooling is having two or more physical printers with the same printer driver share one printer definition in the Printers And Faxes window. The opposite is to have one physical printer have several printer definitions. The different definitions would have different configurations, such as different priorities.

CRITICAL SKILL
15.4 Control a Printer's Queue

As jobs are printed by applications, they are spooled onto a disk and then fed out to the printer at whatever rate the printer can handle. If several print jobs are spooled at close to the same time, they form a queue, waiting for earlier jobs to finish. Controlling this queue is an important administrative function and covers pausing and resuming printing, canceling printing, redirecting documents, and changing a document's properties. These tasks are handled in the printer's window that is similar to Figure 15-5, which is opened by double-clicking the appropriate printer in the Printers And Faxes window.

Pause, Resume, and Restart Printing

As printing is taking place, a situation may occur in which you want to pause the printing. This may be caused by the printer—the need to change paper, for example—in which case you would want to pause all printing. The situation may also be caused by a document, in which case you would want to pause only the printing of that document—for example, for some problem in the document, such as characters that cause the printer to behave erratically. In Windows Server 2003, you can pause and resume printing of all documents, and pause and resume or restart printing of a single document.

Pause and Resume Printing for All Documents

Pausing and resuming printing of all documents is in essence pausing and resuming the printer. See how that is done with these steps:

1. In the printer's window, such as the one shown in Figure 15-5, open the Printer menu and choose Pause Printing. "Paused" will appear in the title bar, and if you look in the Printer menu, you will see a check mark in front of Pause Printing.

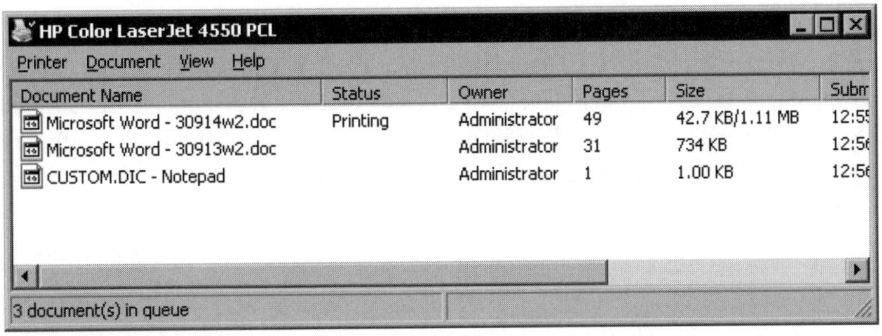

Document Name	Status	Owner	Pages	Size	Subm
Microsoft Word - 30914w2.doc	Printing	Administrator	49	42.7 KB/1.11 MB	12:55
Microsoft Word - 30913w2.doc		Administrator	31	734 KB	12:56
CUSTOM.DIC - Notepad		Administrator	1	1.00 KB	12:56

3 document(s) in queue

Figure 15-5 Documents in a printer's queue can be paused, canceled, resumed, and redirected.

2. To resume printing, again open the Printer menu and choose the checked Pause Printing. "Paused" disappears from the title bar and the check mark disappears in the Pause Printing option in the Printer menu.

Pause, Resume, and Restart Printing for a Single Document

When you want to interrupt the printing of one or more, but not all, the documents in the queue, you can do so and then either resume printing where it left off or restart from the beginning of the document. Here are the steps to do that:

1. In the printer's window, select the documents or document that you want to pause, open the Document menu, and choose Pause. "Paused" will appear in the Status column opposite the document(s) you selected.

2. To resume printing where the document was paused, select the document and choose Resume. "Printing" will appear in the Status column opposite the document selected.

3. To restart printing at the beginning of the document, select the document and choose Restart. "Restarting" and then "Printing" will appear in the Status column.

NOTE

If you want to change the order in which documents are being printed, you cannot pause the current document that is printing and have that happen. You must either complete the document that is printing or cancel it. You can use Pause to get around intermediate documents that are not currently printing. For example, suppose you want to immediately print the third document in the queue, but the first document is currently printing. You must either let the first document finish printing or cancel it. You can then pause the second document before it starts printing, and the third document will begin printing when the first document is out of the way.

Cancel Printing

Canceling printing can be done either at the printer level, which cancels all the jobs in the printer queue, or at the document level, which cancels selected documents. A canceled job is deleted from the print queue and must be restarted by the original application if that is desired. Here's how to cancel first one job and then all the jobs in the queue:

1. In the printer's window, select the job or jobs that you want to cancel. Open the Document menu and choose Cancel. You are asked whether you are sure you want to cancel the selected print job(s). Click Yes. The job or jobs will disappear from the windows and no longer be in the queue.

2. To cancel all the jobs in the queue, open the Printer menu and choose Cancel All Documents. You are asked whether you are sure you want to cancel all documents. Click Yes. All jobs will disappear from the queue and the printer window.

Redirect Documents

If you have two printers with the same print driver, you can redirect the print jobs that are in the queue for one printer to the other printer, even one across the network, where they will be printed without the user having to resubmit them. You do this by changing the port to which the printer is directed:

1. In the printer's window, open the Printer menu, choose Properties, and select the Ports tab.

2. If the second printer is in the list of ports, select it. Otherwise, click Add Port, which opens the Printer Ports dialog box. Choose Local Port, and click New Port, which opens the Port Name dialog box.

3. Enter the UNC name for the printer (for example, \\Server1\HPCLJ4550) and click OK.

4. Click Close and then click Close again. The print queue will be redirected to the other printer.

Change a Document's Properties

A document in the print queue has a Properties dialog box, shown in Figure 15-6, which is opened by right-clicking the document and selecting Properties. This allows you to set the relative priority to use in printing the document from 1, the lowest, to 99, the highest; which logged-on user to notify when the document is printed; and the time of day to print the document.

Set Priority   A document printed to a printer with a default priority setting (see "Printer Priority," earlier in the module) is given a priority of 1, the lowest priority. If you want another document to be printed before the first one, and the "first one" hasn't started printing yet, then set the second document priority to anything higher than 1 by dragging the Priority slider to the right.

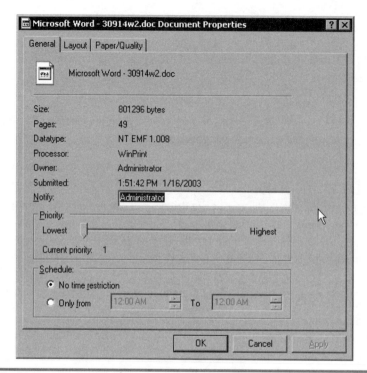

Figure 15-6 Setting a print queue document's properties

Who to Notify The printer can notify the owner of a document of any special situations with the printing and when the document is finished printing. The owner is the logged-on user who sent the document to the printer. Sometimes it is beneficial to notify another logged-on user. You can do that by putting the logon name of the other user in the Notify text box of the document's Properties dialog box.

Also, the server's notification of the client needs to be enabled. Open the Printers And Faxes window and go to File menu | Server Properties | Advanced tab. Then, click Notify When Remote Documents Are Printed to enable it. This isn't on by default.

Set Print Time Normally, a job is printed as soon as it reaches the top of the print queue. You can change this to a particular time frame in the document's Properties dialog box General tab (see Figure 15-6), by selecting Only From at the bottom under Schedule and then entering the time range within which you want the job printed.

This allows you to take large jobs that might clog the print queue and print them at a time when there is little or no load.

CRITICAL SKILL

15.5 Manage Fonts

A *font* is a set of characters with the same design, size, weight, and style. A font is a member of a *typeface* family, all members of which have the same design. The font 12-point Arial bold italic is a member of the Arial typeface with a 12-point size, bold weight, and italic style. Systems running Windows Server 2003 have numerous fonts that you can choose from, including these:

- **Resident fonts**   Built in to printers

- **Cartridge fonts**   Stored in cartridges plugged into printers

- **Soft fonts**   Stored on a disk in the computer to which the printer is attached and downloaded to the printer when they are needed or stored on a disk in the printer

A number of soft fonts come with Windows Server 2003, and there are many, many more that you can add from other sources, including the Internet, or that are automatically added when you install an application. The font management job is to minimize the time taken downloading fonts, while having the fonts you want available. Minimizing download time means that resident and cartridge fonts are used when possible, which is automatically done by the print driver whenever a font that is both resident and available for download is requested. Font availability means that the fonts you want are on the print server's disk and fonts you don't want are not on the disk wasting space and handling time. In this section, you'll look at the fonts in Windows Server 2003, how to add and remove fonts, and how to use fonts.

Fonts in Windows Server 2003

There are three types of soft fonts in Windows Server 2003:

- **Outline fonts**   Stored as a set of commands that is used to draw a particular character. As a result, the fonts can be scaled to any size (and are therefore called *scalable* fonts) and can be rotated. Outline fonts are the primary fonts both used onscreen and downloaded to printers. Windows Server 2003 supports three types of outline fonts: TrueType fonts developed by Microsoft for Windows 95; OpenType fonts, also developed by Microsoft and an extension of TrueType; and Type 1 fonts, developed by Adobe Systems, Inc. All the outline fonts in Windows Server 2003 are OpenType fonts.

NOTE

In Windows 95/98, Microsoft's outline fonts were identified as "TrueType fonts" and a "TT" on their icon was used to identify them. In Windows 2000 and Windows XP, these same fonts were identified as "OpenType fonts with TrueType outlines" and an "O" on their icon was used to identify them. In Windows Server 2003, these same fonts are again identified as "OpenType fonts with TrueType outlines" but a "TT" on their icon is used to identify them.

- **Bitmapped fonts**   Also called *raster fonts*, these are stored as a bitmapped image for a specific size and weight, and a specific printer. They cannot be scaled and rotated. They are included for legacy purposes and are not used in most cases.

- **Vector fonts**   Created with line segments and can be scaled and rotated. Primarily used with plotters and not onscreen or with printers.

You can view and work with the fonts in Windows Server 2003 by opening the Fonts window shown in Figure 15-7. The Fonts window is opened by opening the Start menu and choosing Control Panel | Fonts.

If you haven't installed any other fonts or had them installed by an application, you will see the 66 fonts in Figure 15-7 that are installed by Windows Server 2003 and described in Table 15-1. Fonts with the TT in the icon are OpenType/TrueType fonts, and those with an *A* are either bitmapped or vector. Those fonts that can be displayed with a normal monitor and printed with the majority of printers have a sample of their type shown in Table 15-1. The remaining fonts require special processing either by hardware or software.

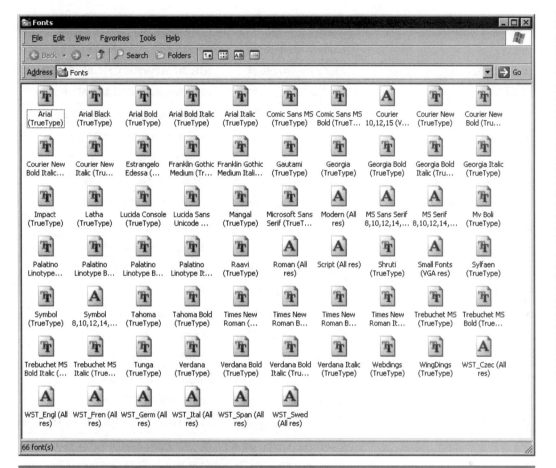

Figure 15-7 Fonts installed with Windows Server 2003

In the Fonts window, you can look at a font by double-clicking its icon. This opens a window for the font showing it in various sizes and giving some information about it, as shown in Figure 15-8. From this window, you can print the font by clicking Print. It is sometimes handy to keep a notebook with printed samples of all the fonts on a print server.

Font	Type	Filename	Type Sample
Arial	Outline	Arial.ttf	abcklmtwABCKLMTW12
Arial Black	Outline	Ariblk.ttf	**abcklmtwABCKLMTW12**
Arial Bold	Outline	Arialbd.ttf	**abcklmtwABCKLMTW12**
Arial Bold Italic	Outline	Arialbi.ttf	***abcklmtwABCKLMTW12***
Arial Italic	Outline	Ariali.ttf	*abcklmtwABCKLMTW12*
Comic Sans MS	Outline	Comic.ttf	abcklmtwABCKLMTW12
Comic Sans MS Bold	Outline	Comicbd.ttf	**abcklmtwABCKLMTW12**
Courier 10,12,15	Bitmap	Coure.fon	abcklmtwABCKLMTW12
Courier New	Outline	Cour.ttf	abcklmtwABCKLMTW12
Courier New Bold	Outline	Courbd.ttf	**abcklmtwABCKLMTW12**
Courier New Bold Italic	Outline	Courbi.ttf	***abcklmtwABCKLMTW12***
Courier New Italic	Outline	Couri.ttf	*abcklmtwABCKLMTW12*
Estrangelo Edessa	Outline	Estre.ttf	(Requires special processing)
Franklin Gothic Medium	Outline	Framd.ttf	abcklmtwABCKLMTW12
Franklin Gothic Medium Italic	Outline	Framdit.ttf	*abcklmtwABCKLMTW12*
Gautami	Outline	Gautami.ttf	(Requires special processing)
Georgia	Outline	Georgia.ttf	abcklmtwABCKLMTW12
Georgia Bold	Outline	Georgiab.ttf	**abcklmtwABCKLMTW12**
Georgia Bold Italic	Outline	Georgiaz.ttf	***abcklmtwABCKLMTW12***
Georgia Italic	Outline	Georgiai.ttf	*abcklmtwABCKLMTW12*
Impact	Outline	Impact.ttf	**abcklmtwABCKLMTW12**
Latha	Outline	Latha.ttf	(Requires special processing)
Lucida Console	Outline	Lucon.ttf	abck1mtwABCKLMTW12
Lucida Sans Unicode	Outline	L_10646.ttf	abcklmtwABCKLMTW12
Mangal	Outline	Mangal.ttf	(Requires special processing)
Microsoft Sans Serif Regular	Outline	Micross.ttf	abcklmtwABCKLMTW12
Modern	Vector	Modern.fon	(Requires special processing)
MS Sans Serif 8,10,12,14,18,24	Bitmap	Sserife.fon	abcklmtwABCKLMTW12
MS Serif 8,10,12,14,18,24	Bitmap	Serife.fon	(Requires special processing)

Table 15-1 Fonts Included with Windows Server 2003

Font	Type	Filename	Type Sample
Mv Boli	Outline	Mvboli.ttf	(Requires special processing)
Palatino Linotype	Outline	Pala.ttf	abcklmtwABCKLMTW12
Palatino Linotype Bold	Outline	Palab.ttf	**abcklmtwABCKLMTW12**
Palatino Linotype Bold Italic	Outline	Palabi.ttf	***abcklmtwABCKLMTW12***
Palatino Linotype Italic	Outline	Palai.ttf	*abcklmtwABCKLMTW12*
Raavi	Outline	Raavi.ttf	(Requires special processing)
Roman	Vector	Roman.fon	**abcklmtwABCKLMTW12**
Script	Vector	Script.fon	(Requires special processing)
Shruti	Outline	Shruti.ttf	(Requires special processing)
Small Fonts	Bitmap	Smalle.fon	abcklmtwABCKLMTW12
Sylfaen	Outline	Sylfaen.ttf	(Requires special processing)
Symbol	Outline	Symbol.ttf	αβχκλμτωΑΒΧΚΛΜΤΩ12
Symbol 8,10,12,14,18,24	Bitmap	Symbole.fon	αβχκλμτωΑΒΧΚΛΜΤΩ12
Tahoma	Outline	Tahoma.ttf	abcklmtwABCKLMTW12
Tahoma Bold	Outline	Tahomabd.ttf	**abcklmtwABCKLMTW12**
Times New Roman	Outline	Times.ttf	abcklmtwABCKLMTW12
Times New Roman Bold	Outline	Timesbd.ttf	**abcklmtwABCKLMTW12**
Times New Roman Bold Italic	Outline	Timesbi.ttf	***abcklmtwABCKLMTW12***
Times New Roman Italic	Outline	Timesi.ttf	*abcklmtwABCKLMTW12*
Trebuchet MS	Outline	Trebuc.ttf	abcklmtwABCKLMTW12
Trebuchet MS Bold	Outline	Trebucbd.ttf	**abcklmtwABCKLMTW12**
Trebuchet MS Bold Italic	Outline	Trebucbi.ttf	***abcklmtwABCKLMTW12***
Trebuchet MS Italic	Outline	Trebucit.ttf	*abcklmtwABCKLMTW12*
Tunga	Outline	Tunga.ttf	(Requires special processing)
Verdana	Outline	Verdana.ttf	abcklmtwABCKLMTW12
Verdana Bold	Outline	Verdanab.ttf	**abcklmtwABCKLMTW12**
Verdana Bold Italic	Outline	Verdanaz.ttf	***abcklmtwABCKLMTW12***
Verdana Italic	Outline	Verdani.ttf	*abcklmtwABCKLMTW12*
Webdings	Outline	Webdings.ttf	✔ ☂ ☐ ✈ ✦ ✦ ! 🏛🏚🏭🏘🚢

Table 15-1 Fonts Included with Windows Server 2003 *(continued)*

Font	Type	Filename	Type Sample
WingDings	Outline	Wingding.ttf	♌♍&☞●○◆♐♒☺☻♦✲✳✠☐▢
WST_Czec	Vector	wst_czec.fon	(Requires special processing)
WST_Engl	Vector	wst_engl.fon	(Requires special processing)
WST_Fren	Vector	wst_fren.fon	(Requires special processing)
WST_Germ	Vector	wst_germ.fon	(Requires special processing)
WST_Ital	Vector	wst_ital.fon	(Requires special processing)
WST_Span	Vector	wst_span.fon	(Requires special processing)
WST_Swed	Vector	wst_swed.fon	(Requires special processing)

Table 15-1   Fonts Included with Windows Server 2003 *(continued)*

Figure 15-8   Double-clicking a font file opens a window that displays the font.

Add and Remove Fonts

You can add fonts to those that are installed by Windows Server 2003 with the following steps:

1. Open the Start menu, and choose Control Panel | Fonts. The Fonts window opens, similar to the one previously shown in Figure 15-7.

2. Open the File menu and choose Install New Font. Open a drive and folder that contains the fonts you want to install (this can be a floppy disk, a CD-ROM, or another hard drive on the network), like this:

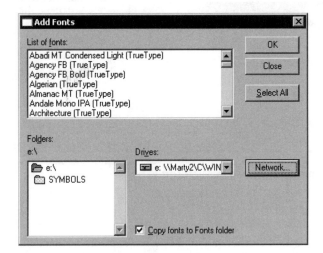

3. Select the fonts you want to install from the list (hold down SHIFT to select several contiguous fonts, or hold down CTRL to select several fonts that are not contiguous) and then click OK. The new fonts appear in the Fonts window.

You can remove fonts simply by selecting them and pressing DELETE. Alternatively, you can right-click the font(s) and choose DELETE. In either case, you are asked whether you are sure. Click Yes if you are. The fonts will be placed in the Recycle Bin, in case you made a mistake and want to retrieve one. If you haven't mistakenly deleted any, you can empty the Recycle Bin.

Use Fonts

Fonts are normally used or applied from within an application. For example, in Microsoft Word, you can select a line of text and then open the font drop-down list, as shown in Figure 15-9.

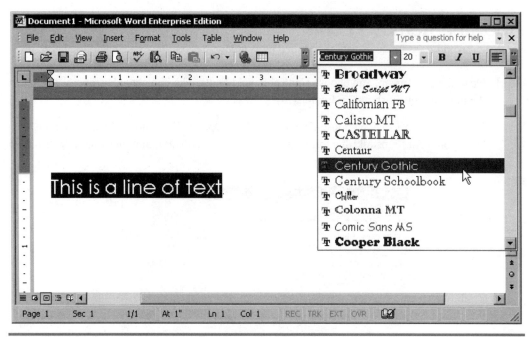

Figure 15-9 Selecting a font to use in Microsoft Word

Every application is a little different, but they all have a similar function. One nice feature of recent versions of Microsoft Word and several other recent applications is that they show what the font looks like in the list, as you can see in Figure 15-9.

Fonts used correctly can be a major asset in getting a message across, but they also can detract from a message if improperly used. Two primary rules are to not use too many fonts, and to use complementary fonts together. In a one-page document, two typefaces should be enough (you can use bold and italic to have as many as eight fonts), and in a longer document, three—and at most four—typefaces is appropriate. Complementary fonts are more subjective. Arial and Times Roman are generally considered complementary, as are Futura and Garamond, and Palatino and Optima. In each of these pairs, one typeface (for example, Arial) is *sans serif* (without the little tails on the ends of a character) and is used for titles and headings, while the other typeface (for example, Times Roman) is *serif* (it has the tails) and is used for the body text. There are of course many other options and considerations in the sophisticated use of fonts.

The Fonts window View menu has two options that help you look at similar fonts. The List Fonts By Similarity option re-sorts your fonts according to similarity to a selected font, and the Hide Variations option hides the bold and italic variations of a font, making it easier for you to look at just the typefaces (see Figure 15-10).

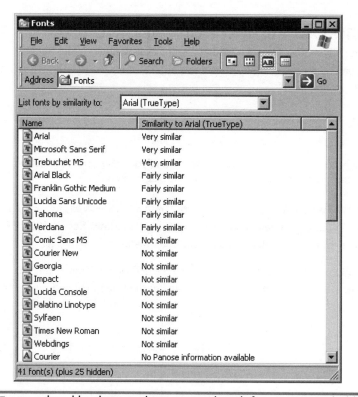

Figure 15-10 Fonts ordered by their similarity to Arial, with font variations hidden

CRITICAL SKILL
15.6 Set Up and Use Faxing

A capability to send and receive faxes has been included in Windows Server 2003 as part of its printing functionality. This allows an application such as Microsoft Word to "print" to a remote fax by specifying a "fax" as a printer and having the software for that printer ask for a phone number, interface with a modem in the computer to dial the phone number, and then work with the fax on the receiving end to transfer the information and print it out. In addition, there is a Fax Console that lets you directly send and receive faxes as you would an e-mail message. This service requires that you have a fax/modem in your computer and a phone line connected to it (see Module 10 on setting up and working with modems). This Fax Service is not fully installed by default when you install Windows XP, but you can easily install it from the Printers And Faxes window. In this section, you'll see how to set up and use the service to send faxes from an application and then how to set up and use the Fax Console to receive faxes.

Set Up and Use Faxing from Applications

Setting up faxing is done from the Printers And Faxes window using Set Up Faxing in the File menu. You can then use faxing by starting an application and "printing" to the fax printer. Here's how:

TIP

If you do not have Set Up Faxing in the File menu and you have Send Fax instead, then faxing has already been set up on your computer. Skip to Step 3.

1. Open Start | Printers And Faxes. In the Printers And Faxes window, open the File menu and click Set Up Faxing. When requested, insert your Windows Server 2003 CD and click Exit to close the introductory Windows Server 2003 Installation window.

2. When Setup is done copying files, you are returned to the Printer And Faxes window, where a new Send Fax option has been added to the File menu and a fax "printer" icon appears like this:

3. Open the File menu and click Send Fax. The first time you do that, an abbreviated Fax Configuration Wizard opens. Click Next. Enter your name, your fax number, and other information that you want associated with faxes that are sent. Click Next and then Finish.

4. The Send Fax wizard will appear. Click Next. Enter the recipient information, click Next, select the cover page template you want, enter the cover page information, and again click Next. Enter the schedule and priority, click Next, preview the fax if you wish, and click Finish to actually send the fax.

   You should hear the modem dial and the fax transmission begin. You'll see more about how to get the status of the fax in a moment.

5. Open a document in an application such as Microsoft Word (or WordPad). Open the File menu and choose Print. Open the Printer Name drop-down list, choose Fax, and click OK.

6. The Send Fax Wizard will open. Click Next. Enter the recipient's name and fax number, and click Next. If you want to send a cover page, click Select A Cover Page Template, choose the template, fill in the information you want on the cover page, and click Next.

7. Enter when you want to send the fax, enter the priority, and click Next. You are shown the settings you have made. Use Back to make any corrections and then click Finish. Again you should hear the modem dial and the initial fax transmission. Close your word processing program.

Use the Fax Console

Windows Server 2003 has several tools to help you manage and configure faxing, all of which are available from the Fax Console. Double-click the Fax icon to open the Fax Console from the Printers And Faxes windows. Alternatively, you can open the Fax Console by opening Start | All Programs | Accessories | Communications | Fax | Fax Console.

In the Fax Console's Tools menu, you can change the Sender information you originally entered in the abbreviated Fax Configuration Wizard. You can also create and edit fax cover pages, and look at the fax status. Additionally, you can open the full Fax Configuration Wizard by choosing Configure Fax, which you should do now and continue with these steps:

1. Click Next. You will see the Sender Information you already entered. Click Next. Your modem should be selected. Click Next. Enter your Transmitting Subscriber Identification (TSID), normally some combination of your fax number and business name.

2. Click Next. Select the device for receiving faxes, normally your modem, whether to manually or automatically answer when a call comes in, and if automatically, the number of rings to wait. Click Next. Enter your Called Subscriber Identification (CSID), again usually some combination of your fax number and business name.

3. Click Next. Decide what to do when a fax is received. By default, it is stored in the Fax Console. Decide if you want it printed on a printer you choose and if you want to have a second copy stored in a selected folder.

4. Click Next. A configuration summary is presented. If you want to change it, click Back and make the desired changes. When you are ready, click Finish.

5. Back in the Fax Console Tools menu, you can look at the Fax Service Manager, which is not very useful, and Fax Printer Configuration, which you should open now. Enter the name you want to use for your fax device, how you want to share the device over the network (as you would share a printer), and the security permissions you want to set up. Then click the Tracking tab (the Configuration tab just takes you to the Fax Configuration Wizard you have already gone through).

6. In the Tracking tab, you can confirm the fax device to monitor and then set the notification that you want and when you want the Fax Monitor to open. I personally like to know what is going on and so turn all of these on, including the sound. When you are ready, click OK.

7. Back in the Fax Console Tools menu, click Fax Monitor. The Fax Monitor will open, and if you click More, you will see the history of your first fax and the progress (if it is still going) or history of the second fax: Dialing, Sending, Completed, as shown in Figure 15-11.

Receive Faxes

With the fax set up as described in the preceding sections, you are ready to receive faxes using the Fax Console.

1. Open the Fax Console by one of the methods described in the preceding section.

2. If you choose Manual Answer Mode in the Fax Configuration Wizard (preceding Step 2), you must wait until you hear the phone ring with the fax message and then click the Receive Now button on the toolbar or open the File menu and choose Receive A Fax Now. A third method for manually answering a fax call is, prior to the call, to open the Tools menu and choose Fax Monitor. The Fax Monitor will appear and wait on the desktop. When a call comes in, click Answer Now.

3. If you chose Automatic Answer Mode in the Fax Configuration Wizard, any calls on that line will be automatically answered after the prescribed number of rings.

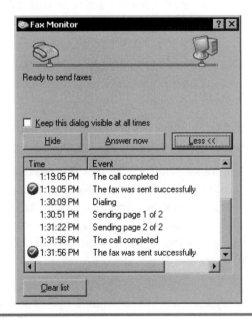

Figure 15-11 History of a fax transmission

4. In all cases of receiving a fax, the Fax Monitor will handle the call. Given that there is a fax machine (or a computer impersonating one) on the other end, a fax will be received and the Fax Monitor will display the progress. When the call is complete, the Fax Monitor will hang up and the received message will appear in the Inbox of the Fax Console, as you can see here:

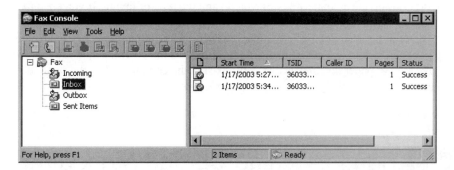

5. Double-click the fax in the Inbox to view it. Right-click the fax and choose to View, Delete, Save As (it is already saved in the Inbox), Mail To (attaches to an e-mail message you address), or Print. When you are ready, close both the Fax Console and Printers And Faxes.

Progress Check

1. Can you pause and restart a print job to insert a higher-priority job?

2. Is the Fax Service a part of the default Windows Server 2003 installation?

3. What do TSID and CSID stand for, and how are they used?

4. How can you answer a fax call?

---

1. No, you would have to cancel and restart the current job, or wait until it is finished.

2. No, it is normally not installed when you install Windows Server 2003, but a command is placed on the File menu of the Printers And Faxes window to do the installation.

3. TSID stands for Transmitting Subscriber Identification and identifies the sender of a fax to the person receiving it. CSID stands for Called Subscriber Identification and identifies the recipient of a fax to the sender.

4. A fax call can be answered either manually at the moment of the call or automatically when the call occurs. To answer a call manually, you can use the Fax Console with the Receive Now button on the toolbar, with the File menu Receive A Fax Now option, or by putting the Fax Monitor on the desktop with the Tools menu Fax Monitor option.

Ask the Expert

Q: Why would we need a regular fax machine if we have a computer fax capability?

A: It depends on the amount of faxing you do and the type of faxing. If you are only occasionally faxing and it is usually a document that is created on your computer, then "printing" that document to a fax is easier than printing it to paper and reading that paper back in to a stand- alone fax machine. On the other hand, if you frequently have a lot of paper documents that don't exist in the computer, then the stand-alone fax machine, especially with a paper feeder, is preferable.

Project 15 Plan for Setting Up and Managing Printing and Faxing

Printing and faxing are not terribly exciting subjects because today you can pretty much plug in a printer and expect it to set itself up and print. Nevertheless, there are always the exceptions, including older printers, printers on the network, printers across the network, and faxing to provide some excitement. Run down this project to make sure you have all the necessary decisions considered in your plans for this area.

Step by Step

1. Determine the computer(s) to use print servers:

   a. Windows Server 2003

   b. Windows XP Professional

   c. Consider the amount of disk space available for spooling

   d. Consider the amount of memory available

   e. Consider the current load availability

2. Determine the type and setup of print servers:

   a. Local printers:

      i. Printer port to be used

      ii. Default printer

      iii. Share printer

b. Network printers on other computers:

   i. UNC printer name

   ii. Default printer

c. Stand-alone network printers:

   i. IP address or DNS name

   ii. Default printer

3. Determine how you want the printer(s) configured:

a. Name and location

b. Paper layout and quality

c. Spool print jobs:

   i. Start printing after last page

   ii. Start printing immediately

d. Print directly without spooling

e. Use separator page

f. Assign permissions

g. Assign paper to trays

h. Use printer pooling with two or more printers

i. Set printer priority

j. Have multiple printers on one port

4. Determine the types of fonts you will use:

a. Resident fonts

b. Cartridge fonts

c. Soft fonts:

   i. Fonts with Windows Server 2003

   ii. Fonts with Microsoft Office

   iii. Fonts with _____

   iv. Fonts with _____

(continued)

    5. Determine how fax will be set up:

        a. Who will the faxes be from (Sender Information)?

        b. Identify the modem to use.

        c. Identify what your TSID and CSID are.

        d. What printer do you want to use with faxes?

        e. Do you want to store a copy of the fax other than in the Fax Console?

        f. Set how you want the fax monitored and you notified.

Project Summary

As mundane as printers may be, it is very important that they function well and without a hassle. Careful installation will help make that possible.

Module 15 Mastery Check

  1. As a general rule, should you use the CD that came with your printer or Windows Server 2003 to install your printer?

  2. What are some of the things you should do before installing a printer?

  3. What are the two kinds of network printers?

  4. What are the tasks that are part of controlling a printer queue?

  5. What is a good method for handling several printing priorities?

  6. What is the one thing you have to do if you have multiple printers?

  7. What is a font, what is a typeface, and how do they differ?

  8. What are the three kinds of fonts?

  9. What types of fonts come with Windows Server 2003?

 10. What are the two ways of opening the Fax Console?

Module 16

Managing Windows Server 2003

Ome of Windows Server 2003's greatest strengths is the variety of management tools that are available to control the many facets of the operating system. The purpose of this module is to look at the general-purpose tools, those that are not part of setting up, networking, file management, or printing. The discussion of these tools is broken into system management tools and user management tools. System management tools are those tools that facilitate running the parts of the operating system and the computer that are not discussed elsewhere. Managing computer users with their varying needs and peculiarities, both in groups and individually, is a major task and one to which Windows Server 2003 has committed considerable resources.

CRITICAL SKILL

16.1 Use the Control Panel

The Control Panel in Windows Server 2003 has by default become a submenu to the Start menu, as shown in Figure 16-1. The classic Control Panel window shown in Figure 16-2 has been a part of Windows for a long time. It is a folder that holds a number of tools that control and maintain configuration information, mainly for system hardware. Here, we'll look at the following Control Panel tools:

- Accessibility Options
- Folder Options
- Keyboard
- Mouse
- Regional And Language Options
- Scheduled Tasks
- System
- Taskbar And Start Menu

Many of the other Control Panel tools are discussed in other places in this book. Add Hardware, Add Or Remove Programs, some Administrative Tools, Date And Time, Display, and Licensing features are discussed in Part II. Other Administrative Tools features are discussed in Part III, while still others are discussed in Module 14. Game Controllers, Scanners And Cameras, Sounds And Multimedia, and Speech deal with applications outside the scope of this book. Fonts and Printers And Faxes are discussed in Module 15. Internet Options and Phone And Modem Options are discussed in Module 10. Network Connections is discussed in Parts III and IV.

Before looking at any of the specific tools, open your Control Panel and look at the tools you have available. You may have slightly different tools than those shown in Figures 16-1 and 16-2, depending on the hardware and software you have and the components of Windows

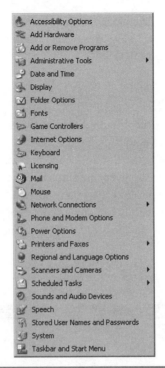

Figure 16-1 The Control Panel menu as it appears by default in Windows Server 2003

Figure 16-2 The Control Panel window as it appeared in prior versions of Windows

Server 2003 that you have installed. Open the Control Panel menu by opening the Start menu and choosing Control Panel. Open the Control Panel window by opening the Start menu, right-clicking Control Panel, and choosing Open.

Accessibility Options

Accessibility
Options

Accessibility Options allows a user with physical limitations to more easily use Windows Server 2003. The Accessibility Options dialog box, shown in Figure 16-3 and opened by selecting Accessibility Options in the Control Panel, provides four tabs (Keyboard, Sound, Display, and Mouse) in which you can enable and configure options to improve accessibility. A description of each of the options in each area is provided in Table 16-1.

The General tab of the Accessibility Options dialog box provides settings for managing the options, including when to automatically turn off the options and whether to give a warning when turning on an option.

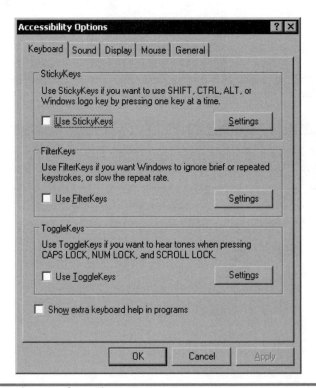

Figure 16-3 Making the use of Windows Server 2003 easier

Area	Option	Description	Turn On or Off
Keyboard	StickyKeys	Enables the user to simulate the effect of pressing a pair of keys, such as CTRL-A, by pressing one key at a time. The keys SHIFT, CTRL, and ALT "stick" down until a second key is pressed, which Windows Server 2003 then interprets as the two keys pressed together.	Press either the left or right SHIFT key five times in succession
Keyboard	FilterKeys	Enables a user to press a key twice in rapid succession and have it interpreted as a single keystroke, and also slows down the rate at which the key is repeated if the user holds it down.	Hold down the right SHIFT key for eight seconds
Keyboard	ToggleKeys	Plays a tone when CAPS LOCK, NUM LOCK, or SCROLL LOCK is pressed.	Hold down NUM LOCK for five seconds
Sound	SoundSentry	Displays a visual indicator when the computer makes a sound. The indicator can be a flashing active caption bar, a flashing active window, or a flashing desktop.	Open Accessibility Options and click Use SoundSentry in the Sound tab
Sound	ShowSounds	Tells compatible programs to display captions when sound and speech are used.	Open Accessibility Options and click Use ShowSounds in the Sound tab
Display	HighContrast	Uses high-contrast colors and special fonts to make the screen easy to use.	Press together: left SHIFT, left ALT, and PRINT SCREEN
Display	Cursor Options	Changes the rate at which the cursor blinks and width of the cursor or insertion point in text.	Always on
Mouse	MouseKeys	Enables the user to use the numeric keypad instead of the mouse to move the pointer on the screen.	Press together: left SHIFT, left ALT, and NUM LOCK

Table 16-1 Accessibility Options

Folder Options

Folder Options

Folder Options in the Control Panel allows you to customize the way folders and files are displayed and handled in various Windows Server 2003 windows, including My Computer and Windows Explorer. The Folder Options dialog box, shown in Figure 16-4 and opened by selecting Folder Options in the Control Panel, can also be accessed by opening the Tools menu and choosing Folder Options in either Windows Explorer or My Computer. The Folder Options dialog box has four tabs: General, View, File Types, and Offline Files.

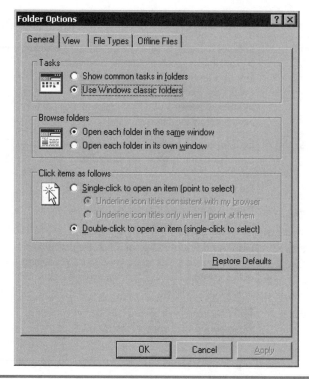

Figure 16-4 Determining how folders are displayed and handled

NOTE

There is one important difference between opening Folder Options from the Control Panel and opening it from My Computer or Windows Explorer. From the Control Panel, it sets the default for all folders; from My Computer or Windows Explorer, it sets the properties for the current open folder unless you click Apply To All Folders in the View tab.

General

The General tab allows you to choose how you want to handle three different questions.

The first question, Tasks, asks whether you want to show the task pane on the left of a window and in file folders or, alternatively, use the classic displays. This is a matter of personal choice. The task pane gives you an easy means to execute common tasks, such as copy or move a file or folder, but it also takes up more room and can't be shown with the folder pane.

The second question, Browse Folders, asks whether you want to open a new window each time a new folder is opened, or repeatedly use the same window. Opening a new window with each folder is convenient if you want to compare two folders, but it also clutters the screen. The default and most popular choice is to use the same window.

The third question, Click Items, asks whether you want to single-click, as you do in a web browser, or double-click, as you do classically in Windows, to open a folder or a file. If you choose single-click, then simply pointing on the item selects it. If you choose double-click, then single-clicking selects the item. If you are a newer user, single-clicking saves you time and the confusion between single- and double-clicking. If you have been double-clicking for very many years, it is hard to stop, and so trying to single-click can be confusing.

View

The View tab, shown in Figure 16-5, determines how files and folders and their attributes are displayed in Windows Explorer and My Computer. The Advanced Settings list has a number of settings that you can turn on or off and that are a matter of personal preference. I like to see everything, so I turn on the display of the full path in either the address bar or the title bar; I show hidden files; I turn off both the hiding of file extensions and the hiding of protected files. You may have other preferences. It is easy to try the different settings to see what you like by opening Folder Options in Windows Explorer. You can always return to the default settings by clicking Restore Defaults.

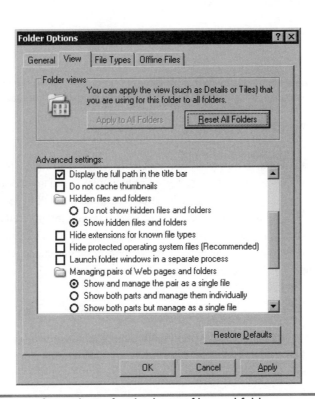

Figure 16-5 Setting specific attributes for displaying files and folders

16

Managing Windows Server 2003

File Types

The File Types tab allows you to specify which application is associated with, and will open, a particular type of file, as identified by the file extension. When Windows Server 2003 is installed, a number of file associations are registered, and each time you add an application, more file associations are added. You can register additional file types or change existing associations in the File Types tab. By clicking New, you can enter a new file extension. If you click OK, the file extension will be registered as that extension's file type. For example, if you were to register the extension MSM, the file type would be "MSM file." In the Create New Extension dialog box, you can click Advanced and select from a long list of file types. Neither of these steps associate the file with an application that can open the file. To do that, you must select the file and click Change. This opens the Open With dialog box, which allows you to select an existing application to open the file, or you can enter a new application by clicking Browse and browsing for it.

In the File Types tab, you can select an extension and then click Advanced to open the Edit File Type dialog box. Here, you can change the icon and specify the actions, such as Open, Print, and Preview, that you want to set up for a type of file. For each action, you can specify an application to be used for that action.

TIP

A fast way to associate a file type with an application is to double-click a file of that type in Windows Explorer. If no application is associated with the file, the Open With dialog box opens, in which you can select the application.

Offline Files

The Offline Files tab sets up how you want to handle working with network files when you are offline or disconnected from the network. For example, if you are working on a document stored on the server and you have enabled Offline Files, the file will be temporarily stored in a folder named Offline Files. If the network goes down or you intentionally disconnect from the network, you can continue to work with the copy in the Offline Files folder. When you reconnect to the network, you can choose to have the file synchronized with the copy on the network. If Remote Desktop is enabled on the computer, Offline Files cannot be.

Keyboard

Keyboard

Keyboard in the Control Panel allows you to set the configuration of your keyboard. As Figure 16-6 shows, the Speed tab allows you to set both how long to wait before repeating a key and how fast to do the repeating once it is started. You can click in the text box on that tab and try out

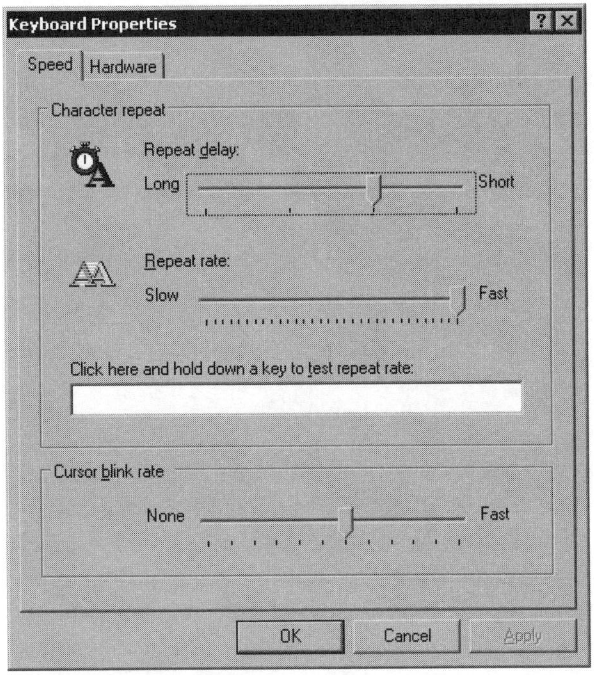

Keyboard Properties ? X

Speed | Hardware |

Character repeat

Repeat delay:

Long |———————————————J——————|Short

Repeat rate:

Slow |——————————————————————J| Fast

Click here and hold down a key to test repeat rate:

[   ]

Cursor blink rate

None ———————————J——————— Fast

OK   Cancel   Apply

Figure 16-6 Configuring the keyboard (and the cursor)

your settings. Also on that tab, you can set the cursor blink rate (although the relationship between that and the keyboard is tenuous).

The Hardware tab shows the description of the device, allows you to troubleshoot the keyboard, and, through Properties, gives you access to the drivers that are being used with it.

Mouse

Mouse

Mouse in the Control Panel allows you to set the configuration of the mouse, as shown in Figure 16-7. The Buttons tab lets you choose whether you want to use the mouse with your right or left hand. This reverses the effect of the two primary buttons on a mouse. You can also choose the speed at which a double-click is interpreted as a double-click, and you can turn on ClickLock, which lets you drag without holding down the mouse button.

The Pointers tab lets you choose or create a scheme for how the mouse pointer looks in various situations. The Pointer Options tab lets you set how fast you want the pointer to move, whether you want the pointer to automatically go to the default button when a dialog box opens, display pointer trails as you move the mouse, hide the pointer while typing, and show the location

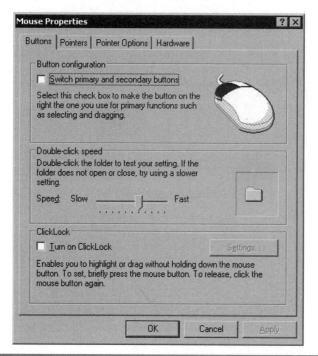

Figure 16-7 Configuring the mouse

of the pointer when the CTRL key is pressed by itself. I find this last option very handy on a laptop where I tend to lose the pointer. Like the Hardware tab in the Keyboard dialog box, the Mouse Hardware tab shows the description of the device, allows you to troubleshoot it, and, by clicking Properties, gives you access to the drivers that are being used with it.

Regional and Language Options

Regional and Language ...

Regional And Language Options in the Control Panel lets you determine how numbers, dates, currency, and time are displayed and used on your computer, as well as the languages that will be used. By choosing the primary locale, such as French (France), all the other settings, including those for formatting numbers, currency, times, and dates, are automatically changed to the standard for that locale. You can then change the individual settings for numbers, currency, time, and so on and customize how you want items displayed. The Languages tab lets you select the language in which you will be typing by default and whether you want to install supplemental support for East Asian and/or complex script languages. The Advanced tab allows you to set the language used with programs that do not use Unicode and to identify the code page conversion tables that are available.

NOTE

The custom settings for numbers, currency, time, and dates will remain set only as long as you maintain the same locale. When you change to a new locale and then change back to the original one, your custom settings will be gone, although you can use a separate profile to prevent this from occurring. See "Employ User Profiles," later in the module.

Scheduled Tasks

Scheduled
Tasks

Scheduled Tasks allows you to set up certain tasks, such as performing a backup or disk defragmentation, on a periodic basis and have those tasks carried out automatically. Selecting Scheduled Tasks in the Control Panel opens the Scheduled Tasks windows where, after they are identified, you see the scheduled tasks. Double-clicking Add Scheduled Task in the Scheduled Tasks window opens the Scheduled Task Wizard, with which you can select the program you want to run from among all the installed programs that are either part of the operating system, such as Backup, or independent, such as Veritas's Backup Exec. Then, you select the frequency with which you want to do the backup, the time of day and day of the week to do it, and finally the username and password of the person authorizing the running of this program. You then are shown what you have scheduled. If you made an error, click Back and make the correction; otherwise, click Finish to establish the scheduled task. An icon for the newly scheduled task will appear in the Scheduled Tasks window. If you want to make a change in the task, double-click its icon, which opens a dialog box that allows you to change everything from the program that is run to the schedule, date, and time.

System

System

Selecting System in the Control Panel opens the System Properties dialog box, the central place to establish, view, and change hardware settings. The System Properties dialog box can also be opened by right-clicking My Computer and choosing Properties. The first two tabs provide general and network identification. If the computer is not a domain controller, you can change the network name and join a domain from the Computer Name tab.

Hardware

The Hardware tab enables you to start the Add Hardware Wizard, which also can be started by double-clicking Add Hardware in the Control Panel. You can also open the Hardware Profiles dialog box, in which you can set up and manage multiple hardware profiles, such as those used with laptops and their docking stations. Driver digital signing gives you assurance of who created the driver and other installation files, and that they have not been changed. The Driver Signing option opens a dialog box where you can determine whether you want to be prevented from using, be warned about, or ignore files that are not digitally signed.

Device Manager

The Device Manager, shown in Figure 16-8, is the most important facility in System, enabling you to look at and configure all of your hardware in one place. You can immediately see whether you have a hardware problem; for example, the audio adapter (Multimedia Audio Controller) in Figure 16-8 has a problem, as indicated by the exclamation point icon. You can then directly open that device by double-clicking it, and attempt to cure the problem. In many cases, the Reinstall Driver, which opens the Hardware Update Wizard, will assist you. Two common problems that often can be cured are a wrong or missing driver (the case in Figure 16-8), or incorrect resources being used, often because the correct ones weren't available. If you open the Properties dialog box for a device and look at the General tab, you will get a quick device status. The Driver tab will then allow you to reinstall or update the driver, and the Resources tab will

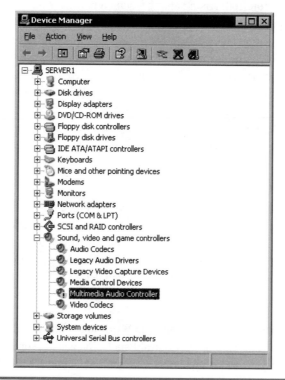

Figure 16-8 Scanning all hardware devices in the Device Manager

show you where the problem is and allow you to select different resources (resources include interrupt request lines, or IRQs, and input/output ports).

NOTE

You can print a System Resource Summary that shows all the resource assignments (IRQs, DMAs, and I/O ports) on the computer by opening the Action menu and choosing Print in Device Manager.

Advanced Tab

The System Properties dialog box's Advanced tab provides access to the settings for two operating system features:

NOTE

If you have installed multiple user profiles, you will also have a User Profiles section, which is discussed later in this module under "Employ User Profiles."

- **Performance**   Optimize performance between running applications or running background services, as are required in a file or print server; you also can identify the visual effects you want and determine the amount of disk space you want to set aside for temporary page files, the storing of memory on disk.

- **Startup and Recovery**   Select the default operating system (OS) to use on startup, how long to wait for a manual selection of that OS, and what to do on a system failure.

TIP

The System Startup area is where you can change the amount of time the computer sits idle during startup waiting for you to pick an OS. You might want to change it to something shorter, such as five seconds.

Taskbar and Start Menu

Taskbar and
Start Menu

Taskbar And Start Menu Properties, shown in Figure 16-9, can be opened either by selecting it in the Control Panel or by right-clicking the taskbar and choosing Properties. It allows you to determine how the taskbar is displayed, what is on the taskbar, whether the most recent or the classic Start menu is used, and to customize both the look and content of the Start menu.

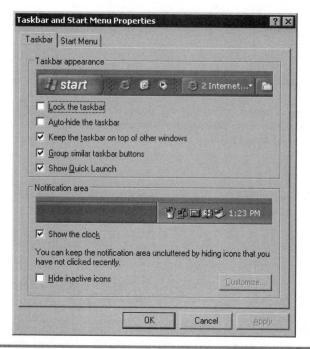

Figure 16-9 Determining how the taskbar and Start menu are displayed

CRITICAL SKILL
16.2 Use the Task Manager

Windows Task Manager allows you to look at and control what is running in Windows Server 2003. You can start Task Manager, shown in Figure 16-10, either by right-clicking a blank area of the taskbar and choosing Task Manager or by pressing CTRL-ALT-DEL and choosing Task Manager. The Applications tab shows you the application tasks that are currently running and allows you to terminate a task; switch to a task; or create a new task by opening a program, folder, document, or Internet resource.

The Processes tab shows the processes that are currently loaded. These include the programs needed for the applications that are running, as well as the OS processes that are active. You can display a large amount of information for each of the processes, and you can select what you want to display by choosing View | Select Columns, as shown next. After you choose the columns you want to display, you can arrange the columns by dragging the column headers, and you can sort the list by clicking the column you want sorted. You can end any process by selecting it and clicking End Process.

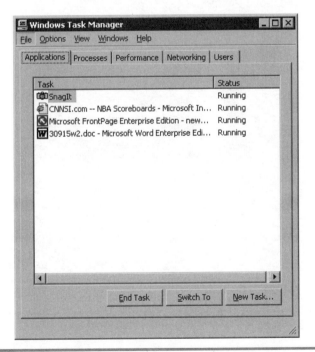

Figure 16-10 Looking at the applications that are currently running

The Performance tab, shown in Figure 16-11, shows you how the tasks being performed by the computer are using the CPU and memory, and what are the components of that usage. This information is particularly important in heavily used servers. You can see if either the CPU or memory (or both) is reaching its limit and what the system is doing to handle it. If you have multiple CPUs, you can see how each is being used, and assign processes to particular processors by right-clicking the processes in the Processes tab. You can also set the priority of a process by right-clicking it in the Processes tab.

The Networking tab shows how a particular connection to the network is being used. If there are multiple network interface cards (NICs) in the computer, they will be listed at the bottom of the window and you can select the one you want to look at. The scale on the graph automatically changes to give you the most precise reading possible. The Users tab lists the users currently logged on to the server. You can disconnect, log off, or send a message to a selected user.

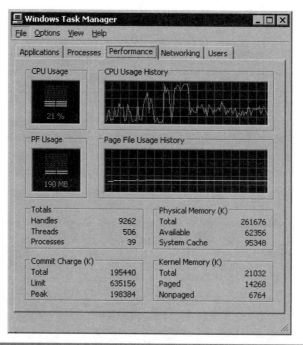

Figure 16-11 Seeing how CPU and memory are being used

CRITICAL SKILL
16.3 Use the Microsoft Management Console

The Microsoft Management Console, or MMC, is a shell to which you can add, and then customize, management tools that you want to use. You can create several different *consoles* containing different tools for different administrative purposes and save these consoles as MSC files. There are two types of management tools that you can add to an MMC: stand-alone tools that are called *snap-ins,* and add-on functions that are called *extensions.* Extensions work with and are available for particular snap-ins. Extensions are automatically added with some snap-ins, whereas other snap-ins require you to select the extensions. An example of a snap-in with automatic extensions is Computer Management, and one of its many extensions is the Disk Defragmenter. There are two modes in which you can create consoles: *Author* mode, in which the consoles can be added to and revised, and *User* mode, in which the console is frozen and cannot be changed. User mode also has full-access and two limited-access options.

Windows Server 2003 comes with a number of consoles already created that you have used in earlier modules. These consoles, which I have called "windows" (because that is what they are), are located in the Administrative Tools folder (Start | Administrative Tools) and include Computer Management, DHCP, Distributed Files System, and many others. All of the built-in consoles are in User mode and cannot be changed or added to.

Create an MMC Console

A console that I have found to be handy is one to manage several remote computers on my network. In this one console, I have added Computer Management for these computers. Therefore, as the administrator on the server, I can remotely look at most of the administrative information on these computers, as you can see in Figure 16-12. Use the following instructions to create a similar console:

NOTE

This set of steps, as most in this module, requires that you be logged on as an Administrator.

1. Open the Start menu and click Run. In the Run dialog box, type **mmc** and click OK. The MMC will open showing only a console root, the window in which you add snap-ins.

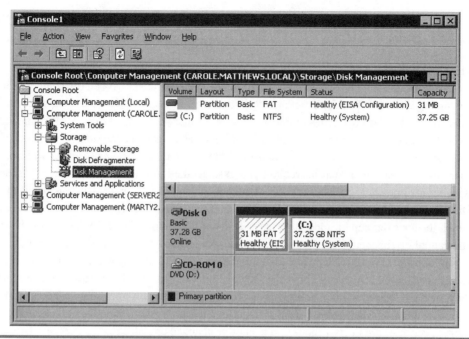

Figure 16-12 Reviewing administrative information on several remote computers

2. Open the File menu and choose Add/Remove Snap-In. In the Add/Remove Snap-In dialog box that opens, click Add. The Add Standalone Snap-In dialog box will open.

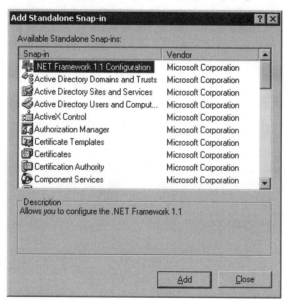

3. Click any of the snap-ins that are not familiar to you and look at the description in the lower part of the dialog box.

4. After you look at all the snap-ins that you want to, double-click Computer Management. The Computer Management dialog box opens, asking you to choose between the local computer you are on and another computer. You may or may not want to include the local computer in this console. Assume you do for these instructions, and click Finish. Computer Management (Local) will appear in the Add/Remove Snap-In dialog box.

5. Double-click Computer Management a second time, click Another Computer, browse for the other computer, and, after it is found, click Finish. Computer Management for the second computer will appear in the Add/Remove Snap-In dialog box.

6. Repeat Step 5 for as many computers as you want to manage in one console. After you add all the snap-ins that you want, click Close in the Add Standalone Snap-In dialog box.

7. In the Add/Remove Snap-In dialog box, click Extensions. The list of extensions is displayed, as shown next. You can see that the default is to add all the extensions, which has been done. If you want to remove some of the extensions, uncheck the Add All Extensions check box and then uncheck the extensions you don't want (doing this once will apply to all Computer Management snap-ins).

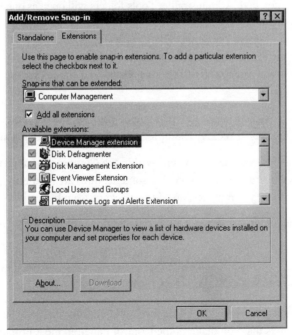

8. After you complete all the changes you want to make to the extensions, click OK. You are returned to the MMC and your snap-ins appear in the left pane. Open several of the snap-ins and their extensions to get a view, similar to Figure 16-12.

9. In the MMC, open the File menu and choose Options to open the Options dialog box. Here, you can choose either Author mode or User mode. Look at the description of what each mode means and what each of the User mode's options means.

10. When you have chosen the mode you want to use, click OK to close the Options dialog box and return to the MMC.

11. Again open the File menu and choose Save As. Enter a name that is meaningful to you and click Save. Finally, close the MMC.

Use an MMC Console

Your custom consoles are kept in the Administrative Tools folder in the shared Administrator area of your hard disk (C:\Documents and Settings\Administrator\Start Menu\Programs\Administrative Tools). If you haven't created one or more custom consoles, you won't have an Administrative Tools folder here, but after you create your first custom console, that folder is created and the console is automatically placed in it. This is not the same as the Administrator Tools folder containing all the built-in consoles, which is in the shared All Users area of your hard disk (C:\Documents and Settings\All Users\Start Menu\Programs\Administrative Tools), but when you log on as Administrator, both Administrative Tools folders will open as one from the Start menu. See how that works by following these steps:

1. Open the Start menu and choose All Programs | Administrative Tools. If necessary, expand the menu so that you can see all the options. On it, you should see the new console you have created.

2. Click your new console to open it. Open one of your remote computers and then continue to open the extensions to see, for example, a particular hardware resource, such as IRQs.

3. Continue to open the various extensions within the Computer Management console and see the capabilities that are available; note that some features are read-only, and that to do remote disk defragmentation, you must buy an add-on package from Executive Software International.

4. After you finish looking at what you can see and do within your new console, close it.

CRITICAL SKILL
16.4 Explore the Registry

The Registry is the central repository of all configuration information in Windows Server 2003. It contains the settings that you make in the Control Panel, in most Properties dialog boxes, and in the Administrative Tools. Almost all programs get information about the local computer and current user from the Registry and write information to the Registry for the OS and other programs to use. The Registry is a complex hierarchical database that in most circumstances should not be directly changed. The majority of the settings in the Registry can be changed in the Control Panel, Properties dialog boxes, or Administrative Tools.

CAUTION

If you directly edit the Registry, it is very easy to make an erroneous change that will bring down the system, so you are strongly advised to directly edit the Registry only as the last alternative used in trying to change a setting.

With the preceding caution firmly in mind, it is still worthwhile understanding and looking at the Registry. Windows Server 2003's Registry Editor enables you to view the Registry, as well as make changes to it if you have to.

TIP

If you make a change to the Registry that doesn't work, you can restore the Registry to the way it was the last time the computer was started by restarting the computer and pressing F8 immediately after you are asked about booting from a CD. Select Last Known Good Configuration and press ENTER. The most recent backup of the Registry will be used to start the computer.

Start the Registry Editor by opening the Start menu, choosing Run, typing **regedit**, and clicking OK. The Registry Editor will appear, as shown in Figure 16-13.

Keys and Subtrees

The Registry consists of two primary keys, or *subtrees* (HKEY_USERS and HKEY_LOCAL_MACHINE), and three subordinate keys, also called subtrees (HKEY_CURRENT_USER, HKEY_CURRENT_CONFIG, and HKEY_CLASSES_ROOT). HKEY_CURRENT_USER is subordinate to HKEY_USERS, and HKEY_CURRENT_CONFIG and HKEY_CLASSES_ROOT are subordinate to HKEY_LOCAL_MACHINE. Each of the five subtrees is a folder in the Registry Editor, and they all are shown at the same level for ease of use. The purpose of each subtree is as follows:

HKEY_USERS

Contains the default information common to all users and is used until a user logs on.

- **HKEY_CURRENT_USER**   Contains the preferences, or *profile,* of the user currently logged on to the computer. This includes the desktop contents, the screen colors, Control Panel settings, and Start menu contents. The settings here take precedence over those in HKEY_LOCAL_MACHINE, where they are duplicated. Later in this module, under "Employ User Profiles," you'll see how to set up and manage user profiles.

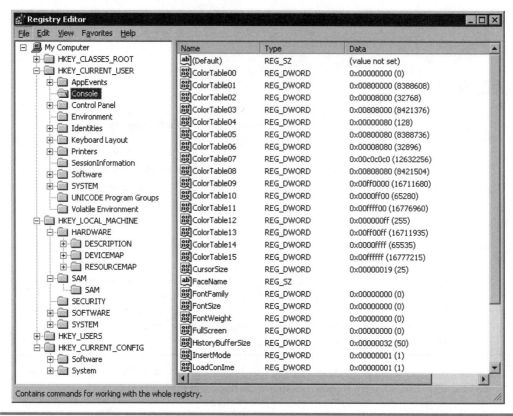

Figure 16-13 Looking at the Registry

HKEY_LOCAL_MACHINE

Contains all the computer and OS settings that are not user-related. This includes the type and model of CPU; the amount of memory; the keyboard, mouse, and ports available on the hardware side; and the drivers, fonts, and settings for individual programs on the software side.

- **HKEY_CURRENT_CONFIG**   Contains the hardware profile for the current computer configuration. This includes the drives, ports, and drivers needed for the currently installed hardware. This is important with mobile computers and their docking stations.

- **HKEY_CLASSES_ROOT**   Contains the file type registration information that relates file extensions to the programs that can open them.

Keys, Subkeys, and Hives

Within each of the primary keys or subtrees are lower-level keys, and within those keys are subkeys, and within the subkeys are lower-level subkeys, and so on for many levels. For example,

Figure 16-14 shows a subkey nine levels below HKEY_LOCAL_MACHINE. You can think of keys and subkeys as folders that have folders within them and folders within those folders.

Several of the keys immediately beneath the two primary keys (HKEY_LOCAL_MACHINE and HKEY_USERS) are deep groupings of keys and subkeys. These keys (Default, SAM, Security, Software, and System), called *hives,* are stored as separate files in the C:\Windows\ System32\Config folder (assuming the default installation). Each hive has at least two files, and most often three or more. The first file, without an extension, is the Registry file that contains the current Registry information. The second file, with the .log extension, is a log of changes that have been made to the Registry file. The third file, with the .sav extension, is the Last Known Good backup of the Registry (known to be good because the system was successfully started with it). The final Registry file type, with the .evt extension, tracks events as they are occurring with the Registry.

NOTE

The SAM key stands for Security Account Manager. It is used for storing the username and password in stand-alone computers.

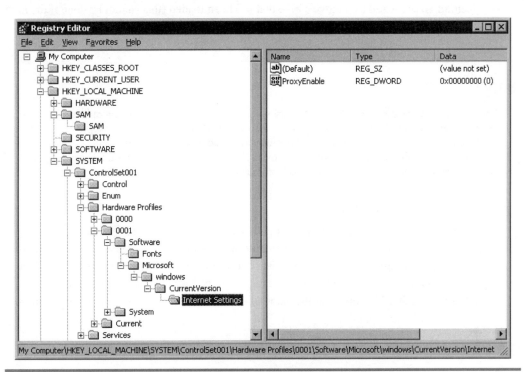

Figure 16-14 There are often many subkeys within each key in the Registry.

You can work with the hives to save a particular group of settings, make changes to the settings, and then either restore the original settings or add the original settings to the new ones. Here are the Registry Editor's File menu commands to do that:

- **Export**   Used to save a selected hive to your disk or a floppy. To use this command, select the hive, open the File menu, choose Export, select a folder, enter a name, and click Save. A saved hive can be either restored or loaded. You can also right-click a hive and choose Export to accomplish the same objective.

- **Import**   Used to replace an existing hive in the Registry. To use this command, select the hive to be replaced, open the File menu, choose Import, select a drive and folder, enter or select a name, and click Open. The restored hive will overwrite the current one.

- **Load Hive**   Used to add a saved hive to an existing one. To use this command, select either HKEY_LOCAL_MACHINE or HKEY_USERS, open the File menu, choose Load Hive, select a drive and folder, enter or select a name, and click Open. When asked, enter the name that you want to give the additional hive, and click OK. A new subkey is created with the name you have given it. This can then be used by software that knows about the new name.

- **Unload Hive**   Used to remove a hive that has been loaded (this cannot be done if the hive was restored). Unload a loaded hive by selecting it, opening the File menu, and choosing Unload Hive.

NOTE

You can make a complete copy of the Registry without having to find the individual files using the Backup utility (Start | All Programs | Accessories | System Tools | Backup). Start the Backup Wizard (Advanced) and back up the System State data. (See the discussion under "Run Automated System Recovery," later in the module.) This backup can be stored on removable media or on a local hard disk.

Entries and Data Types

At the lowest level of the Registry tree, you will see a data entry in the right pane for the selected key. All data entries have three elements: a name on the left, a data type in the middle, and the data on the right. You can see two data entries on the right of Figure 16-14. The data type determines how to look at and use the data. Also, the Registry Editor has an editor for each data type. Table 16-2 provides the name of each data type, its editor, and its description.

TIP

You can automatically open the correct editor for a particular data type by double-clicking the name on the left of the data entry.

Data Type	Editor	Description
REG_BINARY	Binary	A single value that is expressed in the Registry Editor as a hexadecimal number, generally a complex number that is parsed and used to set switches
REG_DWORD	Dword	A single value that is a hexadecimal number of up to eight digits, generally a simple number such as decimal 16, or 60, or 1024
REG_SZ	String	A single string of characters, such as a filename; it can include spaces
REG_EXPAND_SZ	String	A single string of characters that contains a variable that the OS replaces with its current value when the value is requested; an example is the environment variable *Systemroot* that is replaced with the root directory of Windows Server 2003 (by default, C:\Windows)
REG_MULTI_SZ	Multi-String	Multiple strings of characters separated by spaces, commas, or other punctuation, so each string cannot contain spaces, commas, or other punctuation
REG_FULL_RESOURCE_DESCRIPTOR	Array	A series of hexadecimal numbers representing an array used to store a list of values

Table 16-2 Data Types Used in the Registry

Ask the Expert

Q: How do you know where to go to find the particular Registry entry you want to modify?

A: That is the most pertinent of questions. The quick answer is that it is extremely difficult and you should use the Control Panel, Administrative Tools, and every dialog box available before trying to use the Registry Editor. The Registry Editor does have a Find command (Edit | Find or CTRL-F) that lets you search keys, values, and data and locate entries that contain some or all of your search criteria. Since there are often several or even many entries found, you can display them one after the other (Edit | Find Next or

(continued)

press F3). If you do find the entry you want, you can store it for future reference in the Registry Editor's Favorites list so that you can quickly get to the entry in the future. *But,* how do you know what to search for in the first place; how do you know which of several entries found is the entry you want to change; and how do you interpret the hexadecimal and binary entries into values that are meaningful to you? The answers to these questions are very difficult to find and are different for each of the hundreds of values in the Registry. Many books have been written on this subject (a search of Amazon.com produced 43 books); one of the best is by Kathy Ivens, *Admin911: Windows 2000 Registry* (McGraw-Hill/Osborne Media Group, 2000).

Progress Check

1. What are the four groupings of system management tools discussed so far in this module?

2. What are Accessibility Options?

3. How can you get a printout of the hardware resources being used in a computer?

4. What is a major caution to keep in mind with the Registry?

CRITICAL SKILL
16.5 Understand the Boot Process

The Windows Server 2003 startup or *boot* process is reasonably complex and can have problems. Therefore, it is worthwhile for you to understand what is taking place during booting, what you see on the screen, and what files are being used. Armed with this information, hopefully you'll be able to correct or work around any problems that occur.

Boot Files

Booting uses nine primary files and however many driver and other files that are needed for the particular hardware being used. Table 16-3 describes these files, shows in which stage of the boot process each file is used, and lists the default location in which each file is stored.

---

1. The four groupings of system management tools discussed so far are the Control Panel, the Task Manager, the MMC, and the Registry.

2. Accessibility Options allows a user with physical limitations to more easily use Windows Server 2003.

3. Print a System Resource Summary that shows all the resource assignments (IRQs, DMAs, and I/O ports) on the computer by opening Start | Control Panel | System, clicking the Hardware tab and then Device Manager, opening the Action menu, and choosing Print.

4. If you directly edit the Registry, it is very easy to make an erroneous change that will bring down the system, so you are strongly advised to directly edit the Registry only as the last alternative used in trying to change a setting.

Managing Windows Server 2003

Filename	Description	Stage Used	Stored In
Ntldr	Basic operating system loader	Preboot	C:\
Boot.ini	Identifies the optional OS's into which you can boot, as well as the timeout seconds; this file is directly editable	Boot	C:\
Ntdetect.com	Detects and prepares a list of currently installed hardware components	Boot	C:\
Ntoskrnl.exe	The operating system kernel; creates the current hardware Registry key, loads device drivers, and starts Session Manager	Load	C:\Windows\System32
Hal.dll	Hardware abstraction layer; provides the interface between the operating system and the specific set of hardware in the computer. This in turn loads all of the needed hardware drivers.	Load	C:\Windows\System32
Smss.exe	Session Manager; loads basic services, creates the pagefile, starts the Win32 I/O subsystem, and begins the logon process	Initialization	C:\Windows\System32
System	Registry file providing the primary operating system parameters	Initialization	C:\Windows\System32\Config
Winlogon.exe	Handles the logon process and starts the Local Security Authority	Logon	C:\Windows\System32
Lsass.exe	Local Security Authority; provides the security-checking mechanisms	Logon	C:\Windows\System32

Table 16-3 Files Used in the Startup/Boot Process

TIP

To see the preceding system files in Windows Explorer or My Computer, you need to set the appropriate options in the Tools | Folder Options | View tab (Show Hidden Files And Folders should be selected, and Hide Protected Operating System Files should not be checked).

Steps in the Booting Process

As you can see from Table 16-3, the boot process has five major stages: preboot, boot, load, initialization, and logon. Within each of these stages, several steps take place that load and use the files in Table 16-3. In each of these stages, look at the process that is taking place, how the particular files are used, and what you see on the screen.

Preboot   Preboot is the hardware-dependent, BIOS-enabled startup process. It is started either by power coming on or the system being reset. The first step is to see what hardware is available and its condition by using the power-on self test (POST) routines. Next, the boot device is located and the master boot record (MBR) is read. From it, the active partition is found on the partition table and its boot sector is read. Because Windows Server 2003 Setup has written it there, the active partition's boot sector specifies that the Ntldr file should be loaded and run. On the screen, you see the memory check, the identification of hardware, and the search for a boot device.

Boot   Boot is OS-dependent. For Windows Server 2003, it is controlled by Ntldr (the NT loader), which begins by reading the Boot.ini file and, if applicable, asking the user to choose the OS that user wants to use. If a choice is not made before the timeout, the default OS in Boot.ini is loaded. If a Boot.ini file is not found, Ntldr uses the first disk, first partition, and \Windows folder from which to load the operating system.

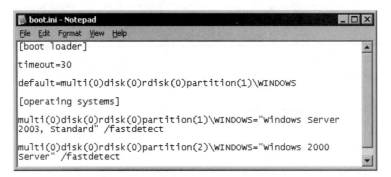

Next, the Ntdetect.com file is loaded, which determines what hardware and drivers are available. Ntldr then switches from real mode to 32-bit mode and loads a miniature file system that can operate with either FAT- or NTFS-formatted disks.

If you are booting Windows Server 2003 and have set up two or more hardware profiles, you are given the option of pressing the SPACEBAR to select a hardware profile you want to use; for example, if you have a laptop that you sometimes use with a docking station. If you press the SPACEBAR, you can choose the hardware profile you want; otherwise, the default profile is used.

Load   Following the operating system and hardware profile selection, the Windows Server 2003 "splash" screen is displayed with the moving bars in the center. While this is happening, Ntldr loads the following:

- **Ntoskrnl.exe**   The operating system kernel

- **Hal.dll**   The hardware abstraction layer that provides the interface between the operating system and a particular set of hardware

- **System**   Registry file from HKEY_LOCAL_MACHINE

- **Device drivers**   Drivers for basic hardware devices, such as the monitor, as specified in System

Initialization   Ntoskrnl.exe is initialized and takes over from Ntldr, bringing up a graphical display with a status bar. Ntoskrnl.exe then writes the HKEY_LOCAL_MACHINE\HARDWARE key and HKEY_LOCAL_MACHINE\SYSTEM\SELECT subkey (called the "Clone Control Set") and loads the remainder of the device drivers. Finally, Smss.exe, the Session Manager, is started. Smss.exe executes any boot-time command files, creates a paging file for the Virtual Memory Manager, creates links to the file system that can be used by DOS commands, and finally starts the Win32 subsystem to handle all I/O for Windows Server 2003.

NOTE

Figure 1-1, the Central Components of Windows Server 2003, shows and relates the Kernel, Win32 Subsystem, and HAL.

Logon   The Win32 subsystem starts the final Windows Server 2003 GUI and then Winlogon.exe, which displays the logon dialog box. After a successful logon, the necessary services are started and the Last Known Good control set is written on the basis of the Clone Control Set.

Correct Booting Problems

Numerous situations can cause a computer to not boot. To counter this fact, Windows Server 2003 has several features to help you work around the problem and to help you fix it. Among these features are the following:

- Returning to the Last Known Good Registry files

- Using Safe Mode and Advanced Options

- Using the Recovery Console

- Repairing the boot sector

- Running Automated System Recovery

Return to the Last Known Good Registry Files

If a computer doesn't successfully complete the boot process, and you have just tried to install a new piece of hardware or software or have otherwise changed the Registry, the problem often is due to the Registry's trying to load a device driver that doesn't work properly, or the result of some other Registry problem. You would normally learn of this problem late in the boot process, probably in either the Initialization or Logon stages. The fastest cure for a Registry problem is to return to the Last Known Good Registry files, by following these steps:

1. Restart the computer, and press F8 immediately after the selection of a boot device (if I don't have a bootable floppy or CD in its drive, I press F8 when I see the system doing the search for a boot device).

2. Use the arrow keys to select Last Known Good Configuration, and press ENTER. The Last Known Good Registry files will be used to start up Windows Server 2003.

The Last Known Good Registry files were saved the last time you successfully completed booting and logged on to Windows Server 2003.

Using the Last Known Good Configuration and Automated System Recovery are the only automated means to try to repair a problem starting Windows Server 2003. All other techniques require that you manually work on the files that are required to start Windows Server 2003.

Use Safe Mode and Other Advanced Options

Safe Mode uses only minimal default drivers to start the basic Windows Server 2003 services, with the idea that, in that mode, you can fix the problem that's preventing the full startup. You start Safe Mode with the same steps used to start Last Known Good Configuration, except that you choose one of three Safe Modes: Safe Mode, Safe Mode With Networking, and Safe Mode With Command Prompt. Basic Safe Mode does not include networking and comes up with a minimal Windows graphics interface. The second Safe Mode option adds networking capability, and the third option places you at a command prompt; otherwise, these two options are the same as Safe Mode.

As you start Safe Mode, you see a listing of the drivers as they are loaded. If the boot fails at that point, you are left looking at the last drivers that were loaded. Once you get into Windows, you might not have a mouse available, so you'll need to remember the shortcut keys for important functions, as shown in Table 16-4.

While working in Safe Mode, the System Information window is very handy, as shown in Figure 16-15. Open the System Information window by opening the Start menu and choosing All Programs | Accessories | System Tools | System Information. Within System Information, Hardware Resources | Conflicts/Sharing, Components | Problem Devices, and Software Environment | Running Tasks are particularly of value.

Function	Shortcut Key
Open Start menu	CTRL-ESC
Open context menu	SHIFT-F10
Close active windows	ALT-F4
Open Help	F1
Open Properties	ALT-ENTER
Search for files or folders	F3
Switch tasks	ALT-ESC
Switch programs	ALT-TAB
Switch tabs	CTRL-TAB
Turn on MouseKeys	Left-SHIFT-left-ALT-NUM LOCK
Undo last operation	CTRL-Z

Table 16-4 Shortcut Keys of Use in Safe Mode

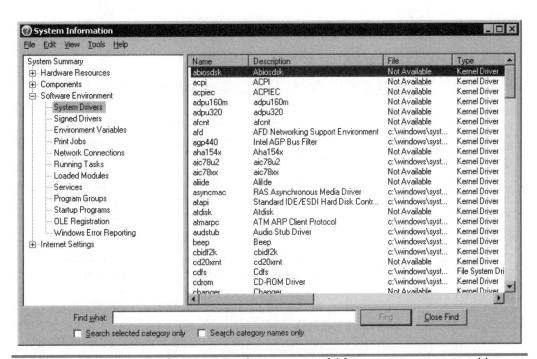

Figure 16-15 The System Information window is very useful for correcting startup problems.

In addition to Safe Mode and Last Known Good Configuration, the Advanced Options menu has the following options. These are in addition to the options, Start Windows Normally, Reboot, and Return To OS Choices Menu (where you can select the Recovery Console, see the next section), which do not need explanation:

- **Enable Boot Logging**   Logs all the events that take place during startup in the file Ntbtlog.txt, located by default in the C:\Windows folder. The loading of all system files and drivers is logged, as shown next, so that you can see if one failed while it was being loaded. Boot logging is done in all advanced startup options except Last Known Good Configuration.

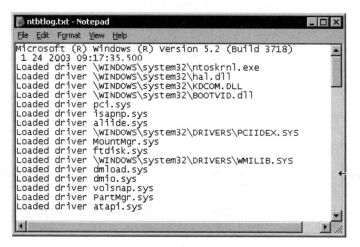

- **Enable VGA Mode**   Sets the display for a minimal video graphic adapter (VGA) with 640×480 resolution using a known good default driver. All other drivers and capabilities are loaded normally. The VGA mode is also used in Safe Mode.

- **Directory Services Restore Mode**   Restores Active Directory in domain controllers and then goes into Safe Mode, except that the mouse is available and normal video display mode is used (not VGA mode). In computers that are not domain controllers, this option is the same as Safe Mode.

- **Debugging Mode**   Turns on the debugger and then boots up into the normal configuration for the computer. This allows you to work on scripts that might be getting in the way of a proper startup.

Use the Recovery Console

The Recovery Console is a DOS-like command-line interface that allows you to read, write, format, and partition or delete partitions on both FAT and NTFS disks, as well as repair the boot and master boot records on a disk. The Recovery Console is started from the Windows Server 2003 Setup CD used for installing Windows Server 2003. Boot from the CD and follow the instructions to repair a Windows Server 2003 installation using the Recovery Console. If you have several partitions with different operating systems in them, you are asked to choose which you want to log on to by typing a number of the drive (the drive numbers are listed for you) and pressing ENTER. You then must enter the Administrator's password and press ENTER. The command prompt will appear, such as C:\Windows.

TIP

If you have copied the Windows Server 2003 Setup CD's I386 folder onto your hard disk, you can install the Recovery Console as a startup option by typing at the command prompt the command **c:\i386\winnt32 /cmdcons**, given that C:\i386 is the folder in which you placed your Setup files. You can then select Windows Server 2003 Recovery Console from the OS Choices menu during startup.

At the Recovery Console's command prompt, you can type many familiar DOS commands, such as Attrib, Cd, Chkdsk, Cls, Copy, Del, Dir, Format, Md, More, Rd, and Ren. You can get a complete list of commands by typing **Help** and pressing ENTER. You can also get an explanation of any of the commands by typing the command followed by **/?**, or you can type **Help** and a command name, and pressing ENTER after any entry.

You can also use commands that are unique to the Recovery Console, some of which are quite powerful. Among these commands are the following:

- **Batch**   Executes a set of commands in a text file.

- **Disable** and **Enable**   Stops and restarts, respectively, a device driver or Windows system service. (You use Listsvc to get the drivers and services that are available.)

- **Diskpart**   Adds and deletes disk partitions.

- **Expand**   Decompresses a compressed file.

- **Fixboot** and **Fixmbr**   Correct problems with the boot and master boot records, respectively. (See the next section for more details.)

- **Listsvc**   Lists the device drivers and system services available on the computer.

- **Logon**   Logs on to a different Windows Server 2003 installation.

- **Map**   Shows the drives (and their drive letters) that are available on the computer.

- **Systemroot**   Changes the directory to the system variable Systemroot, which by default is C:\Windows.

TIP

The Recovery Console's Diskpart is Windows Server 2003's answer to Fdisk that was available in MS-DOS and Windows 95/98.

When you are done with the Recovery Console, type **Exit** and press ENTER.

Repair the Master Boot and Boot Sectors

Two commands in the Recovery Console are particularly significant to fixing problems when booting:

● Typing **fixboot** *drive id* and pressing ENTER at the command prompt in the Recovery Console writes a new boot sector in the identified drive. The *drive id* is optional, and if not stated, the first partition or system partition of the boot device is assumed.

● Typing **fixmbr** *device name* and pressing ENTER at the command prompt in the Recovery Console repairs the master boot record in the boot partition of the named device. The *device name* is optional, and if not stated, the boot device is assumed. If the partition table is not usable, you will be prompted for further information.

Run Automated System Recovery

The most complete way to try to repair a problem with the operating system is to use Automated System Recovery (ASR), which replaces your entire system. This should be a last resort, because *the boot partition of the primary hard drive is reformatted,* all the files are reloaded, and it takes almost as long as running Windows Server 2003 Setup from scratch except that you don't have to enter any information and your system is completely restored to the same condition it was in when you initially ran ASR. To do this, you need an ASR floppy disk and a complete external copy of all information on the drive or partition used to boot and run Windows Server 2003. The ASR floppy disk and the external copy of the boot partition are created in the Backup utility, as discussed in Module 14. Create the ASR floppy and external copy of the boot partition here so that you have it ready. First you need to format a floppy disk:

1. Insert a floppy disk whose contents are of no value, and then open My Computer.

2. Right-click the floppy disk icon, choose Format in the context menu, click Start, and click OK when warned that formatting will erase all data on the disk. Finally, click OK when told that formatting is complete, and then click Close.

3. Leave the floppy disk in its drive and start the Backup utility by opening the Start menu and choosing All Programs | Accessories | System Tools | Backup.

4. If the Backup Or Restore Wizard opens, click Advanced Mode. In the Welcome tab of the Backup window, click the Automated System Recovery Wizard button and then click Next.

16

5. Identify the media type and filename, click Next, and click Finish to start the backup.

6. Click OK when you are told that ASR was saved successfully. Remove the floppy, label it, and store it in a safe place that you can easily find and get to in an emergency.

Automated System Recovery is started from the Windows Server 2003 Setup CD used for installing Windows Server 2003:

1. Restart the computer and boot from the Setup CD. You will see the normal Setup startup take place onscreen.

2. When asked whether you want to start Automated System Recovery, press F2 to do that.

3. When asked, insert the ASR disk in the floppy drive and press ENTER. The basic system information on the floppy will be read, and then Setup will continue with its normal loading. The primary partition of the boot hard disk is reformatted, files are copied, the system is restarted (you should remove the floppy before this happens), and Setup progresses as you saw in Modules 4 and 5.

4. Part way into Setup, after the necessary foundation files have been copied and loaded, the Backup Utility will automatically load and start the Restore process using the external copy of the boot partition made by ASR.

5. When the restore is completed, your system will reboot, and after pressing CTRL-ALT-DEL and entering your password, you will find your system the way it was backed up.

TIP

While ASR is a last resort, it is great to have when you need it, and I strongly recommend that you periodically make an ASR backup. Don't delay, do it today!

CRITICAL SKILL

16.6 Use Group Policies

Group policies provide the means to establish the standards and guidelines that an organization wants to apply to the use of its computers. Group policies are meant to reflect the general policies of an organization and can be established hierarchically from a local computer at the lowest end, to a particular site, to a domain, and to several levels of organizational units (OUs) at the upper end. Normally, lower-level units inherit the policies of the upper-level units, although it is possible to block higher-level policies, as well as to force inheritance if desired. Group polices are divided into *user policies* that prescribe what a user can do, and *computer policies* that determine what is available on a computer. User policies are independent of the computer on which the user is working, and follow the user from computer to computer. When a computer is started (booted), the applicable computer group policies are downloaded to it and stored in the Registry HKEY_LOCAL_MACHINE. When a user logs on to a computer, the applicable user group policies are downloaded to the computer and stored in the Registry HKEY_CURRENT_USER.

Group policies can be very beneficial to both an organization and the individuals in it. All the computers in an organization can automatically adjust to whichever user is currently logged on. This can include a custom desktop with a custom Start menu and a unique set of applications. Group policies can control the access to files, folders, and applications, as well as the ability to change system and application settings, and the ability to delete files and folders. Group policies can automate tasks when a computer starts up or shuts down, and when a user logs on or logs off. Group policies can also automatically store files and shortcuts in specific folders.

Create and Change Group Policies

Group policies can exist at the local computer level, the site level, the domain level, and the OU level. Although the process to create or change group policies is the same at the site, domain, and OU levels, it is sufficiently different at the local computer level to merit discussing this level separately.

Change Group Policies at the Local Computer Level

Every Windows Server 2003 computer has a single local group policy created by Setup during installation and stored by default in C:\Windows\System32\GroupPolicy. Since there can be only one local group policy, you cannot create another, although you can edit the existing one by following these instructions:

1. Open the Start menu, choose Run, type **gpedit.msc**, and press ENTER or click OK. The Group Policy window will open.

2. Open several levels of the tree on the left so that you can get down to a level that shows policies and their settings on the right, as shown in Figure 16-16.

3. Double-click a policy to open its dialog box. Here you can change the local policy settings by adding or removing users or groups.

4. Add additional users or groups to a policy by clicking Add and selecting one or more users and/or groups that you want to add.

5. Expand User Configuration | Administrative Templates | Windows Components | Internet Explorer, Windows Explorer, Start Menu & Taskbar, and Desktop. Note how they are all "Not Configured" and the variety of functions and features that you can control.

6. When you are done making the changes that you want to make to the local computer group policies, close the open dialog boxes and the Group Policy window.

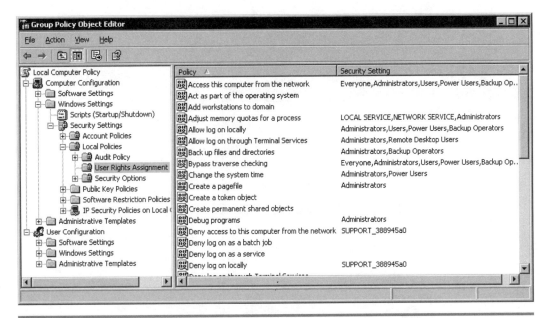

Figure 16-16 Editing the local computer group policies

Although group policies can be implemented at the local computer level and are by default for the computer, they are expected to be overridden at the site, domain, or OU levels.

Create and Change Group Policies at the Site, Domain, and OU Levels

Group policies above the local computer level are Active Directory objects and are therefore called *group policy objects (GPOs)*. They are created as one object, but they are stored in two pieces: a group policy container, and a group policy template. *Group policy containers (GPCs)* are stored in Active Directory and hold smaller pieces of information that change infrequently. *Group policy templates (GPTs)* are a set of folders stored by default at C:\Windows\Sysvol\ Sysvol*domainname*\Polices\ and have both machine and user components, as shown in Figure 16-17. GPTs store larger pieces of information that change frequently.

You can create and change a GPO linked to a site by opening Active Directory Sites And Services, and you can create and change a GPO linked to a domain or OU by opening Active Directory Users And Computers. See how to do both of these next:

1. Open the Start menu and choose Administrative Tools | Active Directory Users And Computers. The Active Directory window opens.

2. In the left pane, right-click the domain that the policy is or will be linked to, and choose Properties. The domain Properties dialog box opens.

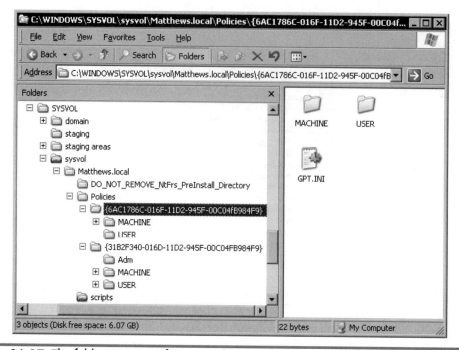

Figure 16-17 The folder structure of group policy templates

3. Click the Group Policy tab. You will see a default domain policy listed that you can look at and edit. In the Group Policy tab of a domain, you can create a new group policy linked to that domain; add a link from a group policy in another domain; edit an existing group policy; disable the policy or prevent it from being overwritten using Options; and delete the policy or change its properties.

4. Select Default Domain Policy and click Edit. The Group Policy window opens. Open several levels of the tree on the left so that you can get down to a level that shows policies and their settings on the right. Notice that there is a great deal of similarity with the group policies at the local computer level, as you saw in Figure 16-16. There are some significant differences, though, as you can see in Figure 16-18.

The icons below Computer Configuration | Windows Settings | Security Settings are different for similar sets of policies; there are some new sets of policies at the domain level; in the default policy at the domain level, all the policies are not defined, as it is originally installed by Setup; and there are some differences between the policies at the local and domain levels.

5. Double-click several of the policies, and you see that there are no detail policy settings, unlike the policies at the local computer level.

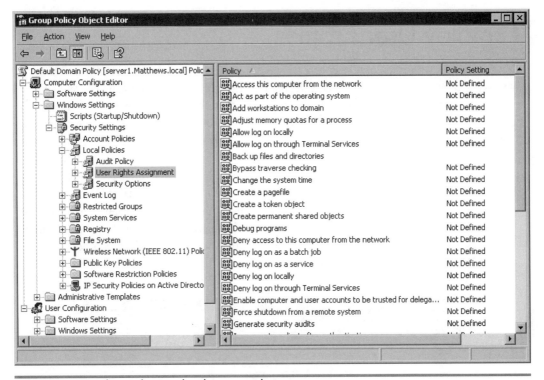

Figure 16-18 Editing domain level group policies

6. As an example of how a policy is set, expand Computer Configuration | Windows Settings | Security Settings | Local Policies | User Rights Assignment and then double-click Back Up Files And Directories. The policy's Properties dialog box will open, and if it is still in its default condition, the Security Policy Setting tab will be empty. (The default condition is assumed in the remaining steps.)

7. Click Define These Policy Settings and then click Add User Or Group. In the Add User Or Group dialog box that opens, click Browse. The Select Users, Computers, Or Groups dialog box will open.

8. Click Advanced and then Find Now. Double-click the users and/or groups that you want to add, and then click OK three times to return to the Group Policy window. You see that now there is a policy setting for Back Up Files And Directories.

9. When you are done making changes to the group policies at the domain level, you can use the same steps to add and change policies at the site and OU levels. Close the Group Policy Object Editor and Active Directory Users And Computers when you are ready.

Employ User Profiles

An individual who is the only user of a computer can tailor the desktop, Start menu, folders, network connections, Control Panel, and applications to his or her individual taste and needs. If several users are on the same computer, however, they could potentially upset each other by making those changes. The way around this is to create a *user profile* for each user that contains individual settings for that user and that loads when the particular user logs on to the computer.

When a new user logs on to a Windows Server 2003 computer, a user profile is created automatically, and when that user logs off the computer, his or her settings are saved under that profile. When the user logs back on, his or her settings are used to reset the system to the way it was when the user last logged off. When Windows Server 2003 is installed, it establishes the Default User profile that is then used as the default for all new users and saved with any changes under the user's name when the user logs off. A user's profile is a set of folders stored in the Documents And Settings folder on the hard disk. Figure 16-19 shows the folders within

Figure 16-19 Set of folders containing the user profile for Administrator

a user profile for a user named Administrator. In the same figure, you can see a folder for All Users, which contains files, folders, and settings applicable to all users, and a folder for Default User.

There are three types of user profiles: local user profiles, roaming user profiles, and mandatory user profiles.

Create Local User Profiles

Local user profiles are automatically created when a new user logs on to a computer, and they are changed by the user making changes to his environment, such as changing the desktop or the Start menu. When the user logs off, any changes that were made are saved in the user's profile. This is an automatic and standard process in Windows Server 2003. A local user account, though, is limited to the computer on which it was established. If the user logs on to a different computer, a new local user profile is created on that computer. A roaming user profile eliminates the need to have a separate profile on each computer.

Create Roaming User Profiles

A *roaming* user profile is set up on a server so that when a user logs on for the first time to a computer on the same network as the server, the user is authenticated by the server and his complete user profile is sent down to the computer, where it is saved as a local user profile. When the user logs off the computer, any changes that he made to the settings in the profile are saved both on the computer and on the server. The next time he logs on to the computer, his profile there is compared to his profile on the server, and only the changes on the server are downloaded to the computer, thereby reducing the time to log on.

The process of creating a roaming user profile has five steps:

1. Create a folder to hold profiles.

2. Create a user account.

3. Assign the profiles folder to the user's account.

4. Create a roaming user profile.

5. Copy a profile template to a user.

Create a Profiles Folder

Roaming user profiles can be stored on any server—they do not have to be on a domain controller. In fact, because of the size of the download the first time a user signs on to a new computer, it might make sense to not store the roaming user profiles on the domain controller. There is not a default folder to hold roaming profiles, so you must create one as follows:

1. Log on as Administrator to the server where you want the profiles folder to reside, and open Windows Explorer (Start | Windows Explorer).

2. Open My Computer and click Local Disk (C:) in the folder list. Right-click in a blank area of the right pane and choose New | Folder.

3. In the new folder's name box, type the name you want to give to the folder that will hold your profiles. This should be an easily recognized name, such as "Profiles."

4. Right-click the new folder and choose Sharing And Security. Click Share This Folder, accept the folder name as the share name, and click Permissions. The Everyone group should have Full Control, as well as Change and Read permissions.

5. Click OK twice to close the Permissions and Properties dialog boxes. Leave Windows Explorer open.

Create a User Account

Every user in a domain must have a user account in that domain. You have seen how to create a user account in earlier modules (Modules 4 and 9) and we talk about it again in Module 17, but as a refresher, here are the steps:

1. While still logged on as Administrator, open the Active Directory Users And Computers window (Start | Administrative Tools | Active Directory Users And Computers).

2. Open the domain within which you want to create the account, and then open Users. Scan the existing users to make sure the new user is not already a user.

3. Open the Action menu and choose New | User. The New Object – User dialog box will open. Enter the user's name and logon name, and click Next.

4. Enter the user's password, choose how soon the password must change, and click Next. Review the settings that you have made. If you want to change any of them, click Back and make the changes. When you are happy with the settings, click Finish.

For the purpose of these exercises, make several new accounts: at least one that will have a regular roaming profile, one that will be a template for a preconfigured profile, and two that will share a preconfigured roaming profile. Leave the Active Directory Users And Computers window open when you are done.

Assign the Profiles Folder to a User's Account

To utilize a roaming profile, the user's account must specify that their profile is stored in the profiles folder that you established earlier. Otherwise, Windows Server 2003 will look in the Documents And Settings folder of the computer the user is logging on to. The following steps show how to assign the profiles folder to a user's account:

1. In the Users folder in which you added the new users, right-click one of the new users that you added, and choose Properties. The user's Properties dialog box opens.

2. Click the Profile tab. In the Profile Path text box, type *servername**foldername**logonname*. For example, if the server name on which the profile is stored is Server1, the folder is Profiles, and the logon name is Mike, then you would type **Server1****Profiles****Mike**.

3. Close the Properties dialog box and repeat this process for the second user you created. Do not assign a folder for the third and fourth users you created.

Create a Roaming User Profile

Once you have set up a shared folder on a server and specified in a user's account that the user's profile is in the specified folder on the server, then the actual user profile will be created and stored on the server simply by having the user log on to any computer within the network. Try this with these steps:

1. Log on one of the new users with her own profile to a computer in the network. Make some changes to the desktop and the Start menu, and then log off that computer.

2. Look at the folder you created on the server to hold profiles. You will see a new profiles folder named after the logon name of the user in Step 1.

3. Log on this same user to another computer in the network. The changes to the desktop and Start menu will follow you to this computer.

While the preceding technique is fine for someone who you want to give free rein to the system and who is knowledgeable about how to tailor it to his or her needs and desires, if you want to put limits on a user, or on someone who does not have a lot of knowledge about how to change the system, you want to create a template profile and then assign it to one or more users.

To build a template, you simply log on the "template" user that you created to the computer you want to use for the profile, and then make the necessary changes that you want reflected in the profile. If the template will be assigned to several people, be sure that the hardware and applications are the same both among the group that will use the profile and on the computer you used to create the template.

Copy or Assign a Profile Template to a User

You can handle a template in one of two ways. You can "copy" it to create a new profile that you assign to a user, or you can assign the template as is to several users. See how both of these are done in the following steps:

NOTE

The "copying" in this case uses a special technique and cannot use the Windows Explorer or My Computer Copy command.

1. Open the Start menu, choose Control Panel | System. The System Properties dialog box opens.

2. Click the Advanced tab, in the User Profiles area click Settings, select the template profile, which I called "Roam," and click Copy To, like this:

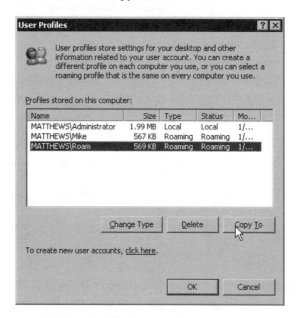

3. In the Copy To dialog box, browse to or enter the path to which you want the template profile copied (C:\Profiles*username* in this example; use one of your new user names), and click OK. Do this twice.

4. To assign a template to several users, open Active Directory Users And Computers, and open the domain and Users in the tree on the left.

5. Scroll the list of users until the first of the users who will share a profile is shown, and then double-click that user. Click OK twice to close User Profiles, and System Properties.

6. In the user's Properties dialog box, click Profile and enter the full path to the template profile that you created (*\\servername*\Profile*username*). Click OK to close the Properties dialog box, and close the Active Directory Users And Computers window.

7. Log on each of your new users to one or more computers and make sure they work. One possibility if the logon doesn't work is that there is a typing error in the path of the profile in the user's Properties dialog box.

Use Mandatory User Profiles

A *mandatory* user profile is a roaming user profile that cannot be changed; it is read-only. This is particularly valuable when several users are sharing the same profile. When a user logs off a computer where a mandatory profile has been used, the user's changes are not saved. The profile does not prevent the user from making changes while logged on, but the changes aren't saved. A mandatory user profile is created by taking a roaming user profile and, in the folder with the user's name (for example, C:\Documents and Settings\Administrator in Figure 16-19), renaming the system file Ntuser.dat to Ntuser.man.

CRITICAL SKILL
16.8 # Update Windows Server 2003

When you complete installing Windows Server 2003, and periodically thereafter, you are reminded to "Stay current with automatic updates" in a little balloon in the lower right of your screen. If you choose to turn on Automatic Updates, it will automatically determine if any updates are available for Windows Server 2003, either automatically or manually download the updates over the Internet, and either automatically or manually install updates on a periodic basis. This gives you the advantage of the latest fixes from Microsoft. If you choose not to install automatic updates, you can still download and install the updates manually.

Manual Updates

To manually get and install updates, you have to open the Windows Update web site and let it scan your system to determine if updates are needed, downloading and then installing the updates. Use the following steps to do that:

1. Open the Start menu and choose All Programs | Windows Update. You will be connected to the Internet and the Windows Update web page will be displayed, as shown in Figure 16-20.

2. Click Scan For Updates. The system software on your computer will be compared against known updates, and if there are any updates you don't have installed, you will be told.

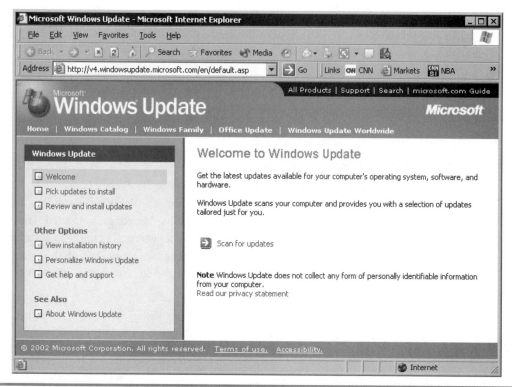

Figure 16-20 Microsoft web site for manually getting updates to download

3. If you have updates that need to be or can be installed, click the type of updates (Critical Updates, Windows Server 2003 Updates, or Driver Updates) to see the explanation of the specific updates and be given the option to download them. For those updates you want to download, click Add.

4. When you have selected all of the updates that you want to download, click Review And Install Updates. Your selections will be displayed, and if you want to go ahead, you can click Install Now.

5. Click Accept when the license agreement is displayed, and then downloading will commence. When downloading is complete, the updates will automatically be installed. When the installation is complete, depending on the update, you may be told that you need to restart your computer. If asked, click OK.

6. If you don't have to restart your computer, close the Internet Explorer window. The updates are in place and ready to use.

Automatic Updates

If Automatic Updates is turned on, Windows detects when you are online and not particularly busy. It then goes out to the Windows Update web site you saw in the preceding section and determines if there are updates you need to download. If so, Automatic Updates will, at your choice, either notify you of the update availability or just automatically download the updates. You can then choose to either automatically install the updates or just be told they have been downloaded and you can install them manually. If you choose to do all three steps (detect updates needed, download them, and install them) automatically, you can schedule a time to do it.

Turn On Automatic Updates

Automatic Updates can be turned on in two ways. Shortly after installing Windows Server 2003, the Stay Current With Automatic Updates balloon appears. This opens the Automatic Updates Setup Wizard. By following its instructions, you can turn on Automatic Updates. You can also access Automatic Updates at any time through the Control Panel. Here's how to turn on Automatic Updates in that way:

1. Open the Start menu and choose Control Panel | System. In the System Properties dialog box that opens, click the Automatic Updates tab, which is then displayed, as you can see in Figure 16-21.

2. Determine the amount of automation you want and click one of the three choices:

   a. The first choice automatically determines if there are updates that are needed and then asks you before downloading, and asks you again before installing them.

   b. The second choice automatically determines if there are updates and automatically downloads them; it then asks you before installing them. (This is the default.)

   c. The third choice does everything automatically on a schedule you determine.

3. Click OK when you are finished.

Use Automatic Updates

If you choose either the first or second choice, you will get a notice when updates are ready to download and/or install. When you click the icon pointed to by this balloon, the Automatic Updates dialog box opens. If you click Details, you will see the specific updates that are being proposed, along with a description of each. You can choose to download and/or install each update by clicking the check box. When you are ready, click either Download or Install or delay the download and/or installation by clicking Remind Me Later and specifying a time. If you click Download or Install, that process will be carried out.

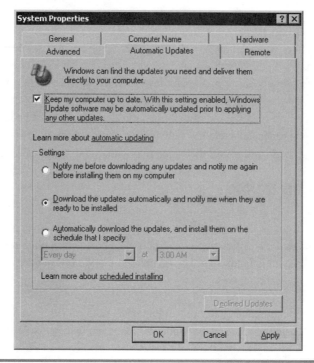

Figure 16-21 Choices for Automatic Updates

Maintain Automatic Updates

Once you have installed Automatic Updates, the Automatic Updates tab in the System Properties dialog box (Start | Control Panel | System |Automatic Updates) allows you to maintain Automatic Updates, including turning this feature off and changing your selection of how automatic to make the downloading and installation.

Ask the Expert

Q: Is it really necessary to fool with Automatic Updates?

A: In my mind it is very necessary, if for no other reason than to keep up with the fast pace at which security loopholes are found and then patched. Automatic Updates is probably the software delivery mode of the future, if Microsoft has anything to say about it. You'll pay an annual fee and get a constant stream of updates instead of one major revision every couple of years.

Progress Check

1. What are the major stages of the Windows startup or boot process?

2. What is the first step in the boot process, and what is it called?

3. What is a good fallback procedure to keep in mind when using Safe Mode, and what are a couple of examples?

4. What are the three types of user profiles, and how do they differ?

5. What are Automatic Updates, and how are they used?

Project 16 Plan the Management of Windows Server 2003

The management of all the complexities that make up Windows Server 2003 is a major undertaking. This project will help you plan how to best use the many tools that Windows Server 2003 has available for its management.

Step by Step

1. Determine if any of the accessibility options will assist in the use of the computer:

   a. StickyKeys to help pressing two keys at once

   b. FilterKeys to help prevent multiple keystrokes

   c. ToggleKeys to indicate when CAPS LOCK and other keys are pressed

   d. ShowSounds to display captions when sounds are used

(continued)

---

1. The boot process has five major stages: preboot, boot, load, initialization, and logon.

2. The first step in the boot process is to see what hardware is available and its condition by running the power-on self test (POST) routines.

3. In Safe Mode, you may not have the mouse available, so it is good to keep several shortcut keys in mind to get around the screen. Some examples are: to open the Start menu, use CTRL-ESC; to open a context menu, use SHIFT-F10; to open Help, press F1; and to turn on MouseKeys, press left-SHIFT-left-ALT-NUM LOCK.

4. The three types of user profiles are local user profiles, which are used on a single computer, roaming user profiles, which are set up on a domain controller for use throughout a network, and mandatory user profiles, which a user cannot change.

5. Automatic Updates automatically determine if any updates are available for Windows Server 2003, either automatically or manually download the updates over the Internet, and either automatically or manually install updates on a periodic basis.

    e. HighContrast to make the screen easier to read

    f. Cursor Options to make the cursor easier to see

    g. MouseKeys to move the mouse pointer with the numeric keypad

2. Determine the settings to use in the Folder Options that are correct for you:

    a. Replace the task pane with file folders.

    b. Use the same window when opening new folders.

    c. Use double-click to open a folder or start a program.

    d. Set how files and folders are displayed.

    e. Specify how applications are associated with file extensions.

    f. Use files offline.

3. Determine the other Control Panel settings in this module:

    a. Determine the settings for the keyboard.

    b. Determine the settings for the mouse.

    c. Determine what region you want to use for formatting numbers, etc.

    d. Set up the tasks, such as Backup, that you want run on a scheduled basis.

    e. Review the hardware status in the Device Manager.

    f. Determine how the taskbar and Start menu are displayed.

4. Determine how you will use the Task Manager:

    a. Review the status of loaded applications.

    b. Review the status of loaded processes.

    c. Review the CPU and memory performance.

    d. Review the network performance.

    e. Review the users currently connected to the computer.

5. Create the Microsoft Management Consoles you need to manage the system.

6. Become familiar with the Registry and how it is edited.

7. Become familiar with the boot process and the steps it goes through.

8. Determine when you would use each of the boot correction procedures:

    a. Return to the Last Known Registry files.

    b. Use Safe Mode and Advanced Options.

   c. Use the Recovery Console.

   d. Repair the boot sector.

   e. Run Automated System Recovery (ASR).

9. Determine how you want to use and possibly change Group Policies:

   a. Review, add, and change Group Policies at the local level.

   b. Review, add, and change Group Policies at the domain level.

   c. Review, add, and change Group Policies at the other levels.

10. Determine how you want to implement User Profiles:

   a. Create local user.

   b. Create roaming user profiles.

   c. Create mandatory user profiles.

11. Determine how you want to implement Automatic Updates:

   a. Do manual updates when I choose.

   b. Enable Automatic Updates:

   i. Notify both before downloading and before installing.

   ii. Download automatically and notify before installing.

   iii. Automatically download and install on a set schedule.

Project Summary

Having a good handle on the management tools that Windows Server 2003 has available and using those tools proactively will make the sizable task of managing a server more reasonable.

Module 16 Mastery Check

1. What are StickyKeys?

2. What are Folder Options, and how do you get to them?

3. What are Regional And Language Settings, and how are they set?

4. How can you look at the status of all the hardware components in a system in one place?

5. How can you see what software is running on a computer, and how can you open that component?

6. What is the Microsoft Management Console, or MMC, and how is it used?

7. What is the central repository of all configuration information in Windows Server 2003, and how is it used?

8. What are some of the ways to work around or fix a problem that causes a computer to not boot?

9. What is the most complete way to repair a problem with the operating system and the boot process?

10. What are group policies, and how are they used?

11. If there are multiple people using the same computer, what is the best way to keep them from interfering with each other?

Module 17

Controlling Windows Server 2003 Security

CRITICAL SKILLS

17.1   Authenticate the User

17.2   Control Access

17.3   Secure Stored Data

17.4   Understand Private/Public Key Encryption

17.5   Secure Data Transmission

Security is one of those topics that is so large that it is hard to get an overall picture of it. One way to try to achieve this overview is to look at the demands for security in a computer network. Once the demands are defined, you can look at how Windows Server 2003 handles the demands. Security demands include the following:

- **Authenticating the user**   Knowing who is trying to use a computer or network connection

- **Controlling access**   Placing and maintaining limits on what a user can do

- **Securing stored data**   Keeping stored data from being used even with access

- **Securing data transmission**   Keeping data in a network from being misused

- **Managing security**   Establishing security policies and auditing their compliance

Windows Server 2003 uses a multilayered approach to implementing security and provides a number of facilities that are used to handle security demands. Central to Windows Server 2003's security strategy is the use of Active Directory to store user accounts and provide authentication services, although security features are available without Active Directory. Active Directory, though, provides a centralization of security management that is very beneficial to strong security. In each of the following sections, a security demand is further explained and the Windows Server 2003 facilities that address that demand are discussed, as are the ways to implement those facilities.

 NOTE

Most sets of steps in this module require that you be logged on as Administrator.

 CRITICAL SKILL
17.1 Authenticate the User

Authentication is the process of verifying that users or objects are as they are represented to be. In its simplest form, computer user authentication entails validating a username and password against a stored entry, as is done in a stand-alone computer. In its fullest form, user authentication entails using the *Kerberos* authentication protocol to validate a potential user, possibly using a smart card or biometric device anywhere in a network against credentials in Active Directory. For objects, such as documents, programs, and messages, authentication requires using Kerberos certificate validation. In Windows Server 2003, all three forms of authentication are available, and both user forms employ a single sign-on concept that allows a user, once authenticated, to access other services within the local computer or the network, depending on their environment, without having to reenter their username and password.

In the normal default installation, when a Windows Server 2003 computer is started, there is a request to press CTRL-ALT-DEL. This stops all programs running on the computer except the request to enter your username and password. The purpose of stopping all programs is to prevent a Trojan horse program from capturing your username and password. If the username/password combination that is entered is not correct, you are given five opportunities to correct it, after which the computer is frozen for 30 seconds. You are then alternatively given one opportunity and then five opportunities, separated by 30 seconds of inactivity, and then the pattern is repeated to correctly enter a username and password. This pattern makes it more difficult to break a password because you can't just repeatedly try a new password.

Once a username and password are entered, they must be authenticated. This can be done at either the local computer, where the user will be limited to that computer, or at a server supporting a network, possibly with Active Directory, in which case the user will have access to the network.

Local Computer User Authentication

To have a username and password accepted on a local stand-alone computer, a *user account* with that username and password must have been previously entered into the Local Users and Groups database, which is in the Security Account Manager (SAM) file of HKEY_LOCAL _MACHINE in the Registry. Here are the steps to set up a user account:

1. While logged on as an Administrator, open the Start menu, choose Administrative Tools | Computer Management. The Computer Management window opens.

2. In the left pane, open System Tools | Local Users And Groups | Users, right-click in the right pane, and choose New User to open the New User dialog box.

3. Enter a username of up to 20 characters. It cannot contain just periods, spaces, or the @ symbol; it can't contain " / [ ] : ; | = , + * ? < >; and leading spaces or periods are dropped.

4. Enter a full name, a description (optional), and a password with its confirmation, and then select what the user must do with the password, as shown in Figure 17-1.

5. When you have successfully entered the information, click Create and then click Close. You will now be able to log off as Administrator and log on as your new user. Try that to make sure it works.

With the entry of this single username and password, the new user will be able to do anything that is within that user's level of permission on that single computer. If the computer subsequently is connected to a network, the account has to be reestablished there for the user to be able to use the network.

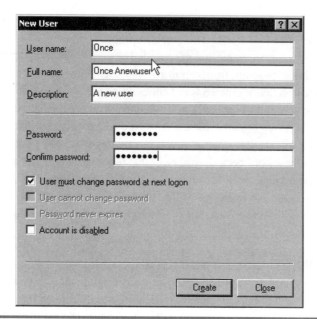

Figure 17-1 Entering a new user account on a local computer

Ask the Expert

Q: What is a "strong password," and how does it differ from any other passwords?

A: A strong password is simply one that is harder to break because it follows some rules that make it that way. People tend to pick passwords that are easy to remember, like their child's name, their pet's name, their birthday, or their anniversary. People trying to break in can easily guess these passwords and negate them. The rules for a strong password are:

- It is at least seven or more characters long
- It is a mixture of letters and numbers
- It includes both uppercase and lowercase letters
- It includes one or more special characters
- The letters should not make a word in the dictionary
- The letters and numbers should not be related

(continued)

Examples of strong passwords are: sd4Y92i#j, 63gT*7p, n7$w819E (unless W. 819 E. is an address somehow related to you). The longer a password is, the harder it is to break, but also the harder it is to remember. Therefore smart cards that store very large passwords are being used in place of passwords (see a discussion of smart cards later in this module under "Replacements for Passwords"). Other rules for strong passwords include:

- Passwords should be changed every 30 to 90 days

- Passwords should not be reused

- Passwords should not be shared

- If a password is written down, store it in a secure place

Network User Authentication

In a network environment, user authentication can be handled by one of several protocols. If Active Directory is not being used, then the authentication protocol on Windows NT 4 (Windows NT LAN Manager, or NTLM) is the default. If Active Directory is in use, then Kerberos Version 5 is the preferred protocol in Windows Server 2003. If users are coming in over the Internet, they can use either Kerberos, or certificates and the Secure Sockets Layer (SSL) or Transport Layer Security (TLS) protocols for authentication. In the case of certificates, Windows Server 2003 can take an authenticated certificate and map it to a user account for integration with the rest of the system (see "Certificate Authentication," later in this module).

In all the preceding cases, a user account must first be established on the server before authentication can be accomplished. With NTLM, the procedure for setting up a user account is exactly the same as with the local computer, discussed in the preceding section, except that it must be done on each server in the network. With Kerberos and the certificate protocols, all of which require Active Directory for full use, the procedure is a little different. Here are the steps:

1. Open the Start menu, choose Administrative Tools | Active Directory Users And Computers. The Active Directory Users And Computers dialog box opens.

2. In the left pane, open the applicable domain and then the user's folder. Open the Action menu and choose New | User.

3. In the New Object – User dialog box, enter the user's name and username, as you can see in Figure 17-2, and then click Next.

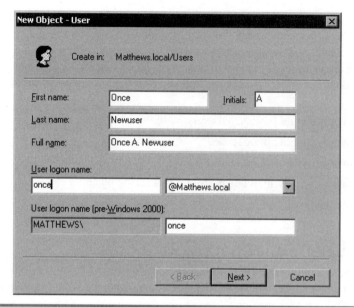

Figure 17-2 Establishing a user account with Active Directory

4. Enter and confirm the password, choose how you want the user to change the password, and then click Next.

5. Review your choices, use Back if you need to make any changes, and click Finish when the account is the way you want it.

By establishing this one user account in Active Directory, with the appropriate policies, the user can sign on anywhere on the network, which may extend over the Internet, and be authenticated.

Kerberos Authentication

Kerberos Version 5 is the default authentication protocol in Windows Server 2003, and Kerberos, in several versions, is the default authentication protocol over much of the Internet. This means that the same authentication routines in Windows Server 2003 can validate both a local Windows Server 2003 client and an Internet-connected UNIX client. Kerberos was originally developed by MIT for Internet authentication, and an implementation is available for free from MIT (http://web.mit.edu/kerberos/www/). The specification for Kerberos Version 5 is maintained by the Internet Engineering Task Force (IETF) and, along with an overview, is contained in Request for Comment 1510 (see Module 7 for a discussion of RFCs), which is available online at http://www.ietf.org/rfc/rfc1510.txt.

In addition to commonality with the Internet and numerous systems, Kerberos provides another major benefit to Windows Server 2003 users. In other authentication schemes, such as NTLM, each time a user attempts to access a different network service, that service has to go to the authentication server to confirm the authenticity of the user. This doesn't mean the user has to log on again, but each service has to get its own confirmation, creating a fair amount of network traffic. That is not the case with Kerberos, which provides each user with an encrypted *ticket* with the user ID and password that network devices can use both for identity and for validity. The Kerberos ticket system also validates the network service to the user, providing mutual authentication between user and service.

NOTE

The Kerberos ticket is also referred to as a service ticket and as a user ticket. They are all the same object.

Kerberos uses a Key Distribution Center (KDC) on each domain controller that stores the user accounts that have been entered into the network's Active Directory. When a user attempts to log on and use any part of the network, the following process takes place:

1. The username and password are encrypted and sent to the KDC.

2. The KDC validates the username/password combination.

3. A ticket is constructed containing the encrypted username and password plus an encryption key that can be used to transfer information between the user and any network service.

4. The ticket is returned to the user's point of logging on, where it is presented to the network service, thereby proving the authenticity of the user.

5. The ability of the service to accept and utilize the ticket proves the authenticity of the service to the user.

6. Any information transferred between the user and the service is done using the encryption key in the ticket.

7. If, while still logged on to the first network service, the user reaches out to another network service, the ticket is automatically presented to the second service, providing immediate mutual authentication and the ability to securely transfer information.

You can see in the preceding steps another major benefit to Kerberos: the inclusion of an encryption key in the ticket that allows the user and a network service to securely transfer information. This automatically solves another of the security demands, securing data transmission.

Kerberos is a very powerful means for authentication and a major asset to Windows Server 2003.

Replacements for Passwords

The weakest link in the Windows Server 2003 security scheme is probably the use of passwords. Users give their passwords to others or forget them, and passwords are stolen or just "found" in many different ways. There is nothing to tie a password to an individual. With someone's password in hand, nothing can stop you from impersonating that person on a password-protected system. Two potential means of replacing passwords are smart cards and biometric devices.

Smart Cards   Smart cards are credit card–sized pieces of plastic that have a tamper-resistant electronic circuit embedded in them that permanently stores an ID, a password, a digital signature, an encryption key, or any combination of those. Smart cards require a personal identification number (PIN), so they add a second layer (smart card plus PIN in place of a password) that an impersonator would have to obtain to log on to a system. Also, smart cards can be configured to lock up after a few unsuccessful attempts to enter a PIN.

Windows Server 2003 fully supports smart cards and lets them be used to log on to a computer or network or to enable certificate-based authentication for opening documents or performing other tasks. Smart cards require a reader attached to the computer through either a serial port or a PCMCIA slot. With a smart card reader, users do not have to press CTRL-ALT-DEL. They only need to insert their card, at which point they are prompted for their PIN. With a valid card and PIN, users are authenticated and allowed on the system in the same way as they would be by entering a valid username and password.

Currently, Windows Server 2003 lists 19 smart card readers that are Plug and Play–compliant and that Microsoft has tested with Windows Server 2003. The drivers for these devices are included with Windows Server 2003, and installing them requires little more than plugging them in.

With a smart card reader installed, set up new accounts (as previously described) and then, for both new and old accounts, open the user's Properties dialog box by double-clicking a user in the Active Directory Users And Computers window (see "Network User Authentication" earlier in this module for directions on opening this window). In the user's Properties dialog box, click the Account tab and scroll the Account Options list and check Smart Card Is Required For Interactive Logon.

NOTE

In case you wondered, the PIN is encrypted and placed on the smart card when it is made. The PIN is not stored on the computer or in Active Directory.

Smart cards are particularly valuable for remote entry to a network, and they can be used by a traveling staff member with a laptop, probably using virtual private networking (VPN) over the Internet. Smart cards are also frequently used in the issuance of certificates of authenticity for documents and other objects (see the discussion of certificates later in the module under "Secure Data Transmission").

Biometric Devices   Smart cards do provide an added degree of security over passwords, but if someone obtains both the card and the PIN, that person is home free. The only way to be totally sure that the computer is talking to the real person is to require some physical identification of the person. This is the purpose of *biometric devices,* which identify people by physical traits, such as their voice, handprint, fingerprint, face, or eyes. Often, these devices are used with a smart card to replace the PIN. Biometric devices are only slowly moving from the experimental to the production stage, and nothing is built into Windows Server 2003 specifically to handle them. Devices and custom installations are available from under $100 for a fingerprint scanner to several thousand dollars for a face scanner. In the next few years, these devices will be everywhere, so, depending on your needs, you may want to keep them in mind.

Certificate Authentication

If you want to bring users into a network over the Internet, but you are concerned that sending usernames and passwords in that public way might compromise them, then you can replace them with a digital certificate. A *digital certificate* (or just "certificate") is issued by a certification authority (CA), who digitally signs it and says that the bearer is who he or she claims to be, or that an object and sender are as represented. There are both private and public CAs. An organization can be its own private CA and issue certificates to its employees, vendors, and/or customers, so that those people can be authenticated when they try to enter the organization's network. Also, a well-trusted public CA, such as VeriSign (http://www.verisign.com/), can issue a certificate to a person, object, organization, or web site. A person or organization receiving the certificate, if they trust the CA, can be reasonably certain that the presenter is as represented. Besides a certificate, most CAs provide the bearer with an encryption key in the certificate, so that secure data transmissions can occur.

To set up certificate authentication, these steps must take place:

1. The user must obtain a certificate.

2. A user account must be established for the user.

3. The certification authority must be listed in the Certificate Trust List.

4. The certificate must be mapped to the user account.

Set Up Certificate Services   The user can obtain a certificate in several ways, one of which is through a Windows Server 2003 domain controller with Certificate Services installed. Certificate Services is not part of the default server installation and must be specifically set up. Here are the steps to do that:

1. Open Start, choose Control Panel and click Add Or Remove Programs. The Add Or Remove Programs dialog box opens. Click Add/Remove Windows Components to open the Windows Components Wizard dialog box.

2. Select Certificate Services if it isn't already checked (if it is, Certificate Services is already installed on this computer and you can jump to the next section). Click Yes when you are told that if you install Certificate Services, you will not be able to rename the computer, and then click Next.

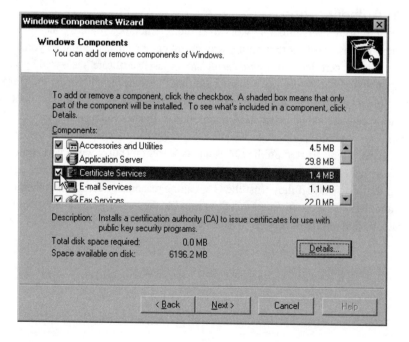

3. Select the type of certificate authority (CA) to be installed from the following choices:

- **Enterprise Root CA** if you are using Active Directory (AD) and this is the first CA in the network

- **Stand-alone Root CA** if you are not using AD and it is the first CA in the network

- **Enterprise Subordinate CA** if you are using Active Directory (AD) and this is not the first CA in the network

- **Stand-alone Subordinate CA** if you are not using AD and it is not the first CA in the network

4. Select Use Custom Settings to consider changing the settings for the generation of key pairs and CA certificates and click Next. The custom settings allow you to select the cryptographic service provider (CSP) that you want to use, the hash algorithm (explained under "Challenge Handshake Authentication Protocol" in Module 12), the key length, and whether you want to use an existing key. Under most circumstances, except if you are using smart cards, you want to leave the defaults. If you are using smart cards, you may need to select a CSP that is used by the smart card.

5. Click Next, enter the name for the CA, and click Next again. You are shown where the certificate database and log will be stored. Once more click Next, and click Yes to temporarily stop Internet Information Services (IIS). (You may need to insert your Windows Server 2003 CD and click Exit to close the automatic Welcome message.)

6. Click Finish when you are told that you have successfully completed installation. Close Add Or Remove Programs. Restart the computer.

Once you have installed the certification authority, you can review it with these steps:

1. Open the Start menu and choose Administrative Tools | Certification Authority. In the left pane, open the new CA you just created and click Issued Certificates. You should see one or more certificates, like this (if you don't see any certificates and you restarted the computer, click Refresh in the Action menu):

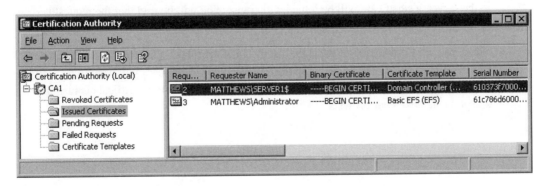

2. Double-click one of the certificates to open it, click the Details tab, and click the various fields to see the details within the open certificate. Click OK when you are done looking at the certificate.

3. Back in the Certification Authority window, click Certificate Templates in the left pane. On the right, you can see the types of certificates that are available and their intended purpose.

4. Double-click one of the templates to open its Properties dialog box. When you are finished looking at the properties, close the dialog box and the Certification Authority window.

Request a Certificate   With Certificate Services installed, users, computers, and other services can request certificates to identify themselves. Normally, certificates are automatically given to computers and users who are known and trusted entities on the network. The two certificates that were automatically created when Certificate Services was installed were issued to the server on which Certificate Services resides and to the Administrator who was currently logged on. (If you didn't get a user certificate, you'll create one here.) It is also possible to explicitly request a certificate over either an intranet or the Internet, or on the server with Certificate Services.

Over the Internet or an intranet is the most common way that a user requests a certificate for their use. In doing this, the user accesses a web page that is created and maintained by Certificate Services. Use these steps to request a certificate over an intranet or the Internet:

1. Open your browser and enter the URL or address of the server with Certificate Services. The address should look something like http://*servername*/certsrv/. The page should appear as shown in Figure 17-3.

2. Select Request A Certificate and click User Certificate. If you want the user to have a smart card, click More Options, where you can select a Cryptographic Service Provider (CSP) and the request format.

3. Click Submit. You are told that the web site is requesting a new certificate for you and asking if you want to go ahead. Click Yes. If the user and/or computer are already known to the server, a certificate will be issued. Otherwise, you will be told that the request is pending.

4. When you see Certificate Issued, click Install This Certificate. You are told that the web site is adding a certificate to the computer and asked if you are sure you want to do that. Click Yes, given that is what you want to do. You are told that the certificate is installed and you can close your browser.

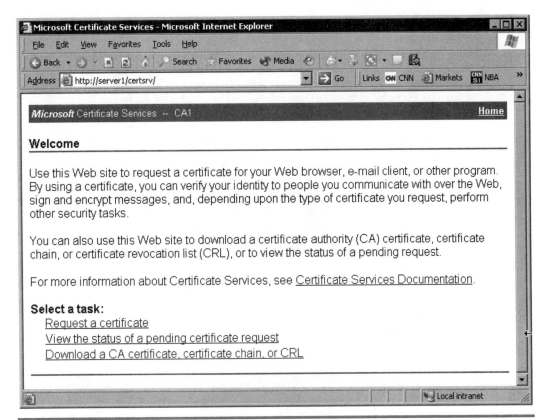

Figure 17-3 Requesting a certificate over the Internet or an intranet

Directly requesting a certificate from Certificate Services is most commonly done for documents or other objects, or for services. It requires the Certificate console in the Microsoft Management Console (MMC). Here is how to set up the Certificate console (assuming that it hasn't been done before) and request a certificate from it:

1. Open the Start menu, choose Run, type **mmc**, and click OK. The MMC shell opens.

2. Open the File menu and choose Add/Remove Snap-In. In the Add/Remove Snap-In dialog box, click Add, click Certificates, and click Add again. Select My User Account for where you want to manage certificates, and click Finish.

NOTE

If you choose to manage certificates for My User Account, the snap-in you create will create certificates only for you. If you choose to manage certificates for Service Account or Computer Account, you must pick a service or computer to manage, such as the web server or the local computer, and you will be able to issue certificates for the service or computer.

3. Click Close and then click OK to complete the Add/Remove Snap-In process. In the console on the left, open Certificates – Current User | Personal | Certificates, as shown here:

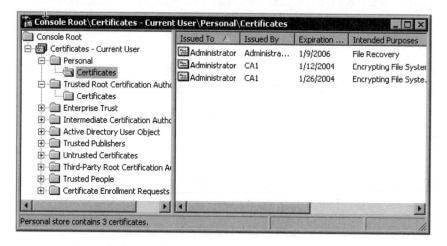

4. Open the Action menu and choose All Tasks | Request New Certificate. The Certificate Request Wizard opens.

5. Click Next, choose a certificate type to support the purpose of the certificate you want to issue (select Administrator for at least one certificate), and click Next again. Enter a friendly name (call the Administrator certificate **Signature**) and a description and click Next.

6. Review the settings you have selected. If you want to make changes, click Back and make the necessary corrections. When you are ready, click Finish. A new certificate will be issued and you will be told that the certificate request was successful. Click OK.

7. Close the Certificates console, click Yes to save the settings for this new console in a file named Certificates.msc, click Save, and finally close the MMC.

List Certificate Authorities   To accept certificates that are presented to the network, the CA must be known to the network. This is accomplished by being listed as a trusted CA in the Certificate Trust List (CTL), which is maintained as part of the group policy. The following steps show you how to open the group policy, which you worked with in Module 16 (see "Use Group Policies"), create a CTL, and make an entry into it (these steps assume that you want to work with the CTL at the domain level, but you could also do it at the local computer level and at the OU level):

1. Open the Start menu and choose Administrative Tools | Active Directory Users And Computers. The Active Directory Users And Computers window opens.

2. Right-click the domain where the policy will reside, choose Properties, click the Group Policy tab, select the policy you want to use, and click Edit. The Group Policy Object Editor window opens.

3. In the left pane, open Computer Configuration | Windows Settings | Security Settings | Public Key Policies | Enterprise Trust. Open the Action menu and choose New | Certificate Trust List. The Certificate Trust List Wizard opens.

4. Click Next. If you so choose, enter an identifying prefix for the CTL, enter the months and/or days that it is valid, select the purposes of the CTL, and click Next.

5. In the Certificates In The CTL dialog box, click Add From Store. The Select Certificate dialog box opens, in which you can select those certificates whose issuers you want to include in the CTL. Early in the list, you will find the certificates that your new CA issued as you followed the steps earlier in this module.

6. Double-click one of the certificates you created. When it opens, you may find that it is not trusted, even though it was created on the same computer. You are told that it must be added to the CTL to be trusted.

7. Select the certificates whose issuers you want on the CTL, holding down CTRL while selecting more than one certificate. Click OK. The new list of certificates will appear in the Certificate Trust List Wizard.

8. Click Next. You must attach a certificate, probably your own, for the purpose of a digital signature for the CTL, and the encryption key used with the signature certificate will be used with the file that contains the CTL.

NOTE

The certificate that you select for the purpose of adding the digital signature to the CTL must be created for the current user with the Administrator template, similar to the Signature certificate you created previously in "Request a Certificate."

9. Click Select from Store, select the certificate you want to use, click OK, and then click Next. If you wish, you can add a timestamp; then, click Next again.

10. Enter a friendly name and description for this CTL and click Next. Review the settings you have chosen, click Back if you need to correct something, and then, when ready, click Finish. You will be told whether the CTL was successfully created.

11. Click OK. The new CTL appears on the right of the Group Policy Object Editor window. Double-click it. The CTL opens, and in the Trust List tab, you see a list of the certificate authorities that you have added to your CTL.

12. Click a CA. You can see some of the details behind a certificate, as shown in Figure 17-4, and if you click View Certificate, you can see the entire certificate. Close the CTL, the Group Policy Object Editor, and the domain's Properties dialog box. Leave Active Directory Users And Computers open for use in the next section.

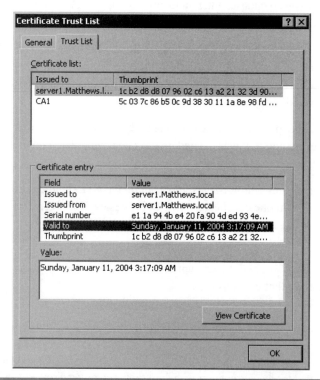

Figure 17-4 A Certificate Trust List

Map Certificates to User Accounts   The core of Windows Server 2003's user-oriented security are user accounts, which require a username and password to log on and are the basis for the permission system that controls access to computer and network resources. Someone who comes into Windows Server 2003 with a certificate doesn't have a username and password to be attached to a user account and the permissions that go with it. The solution is to map or relate a certificate to a user account, so that someone who presents an acceptable certificate will be attached to a user account and given the permissions he or she would acquire by logging on with a username and password. Windows Server 2003 does certificate mapping in two ways: through Active Directory services, and through Internet Information Services (IIS). Also, mapping can be done from one certificate to one user account (one-to-one mapping) or from several certificates to one account (many-to-one mapping). Mapping through IIS was discussed in Module 11.

Certificate mapping through Active Directory services can be done with the following steps (Active Directory Users And Computers should be open from the preceding steps; if it is, skip Step 1):

1. Open the Start menu and choose Administrative Tools | Active Directory Users And Computers.

2. Open the View menu and click Advanced Features (if it is not already checked).

3. In the console on the left, open the domain with the user account to which you want to map, and then open Users.

4. In the list of users on the right, select the user account to which a certificate will be mapped.

5. Open the Action menu, choose Name Mappings (if you don't see it, redo Step 2) to open the Security Identity Mapping dialog box, click the X.509 Certificates tab, and click Add to open the Add Certificate dialog box.

6. Search for and identify, or type, the path and name of the certificate that you want to use, and then click Open. Often the certificates, which have the extension .cer, are in the C:\Windows\System32\Certsrv folder.

   If you don't find a CER file, you may need to export one from the MMC Certificates console. To do so, select Start | Run, type **mmc**, press ENTER. Then open the File menu, choose Open, select the Certificates.msc file, click Open, open Console Root | Certificates – Current User | Personal | Certificates, and select the certificate to use. Next, open the Action menu, choose All Tasks | Export, click Next, choose No, Do Not Export The Private Key, click Next, accept the default DER Encoded Binary format, click Next, enter a useful filename, browse to where you want it stored, click Next, click Finish, and click OK when told that the export was successful. Close the Certificates console.

7. Double-click the certificate you will use and it is displayed in a second Add Certificate dialog box.

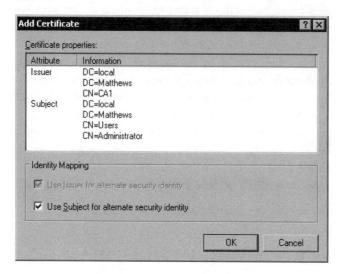

8. If you want one-to-one mapping, both Use Issuer For Alternate Security Identity and Use Subject For Alternate Security Identity should be checked (Use Issuer For Alternate Security Identity is always checked by default and is grayed in most instances, so you can't change it). If you want many-to-one mapping, only Use Issuer For Alternate Security Identity should be checked.

9. Click OK. The certificate is displayed again in the Security Identity Mapping dialog box; click OK again. Close the Active Directory Users And Computers window.

Now, when a user presents this certificate, she or he will be mapped to the related user account and given the permissions that are associated with it.

CRITICAL SKILL
17.2 Control Access

User accounts identify people and allow them to log on to a computer and possibly to a network. What they can then do depends both on the permissions given to them or given to groups to which they belong, and on the ownership of the object they want to use. Windows Server 2003, when using the NT File System (NTFS), allows an administrator to assign various levels of permission to use an object (a file, a folder, a disk drive, a printer), as well as assign ownership and the rights of ownership. (You cannot do this with the FAT or FAT32 file system.)

When you initially install Windows Server 2003, most files, folders, disk drives, and printers withhold permission from most users except for administrators to do most tasks with these objects. You can change the default permission rather quickly by using a property called *inheritance* that says all files, subfolders, and files in subfolders automatically inherit (take on) the permissions of their parent folder. Every file, folder, and other object in Windows Server 2003 NTFS, though, has its own set of *security descriptors* that are attached to it when it is created, and with the proper permission, these security descriptors can be individually changed.

Ownership

Initially, all permissions are granted by the creator of an object or by an administrator. The creator of an object is called its *owner*. The owner of an object has the right to grant and deny permission, as well as the right to grant the Take Ownership permission to others, allowing them to take ownership. An administrator can take over ownership from someone else, but an administrator cannot grant others ownership to objects the administrator did not create.

You can check the ownership and change it through the object's Properties dialog box. For a file or folder, open the Properties dialog box through Windows Explorer and see how you would change the ownership with these steps:

1. Open the Start menu and choose Windows Explorer.

2. In the left pane, open the disk and folders necessary to see in the right pane the folder or file that you want to look at or change the ownership for.

3. In the right pane, right-click the subject folder or file and choose Properties.

4. In the Properties dialog box, click the Security tab and then click Advanced. The Advanced Security Settings dialog box opens.

5. Click the Owner tab, in which you can see who the current owner is and the people to whom the ownership can be transferred. When you are finished, click OK twice to close the two dialog boxes still open. Also close the Windows Explorer.

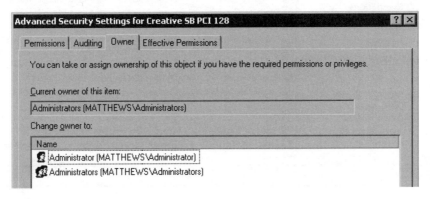

Giving permission to take ownership is described in "Permissions" later in this module.

Groups

Groups, or *group accounts,* are collections of user accounts and can have permissions assigned to them just like user accounts. Most permissions are granted to groups, not individuals, and then individuals are made members of the groups. It is therefore important that you have a set of groups that handles both the mix of people in your organization and the mix of permissions that you want to establish. A number of standard groups with preassigned permissions are built into Windows Server 2003, but you can create your own groups, and you can assign users to any of these.

Look at the groups that are a standard part of Windows Server 2003 and see what permissions they contain, and then create your own if you need to. Like user accounts, you look at groups differently depending on whether you are on a stand-alone server or on an Active Directory domain controller.

Groups in Stand-Alone Servers and Workstations

To view and add groups in stand-alone servers or workstations, you need to use the Computer Management window, as follows:

1. Open the Start menu and choose Administrative Tools | Computer Management.

2. In the left pane, open System Tools | Local Users And Groups | Groups. The list of built-in groups will be displayed, like this:

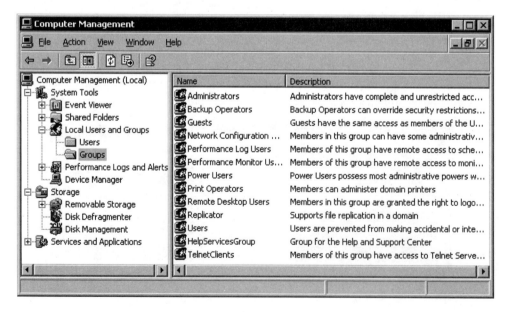

3. Double-click a few groups to open their respective Properties dialog boxes, in which you can see the members of each group.

4. Open the Action menu and choose New Group. The New Group dialog box opens.

5. Enter a group name of up to 63 characters. It cannot contain just numbers, periods, or spaces; it can't contain " / [ ] : ; | = , + * ? < >; and leading spaces or periods are dropped. Enter the description of what the group can uniquely do, and click Add. The Select Users, Computers, Or Groups dialog box opens.

6. Click Advanced, enter a username and password if asked, click Find Now, hold down CTRL, and select the users that you want to include in the group. Click OK. When you have selected all you want to include, click OK. Your new group should look similar to this:

7. When your group is the way you want it, click Create and then click Close. The new group will appear in the list on the right of the Computer Management window. Close that window when you are ready.

Groups in Active Directory Domain Controllers

To view and add groups in an Active Directory domain controller, you need to use the Active Directory Users And Computers window. Within that window, you will find two sets of groups: those in the Builtin folder, which are similar to what you saw in the stand-alone server, and those in the Users folders, which are created by Active Directory. The Builtin groups are limited to the local domain (called a *domain local scope*), while the Users groups can be either domain-limited or not limited (called a *global scope*). Look at both sets of groups and add a new group to Users with the following steps:

1. Open the Start menu and choose Administrative Tools | Active Directory Users And Computers. The Active Directory Users And Computers window opens.

2. In the left pane, open the domain in which you want to work, and then open the Builtin folder. You will see a list of groups that has many of the same groups that you saw on the stand-alone server.

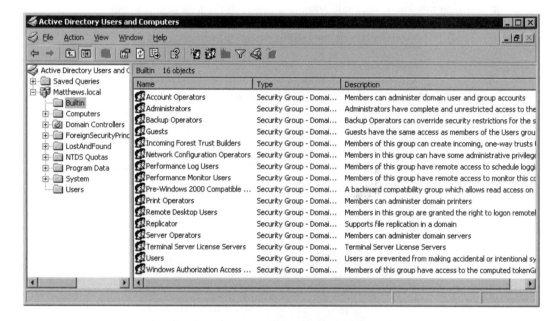

3. Click Users in the left pane. You will see a mixture of users and groups, but a different set of groups that are supporting Active Directory and network operations.

4. Open the View menu and choose Filter Options. Click Show Only The Following Types Of Objects, click Groups, as shown next, and click OK. Once again, open the Users folder, and your Active Directory Users And Computers window should look similar to Figure 17-5.

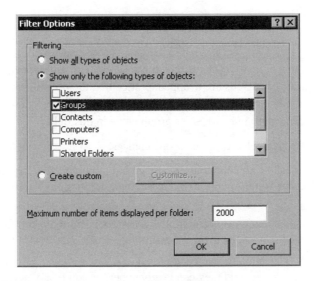

5. Double-click several of the groups to open them. They contain substantially more information than the groups on the stand-alone servers and workstations.

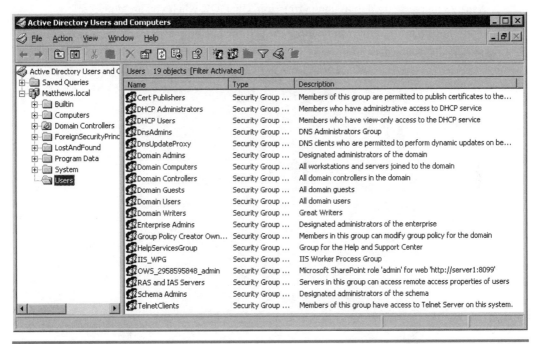

Figure 17-5 Standard Users groups in an Active Directory domain controller

6. While Users is still selected in the left pane, open the Action menu and choose New | Group. The New Object – Group dialog box opens.

7. Enter a Group name of up to 63 characters. It cannot contain just numbers, periods, or spaces, and leading spaces or periods are dropped. Notice that the pre–Windows 2000 name is automatically filled in for you. Only the first 20 characters of this name will be used, so if you want, you can enter your own short group name in this field.

8. Choose the group scope. Here are the scope choices:

   - **Domain Local** Can contain users and global or universal groups from any Windows Server 2003 or Windows NT domain, but their permissions are limited to the current domain.

   - **Global** Can contain users and global groups only from the current domain, but they can be given permissions in any domain.

   - **Universal** Can contain users and global or universal groups from any Windows Server 2003 domain, and they can be given permission in any domain, but they are limited to distribution groups.

9. Choose a group type. Distribution groups are used for e-mail and fax distribution, whereas security groups are used to assign permission. Click OK when you are done.

10. Right-click your new group and choose Properties. The Properties dialog box opens. Enter a description and e-mail address, as shown here:

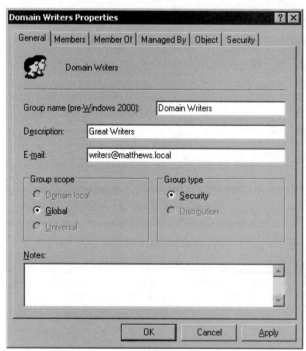

11. Click Members, click Add, click Advanced, click Find Now, and then hold CTRL and select the user accounts that you want included in the group. When you are done, click OK twice. Look at the other tabs and make any necessary changes. The Security tab is discussed in the next section.

12. When you have completed the group the way you want it, click OK, and close Active Directory Users And Computers.

Permissions

Permissions authorize a user or a group to perform some function on an object. Objects, such as files, folders, disks, and printers, have a set of permissions associated with them that can be assigned to users and groups. The specific permissions depend on the object, but all objects have at least two permissions: Read, and either Modify or Change. Permissions are initially set in one of three ways:

● The application or process that creates an object can set its permissions upon creation.

● If the object allows the inheritance of permissions and they were not set upon creation, a parent object can propagate permissions to the object. For example, a parent folder can propagate its permissions to a subfolder it contains.

● If neither the creator nor the parent sets the permissions for an object, then the Windows Server 2003 system defaults will do it.

Once an object is created, its permissions can be changed by its owner, by an administrator, and by anybody else who has been given the permission to change permissions. The following sections look at the default permissions for three commonly used objects—folders, shares, and files—and at how those defaults are changed.

Folder Permissions

Folder permissions are set in the Security tab of the folder's Properties dialog box, shown in Figure 17-6. You can open this tab and change the permissions with these steps:

1. Open the Start menu and choose Windows Explorer. Windows Explorer opens.

2. In the Folders pane on the left, open the boot drive, right-click in a blank area of the right pane, and choose New | Folder. Type a name for the new folder and press ENTER.

3. Right-click the new folder and choose Properties. In the Properties dialog box, click the Security tab. You should see a dialog box similar to Figure 17-6.

Figure 17-6 Default folder permissions

You can see that with a default installation of Windows Server 2003, four groups are available to be given permissions. Two of these groups are domain groups (Administrators and Users), and two are system groups, one for internal operating system (OS) functions (System) and one representing the owner or creator of the object. If you click each of the groups and look at its permissions, you can see that Administrators and System have permission for everything, Users have limited permissions, and the Creator Owner has no permissions (although in my case an administrator is the creator/owner, so it doesn't matter). All of the permissions that are shown here are grayed, meaning that they are inherited from a parent object (the root folder in this case) and have not been set specifically for this object.

NOTE

The default permissions in Windows Server 2003 are substantially different than those in Windows 2000 and earlier versions of Windows NT, where the Everyone group had full permission to do everything in all but a few of the OS folders. Windows Server 2003 starts out with the opposite philosophy, where only Administrators have permission to do everything, and Users (everyone else) have limited permission. This is an intentional tightening of security on the part of Microsoft.

To add new permissions:

1. Click Add in the middle of the Security tab. In the Select Users, Computers, Or Groups dialog box, click Advanced, click Find Now, double-click a single user, group, and/or computer to whom you want to grant permission, or hold CTRL while clicking several objects and then click OK. Click OK once more. If you selected the new group that you created earlier in the Groups section to be added here, as I did, you will see that group automatically picked up the same permissions as those for the Users group because the new group you created is automatically a member of that group.

2. Select one of the new users, groups, or computers that will be given permission, and then click Allow for the permissions that you want that entity to have, or click Deny to specifically exclude a permission. The tasks that can be performed with each permission are as follows:

   - **Full Control**   The sum of all other permissions, plus delete subfolders, change permissions, and take ownership

   - **Modify**   The sum of the Read & Execute and the Write permissions, plus the delete the folder permission

   - **Read & Execute**   The same as List Folder Contents, but inherited by both folders and files

   - **List Folder Contents**   Read permission, plus view the list of subfolders and files in a folder, as well as execute files, and move through folders to reach other files and folders, where the user may not have permission to access the intervening folders (inherited only by folders)

   - **Read**   View the contents of subfolders and files in the folder, as well as view the folder's attributes (Archive, Hidden, Read-only), ownership, and permissions

   - **Write**   Make subfolders and files inside the folder, plus view the ownership and permissions for the folder and change its attributes

   - **Special Permissions**   Detail permissions that are contained in the other six permissions

3. After selecting the permissions that you want to use, click Advanced. The Advanced Security Settings dialog box opens, as shown in Figure 17-7. Notice that the majority of the permissions are inherited and that the Creator Owner here is shown as having Full Control permission. This seeming inconsistency is due to the original parent permission being applied to subfolders and files only.

4. Select a user or group and click Edit. The Permission Entry dialog box appears, as shown next. This contains a more detailed level of permissions, called Special Permissions, which are contained within the primary permissions described in Step 2. The Special Permissions that are granted by each primary permission are shown in Table 17-1.

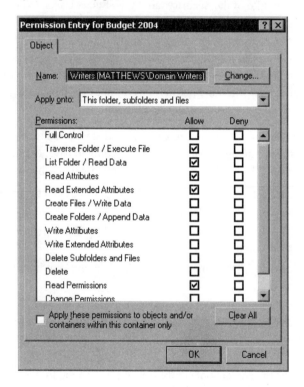

NOTE

Synchronize isn't a default permission unless the folder is set up for it.

5. Make any changes that you want to the detail permissions, check the check box at the bottom if you want the permission to be propagated to the subfolders and files of this folder, and click OK three times to close all dialog boxes.

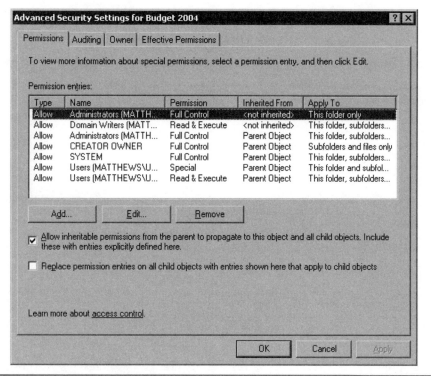

Figure 17-7 Reviewing the detail behind folder permissions

	Primary Permission					
Special Permission	**Read**	**Write**	**List Folder Contents**	**Read and Execute**	**Modify**	**Full Control**
Transverse Folder/ Execute File			Yes	Yes	Yes	Yes
List Folder/ Read Data	Yes		Yes	Yes	Yes	Yes
Read Attributes	Yes		Yes	Yes	Yes	Yes
Read Extended Attributes	Yes		Yes	Yes	Yes	Yes

Table 17-1 Special Permissions Granted by Primary Permissions for Folders

Special Permission	Primary Permission					
	Read	Write	List Folder Contents	Read and Execute	Modify	Full Control
Create Files/ Write Data		Yes			Yes	Yes
Create Folders/ Append Data		Yes			Yes	Yes
Write Attributes		Yes			Yes	Yes
Write Extended Attributes		Yes			Yes	Yes
Delete Subfolders and Files						Yes
Delete					Yes	Yes
Read Permissions	Yes	Yes	Yes	Yes	Yes	Yes
Change Permissions						Yes
Take Ownership						Yes
Synchronize	Yes	Yes	Yes	Yes	Yes	Yes

Table 17-1 Special Permissions Granted by Primary Permissions for Folders *(continued)*

TIP

Denying Everyone the Full Control permission prevents anybody from doing anything with the folder, including administrators. The folder looks like it is permanently locked from everybody, and if you try to delete it, for example, you will be denied access. An administrator, though, can still go in and change the permissions to something more reasonable and then the folder can be deleted.

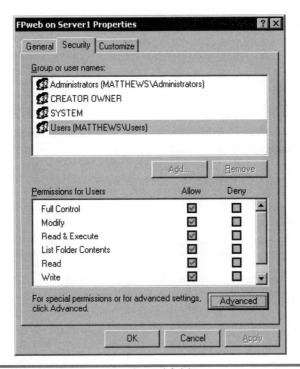

Figure 17-8 Default user permissions on a shared folder

Share Permission

Shares are shared folders, and for those who do not own or administer the folders, a slightly different set of permissions exists. As with regular folders, shared folder permissions are set in the Security tab of the folder's Properties dialog box. The first three of the standard groups look the same, but Users now have full control, although they cannot add or change the permissions as shown in Figure 17-8. An administrator can open this dialog box and change the permissions in the same way as he or she could with unshared folders.

File Permissions

File permissions are set in the Security tab of the file's Properties dialog box, shown in Figure 17-9. As you can see, it is very similar to folder permissions except they are limited to files. This means that the List Folder Contents permission is no longer available and definitions of the individual permissions change slightly.

- **Full Control** The sum of all other permissions, plus change permissions and take ownership

- **Modify** The sum of the Read & Execute and the Write permissions, plus delete and modify the file

- **Read & Execute** The Read permissions, plus execute applications

- **Read** View the contents of the file, as well as view its attributes (Archive, Hidden, Read-only), permissions, and ownership

- **Write** Write to the file, plus view the file's permissions and ownership, and change its attributes

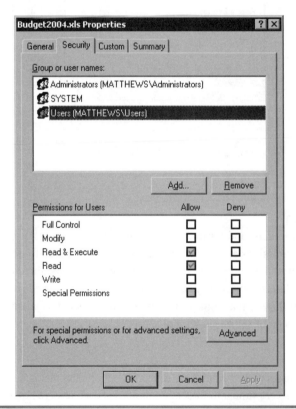

Figure 17-9 Default File permissions

Progress Check

1. What must happen to have a username and password accepted on a local stand-alone computer?

2. What are some examples of strong passwords?

3. What are permissions, and how are they used?

4. What does inheritance, as it is used with permissions, mean?

CRITICAL SKILL
17.3 Secure Stored Data

User authentication puts a lock on the outside doors of the computer, and controlling access puts locks on the inside doors, but if someone breaks through or gets around those barriers, the data inside is available to anyone who wants it. For example, someone may take a disk drive and access it with another operating system, or steal a laptop and methodically break through the passwords. Or, much simpler and more common, an employee either purposefully gets or mistakenly is given access to data that employee should not have and decides to misuse it.

The answer to all of these scenarios is to make the data itself unusable without a key. This is done by encrypting a file or folder so that no matter how it is accessed, by another operating system or a low-level utility, it is encrypted and cannot be read without the key, and the key is itself encrypted so that it is exceptionally difficult to obtain and use.

File and Folder Encryption

File and folder encryption has been built into Windows Server 2003 NTFS and is called the *Encrypting File System (EFS)*. Once EFS is turned on for a file or a folder, only the person who encrypted the file or folder will be able to read it, with the exception that a specially appointed administrator will have a recovery key to access the file or folder. For the person

---

1. To have a username and password accepted on a local stand-alone computer, a user account with that username and password must have been previously entered into the Local Users And Groups database, which is in the Security Account Manager (SAM) file of the Registry.

2. Examples of strong passwords are: sd4Y92i#j, 63gT*7p, n7$k819E.

3. Permissions authorize a user or a group to perform some function on an object. Objects, such as files, folders, disks, and printers, have a set of permissions associated with them that can be assigned to users and groups.

4. Inheritance, as it is used with permissions, means that all files, subfolders, and files in subfolders automatically inherit (take on) the permissions of their parent folder.

who encrypted the file, accessing it requires no additional steps, and the file is re-encrypted every time it is saved. All of the encrypting and decrypting is done behind the scenes and is not obvious to the user.

NOTE

Neither system files or folders nor compressed files or folders can be encrypted. You can decompress a compressed file or folder and then encrypt it.

The Encryption Process

The actual encryption of a file or folder is done with a *symmetric encryption key,* which is the same for both encryption and decryption and is very fast. The symmetric encryption key (also called a *secret key*) is itself encrypted using the file owner's public key that is contained in his or her EFS certificate. (See "Understand Private/Public Key Encryption," later in this module.) Therefore, the owner with her or his private key matching the public key is the only one who can open the encrypted file—except for the recovery administrator. When the file is created or re-created and a symmetric key is made, the key is actually encrypted twice, once for the owner and once for the recovery administrator. Then, if the need arises, the recovery administrator can use his or her private key to decrypt the file.

The encrypted symmetric key is stored as a part of the file. When an application requests the file, NTFS goes and gets it, sees that the file is encrypted, and calls EFS. EFS works with the security protocols to authenticate the user, use his or her private key to decrypt the file, and pass an unencrypted file to the calling application, all in the background, without any outward sign that it is taking place. The encryption and decryption routines are so fast that on most computers that can run Windows Server 2003, you seldom notice the added time.

TIP

Because many applications save temporary and secondary files during normal execution, it is recommended that folders rather than files be the encrypting container. If an application is then told to store all files in that folder where all files are automatically encrypted upon saving, security is improved.

Encryption Considerations

Several requirements must be met to use file and folder encryption:

- Windows 2000, Windows XP, or Windows Server 2003 NTFS must be in use. Any other file system, whether Windows NT 4 NTFS or FAT, will not work with EFS.

- Certificate Services should be installed and running either on a stand-alone computer or within a domain. If Certificate Services is not running, EFS will issue its own certificates, but these are considered "not trusted" by Windows Server 2003.

- The user of the file or folder must have an EFS certificate. If one does not exist, it is automatically created.

- There must be one or more certificated recovery agent administrators. If one does not exist, a default administrator is automatically appointed and a certificate is issued. The default administrator on a stand-alone computer is the local administrator, while in a domain, it is the domain administrator on the first domain controller that is installed.

Recovery Agent Administrators   The reason a recovery agent administrator is required is shown by the situation in which someone leaves an organization, maybe through an accident, and his or her encrypted files are needed. Another situation is one in which a disgruntled employee encrypts shared files before leaving the organization. EFS is disabled without a recovery agent, so that files cannot be encrypted without a means to decrypt them. Several recovery agents may be assigned to an EFS file or folder, but there must be at least one. For each recovery agent, as well as the user, a copy of the symmetric encrypting key encrypted with the person's public key is stored with the encrypted file. Whoever decrypts the file reveals only the data and not any of the other keys.

Copy and Moving EFS Files   Copying and moving EFS files and folders has special significance. Here are the rules:

- If you copy a file or folder to an encrypted folder, the item copied will be encrypted.

- If you move a file or folder to an encrypted folder, the item moved remains as it was prior to moving. If it was unencrypted, it remains so, and if it was encrypted, it is still encrypted after moving.

- Copy or moving encrypted files or folders to another file system, such as Windows NT 4 NTFS or Windows 98 FAT32, removes the encryption, although only the owner or recovery agent can do this. Everyone else will be denied access.

- Backing up encrypted files or folders with Windows Server 2003 Backup leaves the items encrypted.

NOTE

When you back up encrypted data, make sure that both the user and the recovery agent keys are also backed up, which can be done with Certificate Services.

Use File and Folder Encryption

The actual process of encrypting a file or folder is very easy; you simply turn on the Encrypted attribute. Given that there is a certificated recovery agent administrator and that the user turning on the encryption has an EFS certificate, there is very little else to do. Look at the full process, including the certification, in the next sections.

Create EFS Certificates

Earlier in this module, under "Certificate Authentication," there is a discussion of setting up Certificate Services and requesting a certificate. The following steps show specifically how to request an EFS Recovery Agent certificate:

1. While logged on as the administrator who will be the recovery agent, open the MMC by opening the Start menu, clicking Run, typing **mmc**, and clicking OK.

2. In the Console, open the File menu, choose Open, and double-click your Certificates console. In the left pane, open Console Root | Certificates – Current User | Personal | Certificates.

3. Open the Action menu and choose All Tasks | Request New Certificate. The Certificate Request Wizard opens. Click Next.

4. Select EFS Recovery Agent as the Certificate Template, as shown next, and click Next. Enter a friendly name and description, and click Next again.

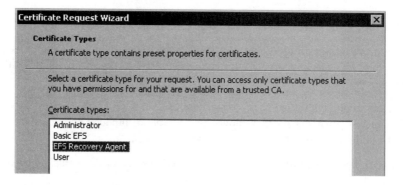

5. Review your selections, use Back to make any corrections, and click Finish. When you're told that the certificate request was successful, click OK. Close the MMC.

Encrypt a File and a Folder

Encryption of either files or folders can be done from Windows Explorer or from the command prompt.

ile from Windows Explorer   Here are the steps to encrypt a file from
plorer:

ndows Explorer by opening Start and clicking Windows Explorer.

lders tree on the left, open the drive and folders necessary to display on the right
you want to encrypt.

lick the file and choose Properties. In the General tab, click Advanced. The Advanced
tes dialog box opens.

Encrypt Contents To Secure Data.

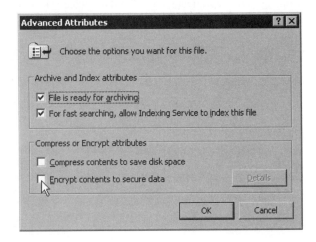

5. Click OK twice. You get an Encryption Warning that the file is not in an encrypted folder,
which means that when you edit the file, temporary or backup files might be created that
are not encrypted.

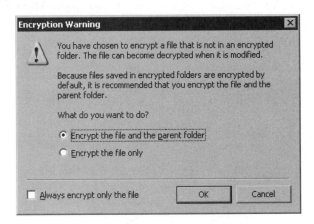

6. Make the choice that is correct for you. If you don't want to see this warning in the future, click Always Encrypt Only The File. Click OK.

Encrypt a Folder from Windows Explorer Encrypting a folder from Windows Explorer is very similar, as you can see in these steps:

1. Open Windows Explorer and display in the right pane the folder you want to encrypt.

2. Right-click the folder and choose Properties. In the General tab, click Advanced. The Advanced Attributes dialog box opens.

3. Click Encrypt Contents To Secure Data, and click OK twice. The Confirm Attribute Changes dialog box opens.

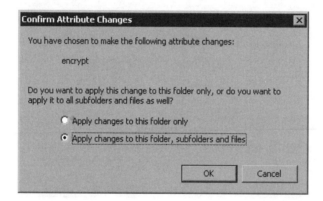

4. You are asked whether you want to apply the encryption to this folder only or to the folder, its files, and its subfolders. If you choose This Folder Only, *existing* files and folders in the folder being encrypted will *not* be encrypted, while files and folders created or copied to the encrypted folder after the fact will be encrypted. If you choose This Folder, Subfolders And Files, existing files and folders, as well as those created or copied in the future, will be encrypted.

5. Choose the settings that are correct for you and click OK.

CAUTION

If you choose This Folder, Subfolders And Files for a shared folder that has files or subfolders belonging to others, you will encrypt those files and subfolders with your key, and the owners will not be able to use their property.

Encrypt a File and a Folder from the Command Prompt

At the command prompt, you can use the Cipher command to encrypt and decrypt files and folders. The following exercise encrypts a file and then a folder that contains the file plus another unencrypted file, looks at the results, and then decrypts the folder and its contents.

NOTE

Close Windows Explorer before you use the command prompt, and make sure your file and folder names do not have embedded spaces. Failure to follow either of these guidelines can cause problems with the following steps.

1. Open the command prompt by opening the Start menu and choosing Command Prompt.

2. Type **cipher /?** and press ENTER to see the parameters that are available with the command, as shown in Figure 17-10.

   In the Cipher parameters, using **/E** by itself encrypts only the folder, not the files and subfolders it contains. This is the same as choosing Folder Only in Windows Explorer. If you want to encrypt the folder and its subfolders, you must use both **/E** and **/S** with a space between them. If you want to encrypt the folder, its subfolders, and the files they contain, use **/E /S /A**. To encrypt a file by itself, you must use **/E /A** with a space between them; only **/E/A** will not encrypt the folder.

3. Type **cipher /e /a** *path\filename* and press ENTER to encrypt just the file *filename.* You are told that the file was encrypted and that you may need to clean up the directory after all encrypting is completed.

4. Type **cipher /e** *path\foldername* and press ENTER to encrypt just the folder *foldername.* You are told the directory is encrypted.

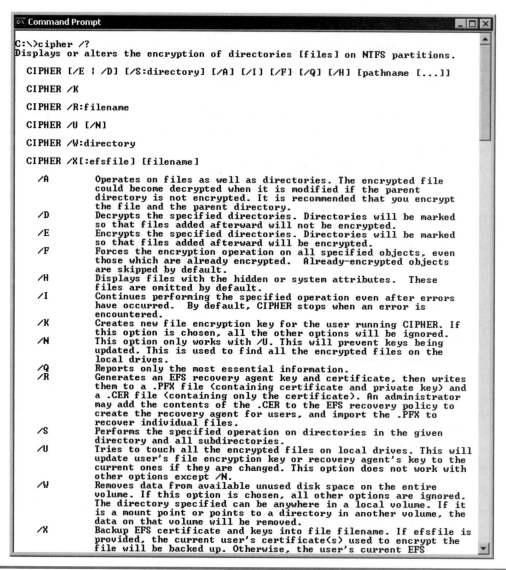

Figure 17-10 Many of the parameters that can be used with the Cipher command

5. Open Windows Explorer and look at the attributes for the two files and the folder. (If Show Encrypted Or Compressed NTFS Files In Color is enabled in Folder Options, the file and folder will be in color.) When you are done looking at these files and folder, close Windows Explorer.

6. Type **cipher /d /s:***path\foldername* ***/a*** and press ENTER to decrypt both the folder and the file it contains, as shown here:

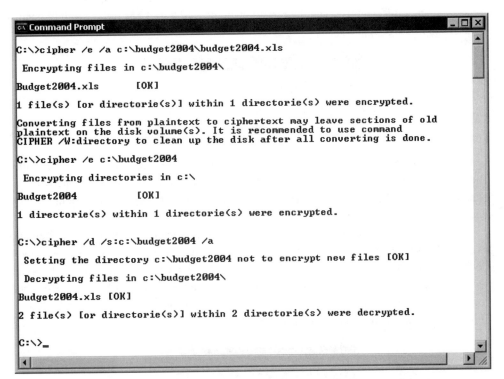

```
C:\>cipher /e /a c:\budget2004\budget2004.xls

 Encrypting files in c:\budget2004\

Budget2004.xls        [OK]
1 file(s) [or directorie(s)] within 1 directorie(s) were encrypted.
Converting files from plaintext to ciphertext may leave sections of old
plaintext on the disk volume(s). It is recommended to use command
CIPHER /W:directory to clean up the disk after all converting is done.
C:\>cipher /e c:\budget2004

 Encrypting directories in c:\

Budget2004           [OK]
1 directorie(s) within 1 directorie(s) were encrypted.

C:\>cipher /d /s:c:\budget2004 /a

 Setting the directory c:\budget2004 not to encrypt new files [OK]

 Decrypting files in c:\budget2004\

Budget2004.xls [OK]
2 file(s) [or directorie(s)] within 2 directorie(s) were decrypted.

C:\>_
```

7. Close any other open programs, type **cipher /w:***path\foldername*, and press ENTER to clean up the folder. This is a fairly slow process taking as long as a half hour if you have a large disk and a slower system.

8. Type **Exit** to close the command prompt and then open Windows Explorer to check out the attributes on the files and folder you have been using.

TIP

If you are giving someone a computer of yours and you are concerned about private information that you have or had on the computer, first delete all the information and applications you do not want to transfer and then run **cipher /w:**. You will totally wipe clean and then write random numbers over all areas of the disk not being used. Even if you reformat the hard drive and reinstall Windows, it is worth running **cipher /w:** to be totally sure no information can be read, even by experts.

Test File Encryption

So what happens when someone tries to access an encrypted file? Try it yourself. Log off and log back on as a different user and then try to open the file. It looks as if it's going to open, and then a little message appears:

The actual message varies depending on the application you are using to try to open the file, but it is purposely understated—one of those little access problems; call the network administrator and she'll work it out. If access is appropriate, the recovery agent administrator can solve the problem and no one is offended.

Okay, what about copying the file to a non–Windows Server 2003 NTFS file system, such as a Windows 98 FAT32 machine on the network? The file is no longer encrypted when you do that, correct? Again, try it, first while logged on as the one who encrypted the file. Everything will work as it is supposed to—the file will be copied and will no longer be encrypted. Then, log off and log back on again as someone else and try copying the file. Once more, it looks as if it's going to work, and then another little message appears:

This too is understated, and in my case, nothing was using the file. The entire encryption system is meant to be unobtrusive, remaining in the background while doing its job.

CRITICAL SKILL
17.4 Understand Private/Public Key Encryption

Several encryption schemes for securing data transmission are in use: private key encryption, public key encryption, and combinations of the two. The set of these three schemes and the technology and standards or protocols that surround them collectively is known as the *public key infrastructure (PKI)*. Windows Server 2003 has made PKI an integral part of the operating system, especially in Active Directory. Windows Server 2003 has implemented all three encryption key schemes and fully supports them with Certificate Services.

Private Key Encryption

Private key encryption, or *symmetric cryptography* (which is also what is used with file and folder encryption, as previously discussed), is relatively old and uses a single key to both encrypt and decrypt a message. This means that the key itself must be transferred from sender to receiver. If this is done over the phone, the Internet, or even a courier service, an unauthorized person simply needs to intercept the key transfer to get hold of the key and decrypt the message. Private key encryption, though, has a major benefit in that it is much faster (as much as 1,000 times faster) than the alternatives. Private key schemes are therefore valuable in situations where you do not have to transfer the key or can do so with security—for example, for personal use such as data encryption, as just discussed, or sending information to someone that you first met face to face. Several private key encryption schemes are being used with the Internet, including the U.S. government's Data Encryption Standard (DES) and the private RC2 ("Rivest Cipher" or "Ron's Code" [for Ron Rivest] 2) and RC4, both from RSA Laboratories.

Public Key Encryption

Public key encryption, or *asymmetric cryptography,* which was developed in the mid-1970s, uses a pair of keys—a public key and a private key. The public key is publicly known and transferred, and is used to encrypt a message. The private key never leaves its creator and is used to decrypt the message. For two people to use this technique, each generates both a public key and a private key, and then they openly exchange public keys, not caring who gets a copy of it. Each person encrypts their message to the other by using the other person's public key, and then sends the message. The message can be decrypted and read only by using the private key held by the recipient. The public and private keys use a mathematical algorithm that relates them to the encrypted message. By use of other mathematical algorithms, it is fairly easy to generate key pairs, but with only the public key, it is extremely difficult to generate the private key. The process of public key encryption is relatively slow compared to private key encryption. Public key encryption is best in open environments where the sender and recipient do not know each other. Most public key encryption uses the Rivest-Shamir-Adleman (RSA) Public Key Cryptosystem, called RSA for short, developed and supported by RSA Laboratories.

Combined Public and Private Key Encryption

Most encryption on the Internet actually is a combination of public and private key encryption methods. The most common combination, Secure Sockets Layer (SSL), was developed by

Netscape to go between HTTP and TCP/IP. SSL provides a highly secure and very fast means of both encryption and authentication.

Recall that private key encryption is very fast but has the problem of transferring the key, whereas public key encryption is very secure but slow. If you were to begin a secure transmission by using a public key to encrypt and send a private key, you could then securely use the private key to quickly send any amount of data you wanted. This is how SSL works. It uses an RSA public key to send a randomly chosen private key using either DES or RC4 encryption, and in so doing sets up a "secure socket" through which any amount of data can be quickly encrypted, sent, and decrypted. After the SSL header has transferred the private key, all information transferred in both directions during a given session—including the URL, any request for a user ID and password, all HTTP web information, and any data entered on a form—is automatically encrypted by the sender and automatically decrypted by the recipient.

Several versions of SSL exist, with SSL version 3 being the one currently in common use. SSL 3 is both more secure than, and offers improved authentication over, earlier versions.

Another combination of public and private key methods is Transport Layer Security (TLS), which is an open security standard similar to SSL 3. TLS, which was drafted by the Internet Engineering Task Force (IETF), uses different encryption algorithms than SSL. Otherwise, TSL is very similar to SSL and even has an option to revert to SSL if necessary. Both SSL 3 and TLS have been proposed to the World Wide Web Consortium (W3C) standards committee as security standards.

Encryption Keys and Certificates

The PKI in Windows Server 2003 and in general use on the Internet depends on digital certificates to issue, authenticate, and maintain encryption keys. (See "Certificate Authentication," earlier in this module, for a discussion of certificates and how to issue and use them.) To get an encryption key, you get a certificate, of which the key is a part. To authenticate the key, you use the certificate that it is a part of. The key is stored in a certificate, which is the means by which keys are maintained in an organization. Certificate Services in Windows Server 2003 provides all of these services.

CRITICAL SKILL
17.5 Secure Data Transmission

The discussion so far in this module has dealt with securing computers and their contents and has been silent about securing the transmission of data among computers, using e-mail, or otherwise transferring information either within a LAN directly or using an intranet or the Internet. Yet, the need to extend a network to outlying parts of an organization and to customers and suppliers is very real and requires secure data transmission. Securing data transmission means the encryption of the information being transmitted so that it cannot be read and misused by those who don't have the ability to decrypt it. Encrypting information is probably as old as the human race and has really blossomed with the advent of computers. Data encryption has become so sophisticated that the U.S. government, worried that it won't be able to decrypt the data (can you imagine that!), hasn't until very recently allowed the better technology to be exported (everyone was getting it over the Internet anyway).

Implement Data Transmission Security

You may be thinking that SSL and TLS sounds great, but also sound complex to use. In fact, both are easy to use, either across the Internet or internally in a LAN.

Implement Secure Internet and Intranet Transmissions

To implement secure Internet and intranet transmissions, you need a web server that supports SSL or TLS, such as Microsoft IIS 6, plus a supporting web browser, such as Microsoft Internet Explorer 6, both of which are included in Windows Server 2003. From the browser, to visit a web site that has implemented SSL or TSL, you simply need to begin the URL with **https://** rather than http:// (see Module 11 on IIS for details on how to implement secure web sites). SSL will then kick in, and without your even being aware that it's happening, the browser and server decide whether to use DCS or RC4, use RSA to transfer a private key, and then use that key and the chosen private key encryption scheme to encrypt and decrypt all the rest of the data during that session. The only thing that you see is a message saying you are about to begin to use a secure connection, similar to this:

    Once you are connected using SSL, your browser will indicate that a secure connection is established. Netscape and Microsoft display an icon of a padlock in the browser's status bar.

NOTE

Even though the combination of public and private encryption is relatively fast, it is still significantly slower than no encryption. For that reason, it is recommended that you use SSL only when you send sensitive information, such as financial or credit card data, and not for an entire web site.

Implement Secure LAN Transmission

Although SSL can be used within a LAN and in an intranet, it requires a security server (which function IIS fulfills) and can get in the way of applications that are working across a LAN. The answer to this is *Internet Protocol Security (IPSec),* which works between any two computers over a network to supply encrypted transmission of information without a security server and without getting in the way of applications. IPSec is a part of IP and works at the third (Network) layer, below any applications, and therefore seldom interferes with them (see the discussion of networking layers in "The OSI Model" in Module 7).

The IPSec Process   IPSec is almost totally automated, and once group policies are established for its operation, network users don't realize that their network communication is taking place securely. The process for establishing and carrying out IPSec is as follows:

1. Domain or local computer policies are established that specify what network traffic needs to be secure and how that security will be handled.

2. Based on the policies, IPSec establishes a set of filters to determine which network packets require secure transmission.

3. When IPSec receives from a sending application a series of network packets that require secure transmission, the sending computer passes this fact to the receiving computer. The two computers exchange credentials and authenticate each other according to IPSec policies.

4. Given authentication, the two computers work out an algorithm whereby each computer can generate the same private key without having to transmit the key over the network, again according to IPSec policies.

5. The sending computer uses the private key to encrypt the packets it is transmitting, digitally signs them so that the receiving computer knows who is sending the packets, and then transmits the packets.

6. The receiving computer authenticates the digital signature and then uses the key to decrypt the packets and send them on to the receiving application.

Set Up IPSec   To set up and use IPSec, you need only establish or revise default IPSec policies. You can do that through the IP Security snap-in to the MMC with these steps:

1. Open the Start menu, choose Run, type **mmc**, and press ENTER. The MMC shell opens.

2. Open the File menu, choose Add/Remove Snap-In, click Add, scroll down, and double-click IP Security Policy Management.

3. Select whether you want to manage security policy for the domain this computer is a member of, or the local computer (I'm using a domain in this example), and click Finish.

4. Close the Add Standalone Snap-In dialog box and click OK to close the Add/Remove Snap-In dialog box. Open the Console Root and select IP Security Policies On Active Directory, so that your MMC looks like this:

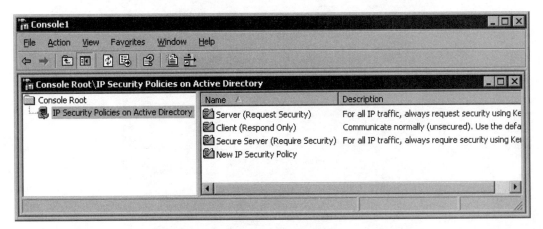

5. Right-click Secure Server and choose Properties. In the Rules tab, you will see a list of IP Security Rules, as shown here:

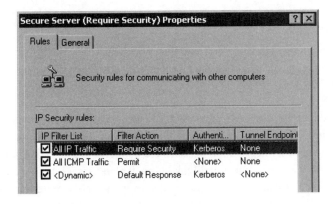

6. Select the All IP Traffic rule and click Edit. The Edit Rule Properties dialog box opens. Look at each of the tabs and then return to the Filter Action tab.

7. Select Require Security and click Edit, which displays a list of security methods similar to the list in Figure 17-11. You can select each of these and click Edit again to select the particular security method you want for a given situation.

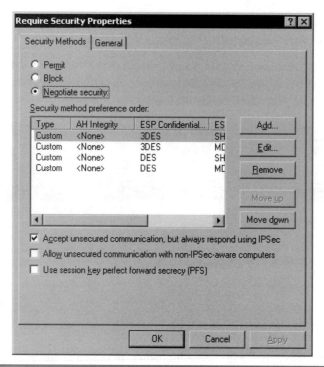

Figure 17-11 Selecting security methods for use in IPSec

8. When you are done, click OK twice and then click Close twice to return to the IPSec console, where you can also click the Close button, answering Yes to save the console settings with the name IPSec.

You can see that the Windows Server 2003 IPSec default is to require security on all IP traffic. This is a safe default; your data will be better protected. The negative side of this default is that the security negotiation between the computers, encrypting and decrypting the data, and the extra bits to transmit all take time. It also uses a lot more bandwidth on the network. Only you and your organization can determine which is more important—time and bandwidth, or security. The point is that Windows Server 2003 gives you the choice, enabling you to make the determination of which networking aspect has a higher priority.

Progress Check

1. Is it better to encrypt the file you want protected or the folder that contains the file?

2. What is PKI, and what does it cover?

3. What form of encryption is most generally used on the Internet?

4. What is IPSec, and how is it used?

Project 17 Plan Security Implementation

In an ever more connected world, security becomes of paramount importance, and to meet that need, the security in Windows has become ever more complex. This project will help you wade through this complexity to figure out what is important for you to implement in the way of computer and network security.

Step by Step

1. Determine how users will be authenticated:

    a. With local computer user authentication

    b. With network user authentication:

        i. Using Kerberos authentication

        ii. Using smart cards

        iii. Using biometric devices

        iv. Using certificates

(continued)

---

1. Because many applications save temporary and secondary files during normal execution, it is recommended that folders rather than files be the encrypting container. If an application is then told to store all files in that folder where all files are automatically encrypted upon saving, security is improved.

2. PKI (which stands for public key infrastructure) is the set of these three encryption schemes: private key encryption, public key encryption, and combinations of the two, and the technology and standards or protocols that surround them.

3. Most encryption on the Internet actually is a combination of public and private key encryption methods. The most common combination, Secure Sockets Layer (SSL), was developed by Netscape to go between HTTP and TCP/IP. SSL provides a highly secure and very fast means using a combination of public and private key methods for both information encryption and authentication.

4. IPSec, which stands for Internet Protocol Security, works between any two computers over a network to supply encrypted transmission of information without a security server and without getting in the way of applications. IPSec is a part of IP and works at the third (Network) layer, below any applications, and therefore seldom interferes with them.

2. Determine how to control access to files, folders, and devices:

   a. Define the meaning of ownership.

   b. Define the groups that will be used:

      i. In stand-alone servers and workstations

      ii. In Active Directory domain controllers

   c. Determine the permissions that will be used:

      i. For folder permissions

      ii. For share permissions

      iii. For file permissions

3. Determine how data will be kept secure:

   a. Determine the files and folders to be encrypted.

   b. Determine who the recovery administrators will be.

   c. Create the necessary certificates.

   d. What procedures will be used for:

      i. Carrying out the encryption

      ii. Copying and moving encrypted files and folders

4. Determine how data will be transmitted securely:

   a. What type of encryption will be used:

      i. Private key encryption

      ii. Public key encryption

      iii. Combination of private and public key encryption

   b. Implement secure Internet transmissions using:

      i. Secure Sockets Layer (SSL)

      ii. Transport Layer Security (TLS)

   c. Implement secure LAN transmission with IPSec

Project Summary

There are a number of tools in Windows Server 2003 to make computers, their contents, and the network joining them secure. But the people responsible for those computers, their contents, and the network must use those tools to make the security a reality.

Module 17 Mastery Check

1. What does authentication mean in a computer network?

2. What is a strong password, and what are the rules for it?

3. What is Kerberos, and what are some of its key features?

4. What are two replacements for passwords, and how are they used?

5. What is a digital certificate, and how is it used?

6. What are groups in Windows Server 2003, and how are they used?

7. How do the default permissions in Windows Server 2003 differ from Windows 2000 and earlier versions of Windows?

8. What is EFS, and how is it used?

9. What is private key encryption, and how is it used?

10. What is public key encryption, and how is it used?

Appendix
Answers to Mastery Checks

Module 1: Exploring Windows Server 2003

1. The term .NET stands for .NET technologies, which enable the connection among people, systems, and devices for the exchange of information and computer resources using XML web services, which are building blocks of applications that can be used together or with other applications.

2. The four editions of Windows Server 2003 are the Web Edition, a server for hosting smaller web sites, the Standard Edition, a network server operating system that is meant for smaller to moderate-sized organizations, the Enterprise Edition, a network server operating system that is meant for larger organizations and e-commerce, and Datacenter Edition, a network server operating system that is meant for the largest organizations.

3. Windows Server 2003 installs faster because of the automated server configuration in addition to improved Plug and Play capability, an enlarged driver database, and enhancements to the Setup program. Windows Server 2003 provides support for many new hardware devices, including CD writers for burning CDs, new keyboard buttons, high-resolution monitors and printers, multifunction printing/fax/copying devices, and expanded AutoPlay ability.

4. The five component areas of User Mode in Windows Server 2003 are networking on a LAN, communications and the Internet on a WAN, the user and application interface, storage and file management, and printing.

5. To prepare to install Windows Server 2003, you must make sure that your computers meet the requirements of Windows Server 2003, that Windows Server 2003 supports all the hardware in your computers, that you know the choices that provide the best operating environment for each of the installation choices, that your computers have been prepared for an operating system installation, and that you have a solid plan for carrying out the installation.

6. The purposes of networking include exchanging information, such as sending a file from one computer to another, communicating by, for example, sending e-mail among network users, sharing information by having common files accessed by multiple network users, and sharing resources on the network, such as printers and backup tape drives.

7. The types of external connections that can be made with Windows Server 2003 include leased-line and private-line WANs; dial-up line computer-to-computer communications using a modem; direct computer-to-computer using serial, parallel, or infrared ports; RAS for accessing a LAN over a dial-up, leased, or private line; dial-up, leased, and private line connections to the Internet; and VPN to securely access a LAN over the Internet.

8. The programs in Windows Server 2003 that control or utilize communications include Internet Explorer for web browsing, Outlook Express for e-mail, Fax, HyperTerminal for computer-to-computer communications, NetMeeting for multimedia communications, Phone Dialer, and both the Internet Connection Wizard and the Network Connection Wizard to establish connections. In addition, Windows Server 2003 networking includes programs to set up and manage RAS and VPN forms of networking over communications lines, as well as the new Remote Desktop Connection to link two remote computers. Finally, IIS can be used to publish web pages on either the Internet or an intranet.

9. The tools in Windows Server 2003 for handling file system management include Disk Management, Dynamic Volume Management, Distributed File System, Removable Storage Manager, Remote Storage Service, and Disk Backup and Restore.

10. The primary demands for security in a computer network include authenticating the user, controlling access, securing stored data, securing data transmission, and managing security.

Module 2: Migrating to Windows Server 2003

1. The features in Windows Server 2003 that encourage larger organizations to migrate include the scalability, the capability to handle large data storage volumes, Active Directory, which is more useful for a large organization, and management and security features.

2. Two areas where Windows Server 2003 provides benefits for smaller organizations are in reliability and manageability, where it provides some substantial enhancements that are beneficial to all users regardless of size, and in sharing an Internet connection line, using Windows Server 2003's built-in router to perform network address translation (NAT) by mapping multiple local area network (LAN) addresses to one IP (Internet Protocol) address.

3. The hardware improvements in Windows 2000 and Windows Server 2003 include full implementation of Plug and Play, an extensive set of hardware drivers that are stored in compressed form on the computer, online access to the latest drivers at the Microsoft site and a program to check whether you need them, online access to what hardware is and isn't compatible with Windows Server 2003, built-in support for such hardware developments as new keyboards, high-resolution monitors, the universal serial bus (USB) and Institute of Electrical and Electronics Engineers (IEEE) 1394 (FireWire) ports, and built-in support for recording on CDs.

4. The security improvements in Windows Server 2003 are certificate, Kerberos, and IPSec (Internet Protocol–based security) enhancements; secure wireless LANs; and key archival and recovery.

5. Kerberos provides the means to transmit secure data across non-secure networks and is the primary means of authentication on the Internet. Other benefits of Kerberos include transitive trusts that transfer trust relationships from computer to computer, Kerberos tickets that stay with the user throughout a computer session, and mutual authentication, which allows the user to authenticate a service or server, while also allowing the service or server to authenticate the user.

6. The Public Key Infrastructure (PKI) in simplified form gives a certificate to a person known to the security system; along with the certificate, unique public and private keys are given to the user; when the user wants to exchange information with another user, they exchange public keys that are in turn used to encrypt information to be sent to the owner of the key; upon receipt of the encrypted information, the private key is used to decrypt it.

7. The Internet tools in Windows Server 2003 include the Internet Connection Wizard, which leads you through all the steps necessary to set up a modem, obtain an ISP, and configure a connection to that ISP for World Wide Web service, e-mail service, and news service; Internet Explorer, which allows you to search for and go to a web site, navigate within a web site, securely send and receive information to and from a web site, store a web site's address in a list of favorites or in a links toolbar, print a web page, and maintain a history of the web sites you have visited; and Outlook Express, which provides one-on-one communications by sending, receiving, and storing e-mail, as well as enabling participation in newsgroups through sending and receiving linked messages.

8. IIS is Internet Information Services, which is the web server in Windows Server 2003 for both intranets and the World Wide Web of the Internet. Among the features in IIS 6 or in Windows Server 2003 that support web hosting include: Certificate and Permissions Wizards to greatly simplify the process of issuing security certificates and assigning the appropriate user permissions; enhanced Active Server Pages (ASP), which uses scripts to generate a custom web page based on requests received by the server; Distributed Authoring and Versioning (DAV), which allows greater and more direct control of web pages on a server from such tools as Microsoft FrontPage and Netscape Composer; Hypertext Transfer Protocol (HTTP) compression, which speeds the transmission of a Hypertext Markup Language (HTML) document, the text part of a web page; Processor Accounting and Throttling, which allow you to monitor, control, and bill the processor time used by a particular web page; and Integrated Streaming Media Delivery, which allows the reliable and controllable distribution of industry-standard streaming audio and video directly from .NET without using third-party software.

9. Windows SharePoint Services provides a comprehensive set of tools to build and manage an intranet site aimed at team collaboration within an organization.

Module 3: Preparing for Installation

1. The major considerations before installing an operating system are these: Your computers must meet the requirements of Windows Server 2003 or Windows XP Professional, you must be sure that Windows Server 2003 or Windows XP Professional supports all the hardware in your system, you must know the choices that provide the best operating environment for each of the installation decisions, your computers must be prepared for an operating system installation, and you must have a solid plan for carrying out the installation.

2. Among the factors that determine the amount of free hard disk space required in Windows Server 2003 installation are the Windows components that are installed, the type of file system used (NTFS, FAT32, or FAT), whether a network-based installation is used, and whether an upgrade or a clean installation is being done.

3. When you take a physical inventory, you need to gather information including the type of adapter card; make and model of the adapter card; type and position of card slot; settings on the adapter cards; type, make, model, and size of disk drive; and the type of disk drive interface.

4. The major reasons to upgrade are to preserve your current environment including the current settings, applications, and data on your computer, and to make the installation of Windows Server 2003 simpler, since most of the installation decisions are made by the current installation. The major reasons to do a clean install are to get around an operating system that cannot be upgraded, to dual-boot into both the old operating system and Windows Server 2003, and to clean up your hard disks.

5. Dual-booting has significant drawbacks including the fact that you must install Windows Server 2003 in a separate partition, so you must reinstall all the applications you want to run under Windows Server 2003; you must handle some complex file-system compatibility issues; Windows NT 4's Defrag and Chkdsk utilities won't work on Windows Server 2003's NTFS partition; and the Plug and Play features of Windows 95, Windows 98, and Windows Server 2003 could cause a device not to work properly in one operating system because the other operating system reconfigured it.

6. The reasons to choose NTFS over either the FAT or FAT32 file systems include NTFS supporting the use of disk volumes up to 2TB (terabytes) and files as large as the total disk volume; providing much more efficient large file and volume handling, allowing the use of file-level security; supporting Active Directory and domains for improved security, flexibility, and manageability; allowing the encryption of individual files as well as offline files for a very high level of security; providing for sparse files; and supporting disk quotas that control how much space an individual user can use.

7. Per Server licensing determines the number of the concurrent connections to the server. Any workstation can use one of the connections, but you can have only so many connections at any one time. Each connection requires one CAL. Per Seat licensing is licensing each individual computer that accesses the server. This means that each workstation has its own CAL in addition to its own operating system license and can use the CAL to access any number of servers. The servers can have any number of concurrent connections, so long as each connection has its own CAL.

8. The techniques you can use to back up hard disks include the backup programs within previous versions of Windows, and one of several third-party programs, such as VERITAS. Backup media can include tape, removable hard disks, Zip drives, writable or rewritable CDs, optical drives, or even a different hard disk on another system or a new hard disk purchased just for backups. With an additional hard disk, you can make a mirror copy of a hard disk using products such as PowerQuest's Drive Copy for a one-to-one copy, or Drive Image for a compressed copy.

9. The steps needed to prepare a computer for a Windows Server 2003 installation include disabling any UPS device connected to the computer's serial port, disabling disk mirroring prior to starting Setup, uncompressing either DriveSpace or DoubleSpace volumes (make sure you have backed up and inventoried the volume first), and stopping all programs that are running, especially any virus-detection programs, before starting Setup.

10. The common steps in preparing a migration plan for installing Windows Server 2003 include identifying what computers and their order are to be upgraded or installed with Windows Server 2003 or Windows XP Professional;

identifying the hardware that needs to be acquired and installed; developing a timeline for completing the tasks; determining a set of installation dates that will provide the minimum amount of disruption; developing a budget for the software, hardware, and labor needed; and identifying realistically the possible disruptions to the company's business and the cost of such disruptions. Identify the benefits of changing over to Windows Server 2003 and how those benefits translate into reduced costs and improved revenues.

Module 4: Installing Windows Server 2003

1. The three ways that Windows Server 2003 can be installed are manually, where a person sits in front of the computer to be installed and, in real time, does the installation; automated, where a script or answer file is used to carry out the installation, so that a person does not have to stay in front of the computer; and remotely, where a person sits in front of a server and performs the installation on a computer across the network.

2. Installing over a network is different than installing remotely. With installing over a network, you are in front of the machine being installed, accessing the network to get the installation files. With remote installation, you are in front of the server installing on a machine across the network.

3. When sitting in front of the machine on which you want to perform the installation of Windows Server 2003, you can start Setup by accessing the installation files on a server across a network, you can directly boot the installation CD, and you can start Setup from most Microsoft operating systems, including MS-DOS and both older and newer versions of Windows.

4. With a newer version of Windows (Windows 95 or Windows NT 3.5*x* and on) running on the computer on which you want to install Windows Server 2003, you can start Setup by simply placing the Setup CD in its drive on most computers built after 1995.

5. The options that are available in the Setup Options dialog box are Advanced Options, which allows you to specify the location of the Windows Server 2003 Setup files and the folder in which you want Windows Server 2003 installed; Accessibility Options, which allows you to turn on a Magnifier to enlarge portions of the Setup screen, and/or turn on a Narrator to read aloud the contents of the Setup screen; and Language Options, which allows you to select a primary language and one of the areas of the world that language is used.

6. If you are starting from an older version (5.*x* or 6.*x*) of DOS or Windows 3.*x* and don't have the DOS SmartDrive disk-caching system loaded, you will be reminded that having it will greatly improve the performance of Setup (although it is still slow compared to other ways of starting Setup). SmartDrive is started with the program Smartdrv.exe that was included with DOS 6.*x* and Windows 3.*x*.

7. The items that you should look at before starting into the server configuration include the folders and files on the hard disk and the view that you see in My Network Places, both seen from Windows Explorer; the boot drive Properties to see how much room you have after installing Windows Server 2003; My Network Places | Entire Network | Microsoft Windows Network to see if you are connected to the network and if you can see other computers to which you can link; Start menu | Administrative Tools to see the tools that are automatically installed and available to you; Start menu | Printers And Faxes to see what is installed; Start menu | Control Panel to see what is available there; Start menu | Control Panel | Network Connections | Local Area Connection to open the Local Area Connection Status dialog box and tell you if you are connected and the speed.

8. Some of the roles you can assign to a server with the Configure Your Server Wizard include file server, print server, application server, mail server, terminal server, remote access/VPN server, domain controller, DNS server, DHCP server, streaming media server, and WINS server.

9. The subnet mask tells the server how much of the IP address has to be searched to determine its uniqueness. If you have a small range, you don't want to waste time searching the full IP address, so the subnet mask limits the search. For a small range, start with a high length such as 28 (it is the number of bits to ignore). If you get a message that the scope cannot be created as entered without creating a superscope, go back and increase the subnet mask until you no longer get that message.

10. No, after creating and activating a DHCP server, it cannot be used until it is authorized. That is done by opening the Start menu | Administrative Tools | DHCP, selecting the server in the left pane, opening the Action menu, and clicking Authorize.

Module 5: Rolling Out Windows XP Professional

1. You cannot delete the partition from which you originally booted the computer. You should be able to do this if you boot into Setup from the Windows XP CD. The simplest way to do this is to boot from the installation CD, start Setup, and choose D at this point in the process.

2. An upgrade to Windows XP Professional may be done from Windows Me, Windows 98, Windows 2000 Professional, or Windows NT Workstation 4. (MS-DOS, Windows 3.1x, Windows 95, Windows NT Workstation 3.51, and OS/2 require a clean install.)

3. The Regional And Language Options dialog box allows you to choose a locale that determines which language is the default; which other languages are available; and how numbers, currencies, time, and dates are displayed and used for the system in general.

4. Automating installation means to run Setup without intervention, to execute a command on a computer and walk away while Setup installs or upgrades to Windows XP. The end objective is to run Setup on a number of machines with a minimum of effort. The two major ways of handling this are command-line parameters and disk imaging.

5. Answer files can contain up to all the information that would otherwise be entered during installation, and are used by Setup to run unattended. Five tools to help in the use of answer files are on the Windows Server 2003 CD (dated tools are also available on the XP Professional CD but aren't recommended): a sample answer file named Unattend.txt, a guide to all the possible parameters in an answer file, help files named Deploy.chm and Ref.chm, articles in Readme.txt in the Deploy.cab file, and a GUI program called Setup Manager wizard to create answer files based on answering questions in Setupmgr.exe in the Deploy.cab file.

6. Setup Manager will create the following four objects in a distribution folder that you specified: an I386 folder containing the Setup files from the I386 folder on the Windows XP installation CD, an Unattend.txt file that is the answer file that was your original objective, an Unattend.bat batch file that implements both the answer file and the distribution folder, and an Unattend.udb optional file used if you have multiple computers to supply the names of the computers.

7. Possible uses for the OEM folder and its subfolders include holding files, folders, and applications that you want placed on a newly installed hard disk; a list of commands, such as application-setup and .inf commands, that will be run at the end of the final GUI phase of Windows XP Setup; files and folders that you want copied into the Windows folder (normally named Windows or Winnt) on the computer being installed; files, such as DLLs, that you want copied to a folder that is normally named \Windows\System32 or \Winnt\System32; files and folders that you want copied to the root directory of the system drive on which Windows is installed; additional device drivers not included in Windows; files and folders that you want copied to the root directory of drive C:, drive D:, and other drives; and hardware-related files, such as SCSI and Fiber Channel device drivers, that are used in the early character-based or text mode of Windows Setup.

8. The Setup command lines and answer files can be implemented in a number of ways, including: typing a Setup command with appropriate parameters and switches at a command prompt, creating a batch file with a Setup command in it and executing the batch file by typing its name at a command prompt or double-clicking it from Windows, copying a batch file with a Setup command in it to another computer and executing it from that computer, and copying a batch file with a Setup command in it along with other files needed for unattended operation to either a bootable floppy disk or a CD and then starting Setup by booting that medium.

9. For disk imaging to work, the systems must be nearly identical. The following items must be identical: the hardware abstraction layer (HAL), which is where the programming code is turned into machine language at the processor level; the Advanced Configuration and Power Interface (ACPI) for power management; the type

of disk controller; the number of processors; and the platform (32-bit versus 64-bit). These items can differ: the processor model (Intel Pentium II-350, PIII-800, or PIV-1.8); RAM size; and Plug and Play devices, such as network interface cards, video cards, modems, and sound cards.

10. The process of creating and using disk images involves the following steps: create a master image of the operating system and applications that you want to replicate; prepare a special answer file and distribution folder for creating a disk image using the Setup Manager wizard; prepare the master image for copying using the SysPrep tool; copy the master image onto other disks using a third-party product, either hardware or software, such as PowerQuest's Drive Image or Symantec's Ghost; start the clone for the first time and run through it in Mini-Setup.

Module 6: Remote Installation Services

1. Among requirements that must be met to run RIS are that you must have Administrator privileges; the server must meet the minimum requirements for running Windows Server 2003; the server must have a separate NTFS 5 or later drive or partition of 2GB; either the RIS server or other servers on the network must have DNS, DHCP, and AD running; the Windows XP files and application programs that you want to install must be on the RIS server; the client that will be installed by RIS must meet the minimum requirements for the operating system being installed; the client must have an NTFS version 5 or later formatted drive on which RIS will install the operating system and other desired software; and the client must have either a NIC that supports the PXE protocol version .99C or later or a NIC that will work with a special boot floppy.

2. A Single-Instance Store (SIS) volume is one of the components set up with RIS. If you create several installation images for different combinations of operating systems and applications, there will probably be a lot of overlap among the files in the various images. SIS is a capability that searches out and eliminates duplicate files, replacing them with a pointer to a single instance of the file stored in the SIS volume.

3. The most common items that can go wrong during a RIS installation include not being able to boot from a floppy, the client network card being unsupported by the RIS boot floppy, and not being able to connect to the RIS server.

4. Under most circumstances, the RIS server knows about only the very latest computers that have a GUID / UUID stored in the computer's BIOS. Therefore, if you click Show Clients, you normally will not see anything. Also for that reason, you don't want to select Do Not Respond To Unknown Client Computers, because the only known ones are those with UUIDs.

5. The summary set of tasks to set up a domain controller for a RIS installation are to set up networking, making sure that TCP/IP is installed and that the DNS and DHCP server(s) have a fixed IP address; to set up DNS and DHCP, making sure that DHCP is running on a domain controller, that it is authorized for the RIS server, and that a scope has been created that covers the clients to be installed by RIS; to set up Active Directory such that the RIS server is a domain controller in the same domain in which the clients are to be installed; to review the policies and permissions for the RIS server and for the client(s) and make sure that nothing stands in the way of doing the remote installation; and to make sure the person logged on to do the RIS installation (you) has domain administrator privileges.

6. RIS gives you two ways to customize the remote installation process: using RIPrep to create an image for remote installation using a completed model installation, including applications and custom settings, and using custom scripts to automate more or less of the installation process.

7. When you do multiple installations of a specifically configured operating system and set of applications, you are assuming that the computers on which you are doing the installation are close to identical in terms of hardware. This is particularly important for newer laptops with the Advanced Configuration and Power Interface (ACPI), which must use their own image.

8. There are actually two copies of the SIF, one in the ...\i386\ folder and one in the ...\i386\Templates folder. Always edit the copy in the ...\Templates\ folder because the copy in the ...\i386\ folder gets copied over by the copy in the ...\Templates\ folder each time RIS is run.

9. No, the OEM folders must be at the same level in the RIS folder structure as the i386 folder and *not* inside the i386 folder as shown in Module 5. Thus in the RIPrep example discussed in the module, the path to the OEM folders would be \RemoteInstall\Setup\English\Images*imagename*\OEM.

10. The initial set of screens that appear when you do a RIS installation, called the Client Installation Wizard, are stored in the \RemoteInstall\OSChooser\English\ folder on the RIS volume. These screens are similar to (but not exactly the same as) HTML-based web pages, and they can be easily modified using Notepad.

Module 7: Windows Server 2003 Networking Environment

1. Network uses include exchanging information, such as by sending a file from one computer to another; communicating, such as by sending e-mail among network users; sharing information by having common files accessed by network users; and sharing resources on the network, such as printers and Internet connections.

2. The dominant networking technology is Ethernet. It is relatively inexpensive, works well for interconnecting many different types of computer systems, and is easy to expand to very large networks. As a result, Ethernet-related equipment and Ethernet support in software, including Windows XP and/or Windows Server 2003, has become pervasive. This fact has brought many vendors into the market to supply equipment, causing the pricing to become most reasonable.

3. The reasons for wireless networking are that it does not require cabling and that it gives users flexibility in where they are when they are networking: they can sit anywhere in a room, roam from room to room, and even be online in some public facilities such as airports. The reasons against it are expense and lack of speed.

4. Small office / home office networking technologies generally refer to one of two types of networking systems that share existing cabling in a home, either telephone cabling or power cabling. Networks using telephone lines simply plug into the phone jacks already installed in many homes and transmit over a frequency that does not interfere with voice communications, so they can be used at the same time a phone conversation is going on. Power-line networking uses the existing power lines that are throughout almost all buildings for networking. While there may be rooms or areas in rooms without phone lines, there are very few without a power outlet.

5. The two primary card buses used with NICs are ISA and PCI. You want to choose PCI. ISA slots are either 8- or 16-bits wide (NICs generally use 16 bits), whereas PCI slots are 32 bits wide and thus have a wider data path and are noticeably faster. Another of PCI's major benefits is that you don't have to worry about the IRQ (interrupt request line), because it is uniquely handled in PCI slots. In ISA slots, you have to figure out what IRQs other cards are using, and hopefully have one left over for the NIC.

6. The interconnection devices are hubs, bridges, routers, and switches. Hubs simply join other components on the network and simply pass all information to all components. Bridges are used to divide two segments of the same network so that information addressed within its originating segment stays in that segment, and information addressed to the other segment gets there. Routers are used to join two networks, such as a LAN and the Internet, keeping the traffic within a network there unless it addresses the other network. Switches are used to divide a network into many segments as a bridge does for two segments; for the most part, they have replaced bridges.

7. The primary topology used today is a star topology that uses a hub from which clients, servers, other hubs, and other connection devices radiate.

8. In a 100BaseT network, the maximum cable length between a hub and a workstation is 100 meters, or 328 feet, the minimum cable type is Category 5, the maximum number of hubs between two workstations or a switch and a workstation is two, and the maximum number of cable segments between two workstations or a switch and a workstation is three, with a maximum total distance of 205 meters, or 672 feet.

9. The primary protocol used in Windows networking is TCP/IP. IP, the Internet Protocol, is used primarily for addressing and the conversion from the logical IP address to the physical hardware address. TCP, the Transmission Control Protocol, establishes the connection with the receiving station, packages the information into digestible packets, and makes sure it is received.

10. Hubs, switches, and routers operate at Physical, Data Link, and Network levels respectively of the OSI model. The portions of a message that is being handled at the Transport, Network, and Data Link levels of the OSI model are called segments, datagrams, and frames respectively.

Module 8: Setting Up and Managing a Network

1. If a NIC is properly plugged into the computer, any of these three things could be causing it to not operate: the NIC driver is either missing or not properly installed, the required resources are not available, or the NIC is not functioning properly.

2. The primary protocol used in Windows networking is TCP/IP. IP, the Internet Protocol, is used primarily for addressing and the conversion from the logical IP address to the physical hardware address. TCP, the Transmission Control Protocol, establishes the connection with the receiving station, packages the information into digestible packets, and makes sure it is received.

3. If you believe that networking is not working correctly, make sure that the network interface card (NIC) is properly set up, the networking functions you want are installed, the cabling is correct, and the networking protocol is installed and properly configured.

4. The primary way to test and determine if a network connection is working is to try to use it by opening Windows Explorer and see if a search for a remote computer returns the computer. The second way is to open the command prompt and type **ping** and a computer name. If the network is working, you will get a response.

5. The three types of network addresses are: the physical address, which is an address that the manufacturer builds onto each NIC, called a MAC address in Ethernet cards; the logical address, which is an address assigned by a network administrator or a server, called the IP address when using TCP/IP; and the Computer name, which is an address used in most applications and in Windows Explorer.

6. The three types of network addressing are used together by having software in the operating system that translates or resolves one type of address into another type of address. A computer name is resolved to a logical address using DNS or WINS, and the logical address is resolved to a physical address using the Address Resolution Protocol (ARP) in TCP/IP.

7. For DHCP to perform its function, the server on which DHCP will be installed must be manually assigned a fixed IP address, DHCP must be enabled/authorized on the server, DHCP must have a scope of IP addresses and a standard lease term defined, and clients must have Obtain An IP Address Automatically selected in the Internet Protocol (TCP/IP) Properties dialog box.

8. A private block of IP addresses used in an internal network can use one of four blocks including 10.0.0.0 through 10.255.255.255, 172.16.0.0 through 172.31.255.255, 192.168.0.0 through 192.168.255.255, and the automatically assigned range from 169.254.0.0 through 169.254.255.255. A public block of IP addresses may be obtained from your local ISP, if it is moderate in size, or you can get it from either a regional ISP or one of three international Internet registries.

9. You can get the physical or MAC address by opening the Command Prompt window (Start | Command Prompt) and typing **ping** *ipaddress,* where *ipaddress* is either the numeric IP address or the computer name of the computer for which you need the MAC address, and pressing ENTER. Then, at the command prompt, type **arp –a** and press ENTER.

10. DNS translates or resolves a computer name to an IP address, in what is called a forward lookup, as well as resolves an IP address into a computer name, in what is called a reverse lookup. It does this with forward and reverse lookup tables. In the process of name resolution, if a local name server cannot resolve a name, it passes it on to the other name servers the local server knows about, including accessing the Internet to query name servers there. As a name server queries for a name, it caches the results, so that it does not have to do the query again in the near future.

Module 9: Using Active Directory and Domains

1. A domain, as used within Windows Server 2003, is a collection of computers that share a common set of policies, a name, and a database of their members. A domain must have one or more servers that serve as domain controllers and store the database, maintain the policies, and provide the authentication of domain logons. A domain, as used within the Internet, is the highest segment of an Internet domain name and identifies the type of organization; for example, .com or .edu. A domain name is the full Internet address used to reach one entity registered on the Internet. For example, www.osborne.com or www.mit.edu.

2. The directory structure used within Windows Server 2003 is based on organizational responsibility, such as marketing, accounting, and manufacturing. The organizational model allows you to store objects (servers, workstations, and printers) in groups, or containers, based on where they are in an organization, which might have its own structure, such as departments within divisions. A particular department might be the first organizational point within an organization. A container holding all the objects in a department is called an organizational unit, or OU, and is itself grouped into higher-level OUs based on the logical structure.

3. FQDN stands for "fully qualified domain name." A server name such as mail.osborne.com that contains all OUs between itself and the root is an FQDN. Every Windows Server 2003 computer has an FQDN. This is a combination of the computer name and the domain name of the domain in which it currently resides. For example, Windows Server 2003 computers in the Osborne domain may very well have a computer name equal to *computername*.osborne.com. However, that same computer may in fact be a member of the subdomain of editorial.osborne.com. In this case, the computer's FQDN would actually be *computername*.editorial.osborne.com.

4. DNS uses a hierarchical directory structure that starts with a root directory, which is described by a single period. The first groups of OUs below the root are the various types of domains that can exist, such as .COM, .NET, and .ORG. The next group of OUs following the ".COMs" consists of domain names, such as coke.com, microsoft.com, and osborne.com. A domain name, such as osborne.com, can contain both additional OUs, called *subdomains,* and actual server objects. For example, in the domain name mail.osborne.com, the mail server is an object in the osborne.com domain.

5. The information that AD stores for a particular directory entry includes the username; contact information, such as physical address, phone numbers, and e-mail address; administrative contacts; access permissions; ownerships; and object attributes, such as object name features; for example, Color LaserJet Printer, 20 sheets per minute, duplex printing.

6. No, AD does not have a PDC. AD is based on the multimaster replication model, and all domain controllers are peers within Windows Server 2003. Nevertheless, the first AD server within a network is the operations master, where some directory services are centralized. Only one Windows Server 2003 domain controller within any forest and within any domain is assigned to become the operations master for that domain or forest. For domain operations, three roles are assigned to the domain's operations master: PDC emulator, looks like a PDC to legacy network members; relative ID master, which assigns blocks of security IDs to the other domain controllers; and infrastructure master, which updates the other domain controllers for changes in usernames and group-to-user references.

7. The schema defines the information stored and subsequently provided by AD for each of its objects. Whenever an object is created in AD, the object is assigned a globally unique identifier, or GUID, which is a hexadecimal number unique to the object. A GUID allows an object's name to be changed without affecting the security and permissions assigned to the object, because the GUID is still the same. Once the object is created, AD uses the schema to create the fields defined for the object, such as phone number, owner, address, description, and so forth.

8. Domains in AD delineate a partition within the AD network. The primary reason for creating multiple domains is the need to partition network information. Other reasons to use multiple domains within a network include providing network structure, such as separating several subsidiary companies from the parent company; simplifying replication and reduce the network traffic consumed by it; improving security and administration by

maintaining separate administrative groups that may or may not be linked together; and delegating administrative authority throughout the network, which makes multiple domains and the network in total easy to handle.

9. A forest is a primary default object in every AD. A forest is the uppermost level of AD's hierarchy and contains any number of trees and domains. All domains within a forest share the same schema and global catalog. In essence, forests are similar to DNS's root container. Most organizations implementing AD will have only one forest, and smaller organizations with only one domain may not even realize the existence of the forest, because all functions appear to exist on the domain level only. In effect, the forest is used as the main directory for the entire network.

10. A trust relationship allows two domains to share user and group resources so that users authenticated by a "trusted" domain can access resources on the "trusting" domain. Transitive trusts allow user accounts within a domain to use a second domain's trust relationships to access resources in a third domain. An example of a transitive trust is: if domain A trusts domain B and domain B trusts domain C, then domain A will trust domain C. Legacy NT domains did not support transitive trust relationships. Domains within a forest are automatically configured with two-way transitive trusts.

11. In AD, replication means copying directory information among domain controllers so that they all have the same information and any of the domain controllers can be queried with the same results. Within an AD domain, four main categories of information require replication: configuration, schema, domain, and global catalog information. Each of these categories is stored in separate directory partitions. These partitions are what each AD server replicates and are used by different servers throughout the forest, depending on their role within the network.

Module 10: Communications and Internet Services

1. A direct cable connection is the most common way to directly connect two computers, other than through a LAN. It is accomplished by using a special serial cable, called a *null modem cable,* or a special parallel cable, both of which are made just for PC-to-PC file transfer. These cables are sometimes called *LapLink* cables, after an early program of that name that was used to transfer information between laptop and desktop computers. The cables have the same connectors on both ends (DB9 female connectors on the serial cable, and DB25 male connectors on the parallel cable), but the wires are crossed in the cable so that the wire connected to the transmit pin on one end is connected to the receive pin on the other end.

2. If you are unable to make a direct cable connection work, there are a number of possible reasons. Is the serial or parallel cable properly installed? Have all the steps for setting up the host, in a domain controller or otherwise, and a guest been properly carried out? Have the same networking protocols been set up on both the host and the guest? Is there an active DHCP server on the network? Is the host computer a member of the RAS And IAS Servers group? Do the users have Allow Access selected under Remote Access Permission in the Dial-In tab of the user's Properties dialog box?

3. A modem (short for "modulator-demodulator") is used to convert a digital signal (patterns of ones and zeros) in a computer to an analog signal (current fluctuations) in a phone line; a second modem is used on the other end to convert the analog signal back to digital for use in the connecting computer. Modems can be internal (inside the computer), in which case the phone line connects to the computer, or external, whereby the phone line plugs in to the modem and the modem plugs in to a serial port in the computer. The fastest modems today receive data at up to 56 Kbps (thousand bits per second) and send data at up to 33.6 Kbps.

4. You check if a modem is working, other than by trying to use it, by opening Start | Control Panel | Phone And Modem Options, clicking the Modems tab, selecting your modem, and clicking Properties. In the Properties dialog box, click the Diagnostics tab, and then click Query Modem. After several seconds, if your modem is properly installed and working, you'll see a set of commands and responses. Not all of the responses have to be positive.

5. Remote Access Service (RAS) provides access to a LAN from a dial-up line, a leased line, or a direct connection. RAS acts as a host or server to a dial-up or direct connection guest or client. RAS is commonly used by travelers whose laptops have a dial-up connection that can be used from a remote location to connect through RAS to the home office LAN.

6. Routers are network devices that are used to join two separate, independent networks, such as a LAN and the Internet. Routers operate at the Network (third) layer of the OSI model and therefore use the full IP address. A router looks at all the traffic on both networks but transfers only those packets that are specifically addressed to the other network. Routers also provide a NAT function, which allows your LAN to use a set of non-Internet-usable IP addresses, such as 10.0.0.9, but when the LAN users access the Internet, they are assigned an Internet-usable IP address, with the router translating between the two. Finally, a router can be used to connect two networks that use two different protocols, such as TCP/IP and IPX.

7. To connect to the Internet, you need to have an existing account with an Internet service provider (ISP), you need to know the phone number for your modem to dial, if you are using a dial-up connection (the ISP's modem phone number), and the username and password for your account. If you want to use Internet mail, you need to know your e-mail address, the type of mail server (POP3, IMAP, or HTTP), the names of the incoming and outgoing mail servers, and the name and password for the mail account.

8. Ways you can locate information on the Internet include navigating within a web site using the links in the site, going directly to a web site by entering the URL in the Address box, searching for a web site, using an entry in Favorites, clicking an entry on the Links toolbar, clicking an entry in History, and setting up a different default home page.

9. The three major ways you can search for a web site are to type in the Address box what you believe is part of the URL, and Internet Explorer will search for a site that has in its URL the text you entered; to click Search in the toolbar, the Search Companion pane will open on the left of Internet Explorer, and you can enter a word or phrase and click Search; and finally, to use another search site such as Google, Yahoo, Excite, Go, Lycos, or AltaVista by typing the search site's name in the Address box.

10. Outlook Express enables you to send, receive, and store e-mail; participate in newsgroups by reading and posting messages; and maintain and use an address book.

Module 11: Internet Information Services Version 6

1. Some of the services that IIS 6 can provide include web hosting based on the Hypertext Transfer Protocol (HTTP), file transfer based on the File Transfer Protocol (FTP), Internet mail handling based on the Simple Mail Transfer Protocol (SMTP), web page automation using Active Server Pages (ASP), and support for emerging web technologies, such as the Web Distributed Authoring and Versioning (WebDAV) protocol and the Extensible Markup Language (XML).

2. IIS is primarily a web server hosting web pages using the Hypertext Markup Language (HTML) for external clients, normally via web browsers and the Hypertext Transfer Protocol (HTTP).

3. Kerberos provides Internet standards–based authentication for accessing Active Directory–managed objects. Kerberos lets a user request an encrypted "ticket" that is used for authentication so that the user's credentials, such as username and password, are no longer needed. Kerberos is based on public key/private key technologies (see the discussion of this in Module 17) and cannot be used by others to access secure network resources. Since Kerberos is an industry standard, Windows 2000 and Windows Server 2003 users can use it to interact with third-party products, as well as other OSs.

4. IIS 6 is managed with the Internet Information Services Snap-In to the Microsoft Management Console (MMC) (the IIS console), and both a Terminal Services ability to remotely access the IIS console (the remote console) and Remote Administration (HTML), a capability for performing some management functions over either an intranet or the Internet connection. Also, IIS 6 has an editable XML-based metabase stored in two easily accessible files. Many of the administrative enhancements in IIS 6 involve the new XML metabase, such as the ability to import and export web site configurations, using command-line scripts to manage web and FTP sites, and including an IIS provider in the Windows Management Instrumentation (WMI).

5. In a new or "clean" installation, Windows Server 2003 Standard or Enterprise Edition Setup does not by default install IIS, while Windows Server 2003 Web Edition Setup does. In the cases where IIS is not installed by default, it can be installed with either Manage Your Server (recommended) or Add Or Remove Programs. Using the default installation of IIS from Manage Your Server or Add Or Remove Programs, different features and settings are installed with each method, and Web Edition Setup installs a third set of defaults.

6. In choosing a migration path, the primary considerations are the risk to the current system and total downtime acceptable, the existing hardware role in the new installation, the content changes expected to the web pages with the new servers, the potential network load and available network resources, and the additional services that the organization is planning on adding.

7. IIS 6 starts locked down. IIS is not installed by default on all Windows Server 2003 editions except the Web Server Edition, dynamic web content is not enabled except for ASP on the Web Server Edition, applications that have not been mapped in IIS are not allowed to run, and direct editing of the IIS metabase is not allowed. Anonymous access, though, is enabled to all but administrative web sites.

8. You differentiate among multiple sites on a single host by giving each site at least one of the three address components: IP address, TCP port, or host header must be unique.

9. Every web site must have a different home directory. The default home directory is C:\inetpub\wwwroot\. When IIS receives a request for a web site it is hosting, it goes to the home directory for that site and gets the default home or first page. Virtual directories allow access to files located in a directory not within the home directory. This is a big advantage when trying to access information to be published on an intranet that is located in multiple locations across the network. Using virtual directories is one way to link that information more easily. For the browser, everything seems to be in one location. For the administrator who has to collect everything, it can be easier to store each person's data in a separate virtual directory.

10. The advantages that Windows Media Services server offers over standard web servers include: more efficient network throughput, better audio and video quality to the user, support for advanced features, cost-effective scalability to a large number of users, protection of content copyright, and multiple delivery options.

Module 12: Virtual Private Networking

1. Virtual Private Networking (VPN) uses an insecure public network to handle secure private networking. Using VPN, you can connect to or extend a LAN using the Internet and so replace dial-up connections or leased lines at a considerable savings. VPN allows a traveling worker to connect to and utilize an organization's LAN by connecting through the Internet. The key ingredient in VPN is security. VPN allows you to use a public network with a high degree of certainty that the data sent across it will be secure.

2. VPN creates a secure "tunnel" by first encrypting the data, including all its addressing and sequencing information, and then encapsulating or wrapping that data in a new Internet Protocol (IP) header with routing and addressing information. The outer package can then weave its way through the servers and routers of the Internet without the inner package ever being exposed.

3. RAS and VPN both require, at a minimum, a network interface card (NIC) and a communications interface device, such as a modem; an ISDN or DSL adapter; or a router on the network with a connection to a DSL, T-1, or frame-relay communications line. Assuming that this hardware has been installed in accordance with the manufacturer's instructions, then it was most likely automatically set up in Windows Server 2003 either when the operating system was installed or when the hardware was installed and detected by the OS.

4. For RAS and especially for VPN, you need to have a static IP address assigned by an ISP. In other words, you need an IP address that is acceptable across the Internet, not one, such as 10.0.0.2, that you assigned yourself.

5. IPSec is a set of authentication and security protocols that can operate without interference and in addition to other protocols being used. As a result of this, IPSec can provide unbroken security over several segments of a network that, for example, begins on a private network, goes out over a public network, and then returns to a private network, so long as all the networks are using IP. IPSec accomplishes this by doing its authentication

and encryption at the third or Network layer of the OSI model, ahead of PPP, which operates at the second or Data Link layer. IPSec can use either a 56-bit Data Encryption Standard (DES) key or Triple DES (3DES), which uses three 56-bit DES keys for the very highest security.

6. VPN, like RAS, has both a client component and a server component. The most common setup is for the client to have a dial-up connection to an ISP, travel across the Internet to the server, where a VPN termination is active and allows access to the LAN.

7. L2TP is more difficult to set up than PPTP because of the need to configure the additional security and authentication infrastructure. Because L2TP uses IPSec and the most common form of IPSec uses computer certificates for authentication, you must have a certification authority active on the network and have it set up to automatically issue certificates to VPN computers.

8. To set up a VPN client, you need to set up a dial-up connection for the client to connect to the Internet and then a connection between the client and the VPN server. Windows 2000, XP, and Server 2003 provide an integrated and automated approach to these two tasks, whereas in Windows 9x/Me and NT, you have to separately set up the dial-up connection to the Internet and then create the VPN connection without the help of a wizard.

9. The reasons VPN may not work include RAS not working (making it important to get RAS working before trying out VPN), client setup not being correct, client dial-up connection not working, connection to the ISP not being made, server connection to the Internet being bad, server setup not being correct, and the policies and permission on the server being wrong. Connecting with PPTP makes the setup on the server and the policies and permissions much easier to do.

10. To install VPN on Windows 95/98/Me and Windows NT 4, you may need to download and install additional files, which you should do before setting up VPN. Windows Me, Windows 98 Second Edition, and Windows NT 4.0 with Service Pack 4 and later all have a VPN client that is compatible with either a Windows 2000 or Windows Server 2003 PPTP VPN server, and so no download is required. Windows 98 original or Service Pack 1 requires that you download Microsoft Virtual Private Networking. Windows 95 and Windows 95 OSR 2 require that you first download and install Dial-Up Networking 1.3 Performance & Security Update, and then that you download and install Microsoft Virtual Private Networking.

Module 13: Terminal Services and Remote Desktop

1. A thin client can be running Windows 95/98/Me, Windows NT 4.0/2000/XP, or, with third-party software, MS-DOS, UNIX, Linux, Mac OS, or Windows for Workgroups 3.11; it can even access the server over the Internet. Only the user interface is running on the client, which returns keystrokes and mouse clicks to the server. The client computer can have a slow processor like a Pentium 100, a small amount of memory, perhaps 8MB, and a small hard disk or even no hard disk.

2. The reasons to use Terminal Services include: utilizing legacy hardware and older operating systems that can't directly run the latest Windows; allowing multiple people to use the same application; centralizing the focus of application deployment, administration, and maintenance; controlling applications that are available to users and how they are configured; accessing a computer remotely, say, one at work from one at home or one on the road; and managing several to many servers remotely with remote administration.

3. The components of Terminal Services in Windows Server 2003 include: Terminal Server, which runs on Standard, Enterprise, and Datacenter Editions of Windows Server 2003 and provides the central component that allows multitasking on a server; Terminal Services Manager, which provides the administrative functions for Terminal Services; Terminal Services Licensing, which provides for client licensing of Windows Terminal Services; Remote Desktop Connection (previously Terminal Services Client), which is preinstalled software on Windows Server 2003, Windows XP Professional, and Windows XP Home Edition that allows the client to connect to and use a terminal server; Remote Desktop Web Connection, (previously Terminal Services Web Connection) which allows hosting Remote Desktop Connections over the Web; 32-bit Terminal Services Client, which is additional client software that can be installed on older versions of Windows.

4. Both Remote Desktop Connection and Remote Desktop are installed by default, while Terminal Services requires installation. The final step that both forms of Terminal Services, as well as Remote Desktop, require to be operational is to be enabled using Control Panel | System | Remote tab.

5. You can connect to a terminal server directly across a LAN, by dialing in across a RAS connection, or through a web connection, either directly or using VPN. To use any of the approaches, you need to set up Terminal Services in the server and Remote Desktop Connection in the client. For RAS, you need to enable Routing and Remote Access in the server and a Dial-Up connection in the client as described in Module 10. For a web connection, you need to have IIS running and set up Remote Desktop Web Connection in the server, and have Internet Explorer 5 or later in the client. To add VPN to the web connection, you need to set it up as discussed in Module 12.

6. Terminal server licenses can be generated by a domain license server or by an enterprise license server, the latter of which is the default. An enterprise license server can handle the terminal servers in several domains so long as the domains use Windows 2000 or Windows Server 2003 Active Directory. Enterprise license servers are polled by terminal servers every 60 minutes, even after they are located. A domain license server can handle only the terminal servers in the same domain the license server is in, but that domain can contain workgroups and be a Windows NT 4 domain. Domain license servers are polled by terminal servers every 15 minutes until they are found, and then they are polled every two hours.

7. You can find out a computer's IP address by opening the Start menu, clicking Control Panel, and double-clicking Network Connections. Right-click the connection you use for your intranet or the Internet and choose Status. In the LAN Status dialog box, click the Support tab, where you will see the IP address.

8. Remote Desktop for Administration uses the Terminal Services environment like Applications Server, but it is limited to a maximum of two users, who must be members of the administrator group, so it does not demand much from the server, does not require licensing, and can be easily used to manage a server without a significant impact on the other processes going on in the server. To do that, it does not include the multiuser and process scheduling components that are present in full Terminal Services.

9. In a default installation of Remote Desktop, cut, copy, and paste are not available, because the local client's disks are not available. You can activate the local client's disks by selecting Options in the Remote Desktop Connection dialog box and opening the Local Resources tab.

10. Clicking Close in the connections bar closes the Remote Desktop windows but leaves you logged on, and any programs you have will remain running. If you restart Remote Desktop, you will resume the preceding session. Logging off terminates your Remote Desktop session, and all programs are stopped. If you restart Remote Desktop, you will begin a new session.

Module 14: Managing Storage and File Systems

1. The two types of partitioning in Windows Server 2003 are primary partitions and extended partitions. Primary partitions are given a drive letter, are separately formatted, and are used to boot or start the computer. There can be up to four primary partitions on a single drive, and one partition at a time is made the active partition that is used to start the computer. One partition on a disk drive can be an extended partition in place of a primary partition. An extended partition does not have a drive letter and is not formatted; rather, it is divided into logical drives, each of which is given a drive letter and separately formatted. An extended partition with logical drives allows you to divide a disk into more than four segments.

2. The five different types of volumes are: simple volumes, which are the same as partitions; spanned volumes, which identify a common disk space on 2 to 32 disk drives; mirrored volumes, which are a pair of simple volumes on two separate disk drives on which the exact same information is written simultaneously; striped volumes, which identify disk space on 2 to 32 disk drives, where a portion of the data is written on each drive at the same time; and RAID-5 volumes, which are striped volumes on at least three disks where error-correction information has been added such that if any disk fails, the information can be reconstructed.

3. Some of the more important reasons you should use NTFS rather than FAT and FAT32 are that NTFS provides file- and folder-level security, whereas FAT and FAT32 do not; NTFS is both a more efficient user of disk space

and is faster in retrieving information; NTFS provides both file-level encryption and file-level compression; and NTFS in Windows 2000 and 2003 provides remote storage management, as well as disk quotas.

4. You can convert a FAT or FAT32 partition, volume, or drive to NTFS in either of two ways: by formatting the partition, volume, or drive, or by running the program Convert.exe.

5. The tools that Windows Server 2003 has to manage storage systems, folders, and files include Disk Management, Dynamic Volume Management, Distributed File System, Removable Storage Manager, Remote Storage Service, and Disk Backup and Restore.

6. Disk management is handled by the Disk Management pane of the Computer Management window. Disk Management provides a means for managing both local and remote network drives, which includes partitioning, disk compression, disk defragmentation, and disk quotas.

7. The first step in preparing a disk for use is to partition and then format it. Partitioning can be done only when there is unallocated space on the drive—space that is not currently used for an existing partition. If you have no unallocated space, then the only way to create a new partition is to delete an existing one. The major caution to be considered with this step is that partitioning and formatting deletes all information in the partitioned area.

8. Automatic archival compression is a routine that automatically compresses any file that goes unused for a period of time that you set. This gets around the worst problem of compression: if you are regularly using a file, it remains uncompressed and therefore faster to access. If a file is primarily just being stored, it can be compressed without much penalty. Automatic archival compression can be turned on as a part of Disk Cleanup.

9. Dynamic Volume Management enables you to create, change, or mirror partitions or volumes without rebooting (except for the initial conversion), by using dynamic storage and disks. A dynamic disk has a single partition within which you can create volumes. Simple volumes are the same as partitions except that they are dynamic (can be changed on the fly), can span disks, and include additional types for advanced hardware (striped, mirrored, and RAID-5).

10. The Distributed File System (DFS) provides for the creation of a directory that spans several file servers and allows users to easily search and locate files or folders distributed over the network. To users of DFS, files spread throughout a network appear as though they are on a single server, which makes their use much easier than if they appear on their actual servers. Users need to go to only one place on the network to access files located in many different places. DFS also assists in load balancing across several servers, by allowing the distribution of files over those servers without penalizing the end user.

11. Removable Storage manages media, such as tapes and disks, not the data on the media. Removable Storage works with programs such as Backup, which controls the data on the removable media, to organize and track the media that are used for the program. The media are placed into *media pools* in such a way that a media pool provides enough storage space for a given operation, such as a recurring backup.

12. The five types of backup are: normal backup, which copies all the files that have been selected to the backup media and marks the files as having been archived; differential backup, which copies all the files that are new or changed since the last normal or incremental backup without clearing the Archive bit; incremental backup, which copies all the files that are new or changed since the last normal or incremental backup and clears the Archive bit; copy backup, which copies all the files that have been selected without clearing the Archive bit; and daily backup, which copies all the files that have changed on the day of the backup without clearing the Archive bit.

Module 15: Setting Up and Managing Printing and Faxing

1. As a general rule, it is better to use the driver and printer setup provided by Windows than it is to use the CD that comes with the printer. The two exceptions are if the printer came out after Windows Server 2003 (April 2003), and if Windows Server 2003 does not have a driver for the printer.

2. Before installing a printer, make sure it is plugged into the correct connector (port) on your computer, is plugged into an electrical outlet, has a fresh ink or toner cartridge (which, along with the print heads, is properly installed), has adequate paper, and is turned on.

3. The two kinds of network printers are printers connected to a dedicated printer server, and printers directly connected to a network.

4. The tasks that are a part of controlling a printer queue include: pausing and resuming printing, canceling printing, redirecting documents, and changing a document's properties.

5. One of the best ways to handle ongoing different printer priorities is to have two or more printer definitions for the same printer and to have each definition have a different priority.

6. With multiple printers, you must pick one as the default to use if you don't specify a printer.

7. A *font* is a set of characters with the same design, size, weight, and style. A font is a member of a *typeface* family, all members of which have the same design. The font 12-point Arial bold italic is a member of the Arial typeface with a 12-point size, bold weight, and italic style.

8. The three kinds of fonts are outline fonts, which are stored as a set of commands, bitmapped fonts, which are stored as bitmapped images, and vector fonts, which are created with line segments.

9. The majority of Windows Server 2003 fonts are OpenType outline fonts, but a few are Adobe bitmapped or vector fonts.

10. You can open the Fax Console from the Start menu (Start | All Programs | Accessories | Communications | Fax | Fax Console) or by double-clicking the Fax "printer" icon in the Printers And Faxes window.

Module 16: Managing Windows Server 2003

1. StickyKeys enables the user to simulate the effect of pressing a pair of keys, such as CTRL-A, by pressing one key at a time. The keys SHIFT, CTRL, and ALT "stick" down until a second key is pressed, which Windows Server 2003 then interprets as the two keys pressed together.

2. Folder Options allows you to customize the way folders and files are displayed and handled in various Windows Server 2003 windows, including My Computer and Windows Explorer. The Folder Options dialog box is opened by selecting Folder Options in the Control Panel, or by opening the Tools menu and choosing Folder Options in either Windows Explorer or My Computer.

3. Regional And Language Options lets you determine how numbers, dates, currency, and time are displayed and used on your computer, as well as the languages that will be used. When you choose the primary locale, such as French (France), all the other settings, including those for formatting numbers, currency, times, and dates, are automatically changed to the standard for that locale. You can then change the individual settings for numbers, currency, time, and so on and customize how you want items displayed.

4. The Device Manager enables you to look at and configure all of your hardware in one place. You can immediately see whether you have a hardware problem. You can then directly open that device by double-clicking it, and attempt to cure the problem. In most cases, the Troubleshooter will lead you through a problem search. Two common problems that often can be cured are a wrong or missing driver, or incorrect resources being used, often because the correct ones weren't available.

5. The Windows Task Manager allows you to look at and control what software is running in Windows Server 2003. You can start Task Manager either by right-clicking a blank area of the taskbar and choosing Task Manager or by pressing CTRL-ALT-DEL and choosing Task Manager. The Applications tab shows you the application tasks that are currently running and allows you to terminate a task, switch to a task, or create a new task.

6. The Microsoft Management Console, or MMC, is a shell to which you can add, and then customize, management tools that you want to use. You can create several different *consoles* containing different tools for different administrative purposes and save these consoles as MSC files. There are two types of management tools that you can add to an MMC: stand-alone tools that are called *snap-ins,* such as Disk Management, and add-on functions that are called *extensions,* such as the Disk Defragmenter. There are two modes in which you can create consoles: *Author* mode, in which the consoles can be added to and revised, and *User* mode, in which the console is frozen and cannot be changed.

7. The Registry is the central repository of all configuration information in Windows Server 2003. It contains the settings that you make in the Control Panel, in most Properties dialog boxes, and in the Administrative Tools. Almost all programs get information about the local computer and current user from the Registry and write information to the Registry for the OS and other programs to use. The Registry is a complex hierarchical database that in most circumstances should not be directly changed. The majority of the settings in the Registry can be changed in the Control Panel, Properties dialog boxes, or Administrative Tools.

8. Some of the ways to work around or fix a problem that causes a computer to not boot include: returning to the Last Known Good Registry files; using Safe Mode and Advanced Options; using the Recovery Console; repairing the boot sector; running Automated System Recovery.

9. The most complete way to repair a problem with the operating system and the boot process is to use Automated System Recovery (ASR), which replaces your entire system by reformatting the boot partition of the primary hard drive and reloading all the files that were in the partition. Your system is completely restored to the same condition it was in when you initially ran ASR. Making the ASR floppy disk and the external copy of the boot partition is done with the Backup utility.

10. Group policies provide the means to establish the standards and guidelines that an organization wants to apply to the use of its computers. Group policies are meant to reflect the general policies of an organization and can be established hierarchically from a local computer at the lowest end, to a particular site, to a domain, and to several levels of organizational units (OUs) at the upper end. Normally, lower-level units inherit the policies of the upper-level units, although it is possible to block higher-level policies, as well as to force inheritance if desired. Group polices are divided into *user policies* that prescribe what a user can do, and *computer policies* that determine what is available on a computer.

11. When there are multiple people using the same computer, the best way to keep them from interfering with each other is to create user profiles for each user. That way, when one of the users logs on, his or her desktop, Start menu, folders, network connections, Control Panel, and applications are available the way the user set them up. When the first user logs off and another user logs on, all of the settings of the first user are set aside and the settings of the second user are enabled.

Module 17: Controlling Windows Server 2003 Security

1. Authentication in a computer network is the process of verifying that users or objects are as they are represented to be. In its simplest form, computer user authentication entails validating a username and password against a stored entry, as is done in a stand-alone computer. In its fullest form, user authentication entails using the Kerberos authentication protocol to validate a potential user, possibly using a smart card or biometric device anywhere in a network against credentials in Active Directory. For objects, such as documents, programs, and messages, authentication requires using Kerberos certificate validation. In Windows Server 2003, all three forms of authentication are available, and both user forms employ a single sign-on concept that allows users, once authenticated, to access other services within the local computer or the network, depending on their environment, without having to reenter their username and password.

2. A strong password is simply one that is harder to break because it follows some rules that make it that way. The rules for a strong password are that it should be at least seven or more characters long; it should be a mixture of letters and numbers; it should include both uppercase and lowercase letters; it should include one or more special characters; the letters should not make a word in the dictionary; and the letters and numbers should not be related.

3. Kerberos Version 5 is the default authentication protocol in Windows Server 2003, and Kerberos, in several versions, is the default authentication protocol over much of the Internet. This means that the same authentication routines in Windows Server 2003 can validate both a local Windows Server 2003 client and an Internet-connected UNIX client. Kerberos provides each user with an encrypted ticket with the user ID and password that network devices can use both for identity and for validity. The Kerberos ticket system also validates the network service to the user, providing mutual authentication between user and service. Kerberos uses a Key Distribution Center (KDC) on each domain controller that stores the user accounts that have been entered into the network's Active Directory. When a user attempts to log on and use any part of the network, the KDC is referenced, the username and password are validated, and a ticket is generated with an encryption key that is used for the transmission of data.

4. Two replacements for passwords are smart cards and biometric devices. Smart cards are credit card–sized pieces of plastic that have a tamper-resistant electronic circuit embedded in them that permanently stores an ID, a password, a digital signature, an encryption key, or any combination of those and a PIN. Smart cards require a personal identification number (PIN), so they add a second layer (smart card plus PIN in place of a username and password) that an impersonator would have to obtain to log on to a system. Biometric devices identify people by physical traits, such as their voice, handprint, fingerprint, face, or eyes. Often, these devices are used with a smart card to replace the PIN. Biometric devices are slowly moving from the experimental to the production stage, but nothing is built into Windows Server 2003 specifically to handle them.

5. A digital certificate, or just "certificate," is used for authentication either directly to log on to a computer or indirectly to log on to a network over the Internet without sending usernames and passwords in a way that might compromise them. A certificate is issued by a certification authority (CA), who digitally signs it and says that the bearer is who he or she says they are, or that an object and sender are as represented.

6. Groups, or group accounts, are collections of user accounts and can have permissions assigned to them just like user accounts. Most permissions are granted to groups, not individuals, and then individuals are made members of the groups. It is therefore important that you have a set of groups that handles both the mix of people in your organization and the mix of permissions that you want to establish. A number of standard groups with preassigned permissions are built into Windows Server 2003, but you can create your own groups, and you can assign users to any of these.

7. The default permissions in Windows Server 2003 are substantially different than those in Windows 2000 and earlier versions of Windows NT, where the Everyone group had full permission to do everything in all but a few of the OS folders. Windows Server 2003 starts out with the opposite philosophy, where only Administrators have permission to do everything, and Users (everyone else) have limited permission. This is an intentional tightening of security on the part of Microsoft.

8. EFS stands for the Encrypting File System, which provides for file and folder encryption. EFS has been built into Windows Server 2003 NTFS, and once EFS is turned on for a file or a folder, only the person who encrypted the file or folder will be able to read it. The one exception is that a specially appointed administrator will have a recovery key to access the file or folder. For the person who encrypted the file, accessing it requires no additional steps, and the file is re-encrypted every time it is saved. All of the encrypting and decrypting is done behind the scenes and is not obvious to the user.

9. Private key encryption, or symmetric cryptography (which is also what is used with file and folder encryption), is relatively old and uses a single key to both encrypt and decrypt a message. This means that the key itself must be transferred from sender to receiver. If this is done over the phone, the Internet, or even a courier service, an unauthorized person simply needs to intercept the key transfer to get hold of the key and decrypt the message. Private key encryption, though, has a major benefit in that it is much faster (as much as 1,000 times faster) than the alternatives.

10. Public key encryption, or asymmetric cryptography, uses a pair of keys—a public key and a private key. The public key is publicly known and transferred and is used to encrypt a message. The private key never leaves its creator and is used to decrypt the message. For two people to use this technique, each generates both a public key and a private key, and then they openly exchange public keys, not caring who gets a copy of it. Each person encrypts their message to the other by using the other person's public key, and then sends the message. The message can be decrypted and read only by using the private key held by the recipient. The public and private keys use a mathematical algorithm that relates them to the encrypted message. By use of other mathematical algorithms, it is fairly easy to generate key pairs, but with only the public key, it is extremely difficult to generate the private key. The process of public key encryption is relatively slow compared to private key encryption.

Index